# A New History of
# Modern Latin America

# A NEW HISTORY OF MODERN LATIN AMERICA

Third Edition

Lawrence A. Clayton, Michael L. Conniff, and Susan M. Gauss

UNIVERSITY OF CALIFORNIA PRESS

University of California Press, one of the most distinguished university presses in the United States, enriches lives around the world by advancing scholarship in the humanities, social sciences, and natural sciences. Its activities are supported by the UC Press Foundation and by philanthropic contributions from individuals and institutions. For more information, visit www.ucpress.edu.

University of California Press
Oakland, California

Library of Congress Cataloging-in-Publication Data
Names: Clayton, Lawrence A., author. | Conniff, Michael L.,
    author. | Gauss, Susan M., author.
Title: A new history of modern Latin America / Lawrence A.
    Clayton, Michael L. Conniff, and Susan M. Gauss.
Other titles: History of modern Latin America
Description: 3e. | Oakland, California : University of California
    Press, [2017] | Includes bibliographical references and index.
Identifiers: LCCN 2016053808 (print) | LCCN 2016056615 (ebook)
    | ISBN 9780520289024 (pbk. : alk. paper) | ISBN 9780520963825 ()
Subjects: LCSH: Latin America—History—19th century. | Latin
    America—History—20th century.
Classification: LCC F1413 .C63 2017 (print) | LCC F1413 (ebook) |
    DDC 980/.02—dc23
LC record available at https://lccn.loc.gov/2016053808

ClassifNumber    PubDate
DeweyNumber´—dc23                              CatalogNumber

Manufactured in the United States of America

24   23   22   21   20   19   18   17

10   9   8   7   6   5   4   3   2   1

# Contents

# Preface

This third edition, now entitled *A New History of Modern Latin America*, retains the key features that have distinguished it from other general histories of Latin America covering the nineteenth through the twenty-first centuries. With an emphasis on historical narrative and biography, it draws out the richness of the region's past in ways that appeal to the college undergraduate who is learning about Latin America for the first time. This textbook also brings to light recent interpretations and analyses of the past in an entertaining and readable style. It is designed with a survey class in mind, and for instructors with in-depth knowledge of the field. Its narrative approach also makes it useful for those instructors who have less familiarity with the region, who can use the textbook as a guide for organizing the course by assigning one or two chapters per week.

The third edition presents an interpretation of the major events in Latin American history from the Wars of Independence in the early nineteenth century to the democratic turn at the start of the twenty-first within a chronologically organized narrative. The men and women of Latin America are the heart and soul of this history, and the writing style allows their voices to be heard across the years. Each chapter opens with a document from that chapter's period or theme. Thus, a letter penned by the Liberator, Simón Bolívar, introduces chapter 2. Information gleaned from documents—diaries, journals, letters, newspaper articles, legal petitions, notary public records, and the like—help stitch together the record of the past. The use of many document samples gives readers a feel for people who lived in earlier times. Each document is preceded by a short introduction to place it in the context of the chapter.

We have tried to be comprehensive by giving attention to each of the nations of Latin America. While the biggest and most populous nations—Mexico, Argentina, and Brazil—take up a significant amount of our attention, we have highlighted important events in the histories of all nations, from Chile in the south to Cuba in the northern Caribbean. Major themes are woven into these pages, from the age of caudillos in the nineteenth century, to populism in the twentieth century, to globalization and its impact in the twenty-first century. These themes tie together the multitude of individual national histories, adding broader understanding of the whole hemisphere. Certain themes—ethnic strife, populism, social and economic revolutions, and militarism, for example—transcend borders, giving Latin America its unity of experience, even while an extraordinary diversity marks the region's geography, peoples, and cultures.

This edition maintains the key pedagogical features of its predecessors. Textboxes with topical readings and primary documents appear throughout the text. These bring the contents to life with vivid descriptions by the historical players and witnesses themselves. They also highlight basic concepts (e.g., dependency theory, race relations, and political alignments) intrinsically important for a deeper and clearer understanding of Latin American history. This edition also has about one hundred images and maps to enhance and enrich the reader's learning experience. Each of the five parts in this textbook has an updated introduction to give the reader a sense of the flow of events and their significance in the chapters that follow. We have included three new pedagogical features in each chapter: discussion questions, a timeline of events, and an updated keywords list. The bibliographies from each section, as well as the general bibliography, have been updated and are now located at the back of the text. These bibliographies are not comprehensive, but rather are designed to give students a place to begin research on individual topics suggested by the more general treatment afforded in the text.

The third edition includes significant revisions that enhance, update, and expand on the prior edition, in addition to changes to style and organization aimed at improving clarity. It has up-to-date interpretations drawn from advances in fields such as Atlantic World, race, and gender history; adds substantial new material on women and gender; and includes new textboxes to bring in more diverse historical biographies. A chapter on culture in the second edition (chapter 17) has now been broken apart and included in the narrative of other thematic chapters in order to emphasize the critical role of culture and society in large-scale political and socioeconomic changes. The third edition also includes a final chapter (chapter 25) that brings the text into the second decade of the twenty-first century. The revisions to the third edition can be summarized as follows:

### COLONIAL PROLOGUE

New content on the influence of women, gender, and indigenous people in the making of colonial society

More connections to the broader Atlantic World

### CHAPTER 1

Expanded treatment of the leadership of indigenous people and women in nineteenth-century rebellions

### CHAPTER 2

Revised and updated textbox on race and ethnicity in Latin America

New and relocated sections on indigenous leaders and Afro-Mexican participation in the Wars of Independence, including the sources of their grievances

### CHAPTER 3

Streamlined narrative of events of the independence movements

New textbox on Manuela Sáenz and ideas about women in early nineteenth-century Latin America

### CHAPTER 4

Enhanced exploration of the influence of the Enlightenment, capitalism, and religion on new nation-states

New section on women and family after the Wars of Independence

Relocated and revised material on race in the post-independence period

### CHAPTER 5

New textbox on religion and morality under Juan Manuel de Rosas

Streamlined narrative of caudillo case studies

### CHAPTER 6

New images of modern infrastructure

Updated textbox on dependency theory

**CHAPTER 7**

Reorganized and updated sections on indigenous and slave life, with a fresh focus on land and labor relations

Updated interpretations of slavery in the region

New section on women and gender in the age of liberalism

**CHAPTER 8**

Revised and expanded content on liberalism in Mexico

**CHAPTER 9**

Expanded analysis of Colombian historiography

New textbox on war, nationalism, and indigenous participation in late nineteenth-century politics

Expanded coverage of international conflicts in South America

New textbox on abolition in Brazil

**CHAPTER 10**

Significant revision and reorganization emphasizing the themes of nation-building and national identity

**CHAPTER 11**

New textbox on race and Cuba's independence movement

**CHAPTER 12**

New textbox on tango and cultural populism

Incorporation of material on gender and popular reforms

**CHAPTER 13**

New document on Venezuelan insurgence to open the chapter

New textbox on tourism in Cuba

**CHAPTER 14**

Substantial revisions to draw comparisons among the divergent paths to modern nation-states

**CHAPTER 15**

Expanded discussion of the definition of revolution

Enhanced exploration of the Mexican revolution, including the role of women

**CHAPTER 16**

Revised and updated material on race and religion in Brazil

Revised and expanded coverage of postrevolutionary Mexico

**CHAPTER 18**

New introductory discussion of gender and women under Peronism

Expanded history of Bolivia

**CHAPTER 19**

Reorganized and expanded coverage of politics and society in Mexico from World War II to the present

New textbox on violence in Mexico

**CHAPTER 20**

Expanded and revised exploration of guerrillas, the drug wars, and paramilitaries in Colombia to the present

New section on gender and war in Colombia

**CHAPTER 21**

Substantial new and revised content on Guatemala and on the role of the U.S. in the region

**CHAPTER 22**

New material on race, women, and rebellion in Cuba, the Dominican Republic, and Nicaragua

**CHAPTER 23**

More discussion of women and protest in Argentina and Chile

New textbox on music and politics in Brazil

**CHAPTER 24**

Updated and expanded section on neopopulism and neoliberalism in the 1980s and 1990s, including substantial new material on Chile, Peru, and Argentina

New textbox on women and rebellion at the turn of the twenty-first century

New textbox on first woman senator of Brazil

**CHAPTER 25**

New document on Cuba's 1990s economic crisis to open the chapter

Extensive new content on democratization in the twenty-first century

More on women leaders, the environment, sexuality, race, migration, violence, crime, and globalization

## ACKNOWLEDGMENTS

The intellectual debts accrued over the years since the first edition of this book cannot be captured in a short acknowledgments section. Decades of conversations and collaborations with hundreds of colleagues fill these pages, whether overtly or implicitly. Some people played immediate roles, however, and we thank the following people for their assistance.

The idea germinated on a train ride from Manchester to London in the spring of 1982, when William Sherman and Lawrence Clayton talked about a textbook in the style of the one you have before you as "long overdue" in Latin American history. Sherman was to contribute the colonial section, which he began but was not able to finish. We owe him an immense debt of gratitude for giving us a standard of readable, exciting prose—especially as evidenced in his widely read coauthored text on Mexican history.

Our thanks go to numerous colleagues and friends along the way who made helpful suggestions for improvements and additions or who helped in other ways. They include Ximena Sosa, Sandra McGee Deutsch, William P. McGreevey, Pamela Murray, Carleen Payne, Samuel Brunk, Paul J. Dosal, Marshall C. Eakin, Ralph Lee Woodward Jr., Felix Angel, Barbara Tenenbaum, Alan LeBaron, Lyman Johnson, Jorge Ortiz Sotelo, Susan Socolow, David Bushnell, Brett Spencer, Neill Macaulay, Frank McCann, Frank Robinson, Anne Fountain, John Britton, Jorge L. Chinea, Douglas R. Keberlein, Stephanie Smith, and Richard Hamm. We also thank Synneva Elthon, who served as images editor. In addition, we are grateful to Heather McCrea and the anonymous UC Press reviewers for their critical reading and helpful suggestions. We would also like to thank copy editor Sue Carter for her careful reading and incisive revisions.

At the University of California Press, we thank Acquisitions Editor Kate Marshall, Development Editor Nic Albert, and Editorial Assistant and Acting Editor Bradley Depew, all of whom shepherded the text into the third edition you are now reading.

# Colonial Prologue

## Atahualpa and Pizarro

It was November 1532. Earlier, Francisco Pizarro had founded a community, San Miguel de Piura, on the coast, and now the small Spanish expedition that Pizarro commanded, 62 horsemen and 106 foot soldiers, marched south and east, deeper and deeper into the heart of the Inca empire toward the city of Cajamarca. There the Inca emperor Atahualpa was camped outside the city. He had just triumphed in a bloody civil war against his brother Huáscar for dominion of the immense Inca empire. The Tahuantisuyo. The Four Corners of the Earth. It stretched from Ecuador in the north to central Chile far to the south.

On November 15, the Spanish force entered Cajamarca. Atahualpa—together with thousands of warriors, noblemen, women, and courtiers—stayed in his camp outside the city. A small troop of Spaniards approached Atahualpa. Hernando Pizarro, brother of Francisco, said, "Our governor would be delighted for you to visit him." Fearing nothing from these few, although exotic, strangers, Atahualpa agreed.

November 16, 1532. Atahualpa and a lightly armed retinue of five or six thousand noblemen and warriors slowly moved toward Cajamarca. Pizarro's army, pitifully small by comparison, was arrayed for an ambush, hidden in the buildings surrounding the central courtyard. Outside the city, Indians seemed to fill every space as they joined Atahualpa's procession.

"Are you afraid?" young Pedro Pizarro, brother to Francisco, asked an even younger soldier standing next to him in the shadows. The soldier shuddered involuntarily. "No!" he snapped and then quickly followed, "Yes, by God, aren't you? They sound like a swarm of bees out there," he said, gesturing toward the entrance to the city.

"Yes, Bernardo," Pedro said. "But commend your soul to God. He will see us through." Pedro Pizarro crossed himself, and so did his companion. It fortified them. God would not allow Christians to be overcome by pagans.

Atahualpa, carried on a litter, entered the square late in the afternoon. His people soon filled the square completely, squeezing in and pressing against the walls until there was barely room to move. Vicente de Valverde, a Dominican friar, approached Atahualpa. "My governor would like you to come and dine with him."

The Inca shot back at the Spanish friar, "Tell your governor to return everything his men have stolen or consumed since they entered my kingdoms! Then perhaps we can talk."

Valverde ignored the rebuke and called upon the Inca to submit to God and his emissaries, the Spanish. "It is all in this book," Valverde said, handing Atahualpa a prayer book that he carried with him. Atahualpa took the small book and examined it. The Inca then dropped it onto the ground, angry that the priest had handed him something so strange that seemed to question the Inca's intelligence.

Valverde spun on his heel and turned to Pizarro and his men hidden in the low buildings surrounding the square.

"Make ready!" Atahualpa warned his people, rising in his litter as he watched Valverde run back to Pizarro.

"Oh God, oh God," Valverde cried out as he ran back. "See what this Lucifer has done, Your Honor!" he shouted to Pizarro and the other Spaniards waiting in ambush. "Come out, come out, Christians! Come at these enemy dogs who reject the things of God. I absolve you!" A cannon roared from the top of one of the buildings. It was the prearranged signal. "Santiago!" the horsemen shouted as they spurred their mounts out of the buildings straight into the mass of Indians around Atahualpa. Terrorized by cannons and trumpets, by the brutal assault of the war horses, by the slashing of steel swords and lances, Atahualpa's followers reeled under the onslaught.

Atahualpa's litter bearers were cut down. All around him his subjects died, limbs and heads pierced and severed by Toledan steel, trampled and bludgeoned under the war horses, suffocated as they were crushed up against the city walls until finally the walls collapsed. The Spanish pursued the fleeing, terrified Indians into the night, piercing and slashing them in the surrounding fields until a trumpet finally called them off.

"When will you kill me?" the Inca asked his captors that evening.

"Oh, no, Your Highness," Hernando de Soto answered for the Spaniards. "We fight with force and courage, but we don't kill afterward. That's not right."

"You are our guest," Pizarro added.

"But tell me," de Soto inquired of the Inca, "Why did you allow us in so easily? Why did you walk into so obvious a trap?"

Atahualpa smiled ruefully. Perhaps they wouldn't kill him after all. "I meant to capture you," he said.

"God was with us, Your Highness," Pedro Pizarro said quietly.

Indeed, the Spaniards and their Christian God had turned the world on its head for Ata-hualpa and his people. Cajamarca, and the events therein, marked the end of the Inca empire and the beginning of the Spanish empire in Peru.

The story of conquest, however, did not begin with Pizarro in Peru. It began in Spain and Portugal hundreds of years before Christopher Columbus sailed, and it is to the Iberian civilization that we must turn briefly to comprehend the nature of a people who so remarkably transformed America.

## THE RECONQUEST OF SPAIN

Spanish civilization at the end of the fifteenth century was riding a high crest of military success that culminated in the reconquest of the Moorish kingdom of Granada in 1492. For almost five hundred years, an intermittent crusading-style war had occupied the Spanish people as they fought to rid the Iberian Peninsula of Moors from Africa. These African peoples, worshippers of the prophet Muhammad, or Muslims, swept over and conquered much of Christian Spain in the eighth century. The push west across Africa and then north into Europe through Spain marked the high tide of Islam as it rose first in the Arabian Peninsula and quickly spread east and west.

Then, around a thousand years ago, some small Christian kingdoms in the far north along the Cantabrian coast that had survived the Moorish conquest launched a war of reconquest. The Reconquest of Spain lasted until 1492, when the last Moorish ruler, that of Granada, fell to the besieging Christian armies of Queen Isabella of Castile and King Ferdinand of Aragon.

The reconquest was a complicated movement that incorporated many elements—some religious, some of a more secular nature. Basically, Spanish society was permeated with the value of military dominion. It was a society that looked to the warrior as the embodiment of Christian endeavor and worldly fulfillment. Warrior kings, warrior bishops, knights, and other fighting men were admired as the embodiment of the ideal life—fighting Moors for the ultimate end of reconquering Spain for Christianity. There was also another dimension to this society, more secular and worldly. This dimension was the goal of enriching oneself through conquest and the acquisition of booty and slaves. Moorish lands and cities, people and property, all were legitimate spoils of war, and conquest became a way of life for much of Spanish society.

When Columbus returned in 1493 to Spain from his first voyage of reconnaissance and discovery, he came back with some fantastic news—news that he delivered to a king and queen who presided over a warrior people with a deeply inbred conquest mentality. Spanish energies, for so long invested in the Reconquest of Spain, turned to the emerging opportunities in the New World. The warriors formerly engaged in the reconquest swarmed over the newly discovered Americas in the sixteenth century, seeking much the same goals they had sought in Spain: fame and fortune through conquest. They found both in abundance in the New World.

## THE AMERICAS

As has been often observed, America was not discovered by the Europeans. It was truly a meeting of two cultures that had not known each other previously. The native peoples of Latin America—stretched as they were from Tierra del Fuego on the southern tip of South America to the immense spaces of North America to the north—were more diverse in culture, lifestyles, languages, and civilization than the Spanish conquistadors (conquerors) who sailed the Atlantic in the sixteenth century in search of adventure and fortune. When Hernán Cortés and his small Spanish expedition of several hundred men reached the capital—Tenochtitlán—of the Aztec empire in 1519, they mar-

veled as they gazed down from the high passes. The Spanish renamed it "Mexico City" during the colonial period.

The indigenous population of the Americas spanned from Stone Age people of the Amazon to the highly developed cultures of Mesoamerica, Mexico, and Peru. The Spanish encountered skilled fishermen and agriculturalists in the Caribbean and the descendants of astronomers and city builders among the Maya of Central America. It is almost impossible to generalize about the Indians of Latin America at the time of the European encounter because they were as diverse in language, ethnic identity, and political and social organization as all of Europe at the time.[1]

There were perhaps 50 million or more Indians in the Americas at the time of the Conquest: 22 million in Mexico alone, another 10 to 12 million under the dominion of the Incas, and the rest scattered across the region. They ranged from nomadic hunters and gatherers to people who had domesticated crops and developed a sedentary agriculture. The latter, freed from the tyranny of hunting and gathering, built complex civilizations, complete with well-developed religious rituals, political organizations, artisans, and cities in Central America, Mexico, and Peru. The Maya developed a written language; the Incas, an efficient state bureaucracy and empire; and the Aztecs, a formidable war machine. When the Spanish arrived in the late fifteenth century, the stage was set for a meeting between European and American civilizations—a meeting that would be the initiating moment in Latin American history and that would also transform world history.

## THE CONQUEST

In the simplest terms, the Conquest refers to the subjugation of the indigenous population by Spanish and Portuguese explorers, warriors, and missionaries from Europe. It was not only a conquest by arms, but also, from the perspective of the Spanish, a triumph of Spanish religion and civilization over pagan Indian peoples. The term "Encounter" is often used to emphasize the balance in the merits of the cultures and civilizations—one American and one European—that "encountered" each other in the seminal sixteenth century. But the Conquest itself devastated the indigenous population and fueled Spain's rise as a world power.

## THE DEVELOPING COLONY

By the middle of the century, European diseases, harsh labor demands, dislocation, and the demoralization of defeat had combined to destroy more than 50 percent of the indigenous population of the Americas. In 1650, censuses in Spanish America recorded that populations had been drastically reduced from levels that had existed at the time of Columbus's arrival. In the Caribbean islands, virtually no indigenous inhabitants survived the first hundred years after the Spanish Conquest, while in the central valley of Mexico and along the Andean mountains of South America, 80 percent and in some areas 90 percent of the populations perished.

Early on, the Spanish Conquest also meant the conquest of Indian women. Comparatively few European women made their way to the Americas. Racial mixing occurred on a vast scale, and a new people was born: the mestizos, those children born of unions between Spaniards and Indians. During the course of the colonial period, mestizos became an increasing percentage of the population, especially in the great Indian population centers of Mexico, Guatemala, Ecuador, Peru, and Bolivia. Afro-Europeans (Africans and their descendants already in the Iberian peninsula) also arrived with the Spanish conquistadors, sometimes free, but increasingly as slaves. A generation

later, their numbers began to increase dramatically as Spaniards and Portuguese imported first hundreds, then thousands, and finally millions of slaves directly from Africa to the Americas to work the fields and plantations of the New World—a place where Indians had thrived before the demographic decimation of the Conquest.

The Spanish fanned out over much of the continent and found what they sought during the Conquest: fame, wealth, and power. They established for Spain the beginnings of American empires—empires that produced in Latin America its basic character in all the many ways that we measure and describe a civilization, from its religion to its eating habits. Meanwhile, the Portuguese occupied and settled Brazil, gradually forming a unique society and economy. By blending with Indians and Afro-descendants, together they also forged in the New World the beginnings of a civilization distinct from Africa, from America, from Europe. It was an amalgamation of all three. It was, in essence, an expression of something historians have labeled the "Atlantic World"—a paradigm or model for studying the history of how peoples and forces (including economic, social, political, racial, and cultural) of all four major continents bordering on the Atlantic Ocean interacted over the three or four hundred years following the arrival of Europeans to the Americas.

While the Spaniards occupied the apex of American society in the colonial period, there evolved in the colonies a rich and diverse culture. After the initial demographic decline following Conquest, the indigenous population rebounded, especially in heavily populated regions like Mexico and Peru. In these areas, the Nahua and Inca, for example, retained their languages, much of their religion, family practices, and other characteristics—food, domesticated animals, agricultural cycles, and gender arrangements. Some scholars have called this "agency," reflecting how Indians retained much of their ability to determine how they worked, thought, and lived despite the new, European-dominated colonial order.

For example, with the Europeans came their religion, Roman Catholicism. And, as the early European settlement of the Indies occurred in the sixteenth century—a time of deep divisions in Christianity created by the Reformation—the Spanish Catholic Church was completely, and almost fanatically, devoted to the evangelization of all its new subjects in the proper form of Christianity, especially in the face of the rise of the new forms of Protestantism in Europe, all thought to be heretical. It would not do for indigenous peoples to be deprived of eternal salvation as understood by the church, nor to retain any vestiges of their pagan, non-Christian religions that survived the Conquest.

The stage was set for the struggle to enforce Spanish domination not only in the secular world—politics, the economy, and so forth—but also in the spiritual world. Despite the enthusiastic and sometimes forceful evangelization of the Indies by Christian missionaries, many indigenous peoples managed to retain aspects of their earlier forms of worship. They even retained some of their gods, disguised as "saints," which the Catholic Church accepted and venerated in many instances. The Spanish friars learned to tolerate indigenous forms and places of worship as long as they didn't openly question or contradict the central doctrines of the church, such as the sole divinity of Jesus Christ, the meaning of his Resurrection, and so forth. This fusion of indigenous religious practices and Catholic forms of worship was called "syncretism" and represented indigenous agency as European and American civilizations blended.

At the apex of Spanish civilization in America was the sovereign of Spain. Through the Council of the Indies, the sovereign governed the colonies, which were themselves divided into administrative entities called "viceroyalties." The viceroyalty of New Spain included all of Mexico, Central America, and the Caribbean, plus some areas of North America and South America, while the viceroyalty of Peru, with its capital of Lima, extended across the continent of South America, excluding Brazil, which belonged to Portugal. From Mexico City and Lima, Spanish nobles were sent to rule these vast domains as viceroys.

Equal in importance to the viceroys, governors, and other secular administrators were the prelates, missionaries, and priests of the Roman Catholic Church, who arrived in the Americas simultaneously with the conquistadors. The church quickly became—after the government—the most important institution in colonial Latin America, conditioning much of Latin American society in this formative period.

Members of missionary orders spearheaded the church's evangelization of Indians in the sixteenth century. Dominicans, Franciscans, and later Jesuits spread the faith rapidly among their new converts—all of whom had suffered a terrible defeat at the hands of the Spanish conquistadors. Were not the Christian gods (or one god, as the friars insisted), then, better than the Indians' own gods, who had failed them so miserably? The answer was a tentative yes, making evangelization easier for the Christian missionaries.

Missionaries established churches, developed new grammars in indigenous languages to reach the new converts with the basic holy writ in the Bible, and baptized Indians by the thousands. As noted above, many indigenous deities and religious traditions survived the evangelization of the Americas. When these were incorporated into formal church worship, new, syncretized forms of worship evolved. Catholic saints and an assortment of indigenous deities sometimes coexisted in somewhat unusual harmony, a fact that distinguished the church in the Americas from the stricter, more conservative church of the Old World.

The secular clergy followed rapidly in the wake of the missionaries. These secular priests and clerics were involved in the day-to-day affairs of parish life and eventually replaced the members of the missionary orders. They were sometimes labeled the "regular" church because members of missionary orders such as the Dominicans and Franciscans were governed by a special set of regulations.

The secular clergy was directly under the control of the Spanish and Portuguese monarchs through an arrangement called the *patronato real*, or the royal patronage. This gave the crown immense influence in the operation of the church in the colonies—such as the right to name clerics, establish churches, and collect tithes—while endowing the church with the powerful support of the monarchy. The church prospered not only in a spiritual fashion—by converting millions of Indians to Christianity—but also in a material way, accumulating vast wealth in property over the duration of the colonial period. It was claimed, for example, that by the era of independence, the church owned half of the real estate in the vast colony of Mexico.

Later, in the nineteenth century, the church became a focal point of intense controversy. During and after the Wars of Independence, it was attacked by reformers and liberals who sought to break its power not only as an immense property holder but also as the dominant force in providing education and social services such as hospitals and philanthropy. The church was also the principal money lender in the colonies, and in dozens of other ways it controlled and fashioned the way that people thought and acted. The Inquisition, sometimes called the police arm of the church, sought to enforce orthodoxy in both spiritual and secular matters, seeking out and punishing crimes as serious as heresy and treason. Committing bigamy, soliciting women parishioners in the confessional, and other lesser crimes also came before the courts of the Inquisition in its role of spiritual and moral censor and judge of colonial society.

The liberators, as we see in the following chapter, were anti-clerical for two major reasons. First, they were imbued with ideals of the Enlightenment, or the Age of Reason, which ran the course of the eighteenth century and spilled into the nineteenth. Second, they saw the Roman Catholic Church as the primary religious and cultural embodiment of Spain in the Americas. And Spain had become the target of those leading the Wars of Independence in the early nineteenth century.

Yet, if one were to take an informal poll of those first learning about Latin America, asking them which word or phrase comes to mind to characterize Spain's colonies in America, it would likely not be religion or the church, but rather, silver. Others might say something like the gold galleons, when, in fact, the bulk of precious metal wealth that flowed from the colonies to Spain for over three hundred years was silver, not gold.

With regard to material wealth, Spaniards enjoyed an incredible run of luck in their colonial experience. The Spanish claimed that finding and exploiting the greatest silver mines the world had ever known in Mexico and Peru were acts of divine providence. Spain's European rivals—principally England, France, and Holland—viewed Spain's luck in other terms. Whatever the perspective, by the late sixteenth century, the silver mines of Zacatecas in Mexico and Potosí in Bolivia (then known as the province of Upper Peru) were on the way to making Spain the envy of all Europe. Fleets arrived annually at the port of Seville loaded down with silver. "Vale un Potosí" (as rich as Potosí) became a common phrase in seventeenth-century Europe, a metaphor for vast and easy wealth.

Around the great silver mines, a complex agricultural and pastoral system developed to supply the workers and the mines with food, leather, and other supplies. These estates became the models for land ownership in colonial Latin America: large haciendas owned by a small minority of Creoles (Spaniards born in the New World of Spanish parents; *criollo* in Spanish), an elite who represented the top of colonial society's pyramid of power and influence. Indigenous and African forced labor became the workforce on these estates and, along with commerce and mining, landed estates became one of the three pillars of colonial economy and society.

As the economic basis of the colonies gradually diversified to include the production of other export products, such as sugar, cacao (chocolate), indigo (a dye), and tobacco, for example, the great hacienda system spread throughout Spanish America and Brazil. A great hacienda owned by a Creole family, however, was not the only form of land ownership. Some of the regular orders of the church, such as the Jesuits, came to be among the richest and most powerful estate builders in colonial America, while in many parts of Latin America, especially in Mexico, Central America, and Peru, Indians managed to preserve their communal lands intact in spite of the encroachments of Spanish and mestizo landowners. Nonetheless, the dispossession of indigenous lands by Creoles and mestizos—as well as exploitation in other areas—produced much stress in this colonial society. Occasionally, rebellions flared up—rebellions that grew more pronounced and violent toward the end of the eighteenth century.

## THE MATURE COLONY

By the middle of the eighteenth century, we can speak of mature colonies. There was a sense of place and self among colonial Latin Americans that distinguished them from the transplanted Spaniards of the sixteenth century. The Creoles, mestizos (persons whose parents were of European and indigenous ancestry), mulattoes (or *pardos;* persons whose parents were of African and European ancestry), zambos (persons whose parents were of indigenous and African ancestry), and other Americans born of the racial mixture of people originally from Spain, the Americas, or Africa for the most part felt themselves to be Americans or Peruvians, Mexicans or Chileans, for example. They related to the region of their birth much more than to the land of their ancestors. This sense of nationality was more pronounced among the Creole elite and only imperceptibly sensed in those groups largely estranged from power and privilege, such as Indians and slaves. While their sense of identity did not stray far from plantation or village, the Creoles were already developing a proto-nationalism that helped spark the Wars of Independence in the early nineteenth century.

This new sense of nationalism emerged in an increasingly enlightened and complex colonial world. The refined caste categories of the early colonial period had ceded to the reality of a society built from the mixing of Europeans, Indians, and Africans. By the 1700s, mestizos and mulattoes were among the largest social groups, following Indians, and Spaniards increasingly used the term "race" (*raza*) rather than "caste," as the former came to be seen less as a biological category than a flexible social one. Mestizos often played an in-between role in colonial society, serving in occupations ranging from rural farmers, estate managers, or peddlers, to urban merchants and skilled workers. Social class and identity became less and less about one's racial heritage and color and more about habits, language, location of residence, and wealth. As European, indigenous, and Afro-descendant people borrowed each other's customs and beliefs, they created their own unique cultures in the Americas—not necessarily a single American culture, but no longer simply European or African, either.

The lives of women in colonial society changed along with the increasingly diverse and vibrant economy and society. The predominance of patriarchy meant that there was a sexual hierarchy that placed men above women in both their families and society. Wealthy men, in particular, legally ruled over their households and all who lived within them. Their duty was to protect and provide for those who depended on them, and these dependents in turn were obligated to obey. To protect their honor and that of their families, elite women remained heavily protected and monitored by the males in their family or, if living in a convent, by the church. Their honor—measured by sexual chastity—was key to ensuring the family's purity of blood and therefore the whole family's status and wealth. The majority of elite women married and often had as many as eight to ten children. Widows, however, were much freer and often participated actively in colonial society and economy. Nevertheless, many believed that women should emulate the virtues of the Virgin Mary, including her femininity, tolerance, love, docility, and virginity. The worship of the Virgin Mary, *marianismo*, did not detract from the centrality of Jesus Christ in the Christian faith in Latin America, but did celebrate the virtues of motherhood and resignation, and thus reinforced the traditional roles expected of women. The noble ideal was to be submissive and obedient, given to sacrifice and tolerance, submerging one's own feelings in nurturing the family, which was seen as the cradle of values and morality. Sexual submission and fidelity to one's husband was expected, even as machismo encouraged men, including married ones, to prove their masculinity—embodied in their virility, dominance, and power—through having multiple lovers.

Expectations for behavior were tied to a woman's race and status, and women—as the transmitters of blood and honor—were the lynchpins of the complex colonial racial world. Therefore, white elite women ideally lived secluded lives, which protected their families from racial impurity and social dishonor. Middle- and lower-status women, who were almost exclusively mestizo, indigenous, or Afro-descendant, were seen as needing less protection and often spent a great deal of time in public spaces. Marriage was less common, though a significant proportion of Indian women married, and female-headed households made up a quarter or more of all households in cities like Mexico City, Lima, and São Paulo in the 1700s. Many middle- and lower-status women worked in a variety of occupations, including as market women selling food, flowers, or fruit; weavers, domestic servants, or agricultural workers. Some were slaves.

Economically, too, the eighteenth century represented a period of increasing self-sufficiency. While the colonies exported greater and greater amounts of products from field, forest, and mine to European consumers, coincidentally the American colonies of Spain and Portugal also were producing more and more for themselves—textiles, shoes, ships, and myriad other items—that spoke of economic maturation.

Certain areas of the colonial export economy expanded dramatically in the second half of the eighteenth century. Cattle products from Argentina (salted beef and leather), sugar from Cuba, cacao from Venezuela and Ecuador, indigo from Guatemala and Mexico, magnificent woods from tropical Central America, silver from the rejuvenated mines of Mexico, and other products helped double, triple, and sometimes even quadruple trade between the colonies and Europe toward the end of the century. It was a period of rising prosperity.

But the times were changing. New ways of thinking about the world were changing the old order of things. Revolutions in the United States (1776), France (1789), and Haiti (1791) were—by their example and rhetoric—helping Creoles of Latin America fine-tune their own sense of grievance and injustice at being second-class citizens in the Spanish empire. Instead of getting the plum jobs and appointments in the empire's bureaucracy that they felt they deserved in the decades preceding the Wars of Independence, Creoles were systematically denied such appointments in favor of *peninsulares* (Spaniards from the peninsula of Iberia). It was frustrating and disappointing, and led to strong sentiments of rebellion against the Spanish monarchy—the prelude to independence. In September of 1810, Mexico's Creoles and Indians rose up dramatically against the old order. The results, in Mexico and across the Spanish empire, changed the course of Latin America's modern history.

## CONCLUSIONS AND ISSUES

The colonial background to independence was marked by one of the most fascinating endeavors in human history: the making of a new civilization. Previously the American continents had been isolated from the Eurasian and African landmasses for ages, each part of the world developing distinct plants, animals, peoples, and cultures. With the Columbian voyages, European and American cultures came together with a great clash. Principal among the European colonizers were the Spanish and Portuguese. They came with their swords and muskets, with their faith and language, with an immense energy to explore, to conquer, to settle. They encountered equally diverse and energetic indigenous cultures, whose people the Spanish and Portuguese first conquered, then attempted to "civilize" with European values.

The result was the long colonial period. Certainly the Spanish and Portuguese prevailed in political and economic matters, but in the end an immensely varied culture and society developed in Latin America out of the fusion of European, Indian, and African peoples.

Over time, the Spanish and Portuguese empires in the Americas produced an incredibly rich cornucopia of wealth for the colonizing countries. In the Indies themselves, societies developed with the Spanish and Portuguese administrators at the top, closely paralleled by a Creole elite who shared power and resources. Eventually, these Creoles moved to separate themselves from European control, motivated by self-interest, revolutionary models (the American and French revolutions, for example), and the desire to carve out their own destinies.

## Discussion Questions

What was the Reconquest of Spain and how did it shape the colonization of the Americas?
What was American society like when the Spaniards arrived?
What was the impact of the Conquest on the indigenous peoples of the Americas?
What role did religion and the Catholic Church play in the Conquest and the colonial period?
Why was the colonial economy so valuable to the Spanish?
What was life like for women in the Americas?

## Keywords

| | |
|---|---|
| Atlantic World | Jesuits |
| Aztec | marianismo |
| Conquest | mestizos |
| Creoles | patriarchy |
| Dominicans | peninsulares |
| Encounter | Potosí |
| Franciscans | reconquest |
| Inca | Zacatecas |

# INDEPENDENCE AND TURMOIL

Latin America passed through one of its most important historical eras in the first half of the nineteenth century. In a tumultuous twenty-year span, from about 1806 to 1826, almost all of the Spanish and Portuguese colonies broke off from their colonizers and became independent nations. The path that each nation followed to independence was often complicated and marked by fits and starts, periods of intense political confusion, sharp military conflicts, interludes of peace, more battles, and by ethnic and political divisions within the revolutionary movements that defy easy or clear analysis.

In the largest context, the Wars of Independence marked a continuation of the same forces that drove the American, French, and Haitian revolutions of the late eighteenth century, all lumped together into something known as the Age of Democratic Revolutions. In the simplest terms, the old forms of government and rule, largely monarchies across the Western World, were overthrown for republican forms of government. But, as in America, France, and Haiti, the seemingly simple becomes more complex as one probes beneath the surface of these wars in Latin America.

For example, while most of the new nations overthrew the king and replaced political authority with a republic, Brazil did not. It replaced a monarch with another monarch and glided into the nineteenth century without the cataclysmic battles and campaigns that characterized the wars in the Spanish colonies. Other forces at work in the Spanish colonies, especially economic and commercial ones, argued for separating from the crown and getting rid of the monopolies and restrictions long set in place by the monarchy to regulate the colonies. The Creole elites and rising middle classes among the patriots wanted freedom and independence in the growing age of capitalism and new wealth. Ironically, this new age of freedom also fastened slavery even more deeply to some areas of culture and society in Latin America. The age of freedom for the Latin American leaders was also the age of slavery for millions of Africans and their slave descendants in Latin America.[1] But the wars were themselves a liberating agent for the many slaves who fought with the patriots, such as Simón Bolívar, and were given their freedom.

Leaders—mostly Creoles, but also mestizos and mulattoes—in Latin America wished for greater independence and autonomy from Spain. Spain for the most part resisted this wish, and the stage was set for the wars that followed. In some instances, such as in Mexico in 1810, the conflict took on racial overtones that horrified many Creoles. They wanted independence but did not particularly want freedom for all Mexicans, which included a vast majority of Indians, blacks, and mestizos who were subject to Creole domination.

In South America, Bolívar headed the patriot forces of Venezuela, Colombia, Ecuador, Peru, and Bolivia. The long struggle for independence began in 1810 in Venezuela and did not culminate until 1826 in Bolivia. From the south, José de San Martín led patriot armies out of Argentina to sweep up through Chile and Peru, eventually joining with Bolívar's forces in the liberation of Peru.

Brazil marched to its own drummer. Independence came late and largely as the result of the transfer of Portugal's court to Rio de Janeiro in 1807. Brazil became essentially equal with Portugal under the rule of João VI, and when he returned to Portugal in 1821 he left his son Pedro to govern over a colony— Brazil—that now felt itself the equal of its colonizer. In 1822 Brazil declared its independence and accepted Pedro as its first emperor. The ease with which Brazil became independent contrasted vividly with the long and violent road followed by the Spanish colonies.

After independence was achieved, a confusing period of political turmoil followed until about midcentury. Multiple experiments with various political forms of government were initiated, from monarchies to republics, but very few were stable or long-lasting. What did ensue were periods of dictatorial rule by caudillos, such as Antonio López de Santa Anna of Mexico and Juan Manuel de Rosas of Argentina. Caudillos were "men on horseback," self-styled political military leaders who governed by force and charisma and were themselves vulnerable to the competing power of other caudillos. Constitutions seemed to rotate almost as rapidly as caudillos in countries such as Peru and Mexico. Political anarchy in turn stifled economic recovery from the independence wars, and to the observer of the 1830s and 1840s, Latin America appeared chaotic politically and stagnant economically.

Yet, even in this period new forces were at work. Bolívar was among the first to spread a message of nativism, which called for the unity, though not equality, of all American-born men. His desire to unite the former colonies and their people was soon superseded by the emergence of proto-nationalism in many areas, as elites competed to define what it meant to be Argentinian or Venezuelan. Elites then used these new nationalist identities to imagine a whole new political order of liberal nation-states and to support their bids for political authority over them. The Wars of Independence disrupted the old racial and ethnic structures of the colonial period as well. As noted, some patriot leaders, such as Bolívar, emancipated their slaves during the wars, and by midcentury emancipation was in full swing. Liberals desired to free Indians of old bondages such as tribute (a form of taxation levied only on indigenous people) that long chained them to secondary citizenship. The experiments to elevate Indians to equality were, however, marked by as many failures as successes.

Women, too, took part in the Wars of Independence on both sides. From the earliest days of the insurgency, wealthy women eager to support the patriot cause spread anti-Spanish propaganda and used their resources and connections to support the struggle for independence. Women of all classes participated in a variety of roles, at times using the veil of perceptions about female passivity to mask their roles as messengers, propagandists, recruiters, and arms smugglers. Some, typically lower-class, women were camp followers— called *soldaderas* in Mexico or *juanas* in northern South America—who provided support services to the patriot armies, serving as cooks, providers, laundresses, and nurses. On occasion, they took up arms or created women's battalions. Some women patriots even faced prosecution from the Spanish royalists for their activities. On the island of Margarita off the coast of Venezuela, for example, women helped with the artillery defending against a royalist attack, and their skill and dexterity in working the cannon were much praised. In speaking about the women who supported the patriot cause, Bolívar revealed the multiple views of femininity at the time, with women seen as both suspects and victims in the battles. Bolívar pointed out the savagery that fighting patriotic women had had to endure at the hands of the Spanish royalists.

> Even the fair sex, the delights of mankind, our amazons have fought against the tyrants of San Carlos with a valor divine, although without success. The monsters and tigers of Spain have shown the full extent of the cowardice of their nation. They have used their infamous arms against the innocent feminine breasts of our beauties; they have shed their blood. They have killed many of them and they loaded them with chains, because they conceived the sublime plan of liberating their beloved country.[2]

Whether motivated by a sense of tradition, obligation, or loyalty to their cause, women were deeply involved in the politics and fighting of the independence era, even if more enduring change to the condition of women and gender relations would have to wait.

Commercially, merchants in the Americas took advantage of independence to deepen their ties to each other and to British, French, and American merchants. Despite Spanish commercial regulations and monopolies, English merchants had been trading with the merchants of Latin America since before independence, though often in a clandestine fashion known as contraband trade. After the wars, and no longer dependent on, collaborating with, or governed by a colonizer and its representatives, merchant groups from Mexico to Uruguay and Argentina switched their loyalties to the newly independent states and pursued freer commerce and higher profits. In breaking with the Spanish empire, they helped to transform the Atlantic trading world from one dominated by imperial centers and peripheries participating in a transatlantic mercantilist economy to one increasingly characterized in the nineteenth century by independent states engaging in capitalist trade.

# Background to Independence

## The "Grito de Dolores"

Father Miguel Hidalgo sought to define the coming insurrection and rally his parishioners and followers with a clarion call to independence that still resounds in Mexico. Father Hidalgo spoke to his congregation early on the morning of September 16, 1810. To this day, the Mexican president reenacts the "Grito" from the balcony of the National Palace in the heart of Mexico City, every September 16. Read the "Grito"—literally a "cry," or proclamation—as if you were a man, woman, or child in the small crowd, excited, listening to the voice of your priest call you to action:

> My friends and countrymen: neither the king nor tributes exist for us any longer. We have borne this shameful tax, which only suits slaves, for three centuries as a sign of tyranny and servitude; [a] terrible stain which we shall know how to wash away with our efforts. The moment of our freedom has arrived; the hour of our liberty has struck; and if you recognized its great value, you will help me defend it from the ambitious grasp of the tyrants. Only a few hours remain before you see me at the head of the men who take pride in being free. I invite you to fulfill this obligation. And so without a patria nor liberty we shall always be at a great distance from true happiness. It has been imperative to take this step as now you know, and to begin this has been necessary. The cause is holy and God will protect it. The arrangements are hastily being made and for that reason I will not have the satisfaction of talking to you any longer. Long live, then, the Virgin of Guadalupe! Long live America for which we are going to fight![1]

The "Grito de Dolores" (Cry of Dolores) had been proclaimed. Mexico was on the road to revolution.

**Figure 1.1** Father Miguel Hidalgo, Mexican War of Independence hero who set the independence movement into action with his call to arms on September 16, 1810, in his largely Indian parish of Dolores. Each year the "Grito de Dolores" is again renewed by the president of Mexico from the balcony of the National Palace on the broad, central plaza of Mexico City. In this mural, located in the Government Palace, Guadalajara, Jalisco, Mexico (painted in 1939), his call to arms is portrayed by Mexican revolutionary muralist José Clemente Orozco. Authors' collection.

But people rarely break easily with the past. The forces of wealth, power, and tradition, the security and comfort of timeworn ways, and the fear of reprisal and loss restrain radical thinking, preserve old institutions, and discourage exploration of unfamiliar paths to new relationships, be they political, economic, or social. Thus, for over three hundred years, Spain's colonies in America evolved slowly, with little dramatic change, at least to the eye of the contemporary observer. Life was predictable. Born an Indian peasant, one expected to die tilling the same soil as one's ancestors. Born a Creole, one expected more privileges, perhaps an education and marriage within one's own caste and rank, and, if a man, a comfortable job in the government bureaucracy. There was constancy to life.

From the late eighteenth century through the early nineteenth century, new forces buffeted this stable world of colonial Spanish America. These forces erupted between 1810 and 1825 in a series of wars and revolutions that shattered Spain's colonial world into pieces and then put the pieces together again as new nations. One of the greatest empires in modern history ended, and a new era of political independence began for the peoples of Latin America—

peoples who were hardly homogeneous but rather a constellation of different societies.

## CAUSES OF THE WARS OF INDEPENDENCE

### Ideas and the Enlightenment

One of the greatest students of revolutions, the historian Crane Brinton, in referring to the French Revolution, wrote: "no ideas, no revolution." In other words, to break with the past, to make a revolution, a people must have an ideology with goals that cannot be fulfilled unless society first changes radically. The desire to achieve these goals must outweigh the risk and trauma of radical change. However, the ideas behind the goals may be largely unarticulated during the early stages of a revolution. When finally formalized, the ideology that emerges may be an ex post facto ("after the fact") justification of what has already happened. When Thomas Jefferson wrote the American Declaration of Independence in 1776, he, in many ways, was justifying what already had happened. By then the American colonists had broken with the king and Parliament, the Minutemen had engaged the Redcoats in Massachusetts; the Declaration was but the final, legalistic break.

In truth, most revolutions—as in the case of the French and the American revolutions, both of which inspired Latin Americans of the era—embody concepts and ideas already articulated by middle-class thinkers and then gain momentum through spontaneous acts by the masses that are not necessarily tied to those ideas. The Latin American Wars of Independence were no different.

Ideologically, the Wars of Independence were born in the eighteenth-century Age of Enlightenment, also sometimes called the Age of Reason or the Age of Democratic Revolution. New ideas challenged old truths and institutions accepted for centuries in Europe. Some ideas were profoundly subversive, like the notion that the ultimate authority in society resides in the people, not with king or emperor. This idea, called popular sovereignty, denied the divine right of monarchs to rule absolutely.

The idea that all people are created equal in nature and possess equal rights furthermore subverted the privileged nobility, whose rank and power derived from birth. The church as the guardian of morality and the enforcer of social order came under attack by enlightened philosophers who favored reason and rejected religious wisdom found in ancient ecclesiastical manuscripts. Instead of an omnipotent god, the Deists, as they were called, envisioned a benign divine presence who had set things in motion but who allowed people freedom to follow their own destinies. This secular trend undermined traditional authority in society.

In science, the new thinkers challenged old knowledge even more decisively. Prior to the Enlightenment, scientific knowledge had been thought to be complete, immutable, and unchanging; it was usually acquired through study of the teachings of Aristotle and his followers. The enlightened scientists, in contrast, studied nature itself for answers to their questions. For example, Aristotelian thinkers "knew" that the earth was the center of the universe. As this was not borne out by scientific observation, it was cast out by enlightened thinkers. They taught inquiring modern society to observe, to classify, to search for rules in nature rather than blindly to accept hand-me-down "knowledge."

In sum, new ways of thinking produced new points of view, new frames of reference, and new forms of behavior that challenged the old order.

## The Enlightenment in the New World

The Enlightenment had considerable impact in the Spanish colonies, although at first it was more evident in philosophical and scientific thinking than in politics. People like the Mexican Antonio Alzate and the Peruvian Hipólito Unanue were committed to reason and progress as the passwords of a new age. They and others like them fostered scientific investigation in medicine, botany, and agriculture, for example. They saw these as useful tools for building a better society. Universities such as San Carlos of Guatemala became relatively open forums for the discussion and dissemination of the new ways, as did societies of civic-minded citizens, most often called Amigos del País (Friends of the Country).

The Spanish crown itself, especially under the enlightened monarch Charles III (1759–1788), encouraged efficiency and the application of enlightened principles in the management of its vast American empire. This had unforeseen consequences for the Spanish empire. Over the years, Creoles had been given, or had bought, access to governmental offices in the colonies from the lowest municipal posts to offices as high as judgeships on the prestigious *audiencias* (high courts with judicial and legislative powers). In the middle and late eighteenth century, the Spanish crown deliberately began to replace Creoles with native-born Spaniards, known as *peninsulares*, in many offices to help centralize and streamline the imperial administration. However wise and enlightened this was from the perspective of the Spanish crown, Creoles saw only an insensitive and offensive monarchy depriving them of their legitimate and hard-earned rights to be leaders in the colonies in favor of the foreign-born.

In this unsettled environment, it was not surprising that headier, more politically volatile facets of the Age of Reason fueled the imaginations of a few Creoles. Activists like Francisco de Miranda of Venezuela, Antonio Nariño of Colombia, Claudio Manuel da Costa of Brazil, and Francisco Javier Espejo of Ecuador immersed themselves in the ideas of the political Enlightenment and, many years before the eruption of the wars, began to champion the cause of independence and liberty for their homelands. They are called precursors (forerunners) of the independence movement. Although few in number, they exercised a disproportionate influence. They forced their fellow Creoles to think in terms defined by the political Enlightenment, to look to the examples of the American and French revolutions. To them, the writings of the Baron de Montesquieu on the sovereignty of the people and of Jean Jacques Rousseau on the social contract were clarion calls to action.

Wealthy Creoles were not the only ones dissatisfied with the colonial systems of Spain and Portugal. Across the Caribbean and along the coast of Brazil, Afro-descended leaders, some slave but many free, accelerated plans for uprisings against planters and officials. They sought independence and self-government in order to create societies like those of Africa. The vast new arrival of Africans in the late eighteenth century meant that conspirators could recruit veteran soldiers, religious leaders, chieftains, and merchant-kings who enjoyed great prestige among the slave masses. Their uprisings were widespread, and in 1791 the greatest of all the slave revolts, that of Haiti, broke out and forever altered the fate of black people in the Americas. The man who ultimately commanded the victorious Haitian Revolution, former slave Toussaint L'Ouverture, became the most famous black man in the world, both feared and loved by millions and remembered for his fight—a fight that made Haiti the first independent nation-state in Latin America in 1804.

In the Andean highlands, as well, Indian and mestizo laborers and peasants chafed under the oppression of Spanish officials and priests. José Gabriel Condorcanqui, a mestizo descendant of the last Inca king, attempted to redress grievances peacefully through the judicial system. But, pushed by a long series of abuses of power by Spanish and Creole officials of his people, including labor demands and the loss of community lands, he took the ancestral name of Túpac Amaru II and launched the Great Andean Rebellion in 1780. Accompanying him in leading the rebellion was his wife, Micaela Bastidas. Bastidas married Condorcanqui in 1760. Identified in her marriage documents as the illegitimate daughter of Spanish parents, she nevertheless became a respected and capable leader in the rebellion. She played a central role in coordinating and commanding various aspects of the revolt itself, from communications and provisioning to troop movements and recruitment. She and other leaders, some of whom were also women, were caught between trying to motivate Indians to join their cause while also struggling to stop the movement from turning into a caste war targeting the Spanish, not the least because they wanted to attract mestizo and Creole support. Condorcanqui and his family, including Bastidas and a son, were captured and brutally executed in 1781. The rebellion was finally put down in 1783, at a loss of eighty thousand lives, and thereafter Spaniards in the Andes remained wary of further rebellions and bloodshed.[2]

Besides leaders such as L'Ouverture and Condorcanqui, dozens of others struggled to organize liberation movements. In the end, all of these early conspirators failed individually—most were executed or died in prison—yet they paved the way for victory by the next generation of leaders. These precursors are much revered in their countries today. Among the most famous were Hidalgo and José María Morelos of Mexico, Francisco Miranda of Venezuela, Claudio Manuel da Costa and Joaquim José da Silva Xavier (the famed Tiradentes) of Brazil, and Antonio Nariño of Colombia.

## Creoles and *Peninsulares*

In the end, wealthy white Creoles led the movements to separate their lands from Spain during the Wars of Independence. Besides the ideology of the Enlightenment, other, more immediate considerations propelled them to action. A diverse set of economic, ethnic, and nationalistic circumstances added to the general level of discontent and frustration among the Latin American population.

Although no one element was more important than another in bringing about the wars, the antagonism and bitter feelings between American Creoles and those Spaniards born in the Iberian Peninsula (*peninsulares*) who came to Latin America either as government administrators or in private enterprise helped ignite the emotional tinderbox that flared in 1810. Creoles felt abused and offended by peninsulares, whom they increasingly viewed as foreigners in the Americas. Peninsulares, in turn, tended to be contemptuous of Creoles, who, in a world dominated by an obsession with purity of blood, they viewed as tainted by virtue of their American birth. This sense of racial and social difference hardened over the years. Creoles claimed that their legitimate aspirations, not only to hold office, as discussed previously, but also to trade freely and to be full citizens within the Spanish empire, were circumscribed and frustrated by an imperial bureaucracy that invariably favored Spaniards over Creoles. Out of this discontent, a sense of Latin American nationalism evolved, a feeling of distinctiveness that the Peruvian historian Jorge Basadre labeled the *"conciencia de sí,"* or national self-awareness.[3]

## Issues of Trade and Commerce

Creole aspirations to independence were also fed by bread-and-butter issues— issues that added to the already smoldering jealousy and antagonisms marking social and political relations between Creoles and peninsulares. Creoles believed that the Spanish crown and peninsulares unjustifiably favored Spain at the expense of the colonies in matters of trade and commerce. Their dissatisfaction took many forms. In some regions, like those that produced agricul-

## Creoles and Spaniards

Although the difference in temperament and character between Spaniards and Creoles, and between the different American peoples, was already deeply marked at the end of the seventeenth century, its consequences only began to emerge during the eighteenth century. The mutual antipathy between Spaniards and Creoles blossomed forth with unwonted vigor from the beginning of that century onwards . . . Spaniards and Creoles were linked by their feelings of loyalty and respect for the king; but they hated one another. In 1748 Jorge Juan and Antonio de Ulloa remarked in their *Noticias secretas de América:* "To be a European, or *chapetón*, is cause enough for hostility to the Creoles, and to have been born in the Indies is sufficient reason for hating Europeans. This ill-will reaches such a pitch that in some ways it surpasses the rabid hatred which two countries in open war feel for one another, since, while with these there is usually a limit to vituperation and insult, with the Spaniards of Peru you will find none. And far from this discord being alleviated by closer contact between the two parties, by family ties, and by other means which might be thought likely to promote unity and friendship, what happens is the reverse—discord grows constantly worse, and the greater the contact between Spaniard and Creole the fiercer the fires of dissension; rancor is constantly renewed, and the fire becomes a blaze that cannot be put out."

Jorge Juan and Antonio de Ulloa, *Noticias secretas de América*, as quoted in Francisco A. Encina, *Historia de Chile desde la prehistoria hasta 1891* (Santiago: Editorial Nascimento, 1941–1952), vol. 6, pp. 7–15, which in turn appears in R. A. Humphreys and John Lynch, eds., *The Origins of the Latin American Revolutions, 1808–1826* (New York: Knopf, 1965), pp. 245–46.

tural products for export, Creole landowners wanted free trade and an end to the system of Spanish monopoly and controls. In other regions, the interior provinces of Ecuador and Peru, for example, where local manufacturers had to compete with imported products, Creoles wanted more protection. And in regions like Argentina, there were both factions wanting free trade and factions wanting protection. Argentines in the coastal provinces, especially Buenos Aires, produced many cattle products for export and desired free trade; their brethren in the interior produced wines and other products marketed internally and wished to be protected from cheap European imports that undermined their livelihood. Whatever the Spanish crown did was bound to rub someone the wrong way, further eroding loyalties to the monarchy. The friction caused by these commercial differences was increased by the other circumstances that estranged Creoles from peninsulares.

## The Invasion of Spain

Creole exasperation with overbearing peninsular officials was all the greater because Creoles did not see the geopolitical units of the New World as lesser lands subject to Spain. Just as Spain itself was a group of ancient kingdoms (like Valencia, Castile, Aragon, Granada) united dynastically by their allegiance to the same crown, so the New World with its various administrative divisions (Guatemala, Mexico, Peru, Venezuela, Ecuador, and so on) was conceived of theoretically as a roster of new kingdoms, equal with one another and with their fellow kingdoms in Spain. Each owed allegiance to the crown, and none was subordinate to any other kingdom. Their allegiance to the crown, moreover, was highly personal. That is, it ran from the kingdom to the person of the king, and not to Spain itself. As the nineteenth century dawned, King Charles IV sat on the Spanish throne. His son Ferdinand was his heir apparent. In Europe, by 1800 the armies of the brilliant and ambitious Napoleon Bonaparte were on the march, building an empire across the continent.

In 1807 and 1808, Napoleon's army invaded what by then had become a weakened Portugal and Spain. A British fleet rescued the Portuguese royal family and court and whisked them off to safety in Brazil just days before French forces occupied Lisbon. Spain, too, was overrun. Amid popular unrest, King Charles IV was forced to abdicate in favor of Prince Ferdinand. Both were invited to France, where they remained hostage. Napoleon then crowned his brother, Joseph Bonaparte, as king of Spain. The curtain was up on a great drama; the actors were already in place. A usurper, Joseph Bonaparte, sat on the throne of the kidnapped King Ferdinand VII. Spain's new leader and his government lacked legitimacy. What were Spain's colonies to do?

On May 2, 1808, the Spanish people in Madrid rose up spontaneously against the French army of occupation and the French Bonaparte king. This was the opening salvo of a civil war that lasted almost six years, until Napoleon's empire collapsed and Ferdinand returned to Spain. Other Spaniards formed juntas, or committees, to work for the expulsion of the French and to carry on the affairs of state in Ferdinand's name during his exile. The most important of these was the Central Junta of Seville.

This Spanish junta asked the colonies to join them in resisting aggression. Consistent with their concept of co-kingdoms, the Creoles demanded equality and equal representation. Indeed, none of the Spanish juntas were willing to concede that.

Local juntas sprang up in the colonies—in La Paz, Quito, Santiago, and elsewhere—to consider governing local affairs in the absence of the legitimate monarch, Ferdinand VII. These juntas, largely controlled by Creoles acting through their municipal governing bodies, the *cabildos*, were little disposed to obey self-appointed juntas in Spain that sought to govern the whole empire in Ferdinand VII's absence. When the Central Junta that convened in Spain attempted to legislate and govern the American kingdoms, the Creoles rejected its authority. They would obey the king but not a group of Spaniards who purported to rule in the name of the king. This was often a ruse, but it maintained a semblance of legality.

In 1810 the Central Junta was replaced by the convocation of a Spanish parliament, the Cortes, which convened in September in the ancient port city of Cádiz. It included representatives from the colonies. The Cortes decreed radical reforms, such as the equality of all Americans, a free press, and abolishment of Indian tribute (tax paid in coin or kind). But the Cortes, radical and liberal in its makeup and actions, came too late.

Between 1808 and 1810, Creoles in Latin America responded to the crisis and the breakdown of authority in Spain by taking matters into their own hands. Across Latin America, they broke with formal Spanish authority, which was usually represented by a viceroy or captain-general in the Americas who now appeared to stand for the usurper Joseph Bonaparte. Creoles determined to govern themselves in Ferdinand VII's name and to await his restoration.

But beneath these acts lay the long history of Latin American grievances. Dissatisfaction had been given ideological form by the Enlightenment, while the crown and peninsulares had thoroughly antagonized Creoles for decades by denying them what they considered legitimate opportunities. Napoleon's invasion of Spain, by suspending colonial loyalty to the Spanish state, touched off the fuse to the powder keg. Isolated military confrontations soon erupted into war.

For fifteen years the Wars of Independence raged across Latin America from the northern deserts of Mexico to the cold, snowy passes of the Andes Mountains, which divide Chile from Argentina in South America. Spain's effort to maintain its rich American empire was overwhelmed by its colonies' fights for autonomy and freedom from colonialism. Spain was pushed violently out of mainland America, and more than a dozen new nations emerged, committed to independence. Portugal, too, was pushed out of Brazil, but the almost peaceful path toward independence in Brazil differed markedly from the long and violent wars of its Spanish-American neighbors.

Although independence was the final result throughout the former colonies, each region followed a distinctive path after 1810. Some, like Mexico, exploded in an ethnic and social revolution. Many Indians, angered by centuries of oppression and inspired by the rhetoric and passion of the moment, waged war against not only Spaniards but also against all whites, including Creoles. In other colonies, like Argentina, the struggle was relatively bloodless, and independence came easily, although deep divisions among Creoles in that region created unique problems.

Thus, as civil war engulfed Spain after 1808, soaking up its energies, the Latin American colonies took things into their own hands. There was little that Spain could do as Creoles and Spaniards in Latin America jockeyed for position all the way from Argentina to Mexico during this temporary, but crucial, vacuum of power. Matters were complicated by other social, political, ethnic, and economic factors. Perhaps no situation was more complicated than the confusion that reigned in Mexico after 1810.

## MEXICO: THE POWDER KEG EXPLODES

In September 1810 a Creole plot to overthrow the viceroy was revealed, and the conspirators were warned to flee for their lives. But one of them, a priest named Miguel Hidalgo y Costilla, decided to go ahead on his own accord. In the dawn hours of September 16, 1810, he sounded the call for arms at his parish church in Dolores.

Mexico now celebrates its independence on the anniversary of this day. Father Hidalgo's "Grito de Dolores" called on his parishioners, mostly Indians, to overthrow "bad government and the Spanish." He tempered his challenge with the slogan "Long Live Ferdinand VII," professing loyalty to the captive monarch while advocating the overthrow of Spanish government in Mexico. In this, he represented a sentiment that was widespread among Mexican Creoles, who might have risen in his support if not for a major miscalculation. What Hidalgo did not foresee was the smoldering anger of Indians in Mexico, which transformed this initial phase of the Mexican independence movement into a violent bloodbath. The Creole leaders of the insurrection witnessed Indians rise against *all* white oppressors, Creole as well as Spaniard.

Mexico, in fact, was a nation of unequals. A white population of about 1 million people dominated the more numerous Indians (about 60 percent of the total population) and mestizos, or people of mixed racial backgrounds, as well as a smaller population of Afro-descended people who had arrived largely as slaves centuries earlier. The castes were separated by cultural and social differences, but mestizaje, or the spatial and sexual mixture of peoples leading to new and blended cultural forms, led to great fluidity.[4] Nevertheless, colonial-era laws, which outlined distinct rights and responsibilities for each caste, defined sharp legal distinctions between different races that, reinforced by beliefs about racial difference and inequality, ensured white elite dominance. Violent extremes in wealth and social position characterized Mexico on the eve of independence, and indigenous protests against tribute, loss of land, and other injustices were common in the 1700s.

Droughts, loss of land, unemployment, and rising food prices added burdens to the Indian population. When Father Hidalgo, who spoke the Indian dialect and sympathized with the plight of his parishioners, issued the Grito de Dolores, the nearby countryside ignited. Indians and mestizos flocked to his cause. The beloved Mexican saint, the Virgin of Guadalupe, was adopted as the patroness of the movement, and before long a ragtag army of sixty thousand was sweeping across the countryside on its way to Guanajuato, a major city in the region.

> ### Inequality in Mexico
>
> Baron Alexander von Humboldt, the German naturalist who traveled through New Spain at the end of the eighteenth century, observed that a "monstrous inequality of rights and fortunes" characterized Mexico. Manuel Abad y Queipo, bishop-elect of Michoacán, identified two groups of late colonial society: "those who have nothing and those who have everything. . . . There are no gradations of man: they are all either rich or poor, noble or infamous."
>
> Alexander von Humboldt, *Political Essay on the Kingdom of New Spain,* trans. John Black (London: Longman, Hurst, Rees, Orme and Brown, 1811).

What happened at Guanajuato was burned into the memories of Spaniards and Creoles alike. Hidalgo's army stormed the Alhóndiga, or granary, where the Spaniards and some Creoles had taken refuge, and massacred the defenders. Pillaging and looting ensued as the rebels lashed out at all whites (although Spaniards suffered more than Creoles).

To Creoles, whether radical or conservative, pro-Hidalgo or anti-Hidalgo, the Guanajuato massacre signaled an unacceptable direction in the independence movement. It threatened their place in society as leaders and put in jeopardy the entire structure of Mexican society, based on the white Creole elite's privileged position. Thus, a great many Creoles and Spaniards alike turned on Hidalgo and his undisciplined mestizo army.

As the revolution proceeded, Hidalgo's decrees to his followers became more and more radical and threatening. He abolished the hated tribute, a centuries-old institution that forced Indians to pay a tax simply because they were Indians. Other acts, such as abolishing slavery and allowing his armed followers to slaughter Spaniards, further alienated Creoles from the Hidalgo revolt. Perhaps it was inevitable that this first great, spontaneous outburst of desire for freedom and justice would be crushed. It was simply too disorganized and too radical to win the support of the Creole elite. Many of them were certainly in favor of independence, but they were unwilling to yield to Hidalgo's radical demands for social and economic justice.

By early 1811 the small royalist army near Mexico City, reinforced and supported by Creole militia, stopped Hidalgo's followers, now numbering eighty thousand, in a decisive battle. Hidalgo retreated, wreaking havoc in Valladolid and Guadalajara as he went. But his army gradually disintegrated under constant blows from the disciplined Spanish-Creole troops. Some months later, Hidalgo himself was captured while trying to escape to the north and was executed. This first bloody phase of the Mexican Wars of Independence came to an end with Hidalgo's death; but the movement that he sparked was by no means dead.

### Miguel Hidalgo, Revolutionary

"[There were] two Hidalgos, the symbolic figure and the man," wrote Lesley Byrd Simpson. "Of the two the man is infinitely the more interesting."

Hidalgo was not a great man before he was caught up in the insurrection and placed at the head of it. He had lived for fifty-seven years without achieving more than moderate distinction. He taught Latin, theology, and philosophy for some years at the ancient (1540) College of San Nicolás in Valladolid (Morelia, Michoacán), and rose to be rector of it. His unorthodox teaching and his reading of prohibited books was resented by the faculty, and in 1792 he resigned from the College and accepted the curacy of Colima. Ten years later he was posted to the parish of Dolores, Guanajuato. . . .

Hidalgo loved words and had the power to move people. He certainly thought he had been relegated to the unimportant parish of Dolores because he was a Creole—in which he may have been right. Then, as he saw the better posts in the Church go to men who had no greater recommendation than to have been born in Spain, his sense of injury grew to a bitter hatred of all things Spanish. His personal grievances and the miseries of his country he laid to the diabolism of the gachupines [peninsular Spaniards]. As his phobia matured, he practiced a number of innocent compensations. He read forbidden books; he raised forbidden grapes and pressed out forbidden wine; he planted forbidden mulberry trees and spun forbidden silk . . . [then] the Literary and Social Club of Querétaro . . . offered him an outlet for his forbidden learning and eloquence. He acquired a taste and discovered a talent for conspiracy. The Rights of Man, the Social Contract, and the rest of the intoxicating doctrines of the French Revolution became woven in his mind into a beautiful fabric of the perfect republic, from which gachupines should be excluded.

Lesley Byrd Simpson, *Many Mexicos,* 4th ed., revised (Berkeley: University of California Press, 1971 [1941]), pp. 209–10.

In 1811 another priest (and a far better general), José María Morelos, assumed the leadership of the independence movement and continued pushing for Mexico's freedom. Meanwhile, in South America, the greatest liberator of all Latin America rose in Venezuela like a comet. Simón Bolívar left a trail of brilliance, creativity, and audacity that still inspires the modern people of Latin America.

## CONCLUSIONS AND ISSUES

The Wars of Independence evolved from a number of internal and external causes, some related, some independent of one another. At the top of the list were the grievances that Creoles held against peninsular Spaniards. Deep-seated hostility between the two classes of rulers ultimately led Creoles to break their three-hundred-year loyalty to Spain and to move the colonies toward independence.

Other rebellions and revolutions in the Americas either inspired or shocked Latin American Creoles into action in the early nineteenth century. Certainly the American Revolution of 1776 and the French Revolution of 1789, both driven by ideas born in the Age of Enlightenment, encouraged Creoles to emulate their example. But the Haitian Revolution of 1791, with its deep-seated racial divisions, horrified Creoles, who were accustomed to governing over a subordinate population of Indians and blacks. When Indians and mestizos did join the revolution—such as in Mexico in 1810—they shocked independence-minded Creoles into rethinking the perils of true freedom if it were ever to become a reality.

Finally, the events in Spain revealed the weakness of the monarchy and helped precipitate the independence movements. Napoleon's invasion of 1807, the installation of his brother Joseph as the king of Spain, the Spanish resistance, the rise of revolutionary juntas to resist Napoleon, and the convocation of the liberal Cortes in Cádiz all inspired Creoles to take matters into their own hands. It was the beginning of the end of the Spanish American empire.

## Discussion Questions

How did the Age of Enlightenment influence the origins of the Wars of Independence?

What were the grievances of Creoles against Spain and its representatives (peninsulares) in Latin America?

What economic factors divided Spain from its colonies by the early 1800s?

How did events in Europe, especially Napoleon's invasion of Spain and Portugal, spark the Wars of Independence in Latin America?

Why did Mexico's Indians support Father Hidalgo's Grito de Dolores?

Why did Mexico's Creoles ultimately refuse to support the revolt led by Father Hidalgo?

## Timeline

| | |
|---|---|
| 1780–83 | Rebellion of Túpac Amaru II |
| 1791–1804 | Haitian Revolution |
| 1804 | Haitian independence |
| 1807–14 | Napoleon invades Portugal and Spain |
| 1810 | Grito de Dolores |
| 1810–21 | Mexican independence movement |

## Keywords

Age of Reason/Age of Democratic Revolution

Creoles

Enlightenment

Grito de Dolores

Haitian Revolution

juntas

mestizaje

peninsulares

popular sovereignty

Wars of Independence

# The Coming of Independence to South America

## Bolívar the Liberator

Simón Bolívar strides like a colossus across the stage of Latin American liberty and independence. But, as in all life, there were colossal downs as well as triumphant highs for the man called "The Liberator" by five nations of South America. In 1815, Bolívar found himself in exile on the island of Jamaica. Queried by a "gentleman of this island"—later identified as a British resident on the island, Henry Cullen—as to the nature of his war against Spain on behalf of liberty and independence, Bolívar penned one of the most perceptive documents ever produced on the nature of Latin America. Read it not only to learn about the mind and world of Bolívar in 1815, but also to appreciate that this document was forged by wisdom and experience that still have relevance today.

> The Jamaica Letter: Reply from a South American to a Gentleman from This Island
>
> Kingston, Jamaica, September 6, 1815
>
> My dear Sir:
>
> It is . . . difficult to predict the future lot of the New World, or to make definitive statements about its politics, or to make prophesies about the form of government it will adopt. Any idea relative to the future of this land seems to me to be purely speculative. Could anyone have foreseen, when the human race was in its infancy, besieged by so much uncertainty, ignorance, and error, what particular regime it would embrace for its own survival? Who would have dared predict that one nation would be a republic or another a monarchy, that this one would be unimportant, that one great? In my opinion, this is the image of our situation. We are a small segment of the human race; we possess a world apart, surrounded by vast seas, new in almost every art and science, though to some extent old in the practices of civil

society. I consider the current state of America similar to the circumstances surrounding the fall of the Roman Empire, when each breakaway province formed a political system suitable to its interests and situation or allied itself to the particular ambitions of a few leaders, families, or corporations. There is, though, this notable difference, that those dispersed members reestablished their former nation with the changes demanded by circumstances or events, while we, who preserve only the barest vestige of what we were formerly, and who are moreover neither Indians nor Europeans, but a race halfway between the legitimate owners of the land and the Spanish usurpers—in short, being Americans by birth and endowed with rights from Europe—find ourselves forced to defend these rights against the natives while maintaining our position in the land against the intrusion of the invaders. Thus, we find ourselves in the most extraordinary and complicated situation. Even though it smacks of divination to predict the outcome of the political path America is following, I venture to offer some conjectures, which of course I characterize as arbitrary guesses dictated by rational desire, not by any process of probable reasoning.[1]

## VENEZUELA

Venezuela, like Mexico, was a country of competing interests. It was complicated even more by racial divisions that included not only Indians, Spaniards, and mestizos, as in Mexico, but also many blacks and pardos, both slave and free, who played an important role in determining the course of the Wars of Independence. The basic choice in 1810 in Venezuela, as in Mexico, was nonetheless simple. Should the Venezuelan Creoles bend to the will of the various Spanish juntas or seek a different path? When faced with a choice, as they were in 1810, the Creoles chose independence, which was declared on July 5, 1811. By this act, Venezuelan Creoles, who constituted an aristocracy based on their control of the land and nurtured by their sense of rank and responsibility, took the lead in the Venezuelan Wars of Independence. Theirs was the first country to declare itself fully independent of Spain.

But, as the United States had discovered in 1776, it was one thing to declare independence; it was another, more difficult thing to make it stick. The radical Creoles who pushed Venezuela so rapidly toward independence soon discovered the depth of opposition as civil war erupted in 1811. The royalists, as Spanish forces were known during the Wars of Independence throughout Latin America, mounted a determined campaign to crush this insurrection against Spain. Joining the royalists were not only more conservative Creoles, but also many pardos and blacks who were disenchanted by the Venezuelan declaration of independence and the new constitution revealed in 1811. With its strict voting requirements based on property ownership, the constitution essentially disenfranchised the large body of pardos, and it also retained slavery.

Why fight for these Creole landowners, those high and mighty lords of the land who mouthed equality but whose constitution promised so little? The

## A Racial and Ethnic Road Map

The ethnic and racial composition of Latin America was complex in the nineteenth century and has become more so since then. Over the centuries, Latin America has attracted migrations of people from all over the globe, in continuous streams. Together they have created a kaleidoscope of cultures across the region.

But "ethnicity" and "race" can be difficult to define. Ethnicity and race exist in tandem with each other and together shape group and individual identities across Latin America. Yet the two terms have no fixed usage in either scholarly or daily life, and are often used interchangeably. Popularly, ethnicity is often used to refer to cultural differences, while race often refers to physical features. In Latin America and until recently among scholars of the region, "ethnicity" was often used to refer to indigenous people, who were defined by their customs, religion, and place of origin. Race often referred to Afro-descendant people, and frequently was based on a combination of ancestry, physical traits, and status. More recently, scholars have discussed "ethnicity, which may include the concept of race, as a social construct or classification system that is created by people with unequal levels of power." Indeed some now use the term "ethnoracial" to highlight how cultural practices and beliefs are intertwined with ancestry, physical traits, and status (Telles 29–31).

Regardless, social identity—how others identify people and how they define themselves—is made up of a combination of all these factors. Moreover, while race is much more than a function of skin color, recent studies have shown that skin color is a key variable in determining difference in Latin America and "social disadvantages are correlated with successively darker skin tones" (Telles 11).

Cuban poet and nationalist José Martí once said of race in Latin America: "There are no races. There are only a number of variations in Man, with reference to customs and forms, imposed by the climatic and historical conditions under which he lives, which do not change that which is identical and essential" (Mörner 150). On one level Martí seems to be suggesting that race does not in fact exist, emphasizing the essential features common to all humans. But on another level, he is pointing out that rather than having a fixed and permanent meaning, race is a social construct—an idea—whose meaning is created out of the historical context in which people live. Races are created as a way to categorize people and, ultimately, to foster difference. Each society uses those differences in distinct ways, whether to assign explicit rights and responsibilities or in more subtle ways, though almost always as a way to justify hierarchies. The Spanish, as they built their empire in the New World, were no different, creating and categorizing different groups, from Spaniards and Creoles to Indians, blacks, and mixed races.

In the early colonial period, Spanish elites introduced a hierarchy of *castas* (castes) defined by the proportion of Spanish blood a person had. The emphasis on *limpieza de sangre,* or purity of blood, dictated that those with more Spanish blood were of higher status and thus had more rights and opportunities. Whiteness itself became a marker of high status in this caste system, while those of indigenous or African descent were arrayed toward the bottom, and had legal rights and obligations accordingly. *Mestizaje,* or the spatial, cultural, and sexual mixture of peoples leading to new and mixed cultural forms, during the colonial period soon complicated this hierarchy and society became much more fluid. The children of the union of parents of different racial categories themselves occupied a new, distinct category from their parents in this racial hierarchy, so that, for example, the children of whites and Indians were called "mestizos," those of whites and Africans were called "mulattoes," and those of Indians and Africans were called "zambos."

There were other combinations, indeed so many that this rigid lexical hierarchy quickly fell away. Reflecting the complexity wrought by mestizaje, by the 1700s Spaniards increasingly referred to *raza,* or race, rather than caste when identifying someone's ancestry. And while people still used skin color and ancestry to make racial categorizations, they also relied as much or more on social cues such as clothing and education to determine a person's race and therefore status. By the early 1800s, the newly independent nations suspended casta laws altogether (Telles 15–16).

Confounding our understanding of lexicon is that in each country, different nomenclature emerged. In Central America, whites of Spanish descent are often referred to as *ladinos;* in Peru and Bolivia, mestizos and Indians are sometimes labeled *cholos;* in Venezuela, mulattoes sometimes carry the term *pardo,* and the examples multiply if we consider the full range of Latin America, from Cuba to Chile.

Through the nineteenth and twentieth centuries, the discussion of race continued to evolve as elites tried to create unified, modern nations out of highly divided and stratified societies. By the late nineteenth century, as we will see in later chapters, the rise of scientific racism and an emphasis on whitening shaped much of the discussion of race in the region; in the early twentieth century, modernizing nation-states often transformed this into a pride in mestizaje or racial democracy. In modern Latin America, a person's race is determined as much by culture, language, habits, location, and economic situation as by skin color, and there is a great deal of fluidity within and between the categories. In the Andes, Indians who dress and act like mestizos and migrate from the highlands to work in the cities become "cholos." Light-skinned mulattoes move easily in the highest circles of society in Panama, the Dominican Republic, and Brazil, for example, and are sometimes thought of as white. While the color line in Latin America is rarely rigid, whites still prevail in the highest circles of power and wealth, an inheritance from the Spanish and Portuguese colonial past.

In the documentary *Haiti and the Dominican Republic: An Island Divided* (2011), Henry Louis Gates Jr. talks about race in the Dominican Republic with Juan Rodríguez, a Dominican anthropologist who worked at their Ministry of Culture. In this fascinating discussion, Rodríguez explains how in the Dominican Republic, no one self-identifies as black, even though 90 percent of the population is Afro-descendant. Rather, many Dominicans call themselves "Indio." Though all of the indigenous people on the island were wiped out after Conquest, the term "Indio" is used to negate their African heritage and to maintain a link with their Spanish heritage, according to Rodríguez. Only when he went to New York, claims Rodríguez, did he "learn to be black" and to feel his "roots were in Africa, not in Spain."

Edward Telles and the Project on Ethnicity and Race in Latin America (PERLA), *Pigmentocracies, Ethnicity, Race, and Color in Latin America* (Chapel Hill: University of North Carolina Press, 2014), pp. 29–31; see also Peter Wade, *Race and Ethnicity in Latin America,* 2nd ed. (Pluto Press, 2010), chapter 1; Magnus Mörner, *Race Mixture in the History of Latin America* (Boston: Little, Brown, 1967); p. 150 (quote originally published in *El Partido Liberal* [Mexico City, March 5, 1892]).

patriots, or those committed to independence, alienated many groups during the long course of the wars, and many of those groups found comfort and security in the cause of the royalists. In one sense, then, the wars were as much civil wars as revolutions, and much of the bitterness and ferocity of the fighting can be attributed to this division.

The complexity of the wars thus becomes painfully apparent. They were not simple wars of independence with sides easily chosen. Blacks, both slave and free, were slow to join with Creole elites; pardos were suspicious of Creole intentions and reluctant to make a common cause with them to champion independence. The royalists were quick to exploit these deep ethnic and social divisions in Venezuelan society. This complicated independence movement required a leader of remarkably high intelligence and ability—and it found one.

Simón Bolívar, born into a wealthy landowning Creole family on July 24, 1783, has been likened to George Washington for his role in the independence not only of his homeland, Venezuela, but also of four other Latin American nations: Colombia, Ecuador, Peru, and Bolivia. But whereas Washington shared the limelight with equally brilliant and determined cohorts such as John Adams, Thomas Jefferson, James Madison, and the other Founding Fathers, Bolívar towered above his fellows. Bolívar's comet arched alone into the darkening sky of war in 1810.

Santo Domingo gained its
independence from Spain in
1821. Occupied by Haiti in 1822,
it finally regained its independence
in 1844.

Puerto Rico–Spanish

Trinidad–British

British Guiana was founded
in 1831 by uniting Berbice,
Demerara, and Essequibo.

Surinam–Dutch

Guiana–French

The United Provinces of Central
America was dissolved by 1839

Cuba–Spanish

Belize–
British

Jamaica–
British

Mexico
City
Veracruz

Caracas

★ Bogota

★ Quito

Guayaquil

**Latin America
in 1830**

✪ Capitals

States with date of independence:

Mexico, 1821

United Provinces of Central America, 1823,
joined Mexico, 1823–1839

Haiti, 1804

Gran Colombia, 1819–1830

Peru, 1821

Bolivia, 1825

Brazil, 1822

Paraguay, 1811

Uruguay, 1828

United Provinces of La Plata, 1816

Chile, 1817

Lima

Salvador

Asunción

São
Paulo

Rio de
Janeiro

Argentine
Confederacy,
1810–1816

Santiago

Buenos
Aires

Montevideo

Patagonia

**Map 2.1** Latin America in 1830.

### What Makes a Revolutionary?

What makes a revolutionary? What passion or obsession drives men and women to challenge the traditional nature of things? To question what is accepted as right? To lay down that most precious possession of humankind—life—for a cause? For Simón Bolívar, it was not just patriotic zeal and an infatuation with the ideals of the Enlightenment. The inspiration sprang as much from his heart as his mind.

In the following passage he described how he became a revolutionary.

Listen to this: an orphan and rich at the age of sixteen, I went to Europe after having visited Mexico and Havana: it was then, in Madrid, I fell in love and married the niece of the old Marquis del Toro, Teresa Toro y Alaiza. I returned from Europe to Caracas in 1801 with my wife and I assure you that at that time my head was only filled with the mists of the most ardent love, and not with political ideas, for they had not yet touched my imagination. Then my wife died and I, desolated with that premature and unexpected loss, returned to Spain and from Madrid I went to France and then to Italy. At that time I was already taking some interest in public affairs, politics interested me. . . . I saw the coronation of Napoleon in Paris, in the last month of 1804: that . . . magnificent ceremony filled me with enthusiasm but less because of its pomp than for the sentiments of love that an immense public manifested to the French hero; that general effusion of all hearts, that free and spontaneous popular movement, stimulated by the glories, the heroic feats of Napoleon, made victorious by more than a million individuals seemed to me to be, for the one who would receive such sentiments . . . the ultimate desire to the ultimate ambition of man. . . . what seemed to me great was the universal acclaim and the interest which his person inspired. This, I confess, made me think of the slavery of my country and the glory that would benefit the one who would liberate it. . . . The death of my wife put me on the road to politics very early; it made me follow the chariot of Mars instead of following the plow of Ceres.

From Louis Peru de Lacroix, *Diario de Bucaramanga,* ed. Nicolas E. Navarro, trans. Doris M. Ladd (Caracas: Ediciones del Ministerio de Educación Nacional, Dirección de Cultura, 1949), pp. 62–65, quoted in John J. Johnson and Doris M. Ladd, eds., *Simón Bolívar and Spanish-American Independence, 1793–1830* (New York: Van Nostrand Reinhold, 1968), p. 130.

Reared in an atmosphere of privilege, wealth, and learning, Bolívar was imbued with many of the ideals of the Enlightenment, from tutors and his own wide reading. He was passionately committed to reason, freedom, and democracy, and he borrowed freely from the models of the British and American constitutional systems in elaborating his own goals for Latin America.

As a young man in 1799 Bolívar was sent to Europe to round out his education, and the long experience abroad was both devastating and inspiring. He returned to Venezuela with his young Spanish wife, whom he adored, but who died in 1803, less than a year after their marriage. The heartbroken Bolívar returned to Europe and swore never to marry again. It was a vow he kept, although he had numerous mistresses during his career as "Liberator" of Latin America.

Bolívar's intellectual and political genius was sharpened and focused in a Europe dominated by the brilliant French emperor Napoleon Bonaparte. Bolívar lived in Paris for many years, traveled often, and observed Napoleon as he conquered most of Europe.[2] When Bolívar entered the service of Venezuela in 1810 and was sent as an emissary to London to seek support for independence, one of his first acts was to persuade Francisco de Miranda, the most important precursor of Venezuelan independence and a confirmed radical, to return with him and lead the movement.

The royalists of Venezuela under the leadership of Domingo Monteverde formed a coalition of Spaniards, conservative Creoles, pardos, and blacks that overwhelmed Miranda and the patriots. Even nature seemed to oppose the patriot cause. A devastating earthquake rumbled across Venezuela from the mountains to the coast on March 26, 1812, and royalist clergy were quick to interpret the disaster as a sign from God. When Miranda signed a capitulation in July and appeared to have betrayed the cause, Bolívar had him arrested and let Miranda be taken by the Spaniards. It was the end of the First Republic in Venezuela. Bolívar fled across the border to neighboring Colombia to regroup. Yet, defeat only sharpened the Liberator's resolve.

Far to the south of Venezuela, Creoles in Argentina, Chile, and elsewhere in the Southern Cone also rose up against Spanish authority.

## THE SOUTHERN CONE MOVEMENTS

### Argentina

The Argentine independence movement played a critical role in independence struggles throughout the Southern Cone (a region comprised of Argentina, Bolivia, Chile, Paraguay, and Uruguay) and was more deeply affected by foreign conflicts than was either Mexico or Venezuela. In 1806 a British military expedition invaded the Rio de la Plata region, and on July 27 the English occupied Buenos Aires. This action was part of the greater struggle between England and Napoleonic France, and it set the stage for a brief, successful show of force by patriotic Argentine Creoles.

The Spanish viceroy and wealthy Spanish merchants fled to the interior when the English landed. Argentine Creoles, on the other hand, organized a patriot army of Creoles, blacks, mulattoes, and some Spaniards, and ousted the British in August. Another British expedition followed in early 1807, landing at Montevideo and then attacking across the estuary. It, too, was soundly defeated.

Creole pride and nationalism were boosted by the successful defense of Buenos Aires and Montevideo in 1806 and 1807. Some date the beginnings of Argentine independence to these heroic actions.

Soon after, the Creoles deposed the cowardly Spanish viceroy who had fled before the British attack. They then elevated Santiago Liniers, a hero of the defense of Buenos Aires, to lead the viceroyalty. This act definitively marked the beginning of the Argentine independence movement. Subsequently, an attempted royalist coup led by the conservative Spanish soldier-merchant Martín Alzaga failed in early 1809, further reinforcing Creole autonomy and self-confidence.

In mid-1809 the Central Junta in Spain, now attempting to govern in the name of Ferdinand VII and wage war against the French, sent another viceroy to Buenos Aires. But the momentum was clearly with the radical Creoles of Buenos Aires. In May 1810 they forced the issue of power when Buenos Aires received news that the Central Junta had collapsed and that the French were in control of Spain. Led by intellectuals such as Mariano Moreno and backed by Creole militia leaders such as Cornelio Saavedra, Creoles called a *cabildo abierto,* or open city council, to discuss and act on the future of the nation. This cabildo abierto deposed the viceroy and named a revolutionary junta to govern Argentina.

Although formal independence was not declared until six years later, the province of Buenos Aires, which considered itself the representative and leader of Argentina, decided to follow its own destiny. The new government decreed virtual free trade and opened the ports of Argentina to the world. The hallowed relationship between church and state was broken, education was secularized, a free press was encouraged, and other enlightened and liberal measures were decreed. Those who resisted the changes were crushed, some being exiled, others executed.

From 1811 to 1816 the Buenos Aires revolutionaries went through several trying stages. Three basic trends were apparent: the gradual move toward complete and official independence in 1816; the splintering of the old viceroyalty of La Plata into the independent countries of Uruguay, Paraguay, and Bolivia; and the growing rivalry between the city of Buenos Aires and the interior provinces of Argentina, which bequeathed major problems of nation-building to Argentina in the nineteenth century.

The struggle between Buenos Aires and the interior provinces of Salta, Tucumán, and Mendoza had many facets. Basically, the interior provinces did not share the worldview of the *porteños,* or citizens of the port city of Buenos Aires, who so dominated the affairs of the new nation. Porteños looked overseas for their prosperity. They thrived on free trade that included the export of hides, tallow, and other beef products and on the import of goods from Europe, principally England, in the post-1810 period. Trade gave life and great wealth to Buenos Aires, and porteños felt that they ruled Argentina.

The interior provinces, on the other hand, marched to a different beat. Traditionally they raised or manufactured simple commodities—sugar, coarse textiles, wine, furniture, draft animals, and livestock—that were marketed locally or to neighboring provinces like Upper Peru, the province that eventually emerged as modern Bolivia. Self-sufficiency marked the economic life of the interior provinces.

The stage was set for a confrontation between Buenos Aires, which wanted free trade, and the interior, which resisted it. Free trade meant the introduction of cheaper European products—such as textiles—that undermined local economies. Porteños were centralists in the main, demanding that the provinces conform to the leadership of Buenos Aires. Provincials were federalists, determined to protect their interests and power against the metropolis.

Superimposed on this rivalry was, of course, the division between patriots and royalists, each one trying to exploit the weakness of the other. Although Argentina's independence was never seriously in jeopardy after 1811, the form that it would take—geographic and political—was hotly debated and fought over for most of the independence period, and, indeed, well into the nineteenth century.

## Bolivia

Bolivia was a world apart from Buenos Aires. A country of high plateaus, magnificent snow-covered peaks, volcanoes, and steep valleys, its population of Indians was ruled over by a small Creole elite. In many respects it was a feudal society, divided between elites who possessed power, privilege, and land, and those who served the elites as servants and peasants. The elite controlled the principal sources of wealth and power, such as vast estates and the lucrative silver mines, while the Indian and mestizo population labored as peons, or peasants, in the service of the rulers. Feudal values—emphasizing the distance between elites and peasants—were not easily changed in such a rigidly organized and conservative society.

Bolivia's patriots, however, were not immune to the liberating influences of the Enlightenment and to the rhetoric of independence that inspired Creoles elsewhere in Latin America. Beginning in Chuquisaca (modern Sucre) and spreading to La Paz, a revolution led by radical Creoles and mestizos erupted in mid-1809. It called for the liberation of Bolivia from Spanish tyranny, but it failed to gain adherents among the majority of conservative Creoles, who were committed to preserving the social order (that is, their high positions in society above the Indian and mestizo masses). Several massive indigenous uprisings in the preceding half-century—notably the revolt of Túpac Amaru II in 1780—scared Creoles. The lessons of Indians and mestizos in rebellion were not lost on the elites. So this early independence movement sputtered and was crushed by royalist forces sent from Peru and Buenos Aires in 1809.

The successful patriot revolutionaries of Buenos Aires instigated the next stage of the Bolivian independence movement. Eager to inspire and control the movement throughout the former viceroyalty of La Plata, the first of several liberating expeditions was dispatched from Argentina to Bolivia in late 1810. Initially successful in defeating royalist resistance in the major cities of Bolivia, the porteños struggled to gain the support of Bolivian Creoles, who resented how the Argentines behaved like conquering overlords rather than companions in independence. The royalist army soon defeated the movement, and the Argentines pillaged and stole as they retreated from Bolivia.

Between 1813 and 1815, there were a few more efforts by Argentine patriots to liberate Bolivia from Spanish control. While each time they failed to bring independence to Bolivia, under the leadership of a brilliant Argentine soldier named José de San Martín, they were able to repel an attempted royalist invasion of Argentina.

What about the Bolivians themselves? They were caught between the invading armies from Buenos Aires and Lima, each side bent on ruling Bolivia, not the least because of the rich silver mines that each wished to control. Bolivian Creoles were in the main fearful of the radical rhetoric that accompanied the armies from Buenos Aires. Indians were promised emancipation from forced labor and from payment of tribute; in some instances, the Argentine agents promised land redistribution and other radical reforms. Therefore, ruling Bolivian Creoles tended to side with Peruvian royalists, who promised to maintain the social and economic order. For their part, radical Creoles and mestizos had continued to fight against royalist forces between 1810 and 1816. They formed guerrilla bands, or *montoneros,* and continued to plague royalists and foment social discontent until a royalist effort in 1816 finally crushed them.

## Uruguay

Uruguay, the coastal country on the north banks of the Rio de la Plata estuary, followed a road to independence closely tied to the fortunes of Argentina. Uruguay, like Bolivia, was the object of active intervention from beyond its borders as royalists, patriots—and, in the case of Uruguay, Brazilians—sought to influence its destiny.

Uruguay's proximity to Buenos Aires, right across the Rio de la Plata estuary, both stimulated and impeded its independence. Uruguay was inspired by the example of Buenos Aires but inhibited by the determination of Buenos Aires to keep Uruguay as part of the emerging Argentine nation. The situation was complicated further by the Brazilians, who wanted to incorporate the region into Brazil.

Montevideo, Uruguay's capital, was located on the coast of the Rio de la Plata estuary. It was comparatively easy to reach from Spain. Often reinforced by Spanish armies, it became a focal point of royalist resistance to the Wars of Independence in the Rio de la Plata area. Uruguayan Creoles who desired autonomy or independence for their country were often driven into temporary and rotating alliances: sometimes with the patriots of Buenos Aires to oppose the Spanish royalists of Uruguay; sometimes with the royalists to oppose the ambitious Argentines; and sometimes Uruguayan patriots were simply overwhelmed by invading Argentines, Brazilians, and royalists and forced to flee their own homeland. In this era of test and challenge, the gaucho (a cowboy of Argentina and Uruguay) chieftain José Gervasio Artigas emerged as the hero of Uruguayan independence.

Born to a well-to-do Creole family in Montevideo, Artigas took up the life of a gaucho smuggler and cattle rustler on the plains of Uruguay near the Brazilian border. Gauchos lived a semi-nomadic life of cattle droving and herding in Argentina and Uruguay. When the Spanish viceroy in Montevideo declared war on the patriots of Buenos Aires in 1811, Artigas rose to lead the Uruguayan patriots. They issued a call to arms, the "Grito de Asunción," in February 1811, and war erupted. The royalists got the upper hand, with the help of invading Brazilians, who saw a chance to expand their influence and perhaps even territory in the region. In turn, Artigas and his patriot army retreated in disgust across the Uruguay River to the province of Entre Rios.

The retreat proved to be a turning point in Uruguayan independence. This patriotic and nationalistic act symbolized the rejection of interference from abroad. The independence movement gained strength under duress, just as metal is forged by fire. The pattern of the Uruguayan independence struggle over the next few years was set: in their effort to gain control of Uruguay's destiny, Artigas and the patriots fought for Uruguay's independence while maneuvering between Argentines and Brazilians seeking to control the same, all the while fighting off the possibility of a royalist resurgence. Though Artigas was able to return to power in 1815, he was once again ousted by a Brazilian army in 1820, after which he fled to Paraguay, where he took permanent asylum and died in 1850, never to return to his beloved homeland.

Uruguay, like Bolivia, did not become independent until the 1820s, after the issue of independence was settled in Peru. After Peru was liberated, Argentina ousted its Brazilian rivals in Uruguay. This struggle finally brought Uruguayan independence, though the national boundaries between Uruguay and Brazil would not be formally established until the 1890s, after decades of skirmishes, invasions, and boundary wars.

## Paraguay

A quick glance at a map of South America shows Paraguay's isolation. Landlocked a thousand miles up the Rio de la Plata river system, it is far from the continent's centers of power and population. Paraguay's independence movement developed rapidly and successfully, so that by 1811 Paraguay was effectively free of Spanish control. In Paraguay, as in other parts of Latin America, a small group of Creole ranchers ruled over the large mass of mestizos and Indians. The agricultural economy of Paraguay produced tobacco, hides, sugar, and yerba mate, a bitter tea popular throughout South America.

Paraguayan Creoles were inspired by the events of May 1810 in Buenos Aires, which triggered crises throughout the former viceroyalty of La Plata. A cabildo abierto held in July in the capital of Asunción decided to tread the middle ground, recognizing the regency in Spain but refusing to accept any relationship with Buenos Aires other than one of "fraternity." The Argentines reacted aggressively and imprudently, dispatching an army under the command of Manuel Belgrano to bring Paraguay under control. Belgrano and his troops were trounced on the battlefield early in 1811. On May 17 Paraguay declared itself independent, and one of the most remarkable caudillos of the century rose in this dawn of the Paraguayan nation. His name was José Gaspar Rodríguez de Francia. By 1814 he was in firm control and in 1815 he had himself appointed "perpetual dictator." Perpetual he was not, but he nonetheless governed Paraguay absolutely until his death in 1840 at the age of seventy-four.

## Chile

The struggle for independence in Chile was long partly because of Chile's location. Located south of Peru—the bastion of royalist power in South America—and west of Argentina—the site of the most successful of the early independence movements on the continent—Chile became a battleground for the patriots of Argentina and the royalists of Peru. But it was neither Argentina nor Peru that triggered the Chilean thrust to independence. The crisis in Spain produced by Napoleon's invasion and the usurpation of Ferdinand set off waves of unrest in Chile.

Creoles in Chile were predisposed to think of themselves as "Chileans." They had a strong sense of identity with their land and its history. When news of the events in Spain and Argentina reached Santiago, the major actors in the independence tableau acted according to their self-interests and self-perceptions. Creoles manipulated the unsettling circumstances to their advantage and called a cabildo abierto for September 10, 1810. This cabildo abierto appointed a junta to govern while a national assembly was called.

This assembly convened in July 1811, but, in the meantime, the junta took some important actions. It organized an army and opened Chile's ports to trade with all nations—two actions difficult to interpret as anything other than steps on the road to full independence. The national assembly then turned even more radical, abolishing the Inquisition, secularizing education, and passing other measures guaranteed to antagonize Chilean royalists and conservatives.

Revolutionaries in Chile now pushed hard for a complete break with Spain. People like Bernardo O'Higgins were determined to make independence a reality. O'Higgins's military talents and patriotic sentiments marked him as the man of the hour. Born in Chile, the son of a Chilean mother and an Irish-born viceroy of Peru, Ambrosio O'Higgins, he was educated in England, where he met the most radical of the revolutionary precursors, the Venezuelan Francisco Miranda, who converted him to the cause of liberty and independence. O'Higgins returned to Chile in 1802 and in 1810 joined the revolutionary movement in Concepción. Although he paid lip service to Ferdinand VII and Spain's liberal Constitution of 1812, O'Higgins's devotion to a free and independent Chile coursed deeply through his heart and mind.

In 1813 and 1814, the viceroy in Peru, José Fernando de Abascal, dispatched royalist armies to crush the rebellion in Chile. They succeeded because the royalist counterrevolution was gaining momentum throughout Latin America after the return of Ferdinand VII to the throne in 1814, and also because the Chileans were divided. When O'Higgins and the patriot army were defeated at the Battle of Rancagua in October 1814, he fled with his troops across the Andes and eventually joined with Argentine forces led by San Martín.

Chile was drawn back again into the royalist orbit of Peru. A period of repression and terror occurred between 1814 and 1817 as the Spanish sought to extinguish the embers of revolt. Their brutality succeeded only in convincing Chileans even more firmly to forge their own destinies. But they had to await another invading army, this time the patriot army led by San Martín, which struck across the Andes from Argentina into Chile in 1817.

## Colombia and Ecuador

Far to the north of Chile and Argentina, in the viceroyalty of New Granada (comprised of Venezuela, Colombia, and Ecuador), the revolutionary movement began in Quito, the capital of Ecuador. The sequence is familiar. In response to the usurpation of the Spanish throne by Napoleon in 1808, Creoles pushed for autonomy. In Quito this occurred in 1810. A junta of Creoles overthrew Spanish authority. Their victory proved short-lived. Dozens of imprisoned Creole patriots were massacred in a violent royalist reaction in August 1810, and by 1812, the royalists had reestablished control. Quito was not freed from colonial rule until 1822, when patriot troops from Colombia intervened.

Colombia itself fought a long and bitter war before its armies helped liberate Ecuador. The revolution in Colombia broke out in 1809, and by March of 1811, Creoles had declared a republic around Bogotá, the capital. Revolutions erupted in the cities of Tunja and Cartagena as well, challenging not only the Spaniards but also the Creoles of Bogotá for leadership of the revolution. While

Bogotá sought to monopolize the independence movement, each region and major city jealously guarded its prerogatives and privileges. One revolutionary newspaper lamented that "our revolution seems more like a lawsuit over lands than a political transformation to recoup our liberties."[3] The most celebrated of the revolutionaries, Antonio Nariño, struggled to unify his fellow Colombians, but the attempt was futile. Nariño was captured and exiled to Spain in 1814. Even Bolívar, operating in Colombia in 1814 and 1815, left the continent for voluntary exile in Jamaica, disgusted with the extremely divisive Colombians. By 1816, as in Chile, royalists were once again in power, and they dealt brutally with the patriots, executing the captured leaders and exacting a vengeance that only hardened the Colombian resolve to be free.

## Peru

The most conservative of all of Spain's kingdoms in the Americas, Peru proved to be the most resistant to revolutionary sentiments. Under the capable administration of its viceroy, José Fernando de Abascal, Peru survived the crises triggered by events in Spain in 1808 with few disturbances. Most Creoles of Peru were largely satisfied with their lot and were uninterested in changing their status as rulers. Although they may have resented particular Spaniards and aspired to more self-government, they tended to side with the royalists in the preservation of order. This order was put to the test in 1814, however, when a rebellion erupted in the sierra (highlands) led by Mateo García Pumacahua, an indigenous leader and descendant of the Incas.

Pumacahua had been a leader in the royal militia who had helped quash the Túpac Amaru II rebellion in the early 1780s and later the early independence movements in Peru, which earned him the rank of colonel in the royal forces and president of the Cusco audiencia. But his dedication to the viceroy soon soured after he was pushed out of the audiencia by elites who felt it was inappropriate for an Indian to have such a high position. By 1814, Pumacahua had joined with liberal Creoles to challenge royalist control of Peru, in part because of the royalist failure to implement the Spanish Constitution of 1812 and especially its more radical reforms, including the end of Indian tribute. But Cusco's elites failed to back Pumacahua in large numbers, since many feared this army of indigenous poor led by a descendant of the Incas, especially when the rebellion became more radical and managed to win some key victories. Having little elite support, Pumacahua was captured and executed in 1815, but the episode was burned into the minds of Peruvian Creoles.[4]

Peru remained a royalist bastion until the 1820s. And it was a formidable one. Between 1810 and 1816, royalist armies from Peru were dispatched south into Chile and Bolivia and north into Ecuador to suppress the revolutions and restore royal order. To comprehend the behavior of Peruvians in this revolutionary crisis, and indeed that of all Latin Americans, one must keep in

## Race and Rebellion in the Andes

Though Pumacahua at first sought to build alliances with Cusco's liberal elites, Creole fears that the indigenous population would rebel and that "all who have property to lose," namely whites, would be robbed and killed by an "undisciplined" horde of Indians were real. In order to undercut liberal opposition, royalists turned to long-held biases among elites that portrayed Indians as untrustworthy, savagely violent, and simmering with unjust anger toward whites despite the gift of civilization that Spain had brought to the Americas. For example, the administrator of Arequipa (in Southern Peru) saw it as a race war and "exhorted his people to be thankful to their 'liberators' [the royalists who put down the rebellion] who had freed them from the threat presented by . . . thousands of Indians, mobilized with the object of removing these provinces from the rule of Ferdinand VII, best of sovereigns; then, in satisfaction of their hatred toward the other races, they would exterminate all the other non-Indians of this hemisphere. If this assertion appears exaggerated, direct your imagination towards the village of Sicuani, where the ungrateful and infamous Pumacahua developed his horrifying plans, designed to exterminate every white, beginning with those of Arequipa."

John Lynch, *The Spanish-American Revolutions: 1808–1826,* 2nd ed. (New York: Norton, 1986), p. 170.

mind that events in Spain were a constant influence on the Americas, and Spain itself was convulsed by movements as powerful as those revolutionary forces rocking its colonies across the Atlantic.

## SPAIN

The colonizer in 1810 was engaged in a rebellion of another kind: a guerrilla war to overthrow the French usurper imposed as king by Napoleon in 1808. With the legitimate king, Ferdinand VII, absent, liberals and radicals governed in his place. They called a Cortes in 1810 and eventually produced a new constitution in 1812, all the while fighting a war with the aid of an English army to free their homeland from Napoleon's invaders.

During the deliberations for the new constitution, liberals in Spain made common cause with their like-thinking brethren in the colonies. Even Creoles were invited to cross the Atlantic to participate in the Cortes. When the Constitution of 1812 was finally proclaimed, it set in motion a train of reforms that abolished the Inquisition, stripped the nobility of many of its privileges, granted freedom of the press, and decreed other reforms that almost transformed Spanish government into a constitutional republic.

Both royalists and patriots in Latin America were kept off balance by the attempted transition from absolute monarchy to liberal constitutionalism in Spain. Moreover, the new constitution was not popular in the Americas. Among other things, it allowed for only a small representation from the colonies, and many conservative Creoles found the document too liberal for their tastes. Old-line royalists such as Viceroy Abascal in Peru thought the reforms dangerous and foolhardy, although he went through the motions of implementing them to placate moderate Creoles in Peru. But the liberal reforms proved short-lived.

In 1814 a powerful coalition defeated Napoleon and restored Ferdinand VII to his throne. The latter disavowed the Constitution of 1812 and initiated a conservative restoration that included bringing his Latin American colonies to heel. With fresh, seasoned armies released by the end of the Napoleonic Wars, the royalists reasserted control over the colonies. By 1816 Spain was once again in charge of most of its American colonies, with one notable exception—Argentina. This triumph over the revolutionaries was a testament to the continued strength of conservative royalism.

## COUNTERREVOLUTION

This Spanish resurgence of arms and initiative was called the counterrevolution. In Mexico, the restoration of Ferdinand VII came at a most opportune moment for the royalist cause. After Hidalgo was executed in 1811, the revolutionary movement temporarily lost momentum until a brilliant mulatto leader emerged to take up the cause in 1812 and 1813. José María Morelos was born in a modest setting and worked as a muleteer for years before studying for the priesthood. When the revolution erupted, Morelos joined the movement and rose to prominence as a well-organized, intelligent, and temperate leader. A profound Mexican nationalist, he rallied all Mexicans to his cause, calling for equality among his countrymen. He declared in 1810 that "all the inhabitants—except Europeans—will no longer be designated as Indians, mulattoes or other castes, but all will be known as Americans."[5] He abolished slavery and Indian tribute—two institutions that perpetuated inequality in Mexico, as they did in many other emerging Latin American nations.

Morelos was avidly committed to other liberal principles as well. He abolished the compulsory church tithe, advocated the seizure of church lands, and promoted the idea that the land should belong to those who till it. Morelos's program promised a more equal and free Mexico, and the battle to achieve his promises has occupied much of modern Mexican history.

## Afro-Mexicans in the Wars of Independence

Recently scholars have begun to pay more attention to the important role of Afro-Mexicans, or Mexicans of African descent, in the country's history, including their role as leading actors in Mexico's War of Independence (1810–1821). On the basis of the genealogical records of the Church of Latter Day Saints (Mormons), scholar Theodore Vincent found that revolutionary leadership became increasingly Afro-Mexican during the course of the movement. By 1818, most of the leaders were of African descent or Afro-mestizos, Mexicans with both African and Indian backgrounds. José María Morelos and Vicente Guerrero were perhaps the most famous. Morelos succeeded Hidalgo as military leader, while Guerrero eventually became president in 1829. Leaders such as Morelos and Guerrero played down their mixed racial origins, preferring to emphasize the equality of all Mexicans and do away with the racial labels so common at the time—"mestizo," "pardo," "mulatto," and so on. This more broadly inclusive message was key to rallying the ordinary people of Mexico behind a progressive, egalitarian agenda, Vincent noted.

Theodore Vincent, *The Legacy of Vicente Guerrero, Mexico's First Black Indian President* (Gainesville: University Press of Florida, 2001).

Morelos, however, fell prey to the counterrevolution. He was unable to gain the support of Mexico's Creoles, and the royalists, reinvigorated by the return of Ferdinand, regained the upper hand in 1815. They captured and executed Morelos on December 22, 1815, and with his death the Mexican independence movement was crushed, not to rise again for several years.

To the south, Simón Bolívar and the Venezuelans continued the fight for independence. After the First Republic ended in 1812 with a royalist triumph, Bolívar fled to the city of Cartagena and took stock. There he considered the failures and triumphs of the movement, the strengths and weaknesses of its principles measured against reality. He summed up his feelings and conclusions in the Cartagena Manifesto.

In this manifesto, Bolívar called for unity above all other considerations if the war for independence was to triumph. Questions of constitutionality, popular elections, and representative government had to be postponed in favor of militarily prosecuting the war. He was firmly committed to centralism, or central authority, rather than federalism, or the sharing of authority by provinces and states. Latin Americans struggled for most of the nineteenth century to reconcile their deep divisions over centralism and federalism, and Bolívar's perceptions of this future struggle between centralists and federalists proved extremely astute.

**Figure 2.1** Simón Bolívar is known as "the Liberator" of five countries: Venezuela, Colombia, Ecuador, Peru, and Bolivia. Imbued with the ideals of the Enlightenment, he was inspired as a young man and devoted his life to freeing his land from Spanish oppression. Courtesy Library of Congress.

Bolívar also argued that Venezuela was the key to patriot victory in the viceroyalty of New Granada, while northern South America was in turn the key to the rest of the continent. After issuing his Cartagena Manifesto, Bolívar resumed his military campaign. Reinvigorated by victories in Colombia, he struck back into Venezuela in 1813. In a brilliant lightning war, Bolívar defeated the royalists and paraded triumphantly into Caracas, his carriage drawn through the flower-strewn streets by young women. It was a hero's welcome that the vain Bolívar reveled in. But the festivities and flattery were short-lived.

Again, the royalists took advantage of the diversity of Venezuelan society. The patriots had not yet gained the loyalties of pardos, blacks, and members of the lower classes in general, who suspected the haughty Creoles of pursuing only their own interests. And in the plains, or *llanos*, in the south of Venezuela, a brutal and ruthless leader of the fierce *llaneros*—as the cowboys and horsemen were called—arose to fight the Creoles and their patriot cause. José Tomás Boves, a Spaniard, led a band of Indian, white, and black llaneros into the war on the royalist side and forced Bolívar and the patriots into retreat. By the time General Pablo Morillo arrived in Venezuela in early 1815 from Spain with ten thousand veterans of the Napoleonic Wars, the second Venezuelan republic had been crushed, and Bolívar again retreated into exile. By 1816 the counterrevolution was almost complete and, with the exception of Argentina, Uruguay, and Paraguay, royal power once again coursed through the Spanish empire in America. But several factors argued against the permanent success of the counterrevolution.

First, the fierceness of the wars themselves made reconciliation difficult if not impossible. Too much blood had been shed, too many people executed ruthlessly, too many hard feelings born in the struggle. Second, Creoles had tasted power, and they were unwilling to let go of their dream of self-rule and self-determination. If defeat was bitter, victory had been sweet, and they were determined to retrieve it. Finally, many of the castes in Latin American society—pardos, mulattoes, mestizos, blacks, and Indians—had heard leaders such as Bolívar and Morelos commit themselves to redemption, freedom, and equality. Soldiering in the patriot armies produced a new sense of rights and identity that empowered these individuals to claim those promises of their leaders. Yet, although the promises often ran afoul of reality, the expectation of a better, more enlightened and liberal world had been awakened.

## CONCLUSIONS AND ISSUES

The Wars of Independence opened across South America, from Venezuela in the north to Chile in the south, with a flush of enthusiasm. Declarations, manifestos, open cabildos, and other pronouncements marked this rupture from life as usual. But the struggle against the royalists was long and bloody and marked by intense passions.

When Spain was freed from Napoleonic domination in 1814, fresh Spanish armies—veterans of the wars against Napoleon—sailed for the colonies to suppress the various rebellions. Making shrewd alliances with conservative Creoles and with many castes who did not relate to the radical, Creole-led patriots, the royalists crushed the patriots from Mexico to Chile. By 1816 it seemed that the fire of the Wars of Independence had been snuffed out. Bolívar was in exile, Morelos was dead, and the patriot cause was crushed.

### Discussion Questions

In Bolívar's letter written from Jamaica in 1815, how does he justify the independence movements?

Why did some radical Creoles seek independence while conservative Creoles were slow to challenge Spain's dominance of Latin America?

What ethnic and social divisions in Latin America affected the ability of patriots to form independence movements? What were the historical roots of these divisions?

What role did Argentine patriots play in the independence movements in the Southern Cone, and how did their leadership spark new conflicts in Latin America?

How did events in Spain affect the course of the independence movements?

What was the counterrevolution, and why did it succeed, at least temporarily?

### Timeline

| | |
|---|---|
| July 24, 1783 | Simón Bolívar born |
| 1806 and 1807 | Argentine Creoles defeat British invasions |
| 1809 | Independence revolt in Bolivia (failed) |
| 1809 | Independence revolt in Colombia (failed by 1816) |
| September 10, 1810 | Cabildo abierto formed in Chile |
| 1810 | Independence revolt in Ecuador (failed by 1812) |
| 1810 | Collapse of Central Junta in Spain and creation of Cortes |
| 1812 | New liberal Spanish Constitution |
| October 1814 | Chilean patriots defeated at Battle of Rancagua |
| 1810–15 | Argentine invasions of Bolivia to gain Bolivian independence (failed) |
| February 1811 | José Gervasio Artigas uprising and the Grito de Asunción |
| July 5, 1811 | Venezuela declares independence |
| July 1812 | Royalists regain control of Venezuela |
| 1814 | Ferdinand VII restored to Spanish throne |
| 1814–15 | Indigenous revolt led by Mateo Pumacahua in Peru |
| 1816 | Argentina gains permanent independence |
| 1816 | Spain regains control of most of Latin America |
| 1820 | Artigas forced into exile |

## Keywords

cabildo abierto
Cartagena Manifesto
Central Junta
cholo
counterrevolution
free trade
gaucho
Grito de Asunción
Jamaica Letter

llaneros
mestizo
mulatto
pardo
patriots
royalists
Southern Cone
zambo

# The Independence Movements

## On to Victory

### The Wars of Independence

The Wars of Independence cut across all sectors of society, from the poorest Indians to the richest Creoles, from bishops to humble parish priests. In this letter, written in late 1821, José Faustino Pérez, a Creole priest in the parish of Concepción in the interior highlands province of Jauja in Peru, describes his role in Peru's War of Independence. By that time, the war was forcing all citizens to take sides, often with dire consequences for those who chose incorrectly. Note how members of the clergy were intimately involved in secular conflicts.

> I, Don Faustino Pérez, priest of Concepción in the province of Jauja, appear before you gentlemen with respect and have this to say: from the first moment when my soul learned of the education given to me by my parents, I felt an inclination to embrace and protect those natural rights given to me. Yet, having raised my enthusiasm, I was never able to display it until the struggle for liberty forced me to shake loose from the yoke of oppression and tyranny. When the troops of Marshall Juan Antonio Alvarez de Arenales entered the Province of Jauja, I, filled with joy, called together my congregation and preached to them about the goals of this courageous general. From here on the town of Concepción—which decided in favor of our sacred cause—has suffered from the dangers and invasions which the invader enemy has committed on numerous occasions.
>
> My heart not satisfied with these operations, I have also contributed money and seed from my first fruits to maintain the patriot troops while they were in our province. . . . This conduct of mine, inspired by both religion and nature, has been judged criminal by the Chiefs of the King's Armies, and so I have been persecuted and stripped of all my possessions, and have fled on numerous occasions, until this latest one which finds me in the Capital [Lima]. And my family also has

suffered on account of their patriotic acts. . . . I have completed all the obligations of a good man, and true priest, not only in forming Christians, but also in making free citizens.[1]

## AWAKENING OF WORLD INTEREST

As the nineteenth century progressed, some parts of Latin America became closely linked to affairs in other parts of the world, principally in Europe and the United States. By the twentieth century, the affairs of most Latin American nations had become inextricably bound to the ebb and flow of events abroad. But, in 1810, most Europeans and North Americans still knew very little about Latin America. It was a world hidden for three centuries behind a Spanish and Portuguese curtain of dominion and exclusion. All of this changed in the wake of the revolutions.

The two most important nations in this awakening of interest were Great Britain and the United States. English merchants and mariners had long enjoyed profits made by trading illegally with Spain's colonies, and the Wars of Independence promised freer access to new markets. Patriots in Argentina, Chile, and other emerging nations opened their ports to free trade with the English, and the English gladly responded by sending more ships and goods and openly traded with the patriots in the Americas.

From the beginning of the Latin American struggle for independence, the United States was largely sympathetic to the patriot cause. Bolívar and his contemporaries were, after all, committed to the same republican ideals as the United States, and many Latin American patriots looked to the successful American Revolution as their model. Furthermore, many Americans viewed Spain as a degenerate European nation bound to a rigidly conservative monarchy and subservient to the Catholic Church. What better way to trumpet the virtues of the New World—filled with optimism, equality, and liberty—than to assist the Latin American patriots on their long, tortuous road to independence?

However, the United States was not an entirely free agent in its dealings with the revolutionaries. The United States, too, was a relatively new country that had to keep the powerful interests of Europe—especially those of Great Britain—in mind when formulating policy toward Latin America. In 1812 the United States and England went to war, and no clear victor had emerged by 1815. Furthermore, in 1815 Napoleon was finally defeated by England and its European allies. The members of this triumphant alliance, among them Austria, Russia, and Prussia, were very conservative and committed to monarchy. So they were predisposed to help their fellow monarch, Ferdinand VII of Spain, reestablish control over his rebellious colonies. Although the United States favored the patriot cause, it had to pursue a policy of strict neutrality in these circumstances. James Monroe,

**John Quincy Adams on Latin American Independence**

"The republican spirit of our country not only sympathizes with people struggling in a cause, so nearly if not precisely the same which was once our own, but
it is working into indignation against the relapse of Europe into the opposite
principle of monkery and despotism. And now, as at the early stage of the French
Revolution, we have ardent spirits who are for rushing into the conflict, without
looking to the consequence."

*Writings of John Quincy Adams,* ed. Worthington Chauncey Ford (New York: Macmillan,
1913–1917), vol. 6, pp. 275–76.

serving as secretary of state in 1815, wrote candidly of his bias toward the patriots: "When it is considered that the alternative is between governments, which,
in the event of their independence, would be free and friendly, and the relation
which, reasoning from the past, must be expected from them, as colonies, there
is no cause to doubt in which scale our interest lies."[2]

Diplomatic, commercial, and cultural relations between the United States
and Latin America in this early period were exploratory and uneven in part
because events moved so rapidly. Agents from both the United States and the
newly emerging republics passed back and forth, some in a formal capacity,
others in semi-official roles, as the two worlds sought to learn more about each
other and to exploit their mutual self-interests. Patriots and royalists alike
were, for example, intensely interested in buying American arms, gunpowder,
and foodstuffs such as wheat to keep their armies in the field. Meanwhile,
American merchants—from Baltimore, New York, and New England, principally—were eager to sell the products of U.S. farms and workshops in exchange
for Latin American silver and gold, always in short supply in North America.
U.S. merchants did not particularly discriminate between patriots or royalists
when it came to finding good markets.

One of the earliest U.S. agents to Latin America was Joel Roberts Poinsett,
whom President James Madison sent to Buenos Aires, Chile, and Peru in 1810.
Typically, Poinsett defended U.S. commercial interests against the English in
Buenos Aires, and he involved himself deeply in partisan politics in Chile. Others like Poinsett were dispatched to Cuba, to Mexico, and to Venezuela, while
the revolutionaries in Latin America sent such individuals as Diego de Saavedra from Buenos Aires and Telésforo de Orea from Venezuela to the United
States to buy arms, flints, and other supplies to further the patriot cause.

By 1816, however, a combination of circumstances—among them the low
fortunes of the patriot cause and the wariness of the United States with respect

to the clout of the powerful European allies of Spain—forced the United States to maintain a public stance of strict neutrality and watchful waiting.

## BOLÍVAR FREES COLOMBIA AND VENEZUELA

Before leaving his Jamaica exile to take up arms against the royalists in Venezuela, Bolívar wrote a letter of remarkable candor and penetrating insight into the nature of the Latin American people, their aspirations, and their limitations. Frustrated by factionalism among the patriots, he championed a strong central government capable of dealing with crises. Bolívar concluded that the people were not ready for the political freedoms and the democratic, representative style of government that existed in the United States. Instead, they needed strong leadership to overcome all of the handicaps inherited from a colonial system that had deprived the Latin Americans of experience with self-government and free institutions.

In the letter, written in 1815, Bolívar stated, "Events in Tierra Firme [Venezuela and Colombia] have proved that wholly representative institutions are not suited to our character, customs and present knowledge."[3] Bolívar, the young, ardent champion of liberal, representative government deriving its sole powers from the political participation of the people, was becoming Bolívar the older, more experienced military realist, concerned with wielding power efficiently and successfully. It was an important transition that foreshadowed the Latin American dictators who would later dominate nineteenth-century governments.

In late 1815 Bolívar and his ragtag revolutionaries sailed to Haiti, where they were hosted by President Alexandre Pétion. Concerned that the fall of Napoleon and consolidation of the Holy Alliance might lead to European reconquest of the Americas, Pétion supported the cause of hemispheric independence. In exchange for Bolívar's promise to emancipate the slaves on the mainland, Pétion outfitted the revolutionaries with small boats, supplies, and arms. After two unsuccessful attempts, Bolívar finally created a beachhead in the Venezuelan llanos.

After returning to the continent in 1816, Bolívar began a five-year campaign to liberate Venezuela and Colombia. The length of this campaign spoke as much for the durability and popularity of the royalist cause as it did for the political and military maneuvering of Bolívar and his allies, like José Antonio Páez, caudillo of the llaneros and a linchpin in the liberation of Venezuela.

Three factors aided Bolívar in this grueling half-decade of war. First, he based his campaign deep in the heart of Venezuela's plains, guarded by vast malarial rivers and wide spaces, far from the centers of royalist power in Caracas and the coastal provinces. The llanos nourished the patriots in both a

**Bolívar's "Jamaica Letter"**

In the Jamaica Letter, cited at the beginning of chapter 2, Bolívar expressed him-self candidly on the nature and form that governments should take:

> Until our compatriots acquire the political skills and virtues that distinguish our brothers to the north, entirely popular systems, far from being favorable to us, will, I greatly fear, lead to our ruin. . . . This nation would be named Colombia in fair and grateful tribute to the creator of our hemisphere. Its government might be modelled on the English, though in place of a king there would be an executive power elected for life, never hereditary, assuming that a republic is the goal. The senate or upper legislative body would be hereditary, and during times of political turmoil it would mediate between the frustrations of the people and unpopular governmental decrees. Finally, there would be a legislative body, freely elected, as unencumbered by restrictions as the English House of Commons.

David Bushnell, ed., *Simón Bolívar: El Libertador; Writings of Simón Bolívar,* trans. Frederick H. Fornoff (Oxford: Oxford University Press, 2003), pp. 23, 26.

physical and spiritual sense, vast herds of cattle providing for the former and the sanctuary and safety of the llanos providing the latter. Second, professional English and Irish soldiers, casting about for employment after the end of the Napoleonic Wars, found their way into Bolívar's army, and these legionnaires added a constancy and experience that helped sustain the army. Third, Bolí-var's genius and charisma held together and inspired a situation of incredible complexity that called for consummate tact in some instances and ruthless discipline in others.

By 1819, and still unable to expel the royalists from Venezuela, Bolívar fash-ioned a new strategy. He struck audaciously across the Andes into Colombia. The results were spectacular: by boldly switching the main theater of campaign, he surprised the Spaniards in Bogotá. This lightning campaign led to the libera-tion of Colombia. His army defeated the royalists at the Battle of Boyacá on August 7, 1819, and three days later Bolívar entered Bogotá. The viceroy fled and Colombia was free. With this newfound base of independent support, for the next two years Bolívar maneuvered to oust the royalists from Venezuela. He finally accomplished this during a successful campaign at the Battle of Cara-bobo on June 24, 1821. Spanish power was now broken across all of northern South America. Venezuela and Colombia were declared independent as one nation, Gran Colombia, by the Congress of Angostura in 1819. Two years later, a congress met at Cúcuta and wrote a constitution to govern the new nation. The new president of Gran Colombia was, naturally enough, Simón Bolívar.

The constitution was a mixture of liberal and conservative sentiment typical of national charters being written by newly independent nations throughout

**Figure 3.1** Reprint of a painting by Venezuelan artist Martín Tovar y Tovar depicting the signing of the Venezuelan Act of Independence, with Francisco de Miranda making a speech. Courtesy Library of Congress.

Latin America. It abolished Indian tribute, guaranteed civil freedoms, and provided for the gradual abolition of slavery. But it also mandated a strong president and limited the vote to literate males who owned substantial property. Bolívar, however, did not linger to govern the new nation. He rode south to liberate Ecuador from royalist control and to incorporate it into the nation of New Granada.

In early 1821 Bolívar's brilliant lieutenant, General Antonio José de Sucre, preceded his commanding officer into Ecuador and Bolívar soon followed. Through a strategy of envelopment, they forced the royalists to yield. While Bolívar battled through the royalist strongholds of Pasto and Popayán in southern Colombia, Sucre struck at Quito. Their campaign culminated on the slopes of the extinct volcano of Pichincha, which overlooks Quito. There, on May 24, 1822, Sucre defeated the royalists and freed Ecuador. Bolívar proceeded to the coastal city of Guayaquil to meet San Martín, who had sailed up from his campaigns in Peru.

## COMPLETION OF RIO DE LA PLATA'S INDEPENDENCE

As Bolívar had been fighting to defeat the royalists in northern South America, José de San Martín had been busy building patriot support and strategy in the south. His strategy was simple. From the province of Mendoza in western Argentina, he built his forces and prepared for a secret crossing of the high Andes into Chile to take the royalists by surprise. He knew that Peru was the center of Spanish control in South America, with royalists able to sustain their power using the profits from the silver mines. For this reason, no frontal assault on Lima or the mining district in Bolivia would ever succeed. By the same token, Spanish power had to be destroyed in Peru, or else the other revolutions would never be safe.

San Martín's plan was to hit at the heart of Spanish support through a different path. He planned to capture Chile by surprise and then send an amphibious expedition to blockade Lima. In the meantime, led by Buenos Aires, elites formally and finally declared Argentina independent on July 9, 1816. Their first constitution, ratified in 1819, provided for a strong central government and favored Buenos Aires at the expense of the provinces. While Argentina's struggle to retain some of its distant provinces, such as Uruguay, continued, independence for the country was nevertheless settled.

## SAN MARTÍN, O'HIGGINS, AND THE LIBERATION OF CHILE

San Martín knew that his invasion force was extremely vulnerable while crossing the Andes. All the passes were high in the Andes and completely snowbound except during the middle of the summer, which south of the equator is in January. Even a small defending force could annihilate his troops. His only hope was to keep the exact timing and location of his attack from the Spanish. San Martín managed to fashion an army of five thousand, mostly Argentines and Chileans, including black slaves who were offered their freedom in return for service in the cause of Latin American liberty, a promise that San Martín kept.

While building his "Army of the Andes," San Martín was joined by the Chilean independence fighter Bernardo O'Higgins, who had fled to Argentina after a crushing defeat by royalist forces at the Battle of Rancagua in 1814. In early 1817, San Martín and his forces crossed the high, freezing passes at several different points to confuse the royalists. The ensuing campaign proved the genius of San Martín as an organizer and soldier. Exact timing and attention to detail brought his army into Chile with surprise and coordination, while his strict discipline and the devotion of his soldiers kept order and enthusiasm high. With Chileans fighting alongside him, San Martín defeated the royalists at the Battle of Chacabuco and rode triumphantly into the capital city of Santiago in February 1817. The royalists rallied in southern Chile, and the campaign continued until April 1818, when another victory on the Plains of Maipo near Santiago finally freed Chile. Leaving O'Higgins to take the glory and be named supreme dictator of Chile, San Martín next turned to Peru.

**Figure 3.2** An 1821 painting of General José de San Martín in full military dress, done by Afro-Peruvian portraitist José Gil de Castro, who himself enlisted for a time in San Martín's Army of the Andes. Courtesy Bastique/Flickr.

## FORTRESS PERU: THE LAST ROYALIST BASTION

Peru's Creole elite, which held the keys to revolution and independence, were a fickle lot. Not wishing to give up power in any way, they flocked indecisively between royalists and patriots, searching for a guarantee to their future. San Martín turned to this politically charged situation in Peru in August 1820 at the head of a large expeditionary force of Chileans and Argentines. They traveled on ships of the Chilean fleet commanded by a former English naval officer, Thomas Cochrane.

Successful warfare along the west coast of South America demanded control of the sea. Cochrane and other English and American officers and sailors provided the backbone of the expeditionary force. It enabled San Martín to transport his army to the Peruvian coast in 1820 and begin his campaign to liberate Peru.

---

### San Martín

Commander William Bowles described his friend San Martín as "tall, strongly formed, with a dark complexion and marked countenance. He is perfectly well bred . . . simple and abstemious." Bowles further noted that "he was liberal in his instincts, knowledgeable and widely read, with a fanatical devotion to work, yet without personal ambition or acquisitiveness."

Bowles to Croker, February 14, 1818, in Gerald S. Graham and R. A. Humphreys, eds., *The Navy and South America, 1807–1823: Correspondence of the Commanders-in-Chief on the South American Station* (London, 1962), p. 227, quoted in John Lynch, *The Spanish-American Revolutions: 1808–1826,* 2nd ed. (New York: Norton, 1986), p. 139.

---

Cochrane wanted to attack Callao and Lima and deal the royalist army a decisive blow. San Martín, by contrast, wanted to gradually attract Peruvian Creoles to the cause of independence. He was aided when in 1820, Ferdinand VII was forced to accept the liberal 1812 Constitution, leading conservative Creoles in Lima to turn to independence as a conservative cause. By 1821 San Martín appeared to be successful, winning the allegiance of many Peruvians. The Spanish, nonetheless, proved intransigent, unwilling to bargain even when San Martín offered to place a prince of Spain at the head of Peru, keeping it a monarchy. San Martín was a monarchist, having viewed the chaos caused by attempts at broadly representative government, but he was totally committed to independence. Faced with growing patriot support for San Martín and blockaded at sea by Cochrane's forces, the viceroy of Peru, José de la Serna, evacuated Lima.

San Martín entered Lima in early July and proclaimed Peru's independence on July 28. However, independence was not yet won. The royalist troops still numbered nearly seventeen thousand and controlled the silver-mining district. Although they were harassed in the highlands by bands of montoneros, they had not been defeated on the battlefield. With his support falling away and factionalism once again on the rise for various reasons, San Martín sailed up to Guayaquil in 1822 to meet with Bolívar. The two greatest Latin American liberators met in July. For Bolívar, it was a triumphant encounter, fresh as he was from victory. For San Martín, it was the bittersweet end of a long campaign that had begun in 1814 when he was named general of the Argentine armies. After their meeting, San Martín withdrew from the field and abdicated leadership to Bolívar. But between 1814 and 1822, the brilliant Argentine soldier had matched Bolívar's record with campaigns and victories in Argentina, Chile, and Peru that were no less grand and enduring in the minds and hearts of those people. Martín went into exile in Europe and he died in 1850 without ever returning to the continent that he had helped liberate.

Why did San Martín bow out? We will never know for certain, but historians generally agree that San Martín recognized the futility of competing with the charismatic Bolívar. There were other equally compelling reasons. Bolívar would not tolerate monarchy in Latin America, and San Martín could not reverse that deeply ingrained commitment in the Liberator. Bolívar was at the height of his powers, having just freed Ecuador; San Martín had just left a quarreling, faction-ridden Peru with little hope of enforcing order on the nation. San Martín suffered from an obscure illness and had become addicted to narcotics to relieve the pain. Without aid from Bolívar, his cause was probably lost. Nevertheless, San Martín, "the Protector of Peru," remains revered by millions of Latin Americans today who continue to recognize his bold actions and achievements in pursuit of Latin American independence.

## MEXICO: MARCHING TO DIFFERENT DRUMMERS

While Bolívar, San Martín, and their lieutenants completed their pincer movement on royalist Peru, Mexico was marching on the road to independence at its own pace. As frequently happened during the Wars of Independence, foreign events triggered changes in the Americas that proved lasting. In this case, political changes in Spain set off a reaction in Mexico that finally culminated in its independence. Ironically, the leaders of Mexican independence were conservative Creoles—most unlikely revolutionaries. But the old adage that reminds us that politics makes for strange bedfellows was richly borne out in the Mexican independence movement.

In 1820, liberals in Spain forced Ferdinand VII to restore the Constitution of 1812 and to call the Cortes, the Spanish parliament, into session. The Cortes attacked religious institutions, striking directly at the vested interests of the conservative Creole elite in Mexico. In the same liberal vein, enlarging the franchise, or the right to vote, struck at Creole control of political power. Other acts undermined their economic privileges. The result was predictable. As in Lima, conservative Creoles in Mexico rejected the new liberal reforms and began to look more favorably on independence.

Mexico had been generally quiet since Morelos's capture and execution in late 1815. A policy of amnesty by Spanish authorities and the tendency of Mexican Creoles to desire tranquility and order after the threat of social disorder brought by Father Hidalgo and his followers both helped keep the peace. This delicate balance was upset in 1820 with the liberal revolt in Spain. Mexican Creoles did not accept the unbridled attacks on their privileges, their power, and the church. Into the act stepped a well-born Creole, Agustín de Iturbide, an ardent Catholic and conservative who had fought against independence since 1810. Now he intended to lead the revolution against the liberals in control of Spain.

---

### His Highness, Emperor Agustín I of Mexico

"With the throne thus occupied, the congress set to work, not on the conspicuous demands of the Mexican nation but on defining proper etiquette and protocol in an obvious attempt to emulate the greatest imperial regime the world had ever known. . . . the congress refined the organizational structure of the monarchy, declaring it to be hereditary and assigning titles of nobility to his immediate family. May 19, the day of Iturbide's proclamation, was declared a national holiday, as were his birthday and the birthdays of his children.

"The greatest preparations of all were made for the official coronation ceremonies in July . . . The efforts were all based on a French model, and the congress hired a French baroness who had designed the costumes for Napoleon Bonaparte some twenty-two years before. . . . jewelry was borrowed, thrones were erected, banners and flags were hung from church towers, and teams of peasants were engaged to scour the streets. The citizenry of the capital was being prepared for the most pretentious spectacle ever to occur in Mexico City . . .

"While the outer trappings of the empire were pretentious to an absurd degree, they were not entirely without purpose and meaning. Iturbide's understanding of Mexico's past, while by no means profound, was acute enough. He realized that the entire governmental system of the colonial period had been predicated upon loyalty to the king and the crown."

Michael C. Meyer, William L. Sherman, and Susan M. Deeds, *The Course of Mexican History,* 10th ed. (New York: Oxford University Press, 2014), pp. 232–33.

---

In late 1820 Iturbide led a royalist army into the field to destroy the last vestiges of a revolutionary band led by Vicente Guerrero. This old fighter had kept the faith with Hidalgo's and Morelos's revolution. Instead of warring on Guerrero, however, Iturbide joined forces with him. He rallied other Creoles to the cause of independence for Mexico under his banner, which he called the Plan of Iguala. If Spain could not guarantee the sanctity of the church or the safety, property, privileges, and powers of the Creoles, then Mexicans would take matters into their own hands. Iturbide was the instrument of this movement that blossomed into independence.

Aimed at quelling any fears that conservatives or Creoles might have, the Plan of Iguala is often referred to as the Plan of the Three Guarantees, in this case of religion, independence, and unity. It called for the restoration of the church and all its rights and privileges, independence under a constitutional monarchy, and equal treatment of Creoles and Spaniards in the new nation. On September 28, 1821, Mexico's Creoles formally declared independence. But,

finding no suitable European prince to assume the throne of the newly independent Mexican empire, Iturbide had himself declared emperor less than a
year later. The reign of Agustín I was not, however, destined to last very long.
Iturbide was unable to cope with the problems of a newly independent nation.
Republicans in the new Congress distrusted him. Furthermore, Iturbide's
excessive spending as he acquired the trappings of monarchy was repugnant to
many.

When Iturbide suspended Congress, his irritated opponents rose in revolt,
rallied by the rising young commander of the Veracruz garrison, Antonio
López de Santa Anna. Iturbide tumbled from power in 1823, and a republican
constitution was enacted in 1824. An old revolutionary, Guadalupe Victoria,
was elected the first president of Mexico. Mexico was now an independent constitutional republic.

## CENTRAL AMERICA FOLLOWS THE LEADER

Independence came to Central America almost as an afterthought. There was
virtually no independence movement until events in Mexico in 1821 forced the
issue. Guatemala, the largest of the Central American colonies and the seat of
government for the entire isthmus, declared independence on September 15,
1821. The next year, Central American leaders joined Iturbide's new Mexican
empire as Spanish authority crumbled throughout the Americas. When the
union with Mexico failed, Guatemala withdrew, and in July 1823 the United
Provinces of Central America became independent of Mexico as well. The
United Provinces included the future nations of Guatemala, Honduras, El Salvador, Nicaragua, and Costa Rica.

The principal issues in the new Central American nation, which was destined to last only to 1838, were largely regional and local. The Creoles "came to
blows over Church-State relations, fiscal policies, office holding, economic
planning, trade policy, and general philosophy of government"—everything, it
seemed, except independence.[4] Though independence came easily, Central
America was in no way spared from the instability and conflict of the 1820s
and 1830s that afflicted most of its Latin American neighbors.

## FINAL PATRIOT VICTORY IN PERU AND BOLIVIA

When San Martín left Peru in 1822, the road to final victory was opened to
Bolívar. Yet even the imperious and commanding Liberator hesitated to take
up the challenge of Peru, where quarreling Creole factions in the north and a
strong and unbowed royalist army in the south made the road rocky and

### Bolívar's Constitution

"The Bolivian Constitution pleased no one. Sucre, the only leader who ever attempted to act under its authority, damned it roundly. Humboldt dismissed it as an inexplicable madness. Scholars have concluded that it united all the defects of all political systems. Víctor Andrés Belaúnde has observed that it took life tenure from absolutism, the demagoguery of electoral assemblies from democracy, and absolute financial centralization from unitarianism. It combined the worst of centralism with the worst of federalism. British constitutionalism was scrapped in favor of Napoleonic despotism or democratic imperialism."

John J. Johnson and Doris M. Ladd, eds., *Simón Bolívar and Spanish-American Independence: 1793–1830* (New York: Van Nostrand Reinhold, 1968), pp. 96–97.

dangerous. Bolívar traveled to Lima in September 1823, preceded by a portion of his army commanded by the ever loyal and talented General José Antonio de Sucre.

Bolívar soon accepted the title of dictator offered by a Peruvian Congress desperately in need of leadership and unity above all else. Since San Martín had declared Peru independent in 1821, some members of Peru's Creole aristocracy, like the marquis of Torre Tagle, had changed sides three times, even turning Lima over to the royalists at one point. Bolívar called Peru a "chamber of horrors" where loyalty to independence was often determined by self-interest and where today's Creole patriot was apt to metamorphose into a royalist by morning.[5] Yet his strong hand stayed the centrifugal forces long enough to free Peru by 1824.

Bolívar and Sucre had fashioned a formidable army, especially a seasoned cavalry drawn from gauchos of Argentina, *huasos* (cowboys) of Chile, and llaneros of Venezuela and Colombia. The royalists themselves were divided between those who supported the liberal Cadiz Constitution and reforms of 1820 and those who supported the absolutism of Ferdinand VII, who had been restored to full power in late 1823. The patriot army under Sucre and Bolívar met the royalists under General José de Canterac on the high plains of Junín on August 6, 1824, and the patriot cavalry carried the day. Lances and swords thrust and slashed in the cold, treacherous Battle of Junín, where not one shot was fired. The victory at Junín paved the way for one last momentous battle between royalists and patriots on the continent of South America. On December 8, 1824, Sucre's army defeated Viceroy José de la Serna's royalists at the Battle of Ayacucho. Effective Spanish power on the continent of South America was over. Peru was free.

Fresh from his victory at Ayacucho, Sucre traveled to Upper Peru to liberate the highland province, which soon emerged as the independent nation of

## Manuela Sáenz, The Liberator of the Liberator

Bolívar was accompanied in much of his work and travels in the 1820s by Manuela Sáenz, a woman deeply committed to the patriot cause. Though she was already in a marriage to a much older Englishman, she courted Bolívar instantly, and many said outrageously, when she met him. She left her husband behind and followed Bolívar to Lima and on to various military campaigns, playing a prominent social and political role along the way. Known as the Liberator of the Liberator, Sáenz was much more than Bolívar's mistress. In 1828, she saved Bolívar from an assassination plot in Bogotá, and vehemently attacked his enemies. She defended him and his faction even after his death—and paid a dear price for it. In 1833, Sáenz was exiled to the small fishing port of Paita in northern Peru, where she lived simply, selling sweets, until her death in 1856. She was criticized long after her death for her scandalous affair and for what many saw as political activities inappropriate for a woman at the time. However, in recent years, she has received a more positive reception for her actions. Countries such as Argentina and Colombia have erected monuments and museums in her honor, and in 2007, Ecuador awarded Sáenz the rank of general in its army for her military contributions to the independence movements. In 2010, her "symbolic remains" were reburied next to Bolívar's grave in Venezuela at a state ceremony attended by the presidents of both Venezuela and Ecuador.

Despite the recent revival of her memory, for more than a century after her death, stories of Sáenz were most often critical of her behavior: she was outspoken, wore men's clothing as she rode into military battle, and of course had an extramarital affair. In an essay by Peruvian writer Ricardo Palma, she is compared to Rosa Campusano, the lover of San Martín and dubbed "La Protectora." Palma used oral traditions, chronicles from the 1820s, and a good deal of imagination to write the essay. Read it for what it tells us about Sáenz and Campusano, but also about traditional views about women and femininity:

"Because I had the good fortune of knowing both Bolívar's favorite lady, and San Martín's, as well, I can establish cardinal differences between them. Physically and morally, they were opposites.

"I saw in Rosa Campusano a woman with the delicate sentiments and weaknesses proper in her sex. In Rosa's heart there was a trove of tears and tenderness, and God even allowed her to become a mother, something He denied Manuela Sáenz. Doña Manuela, in contrast, was a mistake of Nature, the spirit and ambition of a man in a woman's body. Like tough men, she couldn't cry, only get angry.

"La Protectora loved home life and the comforts of the city, while La Libertadora felt at home in the hurly-burly of a barracks or bivouac. The former never went out unless it was in a carriage, and the latter could be seen in the streets of Quito or Lima riding a stallion—astride, like a man—wearing a red military uniform with gold trim and white pants, escorted by two lancers of Bolívar's Colombian army.

"Sáenz renounced her gender, while Campusano was proud to be a woman, fussing over the fashion of her garments. Sáenz put on whatever the seamstress gave her. Doña Manuela wore only two small gold and coral earrings, while Camusano dazzled the senses with her profusion of fine jewelry. Sáenz, educated by nuns in the austerity of their convent, was a freethinker. Campusano, raised amid agitation that challenged the church, was a devout believer.

"Sáenz could control her nerves, remaining calm and energetic amid flying bullets and charging lancers, or facing bloody swords and assassins' daggers. Campusano fainted as the skirt-wearing tribe will do when frightened by the ominous hoot of an owl or the squealing escape of a little mouse.

"The one perfumed her handkerchief with the most exquisite English extracts. The other used masculine verbena water."

Ricardo Palma, *Bolivar en las tradiciones peruanas* (Madrid: Compañía Ibero-Americana de Publicaciones, 1930), pp. 115–20, taken from Sarah C. Chambers and John Charles Chasteen, eds., *Latin American Independence: An Anthology of Sources* (Indianapolis: Hackett, 2010), pp. 226–27.

Bolivia. The royalists had very little choice but to yield to the conquering patriots. A battle at Tumusla on April 1, 1825, confirmed the hopelessness of their cause. The royalists capitulated and Bolivia too was free. In July 1825 a congress convened in Chuquisaca to decide on the country's future. It formally declared independence on August 6 and named the country after the Liberator himself. Bolívar traveled to the new nation late in the year and made a triumphal procession. He then retired to Lima and drew up one of the most extraordinary documents to emerge from the revolutionary period: the Bolivian Constitution of 1826.

In that constitution Bolívar sought to reconcile his old liberal values with his instincts for order and authority, so severely tested in Peru. At the heart of the constitution was a president named for life, who controlled the army. Other features included the guarantees of civil rights; a strong, independent judiciary; and ministers responsible to the national legislature. While Bolívar had great faith in the constitution, it has been criticized over the years as an awkward, unworkable instrument, a noble effort that strove and ultimately failed to provide Bolivia with the foundations for its life as a new nation. It combined contradictory and unfamiliar elements, and faced great opposition as the various forces in the region soon began to pull apart amid factionalism and political chaos.

## BRAZIL TAKES ITS OWN PATH TO INDEPENDENCE

Brazil was a colony of Portugal rather than of Spain, a difference that charted a route to independence quite distinct from that followed by the Spanish colonies. In 1807 Napoleon's armies, already in Spain, surged across the Iberian Peninsula to Portugal, reaching the capital of Lisbon only four days after crossing the frontier with Spain. The Portuguese could not resist militarily. The French issued an ultimatum to Prince Regent Dom João to surrender, but instead the royal family and the entire Portuguese court fled by sea on ships of the English and Portuguese fleets.

The fleets ferried João and more than ten thousand courtiers, bureaucrats, officials, and family members to Brazil. Rio de Janeiro became the de facto capital of the Portuguese empire in 1808. Six years later, when the queen died, the prince became King João VI in his own right. He declared Brazil to be a kingdom equal to Portugal, rather than a colony. Brazil was thus spared the brutal warfare that was under way in Spanish America.

Along with the court had come not only equality with Portugal but also the privilege of freer trade and the rapid elevation of Rio from a provincial backwater to an imperial capital. Its new status warranted new institutions, like a botanical garden, a naval academy, a medical school, a royal museum, the nation's first newspaper, and other accouterments of civilization. João was happy in Brazil. In 1821, however, seven years after Napoleon had been forced by British, Portuguese, and Spanish troops to abandon his invasion of the Iberian peninsula, João was forced to return to Portugal to preserve his crown. He left his son Pedro as prince regent in Brazil. Soon, rising nationalism pushed Brazil toward independence.

The presence of the Portuguese court in Brazil between 1808 and 1821 had not been an entirely happy experience for the Brazilians, and even less so for the Portuguese who remained behind in Europe. Many Brazilian landowners and urban elites welcomed the monarchy, particularly the stability it brought as the rest of the Americas waged wars of independence. But with the court also came thousands of Portuguese officials who replaced many Brazilian administrators and officials. In most matters, João favored Portuguese advisors at the expense of Brazilians. And new taxes to fund the growing bureaucracy and the emerging power of Rio de Janeiro left even more Brazilians dissatisfied with the Portuguese monarch. Many Brazilians soon began to clamor for a constitutional monarchy or even a republic. Discontent welled up in scattered revolts that were put down by King João's forces. The final break with Portugal was triggered by a crisis brought on by the Portuguese Cortes.

In 1821 the Portuguese Cortes, to reestablish Portugal's primacy over Brazil, effectively returned Brazil to colonial status and ordered Prince Pedro to return to Lisbon. Brazilian Creoles, led by José Bonifácio de Andrada e Silva and by Pedro's wife, Princess Leopoldina, rejected these humiliating measures and urged Pedro to lead the independence movement in Brazil.

Pedro was already thinking along the same lines. Before João left Brazil, he counseled his son to do that very thing if Brazil decided on independence. On September 7, 1822, Pedro issued his famous "Grito de Ipiranga." Traveling by the banks of the Ipiranga River, he received news from the Portuguese Cortes once again challenging his rule. He then apparently ripped the Portuguese colors off his uniform, drew his sword, and shouted, "The hour is now! Independence or death!" before sheathing his sword and continuing his journey. Portuguese garrisons scattered throughout Brazil resisted the independence movements for a while. Lord Cochrane, the English officer who had served the Chilean and Peruvian causes of independence, led the Brazilian Navy as it fended off Portuguese counterattacks. By early 1824, after forcing the Portuguese to surrender, Brazil was in effect free.

Pedro convened a constitutional assembly in 1823 to write a charter for the new empire. Radicals used the body as a forum to denounce monarchy and to limit the emperor to the role of a figurehead. Pedro disbanded the assembly and formed a smaller one to write a constitution more to his liking, which it did in 1824. The new constitution was very conservative and provoked consternation among freedom-minded Brazilian Creoles. A republican-inspired revolt broke out again, in the northeastern state of Recife, but was crushed.

By comparison with Spanish America, Brazil had a relatively peaceful transition to independence. Pedro's presence helped set the stage for a unified and politically stable Brazil for much of the rest of the nineteenth century. Given the dismal record of chaos, caudillos, and militarism in Spanish America, it was no small or insignificant legacy to have a ready-made and generally acceptable member of a royal house on the throne of Brazil in 1822.

## U.S. RECOGNITION AND THE MONROE DOCTRINE

The halting but inexorable progress of the Wars of Independence between 1817 and 1824 naturally attracted the attention of the United States. This was the formative period in U.S.-Latin American relations, and much of the future of those relations was foreshadowed by the early intercourse between these two parts of the Americas. Although the United States and Latin America shared the bonds of geography (the Western Hemisphere) and colonial origin (descended partly from European settlers), they were strikingly dissimilar in other ways, such as ethnic makeup, political and economic institutions, and religious patterns. Much of the history of U.S.-Latin American relations reflected these dissimilarities, which were accentuated as the nineteenth century advanced.

Of the many issues between the United States and Latin America in the early period, none was more significant than that of recognition. The United States wished to encourage the twin virtues of independence and republicanism in Latin America but had to proceed deliberately and cautiously so as not to antagonize Spain.

In 1819 Spain ceded Florida to the United States according to the Adams-Onís (or Transcontinental) Treaty. The United States gave up its claims to Texas, acquired Spain's claim to the Oregon Territory north of the Forty-Second Parallel, and paid Spain $5 million as well. The treaty was not ratified until 1821. Meanwhile Spain's colonies were breaking out in rebellion. While the United States negotiated with Spain, it would have been awkward to recognize the independence of Spain's former colonies. Besides, until 1821 to 1822, independence had not been clearly won throughout Latin America.

The Wars of Independence were an ongoing process rather than an accomplished fact, and President James Monroe (1817–1825) and his secretary of state, John Quincy Adams, waited until 1822 to recognize the independence of Mexico, Gran Colombia, Peru, Chile, and Argentina. In doing so, they set a precedent of unity and solidarity with their fellow American nations.

Recognition by the United States came none too soon. Early in 1823, France, backed by a reactionary bloc of European monarchies (the Holy Alliance), marched troops into Spain to overthrow the liberals and to restore Ferdinand VII's conservative, monarchical regime. Many feared that this was the first step toward the restoration of Spain's empire in the Americas. The specter of French armies crossing the Atlantic to help Spanish royalists crush the newly independent Latin American nations was abhorrent to most Americans and unacceptable to a great many English people as well.

Late in 1823 President Monroe read a remarkable address before Congress. Although not much noticed and largely unenforceable at the time, it set the tone for U.S.-Latin American relations for the next two centuries. The British foreign secretary, George Canning, paved the way for Monroe's address by actively opposing the French effort to restore royalist power in Latin America. Canning and the British cabinet wished to preserve the independence of the new nations, whose open ports and markets welcomed English merchants and English goods. It was certainly not in the English interests to allow a restoration of Spain's monopolistic empire in the Americas, and Canning made his views known to the Americans candidly.

Russian czar Alexander I also played a role in the formation of the Monroe Doctrine. From their colony of Alaska, the Russians claimed a wide sphere of influence south into the Oregon country—a sphere that challenged U.S. claims in the same region. The establishment of Russian trading posts as far south as California especially provoked the ire of the Americans. They were dead set against a Russian czar who championed despotic monarchy instead of those principles so dear to Americans—the ideals of revolution and republicanism—and a Russian regime that threatened the more practical issues of profits and territorial security.

## Monroe Doctrine

"The American continents, by the free and independent condition which they have assumed and maintain, are henceforth not to be considered as subjects for future colonization by any European Powers" (the noncolonization principle), and "the political system of the allied powers [the Holy Alliance] is essentially different . . . from that of America. . . . We owe it, therefore, to candor and to the amicable relations existing between the United States and those powers, to declare that we should consider any attempt on their part to extend their system to any portion of this hemisphere as dangerous to our peace and safety. With the existing colonies or dependencies of any European power we have not interfered and shall not interfere. But with the Governments who have declared their independence and maintain it, and whose independence we have, on great consideration and on just principles, acknowledged, we could not view any interposition for the purpose of oppressing them, or controlling in any other manner their destiny, by any European Power in any other light than as the manifestation of an unfriendly disposition towards the United States."

Transcript of Monroe Doctrine, President Monroe's Seventh Annual Message to Congress, December 2, 1823, http://www.ourdocuments.gov/doc.php?doc = 23&page = transcript.

Buttressed by the knowledge that the British would use their navy, the greatest in the world, to oppose the French, and feeling the urgency to respond to the Russian threat, Monroe elaborated two basic principles in his address to Congress. He declared that henceforth the American continents were closed to future colonization by European powers (the noncolonization principle) and that the American continents and political systems were unique and different from the European systems. Consequently, the United States would resist any attempt by the old European monarchies (Spain, France, and Russia, for example) to enforce or expand their systems of government in the New World.

Although the doctrine was specifically written to warn off the Russians and the French, its principles became cornerstones of future U.S.-Latin American relations. The Western Hemisphere was asserted as unique, and the United States vowed to protect the hemisphere's independence and to fend off European interference. Some Latin American nations, such as Colombia and Brazil, officially endorsed the doctrine. Others were negative or coolly indifferent. The Creole elites of Buenos Aires, much under the influence of the English, and many Mexicans, who feared the territorial ambitions of their neighbor to the north, had little taste for Monroe's doctrine.

In this new era, Latin Americans, especially Simón Bolívar, took just as much initiative as President Monroe to define the international relations of the new countries. Latin Americans sought some unity even as they fought for their independence as separate nations from Spain. This unity has been labeled "pan-Americanism." Its origins lay in the Wars of Independence period and, very specifically, are associated with the vision of Simón Bolívar. In 1824 Bolívar called for a meeting of all Latin American nations to consider matters of security and possible confederation. Bolívar acted on the old proverb that "in unity there is strength," and pan-Americanism was the expression of that ideal. After two years of preparation, the delegates gathered in Panama, although Bolívar himself did not attend.

The Congress of Panama was notable for two reasons. One, it was the first of many efforts by Latin American nations to act in concert to defend their rights and to develop international mechanisms to solve common problems. Two, it failed to accomplish anything because, with the exception of Gran Colombia, no other nation ratified the treaty that emerged from the congress. One must recall that international treaties and agreements reached at such congresses and conferences ultimately must be ratified at home. In fact, not all Latin American nations had been represented at the congress, with delegations coming only from Mexico, Central America, Gran Colombia, and Peru. Although the United States was invited as well, the Americans were tardy in naming a delegation, instead arguing over the nature of the Congress of Panama and how much or how little the United States should commit to international agreements. One American delegate died en route, and the other discovered that the congress had ended before he even reached it! The Congress of Panama was also frustrated by the factionalism and jealousies that were painfully apparent to those who shared a vision of pan-Americanism with Bolívar. For over a century, it remained an ideal difficult to translate into action.

In the next chapter we will analyze the meaning of independence. Latin America strode into a new world filled with both promise and uncertainty. The promise was the chance to create new and improved ways of life as independent nations. Yet, the legacies of the colonial past were not so easily discarded, and these same nations soon struggled with the uncertainty of how to incorporate these legacies into their visions for the future.

## CONCLUSIONS AND ISSUES

The second half of the Wars of Independence occurred between 1816 and 1826. In many ways, the stage was set by the first half of the wars, from 1810 to 1816. The declarations were made then, the issues clarified, the battles joined, and the differences frozen into hatreds by the passions of war. Even though Spain temporarily prevailed again by 1815—of course with a few exceptions, Argentina the most significant—the embers of the revolutions were never doused.

From Argentina in the south and Venezuela in the north, San Martín and Bolívar led patriot armies to victory, meeting in the Ecuadorian port city of Guayaquil in 1822 to determine how to liberate the last great Spanish royalist stronghold of Peru. And in Mexico, conservative Creoles such as Iturbide persuaded old radical leaders like Guerrero to join them in the final overthrow of Spanish authority.

The United States responded to the Latin American independence movements with enthusiastic support. Recognition was one of the most effective means of support, while the Monroe Doctrine of 1823 expressed both short- and long-term goals of U.S. policy toward Latin America. The Congress of Panama of 1826 attempted to formulate a vision of pan-Americanism based on Latin American solidarity and cultural affinity.

At the end of the Wars of Independence, the patriots looked back on their recent achievements with immense pride. They had thrown off a three-hundred-year-old colonial rule and moved the countries of Mexico, Central America, and South America to independence. As they would soon learn, however, the legacy of the long colonial rule, and of the violent fifteen-year wars, was mixed.

### Discussion Questions

How did the United States view the independence movements in their early years, and what factors shaped how the U.S. interacted with the independence movements? How and why did this change by the 1820s, and what was the meaning of the Monroe Doctrine?

What type of government did Bolívar envision for post-independence Latin America and why?

What factors changed the tide of the independence movements in favor of the patriots after Bolívar returned from exile in Jamaica?

What factors made winning the struggle for independence in Peru so difficult for the patriots?

How did events in Spain and Portugal affect the independence movements?

How did the Plan of Iguala help the independence fighters build a broad coalition in favor of independence in Mexico?

How and why was Brazil's independence struggle so different from that of Spanish America?

What was pan-Americanism and why did it fail?

### Timeline

| | |
|---|---|
| 1815 | Bolívar in exile in Jamaica |
| July 9, 1816 | Argentina becomes independent |
| February 1817 | Battle of Chacabuco |
| August 7, 1819 | Battle of Boyacá |
| 1819 | Creation of Gran Colombia |
| 1820 | Ferdinand VII forced to accept liberal Constitution of 1812 |
| June 24, 1821 | Battle of Carabobo |

| July 28, 1821 | Peru declares independence |
| September 28, 1821 | Mexico becomes independent |
| July 1822 | Meeting of Bolívar and San Martín |
| September 7, 1822 | Grito de Ipiranga |
| 1822–23 | Reign of Emperor Agustín I in Mexico |
| 1823 | Ferdinand VII restored to full power |
| 1823 | Monroe Doctrine |
| December 8, 1824 | Battle of Ayacucho |
| August 6, 1825 | Bolivia becomes independent |
| 1826 | Congress of Panama |

## Keywords

Adams-Onís Treaty
Army of the Andes
Battle of Ayacucho
Bolivian Constitution of 1826
Boyacá
Congress of Angostura

Congress of Panama
Grito de Ipiranga
Jamaica Letter
Monroe Doctrine
Plan of Iguala

# The Aftermath of Independence

## William Tudor and Simón Bolívar

In 1824, William Tudor, a New England writer, was sent as the first U.S. consul to Peru, then still fighting to establish its independence from Spain. Tudor met all the principals in Peru's war for independence, including Simón Bolívar, whom he observed closely for a number of years. This was at the dawn of the long, and continuing, close relationship between the United States and the other nations in the Western Hemisphere. Tudor saw Bolívar as a tyrant and dictator rather than a democrat and republican. Read his description to see early U.S. stereotypes about Latin America. Americans have long seen Latin America as an area of weak democratic traditions and rife militarism, which this description shows is a view dating from the time of the great Liberator, Simón Bolívar.

> It is not without the most painful feelings, that I have come to the conclusions explained in this letter. I have believed Gen. Bolívar, animated by the most pure & lofty ambition, & that notwithstanding some defects of private character, & personal traits & habits wholly dissimilar, that he had taken a model [George Washington] in view, of which we are so proud, & the world so admiring. Nor am I ashamed of my credulity; the fame within his reach was so glorious, that I could never believe any man would descend from that lofty eminence where posterity would have recognized him, to confound himself with the ignoble herd of ambitious, usurping, military chieftains. . . .
>
> This unfortunate state of things has partly been brought on by the base & excessive adulation that he has admitted, until it has become necessary to him. There is no individual among those about him, who dares tell an unpleasant truth, & at the slightest opposition he gives way to an unrestrained violence. At the present moment when they are in such distress for money, the only public work that is going

on, is an equestrian statue of himself. . . . A great number of gold medals have been distributed with the arms of Peru on one side, & his bust on the other.[1]

As we return to our historical narrative, one of the most intriguing questions in modern Latin American history surfaces: what were the consequences of the Wars of Independence? Bolívar, San Martín, Hidalgo, O'Higgins, Páez, Morelos, and others certainly transformed the political landscape. But what else had changed?

Some historians claim that the wars wrought profound changes, whereas others deny that anything significant changed. For the latter group, and as an old Mexican adage claimed, after fifteen years of war and revolution, it was the same tired mule with a different rider. Instead of Spaniards, the Creoles were now in control. Little else changed because Indians were still exploited, women were still unequal, and the wealth was still in the hands of a powerful white elite.

In fact, much had changed. At the very least, the Wars of Independence destroyed many old relationships, institutions, and traditions. This cleared the way for changes and experimentation with new institutions and ways, including the following:

Democratic constitutions replaced the inherited Spanish monarchy.

Great Britain took Spain's place as the dominant foreign economic influence.

Caudillos, often coming to power by force, replaced bureaucrats sent from Spain to govern.

Slaves were often freed or put on the road to freedom.

These changes did not take place overnight. As many historians now argue, nineteenth-century phenomena like the shift to a capitalist economy, the emergence of republican ideas, and even new opportunities for long-oppressed groups like mestizos and women had their origins in the rise of the Enlightenment beginning in the mid to late 1700s. But the Wars of Independence unleashed new forces that accelerated these changes, ultimately altering the political and social landscape and transforming the region in the nineteenth and early twentieth centuries.

## NEW FORMS OF LEGITIMACY

Among the most obvious results of the wars was the exchange of rule by Spain for self-government. Before, power flowed from the Spanish monarchy and the divine right it had to lead its colonies. After the wars, power flowed from another source: the constitutions created in each new country. This is not a subtle or merely legalistic distinction. It meant that if new governments wanted to be effective and legitimate, they had to cultivate new political loyalties that replaced the obedient loyalty of subjects to the monarchy with that of citizens to a constitutionally derived state, a concept known as popular sovereignty. The king was the source of legitimacy in the old system. People believed in and obeyed the monarchy. When this was removed, a new source of legitimacy had to be created to validate the lawfulness of the new nation-states. In almost all instances, constitutions replaced the monarchy, but the people neither automatically trusted nor gave their loyalty to constitutions as they had trusted and given their loyalty to the old monarchy. Moreover, elites needed the support of the masses but at the same time did not trust them to be responsible citizens and voters of these new nation-states. Some places, such as Mexico City in the late 1820s, briefly experimented with mass political participation, but political radicalism—for example, the 1828 Parián riot in Mexico City, where a group of about five thousand lower-class residents looted some luxury shops in the city center after a number of days of political protests against the country's president—and the elite's inability to control electoral outcomes led these places to just as quickly abandon it in favor of elite-controlled politics.[2]

Constitutions were, after all, instruments made by humans, perishable and changeable like everything else made by humans. Monarchies were thought to be sanctioned by God and were reinforced by the custom of centuries and by the habit of obedience. Constitutions could be and were altered and replaced with alarming rapidity as competing elites fought for control of the emerging nations, with countries such as Ecuador, Bolivia, Peru, and Colombia cycling through more than seven constitutions each in the nineteenth century. The presidency changed hands often, usually before the president had served his full term in office. This contributed to a rather bewildering political scene in the years from 1820 to midcentury.

Little stability in government was apparent, prompting Bolívar to throw his hands up in disgust and claim that chaos prevailed because the good leaders had disappeared and the bad had multiplied. Into this vacuum of political legitimacy moved leaders who ruled more by force than by law. The militarism that consequently came to characterize Latin America after the wars was one of the most enduring legacies of the era. A region torn apart by wars for more than fifteen years ultimately learned to depend upon the power of the sword for order and authority in times of great turmoil. From Bernardo O'Higgins in Chile to Agustín de Iturbide in Mexico, the man on horseback emerged as the hero, the winner of victories on the battlefield, the writer of constitutions, and the guarantor of peace and tranquillity. He could be a Creole, such as Simón Bolívar, or a mestizo, such as Andrés Santa Cruz of Bolivia. As the new nations emerged, it was this militarism that came to dominate politics for the next three decades.

<hr />

**Competing Political Systems**

Some have speculated that constitutional democracy as it was developing in North America was not workable in Latin America. They argue that the ancient habits of authoritarianism and centralism inherited from Spain could not be supplanted easily by democracy and federalism—principles that the new Latin American constitutions generally embodied. In practice, Latin Americans were more disposed by habit and history to seek strong leaders and to govern their new nations with a strong hand from the countries' capitals. In the wake of independence, the conflict between liberal democracy, characterized by decentralized, or federal, governments, and Hispanic authoritarianism, with strong central states, should be considered in accounts of the political instability that followed the wars.

<hr />

## ECONOMIC INDEPENDENCE

The Wars of Independence exacted an enormous economic toll on the countries of Latin America, destroying mines, plantations, and communities with violence, looting, and devastation. The high cost in human lives in areas with heavy fighting—for example, in central Mexico or in Venezuela—decimated communities and workforces. Moreover, many wealthy people abandoned rural areas in favor of the relative safety of the cities or, in the case of peninsulares, of Spain. But military victory and political independence brought new opportunities as well, including the opening of ports to foreign trade. As Spanish power and influence receded, and peninsulares fled the region, taking their wealth with them, foreigners stepped into the void. Englishmen and Americans eagerly pushed into the ports and provinces of Latin America, bringing with them merchandise to be peddled and capital to be invested, while at the same time seeking the goods of Latin America, principally specie (silver and gold), but also the products of plantations and ranches, such as hides, tobacco, sugar, and coffee.

The experience of Brazil was typical. When it opened its ports to Great Britain—Portugal's historic ally and recent savior of the monarchy—trade flourished. Between 1806 and 1818, the annual value of English goods imported into Brazil rose from £1,000 to over £3 million, a spectacular increase. English merchants were given preferential treatment, and imports soared. One observer in Rio de Janeiro claimed that more English goods were available in the crowded marketplace of Rio than in London's Cheapside markets. Similar increases occurred in other areas; English imports in Chile jumped from

**Figure 4.1** Goods arriving at Chile's largest and bustling port, Valparaíso, in 1914. Courtesy Library of Congress.

£37,000 in 1817 to £400,000 in 1822, and English imports to Mexico grew from £21,000 in 1819 to over £1 million in 1825.

The leaders of the new nations sought to advance their economies and recover from the wars by attracting capital, new technology, and skilled European labor. Although few of these goals were accomplished in the first half of the nineteenth century, the phenomenal expansion of the English merchant communities in Latin America laid the foundation for a more intense period of foreign investment and influence in the second half of the century.

By the early 1820s English merchants throughout Latin America had glutted the market. In Buenos Aires, where over three thousand British lived, the saturated market and political anarchy of the years 1819 to 1820 left over £1 million worth of English products piled up in the warehouses of Buenos Aires. In Chile, many English merchants living sumptuous lives in Santiago were forced to move to the port of Valparaíso as shrinking profits reflected the glutted market. The limited Latin American markets could absorb just so much English hardware and textiles. Not only did this mean a glut, but the influx of

European goods also drove domestic producers out of business as commercial opportunities were snapped up by imports.

The early and decidedly impressive English presence in the new countries was not limited to merchants. The British, then leading the world in the accumulation of capital, sought other outlets for their money in Latin America. One outlet was to lend money directly to the new governments, which needed to pay for the immense costs of war and to rebuild their countries in the aftermath. Loans totaling more than £20 million were made to Mexico, Gran Colombia, Peru, Chile, Argentina, and Brazil while the wars were still going on. A large percentage of these loans never reached Latin America, absorbed by commission payments and fees. For example, while the face value of the bonds sold to generate the Mexican loan was £7 million, the bonds sold for only £3,000,732, and of this amount, only £2,800,000 actually reached Mexico. Yet, the Mexicans were bound by the obligations of the contract to pay interest on the principal of £7 million. The same situation prevailed for loans made to other new countries. Latin America, fragile and war-torn, simply could not service the immense new debts, and by 1827 all of the loans were in default. A half a century elapsed before English lenders again viewed Latin America as a good investment opportunity.

This early optimism also persuaded the British to invest heavily in the mining industry of Latin America. After the devastation caused by war, Latin American leaders were desperate to restore the mines, principally silver, to their prewar production and reclaim the taxes and earnings that they made from mining production. After Spanish capital fled the country during and after the wars, leaders such as José Antonio de Sucre in Bolivia actively sought British capital and technology to help them redevelop the mining sector. The British responded with enthusiasm, establishing more than twenty mining companies to develop the languishing mines of Mexico, Peru, Bolivia, Chile, and Argentina. The Potosí, La Paz, and Peruvian Mining Association was typical. Although capitalized at £1 million, only a fraction of this ever reached Bolivia. The few British miners who actually traveled to Bolivia and Mexico under these circumstances discovered immense obstacles, principally the necessity of major work to restore the mines to production after the destructive flooding and neglect of the war years. Unable to raise the necessary capital and to introduce the newest steam technologies, and stymied by the vast distances, poor communications, and general lack of skilled labor, the English mining effort collapsed early on.

Both capital and skilled labor had fled with the Spanish after the wars, and the dreams of English speculators went aground on hard reality. The mines of Latin America, not to mention its centers of agricultural production, both such a rich source of income during the colonial period, continued to languish until well past midcentury. This financial and economic disaster fueled political instability until midcentury and proved to be one of the most difficult legacies to overcome in the nineteenth century.

## NEW WAYS AND OLD

The Wars of Independence opened the doors to many novel ways of political, social, and economic thinking, some of which directly challenged a very traditional society. For example, liberals wanted an individual's free will and "natural" rights (freedom of speech, right to compete, equality before the law) to be the primary values in society and to be guaranteed by constitutions. These new ideas were seen by conservatives and the Roman Catholic Church as a direct challenge to the conservative faith and tradition that had dominated in Latin America since the beginning of the colonial period.

The church had been allied to the Spanish monarchy for three hundred years, and Latin America's transition from colony to nationhood upset this relationship. After independence, the church persistently blocked liberal reforms that threatened to strip its wealth and power. Indeed, the church was one of the largest landowners in Latin America at independence, owning thousands—even millions, of acres—much of it left untilled or underutilized. The church owned even more property through its mortgages. Large percentages of extremely valuable urban property were dedicated to monasteries and nunneries as well.

The foundations of church authority went much deeper than political alliances and wealth, however; it had long been the arbiter of morality, the educator of children, the banker to the wealthy, and the philanthropist to the sick, the poor, and the needy. After independence, while the monarchy may have been usurped as the primary legal force in Latin America, loyalty to the church remained strong, which in the view of liberals threatened the power of the new states. Driven by Enlightenment ideals and a desire to supplant church and conservative authority, liberals promoted a secular society not only by enacting new republican constitutions that proposed a direct relationship between the state and its citizens, but also by stripping the church of its special privileges and tax exemptions. Radicals abhorred the secluded, cloistered life of monks and nuns who to their mind kept citizens mired in backwardness and ignorance. The life of contemplation seemed to represent nothing more than self-indulgence and waste. The liberal creed also sought to strip away the church's traditional role as educator, preferring a secular and public education administered by the state. Public schools would teach children the liberal doctrines of individualism and constitutionalism and the values of republicanism and free speech—all principles dear to the reformers. In effect, liberals wanted to eliminate what they considered to be the church's suffocating, hidebound ways—ways that challenged their authority and the modernization of society that they envisioned. The church and its supporters, for their part, resisted what they considered deranged and ungodly reformers who attacked the very backbone of morality and order as ordained by God. Some of the issues may seem arcane and irrelevant to us today—such as the liberals' insistence on secularizing the cemeteries and

## Liberals and Conservatives

In studying Latin America one is often faced with terms such as "conservative" and "reactionary" to describe the attitudes and actions of certain people and institutions. On the other hand, "liberals" stand in contrast to conservatives. What do these terms mean? Sometimes very few specifics are supplied about what it means to be a conservative or a liberal in the nineteenth century. The Chilean Constitution of 1833 is a near-perfect example of a conservative instrument. It is often described as authoritarian, centralist, and conservative. Its executive powers—those given to the president—were wide and sweeping, resembling in some ways the broad powers of a monarch. This was certainly conservative. The Roman Catholic Church was made the official religion, reinforcing the alliance between the church and state, another old conservative relationship. The right to vote was severely restricted to just a small percentage of Chileans—those who were literate and who owned property. Enforcing strict law and order, preserving the status quo inherited from the colonial period (including slavery and forced labor), and regulating morality were primary ends of conservatives. To be a conservative was, in many ways, to value the forces of tradition and continuity more than those that encouraged change and experimentation.

To be a liberal, by contrast, was to esteem change and to champion a number of values and goals that flew in the face of conservatism. Liberals desired to reduce the power of the Roman Catholic Church and to secularize society, especially education. Liberals wanted more freedom for more individuals, extolling the virtues of a free citizenry who fully participated in the governing of the nation. Liberals wanted free trade, as opposed to the protections for local industry and production that conservatives wanted to maintain. Liberals desired an end to all institutions, such as slavery and Indian tribute, that subordinated individuals in society.

Yet, for both sides these were not hard and fast distinctions, and very often liberal and conservative governments were indistinguishable from each other. Sometimes liberals acted in astonishingly conservative ways, and vice versa. But these definitions help us understand some of the passions that marked relations between conservatives and liberals, and help to explain why elites who acted very similarly engaged in such bitter conflicts in the nineteenth century.

requiring civil marriage ceremonies—but to Latin Americans of the early nine-teenth century, the battle lines clearly divided the forces of good and evil. The early conflicts between conservatives and liberals for control of the new states was driven in part by this disagreement about the rights and role of the church in society, and set the stage for violent confrontations between secular liberals and traditional conservatives later in the century.

These challenges to the Roman Catholic Church advanced at different rates through Latin America. In some areas, such as Brazil, the preservation of the monarchy left the privileges and power of the church basically intact. In Bolivia, on the other hand, José Antonio de Sucre systematically attacked the church in the mid-1820s in a typically reformist and liberal fashion. Sucre, like Bolívar and many other leaders, was thoroughly imbued with the secularism of the Enlightenment. He wanted to strip the wealth of the church to advance the interests of the new states. And, as seen, church resources were considerable.

Sucre went after the church in Bolivia with vigor, setting an example for other liberal leaders across Latin America. He took over collection of tithes, confiscated church-held mortgages and other income-producing activities, closed all monasteries and convents with less than twelve members, and con-fiscated the estates of the remaining monasteries and put their members on state salaries. In sum, Sucre permanently diminished the power of the church in Bolivia so that it ceased to have a major economic or political influence. By good fortune, this also spared Bolivia from the ravages of religious conflict that engulfed Mexico, Colombia, and Ecuador later in the century.[3]

## WOMEN AND FAMILY AFTER THE WARS OF INDEPENDENCE

Despite these attacks on the power and influence of the church, as well as the liberal emphasis on individualism and natural equality, ideas about women and femininity did not change greatly after the wars. Leaders such as Bolívar may have celebrated and even publicly recognized the contributions of women to the patriotic war effort, but women were still ideally expected to be pious, humble, and obedient, and to leave the work of building a new state and society to men. Once the fighting was over, women were expected to return to their homes to fulfill their natural roles as wives and mothers. In a letter to his sister, Bolívar even stated that it was "improper" for women to involve themselves in politics. Women remained legally unequal and without political rights. Yet both in idea and in practice, there were new places for women in society, some of which opened up new opportunities to them and others that merely reshaped older ideas about female subservience into a new liberal mold.

Scholars are now beginning to examine how liberals used the metaphor of the family to understand the Wars of Independence. Men like Bolívar portrayed Ferdinand VII as an irresponsible father who ruled over his colonies illegitimately. In this, the children/patriots had to defy the father figure in order to protect and defend the fledgling nations. But this left liberals in an awkward place: while they used patriarchal values and the metaphor of the family to challenge the legitimacy of the monarchy (portraying Ferdinand VII as a failed patriarch, or father figure), they in no way wanted to challenge the structure of the family itself. While they were eager to free the men of Latin America from the hold of monarchy, they were much less willing to free the women from the bounds of patriarchy. Thus women were not just told to return to their lives of domesticity and passive subordination after the wars; their inequality was written into republican law. Men, in turn, were expected to use this newfound patriarchal legitimacy to become equal, responsible, honorable citizens participating in the public life of the new republics. Politics may have changed dramatically after the wars, but patriarchy, and especially male authority over the home, did not. In fact, in places like Mexico and Brazil, married men were entitled to become legal citizens at a younger age than unmarried men. In many places, as well, no longer were wives guaranteed marital inheritance rights, as they had been during the colonial period. This ensured that, when her husband died, a woman would need to rely on another male family member, sometimes even a son, who would inherit the estate instead of her. As stated by historian Rebecca Earle, "The patriarchal family, in other words, lay at the center of the new republic, and a man's public role was modeled on his role within the family."[4]

Yet, one of the most immediate effects of war was the devastation of families and communities. The burdens of fighting fell disproportionately on men, and after the wars, there were simply more women than men in many areas. Both marriage and birthrates dropped, and the number of single women grew. Whether widowed with children or single and alone, more women now faced the need to make ends meet on their own, without either the income or protection of a partner. Many ended up in cities, working most often as domestic servants, a low-paid and highly exploitative occupation. For example, in Mexico City, almost 60 percent of employed Indian and mestiza women were domestic servants.[5] While legally women enjoyed few rights in the first half of the nineteenth century and the growing population of single women often lived in desperately poor and dangerous situations, some scholars point to a growing independence as women were forced by circumstance to take on new roles and challenges. In a world where women were so politically unequal and economically disadvantaged, we cannot call this feminism, but these new roles and habits set the stage for the much bigger changes that would come later in the century.

## NEW NATIONS, NEW RACES

From Simón Bolívar at the dawn of the nineteenth century to Brazilian writer Euclides da Cunha at its dusk, Latin Americans struggled to explain their mixed racial heritage. Like so many Latin Americans, Bolívar waxed and waned on the subject. At one moment he expressed pride in people of mixed race, but at other moments he was weighed down with shame and contempt at carrying the stigma of mixed blood himself.

In his 1819 address to the Congress of Angostura, he spoke candidly and proudly of Latin America's heritage.

> We must bear in mind that our people are neither European nor North American; they are a mixture of Africa and America rather than an emanation of Europe. . . . It is impossible to determine with any degree of accuracy to which human family we belong. The greater portion of the native Indian has been annihilated. Europeans have mixed with Americans and Africans, and Africans with Indians and Europeans. While we have all been born of the same mother, our fathers, different in origin and in blood, are foreigners, and all differ visibly as to the color of their skin, a dissimilarity which places upon us an obligation of the greatest importance.[6]

That Bolívar was dark skinned and that his great-grandmother may have been mulatta were sources of both pride and anxiety for the Liberator. Were these ennobling factors in his background? Was it good to be descended—no matter how little—from Africa? Blacks, just as surely as whites and Indians, made a deep imprint in the racial composition of many parts of Latin America. A part of Bolívar answered yes.

Yet, toward the end of his life, Bolívar spoke more as a member of the ruling Creole elite, who felt guilt, suspicion, and even fear toward the masses. In 1826 Bolívar expressed anguish and doubt about people of mixed heritage—whose origins arose from the conquest and rape of the New World—and the impact of this heritage on Latin America's ability to rule itself.

> We are very far from the wonderful times of Athens and Rome, and we must not compare ourselves in any way to anything European. The origins of our existence are most impure. All that has preceded us is enveloped in the black cloak of crime. We are the abominable offspring of those raging beasts that came to America to waste her blood and to breed with their victims before sacrificing them. Later the fruits of their unions commingled with slaves uprooted from Africa. With such physical mixtures and such elements of morale, can we possibly place laws above heroes and principles above men?[7]

In his despair of ever getting his beloved nation, which to him included all of South America, to embrace republicanism, rationalism, and the other principles of the Enlightenment that had inspired him in his early life, Bolívar turned against those who were not Creole. The Swedish historian Magnus Mörner observed: "In shocking contrast to his optimistic [pro-Indian Letter from Jamaica] of 1815 Bolívar now speaks of the 'natural enmity of the colors,' prophesying gloomily about the day 'when the people of color will rise and put an end to everything.'"[8] The remark was reminiscent of Bolívar's "plowing the seas" metaphor when, frustrated and brokenhearted near the end of his life, he summarized his efforts to transform Latin America into the vision of his youth. Like the wake of a ship, cresting, foaming, beautiful to watch but entirely ephemeral, Bolívar's efforts to bring political unity and order to Latin America also appeared to be ephemeral and short-lived, just "plowing the seas" in the memorable phrase of the Liberator.

The conflagration between the races did not occur as Bolívar had predicted. Occasional wars and insurrections caused by grievances rooted in racial inequities did flare up in the nineteenth century in scattered areas from Brazil to Mexico (the Caste War of Yucatán of the mid-nineteenth century, for instance). None, however, was massive enough to destroy the prevailing racially stratified system, itself a good deal more flexible and responsive than Bolívar realized. As Latin America steered through the political and economic instability of the age of the caudillos through midcentury, the very mixed racial nature of Latin American society tended to blur the sharp edges between the races. While race-based inequality remained very much in place, mestizos, mulattoes, and zambos all found room to maneuver in the more fluid, postindependence societies; from cowboys in Argentina, to small merchants in the Andean highlands, to landowners and politicians across the region, opportunities grew for these groups in the post-independence period. This fluidity meant that group allegiances were often determined by things other than race, such as location, vocation, or political and personal affiliations. Other than slaves in places like Brazil and Cuba, the least favored of all the various peoples in the nineteenth century were Indians.

## LIBERALISM AND THE ENDURING INDIAN NATIONS

While ideas about race remained ambivalent, the radicals and liberals who fought the wars and emerged as leaders in the 1820s and 1830s were dedicated to individualism and the proposition that all people should be free of any past restrictions or bondage that limited their ability to act independently in society, in the economy, or in politics. That meant abolishing slavery and raising indigenous people to full citizenship in the emerging nations. The long march to this ideal state of equality began during the wars, and many of the forces that pushed for a society free of racial and social barriers were set in motion by the wars themselves. But, progress toward this ideal—as elsewhere in the "enlightened" world—was nonetheless very uneven, and it often produced as much hardship and loss for its intended beneficiaries—especially indigenous people—as progress. Indeed, the liberal ideal of liberating Indians and assimilating them into mainstream culture often contributed to the destruction of Indian villages and practices.

The long-range impact of the Wars of Independence on Indians was ambivalent. They technically stood to benefit far more than any other group because the liberators—Bolívar, Sucre, Morelos, and others—elevated Indians to full citizenship within the new nations. Tribute—the tax that the Spanish crown placed only on Indians—was abolished, and Indians were promised equality before the law. The words and intentions of the heroes and leaders of the independence era are clear, powerful, and unambiguous.

Morelos proclaimed in Mexico in 1810 that from then on, "all the inhabitants except Europeans will no longer be designated as Indians, mulattos or other castes, but all will be known as Americans."[9] In Peru, the Congress of 1822 made the following exhortation and promise to the indigenous people: "Noble children of the sun, you are the first object of our concern. We recall your past sufferings, we work for your present and future happiness. You are going to be noble, educated, and owners of property."[10] Others were no less insistent in championing Indians as the great beneficiaries of liberal doctrine brought about by the Wars of Independence.

But well-meaning liberal leaders were confounded by circumstances. For a variety of reasons, Indians did not transform into the image that liberals preferred—that of independent, small farmers cultivating their own plots of land and developing good democratic and republican instincts. Some rural poor in Mexico and other areas of Latin America used the opportunity of the abandonment of large estates by the Spanish to return to communal (seen as backward by liberals, and thus an obstacle to modernization) and other farming; they took advantage of the post-independence economic decline and political disarray to "alter old roles of subordination," though not necessarily in the ways that liberals wanted, with some indigenous communities even managing to gain local autonomy.[11] Others fell prey to unscrupulous Creoles and mestizos who used legislation meant to benefit Indians and promote modernization, and instead despoiled them of their lands. The case of Gran Colombia illustrates the failure of liberal doctrine with respect to race and equality.

To enable Indians to become the small landholders that liberals envisioned, the old communal system of land tenure in which villages and groups of villages owned land together had to be ended. The concept of private ownership of village lands was foreign to most Indians, from Bolivia to Mexico, and the case was no less true in Colombia, where they had possessed *resguardos,* or communal lands, from ancient times.

In 1810, legislation in Colombia gave Indians individual property rights over their resguardos and abolished Indian tribute. The full implications of this legislation were delayed by the wars themselves, but the principle of private land-ownership was again confirmed by the Congress of Cúcuta in 1821. The resguardos were abolished, and individual families were given titles to those lands that they worked.

**Figure 4.2** On the windswept plateau (altiplano) of Bolivia, Indian women harvest potatoes as they have for hundreds of years, testimony to enduring traditions among the indigenous populations of Latin America. Courtesy Tulane University Library.

But this process ultimately backfired and Indians most often did not become small, private landowners. When stripped of the protection afforded them by the ancient system of resguardos—which had received protection from the Spanish crown—Indians became susceptible to the ambitions of whites and mestizos desiring to expand their own private landholdings. For many reasons, Indians ended up often selling their small plots of land, whether due to tax burdens, lack of access to water, or because they did not have the skills and resources to survive as small, independent agriculturalists. The same sad sequence of events further impoverished Indians across Latin America as they were cheated and despoiled of their ancient lands by the effects of liberal legislation enacted during the nineteenth century.

Even eliminating Indian tribute, a most obvious stigma of second-class citizenship, proved short-lived in portions of Latin America. In Bolivia and Peru, it was restored in the late 1820s because the new governments simply could not survive without the revenue that the tribute produced. In other places it was replaced by taxes that continued to weigh heavily on the region's poor indigenous communities.

Though there were some legal gains and the experience varied across Latin America, haciendas remained an important part of rural life in many areas, with Indian and Afro-descendant workers serving as the labor force. Slavery was abolished in most of Latin America, with Cuba and Brazil being two key exceptions. But other forms of forced labor grew, including debt peonage, which compelled workers to labor on an estate until they could pay off a debt to its owner, which was often nearly impossible. These forms of labor tied rural peasants to estate labor, frequently in the same places where they had worked before independence. Villages remained an equally important part of rural indigenous life in some areas. As a result, liberal legislation designed to create a class of small, private landholders who could help modernize the economy failed to bring about immediate change to much of Latin America.

As in other areas of the world, the ideals of liberty and equality were qualified by lingering ideas about differences between the races, classes, and sexes. In Latin America, the rhetoric and even the legislation of the Wars of Independence era promised Indians much, yet much of the indigenous population continued to live apart from the new rulers. These Creoles, but also mestizos and mulattoes who had risen to positions of prominence and power through the wars, tended to be liberal in rhetoric but conservative in practice. Indians remained, in a phrase coined during the period of Spanish rule, a "nation within the nations" and did not share in the new power structure.

## CONCLUSIONS AND ISSUES

As the Wars of Independence ended, the political changes in who ruled Latin America were the most evident. Gone were the old Portuguese and Spanish colonial empires. Mexico, the United Provinces of Central America (Honduras, Guatemala, El Salvador, Nicaragua, and Costa Rica), Gran Colombia (Venezuela, Colombia, Panama, and Ecuador), Peru, Chile, Bolivia, Argentina, Paraguay, Uruguay, and Brazil all were independent—some as constitutional republics, others as monarchies—and some were extremely short-lived. By 1831, Gran Colombia had broken up into three nations, and by 1839 the United

Provinces of Central America had also fallen apart, and the five small countries went their separate ways. Cuba and Puerto Rico remained Spanish colonies, while most of the islands of the Caribbean continued to be possessions of European nations; the Guianas in South America and British Honduras in Central America did not change hands.

With independence came new challenges and new problems. English merchants and miners brought not only new wares but also new priorities, new money, and new ideas, disrupting the old economies and traditional ways of commerce. Liberals in Latin America courted the English—who, they felt, represented progress and modernization—as they attempted to reinvent Latin American society. They freed Indians from legal bondage, attacked the church as a conservative institution equated with suffocating, reactionary Spanish rule, and attempted to put into place the high ideals of political equality and economic justice. Through it all, the political disorder and economic disruptions caused by the wars argued in favor of strong, military rulers who could enforce a semblance of order in a region often adrift in civil strife and anarchy.

## Discussion Questions

How did the basis for political legitimacy change after independence? And what were the key differences between the type of government during the colonial period and after independence?

How did elites try to rebuild the economies of Latin America immediately after independence, and what was the tie between economic conditions and political stability?

Why did liberals challenge the economic and social power of the Roman Catholic Church after independence?

What were the key differences between liberals and conservatives?

What was the impact of independence on the role of women in society?

How did the Wars of Independence affect rural land holding? How did the lives of rural peasants and Indians change after independence? How did race factor into the creation of new nations?

## Timeline

| | |
|---|---|
| 1810s–1820s | Growth of British business and investment in Latin America |
| 1819 | Bolívar addresses Congress of Angostura |
| 1820s | Attacks on power and wealth of Catholic Church in Bolivia and rest of Latin America |
| 1821 | Congress of Cúcuta |
| 1828 | Parián riot in Mexico City |
| 1831 | Dissolution of Gran Colombia |
| 1833 | Chilean Constitution of 1833 |
| 1839 | Dissolution of United Provinces of Central America |

## Keywords

centralism
communal land
conservative
constitutionalism
debt peonage
Enlightenment
federalism
individualism

liberal
militarism
Parián riot
patriarchy
popular sovereignty
Roman Catholic Church
tribute

# The Search for Political Order: 1830s–1850s

## Rosas Governs Argentina

Juan Manuel de Rosas ruled Argentina from 1829 to 1852. There is no such thing as a typical caudillo, or dictator, of Latin America in this period, when they ruled from Mexico in the north to Chile and Argentina in the far south. But Rosas showed many of the characteristics of the caudillo type.

The following two selections illustrate two of the many roles caudillos played in Latin America. The first, written by Rosas himself, shows an angry dictator using force and terror to impose his authority. The second was written by Domingo Faustino Sarmiento, one of Rosas's most eloquent critics and Argentina's greatest statesman of the mid-nineteenth century. In this passage, Sarmiento grudgingly admits Rosas's strengths, one of the principal ones being his ability to hold the country together and govern with authority.

> Señor Dorrego was shot at Navarro by the Unitarians. General Villafañe, companion of General Quiroga, was killed by the same people on his journey from Chile to Mendoza. General Latorre was put to the lance after surrender and imprisonment in Salta, without being allowed a last minute to prepare himself. The same fate befell Colonel Aguilera. General Quiroga had his throat cut on 16 February last on his return journey eighteen leagues before reaching Córdoba. Colonel José Santos Ortiz suffered the same fate, as did all sixteen of the party, the only ones to escape being a courier and an orderly who fled through the mountain fastnesses. So! Have I understood or not the true state of the country? But even this is not enough for the men of enlightenment and principles.

> No one knew more shrewdly than General Rosas the social situation of the peoples who surround him. His long tenure of government, and the sharp and penetrating intelligence with which nature has, unfortunately, endowed him and which only mean party prejudice could deny, are sufficient to make him well informed of these things . . .

Raised to command his country by a general insurrection of the masses; sustained in office by the power provided by this insurrection; master of this sector and connoisseur of its strength and instincts; conqueror, if not in battle at least by politics and achievements, of the uneducated and Europeanised part of the Argentine people; he was come to have a complete understanding of the state of society in South America and always knows exactly how to touch the right social chords and to produce the sounds which he wants.[1]

## THE BACKGROUND AND NATURE OF CAUDILLISMO

The lack of state legitimacy and strength after the Wars of Independence meant that many countries descended into decades of infighting among elites as they tried to gain and keep control of the weak nation-states. Economic disarray worsened the fighting, since states could not build militaries capable of asserting the state's will. Whether seen as a political vacuum, anarchy, or simply weakness, this lack of legitimate legal authority left the door open to a new type of leader to emerge after independence: the caudillo. Politically, the nineteenth century was the age of the caudillo, a term best translated as "Latin American dictator." Caudillos came in all shapes and sizes, ruled over small clans and vast countries, could be ruthless or civil, Creoles or mestizos. It has been said that the first great caudillo was Simón Bolívar, the model of the caudillos who emerged in the 1830s as rulers of the newly independent nations. Bolívar ruled by the force of his personality and charisma, identifying another attribute of the caudillo: *personalismo*, or "personalism," which meant finding supporters— whether in government or in business—based on personal connections rather than on legal or nationalist foundations. Furthermore, Bolívar had been a military man. Virtually all caudillos who governed to the mid-nineteenth century were, like Bolívar, veterans of the wars. They were military men (marshals, generals, or guerrilla chieftains)—what some scholars call "men on horseback" who were forged into strong leaders by the campaigns and battles of the early nineteenth century.

Even before the Spanish arrived in the New World, great numbers of Indians obeyed chiefs and leaders known as "caciques," who were similar in some ways to caudillos. During the Conquest, this tendency was reinforced by the great conquistadors themselves, who allowed these local rulers, or caciques, to continue in power in order to use their legitimacy and close personal ties to the indigenous population to establish Spanish rule. Then, during the Wars of Independence, strength of personality once more prevailed in governing. Authority issued not from legal, ethical, or moral structures, but rather from patronage, which was a particular leader's (or patrón's) ability to protect, defend, and provide for the welfare of his soldiers and followers in return for their loyalty and support.

Geography also contributed to caudillismo. Latin America was a vast, sparsely populated land, with the people separated on their ranches, farms, small towns, and hamlets by immense distances. The great haciendas and plantations were ruled by men who dispensed justice and wielded power in the time-honored tradition of the patrón. The bonds between the hacienda owners and their retainers and peasants put a premium on personal ties and loyalties. Caudillos often sprang from this hacienda environment; accustomed to personal power, they bound their peons and followers to them through ties based on fictive kinship.

The Mexican poet Octavio Paz explained the caudillo as the macho who dominates. "One word sums up the aggressiveness, insensitivity, invulnerability, and other attributes of the macho: power. It is force without the discipline of any notion of order: arbitrary power, the will without reins and without a set course. . . . The caciques, feudal lords, hacienda owners, politicians, generals, captains of industry . . . are all machos."[2]

During and after the Wars of Independence, many caudillos emerged from classes other than the old landed aristocracy. Often they were mestizos who had risen through the military ranks. The habit of command was not traditional with them, and they lacked strong political connections; they sought to affirm their newly won power and authority by distinguishing themselves from the common man. A new style emerged that took many forms. In some instances, such as in Argentina and Venezuela, brute physical power characterized the caudillos, men who dominated others by their strength and energy. Violence and terror often accompanied their rule.

To guarantee their strength and to demonstrate their power, they often sought wealth, sometimes acquiring it in subtle ways and other times simply taking it. Perhaps the most notorious examples came from the life of Juan Facundo Quiroga, a charismatic but brutal regional caudillo of Argentina. A skilled military man who defended the federalist cause against the centralizing forces from Buenos Aires, he terrorized his opponents and competitors into submitting to his will. For example, he bid a ridiculously low sum for the right to collect the tithe and dared any others to bid above him. His critics called him a barbarian, and the legacy of Quiroga and others like him endured for many decades.

Later, more discreet ways to get rich evolved, including influence peddling, monopolies on imports and manufacturing, lucrative public works contracts from the state, contraband, and land acquisition through intimidation and back channels. In the twentieth century, as will be seen below, members of the Somoza family of Nicaragua exemplified the caudillo tradition, gaining power and expanding their dictatorship at the expense of people, the state, honesty, and integrity.

Personalism and patronage thrived in the Latin American context of family loyalties. Families and dependents supported the caudillos and expected favors

### The Caudillo Phenomenon

The Peruvian historian Francisco García Calderón (1883–1953) described the cau-dillo phenomenon in rich terms that provide insight from the perspective of Peru, where caudillismo flourished to the end of the twentieth century and beyond.

"The generals [and early caudillos] imposed arbitrary limits upon the peoples: they were the creators of the history of the Americas; they impressed the crowds with pomp and pageantry, by military displays as brilliant and gaudy as the pro-cessions of the Roman Catholic Church, by uniforms, medals, and military order. They labeled themselves Regenerators, Restorers, Protectors. . . .

"The individual acquired an extraordinary prestige, as in the time of the Tuscan Renaissance, the French Terror, or the English Revolution. The rude and blood-stained hand of the caudillo forced the amorphous masses into durable molds. Ignorant soldiers ruled; the evolution of the republics was uncertain. There was no history properly because there was no continuity. There was a perpetual repe-tition caused by successive rebellions. The same men appeared with the same promises and the same methods. The political comedy repeated itself periodically: rebellion, a dictator, a program of national restoration. Anarchy and militarism universally characterized political behavior. . . . The dictators, like the kings of modern states, must defeat local challenges, in the case of the Americas, the pro-vincial generals. Men like Porfirio Díaz [Mexico], Gabriel García Moreno [Ecuador], and Antonio Guzmán Blanco [Venezuela] triumphed. Rebellion followed rebellion until the emergence of a tyrant who dominated the life of a nation for twenty or thirty years. . . .

"They represented the new mixed races, traditions, and agriculture . . . these tyrants created a kind of democracy; they often depended on the support of the people, those of mixed races, the Indians, and Afro-Americans, against the oligar-chies [prefiguring the populists of the twentieth century]. They dominated the former colonial elites, favored the mixture of the races, and liberated the slaves."

Francisco García Calderón, *Latin America: Its Rise and Progress* (New York: Charles Scribner's Sons, 1913), pp. 86–96, from E. Bradford Burns, ed., *Latin America: Conflict and Creation: A Historical Reader* (Englewood Cliffs, N.J.: Prentice Hall, 1993), pp. 64–65.

in return. For example, clients, or supporters of the patrón/caudillo expected protection, most broadly from tradition and local power, though more specifi-cally from things such as rapacious landowners, liberal tax or land policies, or military conscription. The religious duties of godfathering and godmothering (*compadrazgo*) reinforced the personality cults. Caudillos would often be god-fathers to hundreds or even thousands of children, sealing their alliances even more firmly within this religious institution.

The personality cults that developed around caudillos arose from their need to legitimize their source of power. Because they were not born with the majesty of monarchs and the rights of ancient nobilities, they sought other ways to establish their social and moral superiority, and hence their right to govern in the eyes of their followers. They glorified themselves with monuments, theatrical gestures, and extravagant uniforms, attempting to create an aura of magnificence.

In Mexico, Antonio López de Santa Anna edified himself in some of the most egregious examples of pomp and circumstance. In one instance, he had his amputated leg buried in a solemn ceremony. He created an elaborate etiquette, including yellow coaches with valets in green livery and escorts of lancers in red uniforms and plumed hats, to celebrate his person and his power.

The caudillos were not without utility and worth. They were essentially unifiers in vast regions where centrifugal forces pulled things apart after the Wars of Independence. Politically, economically, and socially, they centralized power and suppressed regional tendencies, providing a modicum of rule at a time when national states and political elites were too weak to impose their own authority.

## THE AGE OF CAUDILLOS IN THE SOUTHERN CONE

### Argentina

In 1816, Argentina declared independence. A power struggle lasted until 1829, when Juan Manuel de Rosas took control. Buenos Aires, which had served as the capital of the old viceroyalty of La Plata, attempted to unify the new nation under its leadership. In the 1820s those adhering to this point of view coalesced loosely under the title of centralists (*unitarios*).

The people of the interior of Argentina wished largely to govern themselves autonomously within a loose federation of provinces, and they evolved into the federalists (*federales*). The division between the interests of these two groups impeded Argentina's development as a nation until well into the second half of the nineteenth century, when Buenos Aires finally triumphed over the provinces.

Between 1811 and 1829 a series of presidents, triumvirates, juntas, congresses, and other political configurations confounded the attempts of Buenos Aires to impose its will absolutely. In the course of these two decades, Argentina tried unsuccessfully to keep Paraguay, Uruguay, and Upper Peru (later Bolivia) within the nation, fought a war with Brazil between 1825 and 1828, and finally bowed to the rule of Rosas.

Before Rosas, however, another man represented the modern vision of Argentina. In the early 1820s Bernardino Rivadavia's program for Argentina struck a responsive chord among many urban, modernizing elements of the

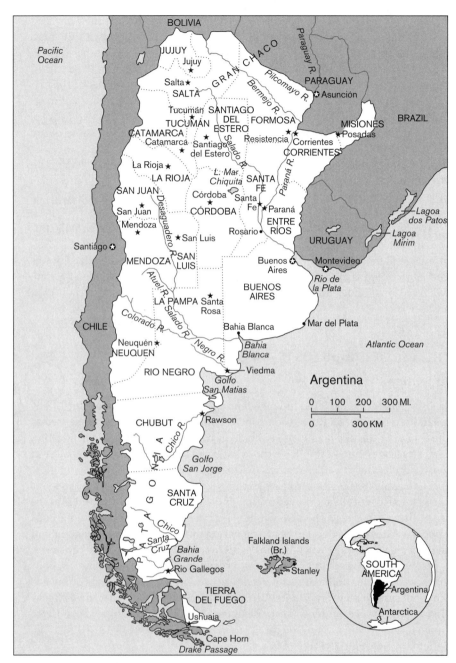

**Map 5.1** Argentina.

population, especially among the porteños, or residents of the port city of Buenos Aires, who looked beyond their shores for commerce and contacts with the countries of Europe and North America.

Rivadavia was born into a wealthy Buenos Aires family and married the daughter of the viceroy. He fought against the British attacks of 1806 and 1807 and then joined the conspirators of 1810. He served in several cabinets during the first decade of independence. Later he continued to serve in a number of capacities until the end of his political career in 1827, including serving as president in 1826 and 1827. He was, in short, one of the founders of the republic and a man of great influence during his career.

An admirer of the English and a believer in the positive influence of foreign contacts, Rivadavia encouraged free trade, foreign investment, and immigration. Irish and Basque sheepherders, English merchants, French shopkeepers, American seamen—they all arrived in considerable numbers during this period, swelling the local population and imparting a more cosmopolitan, outward-looking perspective.

Rivadavia's vision included importing the best intellectual influences from abroad and promoting Argentina's own culture. The University of Buenos Aires was founded in 1821, followed by a public library, a museum, and various other literary, scientific, and charitable societies. Rivadavia also sought to separate church from state with various measures, including the suppression of monasteries and convents. Rivadavia was a liberal and enlightened thinker, devoted to a modern vision of Argentina. He met implacable resistance from a more conservative and traditional Argentina, one embodied in the person of Juan Manuel de Rosas.

In a fashion, Rosas was the typical caudillo of the times. Although not a celebrated veteran of the Wars of Independence, such as Páez of Venezuela, Santander of Colombia, or Santa Cruz of Bolivia (seen later in this chapter), Rosas was, in every other way, a prototype for the Latin American caudillo. Rosas and Argentina can be considered as classic examples of caudillos and the lands they ruled in the nineteenth century.

Rosas was above all else a great landowner in a country where land and cattle formed the twin pillars of wealth. Large ranches and slaughterhouses dominated in the great plains, or pampas, of Argentina. Cattle flourished in this region, and hides and salted or jerked beef were the principal exports of Argentina in the first half of the nineteenth century, with much of the beef destined to feed the slaves of Brazil and Cuba. Between the 1830s and 1850s, exports of hides and salted beef tripled. Exports of tallow—a by-product of the cattle industry—increased sixfold. Wool exports from the burgeoning sheep industry jumped fivefold in the same period, attesting to an even greater growth and dependence upon the pastoral industries in Argentina. Much of the wool was destined for English carpet factories, which were one of the leading engines of

**Figure 5.1** Argentine cowboys (gauchos) on the cattle-rich pampas of their nation. Conservative in social customs and culture, they formed the backbone of support for such leading caudillos as Juan Manuel de Rosas in the first half of the nineteenth century. Gauchos were romanticized by later generations of Argentines as the soul of their nation. Courtesy Tulane University Library.

the Industrial Revolution then stimulating the production and export of many basic commodities from Latin America.

Rosas inherited several ranches and was raised on the land, growing up in the rough-and-tumble society of the gaucho. Rosas was a manager, business-man, entrepreneur, and innovator, but, ultimately, his reputation was based on his leadership of gauchos. The first troop of cavalry he raised in 1820 was made up largely of gauchos and peons who worked on Rosas's ranches. They owed him loyalty, and in return Rosas protected and rewarded them. The rela-tionship between Rosas, the paternal boss, or patrón, and his gauchos and peons, the clients, was fundamental to the way society was organized not only in Argentina but also in many other areas of nineteenth-century Latin America.

The key to Rosas's power in Argentina in the 1830s and 1840s was the struc-ture of society—the very society that Rivadavia wanted to change. Society was profoundly conservative, rooted in the countryside and dependent upon the cattle-ranching class for its prosperity. Change was suspect, especially changes coming from those seeking to centralize power in Buenos Aires. Foreigners threatened ranchers' lifestyles and, ultimately, their control over the country. The Roman Catholic Church represented stability, order, and continuity to the ranchers and thus retained a place of prominence and prestige.

As the 1820s came to an end, Rosas rose to prominence and evolved into a ruthless caudillo. He was the center of Argentina. The ideological battles

**Rosas the Caudillo**

"The relation of patron and client was the essential bond, based on a personal exchange of assets between these unequal partners. The landowner wanted labor, loyalty, and service in peace and war. The peon wanted subsistence and security. The estanciero [rancher], therefore, was a protector, the possessor of sufficient power to defend his dependents against marauding bands, recruiting sergeants, and rival hordes. He is also a provider who developed and defended local resources and could give employment, food, and shelter. Thus a patrón recruited a peonada that followed him blindly in ranching, politics, and war. These individual alliances were extended into a social pyramid as patróns in turn became clients to more powerful men until the peak of power was reached and they all became clients of a superpatron, the caudillo."

Source: John Lynch, *Argentine Caudillo: Juan Manuel de Rosas* (Wilmington, Del.: SR Books, 2001) p. 43.

between centralists and federalists faded in significance in the face of Rosas's consolidation of power. By 1835, Rosas had fought his way to the top, and he remained the supreme caudillo until he was overthrown in 1852. He divided his world between those who supported him, Rosistas, and those who did not, or anti-Rosistas, and he suppressed the opposition ruthlessly. Supporters would wear the color red to symbolize their loyalty to him and often had his picture in their homes. Terror, violent reprisals, and executions against those who opposed him were vicious; this violence reached its peak in the period 1838 to 1842. Decapitations became a ritual form of political execution perpetrated by a secret society called the *mazorca*. Rosas was challenged during his long regime, but only at the high cost of imprisonment, death, or exile for those who opposed him. He ruled with an undisputed sovereignty, well beyond the constitutional rights and guarantees envisioned by the generation of Argentines who fashioned the independence of the country.

In foreign affairs, Rosas meddled in the affairs of Uruguay and provoked crisis after crisis in the 1830s and 1840s, especially with his Brazilian neighbors. The English and the French had commercial interests in the region that were threatened by Rosas's attempt to dominate the Rio de la Plata region. In fact, the French and English between 1838 and 1848 blockaded the port of Buenos Aires several times to force Rosas to yield on a number of issues.

During Rosas's rule, the old cattle-ranching class drew its livelihood from the continued expansion of the salted beef business. But the limits of the business and eventually of Rosas's power were reached in the 1840s and 1850s. The traditional markets—the slave populations of Brazil and Cuba—were on the

### Religion and Morality under Rosas

The life of Maria Camila O'Gorman is one of the best examples of what happened to those who challenged Rosas, and of the role of social norms and values in his dictatorship. Born into a wealthy family in Buenos Aires in 1825, Camila was raised to be a cultured lady of polite Argentine society. She was even a friend of Manuela de Rosas, the caudillo's daughter. At the age of twenty-two, however, Camila fell in love with a Jesuit priest, Father Ladislao Gutiérrez, and they soon started an affair. At the time, the Jesuits were very critical of Rosas for his terror and abuses. Soon, O'Gorman and Gutiérrez ran away to the distant province of Corrientes. Rosas's opponents, men such as Domingo Faustino Sarmiento and other exiles, accused Rosas of allowing moral decay and the corruption of Argentine femininity. Rosas could not allow his political opponents to criticize him in this way, so, when O'Gorman and Gutiérrez were found, Rosas had them arrested and imprisoned. Despite pleas from many, including his own daughter, asking Rosas to show leniency for the now eight-months-pregnant O'Gorman, Rosas insisted that Camila and her lover pay the price for challenging the moral and religious values that he claimed to defend. He ordered their execution, and on August 18, 1848, they, along with their unborn child, were shot by firing squad. Rather than support for his moral rectitude, however, Rosas was roundly condemned by both supporters and enemies for his brutal treatment of the couple.

decline, and overproduction depressed the industry and hurt Rosas's primary source of support. Furthermore, the developing sheep industry, with its infusion of new immigrants, new business ways, and its encroachment on the great cattle ranches, pushed for change.

Soon, Argentines who had been sent into exile by Rosas, led by such men as Estéban Echeverría and Juan B. Alberdi, joined forces with other anti-Rosistas—the Uruguayans, the English, and the French. A powerful coalition of Rosas's enemies finally came together in 1852 and ousted the old caudillo. Ironically, he was rescued by the British and went into exile in England, living the life of an English country squire until his death in 1877 at the age of eighty-eight.

## Brazil

After the "Grito de Ipiranga" of September 1822, Brazil became independent from Portugal. Portugal attempted to resist, but, in truth, its old colony was too strong and determined. A few skirmishes at sea and on land produced far fewer casualties than the Spanish-American wars. The relatively easy transition to independence separated Brazil's independence movement from that of most of the old Spanish colonies—such as Mexico, Venezuela, and Peru—which had suffered through long and agonizing wars for independence.

No less significant for Brazil was the accession of Pedro as the first emperor of Brazil in 1822. Pedro was the son of the king of Portugal, a Braganza, and thus legitimate royalty. He was accepted as such by most Brazilians. Furthermore, Pedro willingly embraced the concept of a constitutional monarchy, reinforcing his initial acceptance and popularity among Brazilians. The peaceful period of Brazilian independence was, nonetheless, short-lived. Between 1824 and 1831 Pedro thoroughly antagonized his Brazilian subjects, leading to his abdication in 1831.

The basic qualm that Brazilians had with Pedro was his Portuguese birth and his tendency to overlook Brazilian priorities in favor of his Portuguese interests. It began with a constitutional assembly in 1823 that produced a constitution too republican and too limiting for Pedro's absolutist leanings. He dissolved that assembly and wrote his own constitution for Brazil in 1824. It gave the emperor broad powers, and indeed lasted until 1889. But in the 1820s, many Brazilian nationalists felt it gave the emperor far too many powers. In 1826 Pedro got involved in a war with Argentina over control of Uruguay. The war proved costly and bitter and, in the end, was resolved by a compromise offered by England: Let Uruguay be a free nation, a buffer to stand forever between Brazil and Argentina. Brazilian nationalists felt that Pedro had dragged the country into a dispute that reflected old Portuguese aggressions and competition with Spain more than the true priorities of Brazil.

Other actions further alienated Pedro from his Brazilian friends. When Pedro's father died in Portugal in 1826, Pedro wished to succeed to that throne as well and to reunite Brazil and Portugal under his rule. Brazilians recoiled at that possibility and told Pedro that, in effect, he could not have his cake and eat it, too. If he insisted on that course, he would have to give up Brazil. He abdicated his claim in Portugal in favor of his daughter, but he continued to manipulate affairs in Portugal, much to the annoyance of Brazilians.

When in 1830 the news came that revolutions were sweeping across Europe, challenging the old monarchies and promoting constitutional republics, Brazilians were electrified. Was not Pedro an absolutist? Were not his Portuguese sympathies out of sync with the Brazilian reality? The movement to get rid of Pedro culminated in April 1831. Hoping to at least preserve the monarchy and his five-year-old son's inheritance, Pedro abdicated in favor of his son, who became Pedro II. A regency was appointed to govern during the boy's minority. Pedro sailed into exile. While still plotting in Portugal, he died a few years later at the age of thirty-six.

In 1840, when he was still just fifteen years old, Pedro II was declared of age to rule and in 1841, he was fully invested with imperial authority, bringing the regency to an end. The decade of the 1830s had been marked by scattered regional rebellions, such as in Bahia in the north and Rio Grande do Sul in the south, regions that sought more autonomy from Rio de Janeiro and a higher degree of federalism. The disruptions of the rebellions led a group of powerful supporters to push for Pedro II's ascension to the throne.

Pedro II's character had much to do with his acceptability to most Brazilians. Brazilian-born, Brazilian-educated, and thoroughly imbued with a strong sense of nationalism by his tutors, he gave no cause to doubt his loyalties and his allegiance, unlike his father before him. Furthermore, he was a serious and highly moral young man who became a dedicated husband and father and was an example that many Brazilians took great pride in. After the declaration of his majority in 1840, Brazil moved into a halcyon period of its history, called the Second Empire. It lasted as long as Emperor Pedro II reigned, which was for almost half a century.

Nevertheless, separatism, regional rebellions, and scattered manifestations of provincialism and federalism kept the regents and Pedro II occupied during the 1830s and 1840s. Moreover, other currents were altering traditions inherited from the long colonial past. None eventually altered Brazil more than the gradual prohibition of the slave trade, which struck at an institution—slavery—that was intimately associated with Brazil's traditional economic mainstay, the production of sugar and coffee.

The basic issue was between the interests of the powerful *fazendeiro,* or planter class, and growing abolitionist sentiments in Great Britain. The planters were committed to slavery as indispensable to their plantation economy, whereas Great Britain, taking the higher moral ground, though also interested in building a global capitalist economy for its wares, was determined to crush the infamous slave trade with its powerful navy. England in 1826 negotiated a treaty with Brazil that called for abolition of the slave trade, and Brazil passed a law to that effect in 1831, but it was widely ignored.

As the illegal traffic in slaves continued in the 1830s and 1840s, the English pressured Brazil to truly eradicate it. British warships increased their patrols off the coasts of Africa and Brazil and often offended Brazilian sensitivities by taking high-handed actions. It was difficult, if not impossible, to withstand the sustained enmity of the world's greatest naval power. In truth, many Brazilians wanted to end the slave trade as well, not the least due to the declining importance of sugar production and a rising coffee economy, which changed the country's labor needs. In 1850 Brazil put real teeth into enforcing the law of 1831, which, together with the vigilance of the English, snuffed out the trade within three years, though slavery itself would continue in Brazil until 1888 (see chapter 7).

The end of the slave trade coincided with a new era in Brazil. Peace was restored to the land as the quarreling regions accepted the rule of Pedro II. Brazil's territorial integrity was preserved, new forces for the economic development of the country were at work, and prosperity became the password for the rest of Pedro II's rule.

**Figure 5.2** *Overseers Punishing Slaves,* by Jean Baptiste Debret (1768–1848). Debret was a French painter who traveled through Brazil between 1816 and 1831, chronicling life there through his images. The brutality and inhumanity of slavery is obvious in this scene. Courtesy www.slaveryimages.org, compiled by Jerome Handler and Michael Tuite, and sponsored by the Virginia Foundation for the Humanities and the University of Virginia Library.

## Uruguay

Uruguay's eventual independence, finally declared in 1828, resulted largely from its strategic geographic position between Brazil and Argentina. It was, nonetheless, a long struggle for autonomy and nationhood between 1811 and 1828, a struggle that was exacerbated both before and after its independence by the continued fighting among caudillos and their opponents for power.

After Uruguay's greatest independence-era leader, José Gervasio Artigas, was driven into exile in 1820, Uruguay was integrated as the Cisplatine province into the Brazilian empire that emerged in 1823. However, neither Uruguayan nationalists nor Argentine centralists were satisfied with its incorporation into the new Brazilian empire. In 1825 a band of Uruguayans led by Juan Antonio Lavalleja—the Thirty-Three Immortals—invaded their homeland, supported by Argentina. War broke out with Brazil, and it rolled back and forth across Uruguay, seriously disrupting trade and commerce along the Rio de la Plata estuary, especially for British and French merchants whose livelihoods and profits depended upon stability. The British government argued for the creation of a buffer state between Brazil and Argentina, and the two powers, unable to defeat each other, agreed. In 1828 a peace treaty was concluded, and

Uruguay emerged as an independent nation, writing its first constitution in 1830.

Uruguay was a small nation with an economy much like Argentina's, dedicated to the cattle industry. Its population, little more than sixty thousand, was made up of Indians, blacks who had drifted south from Brazil, and a sprinkling of European settlers. In the 1880s and 1890s its population increased significantly due to the arrival of European immigrants. Almost fifty thousand came before the turn of the century, mostly from France, Italy, and parts of Spain such as the Canary Islands, contributing to Uruguay's growing racial homogeneity.

Ambitious Argentine and Brazilian rulers continued to interfere in Uruguay's internal affairs, and its growing foreign population almost invited foreign intervention by European powers determined to protect their nationals and their influence in the Rio de la Plata region. In the 1830s a civil war between two of its early leaders—both presidents for a time—not only provoked a series of interventions by foreigners but also caused the formation of Uruguay's two political parties, the *blancos* and the *colorados,* both of which survived as the principal political parties in modern Uruguay. At midcentury Uruguay slowly emerged from this long period of internal warfare, aggravated by the near-constant presence of Argentine armies, French or English supporters, naval blockades, and civil war. Naturally the country suffered, and the cattle industry, its basic livelihood, declined. Nonetheless, significant numbers of immigrants from Europe, especially from Italy, were beginning to transform the country.

## Paraguay

The story of Paraguay from independence to 1840 is largely of one leader, Dr. José Gaspar Rodríguez de Francia. He became dictator of the nation in 1814, consolidated his hold in 1820, and thereafter ruled absolutely until dying from natural causes in 1840. His autocratic regime was cloaked in mysticism and secrets, although he was not simply a ruthless tyrant. He was also imbued with an intense Paraguayan nationalism and an uncompromising honesty. He certainly was a caudillo of the period, although behaving in some ways very differently from those who sprang up in Argentina, Peru, or Mexico, for example. He did rule with the iron will of caudillos, and left an unforgettable mark on his country's modern history.

During a period of intense instability in the Rio de la Plata region, Francia withdrew Paraguay from the international strife and isolated the nation from its neighbors and from foreigners, both commercially and culturally. A well-educated man, he nonetheless distrusted the Argentines, the Brazilians, the English, and the French. He barred them from Paraguay, and if they entered he arrested and detained them. Even though Paraguay was extremely isolated from the currents of the rapidly changing world around it, its independence was guaranteed by Francia's rigid neutrality and xenophobic nationalism. His contributions ran deeper, however, than merely guaranteeing political independence in a region seesawing between the ambitions of the two powers sharing its borders—Brazil and Argentina.

Francia fashioned a regime that eliminated the old ruling elite, made up largely of Creoles and Spaniards. Between 1820 and 1823, he suppressed a conspiracy of his enemies from the old ruling class, executed many, drove others into exile, and confiscated their properties. While destroying the traditional elite, he actively fostered a policy of intermarriage among the mestizos who made up the great majority of the population (descendants of Guaraní Indians and Spanish settlers), and they were the primary beneficiaries of his policies.

Like many caudillos, alongside brute force, Francia also used patronage to build his power. A believer in the Enlightenment, he confiscated church wealth and, combined with assets stripped from the old elites, spread it among the people of Paraguay. He redistributed land to the small farmers and ranchers of the nation and forced them to diversify their production away from traditional export crops of yerba mate and tobacco, which had chained the nation to the whims of a marketplace economy controlled by foreigners. By the 1830s Paraguay was self-sufficient in corn, rice, dried manioc, ham, cheese, and other food products. Francia lowered taxes and made his government extremely efficient, an accomplishment that astounds us today. He never had more than one or two ministers and a few secretaries to do the business of government, instead doing most of the work himself—an incredible commitment of one person as well as a way to build close personal connections to many. He was rigidly honest, sober, and totally dedicated. He championed the principle that "private interest should be subordinated to the common and general welfare."[3] He practiced this principle with conviction and success. Paraguay in 1840 was on the whole a healthier, more prosperous, and more peaceful place to live than were any of its neighbors.

But there was a price to pay for this stability. Francia's successes with Paraguay were achieved at the expense of a total, despotic control that has given Francia the dubious honor of being the model dictator for students of history. When he died in 1840 he left a Paraguay strong and intact, but also subordinated entirely to the will of one person, even when his supporters defended his rule as visionary or successful. It is not surprising that his successors were caudillos, equally ruthless in their rule. They followed the tradition established by Francia, governing the nation molded by a leader known in Paraguayan history as "the Dictator."

Whereas Francia was somewhat of an ascetic, his successor, the corpulent Carlos Antonio López, most certainly was not. A huge man physically with immense appetites, López also was a nationalist like Francia, dedicated to protecting Paraguay in the midst of warlike, bickering neighbors such as Argentina under Rosas. Under López, Paraguay was opened more to the world, and education was improved considerably. His son, Francisco Solano López, succeeded him in 1862. Within three years Paraguay became involved in a disastrous war against Brazil, Uruguay, and Argentina that shattered the small nation and left it in ruins for the remainder of the nineteenth century.

## Chile

Chile has long been thought of as exceptional in Latin America. Following a short period of instability in the 1820s after winning independence, it settled into an era of political stability and economic prosperity that lasted almost to the end of the century. The transfer of power from president to president-elect every five years stood in striking contrast to Chile's caudillo-ridden neighbors. Political order, in turn, helped promote economic development, especially in Chile's mining and commercial sectors, which gave Chile the strength to impose its will on its neighbors and to emerge as a power on the South American continent.

A closer look at Chile produces a slightly less dazzling picture. What emerged in the 1830s was an authoritarian form of government that in truth possessed few democratic or liberal elements. It was fashioned by a coalition of wealthy landowners and merchants, brilliantly led by a man named Diego Portales (1793–1837). It basically denied the average Chilean peasants, miners, and stevedores—the working class, in short—a share of Chile's new wealth and power. In a way, the price of Chile's peace and stability in the nineteenth century was a sacrifice of liberal principles and economic sharing. Yet, Chile's stability stood in such remarkable contrast to that of its neighbors that its history still elicits admiration from students of its past.

To the observer in the 1820s, however, Chile appeared to be no more stable a place to live and work than was any other place in Latin America. Caudillos and their armies rose and fell in a frustrating parody of government. Yet, the instability proved short-lived. A liberal constitution written in 1828 provoked a revolt by more conservative elements. This led to the Constitution of 1833, which survived almost to the end of the century. It was written by Mariano Egaña, a well-traveled man who served Chile as envoy to England in the 1820s and came away with a tremendous respect for the balance of powers among king, lords, and commoners in that nation. The constitution that Egaña wrote for his own country reflected that respect, although Egaña was careful to adapt those principles that he so admired to the Chilean reality. Although Egaña wrote the constitution, the real spirit behind the origins of the "autocratic republic" in the 1830s was Portales.

Born into an upper-middle-class family in 1793, Portales naturally felt a part of the privileged class in Chile. Two of his ancestors had been colonial governors of Chile, and his father enjoyed a royal appointment as superintendent of the mint. Portales went into trade and became a successful businessman. When he plunged into politics in the late 1820s and 1830s, he brought a no-nonsense perspective to bear. He formed a powerful alliance between the church, the military, and the landowners. Together, they emphasized the absolute necessity for law and order, fiscal integrity, and a strong, centralized government. This, in fact, was the type of government that Portales—even though he never served as president—forged in the 1830s.

Portales's attitude toward a government of law and order was best summarized by a statement attributed to him: "The stick and the cake, justly and opportunely administered, are the specifics with which any nation can be cured, however inveterate its bad habits may be."[4] Portales enforced strict honesty and efficiency in government, suppressed banditry and disorder in the countryside, and, in effect, paved the way for the economic prosperity and international success that marked Chile's passage through most of the rest of the century. A successful war waged between 1836 and 1839 against Peru and Bolivia, allied in a confederation, heightened Chile's national consciousness and self-esteem. Economic prosperity meanwhile issued from two vital sectors of its economy: the mines of northern Chile and the great estates of the central valley.

Copper became Chile's leading export in the 1830s and 1840s. Chile's mines were so rich that from midcentury to the 1880s, Chile was the world leader in production. Nitrate exports also increased rapidly after midcentury and helped fuel Chile's rising economic prosperity. The foreign exchange generated by these vital exports in turn promoted political stability during much of the century.

The great haciendas of the central valley also prospered, especially from the export of wheat and flour to their traditional market of Peru, but also to other Pacific rim markets such as California and Australia. Between the 1840s and 1860s, for example, wheat, flour, and barley exports quintupled in value.

As Chile entered this period of economic prosperity in the nineteenth century, the capital city of Santiago and its port of Valparaíso rose to even greater prominence. Valparaíso attracted a large community of foreigners—especially Englishmen—as it blossomed into a center of trade and commerce in the Pacific. Santiago, with a population of over fifty thousand at midcentury, emerged as an intellectual and cultural center in South America. The founding of the University of Chile in 1842 symbolized this role of Santiago. Many expatriates from all over South America found a home in a stable Chile, away from the feuding caudillos and the instabilities of their homelands in this first half of the century.

## CAUDILLOS OF THE ANDES

### Peru and Bolivia

While Chile prospered economically and maintained political order, its two neighbors to the north, Peru and Bolivia, stumbled into independence with considerably less stability. An attempted union in the 1830s between the two nations failed, stagnation rather than growth marked their economies, and they both arrived at midcentury worse off—measured by most indicators—than they had been at the end of the eighteenth century.

Bolivia was a landlocked nation in the interior of South America, which hampered its development during the nineteenth century. Its limited access to the sea—through the remote Pacific port of Cobija or down the long Paraná River to the Rio de la Plata estuary, controlled by other nations on the Atlantic—placed it at the mercy of its stronger neighbors, especially Argentina, Chile, and Peru. Compounding the problem of geographic isolation was the stagnation of its mining economy. Furthermore, immense expenditures on the army, sometimes amounting to 40 and 50 percent of the government budget, strangled efforts to improve the economy. The result was not measured simply in economic terms.

Indian tribute survived from the colonial period and continued to constitute the principal source of government revenue—at least 40 percent—through midcentury. The result was the continued subservience of the great majority of Bolivia's indigenous population to the small white and mestizo elite. In effect, a system of social and racial inequality survived the Wars of Independence, the constitutions, and the fine rhetoric of liberty, republicanism, and equality. More than 80 percent of the population spoke only Quechua or Aymara and lived profoundly rural, agricultural lives far removed from the fashions in the ports and capitals of Bolivia's neighbors. And, of those neighbors, none was more intimately involved in Bolivia's internal affairs than Peru.

Simón Bolívar left Peru in 1826, frustrated by the deceitfulness and disloyalty of Peruvian elites. The Liberator's armies had been victorious on the battlefield, but he could not impose his will on the Peruvians, who plotted and schemed to get rid of him. Peru's politics subsequently dissolved into factions and then chaos. Between 1823 and 1850, for example, six constitutions were proclaimed, and at least thirty men occupied the executive office. The population declined between 1800 and 1850, and the presence of English merchants and capital shrank precipitously in the late 1820s due to glutted local markets and a moribund mining sector. Even the capital city of Lima, once the center of a resplendent viceroyalty that ruled over all Spanish South America, was reported by travelers as tarnished and inward-looking.

From these inauspicious beginnings, however, certain memories of past glories mingled with visions of future glories. Among the most powerful of these ideals was the reunification of Bolivia and Peru. Both General Andrés Santa Cruz of Bolivia and General Agustín Gamarra of Peru shared the desire for strength through unity. Both were mestizos born in the Andes Mountains common to Peru and Bolivia and, although rivals for power, they strove for the same end.

**Figure 5.3** Ships taking guano off the Chincha Islands, Peru. From the 1840s to the 1870s, seabird droppings called guano were exported from Peru to Europe and North America for use as fertilizer. This guano boom fueled the first modernization of Peru. In the background, behind the ships, one can see the guano "stacks" already depleted by the removal of millions of tons. Courtesy of W. R. Grace & Co.

In 1836 Santa Cruz brought Peru and Bolivia together into a confederation and had himself declared its "grand protector." The Peru-Bolivia Confederation, however, proved unacceptable to Chile, which viewed the confederation as a threat to the balance of power in South America. A strong Peru threatened Chile as the rising commercial and military power in the Pacific. Furthermore, Peru meddled in Chilean internal affairs in this period, provoking the Chileans to declare war on Peru and Bolivia. The war lasted three years. Before it was over, Argentina also joined the fray against the Peru-Bolivia Confederation. The Battle of Yungay in 1839 ended the war. A stunning military triumph for Chile, it broke the confederation, and Peru and Bolivia went their separate ways after Santa Cruz fled into exile.

After the passion for the confederation subsided, the combatants, especially Peruvians, were drawn to matters other than political intrigues and military maneuvers. A commercial revolution was beginning on some barren islands off the coast of Peru, and the promise of new wealth mesmerized the latent entrepreneurs in Peru, both native and foreign. The basis of this commercial revolution was a prosaic commodity called "guano"—bird dung. For thousands of years seabirds had been visiting the islands off the coast of Peru after they fed on the teeming sea life in the cold Humboldt Current. Bird droppings had accumulated to depths of hundreds of feet on these islands. Although the ancient peoples of Peru had long realized and carefully exploited the fertilizing properties of guano, it was not until the 1840s that North American and European farmers discovered guano's rich agricultural benefits.

Guano was soon being hauled by hundreds of ships from the islands of Peru to the ports of England and North America and sold to turnip and tobacco planters to replenish their exhausted soils with this remarkable fertilizer. The Age of Guano had dawned in Peru, and before it ended in the 1870s, when the guano piles were depleted, guano had netted over $600 million on the retail markets of the world.

The guano boom transformed Peru. The new wealth not only flowed from taxes into the government's coffers—though much of that ended up funding poorly conceived development projects, war, or corruption—but also hastened the formation of a Peruvian commercial class that sought to modernize the country as rapidly as possible. For example, the Peruvian government abolished slavery in 1854 and compensated slave owners with the new revenues. More important, perhaps, was the abolition of Indian tribute. Liberating black slaves and removing the stigma of Indian tribute did not radically alter Peru's economic and social structures, but these developments did symbolize the new mood of the modern age, which stressed individual and natural rights. They bore testimony to the conspicuous relationship between the application of classic liberal doctrines and Peru's great new wealth, even if the masses were not the primary beneficiaries. This relationship underscored the links between the economic and social consequences of the Age of Guano in Peru.

## Ecuador

By 1830, Bolívar's vision of a Gran Colombia had fallen apart as Ecuador and Venezuela broke away from the union to become independent states. Venezuelan and Ecuadorian leaders were unwilling to accept the authority of a government located in Bogotá, a government perceived as too distant and too unresponsive to their regional needs. Both Ecuador and Venezuela had been governed as separate provinces during the viceroyalty, and both were accustomed to a measure of local rule under Spain. When they broke away, Ecuador, the smallest of the three new nations, was divided by the rivalry of two cities and the competition of two powerful men from 1830 to midcentury. The capital city of Quito, set in a high mountain valley in the Andes, and the Pacific port of Guayaquil had been competing since colonial times. Independence merely changed the players for these two rival cities.

Quito was the seat of government—aristocratic, cultured, proud, and a bit pompous in its attitudes toward the rest of the country. Guayaquil, in contrast, was afflicted with a hot and muggy climate, flooding, and periodic ravages of tropical diseases. Nonetheless, natives of the port city loved it fervently. Their commercial drive, mercantile spirit, and contacts with the outside world bred an independent spirit and a willingness to adapt to new ways and circumstances. In the post-1830 period, Guayaquil emerged as a promoter of change and progress associated with liberalism. Quito embraced conservatism with equal ardor.

The preeminent spokesman for liberalism in Ecuador was Vicente Rocafuerte. Not surprisingly, he was a native of Guayaquil. After a long residence abroad, he returned to Guayaquil in 1833 and emerged as the principal challenger to the conservative rule that Quito wished to impose. Rocafuerte's opponent was President Juan José Flores, elected in 1830 as Ecuador's first president. Flores was born in Venezuela and possessed a distinguished war record. Although born the illegitimate son of a wealthy Spanish merchant who soon abandoned Juan José and his Venezuelan mother to a life of extreme poverty, Flores married into a prominent family and secured a position of prominence in the capital. Furthermore, the army's backing (with many Venezuelans still in it) guaranteed him a powerful base of support. Flores's instincts were to be tough and autocratic at a time when many centrifugal forces—some pro–Gran Colombia, some pro-Peru, and some pro-Spain—threatened the fragile new nation. Conservatives rallied around Flores, especially because Flores supported the church and the landed aristocrats.

Liberal discontent with the Venezuelan-born dictator flared up in 1833 and erupted in a revolt in Guayaquil. Flores defeated the liberals and captured Rocafuerte. But then he surprised his friends and foes alike in one of those about-faces that mystify students of the past. Flores freed Rocafuerte, and in 1835 Rocafuerte was elected president. Thereafter they alternated in the presidency until 1845, when Flores was driven into European exile. From exile in Europe, Flores plotted his return to power and added a novel twist: he would restore monarchy to Ecuador by bringing a European prince to sit on the new throne. Furthermore, Flores was eager to restore what he considered Ecuador's rightful boundaries. These were based on vague territorial divisions inherited from the colonial period. The Ecuadorian claims included provinces now belonging to Peru and Colombia.

Peru, under President Ramón Castilla (1845–1851, 1855–1862), acted decisively. Not only was the restoration of a monarchy repugnant to most Latin Americans, but also, Flores's ambitions at the expense of Colombia and Peru threatened equilibrium throughout the continent. Castilla called for a congress of American nations to convene in Lima in 1847.

Castilla presided over this General American Congress with delegates from Colombia, Ecuador, Peru, Bolivia, and Chile. The Flores plot to establish a monarchy in Ecuador was not their sole order of business. The delegates also wished to cooperate in determining common policies to protect the future integrity and independence of Latin American nations. The backdrop to this congress, which met from December 1847 until March 1848, was the U.S. war with Mexico.

The delegates were of two minds concerning this war, reflecting the ambivalence toward the United States that Latin Americans have felt over the years. Viewing the war as a brazen example of Yankee manifest destiny and territorial aggrandizement, they condemned it thoroughly. Yet, because the United States was involved in a war, the ability of Latin American nations to depend upon the United States to help prevent intrusions from Europe—such as the one being plotted by Flores—was sharply undermined, leaving Latin America more vulnerable and exposed. The Peruvians were unsuccessful in their attempt to buy two steamers from the United States, for example. The United States needed all of its resources to wage war on Mexico. In the end, the delegates produced little more than some nonpolitical decrees regarding commerce, the maritime rights of neutrals, the duties and powers of diplomats, and postal matters. The Flores expedition eventually stalled because Spain and England blocked his plans.

Flores's ambitions and intrigues kept Ecuador off balance during the next fifteen years. No fewer than eleven changes of government occurred during that period before another strong leader, Gabriel García Moreno, imposed order.

## Colombia

Colombia did not challenge the breakup of the short-lived Gran Colombia. It looked to one of its great Wars of Independence heroes, Francisco de Paula Santander, for leadership as it emerged in the 1830s. Santander is generally credited with inspiring formation of the Liberal Party in Colombia. He was elected the first president of Colombia in 1832 and governed until 1837. Mildly anti-clerical, Santander promoted education and economic reforms in the liberal fashion of the day. Yet, he was also a caudillo and hanged members of the opposition who conspired against his rule. This mixture of authoritarianism and liberalism, perhaps odd from the point of view of North American students of Latin America, was perfectly consistent with the temper of the times. Liberalism represented a fashionable and persuasive set of ideals, but a strong hand was seen as needed to fend off chaos and political anarchy. Santander, like Rocafuerte of Ecuador and Santa Cruz of Bolivia, fit the mold.

After Santander stepped down in 1837, political factionalism divided Colombia in the late 1830s and through the 1840s, leading to the formal establishment of the Liberal and Conservative parties before midcentury. No other nation in Latin America suffered more from this basic political division in the nineteenth century than Colombia. Reinforcing the differences between liberals and conservatives in Colombia (see chapter 9 for a more thorough discussion of this phenomenon in Latin America) was Colombia's strong regionalism. Its political and economic power was diffused among three or four regions—principally Santander, Antioquia, Cundinamarca, and the Caribbean provinces. Competition among these regions often led Colombians to feel a stronger sense of identification and affiliation with those regions than with the nation. Liberals, given to federalism, tended to support this feeling; conservatives, centralists in the main, naturally opposed it. With its strong regionalist forces and deep divisions between liberals and conservatives, Colombia struggled to find stability throughout the nineteenth century.

## Venezuela

Venezuela rode into the first stages of its modern history as an independent nation on the strong back of a remarkably able and successful caudillo, José Antonio Páez. Born into a humble family, Páez developed into one of Bolívar's greatest cavalry leaders and, after Bolívar, was Venezuela's preeminent military hero. He not only led Venezuela out of Gran Colombia in 1830 but also dominated the nation until midcentury. Part of his success in imposing order and stability was due to his excellent qualities as a caudillo.

A remarkable transition in agriculture in Venezuela also helped Páez in the reconstruction of his country after the turmoil of the Wars of Independence. Although traditional exports such as cotton, cacao, tobacco, and cattle products expanded considerably after the wars, it was coffee that truly took off and set the pace. Between 1831 and 1841 coffee production tripled, and the subsequent economic prosperity facilitated the political tranquility that Páez imposed.

As one scholar of Venezuela noted, coffee "planters engaged in an orgy of planting and expansion" to take advantage of the growing preference for coffee in North America.[5] Coffee matured faster than cacao, and planters found easy credit among European merchant houses established in Caracas. Thus Venezuela embarked on a strong export economy early in its national life as its bonds to the merchants, markets, and capitalists of Europe and North America developed in the 1830s and 1840s. Páez in turn kept the centrifugal factors of Venezuela at bay, these being largely regionally based caudillos who rose up periodically to challenge the commercial and bureaucratic elites of Caracas. Páez, the greatest of the llanero chieftains during the Wars of Independence, now chief executive, defeated his rivals by the strength of his personality, will power, and brute force.

In the 1840s, however, Páez's rule frayed as the Liberal Party, founded in 1840, challenged the caudillo's rule. As in many places, changes in the global economy had a big impact on the power of caudillos. In Venezuela, a fall in coffee prices on the world market heightened discontent and led to the overthrow of Páez and his followers—now labeled "conservatives"—in 1848. Páez went into exile in the United States. Venezuela plunged into two decades of political turmoil at midcentury, pitting liberals against conservatives, rival caudillos against each other, and Páez (who was in and out of exile) against his enemies.

## CAUDILLOS OF MEXICO AND CENTRAL AMERICA

### Mexico

After the overthrow of Emperor Agustín de Iturbide I in 1823, Mexico declared itself a republic and in 1824 adopted a constitution modeled on the one that the

United States had enacted in 1789. It was a compromise between the conservatives and liberals, who, as in the rest of Latin America, lined up against each other in the politics of their nations. Mexico's problems were shared by most of the newly independent Latin American republics as well. Conservatives and liberals were divided on such traditional issues as the role of the church, centralism versus federalism, the powers of the executive, and land policy for Indians.

Yet other problems buffeted Mexico during the years between independence and midcentury, aptly characterized as teetering between simple chaos and unmitigated anarchy. In this period, it is difficult to follow the tortuous events of revolving-door politics and economic instability that snarled most attempts to bring prosperity and peace to the nation. One caudillo, Antonio López de Santa Anna, dominated the period. In his virtues and in his flaws we can trace much of Mexican history in this age. Santa Anna was president of Mexico, elected or otherwise, six times between 1833 and 1855, while the presidency itself changed hands thirty-six times. The country ran up an immense deficit, and the army continued to be a drain that not only debilitated the treasury but also meddled in politics. Taxes went uncollected, graft and fraud became commonplace, and, in the most disastrous climax to this period, Mexico lost half of its national territory in a war with the United States from 1846 to 1848.

Guadalupe Victoria was elected the first president of Mexico in 1824 but was almost overthrown in a coup in 1827—led by his own vice president! In the election of 1828, the actual winner was displaced by the rival candidate, Vicente Guerrero, who used a combination of force and intimidation to secure his victory. Guerrero was in turn overthrown by his vice president in 1830. Ex-president Guerrero was executed in 1831. Ex-emperor Iturbide had suffered the same fate in 1824 when he returned to Mexico from European exile to offer his services in helping defend Mexico against a rumored Spanish invasion. Accused of treason, Iturbide was executed by a firing squad. And so it went. Santa Anna, a model caudillo, exploited this instability magnificently, both benefiting from it personally and often being the only one seemingly able to manage it.

A Creole from the coastal state of Veracruz, Santa Anna fought for the royalist cause during most of the War of Independence. In 1821, like so many Creoles, he switched sides and worked for independence, and in 1823 he helped to overthrow Iturbide for the republican cause. In 1829 he led the Mexican army in repelling a Spanish invasion at Tampico. By 1830 he was a national hero to whom both liberals and conservatives now turned in order to find some stability, as well as military leadership and courage in the face of repeated foreign invasions between the late 1820s and late 1840s. In 1833, and though always primarily a landowner and military man, he was elected president for the first time. Bored with the tedium of government, he then retired to his estate, Manga de Clavo, in Veracruz. Never a politician in the formal sense, he preferred to leave the reins of government with his vice president, Valentín Gómez Farías.[6]

When Gómez Farías proved too liberal for the conservatives, who objected to his strong anti-clerical measures, Santa Anna stormed back from Veracruz. He threw out Gómez Farías and the liberals, restored those rights of the church that the liberals had tried to eradicate, and established a new centralist constitution more to the liking of his conservative supporters. By 1836, however, Santa Anna was facing another challenge in the north, namely a revolt in the province of Texas, which declared its independence from Mexico.

Texas had been a Spanish colony since the early eighteenth century and naturally became part of Mexico after independence. In order to populate this vast land, which contained fewer than seven thousand inhabitants in the 1820s, the Mexican government allowed American immigrants to come and settle. This decision proved disastrous for Mexico. Those Americans who flooded into Texas in the 1820s and 1830s eventually threw off Mexican rule in 1836, and Mexico lost Texas.

The Americans who came in, led by entrepreneurs such as Stephen F. Austin, also imported their Anglo-American culture, which came into conflict with that of Mexico. They were largely Protestants, although nominally professing Catholicism to satisfy Mexican law. They brought with them their slaves, although slavery was abolished in 1829 throughout Mexico. They came with a different language and vastly different political customs. They balked at their subservience to distant Mexican rule, centered as it was far to the south in Mexico City, especially since the American population of Texas had swelled to more than thirty thousand by 1835.

In 1835, these Texans rose up to proclaim their independence from Mexico. Santa Anna responded to the call to save his country. He led an army north to Texas and overwhelmed a small contingent of Texans holed up in the old Franciscan mission of the Alamo in San Antonio. The entire Texas contingent, including five prisoners, was killed or executed by Santa Anna's army—an unrepentant policy toward prisoners that had been common during the Wars of Independence. This slaughter, plus another mass execution of Texas prisoners at Goliad, hardened feelings on both sides and provoked an immense flow of sympathy, arms, and volunteers from the United States to Texas. On April 21, 1836, Sam Houston, commanding the Texas army, jumped Santa Anna's army, encamped on the San Jacinto River, and routed it. Santa Anna then conceded defeat. He signed a peace treaty with Texas by which he promised to recognize Texans' independence. The Mexican caudillo was repatriated to his homeland. Humiliated by Santa Anna's concessions, Mexico refused to recognize Texas independence. The misadventures in 1836 were but a prelude to a greater Mexican disaster in 1848.

As it often was, Santa Anna's Texas disgrace was short-lived, and he was soon back in the saddle, this time in 1838 to repel a French invasion. The

### Santa Anna's Leg

In perhaps the oddest episode in the career of the eccentric Santa Anna, he had his leg disinterred and reburied in a state funeral in 1842. Lesley Byrd Simpson captured the episode in his *Many Mexicos*. "The year 1842 marked the apogee of the glorious dictatorship. Mexico City enjoyed a continual fiesta: holidays to celebrate Santa Anna's birthday, Independence, and what not; parades of the guard; drums and bugles and salvos of artillery; solemn Masses at the cathedral. . . . On September 27, 1842, occurred the greatest and most solemn celebration of the year. The corpse of Santa Anna's leg was dug up at Manga de Clavo and brought to the city. His Serene Highness's bodyguard, the cavalry, the artillery, the infantry, and the cadets from the military academy at Chapultepec, all dressed for parade, escorted the urn containing the grisly relic across the city to the magnificent cenotaph that had been erected for it in the cemetery of Santa Paula. Ministers and the diplomatic corps attended, hat in hand. Speeches, poems, salvos. A graceful acknowledgment by the Liberator himself, who solemnized the occasion by wearing a new cork leg."

Lesley Byrd Simpson, *Many Mexicos,* 4th ed., revised (Berkeley: University of California Press, 1971 [1941]), pp. 248–49.

origins of the Pastry War, as it was dubbed, dated back to 1828, when a French baker's shop in Veracruz was destroyed in a riot. The Frenchman sued for damages, but trying to collect from Mexico, which was in a state of near political anarchy, proved impossible. The French government finally intervened, demanding an indemnity not only for the French cook but also for other French claims against Mexico. When the Mexicans delayed, the French sent a fleet to Veracruz. The Mexicans agreed to pay, but then the French demanded more money, this time to cover the costs of their blockading fleet. The Mexicans balked, and the French fleet bombarded Veracruz on November 27, 1838. The Mexicans fell back. The indomitable Santa Anna once again offered his services to help the nation defend its honor. In the fighting that ensued between French expeditionary soldiers and the Mexican army, Santa Anna's horse was shot out from under him by a French cannon ball. Shortly thereafter surgeons amputated his left leg below the knee, which Santa Anna had buried in an elaborate ceremony.

Santa Anna reveled in his glory. The French army had been beaten back to its ships by his gallant soldiers, and the Pastry War had been concluded on satisfying terms (the earlier indemnity, without the costs of the blockade). The country was devoted to his service. He did not die, but continued to govern in an extravagant fashion. The army grew in size, new taxes were levied, bribery was practiced on a scale heretofore unknown in Mexican history, and, at the center, Santa Anna grew rich. He became the caricature of a despot, surrounding himself with personal guards called the "Lancers of the Supreme Power," and by the final despotic year of his rule, he had taken the title "His Most Serene Highness."

In 1845 the United States annexed Texas in a wave of intense nationalism and expansionism known as "manifest destiny." Mexico rejected this aggression, which was made doubly insulting in 1846 when Texas and the United States claimed the Rio Grande as the true border with Mexico. Historically, the more northern Nueces River had been considered the border. A quick look at the map shows that by claiming the more southerly and westerly trending Rio Grande, the Americans were asserting that Texas was twice the size that it truly was. When Mexican troops attempted to defend the region between the Nueces and the Rio Grande in May 1846, a skirmish ensued; some American troops under General Zachary Taylor were killed, and the United States declared war.

Five American armies invaded Mexico. One struck into New Mexico and quickly took that province; a second, marching overland from New Mexico, invaded California, only to find that a combined American force under Commodore John D. Sloat and Colonel John C. Fremont had already secured that state; a third, also coming from New Mexico, took Chihuahua; a fourth, under Zachary Taylor, struck south from Texas toward Monterrey; and a fifth, commanded by General Winfield Scott, attacked Veracruz from the sea and then headed directly inland to Mexico City.

Taylor took Monterrey after a fierce three-day battle and then a few months later faced a large Mexican army assembled by none other than Santa Anna. The armies met near Buena Vista in February 1847. It resulted in a stalemate, with Taylor claiming victory. Santa Anna withdrew to the south, carrying some captured battle pennants and also claiming victory. The claim proved false and short-lived. In March, Scott assaulted Veracruz, taking that city after a devastating forty-eight-hour bombardment from the American fleet, and proceeded inland toward Mexico City. The Mexicans defended themselves tenaciously and with courage, but ultimately they could not resist the better-trained and better-equipped American army as it approached the city. Furthermore, political divisions and rivalries among the Mexican defenders of the capital fatally undermined their efforts to oppose the advancing Americans. It was but one more example of the long-standing feud between liberals and conservatives that was afflicting Mexico during this era.

The final battle occurred on the morning of September 13, 1847, when American soldiers and Marines stormed Chapultepec Castle on a hill overlooking the city. Following a furious artillery barrage, the Americans scaled the precipitous walls and breached the defenses, some of which were manned by the young cadets of the Mexican military academy. Enough heroism was displayed and blood spilled by both sides to provide the mythmakers and

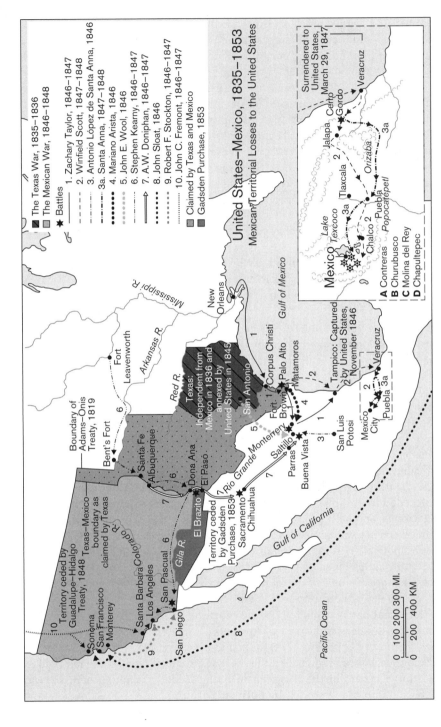

**Map 5.2** United States–Mexico, 1835–1853.

## United States–Mexico, 1835–1853
### Mexican Territorial Losses to the United States

The Texas War, 1835–1836
The Mexican War, 1846–1848

**Battles**

1. Zachary Taylor, 1846–1847
2. Winfield Scott, 1847–1848
3. Antonio López de Santa Anna, 1846
3a. Santa Anna, 1847–1848
4. Mariano Arista, 1846
5. John E. Wool, 1846
6. Stephen Kearny, 1846–1847
7. A.W. Doniphan, 1846–1847
8. John Sloat, 1846
9. Robert F. Stockton, 1846–1847
10. John C. Fremont, 1846–1847

Claimed by Texas and Mexico
Gadsden Purchase, 1853

A Contreras
B Churubusco
C Molina del Rey
D Chapultepec

Surrendered to United States, March 29, 1847

Mexico

Lake Texcoco

Veracruz
Jalapa
Cerro Gordo
Orizaba
Tlaxcala
Puebla
Popocatépetl
Chalco

Boundary of Adams–Onis Treaty, 1819

Mississippi R.

Arkansas R.

Red R.

Fort Leavenworth

Bent's Fort

Santa Fe
Albuquerque
Dona Ana
El Paso

Texas: Independent from Mexico in 1836 and annexed by United States in 1845

San Antonio

Corpus Christi
Fort Brown
Palo Alto
Matamoros

New Orleans

Gulf of Mexico

Tampico: Captured by United States, November 1846

Veracruz
Puebla
Mexico City
San Luis Potosi

Monterrey
Saltillo
Parras
Buena Vista

Rio Grande

Chihuahua
Sacramento
El Brazito
Gila R.

Territory ceded by Gadsden Purchase, 1853

Colorado R.

Gulf of California

Pacific Ocean

Territory ceded by Guadalupe–Hidalgo Treaty, 1848

Texas–Mexico boundary as claimed by Texas

Sonoma
San Francisco
Monterey
Santa Barbara
Los Angeles
San Pascual
San Diego

0  100 200 300 Ml.
0  200  400 KM

songwriters of both nations with tales of courage and sacrifice for generations. In Mexico, the Niños Héroes, the six young cadets who died defending the castle rather than retreating, as their commander had ordered, are now heroes with their own large monument and national holiday. For the U.S., the event is honored in the first line of the official hymn of the U.S. Marine Corps: "From the Halls of Montezuma." The war ended with the surrender of Chapultepec.

The Treaty of Guadalupe Hidalgo, signed on February 2, 1848, stripped Mexico not only of Texas but also of its immense territories of New Mexico and California. Mexico lost, in fact, half its national territory. The United States paid a little over $18 million for this bargain, made possible by its victory at arms. It was followed in 1853 by the Gadsden Purchase, which ceded parts of what are now southern Arizona and New Mexico to the United States so that it could build a southern railroad route across the country in exchange for $10 million. A legacy of distrust and suspicion between Mexico and the United States was sown by this war that so humbled and humiliated Mexico. Throughout, Santa Anna's fortunes and reputation waxed and waned among Mexicans, who were frustrated with his adventures, corruption, and leadership but were unable to impose a stable nation-state to replace him. He fought, plotted, surrendered, and remained a major player, not being overthrown for the last time until 1855.

## Central America

Although independence came easily to Central America in 1823, the unity and prosperity that the region sought in the following decades proved elusive. Central America, too, was wracked by many of the divisions afflicting other areas of Latin America. Conservatives vied with liberals over economic policy, church-state relations, forms of government, and other issues, while Guatemala sought to impose its central leadership on the rest of the region.

The United Provinces of Central America—founded in 1823—consisted of Guatemala, El Salvador, Honduras, Nicaragua, and Costa Rica—or modern Central America (Panama remained a province of Colombia until independence in 1903). As in Gran Colombia, however, the vision of union was soon ruined by realities. Politics, geography, new economic pressures, and administrative configurations that persisted from the colonial period all argued against one central state governed by Guatemala. By the late 1830s, the United Provinces began to split apart, and each province went its separate way as a nation.

But, between 1823 and 1837, Central America probably was more deeply influenced by liberal reform programs than any other new nation in Latin America. Leaders such as Francisco Morazán, a Honduran liberal who became president of the Central American union in the late 1820s, pursued reforms in business, in church-state relationships, in the judicial system, in educational opportunities, and across a wide spectrum of private and public life. These reforms challenged traditions and produced a widespread reaction in the late 1830s that not only split the union but also brought a classic caudillo into power.

The problem for the well-meaning liberals was twofold: one, many of their measures enacted to promote prosperity backfired; and, two, when conservatives criticized and opposed liberal measures, the liberals responded despotically with harshness and force. What were some of the liberal measures? Land reform meant to entrust land to individual landowners tended instead to assist the wealthy to acquire larger properties at the expense of Indians and *ladinos,* as the mestizo population of Central America was known. The church was attacked on a broad front. Church property was seized, many church holidays were abolished, and marriages and education were secularized by allowing for civil marriages and establishing public schools. Clergymen who opposed the reforms were systematically removed, while those who defended the church rallied parishioners to oppose the liberals.

Furthermore, a head tax and mandatory public service were reestablished— as had existed before independence—to raise revenue and to provide a workforce for the new roads and ports that were contemplated. These two measures immediately provoked a public reaction, especially from the peasantry who could not use their wealth and influence to evade these requirements. Liberals, enchanted with the promise inherent in opening Central America to the world, promoted free trade, immigration, loans, and an increase in the production of indigo and cochineal, two dyes that fetched good prices in the English textile industry. Nonetheless, many felt that Central America was being sold out to foreigners whose profits seemed to be gained at the expense of native Central Americans. Many merchants, for example, long accustomed to the protection enjoyed under the old Spanish monopoly, saw their businesses destroyed by free trade, which allowed large amounts of cheap English goods into Central America. They came in mostly through the English colony of Belize and the English-supported Miskito Kingdom, which stretched along the coastline of Nicaragua and Honduras. These enclaves promoted a wide open, commercial, Protestant way of life that many conservatives—still very much inclined to Hispanic, Catholic traditions—found galling. During a revolt that began in Guatemala in the late 1830s, a young ambitious ladino named José Rafael Carrera took its lead.

Carrera was reared in the army, fighting against the liberal forces of Morazán as early as fourteen years of age. He continued his military vocation and rose rapidly, leading peasant uprisings against the liberals. With his pro-Indian rhetoric and policies, he was immensely popular with Guatemala's majority indigenous population. Many indigenous people in Guatemala's highland communities were opposed to the liberal policies that sought to privatize their communal lands and strip their communities of local autonomy, and they resented the increasing regulation of their daily lives. The conservative Carrera challenged these liberal incursions and even returned lands, lowered taxes, and supported Indian leaders over ladinos in rural communities.[7]

A fierce and courageous leader, he was a natural caudillo who eventually rode his talents and the wave of the times to the top in the 1840s, becoming the dictator of Guatemala. He allied himself with the conservatives, who proceeded to undo many of the liberal reforms in the 1840s and 1850s. By then the Central American union had ceased to exist, and conservative regimes had supplanted the liberals who had presided over the union. The conservative reaction proved to be but a temporary dam, however, holding back dynamic forces pressuring Central America for change. These forces were championed not only by liberals but also by foreign entrepreneurs, especially the English and the Americans. These foreigners promoted new, lucrative markets for crops such as coffee that eventually transformed the Central American economy in the nineteenth century. They planned, argued, cajoled, and schemed for the rights and concessions to one of the Western world's grandest dreams— cutting a canal through the Central American isthmus to connect the Atlantic and Pacific oceans. And later, in 1855, an army of American filibusters invaded Nicaragua and established a new rule with an ambitious dreamer from Nashville, Tennessee, as president. The doors of Latin America were in fact being opened to the world after a three-hundred-year period of relative isolation under the Spanish empire.

## CARIBBEAN PATHS

### Cuba and the Caribbean

The story of Cuba and the other Caribbean islands up to the mid-nineteenth century can best be approached by considering two phenomena: the decline of slavery and a booming sugar economy, especially in Cuba. With one major exception—Hispaniola—the Caribbean islands continued as European colonies after the Wars of Independence. The largest of them all, Cuba, remained a Spanish colony until 1898. Independence did not come to the other islands until well into the twentieth century. Hispaniola, however, proved to be a large and important exception.

The Haitian Revolution of 1791 cast off French rule on the western side of Hispaniola, and the black republic of Haiti emerged in the early nineteenth century. The chaos of this revolution and its aftermath ruined the sugar culture of that French colony, and Cuba stepped in to become the principal supplier of sugar for European and North American markets. Between 1810 and 1833 sugar exports from Cuba doubled (from 33,708 to 72,635 tons), and from 1833 to midcentury they tripled (to 208,599 tons). Cuba's remarkable rise to preeminence in sugar was paralleled by the decline of the sugar industry throughout the rest of the British and French Caribbean islands. On these islands, the abolition of the slave trade and finally of slavery itself contributed to the decline of the sugar industry.

The momentum to abolish slavery welled up from many sources, some humanitarian, some political, some economic, but by the early nineteenth century international efforts, especially those of the British, were well under way. The slave trade had been abolished by the British in 1807, and by 1820 most other European nations had followed suit, with the enthusiastic prodding of the English, who led the abolitionist movement.

Slavery itself was abolished throughout the British empire in 1833, but in Cuba slavery survived until 1886. While the sugar economy of the British and French Caribbean islands declined and languished with the end of the slave trade and finally of slavery itself, Cuba's economy prospered, based precisely on slavery and sugar. Even the self-righteous and powerful British, supported by international treaties and the most formidable fleet in the world, failed to stem the illegal flow of slaves into Cuba. In the century after 1763, more than 750,000 Africans arrived as slaves on Cuban shores. In the mid- to late 1850s alone, over a hundred thousand slaves entered Cuba. Even into the 1860s, over four thousand slaves per year arrived at Cuban ports.

Yet, it was not simply slavery that gave Cuba the edge. Cuba also was the first of the Caribbean colonies to begin modernizing its sugar industry. Sugar planters there were quick to adapt to steam power for their mills, to centralize and make their operations more efficient, and to take full advantage of other technological improvements such as the railroads.

Cuba also moved closer to the North American economic and political orbit in this period. Feeling threatened by the powerful British abolitionist movement and unwilling to rely on a weakened Spain for their defense, many Cubans looked to the United States for assistance in maintaining the integrity of Cuba's social and economic system, based on slavery and sugar. The American South, too, perceived its prosperity as flowing from slavery and a single crop—cotton—and annexationist sentiments ran high in the 1840s and 1850s among many Americans and Cubans. Three American presidents attempted to buy Cuba from Spain in the 1840s and 1850s, but these, as well as other, more violent, unofficial efforts, failed. Cuba's destiny, nonetheless, was to be more tightly woven, for better or for worse, into the fabric of American history in the second half of the century.

One other smaller Spanish colony in the Caribbean did follow the more common path during this period. The eastern half of the island of Hispaniola had remained a Spanish colony after Haitian independence, but in 1821 the Dominican Republic declared its independence from Spain. Haiti, however, moved to take it over, and the Dominican Republic freed itself of Haitian rule only in 1844. Puerto Rico remained a Spanish colony, as Cuba did, until the end of the century. It, too, was boosted economically by an expanding, modernizing sugar industry, but its increasing prosperity in the nineteenth century was fueled more by the growth of the coffee industry.

By the middle of the nineteenth century, in fact, new forces were at work not only in the Caribbean—the expanding, modernizing sugar industry, for example, and the demise of slavery—but also throughout Latin America. The key word in the air among Latin Americans was "progress." It meant many things to many people, as we will examine in the next chapter, ushering in a new era in Latin America's relationship to the world. As this relationship developed, it also transformed Latin America.

## CONCLUSIONS AND ISSUES

The search for political order was paramount among leaders in the first two or three decades of independence. But the ideal of constitutional republicanism was belied by the political realities of the region. Brazil did not even bother with a republican form of government but went directly from colony to independent empire. After a discordant start, Brazil took its native emperor, Pedro II, to heart and settled into a long period of political stability and economic progress. In other parts of Latin America, caudillos such as Santa Anna of Mexico presided over a bewitched brew of feuding liberals and conservatives. In Mexico they tore the country apart, leaving it open to Mexico's greatest national disaster, the war with the United States in 1848. Yet, the presence of caudillos was not necessarily a prescription for disaster.

In Chile, a strong centralized and conservative constitution provided for presidents who governed with authority and discipline, and Chile's political trajectory was immensely stable when compared with that of neighbors Peru and Bolivia, for example. Chile, like Brazil, was nonetheless exceptional in an era of feuding liberals and conservatives, centralists and federalists, each with a claimed monopoly on political wisdom and moral truth. More often than not, the feuds—such as in Central America, Venezuela, Ecuador, Peru, and other countries—lessened the ability of their peoples to rise out of the economic stagnation bequeathed by the Wars of Independence.

### Discussion Questions

What were the characteristics of caudillos and why did they rise to power after the Wars of Independence?

Why did caudillos so often have conflicts with liberals?

How did Latin American economies develop in the decades after independence?

Why is Juan Manuel de Rosas often seen as the most iconic example of a caudillo? What were the social and economic bases of Rosas's rule?

Did Indians and slaves tend to support liberals or conservative caudillos? Why?

Why did Brazil not have national caudillos in the nineteenth century?

What were the primary reasons for international wars during the early to mid-nineteenth century in Latin America?

## Timeline

| | |
|---|---|
| 1814–40 | José Gaspar Rodríguez de Francia leads Paraguay |
| 1821–27 | Bernardino Rivadavia leads Argentina (president 1826–1827) |
| 1822–31 | Pedro I is emperor of Brazil |
| 1823–39 | United Provinces of Central America |
| 1824–29 | Guadalupe Victoria president of Mexico |
| 1825–28 | Cisplatine War (Brazil vs. Argentina) |
| 1828 | Uruguay declares independence |
| 1829 | Vicente Guerrero president of Mexico |
| 1829–52 | Juan Manuel de Rosas rules Argentina |
| 1830s–1860s | José Antonio Páez president of Venezuela (1830–1835, 1839–1843, 1861–1863) |
| 1831 | Gran Colombia dissolves |
| 1833–55 | Antonio López de Santa Anna leads Mexico (president six times) |
| 1836 | Texas declares independence |
| 1836–39 | War between Chile, Bolivia, and Peru |
| 1838 | Pastry War in Mexico |
| 1839–65 | Rafael Carrera rules Guatemala |
| 1840 | Pedro II becomes emperor of Brazil |
| 1846–48 | Mexican-American War |
| 1848 | Treaty of Guadalupe Hidalgo |
| 1853 | Gadsden Purchase |

## Keywords

the Alamo
caudillo
centralism
compadrazgo
federalism
Gadsden Purchase
Grito de Ipiranga
guano

hacienda
manifest destiny
Mexican-American War
pampa
patronage
Peru-Bolivia Confederation
Rio de la Plata
Treaty of Guadalupe Hidalgo

# NATION-BUILDING

In part I of this book we briefly reviewed the colonial background of modern Latin America and the Wars of Independence era. These wars brought on many changes, including political and economic instability that lasted for several decades after they ended. Nonetheless, the outlines of a more stable, prosperous region were clearer by midcentury. Several forces influenced the historical evolution of these new nations.

Not the least of these forces was economic development. Throughout the region, the pace of integration into the Atlantic World economic orbit quickened in the second half of the century. Latin American exports to Europe—especially England—and, to a lesser extent, the United States, increased dramatically. Coffee from Costa Rica, guano from Peru, copper from Chile, sugar from Cuba, meats from Uruguay and Argentina, and other products from fields, forests, mines, and ranches produced a remarkable upturn in the economic prosperity of the region. These events, in turn, promoted political stability, bringing to an end the era of the caudillo. With political stability, each country began to more systematically develop true national characteristics.

Along with economic development and political stability came a new devotion to liberal and modern ideals. Very loosely, "progress" meant the desire and willingness to change and adopt new customs, new technologies, and new agendas. The term "modernization" is often associated with this period. While modernization proceeded even more rapidly in the twentieth century, the roots of the process lay in the nineteenth. Part II of this book is devoted to the changes that accompanied the beginnings of modernization.

Progress moves unevenly. In Latin America, for example, it produced excesses of both wealth and poverty. Life was transformed in the cities and countryside by the coming of the railroads, by changes in how one made a living, by immigrants pouring in from Europe, by the emancipation of slaves, and by many other destabilizing influences. New ideas brought change as well, and positivism, scientific racism, and even anarchism were among the many new influences that reshaped how people viewed the social order. Some people prospered, and a small and very real middle class began to emerge. Still, the great majority of people in such nations as Mexico became even poorer and marginalized by these changes. From the disparities of power and influence that arose during this era, the revolutions of the twentieth century were born. These will be dealt with in part III.

Countries began to coalesce as national units, as they fixed their boundaries, developed state bureaucracies, and stabilized issues of authority and power. They also forged a sense of national identity as people developed deeper ties to these new, stronger states, whether through the rhetoric of republicanism that promised citizenship, through education and symbols that sought to create a common history and identity for the citizens, or simply through more extensive markets, better roads and railways, or military conscription—all of which tied people together and to the state in material ways. But these stronger nation-states also came into conflict with one another more often. The resulting wars and international disputes left deep and lasting scars on some of the new nations. The origins of the wars were sometimes legacies of old colonial territorial disputes and border problems, but, even more important, the wars were prompted by the process of modernization itself. The War of the Pacific (1879–1883), between Bolivia, Chile, and Peru, for example, was basically fought over natural resources—principally guano and nitrates—that had become important sources of income as demands in Europe and North America drove up their prices and value.

Throughout this era, and increasing in range and depth in the twentieth century, the United States played a role in the region. Beginning with the ambitious Monroe Doctrine, declared in 1823, U.S. interests in Latin America slowly grew as the century proceeded. Having largely commercial interests in the beginning, the United States expanded its diplomatic and imperialist activities so that by the end of the century, when the last Spanish colonies—Cuba and Puerto Rico—fought *their* wars of independence from Spain, the United States was a principal actor.

Although the Wars of Independence certainly took Latin America down a radically different political road—the one of national independence—they really did not significantly alter some of the basic social, ethnic, and cultural realities of the region. These, however, did begin to change under the impact of modernization. Part II travels down that road.

# Order and Progress

## Overcoming Anarchy

To achieve progress, Latin Americans turned more and more in the second half of the nineteenth century to positivism—a political philosophy that stressed order, peace, and progress. The objective was to overcome the near anarchy and the rule of the caudillos that had followed the Wars of Independence. One of the most vocal and eloquent proponents of positivism was the Mexican liberal political thinker Francisco G. Cosmes, editor of the positivist journal *La Libertad.* In the following passage, look for the positivist buzz words of the times: "order" and "peace." Note how Cosmes insists that without peace and order, the country can never achieve stability and progress.

> Rights! Society already has rejected them; what is necessary is bread. In place of these constitutions filled with sublime ideas, not one of which have we seen realized in practice. . . . I would prefer peace, in whose shade or shelter it would be possible to work tranquilly, with some security for its interests and to know that, instead of launching themselves into the hunt, the flight, of the ideal, the authorities would hang the exploiters, the thieves, and the revolutionaries. Fewer rights and fewer liberties, in exchange for greater order and peace. No more utopias. I want order and peace, even at the price of all the rights which have cost me so dearly. And more, the day is not distant when the country will say, I want order and peace even at the price of my independence.
>
> We have already realized an infinity of rights which produce only misery and distress in society. Now we are going to try a bit of honorable tyranny to see what effect it might produce.[1]

The nineteenth century was called the century of progress. Everywhere, it seemed, business was booming. From cotton and sugar shipped to the United States and Europe to railroads connecting the silver and copper mines to the ports of Peru and Chile and the new buildings and boulevards in the capital cities—all suggested prosperity and progress.

But there was a darker side to progress, as the pursuit of modernization brought a wider array of labor abuses. For example, the Chinese indentured servants brought to Peru by the North American entrepreneur Henry Meiggs to build railroads worked from dawn to dusk in the harsh, cold mountains. Meiggs was not the worst of taskmasters. He made sure his workers were fed well with meat and rice and treated with some tolerance. Meiggs knew his successes were built on the backs of his workers. Each of his Chinese workers had signed a contract, called an indenture, to work for seven years. Upon completing their service, they would be free to return to their homeland with their silver. Others were not so fortunate.

All over Latin America the sounds of progress marked the region. For some, the sounds were of hammers striking rails, and the grunts and groans of the working person. For others, it was the steam whistle of the locomotive blasting through the quiet valleys of the Andes Mountains as Henry Meiggs pulled on the whistle cord that ran along the top of the engine cab. A wisp of steam from the whistle drifted back from the engine, pressing higher and higher into the Andes, following the route where a few months earlier the chants of Chinese swinging hammers had echoed through the canyons. Again Meiggs tugged on the cord, and again the whistle cut through the valley. Children came scampering down from tending sheep and llamas in the high pasture to wonder at the monstrous black locomotive, spewing smoke, steam, and fire. While for many it was a marvelous time to be alive, for millions of workers and peasants, progress was a double-edged sword—one that could cut silver and sweat in vastly different proportions for those who lived in Latin America.

Europe's—and later North America's—influence in Latin America deepened and widened in the second half of the nineteenth century. After the disruptive decades following the Wars of Independence, most countries found a measure of political stability; this, in turn, promoted economic growth and prosperity based on Latin America's exports. Latin American countries exploited their comparative advantage in producing export commodities and dove head first into the circles of trade tying together the expanding Atlantic World economies. The late nineteenth century, a high point of economic liberalism, saw countries across the region drop taxes on exports and imports in order to foster trade. Backed by stronger laws defending the rights of individual property owners, capital also flowed more freely across international borders, as did new types of technology aimed at bringing material progress and economic growth. As foreign markets clamored for Latin American cacao, coffee, silver, and sugar, for example, the economies in the region boomed. In return, European and U.S. investors, manufactured goods, and expertise poured into Latin

**Figure 6.1** Few things symbolized progress better than the arrival of the railroads in the late 1800s. The Metlac Railway bridge (Veracruz, Mexico), seen in this 1872 picture, was a feat of engineering that connected formerly distant markets, communities, and peoples. A. Briquet. Courtesy Library of Congress.

America, bringing with them new consumer habits, modern industries, and better public services.

The foundations of this change in Latin America were a commitment to progress. Liberals were especially dedicated to progress, whereas conservatives considered the liberal obsession with progress and modernization both erroneous and immoral, not the least because of its secularizing tendencies. Liberals wished to unshackle the creative energies of the individual from old institutions and beliefs in order to create new wealth—wealth that would ultimately benefit the entire nation. Conservatives were more cautious, unwilling to part so easily with traditional values and institutions that preserved social order and privilege. Yet, differences between liberals and conservatives were blurred in the second half of the century, especially over volatile subjects such as the church. A majority of Latin America's politically and economically active population embraced progress—and its accompanying profits—with gusto.

What did such an embrace of progress mean for Latin America? We have already seen how the Age of Guano began to transform Peru at midcentury, how growing copper and nitrate exports from Chile fueled that country's growth, and how the modernization of the sugar industry propelled Cuba into an era of unprecedented wealth.[2] So let us first examine the intellectual elements of the modernizing mood that captivated Latin Americans.

Perhaps the underlying assumption was that change is inherently more desirable than continuity—that promoting change would improve the well-being of all individuals. This well-being was not only material, but also political and social. The feeling was that people were advancing toward a better world, as if on a line between the past and the future. The railroad was an apt symbol of this commitment to linear progress. As it penetrated the plains and mountains and valleys of Latin America in the second half of the century (the first tracks were laid in Cuba in 1838), the railroad opened new vistas and markets for Latin Americans.

Two of the greatest obstacles to change were political disorder and the intransigence of some powerful conservative institutions. To overcome these obstacles and to clarify their philosophy, liberals borrowed freely from a persuasive philosophy then in fashion in Europe: positivism.

## THE POSITIVISTS

Positivism sprang from the writings of the French philosopher Auguste Comte, one of the pioneers of modern sociology. His long philosophical treatises published in the 1830s and 1840s essentially outlined three stages in human thought: theological, metaphysical, and the positive. In this last stage, humans would base their thinking and actions on empirical, scientific observations.

Latin American intellectuals, especially in the last quarter of the nineteenth century, embraced positivism with enthusiasm as they sought to modernize their economies and societies and break surviving colonial patterns. Positivism closely linked twin goals so often sought by humanity: social and political order, and material progress. To achieve material progress, one needed social and political order. To establish a true and enduring order, one needed to make material progress. They complemented each other perfectly in the view of Latin American positivists. In Mexico, Brazil, Argentina, Chile, and throughout the hemisphere, the positivists, as the followers of the Comtean philosophy were called, ardently embraced Comte's teachings and adapted them to Latin America.

Positivism took many forms. In Argentina, for example, one of the highest priorities voiced by positivist leaders such as Juan Bautista Alberdi was to promote European immigration to his vast country, not only to populate the seemingly empty spaces with hardworking immigrants and thereby increase national prosperity, but also to revitalize the Argentine people with dynamic European elements, including what positivists claimed were the civilizing virtues of their whiteness. Alberdi wrote that "to govern is to populate," and

Argentina was spectacularly successful in promoting immigration in the second half of the nineteenth century.

Positivists in Chile, such as José Victorino Lastarria and Valentín Letelier, promoted modern, scientific development, which found a ready following in that prosperous country. Chilean positivists remodeled and secularized the educational system. They promoted the restructuring of the government and the economy along scientific principles. They also attributed Chile's unprecedented prosperity in the second half of the nineteenth century to their own actions.

In Brazil, many positivists favored the abolition of slavery (an increasingly outmoded institution that was decidedly not progressive), the separation of church and state (an old liberal creed), and the establishment of a republic. A mathematics professor in the military academy, Benjamin Constant, was especially influential in the pro-republican movement that led to the overthrow of the monarchy in 1889. When the republicans created a flag for their new republic, they could think of no motto more appropriate than Order and Progress, the battle cry of positivists throughout Latin America. To this day, the Brazilian flag carries this motto.

Mexican positivists, labeled *científicos*, also flourished in the latter half of the century and profoundly influenced the course of Mexican history. In Mexican positivism, there were many of the elements common to the positivist movement throughout Latin America, with its emphasis on a practical, scientific approach to the organization of their world, repudiating the unchanging, conservative, almost mystical approach associated with Spanish ways and heritage. In spite of Mexico's defeat in the Mexican-American War of 1846–1848, the country's científicos often looked to the United States for inspiration, believing they saw practicality and rationality that could serve their modernizing vision—not to mention a way to move from anarchy and chaos toward order and progress.

But Mexican positivism was also based on the idea that a dictatorship was needed to promote order and thus facilitate the material progress of the nation. The Mexican positivist Francisco Cosmes called this dictatorship an "honest tyranny," to be distinguished from the chaos that had torn apart Mexico in the first half of the century.[3] The dictator who fulfilled that role, Porfirio Díaz, led Mexico from 1876 to 1911, and he did manage to impose order.

Other Mexican positivists, such as the educator Gabino Barreda, who first popularized positivism in Mexico, and Justo Sierra, one of its foremost promoters, freely adapted the theories of Charles Darwin, especially as reinterpreted by the English positivist Herbert Spencer, to the Mexican reality. Spencer claimed that Darwin's theories of evolution were applicable to society. Society, too, was an organism that was evolving slowly to a higher and better form. The mechanism for this evolution was the constant working of a law expressed by the phrase "survival of the fittest." In a free society, those people and institutions best adapted to making progress would naturally survive and prosper, thereby raising the level of all people with them. This was compatible with the ideas of positivists across Latin America who wished to advance their people scientifically and practically. By applying the rule of order, they encouraged the establishment of strong, often dictatorial governments. By embracing Spencerian principles as the means for achieving material progress, they encouraged competition, free enterprise, and, especially, the introduction of foreign capital, foreign ideas, and foreign initiative.

Positivists also adopted some of the most pernicious racist views then prevailing in the Western world. Across most of Latin America, positivists viewed Afro-descendant and indigenous people as racially inferior and as having degraded their countries' populations through massive mestizaje, or the cultural and sexual mixing of people to produce new cultural forms, over the centuries. Some sought to "improve" the races, like Argentine positivists who encouraged European immigration in order to "whiten" their societies as a prelude to scientific modernization. In other countries, like Mexico and Peru, positivists turned to education as a way to achieve the racial "improvement" of the indigenous or Afro-descendant majorities. At the same time, all sorts of pseudoscientific proofs and theories were concocted—from measuring cranial capacities to associating "substandard" races with tropical climates, for example—to support policies that exacerbated racial inequality.

Positivists often used liberal justifications, such as individualism and free markets, to promote policies that ultimately accelerated the loss of village lands and the expansion of forced labor. They may have incorporated indigenous and Afro-descendant people as citizens in exchange for the latter's political support or military service. Yet they most often treated them as "racial subordinates" who did not have access to full citizenship rights, including suffrage.[4] In doing so, positivists transformed the caste-based stratifications of the colonial period into more exclusionary policies based on a scientific racism that touted the biological bases of inequality.

The positivists of the second half of the nineteenth century claimed to have worked virtual revolutions in their homelands. They "claimed credit for reforming outmoded political institutions, for bringing about the industrial revolution, for beginning the process of mass popular education, for destroying the traditional power of the Church, for giving the military professional status, for reforming penal codes, for expanding national frontiers, for modernizing the cities, for introducing immigration of both men and ideas and, thus, for fomenting the material welfare of the continent." If the intellectual framework provided by the positivists did not produce results as total and as good as they claimed, the economic transformation of Latin America—that "material progress" so dear to the positivists—was nonetheless spectacular in the second half of the century.[5]

## ECONOMIC TRANSFORMATION

In analyzing economic changes that Latin America underwent in the second half of the century, the statistical evidence is impressive. Argentina's exports between 1870 and 1900 increased 500 percent. Between 1833 and 1889 the value of Brazil's foreign trade increased at least sixfold. Between 1879 and 1900, the export of nitrates from Chile increased from 125,000 tons to almost 1.5 million tons. Cuban sugar production rose from 322,000 tons to over a million tons between 1853 and 1894. During the heyday of the positivists in Mexico, from 1877 to 1910, Mexican exports increased in value eightfold, and sevenfold in volume.

Exports fueled the growth of other Latin American nations with similarly dramatic effects: coffee from Colombia and Costa Rica, guano from Peru, minerals (silver, gold, copper) from Chile, Peru, and Mexico, bananas from Central America, rubber from the countries sharing the Amazon basin, tin from Bolivia; the list is long and diverse. Taken as a whole, the effects were not only impressive, but also controversial.

The growth of export economies produced three broad changes: one, the creation of new wealth; two, a deepening and dependent relationship with Europe and North America; and three, a more unequal distribution of that new wealth and income. All three were evident in the second half of the century. Cities grew, banks were founded, railroads pushed into the interiors, industrialization commenced, telegraph and cable lines appeared, a middle class began to develop, education became more public and available, and, in countries such as Argentina and Uruguay, the flood of foreign immigrants considerably altered the demographics and social scene.

The growth of the cities and of railroads was the most visible symbol of the material and cultural transformations taking place throughout the region. By the early twentieth century, many large cities had streetcars, telephones, electricity, sewers, paved roads, beautiful parks, and French-inspired architecture. In San José, the capital of Costa Rica, the crowning jewel in the transformation of that city was set in place in 1897 when the National Theater, modeled on the Paris Opera House, was inaugurated with a production of *Faust*.

The imitation of European architecture, fashions, and culture was a natural extension of the deepening ties between Latin America and the rest of the world. Latin Americans looked abroad not only for their markets and for sources of capital, but also for those trends in politics (positivism) and in culture (from hat styles to the latest in horseless carriages) that marked modern society. And nothing was more modern or progressive to the Latin Americans than the railroad. It was both the preeminent agent and the symbol of progress and modernization.

Peru aptly illustrates the links between the growing export economies and the introduction of the railroads. The boom in guano exports produced a surplus of

**Figure 6.2** The Teatro Nacional, or National Theater, in San José, Costa Rica, 1909. The imitation of European culture—especially French—was very popular in Latin America in the nineteenth century. National Photo Company. Courtesy Library of Congress.

capital, and this capital was in turn invested in building railroads. The railroads began on the coast and penetrated into the highland interior, with the twin goals of making potentially rich mines (silver and copper, for example) accessible and bringing progress to those remote parts of Peru largely untouched by the Industrial Revolution.

Manuel Pardo, a president of Peru in the 1870s, was a typical apostle of the railroads. His arguments are representative of the times. Not only would the railroads catalyze increases in production and commerce, but they would also further an even higher mission in Peru: "to create where nothing today exists, to spawn and stimulate the elements of wealth which today are found only in a latent and embryonic state."[6] In an effusive display of missionary-like optimism, Pardo went on about the impact of the railroads: "Who denies that the railroads are today the missionaries of civilization? Who denies that Peru urgently needs those same missionaries? Without railroads today there cannot be real material progress. And without material progress there can be no moral progress among the masses, because material progress increases the people's well-being, and this reduces their brutishness and misery. Without the railroads, civilization can proceed only very slowly."[7] Pardo was, in effect, a positivist to the core, committed to change and modernization. His counterparts flourished across the rest of Latin America.

**Railroad Fever**

In 1853, the Argentine Juan Bautista Alberdi (1810–1884) wrote about the railroads in a fashion typical of the time, extolling them as the primary agents of modernization and nation-building:

> The railroad and the electric telegraph, the conquerors of space, work this wonder better than all the potentates on earth. The railroad changes, reforms, and solves the most difficult problems without decrees or mob violence.
>
> It will forge the unity of the Argentine Republic better than all our congresses. The congresses may declare it "one and indivisible," but without the railroad to connect its most remote regions it will always remain divided and divisible. . . .
>
> Without the railroad you will not have political unity in lands where distance nullifies the action of the central government . . . Political unity, then, should begin with territorial unity, and only the railroad can make a single region of two regions separated by five hundred leagues.
>
> Nor can you bring the interior of our lands within reach of Europe's immigrants, who today are regenerating our coasts, except with the powerful aid of the railroads. They are or will be to the life of our interior territories what the great arteries are to the inferior extremities of the human body: sources of life.

Juan Bautista Alberdi, *Bases y puntos de partida para la organización política de la República Argentina* (Buenos Aires, 1951), pp. 62–63, 85–88, 90–92, 240–45, in Robert Buffington and Lila Caimari, eds., *Keen's Latin American Civilization: History and Society, 1492 to the Present,* 9th ed. (Boulder: Westview Press, 2009), pp. 308–12.

In Mexico, a frenzy of railroad building occurred from the 1870s to the end of the century, most of these railroads penetrating Mexico on a north-south axis, making it more accessible to the United States. Old silver mines revitalized, and new sources of zinc, lead, and copper came into production, made possible by linking the mining areas with the markets in North America. As early as 1880 it was possible to travel by rail from Chicago to Mexico City, and, perhaps just as important, North American and English capital dominated in the expansion of the railroads. The great names in U.S. capitalism, such as Guggenheim, appeared frequently in the roster of those agents of economic transformation in Mexico.

In the rest of Latin America, railroad fever ran just as high as in Peru and Mexico. Argentina's railroads, largely financed by British capital, promoted economic development based on cattle and agricultural exports. The traditional exports of salted beef, hides, tallow, and wool were supplemented and then superseded by exports made possible by new factors: technological improvements, immigration, and, of course, the railroads. Refrigerated mutton and wheat came to dominate Argentine exports by the turn of the century and promoted a spectacular rise in the prosperity of the nation. A map of the railroads of Argentina at the end of the century looks like a plate of spaghetti strands strung out across the nation, all converging on Buenos Aires.

Along with the railroads came the telegraph, steamships, electricity, and a host of other technological improvements or breakthroughs that promoted the economic transformation of the region. In this era of invention and growth and prosperity, anything was thought possible. Is it any surprise that perhaps the greatest engineering feat ever attempted in Latin America was launched in the second half of the nineteenth century?

The goal of linking the Atlantic and Pacific oceans by cutting a canal through the Central American isthmus had been envisioned ever since the sixteenth century. But the task seemed overwhelming. The various proposed routes were plagued by tropical diseases and blocked by mountains, earthquakes, and flooding downpours. Efforts to dig were quickly swept away in torrents of water that both impeded work and demoralized canal builders. Yet, commencing in the 1870s, Europeans and North Americans launched a series of canal-building endeavors, both in Panama and Nicaragua, that ultimately culminated, after the turn of the century, in an American commitment to complete the canal in Panama. Earlier, in the 1880s, the French undertook the task under the leadership of Ferdinand de Lesseps. But de Lesseps—the builder of the Suez Canal—and his project ultimately failed in Panama, broken by yellow fever and malaria, floods, and finally, bankruptcy.

There were, of course, some catches to the unprecedented burst of prosperity and boundless optimism that propelled and captivated Latin Americans during the age of positivism and economic transformations. A price had to be paid, and in the case of Latin America, it was paid in two broad areas: the wealth was unequally distributed, what historian E. Bradford Burns aptly called the "poverty of progress"; and Latin America became even more dependent upon Europe and the United States. Their effects persist, in one form or another, even to today.

One immediate outcome of this growing prosperity was a maturing sense of nationalism. This nationalism was fueled by old feuds over undefined borders inherited from the colonial era as well as by the increasing value of exports—nitrates, rubber, copper, sugar, coffee, wheat, and so forth—so keenly sought by the industrializing nations of Europe and North America. The result was an increasingly complex and competitive international politics marked by wars across the nineteenth century.

The modern revolutions of Latin America, beginning with the massive Mexican Revolution of 1910, make it apparent that whether one favors dependency or diffusion to describe the relationship between Latin America and England and North America, modernization produced wildly uneven results in Latin America. Although cities were electrified and prosperous middle classes began to emerge, as we will see in the next chapter on social change in this era, many of the common people—the masses—continued to toil in hardship and privation

## The Issue of Dependency

The relationship between Latin America and the rest of the world—principally Europe and the United States in the nineteenth century—has been described as dependent. A dependent relationship is one in which an unequal partnership exists that benefits one partner more than the other. In the theory of dependency that has been developed to explain Latin America's relationship to the rest of the world, Latin America has most often been analyzed as the junior partner whose growth and development were accomplished only by paying the price of becoming more dependent upon Europe and the United States.

Most analyses emphasize the negative effects of this dependency. Furthermore, dependency cut across economic, political, and social categories. Latin America became dependent upon foreign markets for its relatively lower-priced commodity exports, which set it up for repeated cycles of economic boom-and-bust, and upon those same foreign producers for their relatively higher-priced manufactured goods and other imports. But economic clout also carried with it foreign political influence. Wherever the English merchant went, the English consul or minister and the English warship were not far behind. The same was true for the French and Americans, both of whom contributed heavily to the rise of dependency in the second half of the nineteenth century.

Another way of describing dependency—this time in a more historical framework—is to call it "neocolonialism." Formal colonialism existed from the sixteenth century until the Wars of Independence. That is to say, Latin America was a colony of Spain and Portugal—legally, politically, economically, ecclesiastically, and so forth. When those bonds were broken by the wars, Latin America became independent politically, but it continued to be dependent upon Europe, especially Great Britain, for its economic growth and prosperity. This relationship deepened, and the U.S. role in Latin America in the nineteenth century gradually grew at the expense of the British. Although not a formal colony of Europe, Latin America continued to be a neocolony of Europe and North America, increasingly dependent in an economic fashion—hence, neocolonialism.

A third way to describe the dependent relationship has been to invoke the term "imperialism." Again, as in neocolonialism, most of Latin America in the nineteenth century did not form a legal or political part of the expanding British or American empires, but Latin America's subordination to British capital, British investments, American railroad builders, and so forth, in effect spread the British and American empires over Latin America. Thus, imperialism becomes closely associated with a description of the relationship between Latin America and the rest of the world, especially, of course, Great Britain and the United States.

Finally, the student of Latin American history must consider a competing theory, called "diffusionism," which maintains that the spread of European and North American capital, investments, values, technology, and immigrants to

Latin America was positive rather than negative. The benefits of progress and modernization were slowly diffused to Latin America, spreading like ripples on a pond. The center of the ripples, often labeled the "metropolis," was Europe or North America. Here invention and industrialization were proceeding rapidly. The effects of these phenomena gradually spread out to the rest of the world (the "periphery"), promoting change and prosperity in a gradual manner.

that were often more severe than that of their immediate ancestors under the Spanish and Portuguese empires.

## CONCLUSIONS AND ISSUES

One of Isaac Newton's laws of nature is that a body at rest tends to remain at rest, whereas a body in motion continues in motion. Latin American political, social, and economic leaders in the second half of the nineteenth century sought to get their countries into the latter mode, to break the economic stagnation of the post-independence decades. They passionately embraced the notion of progress and took up the tools of positivism to realize their ambitions. They promoted change across the economic spectrum and invited in foreign capital and ideas with enthusiasm. The liberal ideals of creating an egalitarian society, especially providing the political freedoms and economic incentives to advance the indigenous population in the new nation-states, were postponed in favor of economic development. The new modernizing rulers even managed to impose an unprecedented degree of political stability at the end of the century.

Latin American material progress did indeed take off in the era of order envisioned by the positivists. Exports expanded dramatically, railroads reached economically viable areas and connected goods to markets abroad, and old and new products of fields and forests, mountains and deserts such as coffee, guano, and nitrates all powered a new prosperity. With this prosperity came increasing dependency upon European and North American markets, technology, banking, and entrepreneurial and scientific skills. This dependent relationship possessed a number of facets—some considered positive and some negative—in the process of nation-building.

### Discussion Questions

How did Latin American elites understand the motto Order and Progress?
What were the origins and argument of positivism?
What was the impact of the export boom and modernization on the popular masses?

How did Latin American elites apply Darwinist ideas to their thinking about race in Latin America?

What happened to Latin America's relationships with Europe and the U.S. in the second half of the nineteenth century? Why do some scholars point to growing dependency or neocolonialism in that period?

Why was the introduction of railroads so significant to economic development, social order, and the creation of nations?

### Timeline

| | |
|---|---|
| 1872–76 | Manuel Pardo is president of Peru |
| 1876–1911 | Porfirio Díaz rules Mexico |
| 1881–94 | France attempts and fails to build Panama Canal |
| 1889 | End of Brazilian monarchy/Second Empire |
| 1904–14 | Panama Canal built by U.S. |

### Keywords

| | |
|---|---|
| científicos | Order and Progress |
| dependency | Panama Canal |
| diffusion | positivism |
| economic transformation | poverty of progress |
| imperialism | scientific racism |
| neocolonialism | |

# Citizen and Nation on the Road to Progress

## Mariquita's Complaint

María Sánchez de Thompson (1786–1868), or Mariquita, lived through the dawn of Argentina's emergence as an independent nation. She wrote a letter to one of her celebrated friends, the Argentine intellectual and diplomat Juan Bautista Alberdi, at midcentury that captured the dilemma of the cultured and well-educated woman of the nineteenth century. Women of the times were not expected to dwell on serious matters of policy and state; rather, they were to be given over to music and the arts, and the chores of taking care of home and children. Mariquita writes a very candid letter, showing how frustrating it could be to have to conform to a life that did not allow her the full range of freedoms that women of privilege and intelligence desired. Several generations passed before women were legally empowered in Latin America, but the desires—and the social changes that were fueling them—were expressed well by Mariquita.

> Let me tell you what happened. I went to see Gutiérrez' family and they made me play the piano. I wish you could have seen how happy it made María de los Angeles. While remembering you they all decided that I should play the piano like you. Funny that just a few days earlier Luis Méndez had paid me the same compliment. We share so much in common that it's no surprise we play the same kind of music. I have passed through some days of desperation in my sorrow, my heart like in a prison and my soul in solitude. While looking for some ways to relieve this feeling I've been reduced to the piano and other womanly chores, none of which I liked, but, since despotism is in style, even I have submitted myself to sewing, doing silly things like schoolgirls. And so that's the way we live, sometimes like idiots, sometimes soaring into higher thoughts, running through space, seeing that the whole world wants to be better, but each day it's worse. Who will see the end of this universal struggle! What are we to do after so much destruction![1]

## THE PEOPLES OF LATIN AMERICA

Order and Progress brought great change to the peoples of Latin America in the mid- to late nineteenth century. With the power of liberal states on the upswing and booming export economies bringing in new wealth, elites were better able to put into practice ideas of individualism, free competition, and secularism. As a result, the changes promised by the rupture of Spanish authority after the Wars of Independence but largely delayed by the disorder of the caudillo years finally began to move more quickly. Economic progress and political order transformed the way people lived their daily lives, as the privatization of land, the growth of public education, and attacks on the power and privilege of the Catholic Church all became common to varying degrees across the region. The growth of export-oriented plantation agriculture often dramatically altered rural and agrarian ways, and people found new opportunities in the rapidly growing cities. Work, family life, and religious practices were all affected by Latin America's integration into the Atlantic World economy and the rise of the liberal order.

The demographic changes alone in the second half of the nineteenth century were impressive, and marked a departure from earlier in the century. After the Wars of Independence, little changed in the overall racial makeup of the people, but throughout the nineteenth century, due to better sanitation, medicine, urbanization, and other factors, the population of Latin America expanded dramatically. The flow of immigrants from Europe altered the proportion of each ethnic group substantially in some nations—most noticeably in the nations of the Southern Cone and Brazil, where European immigrants swelled the percentage of foreign-born Brazilians from about 4 percent to over 7 percent by the end of the century. In others, the population of mestizos, pardos, and mulattoes (sometimes collectively labeled "castas," though increasingly called "mestizos" by the end of the nineteenth century) expanded proportionally within the overall population at the expense of Indians and blacks. Nonetheless, well into the twentieth century, the indigenous population remained the majority or represented the most significant proportion of the population in the five nations of Mexico, Guatemala, Ecuador, Peru, and Bolivia.

The end of the slave trade during the course of the century contributed to one aspect of these demographic trends. For example, in a population that increased from about 4 million to almost 18 million in Brazil in the nineteenth century, the free population of color constituted more than half (around 58 percent) of the total population by the 1870s. The black slave population declined from close to 2 million to just more than a half-million by 1888, when slavery was abolished and the last were finally freed. As in the rest of Latin America, the era of Order and Progress brought with it major social change.

## LAND, LABOR, AND INDIANS

Indians experienced significant negative consequences from the liberal political philosophy that pervaded Latin America. This philosophy, when enacted in land, labor, and tax laws, especially after midcentury, deprived Indians of colonial protections and restraints, leaving them vulnerable to exploitation born of liberal political ideals and impersonal and often brutal economic forces. Liberals may have freed Indians of ancient shackles, such as the tribute, and broken up indigenous communal lands, giving individuals, usually men, title to their own plot of privately owned land. Liberals hoped that these actions would remake Indians into independent landowners, endowed with their own resources, moving along the road to prosperity and progress, learning the rudiments of self-sufficiency and democracy in the liberal, progressive, modern world then thought to be dawning. It did not work that way.

These new laws that required land to be held privately by individuals cheated and despoiled millions of Indians of their lands in Mexico, Guatemala, Colombia, and the Andean nations of Ecuador, Peru, and Bolivia. To be sure, many indigenous communities held on to their lands tenaciously, owning them collectively in what were called *ejidos* in Mexico and *comunidades indígenas* or *ayllus* in Peru. As many as 40 or 50 percent retained their collective identities and both the communal landholdings and the local autonomy that underpinned them. But many other communities split apart due to growing pressures. Some fell to the pressures of outsiders who, backed by these new laws, swept in to buy up or seize lands previously held communally. Other communities split apart by their own hand, as competition among members to gain ownership of the best lands and irrigation undermined the community.

The demands of a modernizing plantation and hacienda economy further undermined Indians' quality of life. As industrial capitalism developed in Europe and North America, the ever-increasing demands of the industrializing world stimulated the agrarian systems of Latin America to produce more for new foreign markets. New and more efficient ways developed to make money by growing and selling Latin American agricultural products such as sugar, coffee, bananas, wheat, *henequen* (agave fiber), and the like. In essence, this meant transforming the paternalistic hacienda into a capitalist estate.

Such a transformation degraded conditions for Indians and mestizos working on these new, export-oriented estates. Many were pushed into the workforce and became cogs in the production cycle, mere laborers who could be exploited by owners and managers. Although the forms of labor varied widely across Latin America, from the henequen plantations of Yucatán to the wheat-producing estates of Chile's central valley, the net result was its depersonalization. During the long colonial period, the relationship between *hacendado* (hacienda owner) and peon had often been close, dependent, and, in many instances, mutually supportive, based on a paternalistic system that although unequal lessened the distance between owner and worker. When labor became something other than the expression of a legal and social relationship between individuals, the relationship suffered. As plantations and haciendas became larger, more efficient, and more tightly wedded to the demands of an external market, labor became but one more element in the economic formula for boosting profits. Individuals often became mere figures in the equation of capital, resources, and markets that governed capitalist relations. Alienation, rather than paternalism, marked the growing modernization of the haciendas. The redress of these circumstances for most Indians would not begin until the twentieth century.

## THE END OF SLAVERY

Whereas the lot of the indigenous population worsened in the nineteenth century, black slaves won emancipation. The institution of slavery retreated during the century throughout Latin America, although unevenly. First, the slave trade had to be eliminated. Then slavery itself was gradually abolished as humanitarian sentiments and practical political and economic considerations argued ever more persuasively for its end. These political and economic forces became even stronger after midcentury, as states emerged that could ensure social order. Latin America's integration into Atlantic World markets also placed new pressures on plantation owners to free labor and capital from the bondage of the slave-plantation complex.

The process of abolition took close to a century to occur across the region. First, the Wars of Independence dealt a blow to the institution. Not only was human bondage incompatible with the high principles of equality written into the nascent Latin American constitutions, but also blacks, mulattoes, zambos, pardos, and other castes had fought, and fought well, in the wars. In Argentina, for example, thousands of Argentines of African descent, both free and slave, served in the patriot armies, sometimes in segregated units, sometimes well integrated into the general battalions and regiments. They fought for the promise of advancement and freedom, and some rose to high levels in the military or later gained political office. Yet, progress toward emancipation was not inevitable.

As in the United States Constitution of 1789, slavery was not eliminated with one stroke of the pen simply because the principle that "all men are created equal" carried the day. Slavery continued to exist in the United States after 1789, and slavery continued to exist in most of Latin America after

---

**The Weight of the Slave Trade**

"The British poet of the *fin de siècle* who proved the most effective abolitionist was Robert Southey. . . . His simple and poignant ballad, in 1798, 'The Sailor who had served in the Slave Trade,' dealt with a sailor found by a minister in Bristol, groaning and praying in a cowhouse [barn]. The sailor had been ordered by the captain of a slave ship to lash a female Negro slave who had refused to eat. The captain stood by, cursing whenever the sailor paused because of the woman's cries. When she was taken down, the woman groaned and moaned, her voice growing fainter and fainter until she died. No anti-slavery propaganda was quite so effective as the final stanza of Southey's ballad:

They flung her overboard, poor wretch
She rested from her pain . . .
But when . . . O Christ! O Blessed *God!*
Shall I have rest again!"

Eric Williams, *From Columbus to Castro: The History of the Caribbean, 1492–1969* (New York: Vintage Books, 1970), pp. 269–70.

---

1825. Bolívar and other Creoles were troubled by this contradiction. They believed that freedom should be the natural state of all people, but to immediately free black slaves en masse might threaten the predominance of white elites by provoking social disorder and economic disruption due to a loss of labor.

The Haitian Revolution of 1791 and its aftermath haunted Creoles in Latin America. There, white plantation owners either had been massacred or had fled, abandoning the island to its new black and mulatto rulers. And the implications of the Hidalgo revolt in Mexico in 1810 were never far from the consciousness of Creoles. The beginnings of the Mexican independence movement had rapidly spun out of control, as Indians and mestizos rose up in revolt against Creoles and peninsulares. For Bolívar and others to abolish black slavery was to fulfill the high ideals that inspired the Wars of Independence. But to free slaves was to open the door to the possibility of social revolution and anarchy, a state intolerable to Creoles long accustomed to governing their lands without having to share power with the masses. While Creoles vacillated, another strong wind of freedom blew through Latin America, strengthening the abolitionist forces.

In 1833 Great Britain abolished slavery throughout its empire. The British also pressured the rest of the Western world to conform. The British were not simply motivated by humanitarianism, but also by a complex amalgam of

**Figure 7.1** Slaves in a Haitian sugar mill prior to the island's independence in 1804. In Brazil and Cuba, Afro-descended men and women continued to toil as slaves like these until emancipation in the 1880s. Courtesy Library of Congress.

political and economic motives. The result was increasing pressure on the new Latin American nations. In their efforts to persuade Latin Americans, the British played many cards. One, the British were Latin America's principal trading and commercial partners in the nineteenth century and could bring economic pressure to bear. The trump card, however, was the powerful British Navy, undisputed sovereign of the seas in the nineteenth century. The British chased and hounded slave traders from the African coast to the waters of the new American states, lobbying with their cannons as well as with their humanitarianism.

Genuine internal Latin American motivations, combined with British pressures, produced the momentum needed to finally rid Latin America of slavery. By midcentury, the institution had been abolished everywhere in Latin America except Brazil and Cuba (still a colony of Spain). Slavery persisted longest there, where it continued to play an important role in their economies; the ruling planter class stalled as long as possible. Cuban slavery came to an end officially in 1886, followed two years later by the Golden Law, which put an end to slavery in Brazil.

---

### Poets and Slaves

Two Brazilians, Antônio Gonçalves Dias (1823–1864) and Antônio de Castro Alves (1847–1871), wrote some of the most beautiful poetry produced in Brazil in the nineteenth century and contributed significantly to the abolitionist cause. Although Gonçalves Dias was chiefly concerned with Indians, he also touched very eloquently on the theme of slavery. Castro Alves dedicated himself to the cause of antislavery, and "awoke the social conscience of his readers to the injustices inflicted on [slaves]." His poem "O Navio Negreiro" (The Slave Ship) "evoked the inhuman suffering of the captives during the crossing from Africa to Brazil. Life on the slave ship recalled some of the scenes of Dante's *Inferno*." According to Castro Alves in part 4 of "O Navio Negreiro," the ship was a "Dantesque dream . . . the deck with lanterns reddening the glow, washing with blood. Clink of iron . . . snap of a whip . . . Legions of men so black as the night . . . One is delirious with anger, another gets insane and another one, who is brutalized by tortures, sings, moans, and laughs!"

E. Bradford Burns, *A History of Brazil,* 3rd ed. (New York: Columbia University Press, 1992), p. 219.

---

One of the most powerful arguments made against slavery invoked simple economics: free, wage labor was more efficient than slave labor. In the late eighteenth century, the Scottish philosopher Adam Smith declared that slave labor was the least productive of any in the world. His followers, among them the British prime minister William Pitt, reframed that argument as they sought—successfully—to destroy the slave trade and ultimately slavery throughout the Western world.

In Brazil, new immigrant labor and a dwindling slave population, as well as shifting political forces, eroded the institution of slavery so much that even the planter class was willing to abandon it by 1888. The planter class of Cuba, which had long championed slavery for economic and political reasons, abandoned its commitment as new forces upended its universe. One, the end of slavery in the United States after the Civil War broke ties to the American South. These ties had been sustained in the 1840s and 1850s by the possibility of Cuba's being annexed to the United States as a slave state. Many Cubans, from the 1860s to the end of the century, were preoccupied with changing their island's political status in a different way. In pursuit of independence from Spain, they fought multiple wars in the 1860s and 1870s—wars that brought freedom to some slaves who participated in the fighting. As they neared the goal of independence in the 1880s, they also argued for freedom for all Cubans, especially, of course, for blacks, who could be expected to be willing revolutionaries.

## Latin American Slavery in Comparative Perspective

Scholars in the Americas have long compared slavery in the different regions of the hemisphere in an attempt to better understand it and how it influenced the people and historical developments in each context. In the Latin American experience, some have contended that certain mitigating factors lessened the harshness of slave life, and therefore diminished the vast social and racial distance between masters and slaves and, after slavery was abolished, between whites and blacks. Among these factors were the influence of the Roman Catholic Church, the legal protection of slave rights provided for under Spanish colonial law, and the long association of Portuguese and Spanish people with Africans through their trading and exploration there. Due to these factors, slaves in Latin America had the right to marry and gain legal protection from cruel masters. It was also argued that the long history of contact with Africa had made Spaniards and Portuguese less racist against blacks. These factors, and others, supposedly made the black experience in Latin America less harsh than the comparable black experience in North America.

This view received its most notable expression in the 1930s, when the Brazilian social anthropologist Gilberto Freyre stressed the close and intimate personal relationships between masters and slaves in the great houses in Brazil, where he argued that slaves were treated comparatively mildly. Freyre added that this had reduced the friction between blacks and whites and thus explained what he argued were Brazil's more positive race relations. For a generation, Freyre's view shaped other scholarship, which took a more sympathetic view of Latin American slavery compared to that in the United States.

Other scholars later contradicted Freyre's argument, contending that slavery was pretty much the same institution across the Americas, equally brutal and equally exploitative. They based their argument on the idea that the economic needs of the plantation economy were the same across the region, with plantations in the U.S. south, the Caribbean, and Brazil all responding to the needs and pressures of increased production for export in the nineteenth century. From the sugar fields of Brazil to the rice plantations of South Carolina, the exploitation by each was absolute.

More recently, scholars have begun to use the demographics of slavery to develop more concrete evidence about the experiences of slavery in the Americas. They point to the fact that while only 6 percent of Africans arriving as slaves to the Americas were sent to the United States, by 1860, about two-thirds of all slaves in the Americas lived in the U.S. south. They argue that while slavery in the U.S. south was long assumed to be more abusive than the slavery in the Caribbean islands and Brazil, the much higher survival rate in the United States suggests otherwise. By looking more closely at the documents, what scholars have found is that the church and colonial law rarely protected slaves in Latin America, and while manumission was more common there, it was usually of the old or ill. Moreover, slaves in some regions of Latin America were responsible for supplying their own food. Thus, death rates and suicide rates among slaves were much higher in the region. Further influencing these calculations is the fact that fewer female slaves as a proportion of the total were brought to Latin America by comparison with the U.S. south, affecting both quality of life and reproduction rates. Slave families were less common and female slaves gave birth to fewer children on average in Latin America

Yet Spaniards and Portuguese also had a much more fluid view of race, where race mixing was common and, in practice, accepted. In the U.S., by contrast, the color line between black and white was stark. How each society dealt with race relations after the abolition of slavery was influenced by their experiences of slavery as well as by underlying racial beliefs. One need not conclude whether slavery was more brutal in one setting or another, since the ways to define what make it exploitative can vary. But a comparison is useful in forcing us to think in new ways about slavery in each setting, and to appreciate how each continues to deal in distinct ways with the legacy of the impact of slavery on race relations in each country today.

New economic forces also tipped the scales toward abolition in Cuba. Immigrant laborers from Mexico (Indians from Yucatán) and from China were brought in to work in the sugar fields and on the railroads of Cuba. They tended to displace slave labor as the sugar plantations became larger and more efficient. Yet, though abolition brought freedom for the enslaved blacks of Latin America, it did not necessarily result in equality or, in the short term, much of an improvement in their daily lives.

## WOMEN AND GENDER IN THE LIBERAL ERA

Throughout the nineteenth century, home ideally remained the sanctuary where women were regarded to be safe from the temptations of the world and where they could fulfill their natural destinies as mothers and wives. Even the Wars of Independence did little more than recast religious ideals about women as wives and mothers into a republican mold that ensured that women would remain excluded from official public life. In this patriarchal society, men kept legal and moral authority over their wives and families, restricting most wealthy women to a life of domesticity and dependence. Nevertheless, to be wife, mother, sister, or daughter was a complex business:

Although women married early and were encouraged to produce large families, they did make contributions to certain areas of life both in and outside the home. Women engaged in trade and commerce; held large amounts of money and property; collected debts; controlled the female religious orders; sponsored, organized, and financed colegios for girls; sustained charitable activities; contributed to the religious literature of the day; managed and organized their homes; supervised the servants; gave the rudiments of education to their progeny; and moved to exert control over their husbands. The Latin American woman, although homebound much of the time, was not a docile, passive type invested with little responsibility, for she took on much and exerted herself on behalf of her family and society in general.[2]

As in other aspects of Latin American society, a vast gulf divided privileged Creole ladies, surrounded by servants and protected by wealth, from poor Indian and black women subordinated on the basis of their gender and color. In other words, class divided women as well. Upper-class women found numerous avenues for the expression of their desires and skills, but the simple demands of making a living and caring for their families largely bound lower-class women. Despite ideals that confined women to domestic responsibilities, women of all classes engaged in an array of religious, philanthropic, and work activities, bringing them into regular contact with the world outside the home. As in all eras, some women broke with the traditional mold in quite spectacular ways. In Brazil, a small but active feminist press emerged in the 1870s and 1880s, dedicated to such women's issues as improved education, respect, and careers for women, as well as changes in women's legal rights. By the end of the century, even female suffrage—the right of women to vote—was emerging as an issue, though gaining the vote was still decades away for Latin American women. And in Peru, Clorinda Matto de Turner wrote *Aves sin nido* (Birds without a Nest) in 1899, the first major Indianist novel describing the plight of Indians in her country. A trailblazing book, it helped spark the Indianist movement that revolutionized Latin American society in the twentieth century. Equally important, it helped legitimize women as writers and social critics.

Most women did not lead such notable lives. But as Latin America entered the liberal era of order and progess in the mid- to late nineteenth century, opportunities for women grew. The activities that women engaged in took on new meaning in a world where liberalism—with its emphasis on freedom and respect for the individual—was ascendant. Women soon found that laws emphasizing the rights of individuals alongside the growing power of the nation-state provided both new opportunities and new challenges. Two liberal initiatives, in particular, had a dramatic impact on women and their role in society: the rise of public education and of private property.

Most women, including wealthy women, had little access to formal education. Women instead were educated within the home, learning a bit of French, the piano, and perhaps painting. They were taught how to read, though many were kept from learning to write. Fanny Calderón de la Barca, a Scotswoman married to a Spanish diplomat, lived in Mexico from 1839 to 1842, and her recollections of women in Mexico are revealing of her thoughts about the education of upper-class women:

> Generally speaking, then, the Mexican señoras and señoritas write, read, and play a little—sew, and take care of their houses and children. When I say they read, I mean they know how to read; when I say write, I do not mean they can always spell; and when I say they play [music], I do not assert that they have generally a knowledge of music . . . In fact, if we compare the education of women in Mexico with that of girls in England or in the United States, we should be inclined to dismiss the subject as nonexistent. It is not a comparison, but a contrast.[3]

The lack of educational opportunities for women began to shift for middle- and upper-class women in the late nineteenth century, though access to it varied greatly between and even within countries. Women in education were found earliest and with greatest influence in Argentina, a nation that modernized relatively quickly. Domingo F. Sarmiento, who in chapter 5 we saw was a key opponent of the caudillo Juan Manuel de Rosas, was Argentina's foremost educator, a president (1868–1874), a writer, and one of Latin America's best-known apostles of modernization. Inspired by the progressive educational reforms being made in the United States—where he spent several years in exile—Sarmiento introduced reforms into his native Argentina. For Sarmiento, public secular education for citizens was the ultimate weapon for eradicating ignorance, reducing prejudice, and transforming Argentina into a prosperous, civilized nation. A key element in Sarmiento's thinking—as well as that of Juan Bautista Alberdi, another reformer and leader—was to bring women fully into the educational system. The philosophy of Sarmiento and Alberdi was well captured by Cynthia Jeffress Little.

> Alberdi, who coined the motto "to govern is to populate," believed that Argentina would not advance until its women no longer lived under the yoke of Spanish law and customs that subjugated them first to their fathers' and then to their husbands' control. He maintained that with scant opportunities to develop identities beyond wife and mother, most women were no more than mere children. Alberdi advocated that Argentine women should be educated to assume the full duties of citizenship and to contribute to the country's economic growth.[4]

Sarmiento was convinced that the educational models being developed by Horace Mann and others in North America were exemplary. And women played a central role, not simply as persons to be educated to fulfill their new roles of citizens, but as educators themselves, as teachers who could transmit values and knowledge in the new normal schools of Argentina. Sarmiento invited young North American teachers to come to Argentina to be leaders in this movement. Between 1869 and 1898, more than sixty came, bringing with them the newest ways then being pioneered in the United States. They extolled the virtue of universality—little red schoolhouses that taught the basics of reading, writing, and arithmetic, ideally reaching all children. They also stressed practical, vocational education. Under Sarmiento's tutelage, these normal schools deemphasized the traditional method of rote learning, which did not promote education in the broadest sense. Self-discipline, physical fitness, technical training, and manual labor all were stressed in these new normal schools, while home economics became a linchpin of the curriculum. Old church curricula were abandoned for a more secular, scientific course of study. The goal of these new schools was to educate young women to learn new ways in order to improve their lives, the lives of their families, and, ultimately, the life of their nation. The post-independence emergence of liberal freedoms and liberties thus brought many positive changes for women in education.

Yet women also lost the protection of colonial laws and of the church. The era of Order and Progress opened women up to new types of exploitation—especially poorer women—bringing new challenges and limits. For example, new legal codes after independence reinforced the rights of fathers and husbands over the home. With the goal of strengthening the republican family, the new governments took away married women's rights over both their property and their children. Not only did a woman lose rights to marital property after the death of her husband, but men also gained the legal right to choose whether to recognize a child born to them out of wedlock, giving them maximum control over inheritance. Family honor continued to dominate marital and family relations, with a man's obligation to provide for his family and a woman's obligation to be a dutiful and obedient companion forming the foundations of marriage and family laws. The emancipation of wives from their husbands' authority, as one politician in Mexico stated, would "risk the continued mutiny of the population against the established authority, and undermine the stability of the Mexican state."[5]

With greater political stability by the later part of the century, the state became more active in intervening in the affairs of the home, for example, through rulings over divorce and custody arrangements. Seeing marital instability as a forerunner to social disorder, the state was most often paternalistic, with judges decreeing rulings that prioritized family stability over female happiness—sometimes even safety. The laws and decrees favoring the patriarchal family cut both ways. The courts became an important place—one where women sued their husbands for separation, demanded that they fulfill material obligations to the family, or tried to end years of extreme abuse. Yet, laws also stated that if a husband was unfaithful to his wife, it was legal, so long as his actions were not scandalous or injurious to family honor. However, if a wife were caught with another man, it was illegal—even a capital crime in some places. In essence, in their pursuit of order and progress, the new, stronger, liberal states played a more prominent role in regulating gender and relationships between men and women, displacing the historic role of the church or village leaders as the primary moral authorities.

Of course, the power of the state had limits; people who lived in urban areas or were more prominent faced closer scrutiny. For example, scholars have shown how prostitutes were a key target of the moralizing campaigns and expanding regulatory reach of the state. But for many poor women, whether ex-slaves working as domestic servants in Rio de Janeiro or Indian tortilla vendors on the streets of Mexico City, the state continued to be a distant power disconnected from the conditions that shaped their daily lives.

Latin America's integration into global capitalist markets also had a significant influence on gender relations and women in the late nineteenth century. The expansion of haciendas and new land laws enforcing private property rights disrupted village and community life and land relations. At a minimum, the import of new goods threatened the livelihoods of women artisans, with female unemployment growing in some places. In other places, the expansion of export agriculture gave women new opportunities to earn money by setting up small businesses around the new, larger plantations, selling things like food, clothes, or even sex. These disruptions—like the loss of subsistence agriculture as large landowners took land—could also tear apart communities and families by undermining men's ability to care for their families. Traditionally, women were to obey community leaders and male patriarchs in subsistence-based economies; this limitation had also provided a measure of protection and care. With the export boom of the late nineteenth century, many women found themselves pushed by necessity to seek out new ways to earn money and care for their families without the protection of community. The impact of wars and migration on the male population left women increasingly in charge of their own households. Even when men and women joined, they often did so without the official sanction of marriage. Across Latin America, marriage rates among non-elites were low, and out-of-wedlock births were common.

These disruptions could have surprising and ambivalent results. In some places, like various communities in highland Mexico, no women received new land titles when land was privatized, and their only access to land was through men. Yet, in other places, the results were quite different. For example, in Dirioma, Nicaragua, historian Elizabeth Dore has shown that with the expansion of the coffee economy, commercialization and land privatization actually created more economic opportunities for women, including a growing number of female property owners, and marriage rates dropped. Dore concludes, nonetheless, that these changes did not necessarily mean equality or more autonomy for women, as local authorities moved in to regulate women's lives and behavior.[6] Whether their new economic roles were as landowners or urban domestic servants, as food vendors or prostitutes, the export boom of the late nineteenth century was a period of fast change for women and families. The percentage of female-headed households continued to grow in large cities like São Paolo, Brazil, and in small towns such as Diriomo, Nicaragua, disrupting the power of men over the household. Thus, while liberal laws and ideals continued to exert influence over women, and positivist leaders were deeply concerned about the impact on social order of unregulated women, reality meant that women had diverse and active roles in everyday life—roles that reflected their own needs and desires, regardless of what patriarchal norms and religious morality prescribed.

## LIFE IN THE COUNTRY

> [In Mexico] the white is the proprietor; the Indian the worker. The white is rich; the Indian poor and miserable. The descendants of the Spaniards have within their reach all the knowledge of the century and all of the scientific discoveries; the Indian is completely unaware of it. The white dresses like a Parisian fashion plate and uses the richest of fabrics; the Indian runs around almost naked. The white lives in the cities in magnificent houses; the Indian is isolated in the country, his house a miserable hut. They are two different peoples in the same land; but worse, to a degree they are enemies.[7]

This grim observation of Mexican rural life at midcentury was not unusual. Rural life in nineteenth-century Latin America was, in fact, altered substantially by the introduction of new technologies, by the opening of new markets, by more efficient forms of organization, and by improved methods of production. The rural population declined in the second half of the nineteenth century, but it still represented about 80 to 85 percent of the total population, although the ratio of rural to urban population varied tremendously across countries. The social and economic distance that divided the owners from the workers, the hacendados from the peons, and the masters from the slaves tended to widen.

Of the many forms of land tenure prevalent in Latin America, the most common ones devoted to commercial operations were the hacienda and the plantation. Both were large estates—controlled or owned by the few, and worked by the many. At the other end of the land-use spectrum were the small plots and mini-farms that, along with sharecropping, probably predominated in Latin America. In much of indigenous America—such as Mexico, Guatemala, Ecuador, Peru, and Bolivia—Indians still held and worked a significant proportion of land communally.

Haciendas and plantations were basically the same. They were not, however, simple institutions, because they fulfilled several different goals and were shaped by regional differences. They evolved in the rapidly changing conditions of the nineteenth century and were dynamic rather than static institutions. Economically, the haciendas and plantations were among the principal forms of livelihood in nineteenth-century Latin America. In many instances, they were self-sufficient, producing foods, animals, and rudimentary goods for local consumption. Cash crops and animals—from sugar to cattle—also came from the plantations and haciendas to be sold for profit either in domestic markets or through export. Socially, haciendas and plantations were the basic source of wealth to maintain and increase the status of the elites who owned or controlled them. They were also the primary social organization in many rural areas, tying together wealthy and poor through their distinct but connected roles on the hacienda or plantation. And politically, they nurtured the rulers, who by and large shared a common background—commercial landholding—that was their source of power. One has simply to refer to the great and small caudillos of the nineteenth century to witness how closely they resembled one another in their sources of power. Santa Anna of Mexico and Rosas of Argentina, for example, were hacendados who drew strength from fellow hacendados.

The haciendas produced everything from beans for their peons to sugar for export to the emporiums of Europe. Life on the haciendas varied widely. It depended upon who one was. The accounts in the accompanying textboxes give some idea of this variety. The historian James Scobie captured some of this variety in his description of Argentina. *Estancias* was simply another term for ranches, in this instance haciendas geared more for livestock production. Historians Michael Meyer, William Sherman, and Susan Deeds described the flip side of the coin: life on a Mexican hacienda for the peon. Stanley Stein described life for a slave on a sugar or coffee plantation in Brazil.

### The Estancias of Argentina

"A few of the rural population—the wealthy landowner or cattleman—enjoyed the amenities of a civilized existence. By the end of the nineteenth century the *estancia* headquarters had changed from a bare frontier outpost into a Mediterranean villa, a French chateau, or a gabled English country house, surrounded by eucalyptus groves, cropped lawns, rose gardens, and tennis courts. But for these people, country residence was limited to summer or weekend visits, and they were far better acquainted with the streets of Buenos Aires or Paris and the beaches of Mar del Plata than with the land which provided their wealth. Those who actually lived on the pampas led quite another existence."

James R. Scobie, *Argentina: A City and a Nation,* 2nd ed. (New York: Oxford University Press, 1971), p. 126.

### The Haciendas of Mexico

"Working conditions varied considerably from region to region and even from hacienda to hacienda, but they were generally poor. Peones often availed themselves of the talents of a scribe to spell out their gamut of complaints. While it was not uncommon for the peón to be allotted a couple of furrows to plant a little corn and chile and on occasion to receive a small ration of food from the hacienda, he worked from sunrise to sunset, often seven days a week, raising crops or tending cattle. Sometimes he was allowed to cut firewood free; on other occasions he paid for the right. The scant wages he received most often were not paid in currency but in certificates or metal discs redeemable only at the local *tienda de raya,* an all-purpose company store located on the hacienda complex. Credit was extended liberally, but the prices, set by the hacendado or the mayordomo, were invariably several times higher than those in a nearby village. For the hacendado the situation was perfect. The taxes on his land were negligible; his labor was, in effect, free, for all the wages that went out came back to him through the *tienda de raya* with a handsome profit. The peón found himself in a state of perpetual debt, and by law he was bound to remain on the hacienda so long as he owed a single centavo. Debts could be passed on to the children. Should an occasional obdurate peón escape, there was scarcely any place for him to go. Many states had laws making it illegal to hire an indebted peón."

Michael C. Meyer, William L. Sherman, and Susan M. Deeds, *The Course of Mexican History,* 10th ed. (New York: Oxford University Press, 2013), pp. 342–43.

### The Fazendas of Brazil

"'Greater or lesser perfection . . . of discipline determines the greater or lesser degree of prosperity of agricultural establishments.' Constant supervision and thorough control through discipline joined to swift, often brutal punishment were considered an absolute necessity on coffee plantations. Proper function of a fazenda [Portuguese for hacienda] varied directly with the steady application of the working force; in an epoch of little machinery, slave labor, or what Brazilians termed 'organized labor,' had to be guided carefully and supervised closely. . . .

"Most visible of the master's authority over the slave, the whip enjoyed several names: there was the literate term *chicote,* which was usually a five-tailed and metal-tipped lash, colloquially known as the 'codfish' or 'armadillo.' Probably because Portuguese drivers went armed with such cat-o'-nine-tails, slaves tagged it with the name of the favorite article of Portuguese diet—codfish. It was felt that sometimes it was used too much, sometimes too little, for often masters had the 'very poor habit of failing to whip on the spot, and prefer to threaten the vexatious slave with 'Wait, you'll pay for this all at once' or 'The cup is brimming, wait 'til it pours over and *then* we'll see'—and at that time they grab and beat him unmercifully; why? because he paid for his misdeeds *all at once!!!!*' It was difficult to apply legal restraints to the planters' use of the lash. When one of the founding fathers of Vassouras [a Brazilian coffee-producing region], Ambrozio de Souza Coutinho, proposed, as one of the municipal regulations of 1829, that 'Every master who mistreats his slaves with blows and lashes, with repeated and inhuman punishment proven by verbal testimony . . .' be fined, fellow-planters refused to accept it. Not sheer perversity but the desire to drive slaves to work longer and harder motivated liberal use of the lash. 'Many inhuman fazendeiros [Portuguese for *hacendado*],' wrote Caetano da Fonseca, more than thirty years after Souza Coutinho, 'force their slaves with the lash to work beyond physical endurance. These wretched slaves, using up their last drops of energy, end their days in a brief time.'"

Stanley Stein, "Masters and Slaves in Southern Brazil," in Robert G. Keith, *Haciendas and Plantations in Latin American History* (New York: Holmes and Meier, 1977), pp. 94–95.

These accounts of life on haciendas and fazendas provide only a small glimpse into the diversity of the relationships that developed on these estates. Some research has suggested that life was not always as rigidly regulated or as demeaning as the descriptions by Scobie, Meyer et al., and Stein suggest. For example, the system of debt peonage described so well in the passage on Mexico may not have so dominated the relationship between landlord and peon as was once thought, and wage labor was more common in some areas than previously known. In Peru, Indians who were persuaded to travel from the highlands to work seasonally on the sugar and cotton plantations on the coast soon learned to bargain actively for their labor with the hacienda owners. In other countries, slaves could be brutalized by overseers intent on getting the most work out of the slaves' short life spans. Conversely, as described by Gilberto Freyre, slaves may have experienced relatively mild treatment in the context of the intimacy of life within the great houses on the sugar estates of the Brazilian northeast. The variety of arrangements reflected regional differences, as well as the local labor supply, laws, production needs, and even simply individual personalities.

Not all land was owned by the hacendado class in Latin America. Perhaps 30 to 40 percent of the land in the Indian nations (Mexico, Guatemala, Ecuador, Peru, and Bolivia, principally) was still preserved by the ancient communities that owned the land collectively. These communal lands and the communities they sustained were as varied as the haciendas and plantations. They differed greatly in size from a few dozen people to hundreds or more. They produced a variety of things, usually for subsistence but, increasingly over the course of the nineteenth century, goods such as vanilla or coffee that could be marketed beyond the community. Moreover, while some were bastions of cohesion, cooperation, and goodwill, others were riven by conflicts over things like access to land, water, or local power. Like any other community, they were socially stratified, with clear distinctions between rich and poor, old and young, men and women. As the state became more intrusive over the nineteenth century and as export-oriented agriculture played a more prominent role in rural life, the ability of local leaders to manage conflicts within the community was challenged.

In other parts of Latin America, workers on the haciendas might also have been small landowners, or tenants who were allowed to farm a portion of the hacienda's land for their own benefit. Such people were called *inquilinos* in Chile and *parceiros* in Brazil; again, other names were applied in other places. Their lot may or may not have been onerous, depending upon the conditions and the place.

Labor on the haciendas could be permanent or seasonal. Coffee plantations in the highlands of Guatemala or sugar plantations in Cuba or Peru necessitated large amounts of labor at selected times of the year, principally during harvest. In these areas, especially as those crops developed larger markets abroad, migrant laborers tended to be treated more as components in the economic formula that produced profits. As wage laborers, they could be hired and fired at will. This gave the owners surer control over labor, and thus better control over their exports, whose market conditions also varied widely.

To meet changing market conditions abroad, the haciendas and plantations themselves took on different complexions in the nineteenth century. As they shifted to producing more and more for export, they became larger and more commercialized, necessitating greater amounts of labor and capital. If the labor was not available locally, they reached into other parts of the country. As noted earlier, coastal sugar plantations in Peru attracted Indians from the highlands who came as seasonal, paid laborers. In other locations, they might hook a worker into debt labor through a loan, which, depending on the region or owner, could be highly exploitative or merely a way to attract workers through an advance. And in some places, such as Guatemala, there was a return of draft labor, in this case forcing indigenous people to work a certain number of days on a hacienda. In all cases, the growth of export agriculture brought with it growing internal migrations. Workers might migrate to a coastal plantation to work temporarily during the harvest, earning enough to perhaps pay off their taxes, the expenses of religious rites such as marriage or a burial, or even just the daily cost of living, after which they would return to their communities and continue their subsistence farming. In other places, they might be tied more permanently to a plantation or hacienda through debt, leaving behind family and community for great stretches of time. As migrations increased, whether temporary or longer term, the communities and families left behind often had to adjust to a new way of life caused by the disruptions, including new patterns of farming and land usage, the emergence of new rivalries and factions seeking

**Figure 7.2** A typical hacienda in late nineteenth-century Mexico, showing horses, laborers, and a church in the background. Courtesy Library of Congress.

power and resources, the influx of capital from the migrant laborers, and new types of family and marriage arrangements.

When domestic sources of labor were insufficient, hacendados and other employers (such as the great railroad builders in the second half of the century) looked abroad. Hundreds of thousands of Chinese indentured servants were brought to Costa Rica, Peru, Cuba, and other countries in Latin America not only to work on the railroads but also to plant, till, and harvest on the expanding plantations. Many faced deplorable conditions, including extreme physical abuse and a lack of basic food and shelter. Many died, including over half of the indentured servants on Peru's plantations and guano fields, before the Chinese government forced an end to the traffic in the 1870s.[8] Emigrants from Italy swelled the rural population of Argentina and Brazil to allow for the rapid expansion of the wheat and coffee industries, for example. Although the experience of Italians in the coffee groves of Brazil might have been harsh, it was different from the experience of Yucatecan Indians, nearly enslaved by tradition and force on the sugar and henequen plantations of their native homeland.

Throughout the nineteenth century, land tended to be concentrated more and more into larger estates controlled by fewer people, a result of liberal land laws that promoted the privatization of property, the influx of foreign investors looking to profit from expanding economies, new technologies that enabled mass production, market forces that encouraged export-oriented production, and sometimes simply corruption that allowed elites to seize rural lands for their own use. The goal was to make haciendas and plantations more efficient—to produce more with lowered costs for the export market. In Cuba, large, modern sugar mills replaced the smaller and less efficient sugar mills of the past. The same occurred in Peru, where concentration reached such an extreme that, by the turn of the century, most of the sugar industry was controlled by a handful of people. The result, from Chile north to Mexico, from Cuba south to Argentina, was the impoverishment of the people who worked the land, whether tenants, seasonal laborers, immigrants, indentured servants, Indians, mestizos, or blacks.

When one considers that Latin America in the nineteenth century was still overwhelmingly rural, this tendency certainly worked against the majority of people. For every trend, however, there is usually one, under way or just beginning, that contradicts the larger trend—or that argues for a different view in the face of it. As life got tougher in the country, it improved in the cities.

## LIFE IN THE CITY

The Hispanic and Portuguese legacy in Latin America emphasized the city as the center of culture and society. Tendencies set loose by the modernization and industrialization processes in the nineteenth century reinforced urbanization. Cities grew larger and more prosperous, becoming the diadems of progress, crisscrossed by new trams and streetcars clanking along wide boulevards carved out from the narrow colonial alleys and streets.

Opera houses and salons catered to the wealthy, while business and politics hummed in the counting houses and government palaces built to accommodate the new lifestyles. Although there were great differences between nations, overall the number of people living in cities increased dramatically in Latin America from the 1870s through the 1930s; by the early twentieth century, 10 to 20 percent of the population of Latin America was urban.

The influence of Europe was pervasive in the great (and even not-so-great) cities of Latin America. Paris fashions adorned wealthy women, and many adopted English customs. Jockey clubs, cricket clubs, and other trappings of European life popped up in Mexico City, Buenos Aires, and Santiago. If Europe was the center of civilization, then its ways were to be imitated. Sons were sent off to the cities of Europe to be educated, and artists went to escape the suffocating provinciality of Latin America—to breathe in the invigorating streams of innovation and experimentation. Even European political ideals and philosophies (positivism and scientific racism, for example) were imported wholesale into Latin America.

People flocked to the city from the countryside, looking for work, education, or sometimes just excitement. Immigrants further swelled urban populations. For example, in the early twentieth century, half of the population of Buenos Aires was born abroad. Overall, São Paulo's population jumped from 64,000 in 1890 to 240,000 barely a decade later. Santiago's population went from 160,000

> ### Buenos Aires, a Great City in the Making
>
> "[Buenos Aires] was the city that by 1910 even Parisians would claim as the Paris of South America after a Cinderella-like transformation from *gran aldea* [big town] into the beautiful and prosperous queen of the Río de la Plata. Much of the change was physical. . . . Open sewers and dirt streets disappeared from downtown Buenos Aires during the 1880s . . . and by the turn of the century *porteño* ladies were enjoying relatively comfortable carriage rides (aided by the first use of rubber tires) over a steadily expanding network of asphalted streets and avenues. . . . By 1905 electricity had largely replaced the overworked horses of the city's trolley system. . . . How rapidly the city was changing was emphasized in 1911 when work began on the Avenida de Mayo subway. Three years later, the British-built line was opened to its present extension four miles west of the Plaza de Mayo—only a decade after New York City had completed the first major subway in the hemisphere. . . . Office buildings, hotels, and private palaces replaced many of the one- or two-story, patio-style houses in the center of Buenos Aires."
>
> James R. Scobie, *Argentina: A City and a Nation,* 2nd ed. (New York: Oxford University Press, 1971), pp. 164–67.

in 1880 to 400,000 in 1910. Mexico City was swept up in the same trend, its population rising from 200,000 in 1874 to almost 500,000 in 1910. Smaller cities sometimes recorded even more spectacular increases, their populations tripling, quadrupling, and even quintupling as railroads, mining, port improvements, and other incentives promoted growth.

Of the great cities of Latin America, Buenos Aires perhaps underwent one of the most spectacular transformations. Its population jumped fivefold from 300,000 in 1880 to 1.5 million in 1914, much of the growth coming from European immigrants. In Valparaíso, a beautiful Chilean port city rising from a bay into hills that climb steeply from the water's edge, also was transformed, provoking a rave review from one observer in 1885 (see p. 152).

Although madly modernizing their cities, Latin Americans were not insensitive to the need to beautify and humanize as they tore down the old and built the new. Parks, promenades, majestic trees, and shaded walks all were planned into the new cities. Mexico City's great Alameda Park was a gathering place for young and old, rich and poor, while public activities such as bullfights also brought all the classes together in the city.

The Latin American city had a leveling effect on society that did not occur in the countryside, where rigid norms and patriarchal power limited social mobility. Freed from the oversight of rural communities, people flooded into cities and tried to forge their own way, often against incredible odds. Principal beneficiaries

**Figure 7.3** Downtown Buenos Aires, Argentina, 1900. The signs of modernization are easily recognizable: carriages, wide boulevards, architecture inspired by European styles—a city and a nation on the move. Bain News Service. Courtesy Library of Congress.

were members of the expanding, ambitious middle class, a rather vague group that we can begin to define as everybody who was not a member of the elite or of the lower classes, sometimes also called the working class. Who were they?

By profession and economic activity they were bank clerks, government bureaucrats, low-ranking army officers, teachers, clergy, small businesspeople, skilled artisans, journalists, and neighborhood grocers. Ethnically, they could be mestizos, whites, European or Asian immigrants, mulattoes, blacks—all people, in fact, whose economic activity was more important in defining them than was their ancestry. They aspired to move up the economic and social ladder. This meant finding larger, more modern apartments or homes equipped with the best of city life: running water, sewerage, electricity. Shopping at the new, European-style department stores, they dressed for and wished to give evidence of their prosperity. They often spent more than they made to keep up a good front and to give their children the best chances at a good education. They were subject to fluctuations in the economy, being pinched severely in times of inflation and recession. Perhaps most important, they did not have a clearly defined sense of class. They were glad to have risen above the lower classes, and they aspired to be like the upper classes. Their values thus tended to be adopted from the elites. Scattered around the many political groupings in the nineteenth century, they possessed little political cohesion. In numbers, they represented about a tenth of

> **Valparaíso**
>
> "I was struck by the very civilized look of the famous Chilean seaport. . . . In the dining-room of the hotel the electric light was used, as well as in very many of the stores. In the streets is a 'Belgium' pavement, and the sidewalks are smoothly and neatly flagged. The architecture of some of the buildings is very fine, and there are several rich and elegant churches. The principal streets are threaded by tramways. The trams, or cars, are of two stories as in Paris and other European cities."
>
> Frank Vincent, a traveler in Valparaíso in 1885, quoted in E. Bradford Burns, ed., *Latin America: Conflict and Creation; A Historical Reader* (Englewood Cliffs, N.J.: Prentice Hall, 1993), p. 141.

the population, largely concentrated in the cities, where the industrialization and urbanization processes provided opportunities for advancement. They were the epitome of Order and Progress, the human manifestation of the power of positivism to modernize the region and the people who lived there.

Nevertheless, the lower classes constituted the bulk of the population in the growing cities. They were often looked down on by elites for introducing their traditional ways to modern urban life, and were resented for moving so freely across urban spaces. But they did the work that kept the cities growing and moving. They worked in the modern factories that emerged in the late nineteenth century, were stevedores on the piers and wharves, or worked as pick-and-shovel men in the vastly expanding public works sponsored by governments. They were market vendors, flower sellers, seamstresses, domestic servants, or even prostitutes, fulfilling the needs of the rapidly growing urban population. They were, in fact, everywhere where strong backs or nimble fingers were needed to dig ditches, work the looms of textile mills, clean the homes of the wealthy and middle classes, or labor in any other of the many enterprises associated with the growing economies.

And members of the lower classes, be they Indians recently arrived in the coastal cities of Peru, Italians in the cities of southern Brazil, or mestizos migrating from country to city throughout Latin America, received few immediate benefits from their work. They were, in fact, underfed, overworked, exploited, and in the main helpless to protect themselves in a society where laissez-faire was the reigning philosophy. Laws to protect men, women, or children in the workplace simply did not exist, whereas laws and traditions that forbade the formation of labor unions *did* exist, often enforced with brutality by governments largely controlled by the elites. Many newly arrived, including an increasing number of women who headed their own households, found themselves in a world with few protections. Many of the lower classes lived in tenements, where they often shared a single room with a dozen other people, with no running water or bathing facilities. With few public services, the streets in poorer areas would flood with sewage and garbage; the only access to water would be from the nearby fountain. Illiteracy and poverty were associated with life among the lower classes. Infant mortality ran as high as 30 percent among Mexico's lower classes, a dismal statistic to contemplate when translated into the human suffering that dead and dying children meant to mothers and fathers. In Argentina, real wages among the urban poor climbed slightly during the booming 1880s and 1890s, then spiraled downward in succeeding downturns of the economy.

One cannot ignore the gulf that separated the elites, the aspiring middle classes, and the great mass of people called the lower class in these thriving urban centers. Although the *promise* of a better life was inherent in the profound changes being induced by modernization—greater opportunities, new jobs, new industries, new hopes (being best realized by the small middle class)—the great majority of people still led humble lives, prevented from rising out of dire existence by their illiteracy, their poverty, and powerful traditions, institutions, and beliefs. Indeed, the great social movements of the twentieth century in Latin America, covered in succeeding chapters, began when these contrasts in wealth and opportunity could no longer be tolerated.

Amidst all these changes, one principal institution from the colonial period emerged intact from the Wars of Independence into the nineteenth century. It survived liberal assaults on its power, economic assaults on its property, and philosophical assaults on its significance to survive, as it still does today in Latin America, as one of the most significant sources of spiritual and physical solace and comfort for the majority of Latin Americans. That institution is the Roman Catholic Church.

## RELIGION AND THE CHURCH

There was in the Roman Catholic Church a social unity as well as a unity of belief. Catholicism was implanted not only on the coasts, but also in the highlands; not only in the towns but also in the country, among peasants, miners, and artisans. Although the church represented the principal form of organized religion in nineteenth-century Latin America, other religious currents flowed through the spiritual life of the people. Many blacks, for example, developed alternate religious institutions such as Candomblé in Brazil, Vodou (voodoo) in Haiti, and Santería in Cuba. In the heavily populated indigenous regions of Latin America, such as in Mexico, Guatemala, and along the Andes of the west coast of South America, many syncretized (or combined) forms of worship developed. Catholicism was accepted, but the worship of indigenous gods and spirits, often associated with geographic locations and natural phenomena, also coexisted with formal Catholicism. Even Protestantism made some

### Religion of the People

"It has been said of Peru: 'From Spanish cities to the most primitive Indian communities in the bleak *altiplano* [high plains] the same signs and symbols of the Christian faith were recognized and revered, pointing to a unity of religious belief that cut across steep economic, social and linguistic barriers. . . .' [The sacred landscape was] the local world of images and relics, patron saints, vows, shrines and miracles, and all the other spiritual aids which these urban and rural communities invoked against the scourge of plague, earthquake, drought and famine. The religion of the people was expressed in various ways, vows to Our Lady and the saints, relics and indulgences, and, above all, the shrines and sacred sites of local religious life. These were the scenes of cures, miracles and visions, the holy places where prayers were said and heard, the objects of processions and pilgrimages, part of the landscape of the people. Everyday life was pervaded by religion, which appeared to the people in metaphysical truths and physical forms; it answered their questions and satisfied their needs which nature itself could not. The great religious processions, Christ of the Miracles in Lima, Our Lady of Chapi in Arequipa, the Lord of Solitude in Huaraz, Our Lady of Copacabana in Bolivia, Our Lady of Luján in Argentina, Our Lady of Guadalupe in Mexico, these testify to the popular base of the Church and the strength of popular religiosity."

John Lynch, "The Catholic Church in Latin America, 1830–1930," in Leslie Bethell, ed., *The Cambridge History of Latin America* (Cambridge: Cambridge University Press, 1986), 4:553–54.

inroads, largely through the missionary movements of mainline denominations such as Presbyterian and Methodist. The main impact of Protestantism, however, would come in the second half of the twentieth century with the dramatic expansion of the Evangelicals and Pentecostals.

The Roman Catholic Church underwent some drastic changes as it adapted to the conditions brought on by independence and modernization. The formal separation of church and state came about as the new countries broke their ties with Spain. The church also had to meet the challenges of a rising tide of secularism and positivism, which challenged its ancient monopoly on truth and morality. It had to adjust to a world where its word and its jurisdiction were not simply accepted on the basis of faith, law, and tradition. The transition for the church was wrenching in many instances, and its struggle for survival began with the shock of independence.

When the ties between the colonies and the Spanish crown were severed by independence, the centuries-old bond between the church and its principal

**Figure 7.4** Religious procession in Lima, Peru, circa 1935. Thousands of believers surrounded the statue of Christ—*Cristo de los Milagros*—as it was carried through the streets of the capital. Courtesy Tulane University Library.

benefactor, the crown, was also cut. The new national governments in turn quickly assumed the old powers of the crown to appoint church officials, collect and distribute tithes, and, in effect, administer many aspects of church life. Some new governments also moved to strip much of the church's economic wealth by confiscating lands and property while eliminating or cutting back the religious orders, secularizing education, and attacking other rights and privileges of the church. A corollary was that middle- and upper-class women took over some of the welfare functions of the church, including lobbying for material and political support for schools, orphanages, and other charitable institutions formerly run by the church.

For the rest of the nineteenth century, the church essentially adjusted to the harsh conditions forced upon it by liberals, positivists, and nationalists who wanted to gain control over diverse areas such as education and property holding, for example. In a concession to conservatives, in some areas liberals were less aggressive in going after the rights and wealth of the church. Nevertheless, eventually cut loose from the support of the state, the church became more independent by the dawn of the twentieth century. Instead of looking to the crown or to the republic, it became more closely tied to the papacy in Rome. There, popes—especially Pius IX in the 1860s and 1870s and Leo XIII in the 1890s—reasserted control over the church in Latin America and moved to revitalize it.

In the second half of the nineteenth century, reform and renewed evangelization became passwords of the changing church. New priests emerged from the seminaries instilled with a strict morality and a deep commitment to their flocks. Becoming more orthodox, they also fought liberalism passionately, underscoring the tendency of the church to associate with conservative factions in political battles. In 1864, Pope Pius IX reaffirmed the church's antagonism to liberalism with his *Syllabus of Errors.*

The *Syllabus* condemned liberalism, freedom of thought, tolerance, and secular education. The church lashed out at its enemies—those who undermined its authority. Positivism especially drew the church's fire because it seemed to represent an alternative religion, a faith in science rather than in tradition and revelation. Intellectual radicals such as the Peruvian Manuel González Prada (1848–1918) attacked the church directly, calling for it to be eliminated from all public life and for science, as its substitute, to be raised as "the only God of the future."[9]

As the church sought to renew and protect itself, it also had to face a rapidly changing world, marked not only by hostile philosophies such as positivism but also by modernization, urbanization, and industrialization. To meet the challenges of the new working classes in the cities, of immigrants, and of countless other phenomena associated with modernization, Pope Leo XIII in 1891 issued a critical encyclical entitled *Rerum Novarum* (Of New Things). In it he took the revolutionary position that the church must protect the rights of workers and fight the injustices of the liberal system. Catholics had the duty to promote social justice and to ensure that the immense gaps between rich and poor would be closed by state intervention or by the application of justice. While the encyclical denied the validity of socialism, which competed with the church for the allegiance of the masses, it also attacked unbridled capitalism as a source of inequality and injustice. *Rerum Novarum* was, in effect, a modern response by an ancient institution, the church, to challenges to its worth and validity.

As the church adjusted to the demands of the modernizing world, the people of Latin America continued to practice and develop other forms of worship—forms that reflected the immensely diverse ethnic and cultural pop-

### The Church before the Modern World

"Yet the Church in Latin America had adjusted to change. At the beginning of the nineteenth century it was a colonial Church, dependent on a metropolis, Spain or Portugal. A century later it was truly independent, compatible with the nation state yet part of the universal Church. It still fulfilled a basic responsibility of the Church, to bring people to God, and it preserved intact Christian doctrine and religious observance for transmission to future generations . . . the compromising alliance of the altar and the throne, of the church and the state, was gone forever . . . [yet] this new independence . . . enabled the Church to speak more clearly to the poor and oppressed. It sharpened the division between religionists and secularists . . . at the same time the Church expanded materially, increasing its own revenues and strengthening its own institutions."

John Lynch, "The Catholic Church in Latin America, 1830–1930," in Leslie Bethell, ed., *The Cambridge History of Latin America* (Cambridge: Cambridge University Press, 1986), 4:595.

ulation of the region. Candomblé in Brazil combined African spirits and liturgies into a Catholic context where African religious traits, folk Catholicism, and native Brazilian Indian folklore all commingled in novel forms. Haitian Vodou, based on the belief systems of Dahomeans, an African people enslaved and brought to the island in the eighteenth century, focused on spirit worship. It became a focal point in the slave rebellions that eventually overthrew the French colonial authorities and established a free Haiti. And along the Andes and other parts of indigenous America ancient gods and spirits continued to coexist with Christian saints, sometimes subsumed into church ritual, sometimes simply practiced alongside Christian forms of worship. Mountains, streams, and lakes all could be the abode of spirits whose presence far predated the arrival of Christianity.

Religion in Latin America was the natural expression of a desire to understand and live in harmony with the supernatural world beyond people's immediate senses. As we probe the history of Latin America, it becomes evident that the reality is far deeper and richer than simple economic and political approaches, for example, can reveal. Running beneath the surface of political and social realities are rich cultures that open different windows into the human condition. At the same time, the most powerful institution representing religious beliefs, the Catholic Church, was not immune to the pressures that came in the era of Order and Progress, and it adapted in innovative ways, such as calling for social justice for the masses, to the changing world brought on by urbanization, modernization, and rising liberalism.

## CONCLUSIONS AND ISSUES

The booming export economies and liberal nation-states discussed in chapter 6 were part of the broader phenomena of social change that spread across the region in the late nineteenth century. Order and Progress was not merely a political slogan of aspiring liberal politicians, but embodied the spirit of the age of secular individualism—and the policies, practices, and beliefs that came along with it. Population growth, urbanization, public education, and new land and labor laws reshaped the lives of all Latin Americans.

Between the extremes of the white wealthy elite and the powerless and penniless black slaves, there existed a broad stratum of Indians, free blacks, poor whites, and powerful mestizos, mulattoes, and pardos who belied the stereotypical situation of a simple privileged white elite governing a mass of Indians, black slaves, and mestizos. The emerging middle classes alone were testament to the modernizing impulses that characterized this increasingly complex society. Women were not simply passive on this changing stage, but rather actively pursued their own goals and set their own agendas, even if limited within the prevailing laws and cultural norms, and even if, along with the poor, they now increasingly fell under the regulatory gaze of the state. Together, these groups comprised a rich and varied Latin American culture and society that by the late nineteenth century was on the move.

Likewise, we examined the abolition of slavery, some of the major ways in which people related to one another in urban and rural environments, and the role of religion in the region. Each of these topics gives us insight into how people lived, worked, played, and worshipped within complex societies. Extremes did indeed exist within Latin American societies, but there were immense spaces between the very rich and the very poor, spaces occupied by native and African religions, spaces occupied by small but emerging middle classes, and spaces marked by the evolution of a people who possessed a rich and varied culture and society.

### Discussion Questions

What were the major demographic changes in Latin American in the nineteenth century and why are they important for understanding the period?

What were the most significant liberal policies and practices affecting the lives of Indians in Latin America, and what was their impact?

What were the causes of the abolition of slavery in Brazil and Cuba?

How did the emergence of public education and laws enforcing private property affect the lives of women and families in Latin America? Did the liberal era empower women?

How did Latin America's turn to export-oriented production transform rural areas? What were the primary forms of land use, and how did they shape rural social relations?

What can changes to urban life tell us about the liberal era of Order and Progress?
How did the Roman Catholic Church respond to rising secularism?

## Timeline

| | |
|---|---|
| 1833 | Great Britain abolishes slavery in its empire |
| 1840s–1850s | U.S. considers annexing Cuba |
| 1864 | Pope Pius IX issues *Syllabus of Errors* |
| 1868–74 | Domingo Faustino Sarmiento is president of Argentina |
| 1886 | Abolition of slavery in Cuba |
| 1888 | Abolition of slavery in Brazil |
| 1891 | Pope Leo XIII issues *Rerum Novarum* (Of New Things) |

## Keywords

abolition
debt peonage
ejido
elites
estancia
fazenda
hacendado
hacienda
indentured servants

individualism
laissez-faire
mestizos
middle class
Roman Catholic Church
secularism
slave trade
tienda de raya
working class

# The Development of Nations

# 8

## Mexico and Central America

### Mexico's Two Laws

In 1855 and 1856, liberals in Mexico passed two laws, Ley Juárez and Ley Lerdo, that led Mexico into a long and violent civil war, once again highlighting profoundly different visions of nationhood. Ley Juárez struck at many of the privileges of the Catholic Church and the military, while Ley Lerdo proposed to turn over much church and other communally owned property to individual hands, though only church lands were targeted at first.

The immediacy of the documents themselves adds to our understanding of the era, the events, and the people who wrote these laws. Read portions of Ley Juárez and Ley Lerdo to get the feel for how revolutionary ideas get transferred into political statements and finally law. They read rather drily, but their contents ignited the powderkeg beneath feuding liberals and conservatives. Mexico exploded into war—the War of the Reform. Though long and bitter, this war set the stage for Mexico's transition, under the dictator Porfirio Díaz, into one of the wealthiest Latin American nations at the end of the nineteenth century.

Ley Juárez, November 23, 1855

The ecclesiastical courts will cease to treat civil cases, but will continue to treat common crimes committed by individuals enjoying those rights while a law is drawn up which will further define this point. Military courts will also cease to treat civil cases, and will deal only with purely military crimes, or connected crimes, of those individuals enjoying military rights. These statutes apply generally across the entire Republic, and individual States may not change or modify them.

Ley Lerdo, June 25, 1856

Considering that one of the major obstacles to the prosperity and growth of our country is the lack of movement or free circulation of a great portion of our real estate, the fundamental basis for the wealth of public wealth; and that I have been vested with authority by the plan proclaimed in the city of Ayutla, and updated in Acapulco, I have thought it best to decree the following:

Art. 1. All country and city estates now administered or owned by civil and ecclesiastical corporations in the Republic will be judged as property of those who rent them, for the value corresponding to the rent which they are actually paying. . . .

Art. 2. Under the corporate title are included all religious communities of both sexes, cofraternities, congregations, brotherhoods, parishes, councils, colleges and in general all establishments or foundations which have a perpetual character.

## MEXICO

The history of Mexico from the overthrow of Santa Anna in 1855 to the turn of the century is divided into two chronological parts. The first part saw the triumph of the Liberal Party and is called the period of the reform—la Reforma—during which liberals focused on land reform and the separation of church and state. It was most closely associated with the liberal leader Benito Juárez, a revered figure in Mexican history. The second part is known as the Porfiriato, or the long rule (1876 to 1911) of the dictator Porfirio Díaz. It was a period of great economic growth and political stability, but also of rising inequality.

### La Reforma

Benito Juárez, a Zapotec Indian, came from the state of Oaxaca. Born poor in 1806 and illiterate until the age of twelve, he nonetheless strove to improve himself, eventually finishing law school and rising in the ranks of the political order in his native state. His predispositions and training were mainstream liberal, and he naturally enough questioned and subsequently attacked the privileged society of Mexico dominated by wealthy landowners and a profoundly conservative Roman Catholic Church. When Santa Anna was overthrown by a revolution in 1855, Juárez emerged as a leader and was appointed secretary of justice in the new government dominated by liberals.

No other figure in Mexican history is more beloved than Benito Juárez. He rose in life to become a hero, delivered his country from a foreign invader, and became the quintessential activist for liberal causes. That he was Zapotec endowed him with even more affection in a country where more than 90 percent of the population had indigenous ancestry. He was orphaned at the age of three and raised by an uncle in a small village, San Pablo Guelatao, Oaxaca, where Spanish was spoken by very few in favor of their Zapotec

**Figure 8.1** This photo of Benito Juárez, the great liberal leader of his country in the 1850s and 1860s, emphasizes his Indian ancestry, a heritage that helped him forge a strong bond with Mexico's immense Indian population. Perhaps the most beloved of Mexican historic figures, he was an effective advocate of classic liberal doctrines. Courtesy Library of Congress.

dialect. An intrepid spirit governed the boy, and at the age of twelve he walked forty-one miles to the state capital of Oaxaca. There, an older sister gave him refuge and found him a job in the home of a Franciscan lay brother who did bookbinding in his spare time. In return for work, the Franciscan paid for Juárez's first schooling, which eventually led him to study law. Juárez received his certificate in 1831 at the age of twenty-five. Early on he was attracted to letters and to the law, and it was certainly not hard to develop a sense of injustice about Mexico's unequal society and of the need for reform that marked his career.

He soon entered politics in Oaxaca, successively being elected to the city council, state legislature, and eventually the governorship (1848), making him the first Indian elected to a governorship after independence. As a lawyer of that period, he often represented the wealthy, though he also found time to defend poor people exploited by members of the clergy, who demanded exorbitant fees for the sacraments, and to protest the actions of the local landholding elites against the poorer villagers and farmers, most of them Indians.

By the early 1850s, Juárez's liberal credentials were well established, and when Santa Anna returned to power for the last time, he had Juárez arrested

## Juárez, the Redeemer of His People

Justo Sierra, one of Mexico's most well known liberal writers of the late nineteenth century, eloquently captured why Juárez was respected by so many Mexicans and why he would become one of Mexico's most revered historical figures. He stated: "Juárez possessed the great virtue of the indigenous race, to which, without a single drop of admixture, he belonged, and this virtue is perseverance. His fellow believers in Reform had faith in its inevitable triumph. So did he, but success, to him, was a secondary matter. What came first was the performance of his duty, even if the consequence was to be disaster and death. *What he sought, far beyond the Constitution and the Reform, was the redemption of the indigenous people* [italics added]. In his pursuit of this ideal he never faltered; to free his people from clerical domination, from serfdom, from ignorance, from mute withdrawal—this was his secret, religious longing, the reason why he was a liberal and a reformist, the reason why he was great . . . He towers, morally, above any other figure of our civil wars."

Justo Sierra, *The Political Evolution of the Mexican People,* trans. Charles Ramsdell (Austin: University of Texas Press, 1969), pp. 283–85, in John Charles Chasteen and Joseph S. Tulchin, eds., *Problems in Latin American History: A Reader* (Wilmington, Del.: Scholarly Resources, 1994), pp. 49–50.

and exiled to the U.S. Juárez found other liberals in New Orleans, joining them in plotting the overthrow of this last Santa Anna dictatorship. The exiles drew up a statement of principles that evolved into another one of Mexico's well-known plans, the Plan de Ayutla. It was, as usual, a call for insurrection, outlining grievances and offering solutions. For Santa Anna, it was the end. He resigned and went into exile for the last time in 1855. For Juárez and the liberals, it was the beginning of a prolonged period of war, first a brutal civil war with conservatives from 1857 to 1860, and then a French intervention (1861–1867).

It was not long before the liberals and Juárez, then still secretary of justice, struck at some of their favorite conservative targets. Their Constitution of 1857 was a liberal instrument that attacked the church and the rights and privileges (*fueros*) of both the military and the clergy. The conservative reaction was violent and led to civil war. The constitution incorporated two liberal laws that had been passed the year before and that set the tone of the conflicts of la Reforma. The Ley Juárez and the Ley Lerdo both directly attacked the corporate privileges of the military and the church, but it was the reaction to the latter that produced the most acrimony. The Ley Juárez essentially stripped military and ecclesiastical tribunals of their right to try all cases—civil or criminal—involving soldiers and priests in their own private courts. The Ley

---

**The War of the Reform**

"'The Chamber of Deputies,' wrote the Pope, 'among the many insults it has heaped upon our Most Holy religion and upon its ministers, as well as upon the Vicar of Christ on Earth [that is, upon the pope himself!], has proposed a new constitution containing many articles, not a few of which conflict with Divine Religion itself, its salutary doctrines, its most holy precepts, and with its rights. . . . For the purpose of more easily corrupting manners and propagating the detestable pest of indifferentism and tearing souls away from our Most Holy Religion, it allows the free exercise of all cults and admits the right of pronouncing in public every kind of thought and opinion. . . . We energetically reprove everything the Mexican government has done against the Catholic Religion, against its Church, its sacred ministers and pastors, and against its laws, rights, and properties. We raise our Pontifical voice in apostolic liberty . . . to condemn, to reprove, and declare null and void everything the said decrees and everything else that the civil authority has done in scorn of ecclesiastical authority and of this Holy See.'"

Lesley Byrd Simpson, *Many Mexicos,* 4th ed., revised (Berkeley: University of California Press, 1971 [1941]), pp. 274–75.

---

Lerdo forced the church to sell off many of its properties, though its implementation would largely wait until after the fighting had ended years later. The Constitution of 1857 incorporated the Ley Lerdo and the Ley Juárez as well as implementing other liberal principles.

A wide-ranging bill of rights was created, including freedom of the press, of speech, of petition, of assembly, and of education. Slavery was abolished, and the right of habeas corpus guaranteed. None of the provisions sparked more controversy than those attacking the church. Conservatives viewed the entire constitution as a monstrous violation of historical sense and religious order; even the Pope, Pius IX, got into the fray, directly condemning the work of the constitutional assembly.

By the end of 1857, liberals and conservatives were at war again. Both liberals and conservatives rallied their clients. Some indigenous communities backed conservatives in their defense of communal lands, village autonomy, and Catholicism, and other communities fought for liberals and their promises of full citizenship or paternal protection. The fighting spread far and involved many, and cruel acts of violence were committed by both sides. Murders were perpetrated in the name of religion or of freedom and democratic government. When the war finally ended in 1860, the liberals under Juárez emerged triumphant, and the church was even more constrained. In the heat of battle, liberals radicalized their program against the church. They secularized cemeteries and marriage, limited the fees that the church could charge for the sacraments, limited religious holidays and celebrations, nationalized church properties, and confiscated monasteries and nunneries. Weakened by civil war, Mexico was a prime target for European countries—such as France—attempting to rebuild their lost American empires. With the United States immersed in its own civil war between 1861 and 1865, the French occupied Mexico between 1861 and 1867 in the greatest challenge to Mexican independence yet.

The French pretext was that Mexico, torn and tattered by the War of the Reform, had defaulted on its foreign debts and that the European powers thus had the right to intervene and collect those debts. Both European powers and the U.S. repeatedly intervened militarily in the nineteenth century in Latin America to collect debts. And indeed, Mexico could not service its debt and had declared a two-year moratorium on debt payments. Yet, when English, Spanish, and French troops landed at the port of Veracruz on December 8, 1861, to seize the customs house (the principal public revenues at the time came from import and export taxes, or duties, charged at Veracruz), the French were fishing for more than money. Emperor Napoleon III dreamed of reestablishing the French empire in America, and the situation in Mexico seemed ripe. Not only was it fresh out of a war that had damaged the country and its economy, but a number of conservatives in Mexico, including lingering monarchists and the church, were eager to conspire with the French as a means to fight back against the victorious liberals.

The English and Spanish eventually withdrew, but the French stayed and marched inland to consolidate their hold on Mexico. There was a strong effort by Mexican troops to stop the invasion, including a victory at the famous Battle of Puebla on May 5, 1862. On that day, a ragtag and much smaller group of Mexican soldiers surprised and routed a much larger French contingent in a battle that is now celebrated as Cinco de Mayo. Nevertheless, the French continued to fight, and by 1864 had installed a European prince, Ferdinand Maximilian, as emperor of Mexico, although Maximilian's place was secured only by the ongoing presence of French troops on Mexican soil. Maximilian was accompanied on his journey to Mexico by his wife, a Belgian princess named Charlotte; they set up a home in Chapultepec Castle, the famed site of the final battle with U.S. soldiers during their 1847 invasion. By all accounts, both Maximilian and his wife, now known as Carlota, took to their roles as emperor and empress with delight and not a small amount of seriousness.

Resistance to Maximilian came from two quarters: from the Mexicans themselves, led by Benito Juárez, who had been pushed out of the presidency by the French invasion; and after the conclusion of its civil war, from the United States. In 1865, the United States, with almost a million soldiers in the Union armies, had the most powerful war machine in the world, and the American government began to pressure Napoleon III to get out of Mexico. With the

**Figure 8.2** The execution of deposed emperor Ferdinand Maximilian in 1867. Imposed by the French, he ultimately was captured and executed by Mexican patriots, led by Benito Juárez. Here Maximilian is depicted awaiting the final shots as a priest holds up a cross to comfort him. Cover of *Harpers Weekly*. Courtesy Library of Congress.

Monroe Doctrine at its back challenging all foreign interventions in Latin America, it was especially galling to the United States to witness the displacement of a legitimate Mexican government by a foreign monarchy. Furthermore, Juárez's forces were daily growing in strength, bolstered by nationalist resentments against the foreigner running the country. This isolated Maximilian and his French troops.

Napoleon III, now also increasingly preoccupied with threats from Prussia at home, got the message, even though Maximilian did not. The French troops pulled out in 1867. But Maximilian stayed, a critical mistake for a leader who by then had lost conservative backing due to his support for liberal causes such as freedom of religion and an end to debt peonage. An appealing if tragic figure who believed he could truly serve the Mexican people, he refused to run away and escape. He surrendered to Juárez and was executed on the outskirts of Querétaro by a firing squad on June 19, 1867. By this time, the equally tragic and some say insane Carlota had fled back to Europe, where she lived out her years in seclusion, eventually dying in 1927. Following Maximilian's execution, Juárez was elected for a third term in 1868. After backing the French in their invasion, Mexico's conservatives found themselves utterly defeated and discredited.

Juárez moved to consolidate the liberal victory by unifying a nation torn apart by decades of political infighting, racial conflicts, and foreign intervention. During his administration, Juárez initiated a wide variety of activities to help modernize Mexico, especially in education and the economy. For example, in 1872 he inaugurated the first major railroad, running between Mexico City and Veracruz, the principal port of entry on the coast. To reduce banditry and to promote security in a country plagued by disorder, Juárez established a rural police force called the *rurales*. Later, under Porfirio Díaz, the rurales enforced a peace and quiet heretofore unknown in nineteenth-century Mexico. The "Mexican Abraham Lincoln," as many styled Juárez, died in office in 1872. This was not before sparking criticism from some, including from Porfirio Díaz, who increasingly disagreed with Juárez's leadership and claimed he had turned to fraud to win reelection in 1871. Juárez's successor to the presidency in 1872, Sebastián Lerdo de Tejada, proceeded along the same lines as Juárez, laying the foundations for the order and progress of the Díaz period.

## The Porfiriato

Porfirio Díaz came to power through the overthrow of Lerdo de Tejada in 1876, who had just beaten Díaz in another national election. In protest, Díaz rose up and declared the Plan de Tuxtepec, which called for effective suffrage and no reelection. Ironically, Díaz remained in power until 1911, occupying the presidency for the entire period except for the 1880 to 1884 term. His tenure as Mexico's dictator over this long period bears his name, the Porfiriato, and it altered the course of Mexican history dramatically. Under Díaz Mexico reached a material prosperity of unprecedented proportions based on railroading, mining, industrialization, and commerce. The great mass of its people, however, especially its rural laborers, the peons, were ground deeper into poverty.

Like other nations in Latin America, Mexico was part of the export boom that transformed the economies of the region. All of the economic indicators took off, producing a boom in prosperity that Mexico had never known before. Under José Yves Limantour, who from 1893 to 1911 was Díaz's secretary of finance, Mexico balanced its budget, paid off its immense national debt, and improved its reputation abroad, which was critical if it wanted to attract more investors. Previously known as a country of violence, banditry, and political chaos, Mexico became a paragon of tranquility, fiscal stability, and political order. Foreign investors, principally British, French, and American, sank their capital into building Mexico's new railroads, opening new mines, and either modernizing old industries like textiles or pioneering new ones such as petroleum and beer. They also bought up huge swaths of land, especially in the north. For many decades, scholars asserted that Mexico was the "mother of foreigners and the stepmother of Mexicans," suggesting that Díaz sold out the country to foreigners. But recently, historians discovered that while foreign capital surged to new heights, Díaz and Limantour and their cronies were solidly in control. They protected their Mexican friends and often penalized foreign investors as they worked to modernize the economy. Unlike their Central American counterparts who succumbed to extensive U.S. influence and intervention, Díaz was able to use the power of the state to reign in foreign aspirations and to build a diverse economy of mining, agriculture, and industry.

With balanced budgets, surpluses in the treasury, and an expanding economy, Mexico was transformed by prosperity. Mexico City more than doubled in population, and its reputation as a civilized and cultured capital was enhanced by electricity, streetcars, hotels, weekly newspapers, and broad boulevards. The same progress—although not as spectacular as that achieved in the capital—could be measured in Mexico's smaller cities, now tied together by railroads (fifteen thousand miles in 1911 compared to four hundred miles in 1876) that were responsible for the movement not only of materials but also of people and ideas crisscrossing the country. Mexico's burgeoning middle classes made these modern urban centers their home, and they reveled in the delights of the new cosmopolitan culture. The growth of cities and the economy was a boon for mestizos. Grappling with the problem of the large indigenous and mixed-race population, positivists increasingly viewed mestizos less as a sign of racial degradation than as a step toward a new Mexican nation, and they were primary beneficiaries of new schools, government jobs, and economic opportunities.

To accomplish all this, supported by landed elites, the military, and an ever-growing bureaucracy, Díaz forged one of the most enduring dictatorships to govern in modern Latin America. Like other liberal leaders once they rose to power in the late nineteenth century, Díaz and his cronies did not believe that most Mexicans were ready for the responsibility of democracy, and they were unwilling to gamble on modernity for the ideals of liberty and democracy. He relied heavily on the científicos, a cadre of elite intellectuals, technocrats, and professionals who supported economic liberalism and positivism in their quest for modernity, such as Limantour. Díaz and his allies achieved peace and stability in the city and countryside by a combination of rewards and intimidation, the latter enforced through fear, threats, and brutality. To Mexicans at the time, the system was known as pan o palo (bread or stick). By adroitly manipulating his political and military officials, Díaz kept potential opponents off balance while using patronage to reward his most loyal supporters with political positions and economic opportunities. The press was effectively muzzled, elections were rigged, and the rurales kept the peace in the country, earning a reputation for cruelty. Workers might strike, bandits might rob, and political opponents might cry out against censorship and brutality, but they did so at the peril of being beaten, killed, or sent into exile by the rurales. In one of Díaz's most notorious acts of repression, he had about ten thousand Yaqui Indians arrested, virtually enslaved, and sent into exile in Yucatán as punishment for resisting his rule. In such a society, for many, it was best to keep one's mouth shut and suffer silently. That, indeed, was the lot of the Mexican peon under the Porfiriato.

The Roman Catholic Church had become a tacit ally of Díaz's government by the 1880s, helping to forge a broader consensus among Mexico's elite. Although Díaz remained a liberal and did not formalize relations with the Vatican, he did deal quietly with church leaders and assuage their concerns about anti-clericalism. Díaz's wife, doña Carmen, played a major role in this rapprochement, carrying out a backdoor diplomacy that softened her husband's harsh methods when it came to religious matters. Improved relations with the church brought liberals and conservatives into closer proximity and also removed one of the major causes of unrest among the masses of peasants and Indians.

Classically, peons, whether Indian or mestizo, lived on the land, usually on a hacienda. This was especially true after the Ley Lerdo and other laws that illegalized communally owned lands despoiled many villages of their lands, forcing peasants into the labor force. The lot of peons during the Porfiriato was dismal, marked by abject poverty and increasing deprivation. The hacendados (or landowners) were thoroughly imbued with the prevailing racism among the Mexican positivists, who considered the largely indigenous peons to be biologically inferior. This reinforced the hacendados' tendency to view themselves as the natural lords of the land, born to govern and discipline. Hacendado haughtiness and positivist racism combined to make life miserable for Mexico's peons.

The proof was everywhere. The peons' average daily wage—thirty-five cents—did not rise during the nineteenth century, while the cost of their staple food—beans, corn, and chiles—increased between 200 and 600 percent. In terms of diet, peons were worse off in 1910 than in 1810 when still under the rule of Spain. Rural labor relations were varied, from the hired miners and cowboys in the north, to the debt laborers working on large grain and sugar plantations of the central plateau, to the virtual slaves on the brutal henequen plantations in Yucatán. At the worst, they were bound to the hacienda by the pernicious system of debt peonage. The worst hacendados kept their workers perpetually in debt, controlling access to stores and food. Their workers were effectively bound to the land and to the service of the hacendado forever. Debts were inherited by the debt peon's children during the Porfiriato.

The hacendados, on the other hand, ruled the land and reached mind-boggling extremes of wealth. Porfirian policies directly contributed to the expansion of the hacienda system in the late nineteenth century. New land laws, such as a 1883 law designed to encourage foreign immigration, awarded huge tracts—both public lands and communal lands stripped from indigenous villages—to land companies that in turn sold it to the hacendados. The results were spectacular concentrations of land in the hands of the few, with the majority struggling for simple subsistence. Thoroughly excluded from politics and economically marginalized, the rural poor experienced a simmering discontent that periodically broke out in rebellion, only to be put down repeatedly by the rurales.

One family, the Terrazas-Creel clan of the northern state of Chihuahua, had amassed over 7 million acres by 1900! It directed much of its wealth into diversified investments, such as banking, railroads, telephone companies, sugar mills, and the like; controlled local and gubernatorial politics; and sat astride a mountain of privilege and wealth as Mexico passed into the twentieth century. The great gulf between the haves and the have-nots finally ruptured the Porfiriato with the Mexican Revolution, which ignited in 1910.

## CENTRAL AMERICA

Central America's history from the 1850s to the turn of the century was deeply influenced by priorities set beyond its borders. The coffee brokers of London, the canal builders of France, the banana barons of New Orleans and Boston—they and many other foreigners were encouraged by the surge of outward-looking, positivist, and progressive liberal parties in Central America to invest in and develop the region. The broad goal—shared by Central Americans and foreigners—was to integrate the region into the quickening international economy in the second half of the nineteenth century. It was an age of mutual admiration. Central American elites looked to the brokerage and investment houses of London, Paris, and New York for markets and monies, while foreigners made handsome profits in booming new activities, such as the coffee and banana industries. Yet another concern weighed heavily on Central America as it found itself increasingly subject to foreign influence: the preservation of its sovereignty.

### The Walker Invasion

In 1855, liberals in Nicaragua contracted with some North American mercenaries led by a Nashville-born adventurer named William Walker to help them in their battle against conservatives. Walker arrived in Nicaragua in June 1855 with fifty-seven Americans recruited in California. In the space of a few months, the liberals, with the assistance of Walker's small army, soundly defeated the conservatives. What Nicaraguans and other Central Americans did not expect was Walker's vision: to carve out an American empire in Central America. In 1856, Walker took over Nicaragua. He legalized slavery, made English the official language, and offered large land grants. Consequently, hundreds of American adventurers flocked to the country. Central American patriots, in the meantime, prepared to oust the invaders.

In a series of pitched battles that ranged over northern Costa Rica and Nicaragua, causing widespread destruction, patriots, led by President Juan Rafael Mora of Costa Rica, challenged and finally defeated Walker's mercenaries in 1857. Saved by an intervention from the United States, Walker went into exile. Twice he tried to return to Central America and reconstitute his putative empire. On his second return, in 1860, Walker was captured by British marines and turned over to the Hondurans. They executed the "gray-eyed man of destiny" with dispatch. The struggle against Walker united Central Americans and endowed them with a sense of pride and nationalism based on this war of liberation from a foreign invader. Meanwhile, remarkable changes were transforming the economies of these small countries.

## Canals and Coffee

In 1833, a few sacks of coffee beans were shipped to England from Costa Rica's port on the Pacific, Puntarenas. It was a long but highly profitable trip. The English, it turned out, liked good coffee and were willing to pay the price. And Costa Rica, as well as most of its Central American neighbors, possessed excellent highlands for growing the highest quality beans. Coffee growing soon outstripped all other commercial activities in Central America. By the 1880s, it represented 70 to 80 percent of all exports, with profits increasing the overall wealth of Central America by thousands of percent. Foreigners, especially in Guatemala and Nicaragua, moved into the growing industry in large numbers. A new oligarchy prospered from the growing and marketing of the coffee bean, which was called, appropriately enough, the *grano de oro,* or "grain of gold," in Costa Rica.

Coffee profits were in turn plowed into two areas: one, extravagant expenditures by the emerging coffee elites (ornate estates, trips to Europe, expensive imports); and two, the modernization of the countries under a series of liberal presidents, such as Justo Rufino Barrios of Guatemala, José Zelaya of Nicaragua, and Tomás Guardia of Costa Rica. These leaders, like so many others of the era, were somewhat paradoxically liberal in their economic policies but dictatorial in their politics. They were, in fact, apostles of the positivist principle that to achieve economic progress, one needs political order. These presidents, some governing for a decade or more, provided political stability, while the new income from coffee was plowed into those sectors—railroads, telegraphs, and ports, for example—that were associated directly with progress.

Railroads seized the imagination of Central Americans just as they did the imagination of other Latin Americans from Mexico to Argentina in the last third of the nineteenth century. In Central America, the first railroads were begun in the 1870s to bring the coffee-producing regions of the interior into better communication with the ports on both the Atlantic and Pacific coasts. Typical of this effort was Costa Rica's contract with a family of North

**Figure 8.3** Coffee pickers in Costa Rica picking the grano de oro, or the grains of gold that coffee represented for many Latin American countries, from Guatemala to Brazil. This profitable crop was labor intensive and fostered small- to middle-sized landholdings in some countries such as Costa Rica and Colombia. Courtesy Wiki Commons.

American entrepreneurs, the Meiggses, to build a railroad from the highland central valley to the Caribbean port of Puerto Limón. The task fell to a young member of the family, Minor Cooper Keith, who completed the task in 1890. As Keith lay track slowly through the difficult coastal jungle, he constantly experimented with ways to make the railroad pay before it was finished and could transport coffee from the interior to Puerto Limón. Among his experiments was importing some banana trees (actually herbs, but such big ones that we call them trees) from Panama and planting them along the railroad. He began to export bananas in small numbers to New Orleans in the late 1870s. Another American entrepreneur, a ship captain from Boston named Lorenzo Baker, had already experimented as early as 1870 with bringing bananas from Jamaica to Boston.

Keith and Baker in effect pioneered a new industry—bananas from the Caribbean and Central America exported to the United States—whose growth and profitability were startling. In Costa Rica and Honduras, bananas challenged coffee for the lead in exports by the beginning of the First World War, accounting in some years for more than 50 percent of exports. The foreign banana growers in turn merged in 1899 and created the United Fruit Company, an institution that symbolized the widespread penetration and dominance of Central America by foreigners.

While coffee and then bananas powered Central American economies into the next century, the canal-building momentum grew rapidly in the same period. North Americans tended to favor a route across Nicaragua, employing the San Juan River and Lake Nicaragua, whereas the French were persuaded that Panama offered the best conditions. In the 1880s, Ferdinand de Lesseps, the French entrepreneur who built the Suez Canal, launched a massively publicized effort to cut the canal across the isthmus of Panama. Brought down by torrential tropical rains, almost nightmarish engineering problems, diseases, and, finally, bankruptcy, it failed. The North Americans clucked their tongues at the French and prepared to dig in Nicaragua.

A privately sponsored company, the Maritime Canal Company, obtained a charter from the U.S. Congress in 1887, and in 1890 it began operations in Nicaragua. In 1893 it, too, went bankrupt, and the canal between the oceans seemed no nearer to completion in Nicaragua than in Panama. But it was an age of high optimism and rapidly increasing technological and medical breakthroughs. At the end of the century, a coincidence of circumstances related to the Cuban-Spanish-American War of 1898 once again provoked canal fever. The war was waged on two oceans, making Americans extremely conscious of their strategic need for a canal to transfer warships and their supply vessels between the Atlantic and the Pacific. That an isthmian canal would be a boon to maritime commerce by eliminating the long voyage around South America was almost taken for granted.

The question became where to build the canal: Panama or Nicaragua. The Panama lobby, led by a bold French engineer named Phillipe Bunau Varilla, argued that 30 percent of the canal had already been constructed by the French, and the North Americans had only to buy out the French interests and concessions and complete the work. The Nicaraguans and their supporters in the United States, led by the tenacious senator from Alabama John Tyler Morgan, pushed for the route across Nicaragua. This route was thought to pose fewer engineering problems, to be healthier, and, furthermore, it was located nearer to the United States. In the end, however, Panama won the "battle of the routes." In 1902, the U.S. Senate voted to support the Panama route, persuaded in part by a dramatic lowering of the price that Bunau Varilla and his backers were asking for the French investment in Panama.

For Nicaraguans, and most Central Americans, it was a great disappointment, a promise unfulfilled. Yet, as the liberal dictators and their supporters turned the century, they viewed the last half of the nineteenth century as one of unprecedented progress, marked by the building of railroads and ports, the modernization of their capitals, and the increase of the material wealth of Central America, especially that based on coffee and banana exports.

This positivist age in Central America also failed in some significant ways. One, prosperity was not shared by the great body of Central Americans, and many indigenous villages were disrupted by the growth of export-oriented agriculture. Wealth did not trickle down to the masses, to the Maya of Guatemala or to the ladinos of Nicaragua. Indeed, many of them lost lands as rapacious landowners built huge coffee and banana plantations. Traditional social relationships in indigenous communities were damaged as well. From vanilla producers in Veracruz, Mexico, to coffee growers in highland Guatemala, indigenous elites became key brokers between their own communities and large-scale owners, and the indigenous elites often used this new status to gain power and individual wealth, increasing stratification and tensions in their communities. In Guatemala in the late 1800s, for example, K'iche' leaders increasingly relied on Creole elites to help them preserve their local authority and access to wealth, and the K'iche' leaders in turn helped to maintain social peace and facilitate elite access to labor.[1] Two, much of the new economic infrastructure of Central America was dependent upon foreigners, from German coffee growers in Guatemala to North American banana barons in Honduras. This trend made Central America especially vulnerable to foreign meddling in the twentieth century. Three, with the exception of Costa Rica, which continued to invest in education and to lay the foundations of a modern political democracy, public order and tranquility were maintained largely by a series of dictators and caudillos who ruled by force, looking to the military more than to the ballot box for their legitimacy.

## CONCLUSIONS AND ISSUES

Mexico at midcentury suffered through a period of devastating turmoil marked by the War of the Reform and the French occupation. Internal divisions in Mexican politics and society contributed to internecine warfare as Mexicans fought over some immensely controversial issues in society, such as the status of the indigenous population and the proper relationship between church and state. After the liberals won, a stronger Mexico emerged in the 1870s and 1880s under the leadership of Porfirio Díaz, who established a dictatorship that endured until 1911. His emphasis on order and stability encouraged foreign investors, merchants, miners, and railroad builders—all of whom helped produce an unprecedented material prosperity in Mexico during the Porfiriato. However, it was a radically unbalanced prosperity that divided Mexico more deeply between the haves and have-nots. A small percentage of Mexicans and the foreigners took the bulk of the newly developed wealth, alienating the great majority of Mexicans, who viewed the growing disparity as a monstrous injustice. The result would be the monumental Mexican Revolution of 1910.

In Central America, the invasion of an American filibuster, William Walker, at midcentury symbolized the growing interest of the United States in Central America. Walker's defeat helped define Central American nationalism and also symbolized the beginning of a new era in Central American life. In the second half of the nineteenth century, the increasing production of coffee and, later, bananas, began the rapid integration of Central America into the world economy and produced a quickening of the modernization process in these small countries. The desire for a transisthmian canal by the great maritime and naval powers of the world—especially Great Britain, France, and the United States—focused increasing attention on Central America toward the turn of the century.

## Discussion Questions

Why is Benito Juárez considered one of Mexico's great leaders? What changes did he and his liberal supporters enact in the 1850s–1870s?

What were the causes of the War of the Reform?

Why did Napoleon III invade Mexico and place Maximilian on the throne there, and how were the French finally forced out?

What were the signs of Order and Progress during the Porfiriato?

How did rural conditions change for the majority during the Porfiriato?

How did foreign economic interests transform Central America in the late nineteenth century?

## Timeline

| | |
|---|---|
| 1855–1870s | La Reforma (Mexico) |
| 1855 | Ley Juárez (Mexico) |
| 1855–57 | Walker invasion (Nicaragua) |
| 1856 | Ley Lerdo (Mexico) |
| 1857 | Liberal Constitution in Mexico |
| 1857–60 | War of the Reform (Mexico) |
| 1858–72 | Benito Juárez presidencies (Mexico) |
| 1861–67 | French intervention (Mexico) |
| 1876 | Plan de Tuxtepec (Mexico) |
| 1876–1911 | Porfiriato (Mexico) |

## Keywords

| | |
|---|---|
| científico | peon |
| Cinco de Mayo | Plan de Ayutla |
| debt peonage | Plan de Tuxtepec |
| grano de oro | Porfiriato |
| La Reforma | rurales |
| Ley Juárez | Suez Canal |
| Ley Lerdo | United Fruit Company (UFCO) |
| Panama Canal | Walker invasion |
| pan o palo | War of the Reform |

# The Development of Nations

## South America

### The *Huáscar*

In the Battle of Angamos, Peru suffered a deep loss that contributed much to Chile's eventual victory in the War of the Pacific (1879–1883). In this eyewitness account, a young Peruvian naval officer, Manuel Meliton Carbajal, describes the hottest part of the battle. He sees his commanding officer, Miguel Grau, wounded mortally as his ship, the *Huáscar*, is shot to pieces by the Chilean warships. Moments like these helped maintain the vigor of militarism in the minds and hearts of Latin Americans and fueled nationalism in the twentieth century. Listen to this voice of a young officer caught in the heat of battle, and you will hear echoes of loyalty and bravery that, for better or worse, continue to inspire generations today.

> About ten minutes after taking smaller shots, a big one hit us. The projectile struck the conning tower and exploded inside, blowing up Admiral Mr. [Miguel] Grau who had the con, also killing Lieutenant Diego Ferré, his young assistant. The second in command, Lieutenant Commander Elías Aguirre, took charge and the battle raged on as tenaciously as before. The damage to the steering gear prevented *Huáscar* from holding a course, so she simply responded to the thrust of the propellers. This damage allowed the *Blanco* and *Covadonga* to close the distance with the *Huáscar* to about 200 meters off the starboard side. In this situation, having lost her steering, *Huáscar* returned fire at *Blanco* and turned to ram her with her ram. The *Blanco* easily evaded the attack and *Huáscar* continued taking fire from the Chilean monitors, and from the *Covadonga* as well . . .
>
> In these circumstances, the undersigned, finding himself near the right cannon of the turret, was wounded by shrapnel from a shell which penetrated and exploded inside the turret. He was carried down into the engine room where he received care for his wounds.

**Figure 9.1** In a deadly duel in late 1879, the Peruvian warship *Huáscar* was trapped and captured by more powerful Chilean ships in the Battle of Angamos during the War of the Pacific. The defeat of the *Huáscar*, and the death of its brilliant commander, Miguel Grau, gave Chile command of the sea and led to its ultimate victory in the war. Courtesy Wiki Commons.

Lieutenant Pedro Gárezon, in his testimony, will give you the details of how this unequal, sharp battle ended. He had assumed command after the second in command, Lieutenant Commander Aguirre, was also killed.

*Huáscar* fell into the enemy's hands when it was no longer possible to resist, her canons silenced, her steering shot up, and her crew decimated.

As a last effort, the crew opened up her valves to scuttle her and probably would have succeeded if the enemy had not closed so swiftly and if we could have resisted their boarding. Not being able, the Chilean crews took possession of *Huáscar* and managed to keep her afloat even though she already had 4 feet of water in her hold. They put out some fires and took her to Mejillones . . .

All of *Huáscar*'s crew were taken prisoner and taken aboard the Chilean monitors where they were treated with great consideration.[1]

The battle between the *Huáscar* and the Chilean ships was fought early in the War of the Pacific, which erupted in 1879 between Chile on the one hand, and Peru and Bolivia on the other. Economic developments—especially the rapid growth of profitable exports—in the nineteenth century contributed to border disputes and commercial rivalries that sometimes broke out in major conflicts such as the War of the Pacific. This war, like several others, notably the Paraguayan War, also known as the War of the Triple Alliance (1864–1870), between Paraguay and a coalition of its neighbors consisting of Argentina, Brazil, and Uruguay, left deep scars on the losing nations. These international and boundary wars also promoted the growth of nationalistic sentiments that endowed these countries with a stronger sense of identity and national unity.

South America is a vast and diverse region, and its experiences in the late nineteenth century were equally diverse. The liberal mission of Order and Progress spread across the entire region, yet the changes and tensions it brought varied by country. Some, like Brazil, followed a relatively stable path, wherein even the end of the monarchy, the abolition of slavery, and economic growth and urbanization did not disrupt the relative political and social peace. For others, political and economic instability plagued national life. From the bloody civil wars that ravaged Venezuela at midcentury to the guano bust of the Peruvian economy in the 1870s, the period was one of great challenge, as Latin Americans sought to take advantage of the modernizing impulses sweeping across these new nation-states.

## VENEZUELA

Following the ouster of the caudillo José Antonio Páez at midcentury, Venezuela plunged into a period of intense political instability known as the Federal Wars. More than 350,000 people perished during these wars, which lasted until 1863, as caudillos warred against one another for power. A new caudillo, Antonio Guzmán Blanco, emerged out of this civil tumult, and he dominated the country for over a decade.

Guzmán Blanco, the son of a liberal leader, was born to politics and caudillo warfare. He earned his spurs and became a general during the Federal Wars, and then emerged in the late 1860s as the supreme caudillo. Although dictatorial and vain—styling himself the "Illustrious American"—Guzmán Blanco managed to preside over a period of civil order and peace. Having established this most basic of all positivist prerequisites—order—Guzmán Blanco then moved to promote the modernization of the nation.

Caracas—the capital—was rebuilt and modernized with wide boulevards, sewers, electricity, water, and public transportation, reinforcing the dominant role of the city in national life. The coffee trade was revitalized, centered in the Andean states of Táchira, Trujillo, and Mérida. With new foreign loans and credits generated from the export not only of coffee but also of cacao and cattle, Guzmán Blanco encouraged public education, built railroads and telegraphs, and initiated an ambitious public works program, which included statues of the Illustrious American himself as often as it included roads and telegraphs. Yet, his ruthless persecution of the Catholic Church and of conservatives in general—along with the hero worship required to gratify his ego—mark his regime as one of mixed blessings.

Were the changes in Venezuela during this period as broad and profound as they seemed to be? The population, about 2.5 million at the turn of the century, remained largely rural, traditional, and illiterate, having suffered generally from the wasting effects of countless caudillo wars after midcentury. In the 1890s, the residents of Caracas might show off the newest French clothes and have the finest china imported from Paris, and they might discuss the newest ideas coming from Europe. But the great mass of rural Venezuelans— campesinos (rural peasants) on the plantations or llaneros (cowboys) roaming the great, open plains of the interior—still ate and lived and danced in the traditional folkways of their parents and grandparents, cut off from many of the modernizing changes in the cities.

In 1888, Guzmán Blanco abandoned his native country for Paris, drawn irresistibly by the attractions of a city and a nation that many considered the center of the civilized universe. Venezuela drifted politically for a decade before another strong caudillo, Cipriano Castro, came to power in 1899. During this interlude, Venezuela was drawn more tightly into the orbit of European and North American economic and political interests. These, as noted in an earlier chapter, were expanding rapidly in Latin America on many fronts.

In 1894 and 1895 a dispute flared up between Venezuela and Great Britain over the boundary they shared between British Guiana (modern Guyana) and Venezuela. Unable to stand up to Great Britain alone, Venezuela appealed to the United States for arbitration, and the United States obliged, with a roar. Richard Olney, U.S. secretary of state, crowed after Great Britain accepted arbitration that "the United States was practically sovereign in this hemisphere." When the final decision was announced in 1899, Venezuela retained control of the vital Orinoco River delta but had to give up an immense chunk— sixty thousand square miles—of Venezuelan territory to British Guiana. Venezuelans discovered at the turn of the century that appealing to the United States in their disputes with the great powers of Europe could produce mixed results.

Cipriano Castro fought his way into power in 1899 and governed Venezuela with a flair until his overthrow in 1908. Castro possessed a temperamental, bon vivant personality, characterized as much by philandering and dancing as by tending to matters of state. His intense nationalism and Venezuela's foreign debts combined to produce another international crisis in 1902 and 1903 that again drew in the United States.

Irritated by Venezuela's inability to pay off debts contracted largely during the Guzmán Blanco era, Great Britain, Germany, and Italy took matters into their own hands. They blockaded Venezuelan ports in 1902 and 1903 to force Venezuela to pay. The United States stepped in and arranged to lift the blockade and resume debt service. But the intervention of the United States came with a price: the 1904 Roosevelt Corollary to the Monroe Doctrine (see chapter 13), with which President Theodore Roosevelt adamantly rejected *any* form of European intervention in Latin American affairs, asserting that in all instances the United States would instead step in to settle disputes.

During Cipriano Castro's regime, and especially under his successor, Juan Vicente Gómez, a pattern in modern Venezuela emerged. Caudillos such as Cipriano Castro and Gómez had the instincts and skills to forge a more unified modern nation. But they relied on the skills and knowledge of the more sophisticated elites from Caracas for the economic and commercial integration of Venezuela into international markets, especially as oil rose in importance. The dictators and the urban elites—working together—forged the the modern nation-state in Venezuela. Beneath these trends, others also were apparent, especially the formation of a new semi-industrialized workforce, with priorities and agendas that would later challenge the prevailing order.

## COLOMBIA

Colombia, in the second half of the nineteenth century, was beset by more political tumult than perhaps any other Latin American nation in that same period. From the 1860s to the turn of the century, civil war between liberals and conservatives interrupted national life more than ten times, in some instances (1860–1863, 1899–1902, for example) lasting in excess of two or three years and costing thousands of lives. One historian called it "a country of permanent war" in the nineteenth century. The causes of such internal stress still spark lively debate among historians.

The basic alignment between liberals and conservatives at midcentury framed events as they unfolded from the 1860s onward. In 1863, the liberals triumphed in a civil war over the conservatives and wrote a new constitution for the country. By promoting free trade, they encouraged the expansion of the tobacco economy, and a boom in that crop's export helped sustain the liberals in power. When the prices of tobacco began to drop in the 1870s, so did liberal unity.

Liberal leaders quarreled over personal rivalries, but their feuding also represented the continuing competition for power between the regions of Colombia. For example, the dominant personality of the period, Rafael Núñez, divided liberals by frankly promoting his native region, the Atlantic coast, in the forums of power. Núñez was not unique. Each region, from the mountainous region, where about 80 percent of the population lived, to the sparsely populated eastern lowlying flatlands known as the llanos, to the Pacific and Caribbean coasts, competed hotly for power at the national level.

In 1885, conservatives, allied with independent liberals led by Núñez, recaptured power from the liberals. Núñez, a prolific writer and accomplished states-

## Historical Debates

Very often historians themselves cannot agree on how to interpret events in particular nations or periods of time. They may agree on basic facts, the "names and dates" that so often plague students who are first learning history, but then go their separate ways in interpreting those facts. Indeed, this aspect of history is the one that so often makes the past glow with intellectual excitement. A good case is interpreting Colombian historiography (the study of history) in the late nineteenth century.

One school of historians contends that the tumultuous politics of the period, marked by nearly incessant civil war between liberals and conservatives, was caused by the internal differences between the partisans of these two political groups. Deep differences over the role of the church, over whether the country should be federal or centralized, over free trade versus protectionism, and other issues—some particular to Colombia and others shared in general by other Latin Americans of the same generation—proved irresolvable and led to civil war. The War of a Thousand Days (1899–1902) at the end of the century was the most disruptive of these civil wars, laying waste to the land and the people.

Other historians view this period of intense conflict through a different lens, maintaining that the fortunes of the Liberal and Conservative parties were closely linked to events outside of Colombia, especially to the rise and fall of Colombia's principal exports in the period, tobacco and coffee. The parties and their leaders were more apt to respond to these external pressures than to internal, ideological differences. For example, if liberal fortunes were tied to a prospering export—as tobacco was in the 1860s—they were able to use it to dominate the conservatives and maintain power. When the export economy faltered, so did the power of the liberals, and conservatives ascended, blaming the liberals, of course, for depression and bad fortune.

Even the nature of the Liberal and Conservative parties challenges historians. One wrote that "by mid-century the Liberal and Conservative parties had achieved clear definition," whereas another said that "in the realm of ideology, it is vain to seek perfect consistency among nineteenth century Liberals" (Park 2). For this latter group, the liberals and conservatives were not markedly different in terms of ideas, but rather drew upon intense personal loyalties, built through an extensive system of patronage that tied rural bosses (known as *gamonales*) to local communities and to the parties. The fighting was less about politics than it was about personal vendettas between families and communities that remained deeply dependent on the land and on the local bosses who owned the land. For much of the century, they contend, there was no dominant export crop to create a single powerful elite, so no group could rise to the top and develop enough power to squelch the fighting.

Local allegiances were perhaps more important than party politics and ideas in deciding sides in the fighting. But recently, historians have shown how allegiances, while cemented through patronage, were imbued with the different hopes and aspirations of the Colombian people. They joined in these alliances and in the fighting not out of blind loyalty, but as a way to take part in the republican political process. For example, landless workers, many of Afro-Colombian descent, often supported liberals in order to press for better conditions, while Indians living on communal lands often supported conservatives in order to defend their landholdings and traditions from liberal policies (see, e.g., Sanders).

Each of these views can be explained and sustained, and they reflect an exciting dimension of history: its dynamic rather than static nature as we take those names and dates and facts and debate their meaning and significance.

See James William Park, *Rafael Núñez and the Politics of Colombian Regionalism, 1863–1886* (Baton Rouge: Louisiana State University Press, 1985), p. 2; Helen Delpar, *Red against Blue: The Liberal Party in Colombian Politics, 1863–1899* (Tuscaloosa: University of Alabama Press, 1981), p. 190; James E. Sanders, *Contentious Republicans: Popular Politics, Race, and Class in Nineteenth-Century Colombia* (Durham: Duke University Press, 2004).

man, had already served two terms as a liberal president in the early 1880s before he switched allegiances and led the conservatives to power. In 1886, he oversaw the creation of a new constitution that lasted more than a century.

As coffee exports rose dramatically in Colombia, so did the strength of Núñez and the conservatives. By 1896, coffee constituted 70 percent of Colombia's total exports. The new wealth from coffee pumped revenue into the government and fostered the beginnings of modernization in the nation. A fall in international prices after 1896, however, triggered a depression in the coffee industry, and liberals blamed conservatives.

Furthermore, Núñez and his successors thoroughly antagonized the liberals, especially by excluding them from power. The festering feud between the parties came to a head when the activist liberal leader Rafael Uribe pushed for a resolution of the power struggle. The result was the War of a Thousand Days (1899–1902), one of the bloodiest in Colombia's history. Liberals and conservatives rose up to fight for their *gamonales* (rural bosses), spreading fighting across a wide swath of the country.

When the combatants finally called a truce in 1902, the country was nearly prostrate. About one hundred thousand Colombians perished from the fighting, disease, and turmoil brought on by the conflict. Plantations were devastated, families were torn from their lands, the peso was devalued, and business was paralyzed. As one politician stated, "A gust of death had passed over the entire country." Colombia emerged exhausted and weak, the conservatives still in power but unable to withstand another threat, this time from the United States.

In 1903, the United States supported a revolt in the Colombian state of Panama by which Panama became independent and a protectorate of the United States. Colombians were shocked and outraged but could not prevent the loss of Panama, soon to be the site of the transisthmian canal. As the Venezuelans also learned at the turn of the century, closer ties with the United States could bring both gains and losses. It was a rude introduction to the twentieth century for Colombians, but as the price of coffee slowly recovered on world markets after 1900, so did Colombian prosperity.

## ECUADOR

In 1861, Gabriel García Moreno seized power after a decade and a half of political chaos in Ecuador. Born in 1821 into a prominent family of Guayaquil, he studied theology and law in Quito and then married into a well-to-do Quito family. García Moreno was eminently well equipped to govern Ecuador because his roots sprang from both Guayaquil and Quito, the twin poles of power in Ecuador. García Moreno began his political career as a liberal disciple of another native of Guayaquil, Vicente Rocafuerte.

García Moreno governed Ecuador until 1875, demonstrating both liberal and conservative tendencies, which was not unusual in an age in transition. Leaders such as García Moreno championed liberal principles and often acted as liberals economically, but they were just as naturally committed to profoundly conservative political, cultural, and religious causes. Wild as a youth, García Moreno embraced Catholicism as he matured. When he came to power, he recommitted Ecuador to a brand of Catholicism that had not been seen since the colonial period. He invited the Jesuit order to return, normalized relations with the Vatican, and regenerated and enlarged the educational establishment by bringing in members of Catholic French teaching orders. Ecuadorian liberals, inspired by the brilliant Juan Montalvo, raged against this intensely Catholic, conservative caudillo who seemed to have sold the soul of Ecuador to foreign priests and the pope.

But there was another side to García Moreno: he was also committed to modernization. He built the first railroad, encouraged the expansion of exports, and backed native industries, all the while promoting education as the key to progress. He left a decidedly mixed legacy, open and progressive in some respects, dictatorial and repressive in others. He died at the hands of an assassin in 1875, chopped up by a fanatical, machete-wielding liberal.

After García Moreno's assassination, Ecuador's conservatives and liberals fought for control of the national stage until 1895. Then Eloy Alfaro, known as the Old Battler, emerged as the strong leader of a surging liberal movement. Alfaro dominated the country until his brutal assassination in 1912, and he left a deep

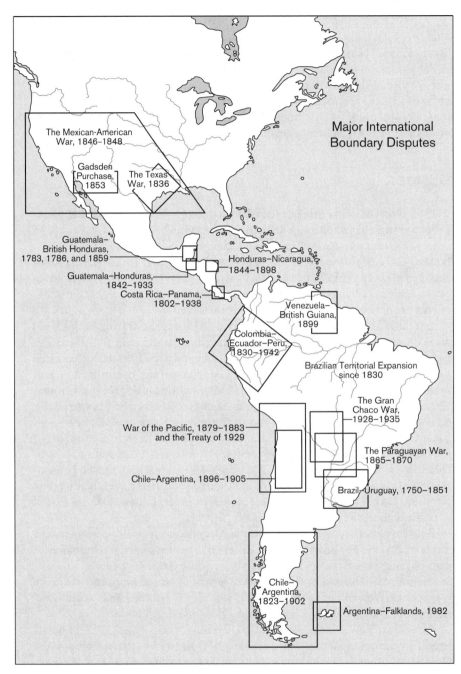

**Map 9.1** Major international boundary disputes.

imprint on the country. His regime was characterized by progressive, pro-United States acts of modernization, all consistent with liberal principles of the time.

A growing export economy paved the way for Alfaro and the liberals to consolidate power at the turn of the century. Cacao, the basic ingredient in chocolate, had been exported since the colonial period, but only after 1870 did the industry really take off. By 1894 Ecuador was producing more cacao than any other country in the world. The general prosperity from the cacao industry contributed to the political equilibrium that the liberals achieved after 1895, and it provided much of the revenues for projects that Alfaro felt were essential to the progress of the nation. The commercial and mercantile classes of the coastal region were especially committed to looking abroad not only for markets but also for inspiration in modernizing the economy and the nation in general.

The old problem of uniting the diverse regions of Ecuador was partially solved under Alfaro by the completion of the Guayaquil-to-Quito railroad in 1908. Regionalism and limited natural resources, however, continued to plague Ecuador even as it entered the twentieth century on a wave of prosperity induced by the cacao boom.

While the division between the coast (Guayaquil) and the mountains (Quito) was most evident and the cause of continuing rivalry, the highlands themselves were broken up into regions isolated from each other by the high Andes. Each region, whether coastal or mountain, sought to better its situation at the expense of those individuals who wished to give the national government more powers to centralize and rationalize the nation's economy. Taxes, which were largely derived from duties on imports and exports, tended to be siphoned off by the regions rather than invested in national improvements. The long struggle between Guayaquil and Quito, and between liberals and conservatives in general, reflected the intensity of this regionalism in Ecuador.

Nonetheless, Ecuador changed significantly under Alfaro and the liberals. The completion of the Guayaquil-to-Quito railroad, itself a symbol of progress to all Latin American modernizers, was accompanied by public works programs that began to modernize the cities with better sanitation, modern communications systems, and, in the case of Guayaquil, the gradual eradication of tropical diseases that had so long plagued its people. When the railroad was completed, the switchback climb into the Andes proved to be one of the engineering marvels of the world.

## PERU

Peru's history in the second half of the nineteenth century resembled a roller-coaster ride. First it rode up to dizzying heights of success on the guano boom, then it was driven down to despair and defeat by the War of the Pacific (1879–1883). From that war until the turn of the century, Peru strove to overcome the

### Henry Meiggs, the Messiah of the Railroads

"Henry Meiggs was perhaps the most remarkable railroad builder who ever appeared on the Latin-American scene," wrote J. Fred Rippy, describing the life of this remarkable North American entrepreneur.

Landing in Chile early in 1855, a stranger and "like a thief in the night," he obtained the first railway contract three years later, and by the end of 1867 had managed the construction of nearly 200 miles, a good part of it across the Chilean coastal range. In 1868 he went to Peru, where the railway era was at its dawn, with less than 60 miles in operation. At his death in Lima on September 30, 1877, Peru had approximately 1,200 miles of track, more than 700 miles of which had been built under Meiggs's direction. . . .

Meiggs knew how to win Latin-American sympathies. He was a great dramatist and a great orator. His banquets, celebrations, and charities were long remembered both in Chile and Peru. . . . He distributed thousands of pesos and soles (Peruvian currency) among the poor and the victims of earthquakes. He spent tens of thousands on ceremonies and entertainments. . . . One of the banquets Meiggs gave in Lima during the celebration that marked the beginning of work on the Oroya Railway was attended by 800 of the double creme of society. On that occasion he promised eternal fame to the top-flight officials who were soon to collaborate in unlocking the treasure vaults of the nation and expanding its role in history:

"This happy event proclaims . . . a great social revolution whose triumph and whose benefits are entrusted to the locomotive, that irresistible battering ram of modern civilization. At its pressure will fall those granite masses which physical nature until today has opposed to the . . . aggrandizement of the Peruvian nation. Its whistle will awaken the native race from . . . [its] lethargy . . . Peru, ever noble and generous, will . . . inscribe in the book of its glorious history, at the head of its lofty benefactors, the names of all the illustrious citizens to whose indefatigable exertions and patriotism [are] due the establishment of this iron road."

The Bolivian minister [to Peru at the inauguration of the Mollendo-to-Arequipa railroad] called Meiggs a "colossus of fortune and credit," a "contractor without fear," a wizard who had come to Latin America to erase the word "impossible" from all the dictionaries, a miracle-man who had joined Valparaíso and Santiago and brought Arequipa down to the sea. . . . After the banquet was over the guests began to dance. . . . In Arequipa . . . Almighty God, President José Balta, and Henry Meiggs were praised and thanked. Handing Balta the hammer and the last spike, Meiggs declared:

"Be certain, most excellent sir, that as you place the last rail . . . the civilized nations will look upon you as the collaborator of Newton, Fulton, and Humboldt in science, and that the history of the fatherland will open to you its pages alongside those of Bolívar and San Martín, because the steam and iron with which you are endowing your country affirm also the liberty and independence of nations."

J. Fred Rippy, *Latin America and the Industrial Age* (New York: G. P. Putnam and Sons, 1944), in Lewis Hanke and Jane M. Rausch, eds., *People and Issues in Latin American History: From Independence to the Present; Sources and Interpretations,* 2nd ed. (Princeton: Markus Wiener, 1990), pp. 110–16.

legacy of an economic boom that had turned sour and of a war that had left it prostrate, embittered, and in debt.

Part of Peru's problems resulted from massive debt incurred in the 1860s and 1870s, as it turned guano profits into railroads. When the guano piles were depleted and the economic boom became bust, Peru turned to mining its nitrate fields in the south. But both sources of income proved incapable of servicing the debt incurred in the European bond market. These loans, in the tens of millions of dollars, not only were directed toward paying for the railroads but also were swallowed up by an expanding, and bloated, bureaucracy and military. Peru's economic problems were exacerbated by a growing dispute with Chile over borders—a dispute that led to war.

On the simplest level, the War of the Pacific was caused by competition among Chile, Bolivia, and Peru for the guano and nitrate riches discovered along the rugged coastal desert shared by all three countries. The value of this wealth was not evident until the middle of the nineteenth century, when Europe and North America, with rapidly expanding populations and increasing agricultural production, stimulated the export of guano and nitrates to be used for fertilizer. Even before then, however, old border disputes and rivalries had produced friction among the countries that shared the near-barren, rainless Atacama Desert.

After Chile defeated the Peru-Bolivia Confederation in 1839, Chile advanced its claims on the Atacama northward into the Bolivian coastal province of Antofagasta. Bolivia and Chile continued to spar over this province, reaching agreements in 1857 and 1866 that gave Chile wide-ranging commercial and mining rights in the region but preserved Bolivian sovereignty over the province. Chilean capital and miners were largely responsible for developing the region and tension soon developed between Chileans and Bolivians. The Bolivian presence was tenuous at best, and conflict arose between those who were working and developing the mines—the Chileans—and those who nominally exercised sovereignty over the province—the Bolivians. Sovereignty, of course, implied the right to tax, and it was this specific issue that triggered the war. Yet, in the Pacific, a further complicating factor existed—Peru.

Chile and Peru had been commercial rivals in the Pacific since the colonial period, and this rivalry intensified in the nineteenth century. Both nations feared that the other was attempting to dominate the region, especially by manipulating the weaker Bolivia. By the 1860s a naval arms race had developed between Chile and Peru. When the Bolivian government imposed a new tax on Chilean business in Antofagasta in 1879, the conflict erupted. Chile and Peru each set out to establish naval dominance. This was strategically imperative given the nature of the long barren coastline shared by the three combatants. If armies were to be moved effectively, the challenges at sea had to be met. To this end, the first, critical stage of the war was fought at sea, as seen in the opening excerpt to this chapter.

Both countries had been modernizing their fleets in the years before the war, and now the ironclads and battle cruisers were put to the test. In a series of sea battles between April and October 1879, naval officers and soldiers of both countries fought fiercely. Ultimately, the more powerful, heavily armed Chilean warships prevailed. At the Battle of Angamos, the Chileans captured the best Peruvian ship, the *Huáscar*, and killed its commander, Miguel Grau. With superiority established at sea, Chile launched a devastating series of military campaigns.

First, Chile gained control of the disputed nitrate provinces and effectively eliminated Bolivia from the war. Then, in a series of seaborne raids commanded by General Patricio Lynch, Chile ravaged the Peruvian coastline. As war fever rose in Chile, demanding that the battle be carried to Lima, the Chilean commanders did precisely that. In 1881, they attacked the Peruvian capital and overwhelmed its defenses. Although some sporadic resistance continued in the interior for the next two years, the capture of Lima effectively broke the main Peruvian armies. The Treaty of Ancón, signed in October, 1883, brought the war to an end.

Chile ultimately took the province of Antofagasta from Bolivia, and, as a result, Bolivia lost the last of its Pacific coast and became a landlocked nation. Peru ceded Tarapacá to Chile, and the territory of Tacna-Arica was left in Chilean control, its future to be decided by a plebiscite. The plebiscite was never held, however, and it took until 1929 for a final disposition of the territory to be made. In that international arbitration, Tacna went to Peru, and Arica to Chile. The War of the Pacific left Peru, and to a lesser extent Bolivia, bankrupt and bitter from the defeat and the loss of both pride and territory to the Chileans. The Chileans, in turn, savored the triumph with relish and emerged as an important power broker on the continent.

As bitter as defeat was, Peru still faced the problem of debt, now increased by the costs of defeat at war. Peru's valuable nitrate-producing province of Tarapacá was stripped away by the Chileans, and as Peru emerged from the Treaty of Ancón in 1883, it faced $260 million in debt.

The careers of many of Peru's national leaders, members of the conservative Civilista Party, had been severely tarnished by the war. The *civilista* movement, Peru's first true political party, formed in 1871 in the attempt to rationalize and modernize Peru's government, and especially to wrest control from military-style caudillos. But the War of the Pacific discredited the civilistas, who had led Peru into that conflict, and they were unable to return to power until the 1890s. The major issue through the 1880s and 1890s remained how to deal with the legacy of the war.

The war not only exacerbated Peru's financial plight but also strained the social order. Peru's society was extremely fragmented along ethnic and class lines, and the country's urban elites shared a disdain for the indigenous population. While in the spirit of liberalism they had abolished colonial-era laws treating Indians as a separate caste, they had subsequently reimagined Indians as an inferior "race" who were unprepared to be modern citizens in the new

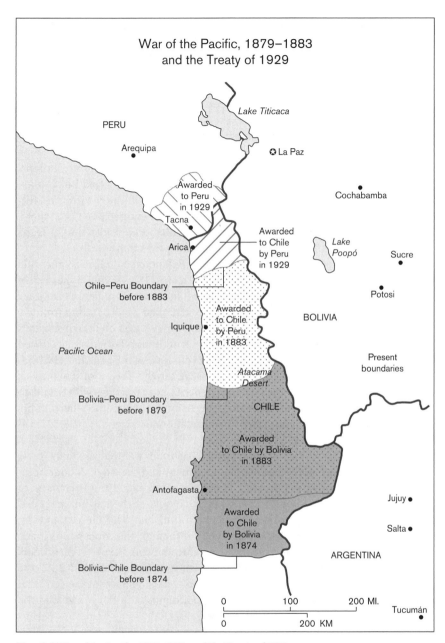

**Map 9.2** War of the Pacific, 1879–1883, and the Treaty of 1929.

nation-state. The "Indian" was no longer a legal or fiscal category but rather a racial problem. The country's much smaller Afro-Peruvian population was treated similarly. The influence of positivism later in the century was predictable in this context, with elites promoting European immigration, education, and other ways to "whiten" or "improve" the population.[2]

The tensions of racial and political conflict opened many avenues for the redress of old grievances, not only by the indigenous people of the highlands but also by blacks, mulattoes, and mestizos along the coast. As the war broke up into guerrilla actions in 1881 and 1882, many of these dispossessed groups took advantage of the chaos and disorder to press for their own rights. Indians, for example, sought to regain indigenous communities that had been taken from them over the past four centuries. Some even collaborated with the Chilean armies in order to challenge the established order and reclaim their rights. Some mineowners, merchants, and hacendados collaborated with the Chileans in an effort to end the fighting that was devastating the country.

Fighting on the side of Peru with his own indigenous and mestizo guerrilla armies was a general named Andrés Avelino Cáceres (1836–1923), a mestizo of Spanish and noble indigenous ancestry. Cáceres had long served in the military and had earned the trust of the Civilista Party after he helped to stop a military overthrow of a civilista in 1873 who was the country's first civilian president. Cáceres fought hard in the war against Chile, and though Peru lost, he earned the trust of his fellow citizens by keeping the war alive against the hated Chileans with courage, honor, and some success. After the Treaty of Ancón was signed in 1883, Peru renegotiated its foreign debt under Cáceres, who would go on to serve as president of Peru on three occasions and become a hero in his country. This debt renegotiation laid the foundation for extending the railroad into the ore-rich highlands.

At the center of settling the debt was an Irishman named Michael Grace, who negotiated between the Peruvian government and the English bondholders who held the largest portion of the debt. He persuaded the Peruvians to turn over to the English bondholders various assets of the nation, principal among them the railroads, both finished and unfinished. This Grace Contract was ratified in 1890. The debt was forgiven in return for the concessions made to the bondholders, now called the Peruvian Corporation. Peru's credit abroad, so vital to any economic recovery of the nation, was reestablished. In 1893 the railroad from Lima into the interior was completed to La Oroya, the center of one of the wealthiest areas of silver and copper deposits in the world, and the economic recovery of Peru was finally under way.

Then, in 1895, the politicians of Peru did a remarkable about-face. The civilistas buried the hatchet with their old antagonists and led a revolt that brought them back to power in 1895. This civilista oligarchy presided over a spectacular growth of the Peruvian economy into the twentieth century, fueled not only by

## War and Nationalism in the Highlands

For many in nineteenth-century Latin America, from Peru and Colombia to Brazil and Mexico, war and military service were the first initiation into the nation-state; they were a sort of school in national politics and nationalism. In Peru, many indigenous people in the central highlands had stayed out of the fighting with Chile due to their sheer distance from the war. For most, the international war over a distant border had little to do with their daily existence. This all changed in 1881 and 1882, when the central sierra witnessed two invasions by Chilean armies. Though hurt by the provisions they were forced to supply to both Chilean and Peruvian armies, many peasants joined with Cáceres simply because his exactions were more reasonable than those of the marauding Chileans. They formed peasant guerrilla forces, called *montoneras,* that kept up the fighting by inflicting casualties and stealing weapons, even when Cáceres and his troops were in retreat.

Many of the local elites found the independent peasant actions to be troubling. They were concerned about the growing "democratic flavor" to participation in the fighting and what it could mean to their regional power once the fighting was over. As historian Florencia Mallon wrote, "It was one thing to resist the invader, but to create an armed, mobilized, and relatively autonomous peasantry and, even worse, to respect them as citizens—that was an entirely different story. The most dangerous part of it, moreover, was that the peasants were beginning to believe in their equality as soldiers. Not only did they keep the booty and ammunition they obtained from the Chileans, but they also entered haciendas asking for provisions." As a result, some local elites collaborated with Chileans simply because they feared that the peasant soldiers taking up arms to fight for Peru threatened the centuries-old social order and elite wealth in the highlands. They chose to fight what they saw as "internal enemies of peace." Peasant leaders responded by calling them traitors to Peru, and Cáceres himself called these collaborators "perverted." They at times became targets of Peruvian guerrillas, who invaded their haciendas and even killed a handful of collaborators, and for a short time, the countryside was largely under peasant control. Once the Treaty of Ancón was signed, the peasant guerrillas were demobilized, with Cáceres himself ordering the execution of a handful of guerilla leaders for their actions against local hacendados.

Source: Florencia Mallon, "Comas and the War of the Pacific," in Orin Stern et al. eds., *The Peru Reader: History, Politics, Culture* (Durham: Duke University Press, 2005), pp. 181–98.

the growing exports of minerals, but also by sugar and cotton produced by modernized plantations along the coast.

## BOLIVIA

Bolivia—like several of its neighbors—was plagued by particularly venal caudillos from midcentury to the 1880s. The most notorious of them all was Mariano Melgarejo (1820–1871). His sexual excesses, alcoholic rampages, and cruelty to his enemies were so beyond the norm that they led to the coining of a new word in Bolivian Spanish—*melgarejismo*.

Good material though he may be for an engrossing history of scandal and despotism, and even madness, Melgarejo unfortunately also dragged down Bolivia's fortunes with his incompetent rule. He negotiated the transfer of disputed lands to Brazil and also focused Bolivia's aspirations on its Pacific coast. There, his major concessions to Chilean entrepreneurs developing the nitrate business became the basis of a protracted dispute between Bolivia and Chile that years later led to Bolivia's disastrous defeat in the War of the Pacific. Melgarejo also attacked the ancient patterns of Indian communal landholding. He broke up the lands and sold them to the highest bidders, further impoverishing an already poor people. He was overthrown and fled to Lima in 1871. There he was assassinated by the brother of his favorite mistress, perhaps an apt end for the debauched life of a despot.

After the War of the Pacific, Chile stripped Bolivia of its only province on the Pacific coast, Antofagasta, and left Bolivia landlocked. Although Bolivia seemed to face a bleak future in the wake of this war, several developments bode well for the country. Bolivian exports of silver, rubber, and tin stimulated the economy and produced social and political changes.

Silver enjoyed a resurgence in the 1860s and 1870s as the industry was modernized, especially through advances in electrification and transportation. Equally important was the discrediting of the military after the war and a return to civilian government from 1880 to the turn of the century. With relatively peaceful transitions of government, energies were directed into developing Bolivia's resources so sought after in Europe and North America.

When the silver boom began to taper off in the 1890s due to depressed prices on the world market, Bolivia was able to take advantage of growing demand for another of its abundant natural resources: rubber. Rubber put the world on soft tires, first as the bicycle craze spread in the 1880s and 1890s and later as the horseless carriage (predecessor of the modern automobile) began to revolutionize transportation at the turn of the century. This product was also important as an insulating material in the burgeoning electric appliance industry. Rubber trees grew naturally in the Amazon rainforest, with especially dense stands in Bolivia's Acre province on the eastern slopes of the Andes.

Brazilians dominated the early decades of the rubber boom, and by the 1890s tappers had penetrated far into Acre. The Bolivian government saw the boom as a potential windfall because it could tax the export of rubber down the Amazon River. Most of the tappers, however, were Brazilians.

The Bolivian government decided that its presence was too weak to enforce tax collection, so it gave a contract to a group of New York–based bankers and industrialists, the Bolivian Syndicate. Presumably, its capital resources, combined with the diplomatic support of the U.S. government, could keep Acre under Bolivian jurisdiction. When Brazilian tappers objected to the arrangement and revolted, Brazil's foreign minister offered to purchase Acre for $10 million plus perpetual Amazon navigation rights. By the 1903 Treaty of Petrópolis, Bolivia ceded the province to its much larger and more powerful neighbor.

Yet, a rise in demand in the industrialized countries for another of Bolivia's products, tin, triggered a more lasting boom. Tin had long been a by-product of the silver-mining industry, and when the demand abroad rose, Bolivia was able to respond quickly. By the 1920s Bolivia was supplying more than a fifth of the world's tin, and exports of the commodity, which quintupled between 1900 and 1915, accounted for more than half of all Bolivian exports.

The tin boom was accompanied by a series of developments similar to those in other export booms in Latin America. Each was characterized by modernization of the industry with capital and expertise from abroad, the construction of railroads connecting key producing areas with ports for export, a growing demand from abroad, and an ambitious group of entrepreneurs who were able to take advantage of all these factors. In the case of Bolivia's tin boom, one name stands out, that of Simón Patiño.

A cholo (as mestizos were known in Bolivia and Peru) of humble birth, Patiño rose in the industry due to hard work, a willingness to take risks, and, of course, luck. He acquired his first mine, La Salvadora, in the 1890s and within a few years struck an immensely rich vein of tin. He was especially adept in drawing in both foreign capital and the best of foreign technicians to help him play out his hunches. In 1905, La Salvadora (located near Oruro) emerged as the largest tin mine in Bolivia, and Patiño's wealth soared. When he died in 1947, he was one of the wealthiest people in the world.

Despite these changes in the nation, Bolivia remained, as one of its most able students wrote, "predominantly a rural and Indian peasant nation well into the twentieth century."[3] Furthermore, the attacks on Indian communal landholdings begun by Melgarejo were continued by the white and cholo elites who controlled the government as conservatives or liberals at the end of the century. The ancient patterns of communal landholding were broken, and Indians were given individual titles to their land. With their solidarity broken, they became easy prey for whites and cholos who bought, or simply stole, their land. Old haciendas were enlarged, new haciendas formed, and Indians were even more impoverished as they now toiled not on the land they owned, but for another owner on their hacienda or in their mine. With tin dominating the economy and the majority indigenous population despoiled of lands, Bolivia would go on to become one of the most unequal countries in Latin America in the twentieth century.

## CHILE

Contradictions marked Chile's history in the second half of the century. Its victory in the War of the Pacific confirmed it as a rising military power in South America. Its economic booms, through the exports of silver, copper, nitrates, and wheat, bespoke a prosperous nation. The evidence was everywhere. Santiago and Valparaíso became modern cities, where the affluence of the nation was evidenced by streetcars and museums, mansions, and great public buildings: all of the artifacts that we have come to associate with modernization and affluence. Railroads and steamships and telegraphs linked its mines, its cities, and its ports with England, Germany, Australia, and the United States. Politically, Chile was a model of stability in a part of the world where instability was the rule. Presidents and congresses were elected on schedule, dissent was tolerated, and exiles from across Latin America arrived to live and work in freedom. The wealth and freedom, however, were enjoyed only by a minority of the elite. Underneath Chilean prosperity, a great mass of agricultural and mining workers lived beyond the reach of electricity, a decent wage, and political liberty. Even the oligarchy—those few who governed the many—were divided rather bitterly along the traditional lines of conservatives and liberals, state interventionists and free enterprisers, centralizers and federalists, authoritarians and democrats. The upshot was a violent conflict in 1891 that took the lives of ten thousand Chileans, including that of the president, José Manuel Balmaceda, who committed suicide.

The Chilean Congress opposed Balmaceda vocally and effectively. It objected to Balmaceda's increasingly high-handed, almost dictatorial style, which coincided fatally with other factors between 1889 and 1891 to trigger the dramatic and tragic end of Balmaceda. A series of differences between Congress and the president over constitutional powers gradually grew more embittered. Instead of searching for consensus and compromise over a host of matters—control of municipal politics, the president's cabinet, and the national budget—the two sides grew more intransigent. A strike among the nitrate workers in the north spread to other sectors of industrialized labor, and Balmaceda antagonized the workers by angrily dispatching the army to restore order by force. When Balmaceda refused to submit the new budget to Congress for approval as required by law, congressmen bolted. They packed their bags, boarded naval vessels in Valparaíso, and set up their headquarters in northern Chile. The battle was on. With the support of the navy and the rich nitrate-mining sector, the congressmen waged an effective and ultimately successful war against the president. When it was over, the traditional power of the strong executive in Chile was broken, and the country entered a period of parliamentary control that lasted until the 1920s.

Chile's transformation into a modern nation progressed along many fronts. Intellectually, people such as José Victorino Lastarria in the middle and second half of the nineteenth century promoted a more liberal and secular society. The historian Diego Barros Arana argued successfully for ridding education of any religious control or affiliation. In Chile the *estado docente,* or "teaching state," emerged and effectively secularized public education. It established Chilean higher education as one of the most progressive and advanced in all of Latin America. It became, in effect, a model of excellence.

The boom in the nitrate industry continued through the turn of the century, and its prosperity rippled out through other sectors of the Chilean economy. When the copper industry recovered after 1900 with the infusion of large amounts of foreign capital, it, too, added to the rippling effect. The industrial base of Chile continued to expand and diversify. Chilean factories and foundries produced cement, paper, sugar, beer, iron, glass, bottles, and chemicals, while the coalfields of southern Chile expanded their production. Increasingly, European immigrants, although never reaching more than 5 percent of the total population, came to control important segments of the economy. And the lifestyle of the Chilean elite—the rich and the famous—was heady, marked by the good life of café society, balls, aristocratic social clubs, theater, opera, and the imitation of the latest fashions from London and Paris, a demonstration of high living in keeping with the new prosperity.

The increase in the size of the labor force, the maintenance of a semifeudal system on the great landed estates, and the exploding population in the growing cities all contributed to another side of Chile, however. One scholar of Chile described its modernization and growth as having "occurred in a country where more than half of all deaths recorded in 1913 were of infants and children under five years of age, and where the infant mortality rate more than tripled that of the United States or the United Kingdom, and significantly exceeded the rates in Egypt, Mauritius, Japan, Argentina, and even Mexico."[4] This was an example of the "social question" that began to concern Chileans with increasing passion after 1900. How could a celebrated prosperity and political stability be reconciled with a population where large and growing segments of the people suffered from deprivation, poverty, and political alienation? This question would continue to preoccupy the country as it experienced one of the most far-reaching populist experiments in the twentieth century.

## ARGENTINA

During the three colonial centuries the territory that is now Argentina was one of the least important of Spain's far-flung dominions in America. By 1910, however, it had become a world leader as a source of foodstuffs, as a field for capital investment, and in railway trackage. Among the twenty Latin American nations, it had taken first place in almost every category: politics, economics, and culture. Most of this remarkable change had come about in the last fifty of the nearly four hundred years since Spanish settlement began, and it was on so large a scale and due to such an extraordinary coincidence of domestic and foreign factors "as *to seem almost a miracle* [italics added]."[5]

The change in Argentina from midcentury, when the dictator Rosas was overthrown, to the turn of the century was indeed extraordinary. One historian identified the sources of this change: "Economic growth . . . resulted from a simple trinity: foreign investment, foreign trade, and immigration."[6] While economic progress was important, it came about only because of the renewed focus by liberals such as Sarmiento on bringing order to the divided region.

The political struggle between Buenos Aires—both the city and the province—and the rest of Argentina continued to plague the country after Rosas fell. Amid the continued conflict, however, a new constitution drawn up in 1853 was eventually ratified by all the provinces, including Buenos Aires; in 1862 Bartolomé Mitre was elected as the first president of the now-unified Argentine republic. In 1880, the city of Buenos Aires was detached from its province and became the federal capital. Argentina, it seemed, had finally settled its borders and unified its provinces into a centrally run republic.

European immigrants swelled the Argentine population in the late nineteenth century. They came first by the hundreds, then by the thousands, and finally by the millions: 5.9 million between 1871 and 1914, in fact. The city of Buenos Aires grew from about 300,000 in the 1880s to over 1.5 million by 1914, the result of immigration from all across Europe, but mostly from the Mediterranean countries of Italy, France, Spain, and the Middle East, with the majority coming from Italy. Why did they come?

In a word, they came for opportunity, the chance to get ahead in a new world where the restraints of the old country did not prevail. In the early years, Argentine positivists encouraged them, welcoming them as a way to both build a more skilled workforce and "whiten" the population. And many did realize their immediate dreams of becoming small landholders. The majority, however, became petty merchants or found employment as wage earners. A great number ended up in the cities, drawn by the pull of factory labor in places such as meat-processing plants and bringing with them the radicalism of the European labor movement. Many others endured great poverty in less esteemed jobs, working as seamstresses, day laborers, or even prostitutes. They settled into the fast-growing cities, occupying overcrowded tenements and contributing to the disorderly, turn-of-the-century urban street life.

Other immigrants took agricultural jobs, working as shepherds in the booming wool business or as tenants and sharecroppers. Their importance was to be measured in many ways, including in the racial identity of the nation. By the time immigrants made their way to Argentine shores, liberal elites, who largely rejected the more positive assessments of mestizaje that were emerging in places like Mexico at the time, had already implemented many changes to transform the country's ethnic and racial makeup through better education, hygiene, and nutrition. They also had "improved" the race through simple reclassification; while in the 1830s, Afro-Argentines made up 25 percent of the population of Buenos Aires, by the late 1880s they made up just 2 percent. To accomplish this, many were simply reclassified as "wheat colored," though this reclassification did little to slow their marginalization as scientific racism took hold.[7] While many immigrants were poorer than liberal elites had hoped, their presence effectively shrank the proportion of indigenous and Afro-descendant people in the Argentine population. But the most significant contribution from immigrants in the period from 1870 to 1910 was to provide a labor force that underlay Argentina's miraculous economic growth. It began with a wool boom in the 1860s.

While immigrants swelled the human population, sheep did the same in the animal population, increasing from 7 million in 1852 to 88 million in 1888! Wool remained the largest export until after 1900. The sheep industry opened up new lands and transformed other segments of the coastal region from immense cattle ranches into small- and middle-sized ranches more intensively worked by sheep ranching. In the same period, wheat farming increased at an equally astounding rate, with exports jumping from seventy-seven tons per annum in the 1870s to more than a million tons annually in the 1890s, prompting observers in the United States to take note of this growing rival.[8] Although the system of *latifundia*, or large (immense, in some instances) land-holdings producing beef, continued to exist, small- and middle-sized farms grew rapidly, especially in the interior provinces of Entre Ríos, Córdoba, and Santa Fe.

The cattle business itself underwent some major changes. Where salted beef, tallow, and hides traditionally formed the bulk of exports, by the turn of the century, new markets and innovations were transforming the industry. When slavery came to an end in Cuba and Brazil (1886 and 1888, respectively), so did the market for salted beef. Meanwhile, a rapidly expanding European population with growing purchasing power and new technologies in seaborne transportation and refrigeration opened up the possibilities of selling vast quantities of meat in Europe. At first, in the 1870s, packing plants sent frozen sheep carcasses to England and the continent in recently invented refrigerated ships. By the end of the century, they began selling frozen beef slaughtered in Buenos Aires fattening yards. The best arrangement, however, proved to be shipments of chilled beef, which aged during the crossing and found eager clients throughout Europe.

The railroad catalyzed the agricultural revolution on the pampas. A railroad-building boom in the 1870s and 1880s increased mileage from 470 in 1870 to over 10,000 by 1900. As in the United States, railroads not only opened new lands for settlement and farming but also triggered an orgy of land speculation, inflation, and feverish expansion that ultimately contributed to a financial crisis in 1890.

Not all people shared in the booming times. As the ranching and farming frontier pushed west and south into the vast, flat, prairie-like land of Patagonia, the advance met the often nomadic, indigenous population of the interior. Many Indians resisted the incursions, and attacked the settlers and stole their cattle. Much like white North Americans as they rolled westward, whites in Argentina made war on Indians to determine who would rule on and profit from the great prairie. In 1879, General Julio A. Roca led a brutal expedition into the southern frontier in an effort to claim the lands in the name of order and progress against what he called the "savages who destroy our wealth." In this final campaign, the "Conquest of the Desert," Roca definitively broke the resistance of the Indians, taking over fifteen thousand captive and massacring another thousand, securing the south for its pioneer white settlers. He also succeeded in making Argentina's claims to Patagonia and its far southern frontier more secure against claims by Chile. Still, the two countries continued to spar over these territories well into the twentieth century.

The booming Argentine free enterprise economy crashed with a loud thud in 1890. Banks closed, credit dried up, inflation devastated the middle class, and an armed revolt against the government flared for three days in the streets of Buenos Aires. Corruption and speculation among public servants further fueled discontent among many Argentines. Rather than a country cynically manipulated by an old oligarchy, they wanted a republic in which suffrage was meaningful and in which democratic institutions could prosper.

In a sense, the crash of 1890 and the subsequent economic recession were but symptoms of laissez-faire capitalism across the world. Triggered by rejection of Buenos Aires–issued bonds underwritten by Baring Brothers Bank in London, the crash forced the Bank of England to bail out Baring and soured the market for all South American bonds. This in turn dashed investor confidence more generally and led to a global depression. Latin America had definitely joined the international economy.

Argentina rebounded sooner than the rest of the Atlantic economies, and by the end of the century it was soaring again with increasing exports of wheat, the continued infusion of immigrants, a renewal of railroad building, new public works, and, ultimately, the restoration of trust in the financial markets of Europe. Similarly, in 1893 the U.S. economy stumbled mightily, and it, too, recovered, not to crash again until 1929.

In Argentina, a new political group, the Unión Cívica Radical (UCR, but generally known as the Radical Party), emerged from the crisis of 1890, and with it, a new leader, Hipólito Yrigoyen. He struggled for the next four decades with the most intriguing question of modern Argentina: its failure to develop a viable and stable political establishment to mirror its spectacular economic

**What Is Argentina?**

"The nation which emerged from the late nineteenth century was, nevertheless, a divided and uncertain people. On the one hand the ports, immigrants, and agricultural products provided Argentina with the trappings of a prosperous and expanding economy. Yet to step from cosmopolitian Buenos Aires into remote Salta or Jujuy was to move backward a hundred years. What was Argentina? Was it the educated, progressive elite who administered the nation, as their patrimony, from the floor of congress or the stock exchange or over an after-dinner brandy at the Jockey Club, the Club del Progreso, or the Círculo de Armas? Or was it the burgeoning middle class so evident as grocers, clerks, office managers, and foremen in the coastal cities? Or was it the Indian working in the cane fields of Tucumán or the quebracho forests of the Chaco, the Italian sharecropper in his hovel on the pampas, the Irish shepherd in Patagonia, or the native peon in the province of Buenos Aires? Or was it the rapidly expanding urban proletariat in the ports—the mestizo cook from Santiago del Estero, the Basque laborer in the slaughter house or packing plant, the porter from Galicia, or the Italian peddler? Little wonder was it that, after a century of independence, Argentines were still searching for identity and that the nation presented simultaneously all shades of prosperity and poverty, progress and reaction, learning and illiteracy."

James R. Scobie, *Argentina: A City and a Nation,* 2nd ed. (New York: Oxford University Press, 1971), p. 135.

development in the late nineteenth and early twentieth centuries. There is another, equally challenging aspect of Argentine life that became apparent at the end of the century. There were in fact two Argentinas for the nation makers to contend with: one rural and one urban. No one has better described this dichotomy than the historian James Scobie.

## URUGUAY AND PARAGUAY

Uruguay and Paraguay followed rather different paths in their national histories in the second half of the nineteenth century, although they shared certain unchanging elements, most noticeably, common borders with Argentina and Brazil. These two larger nations injected themselves with maddening regularity into the internal affairs of Uruguay and Paraguay, and, in fact, during the Paraguayan War of 1864 to 1870, they nearly destroyed Paraguay. Furthermore, the destinies of both small nations were tied—again by geographic reasons—to the mighty Rio de la Plata, which gave them access to the sea and the world through a river and estuary system dominated by Argentina.

Destiny favored Uruguay much more than Paraguay in the second half of the century. Whereas Paraguay suffered a terrible blow delivered by the Paraguayan War, Uruguay prospered and emerged at the end of the century much like Argentina, lifted up by economic forces and, in many ways, transformed by waves of immigrants and modernizing tendencies. Although the two countries were similar, Uruguay's prosperity was narrower than Argentina's. Uruguay is smaller and more limited in natural resources and geology. Ranching, principally cattle and sheep, continued to prevail as the chief economic activity, although wheat exports added to the country's income. As in Argentina, a burgeoning population added to the prosperity. Between 1852 and 1908, the population increased by over 700 percent. Many of those people were immigrants from the Mediterranean countries of Italy, France, and Spain. Improvements in the production of wool and meat (better genetic strains, refrigeration, and so forth), a relatively stable monetary system that benefited the middle classes, and an intense urbanization centered in the capital of Montevideo all contributed to a golden age. On the frontiers, for example with Brazil, caudillos and their gaucho followers continued to struggle for control of territory and to chafe against the centralizing and "civilizing" impact of urban elites. As shown so eloquently by John Chasteen, these "heroes on horseback" spent the waning decades of the nineteenth century trying to preserve a way of life rooted in rural authority, masculine honor, and local customs. Many were killed or marginalized, while others were drawn into the politics of urban elites, though increasingly more as celebrated symbols of an essential Uruguayan national identity than as actual power brokers.[9] A well-merited optimism buoyed the population and added to the feeling of well-being.

It was a period, as one of its native sons phrased it, of "optimism, expansion, accomplishments, and facility. It was a belle epoque characterized by full employment, high salaries, social mobility (especially among first generation immigrants), confidence in equality of opportunity, strengthening of the middle classes and, last but not least, the progressive resolution of social and political tensions through institutional means."[10] By the first decade of the twentieth century, democratically elected regimes were replacing caudillos and military rule. But there were problems.

A high foreign debt (the highest in South America in 1900), contracted largely by the warring caudillos of the nineteenth century, soaked up much of the revenue produced by the prosperous export sector. In 1900 one of Uruguay's most celebrated intellectuals, José Enrique Rodó, published a long essay lamenting the march of materialism and positivism through his country and the Western Hemisphere in general. In *Ariel* he expressed a profound hope and faith that matters of the spirit might balance the rampant secularism and materialism of the times (see also chapter 10). Rodó depicted the United States as perhaps the worst example of the trend that he criticized.

Whereas Uruguayans possessed the luxury of commenting on the sources and consequences of their new wealth and prosperity, the lot of Paraguay was dismal. In 1864, Paraguay went to war against its powerful neighbors, setting off a tragedy of epic proportions for that landlocked nation so carefully nurtured by the dictator Dr. Francia in the 1820s and 1830s. The Paraguayan War, which pitted Paraguay against an alliance of Argentina, Brazil, and Uruguay, nearly destroyed Paraguay as a people and a nation. The war was born of a complicated amalgam of international politics and human ambitions. Before it was over, nearly half of Paraguay's population (about 450,000 in 1865) had perished, and Paraguay survived as an independent nation only because its suspicious larger neighbors—Brazil and Argentina—were unwilling to allow the other a preponderant influence in this river Platine country.

At the vortex of the Paraguayan tragedy was Francisco Solano López. In 1862, he succeeded his father, Carlos Antonio López, to the Paraguayan presidency, and he drew Paraguay into the confrontation with its neighbors in 1864. Solano López was a complex man, modern and even progressive in some ways, a traditional caudillo of large appetites and ambitions in others. He dealt with his enemies, real and imagined, cruelly, employing torture and execution to consolidate his position.

While in Europe as his father's representative in 1853 and 1854, he met Eliza Alicia Lynch in Paris. Smitten by this beautiful Irish courtesan, he brought her to Paraguay and set her up as his mistress. Though they never married, she acted as de facto first lady. She not only bore him six children but also proved to be his most loyal supporter during the war. She urged Solano López to think in terms of greatness, hoping herself to become an empress of the New World. Solano López was a willing believer in himself, especially puffed up by the support of Eliza.

His European experiences also turned Solano López into a more cosmopolitan person. In Paraguay, he sought to raise Asunción from a provincial town to a more European-like city, with theater performances and fashionable events. He encouraged railroad expansion and telegraph construction, and fostered the increase of doctors, teachers, and engineers and a more modern economy. In the meantime, Eliza and Solano López accumulated vast amounts of personal wealth.

In the international arena, he fancied himself a power broker in the complicated politics of the Rio de la Plata region shared by Paraguay, Uruguay, Brazil, and Argentina. He built up the Paraguayan military, established fortifications on the rivers that served as key highways into the interiors of Brazil, Argentina, and Paraguay, and in 1864 warned Brazil to cease meddling in the internal affairs of Uruguay. That was a mistake.

Brazil, under Emperor Pedro II, ignored Solano López's warnings. Solano López then seized Brazilian ships going up Paraguay's rivers en route to Brazilian towns in the interior of that vast country. Soon thereafter, Solano López provoked Argentina into war when he violated Argentine territory that he needed to cross in order to attack a part of Brazil. Brazil and Argentina then joined to declare war on Paraguay, taking Uruguay into the alliance with them. Historians have long debated the causes of the war, often citing Solano López as the primary aggressor, bent on using war to secure his power. Others have focused more on the imperial ambitions of Great Britain and its role in destabilizing the region. Most clearly, all four countries caught up in the war were driven by politics and by their desire to advance their own interests in the region.

The war lasted five years, until 1870, when the Paraguayan people were finally exhausted and left prostrate by the exertions of a hopeless struggle against more powerful enemies. Curiously, Solano López—despite his multiple and flagrant transgressions against social conventions and his paranoid behavior toward the end of the war, when he tortured and executed hundreds of Paraguayans suspected of treason—tapped a deep patriotism among the tens of thousands of Paraguayans who went to war and death for him and the patria (the fatherland). By the end of the war, his ragtag army was made up of as many children and women as men, and they fought valiantly in a cause doomed to failure. Solano López himself struggled to the end and was killed by a Brazilian lancer in 1870 just after his capture, refusing the unconditional terms of surrender demanded by the allies. Eliza, who followed Solano López throughout the war, witnessed his death, as well as that of one of her sons, and was captured and deported by the Brazilians at the end of the war. She returned to Asunción to try to claim her property after a few years, but, failing that, she sailed to Paris, where she died destitute in 1886. Paraguay survived as a nation but was crushed by the defeat and knocked out of international politics for at least a generation.

Argentina emerged more powerful and confident than ever, consolidating its strength and projecting itself beyond its borders. By contrast, one scholar referred to the Paraguayan War as "the Immolation of Paraguay."[11] In fact, Paraguay—having lost half its population, including almost seven out of every ten adult males and having been devastated by the war—simply marked time for a generation. Although Brazil and Argentina occupied Paraguay for six years after the war, and each gained territory in postwar negotiations, neither could take advantage of Paraguay's devastation. In a sense, Paraguay continued to exist because both of the larger powers were wary of each other's intentions, and neither would tolerate Paraguay being dominated by the other. Attempts to promote immigration into Paraguay failed dismally, the politicians ruled arbitrarily, and by 1904, when liberals took power, Paraguay was very little changed from fifty years before.

## BRAZIL

By contrast with Paraguay, Brazil in the second half of the nineteenth century boomed to the rhythm and cacophony of progress. Brazil had passed through a watershed in 1850. Regional rebellions ended, and Brazilians began to unite as one nation. Furthermore, with the end of the slave trade, which prefigured the ultimate abolition of slavery itself in 1888, new forces were released in the nation. Capital, imagination, and energy were poured both into new enterprises and into old industries being revitalized by the inventions and technologies of a century imbued with progress.

The emperor, Pedro II, emerged as a modern, enlightened monarch who governed with tolerance and the approval of most Brazilians. Certain export crops, such as coffee, cacao, and rubber, boomed in value and provided capital that was transformed into railroads, ports, banks, and other elements key to the beginnings of a modern economic infrastructure. In foreign affairs, a string of successes on the battlefields and in diplomatic forums ensured Brazil's emergence as one of the great powers in Latin America.

Of all the changes noted earlier, perhaps none was so dramatic in human terms as the abolitionist movement that finally destroyed slavery in Brazil. No other Latin American nation was wedded more closely than Brazil to slavery as an economic and social system, and no other nation included so many slaves within its population. Indeed, at the beginning of the nineteenth century, slaves constituted a majority of the population, although by midcentury the free black population was gaining on the slaves. The move to abolish slavery gradually gained momentum in the second half of the century. The emperor himself believed in the emancipation of all slaves. He personally had freed his own slaves in 1840. He moved cautiously as the leader of his nation in this regard, however, always conscious of the tremendous economic, political, and social power wielded by members of the sugar and coffee planter class, who continued to defend slavery as essential to their prosperity and way of life.

The Paraguayan War produced deep splits in the slave system. Slaves who volunteered to serve in the Brazilian army were promised their freedom, and over six thousand were liberated in this fashion. Such men, often decorated and honored by the nation for their courage and bravery in battle, pushed for the destruction of an oppressive system whose very existence insulted their patriotism and service to their country.

The officer class of the army also emerged from the war with a new consciousness, a new sense of mission and professionalism gained from its victories in the battlefield. Many of these officers rose from the middle class and did not share the sentiments of the old landed oligarchs who defended slavery. A proud and militant army restlessly argued for a greater role in politics and in determining the course of Brazil's destiny. Many of these officers became ardent abolitionists and republicans. Embracing positivism and imbued with egalitarian sentiments fostered by the shared experience of war, they condemned slavery as an antiquated and irrational remnant of an earlier world.

They were joined in their efforts to abolish slavery by an increasing number of Brazilians who shared their sentiments. The fact that rights and status in Brazil were not rigidly tied to race made opposition to slavery easier. By midcentury, many freed blacks and other nonwhites were landowners, businesspeople, educators, and government officials, some reaching to the heights of political and economic power. Legal discrimination had largely been outlawed, though scientific racism and an enthusiasm for "whitening" the population, including through European immigration, took hold, especially after abolition.

Sugar planters in the north whose declining fortunes made slavery less important in the region were among abolition's biggest supporters by midcentury. By then, coffee planters in the south, whose fortunes were on the rise, remained the institution's greatest defenders. Nevertheless, in 1871, under the leadership of the emperor and his prime minister, the viscount of Rio Branco, the Law of the Free Womb (or Rio Branco law) was enacted to free all children born of slave mothers after the date of the passage of that law. Children were to remain with their mothers' owners until age eight, at which time the owners had the option of freeing the child and receiving payment from the state or keeping and caring for the child while receiving its labor until the age of twenty-one. While slavery did not end immediately, coupled with the end of the slave trade in 1850, the Law of the Free Womb doomed the institution.

For the abolitionists, however, even the end of the slave trade and the Law of the Free Womb were too slow and gradual. Led by such people as Joaquim Nabuco (1849–1910), who founded the Brazilian Anti-Slavery Society, these abolitionists waged a relentless war on slavery based on moral and religious grounds. As in the United States, a number of blacks and mulattoes took part in the campaign, writing, lecturing, raising money, and counseling slaves on their rights and opportunities for freedom.

Although the philosophical repugnance of slavery was the moral foundation of the movement, other factors in the push for total emancipation also drove the abolitionists. The most persuasive of these was the antiquated nature of an institution in a nation so committed to progress. Slavery reminded the abolitionists of a stagnant, elitist way of life that had to be swept away to make room for the railroad, industrialization, and progress.

The rapid expansion of the coffee industry represented one facet of this new, liberal Brazil. The export of coffee began in the eighteenth century, and by the era of independence coffee exports accounted for 20 percent of Brazil's foreign earnings. Spurred on by British traders and entrepreneurs, the coffee culture expanded rapidly in the Paraíba Valley of the state of Rio de Janeiro and spread into the states of São Paulo and Minas Gerais in the second half of the century.

**Joaquim Nabuco**

Joaquim Aurélio Nabuco de Araújo (1849–1910) was a wealthy diplomat and monarchist who worked avidly throughout his life to end slavery in Brazil. He argued against it from all sides—moral, political, economic—stating that it prevented Brazil from being a truly free and modern country. He wrote:

> The use of slave labor not only hinders to the point of stagnation material development, but it deadens the moral progress of civilization . . . Every dimension of our social existence is contaminated by this crime: we grow with it and it forms the basis of our society. From where does our fortune come? From profits produced by slaves. Our state of liberty was rooted in this criminal activity, and now, when we want to free ourselves from it, it holds us fast . . . Slavery corrupts everything, robbing working people of their former virtues: diligence, thrift, charity, patriotism, fear of death, love of liberty.

Joaquim Nabuco, "Slavery and Society," in Robert M. Levine and John J. Crocitti, eds., *The Brazil Reader: History, Culture, Politics* (Durham: Duke University Press, 1999), pp. 143–44.

By the 1890s, coffee dominated Brazil's export trade, accounting for over 50 percent of total exports, producing high profits, and fueling the growth of the economy. Coffee plantations initially were worked wholly by slave labor, and coffee planters remained among its biggest defenders after midcentury. However, they also increasingly hired European immigrants to replace the slave labor, moving gradually at first and then more quickly to a wage labor force. Half of all coffee exports were going to the United States by the end of the century, reinforcing the ties slowly growing between two of the largest countries in the Western Hemisphere.

Coffee earnings stimulated the railroad boom in Brazil as well. The first railroads were strung from the coastal cities of Rio de Janeiro and São Paulo (connected to its port of Santos by a railroad) into the interior coffee-growing regions. The very first railroad began operating in Rio de Janeiro in 1854. By 1889, over six thousand miles of track were in use. In the forefront of this swelling movement was the viscount of Mauá, a pioneer entrepreneur and industrialist. Mauá has been likened to the heroes of American industry—the Goulds, Vanderbilts, and Rockefellers—and could well have fit the Horatio Alger mold. Alger, whose readers were in the millions, wrote stories of poor boys made rich by dint of their hard work, good luck, and fantastic opportunities created by the industrialization of the land and its people.

Other exports, such as rubber, fueled the modernization of Brazil. Charles Goodyear's invention of the vulcanization process in 1839 opened the way to the wide use of rubber in industry. It was used in a variety of processes, from railway mechanics and general engineering to insulation in the new electrical

### Viscount of Mauá, a Brazilian Modernizer

"Irineu Evangelista de Sousa, known as the Viscount of Mauá (1813–1889), was widely recognized as the leading industrial capitalist before the Paraguayan War. At the age of thirteen he [began] working for Richard Carruthers, head of a large English importing firm. This was the turning point in his life: seven years later he became a partner in the firm. And the next year Carruthers retired to England, leaving the future Viscount of Mauá, aged twenty-four, as manager of the Brazilian house, a position through which he amassed a large fortune. He became involved in a wide variety of enterprises, most important of which were a foundry-shipyard, railways, and banks. The initial impetus that led him to broaden his interests and eventually break away from the importing business altogether was a visit to England in 1840. The industrial might of Great Britain greatly excited him, and he dreamed of creating a similarly powerful and industrialized Brazil. Of particular importance was Mauá's visit to an iron foundry in Bristol. He later wrote that 'I was deeply impressed by what I saw and observed, and right there the idea of founding in my country an identical establishment was born in my spirit.' He bought a small iron foundry and shipyard in 1846. It prospered from the first. . . . During its days of prosperity, this establishment was the basis of a business empire. The firm built 72 ships, most of them steam. . . . He also made the pipes and lamps to be employed in the Mauá-owned gas company in Rio de Janeiro. . . . Railroads were one of Mauá's greatest enthusiasms. The very first railroad in Brazil was his creation. . . . Mauá visualized banks as the partners of railways in pushing the country toward economic development. . . . Mauá created, in 1851, the Banco Mauá e Companhia, which was merged into a semi-governmental bank two years later. He then organized the banking house Mauá, MacGregor & Cia. with branches in Buenos Aires, Montevideo, Rio Grande do Sul, Pelotas, Pôrto Alegre, Santos, São Paulo, Campinas, and Belém."

Richard Graham, *Britain and the Onset of Modernization in Brazil, 1850–1914* (Cambridge: Cambridge University Press, 1968), pp. 187–90.

businesses. As these industries grew, they, in turn, stimulated the increasing production of rubber. Exports from the Amazon rose from 1,500 tons in 1850 to 3,000 tons by 1867, and by 1880 over 8,000 tons were being exported annually. Production again doubled between 1880 and 1890 as demand increased in the electrical and engineering industries. By the turn of the century, the rubber boom was in full swing, catalyzed by the bicycle craze and the growing automobile industry, both dependent on pneumatic tires.

The Amazon was transformed by the process. The cities of Belém and Manaus exploded with an influx of immigrants, entrepreneurs, and merchants.

**Figure 9.2** The Manaus Opera House, finished in 1896, was built from wealth generated by the Amazon rubber boom. Made of materials imported from all over Europe, it included 198 Italian chandeliers. It joined the wealth of domestic industry and the embrace of European culture deep in the Brazilian interior and symbolized Brazil's quest for modernity. Courtesy Wiki Commons.

Manaus, located nearly a thousand miles up the Amazon, became the richest and most modern city in all Brazil, sporting an opera house, Paris fashions, electric lighting, and trams. In 1901, rubber accounted for 28 percent of Brazil's total exports, second only to coffee, and constituted one of those fuels for the engines of change that were transforming Brazil.

The growth and modernization of cities alongside the abolition of slavery put ex-slaves in a new and precarious position. In some areas, like the declining northern sugar-producing regions, they struggled to eke out a living with little access to land. Some, both there and in other agricultural areas, found that life before and after slavery looked very much the same, with the biggest change simply being that they now labored for a different plantation. Others joined the urban poor. In Rio de Janeiro in the 1870s, almost two-thirds of free women were domestic servants, while close to 90 percent of slave women were, meaning that about 70 percent of all working women were domestic servants. Their occupations ranged from the more highly esteemed chambermaid and wet nurse to cook, maid, water carrier, and laundress. By 1906, 76 percent of working women in Rio were still domestic servants. While work conditions, living arrangements, and pay varied from house to house, it nevertheless was a difficult and sometimes dangerous life that put them into contact with both the country's wealthiest residents and the city's least sanitary conditions.[12] These urban and rural workers and ex-slaves, with their often unsanitary living conditions and unstable labor arrangements, were as critical to defining Brazil's modernization as its most advanced industries and elegant mansions.

British, American, and native Brazilian entrepreneurs such as the Viscount of Mauá pushed the vanguard of modernization along other fronts as well. Flour mills, sugar mills, and a dynamic textile industry all were established in this period, testifying to the faith in capitalism, risk taking, and, ultimately, industrialization as the key to a progressive, modern Brazil. Rather than subscribing to the static and stable life of old Brazil—characterized by slavery, a plantation economy, and an unwillingness to change or experiment—the entrepreneurs, the abolitionists, the republicans, the military, and the slaves themselves challenged the existing order. In the end, the old empire fell, itself an anachronism that, to most Brazilians, had to be swept away along with slavery. The end of slavery came in 1888, and the empire itself fell in 1889, replaced by the republic of Brazil.

The empire had been undermined by a number of factors. Intellectually, the positivists paved the way, arguing that slavery and monarchy were outdated institutions in a modern, scientific society. Republicans, furthermore, were ascendant in the 1870s and 1880s. Men such as Benjamin Constant, veteran of the Paraguayan War, instructor in mathematics at the military school and tutor of Emperor Dom Pedro's grandchildren, promoted the end of slavery and the establishment of a republic, which he considered to be absolutely necessary reforms for the new, modern Brazil. Religious controversy further added to the stew of discontent in the 1870s and 1880s. The emperor alienated many conservative Catholics by his high-handed regalism, holding that, in Brazil at least, the state would continue to govern the church in spite of Vatican efforts to the contrary.

In this charged atmosphere, the abolitionists were the first to triumph. On May 13, 1888, Isabel, Dom Pedro's daughter, who was ruling as regent while he traveled in Europe, formally abolished slavery in Brazil. She signed the Golden Law, which freed all slaves with no conditions and no compensation to the owners. While slavery came to an end quite abruptly in Brazil, it had been preceded by a consistent and determined campaign by abolitionists. A number of factors worked toward this end: the end of the slave trade at midcentury, the growing antagonism of the urban professional sectors toward an institution that supported the old planter class, the gradual increase in European immigrants to take the place of slaves, and the initiative of the slaves themselves, who fled the plantations in ever-increasing numbers. All of these factors undermined the institution, now considered an anachronism in a progressive, modernizing Brazil. The news of emancipation was greeted joyfully in Rio de Janeiro with fireworks, bands, and speeches. Within eighteen months, the emperor and the empire were toppled as well, and a republic proclaimed. The

**Figure 9.3** Emperor Pedro II ruled Brazil from 1841 until he was overthrown by the army in 1889. He presided over major developments, such as the expansion of coffee, the encouragement of immigration and foreign investment, and a more active role in South American affairs. Princess Isabel, Pedro II's oldest daughter, twice served as head of state in her father's absence. During the second time, in 1888, she decreed the end of slavery. Had the army not deposed Pedro II, she would have succeeded to his throne. Courtesy Library of Congress.

events were inexorably linked, because abolitionists, positivists, and republicans all were rolled into the same movement.

The army led the way. On November 15, 1889, Marshal Manuel Deodoro da Fonseca, the army's ranking general, ordered troops out of the barracks in Rio de Janeiro. They surrounded the royal palace and secured other public buildings, and Deodoro announced the end of the monarchy. Very few people objected. Two days later the royal family went into exile. Dom Pedro lived two more years before dying in Paris in 1891.

An unlikely combination of factions brought the empire to its end. The army felt insulted and ignored by the politicians of the empire. Officers wished to restore credit and prestige to their institution, now also thoroughly imbued with the doctrines of republicanism cultivated by writers such as Benjamin Constant. From a ragtag band of dragoons in the early part of the century, the military had been professionalized by the end of the century, and its leaders saw it increasingly as a progressive and moralizing force wherein Brazilian men were taught the values of a modern republican citizenry at odds with the ways of the past. Church leaders, still very conservative, were put off by Dom Pedro's attitude, which seemed to threaten their autonomy and growing ultramontanism (the idea that the church in all nations must be more loyal to the Vatican and the Pope than to any secular authority). The growing middle classes and the new industrialists—the pioneers of progress and industrialization—all found the monarchy too unresponsive, too anachronistic, and too out of sync with the republican values of the era. Even the planter class, the most powerful conservative supporters of the monarchy, lost faith when it failed to prevent abolition.

Ironically, Dom Pedro himself did more to prepare his nation for the transition to a free society and republicanism than any other single factor. The emperor was an enlightened leader who encouraged republicanism, tolerated dissent, encouraged the sciences, and, in a sense, paved the way for the end of his own regime.[13] That the transition from empire to republic was virtually bloodless testified to the disposition of politically active Brazilians to make this dramatic change in their form of government, although the vast majority of the population stood by inert.

A new republican constitution was approved in 1891, and Deodoro was elected the first president. He resigned in 1892 amidst bitter feuding, and much skirmishing followed before a new president, Prudente de Morais, was elected in 1894, the first of a long line of presidents from the coffee-producing region of São Paulo. They would alternate in the presidency with politicians from Minas Gerais and Rio de Janeiro until 1930, when this first republic was toppled.

Coffee exports continued to increase, the rubber boom reached its peak in the first decade of the twentieth century, and Brazil flexed its muscles as a major power on the South American continent, settling boundary disputes with all of its neighbors. These settlements were always peaceful, but several of Brazil's neighbors, such as Bolivia and Peru, were forced to accept Brazilian demands in the end.

## CONCLUSIONS AND ISSUES

South American countries, like Mexico and Central America to the north, were gradually transformed in the second half of the nineteenth century by forces that continued to change them well into the twentieth century. These forces are generally subsumed under the term "modernization," a process that implies the progressive transformation of economic and social structures. This process sometimes simply emphasized well-established economic practices—such as relying on export crops and products for income—though now with increased production and levels of activity. Such was the case of silver in Bolivia, for example.

Another important phase in modernization was the development of relatively new crops and products. Some, such as coffee in Colombia, cacao in Ecuador, beef products from the Platine countries (especially Argentina and Uruguay), and nitrates from Chile, had been in limited production for decades, but the demands from Europe and North America propelled their production to new heights.

And then there were the new products, such as rubber from the Amazon, tin from Bolivia, and petroleum from Venezuela. The rapidly industrializing nations of Europe and the United States required these products in ever-increasing quantities, leading to booms in the economies of those countries that produced them.

Concomitantly, the increasing exports drove internal improvements and changes from Colombia to Chile. Railroads and new urban developments were but two examples. Cities were transformed by gas lights, then electric street-lights, then trams, and in numerous other ways became more modernized, often refashioned with new boulevards, plazas, and monumental buildings to copy the styles of the great European cities. The other side of this modernizing coin, however, was the great impoverishment of rural indigenous and mestizo populations, who lost lands and communities amid the push for profits and progress. For them—transformed into laborers in the vast new export-oriented haciendas or mines, or migrating to cities to become part of a rapidly growing population of urban working poor—modernization was an ambivalent process of both improvement and loss.

And, as witnessed in Brazil, new fashions and modern ways also swept out old traditions and social structures. Slavery was finally abolished in Brazil because it was an institution made obsolete by the modern world. That slavery held on for so long in Brazil, however, and the fact that for many, rural life changed little with its end, are testimony to the enduring patterns of tradi-tional life that did not yield easily to change.

### Discussion Questions

What were the reasons for international wars in nineteenth-century Latin America and what was their impact?

What were the similarities in the modernizing processes across South America in the mid- to late nineteenth century?

What was modernization like in urban areas? In rural areas?

What was the export boom? What were its advantages and drawbacks for the countries in the region?

How did the Catholic Church fare in the region as liberals gained power?

How did regionalism in places like Colombia, Ecuador, and Argentina influence politi-cal consolidation and economic progress?

How did immigration influence the changes taking place in the late nineteenth cen-tury? How did scientific racism influence the integration of immigrants into Latin American society?

### Timeline

| | |
|---|---|
| 1864–70 | Paraguayan War, or the War of the Triple Alliance |
| 1871 | Law of the Free Womb (Brazil) |

| 1879–83 | War of the Pacific |
|---|---|
| 1870s–1884 | Conquest of the Desert (Argentina) |
| 1883 | Treaty of Ancón (Chile and Peru) |
| 1888 | Abolition of slavery, or the Golden Law (Brazil) |
| 1889 | End of Brazilian empire |
| 1899–1902 | War of a Thousand Days (Colombia) |
| 1904 | Roosevelt Corollary |

## Keywords

campesinos

Conquest of the Desert

conservatives

gamonales

latifundia

Law of the Free Womb (Rio Branco Law)

liberals

llaneros

melgarejismo

modernization

nitrates

Paraguayan War, or War of the Triple Alliance

Roosevelt Corollary

rubber

silver

tin

Treaty of Ancón

ultramontanism

Unión Cívica Radical (UCR, Radical Party) (Argentina)

War of the Pacific

# Inventing Latin America

## The Paradox of North America

In the following poem, "To Roosevelt," Nicaraguan poet Rubén Darío (1867–1916) strikes out at the paragon of imperialism in the early twentieth century, President Theodore Roosevelt. Darío catches the ambivalence of Latin Americans toward North America, at once admiring of the march of progress and inventiveness and shuddering at the sacrifice of soul and religion. Read Darío for the sense he transmits, and for how Latin American intellectuals felt toward the United States in the early twentieth century. In Darío's poetry we see the invention of the new Latin America, a people set apart from North America by culture, religion, and history.

### TO ROOSEVELT

The voice that would reach you, Hunter, must speak
in Biblical tones, or in the poetry of Walt Whitman.
You are primitive and modern, simple and complex;
you are one part George Washington and one part Nimrod.
You are the United States,
future invader of our naive America
with its Indian blood, an America
that still prays to Christ and still speaks Spanish.

You are strong, proud model of your race;
you are cultured and able; you oppose Tolstoy.
You are an Alexander-Nebuchadnezzar,
breaking horses and murdering tigers.
(You are a Professor of Energy,
as current lunatics say.)

You think that life is a fire,
that progress is an irruption,
that the future is wherever
your bullet strikes.
No.

The United States is grand and powerful.
Whenever it trembles, a profound shudder
runs down the enormous backbone of the Andes.

If it shouts, the sound is like the roar of a lion.
And Hugo said to Grant: "The stars are yours."
(The dawning sun of the Argentine barely shines;
the star of Chile is rising.) A wealthy country,
joining the cult of Mammon to the cult of Hercules;
while Liberty, lighting the path
to easy conquest, raises her torch in New York.

But our own America, which has had poets
since the ancient times of Nezahualcóyotl;
which preserved the footprint of great Bacchus,
and learned the Panic alphabet once,
and consulted the stars; which also knew Atlantic
(whose name comes ringing down to us in Plato)
and has lived, since the earliest moments of its life,
in light, in fire, in fragrance, and in love—
the America of Moctezuma and Atahualpa,
the aromatic America of Columbus,
Catholic America, Spanish America,
the America where noble Cuauhtémoc said:
"I am not in a bed of roses"—our America,
trembling with hurricanes, trembling with Love:
O men with Saxon eyes and barbarous souls,
our America lives. And dreams. And loves.
And it is the daughter of the Sun. Be careful.
Long live Spanish America!
A thousand cubs of the Spanish lion are roaming free.
Roosevelt, you must become, by God's own will,
the deadly Rifleman and the dreadful Hunter
before you can clutch us in your iron claws.

And though you have everything, you are lacking one thing:
God![1]

The Wars of Independence released new energies and promoted new ways of thinking, as Latin Americans examined themselves to determine who they were and where they were going as a distinct civilization. The first important novel in Latin American literature was produced during the wars. Written by José Joaquín Fernández de Lizardi, *The Mangy Parrot* (El periquillo sarniento) appeared in 1816 in Mexico, condemning many social wrongs of the day through the picaresque adventures of its hero. Lizardi's life transcended the epoch, because he began his writing career during the vice-royalty and lived to 1827. Not a revolutionary, he nonetheless was an ardent reformer and satirist. Lizardi condemned the excessive powers of the church, defended freedom of the press, and was often in trouble with the Spanish authorities.

Others were to search more deeply for the Latin American heritage soon after the wars were over. If Spanish things—the monarchy, the Inquisition, despotism—were to be rejected, then an alternative culture had to be discovered or invented. This became one of the principal goals of Latin American intellectuals for the rest of the century. The influences shaping the search for identity were many. Latin America is a large area with many different cultures, from the slaves of Bahía in tropical Brazil to the indigenous people of highland Mexico to the privileged Creole elites of Santiago in temperate Chile. The colonial hispanic legacy, the intellectual influences coming out of nineteenth-century Europe, and the growing power and materialism of the U.S. all shaped the search for identity as well. The impermanence and political instability made cultural inventiveness and creativity difficult in the early to mid-nineteenth century, leading Latin Americans to look abroad for intellectual and cultural values, especially to Europe. This tendency often suffocated the earnest attempts of Latin Americans to explore and define their own native culture and to establish their own national identities. But, by midcentury, political order and economic progress brought with it a flowering of new voices seeking to define the nations of the Americas. As they engaged in this nation-building project, these voices drew from the past and from the region's diversity while looking to the future to identify what was unique about Latin America in an increasingly modern world.

## MENTAL EMANCIPATION

> We shall be Argentines when we feel in ourselves the attachment to the soil that the Indian had, making it the source of his art and myths; when we feel the urge to create civilization which the Spanish founders of cities possessed; when we feel the plasticity of the gaucho on the limitless pampas and his inspiration to rise above his environment and to tell of it in song; when we have the capacity for disciplined work, like the gringo; when we are neither Indians, nor gauchos, nor Spaniards, nor gringos, but Argentines.[2]

So wrote Domingo Faustino Sarmiento, the great Argentine man of letters, educator, and political leader of his generation, as he sought to give form to the new nation of Argentina. Contemporaries across Latin America echoed Sarmiento's concerns as they faced the task of creating and defining a national consciousness and a national culture—a national identity—to accompany the political emancipation that the wars themselves achieved.

In moving toward this goal, many Latin Americans repudiated their Hispanic heritage with scorn. Catholicism and feudalism were vilified as twin evils inherited from Spain. One of the champions of this anti-Hispanic view created a tremendous stir in 1844 when he delivered an address before the University of Chile entitled "Investigations of the Social Influence of the Conquest and the Colonial System of the Spanish in Chile." José Victorino Lastarria minced few words in this famous polemic: "'The Spaniards conquered America, soaking its soil in blood, not to colonize it, but rather to take possession of the precious metals that it produced so abundantly.' America was just a booty of war. . . . When Spain attempted to colonize it, it transplanted into Hispanic America 'all the vices of her absurd system of government, vices that multiplied as a result of causes that had their origin in the system itself.'"[3]

Lastarria's thinking was echoed by fellow Hispanophobes, such as Sarmiento himself in Argentina and José María Luis Mora in Mexico. Mora, a priest and historian, hotly criticized the clergy and the military of Mexico for prolonging the crisis that followed Mexico's independence, labeling both institutions as hopelessly archaic. Furthermore, he faulted the tendency to sacrifice the national interests to those of corporations whose structure was inherited from Spain and the colonial world. A corporate view and structure of the world simply meant that individuals were not as important as the corporate entity—the church, the military, the merchant guild, or the Indian village—to which they belonged or with which they identified. Mora argued that this corporatist legacy of the colonial era continued to block the modern changes that would free Mexico from its backward past and allow it to become a truly modern, liberal, independent nation.

Sarmiento raged with venom, and not a little humor, against the Spanish legacy. Citing the physiological fact that little-used organs tend to wither and grow weak, Sarmiento said that the Spanish brain had not advanced since the fourteenth century, when the Inquisition began. He added that the nineteenth-century Latin Americans' ability to deal with the concepts of liberty and freedom was almost dead from lack of practice.

Other potshots were leveled at all things Hispanic across the Americas. In Mexico, poets, composers, and writers creatively condemned the inheritance of Spain, which they typified as being made up of equal parts avarice, inhumanity, and bigotry. The Mexican composer José Mariano Elízaga dropped the title "don" from his name because it was an ancient Spanish practice that denoted a gentleman. Others argued successfully to change the spelling of "Méjico" to "México," figuring that the letter $x$ was more truly Mexican and Indian than was the Spanish $j$.

Not everyone was as quick to condemn everything Spanish. In the search to forge the new Latin American identity and culture, one simply could not ignore three hundred years of history. The blood, language, and faith of Spain coursed through Latin America, a fact that the intellectual Andrés Bello recognized

## An Indictment of Spain and Hispanicism

Javier Prado y Ugarteche (1871–1921), a Peruvian educator and politician, condemned Spain for much of Peru's backwardness. In the following passage, Alejandro O. Deustua reviewed the 1941 edition of Prado's book, which originally appeared under the title *Estado social del Perú durante la dominación española: Estudio histórico-sociológico* (Lima, 1894):

> Politically, it [the colonial period] bequeathed to us the vices of totalitarianism, the enemy of all social liberty. . . . We have received traditions of incorrigible bureaucratic abuses in public administration; bribery nourished by avarice and impunity that extended even to the highest officials; and, as Prado puts it, "a sick obsession with wealth, no matter how acquired, that became an all-pervasive and incurable disease. . . ."
>
> What has been our inheritance in the economic order? As Prado explains it, "The immediate exploitation of our sources of wealth without long-term planning and with only immediate results in mind." In short, we have inherited a most pernicious system that in Peru has produced abominable and destructive habits persisting even to the present day because of the immutable law of psychological inheritance.
>
> The colonial ecclesiastical heritage has left in our church officials an unbridled ambition to govern, even in the temporal order; an instransigent fanaticism, developed to the most refined point of cruelty by the Holy Office of the Inquisition . . . clergy, whose individual morals are weakened by the abundance of pleasures attaching to their positions. . . . All they did during three hundred years was to abuse their power. As teachers, they suffocated the spirit of scientific investigation. As models of perfect men, they served only to weaken the ties of social morality. They poisoned the atmosphere with superstition, pride, wrath, impurity, and their terrible train of consequences. Cloaked in a primitive doctrine of charity and chastity, they proceeded actually to institute a policy of hatred, extermination and profligacy. . . .
>
> Under colonial influences, intelligence atrophied and the practical spirit of work and economy disappeared, along with concern for political rights. All that remained were absurd ideals, aggressiveness, hallucinatory fanaticism, and a reverential form of homage to the king and his government. Such was the spirit of the race to which the conquerors belonged. Such was the spirit that they imparted to the blood of our creoles.

Quoted in Frederick B. Pike, ed., *Latin American History: Select Problems, Identity, Integration, and Nationhood* (New York: Harcourt, Brace and World, 1969), pp. 199–200.

quite well.[4] Bello was a Venezuelan by birth who spent many years in Chile; he also served as teacher to Simón Bolívar for a time and accompanied him on his trip to London in 1810. Many revered him as an educator, philosopher, poet, and statesman.

To Bello, the evidence of the positive Hispanic heritage was perfectly clear. One had but to consider the sacrifices, the nobility, the courage, and the steadfastness shown by the patriots during the Wars of Independence to witness the strength and virtues that Latin Americans had inherited from Spain. The very ability of Latin Americans to rise up and overthrow Spain was an ability born within the Hispanic bosom. The vices attributed to the Spaniards—injustice, treachery in war, atrocity—were vices common to humanity, and certainly not uniquely Spanish.

Bello, Sarmiento, and others such as the Mexican conservative historian Lucas Alamán were not content with a simple condemnation of Spanish culture and practices, which, despite widespread resentments against the former colonizer, they saw as being just as fundamental to the creation of Latin America as the region's indigenous roots. After political emancipation had been achieved through the Wars of Independence, they sought what the modern Mexican philosopher Leopoldo Zea called "mental emancipation." It proved to be a difficult task, because one is never truly freed of one's past; rather, the search for identity was a creative process spanning the nineteenth century and beyond, in which an array of Latin Americans participated in forging a distinct consciousness and culture.

## INVENTING TRADITIONS

The search for identity led Latin Americans to concern themselves for the first time with the region's unique cultural, racial, and intellectual features. As governments became more stable and states became stronger, the need to identify habits, culture, and symbols that could unite the people as a nation grew more important. It was not an easy task, since the region was so diverse and elites so distanced from the masses. Many struggled with how to celebrate what was American while rejecting what they saw as the region's backwardness and brutality. The first generation of writers to engage in writing the nation, to create what scholar Doris Sommer termed "foundational fictions," were heavily influenced by the romanticism that emerged out of the Enlightenment, though they were not always strictly romantics in the intellectual sense.[5] Rather, for many, their message was often explicitly political and favored American themes. These themes were based in the realities of nineteenth-century life, though they were reinvented to fit the nationalist purpose and recast as historical traditions and symbols that united the people of the nation in a single community.

Rejecting forces that ran against this nationalist project was part of their mission. For example, although the Argentine poet and writer Esteban Echeverría sought during his life to be a romantic, he is best remembered for a work that appeared posthumously, a quickly written piece of prose fiction with a political message. Echeverría's *El matadero* (The Slaughter Yard), composed about 1840, was a thinly disguised attack on the Rosas regime. The story is best synopsized by Jean Franco:

It relates an incident at the abattoir [slaughter yard] in Buenos Aires where, during the slaughtering of the animals, a bull escapes, killing a boy as he does so. The bull is recaptured and the butchers, excited by the thrill of the pursuit and capture, make a bloodthirsty ritual of the killing. As they finish off the animal, a refined-looking young man passes on horseback. They turn against him, drag him down from his horse and torment him. The youth struggles valiantly against the attackers but has a hemorrhage and is left for dead. The reason for the attack on him is that he is "unitarian" (that is, in opposition to Rosas and the federalist party). The butchers know this because their victim carries no outward sign of support for the Rosas regime and also because he rides with a foreign saddle. He is thus identified with an "un-American" way of life. Echeverría's own sympathies are not left in doubt. He is unmistakably on the side of refinement and civilization, against the native "butchers."[6]

Even more well known for his attacks on Rosas was Domingo Faustino Sarmiento. In his novel *Facundo: Or, Civilization and Barbarism* (1845), Sarmiento told the story of the rise and fall of an Argentine gaucho caudillo named Juan Facundo Quiroga. Facundo represented all that was rough and wild and untamed in Argentina. Opposed to Facundo were the forces of civility, education, and progress, represented by Buenos Aires and the civilization from abroad that inspired it. *Facundo* is Sarmiento's statement of the classic battle between civilization (the city, education, and European influences) and barbarism (untamed nature, unbridled passions, and the gauchos) that he felt Argentina, and indeed much of Latin America, was fighting. To Sarmiento, who later became president and worked to implement his vision of a progressive, modern society, Rosas, Facundo, and other caudillos had to be destroyed or, at the least, reined in, if Latin America was ever to rise above the political anarchy that tore it apart in the first part of the nineteenth century.

In *Facundo* and other works, we see the power of creation at work. Although *Facundo* and *The Slaughter Yard*, for example, borrowed from the romantic style, they were essentially American works, inspired by the strengths and failures of their traditions, describing the sweep of plains and mountains and forests and their inhabitants in a vital, American prose. *Facundo* went through several editions and was translated into English, and its impact on nineteenth-century Latin America was long-lasting.

Not all Argentines were so quick to condemn the gauchos. Instead, they sought to create a tradition around the gaucho way of life as a way to build a common identity and history for Argentina. For example, in response to the denigration of the gaucho and his way of life, José Hernández wrote *Martín Fierro* (published in two parts in 1872 and 1879), the greatest epic poem in Argentine history. It depicted the gaucho as a victim of the new, modern world that was gradually stripping him of his freedom and way of life. Fences, railroads, unscrupulous politicians, and greedy ranch owners drove gauchos such as the hero of the poem, Martín Fierro, to become an outlaw. In the poem, Hernández especially protested the sending of gaucho conscripts to fight on the Indian frontier, depriving them of their rights and denying them of their traditional livelihoods, which sprang from being born on and living freely in the wide expanses of the pampas.

Hernández wrote *Martín Fierro* as the gaucho himself might have spun his story, in a language familiar to most Argentines, interlaced with idioms, proverbs, and folk imagery. It became immensely popular, from being read by wide sections of the public to being recited in remote farmhouses. It reached across the country as no other work had before it, and helped Argentina identify and celebrate a common and unique tradition and history.

Other writers, such as Ricardo Palma of Peru, found equal inspiration in the rich past of their homelands. Palma wrote his *Tradiciones peruanas* (Peruvian Traditions) over the course of forty years, from the 1870s to 1910. They were stories based on his intense curiosity about the human condition in the colonial period. Still the most widely read of his country's writers, Palma ransacked libraries and archives for the manuscripts that illuminated the viceroyalty's past, filled with stories of glory, intrigue, debauchery, love, and murder, all drawn from true life and rewritten by Palma for his readers. Palma is, in fact, credited with creating this new genre of literature, called "the traditions," although it was a genre not unknown both in Spain and Latin America before him. Yet, perhaps even more important, it was an American theme, and an American form that Palma dealt with and created, respectively. He provided for his people a continuity with the past, looking to the viceroyalty not as an iniquitous period of Spanish occupation, but rather as the cradle of Peruvian traditions. Many of these traditions include miracles and incredible acts that contradicted the laws of nature. In some ways, then, they prefigured the literature of magical realism of the mid-twentieth century, which earned Latin American authors praises and prizes from around the literary world for creativity and genius.

As elites attempted to forge new, modern nations, they ran up against the fact that the majority of Latin Americans lived impoverished, illiterate, and often brutally short lives. Just as the presence of the rural, uneducated gauchos so preoccupied Argentine poets such as Hernández, so Peruvians and other Latin Americans were concerned about the deplorable condition of the indigenous people in their homelands and what it said about their chances to be a modern nation. The ennoblement of Indians as a major and positive contributor to Latin American civilization would not reach full-blown proportions until the twentieth century, especially after the Mexican Revolution of 1910. But already in the late nineteenth century, writers were being drawn to the subject, sparking an entirely new intellectual trend that was a precursor to *indigenismo.*

The most acerbic and polemical of these writers was the Peruvian Manuel González Prada. After a sojourn in Europe, González Prada returned to his native Peru a confirmed anarchist and atheist. Unlike Ricardo Palma, González Prada attacked the colonial heritage and became a radical defender of Indians.

Clorinda Matto de Turner

**Figure 10.1** Clorinda Matto de Turner was the author of *Aves sin nido*, the first Indianist novel of Peru that presaged the rise of indigenismo, or Indianism, across Latin America in the twentieth century. This movement, given power by the Mexican Revolution (1910–1920), elevated Indian culture to equal status with the reigning Hispanic values inherited from Spain. Courtesy Wiki Commons.

He advocated a thorough purge of Peru by destroying the old system of social order and economic privilege, and he championed Indians as the truly dynamic and potentially redeeming force in Peruvian society. Untouched by the greed of capitalism and made virtuous by a collective lifestyle that emphasized sharing and the well-being of the community rather than the individual, Indians represented the ideal to González Prada.

As González Prada was extolling the virtues of the indigenous population, a compatriot who was considered a naturalist writer, Clorinda Matto de Turner, published *Aves sin nido* (Birds without a Nest) in 1899. It was the first Indianist, or *indigenista*, novel. With its forthright description of the plight of Indians, Turner's book earned her the contempt of the Catholic Church and Peruvian elites, both of whom were held to account for the oppression of Indians. But the novel became a landmark in the Indianist movement. A short novel published in Colombia in 1896, *El alma de Pablo Suesca* (Pablo Suesca's Soul), belonged to the same genre. Its author, Enrique Cortés Holguín, shared the sentiments of the better-known Peruvian Indianists.

Brazil's struggle to resolve the conflict between past—embodied in rural and traditional lifestyles—and future found its greatest expression in the naturalist and realist Brazilian writer Euclides da Cunha (1866–1909). Da Cunha wrote *Os Sertões* (Rebellion in the Backlands, 1902), considered to be a classic in Brazilian letters. It is the story of the government suppression of a commune in the backlands (the rough, arid interior regions of northeast Brazil called the *sertão*) at the end of the century. Like Sarmiento's *Facundo*, it is a story of the epic conflict between civilization and barbarism.

Da Cunha was born in Rio de Janeiro. He was trained in the army as an engineer but in 1896 mustered out and took up journalism. As a correspondent for the prestigious newspaper *O Estado de São Paulo,* he was assigned to cover the last stages of a remarkable conflict between peasants, led by their messiah, Antônio Conselheiro, and the federal government, represented by the army. From this conflict da Cunha spun out the story that emerged as *Rebellion in the Backlands.*

Conselheiro was born into a middle-class family that had fallen on hard times. After running afoul of local authorities and losing his wife, he began to wander the Brazilian backlands. He lived off charity and preached folk religious sermons to anyone who would listen. Because most villages in the interior had no priest, Conselheiro (a pseudonym meaning "the Counselor") became a religious messenger. By the early 1890s he had gathered a small following, and he settled on an abandoned ranch called Canudos. Gradually his fame as a healer and provider spread, and peasants by the hundreds flocked to join his informal congregation. A description of Conselheiro in 1876 was included in *Rebellion.* "In the year 1876 . . . the 'Counselor' made his appearance in the town of Itapicurú de Cima. His renown at this time was already very great, as is shown by an account which was published that very year, in the capital of the Empire":

> There has appeared in the northern backlands an individual who goes by the name of Antonio Conselheiro, and who exerts a great influence over the minds of the lower classes, making use of his mysterious trappings and ascetic habits to impose upon their ignorance and simplicity. He lets his beard and hair grow long, wears a cotton tunic, and eats sparingly, being almost a mummy in aspect. Accompanied by a couple of women followers, he lives by reciting beads and litanies, by preaching, and by giving counsel to the multitudes that come to hear him when the local Church authorities permit it. Appealing to their religious sentiments, he draws them after him in throngs and moves them at his will. He gives evidence of being an intelligent man, but an uncultivated one.[7]

Da Cunha's own powerful and evocative description of Conselheiro highlights not only the mystical power of Conselheiro but also the brilliance of da Cunha. He draws upon contemporary scientific theories, including positivism and social Darwinism, and his own native insight to portray the ways of Conselheiro, and especially the willingness of peasants to be controlled and led by such a person.

It is not surprising, then, if to these simple folk he became a fantastic apparition, with something unprepossessing about him; nor is it strange if, when this singular old man of a little more than thirty years drew near the farmhouses of the *tropieros* [ones who drive a packhorse or mule], the festive guitars at once stopped strumming and the improvisations ceased. This was only natural. Filthy and battered in appearance, clad in his threadbare garment and silent as a ghost, he would spring up suddenly out of the plains, peopled by hobgoblins. Then he would pass on, bound for other places, leaving the superstitious backwoodsmen in a daze. And so it was, in the end, he came to dominate them without seeking to do so.

In the midst of a primitive society which, by its own ethnic qualities and through the malevolent influence of the holy missions, found it easier to comprehend life in the form of incomprehensible miracles, this man's mysterious way of living was bound to surround him with a more than ordinary amount of prestige, which merely served to aggravate his delirious temperament. All the legends and conjectures which sprang up about him were a propitious soil for the growth of his own hallucinations. His insanity therewith became externalized. The intense admiration and the absolute respect which were accorded him gradually led to his becoming the unconditional arbiter in all misunderstandings and disputes, the favored Counselor in all decisions. . . . The multitude created him, refashioning him in its own image. . . . The people needed someone to translate for them their own vague idealizations, someone to guide them in the mysterious paths of heaven.

And so the evangelist arose, a monstrous being, but an automaton. This man who swayed the masses was but a puppet.[8]

The rebellion that Conselheiro led was essentially one of resistance by peasants and backlanders to conformity to a "civilized" standard. Organized in small communities, they raided neighboring landowners, evaded taxes, and refused to submit to the authority of the Catholic Church. Four expeditions were sent by the government in the 1890s, and only the fourth succeeded in quashing the rebels in their stronghold of Canudos. It was with this fourth expedition that da Cunha arrived to observe the final defeat of the rebels.

*Rebellion in the Backlands* is above all else a first-rate narrative that draws the reader into the world of the sertão, a story told with full attention to the geographic and political setting before it focuses with clarity, and not without sympathy, on the protagonist Conselheiro. The book obviously champions the forces of light and civilization over the ignorance and brutality that the rebellion represented. Da Cunha is quite clear on this.

This entire campaign [to destroy Canudos and the rebels] would be a crime, a futile and a barbarous one, if we were not to take advantage of the paths opened by the artillery, by following up our cannon with a constant, stubborn, and persistent campaign of education, with the object of drawing these rude and backward fellow countrymen of ours into the current of our times and our own national life. . . . We are condemned to civilization. Either we shall progress or we shall perish. So much is certain and our choice is clear.[9]

Yet Da Cunha is ambivalent about the forces of modernity and what he sees as their brutality and irrationality. He does not spare the barbarity shown by the

## Machado de Assis and Self-Definition

The struggle to define the nation was, for many intellectuals, also a struggle to define the self. Considered one of the greatest writers in Brazilian history, Joaquim Maria Machado de Assis (1839–1908) remains today a world-respected writer. He was a monarchist who, despite his distaste for republicanism, largely stayed out of politics. Yet his writings reflect the reality of a complex civilization and nation that was emerging in modern Brazil, a fascinating amalgamation of different cultures and peoples.

Machado de Assis was born to a mulatto housepainter and a Portuguese mother in Rio de Janeiro in 1839. He was an avid reader and educated himself at the library. He became an apprentice typographer early in life and rose through the government bureaucracy to eventually help found and become the first president of the Brazilian Academy of Letters in 1897. He married a refined Portuguese woman and lived a modest middle-class life, superficially humdrum and perhaps even boring. Yet his liabilities—having been born a mulatto in a racist society and subject to epileptic seizures—affected his literature profoundly.

He began writing poems when he was sixteen, and by the end of his life, his works filled thirty-one volumes. He pointed out the follies and foibles of his world with wit and sarcasm. A near-total disillusionment with humankind produced few "good" characters in his books; most of his characters were tormented by doubts and demons, caught in a web of fears and dreams. His finest work is considered to be *Dom Casmurro* (1900). It is the classic story of the husband who suspects adultery and of his obsession with revenge: on his wife, her lover, and his son, who may or may not have been the son of the lover. The novel is told by the tortured narrator himself, and its involved and ironic style of writing presaged the brilliant flowering of the Latin American novel in the twentieth century. So eminent was his writing that the Brazilian Academy of Letters created a prize in his honor.

army in its extermination of the Canudos rebels, nor does he fail to point out the grandeur of Conselheiro, a man whose life both attracted and repelled him.

Da Cunha's ambivalence crops up in other great literary interpreters of national developments in the nineteenth century. Although a commitment to progress and change is quite evident, there is also an unwillingness to forego the bittersweet, powerful, and earthly life of gauchos and peasants, of Indians and mulattoes. The vastness and wildness of the land profoundly shaped the lives of people with its own nature. These elements were not so easily dismissed by writers who wished to both send a message of culture and civilization and also represent life for what it was: still wild and even unknown in many parts of Latin America. In the end, all of these authors, whether critical of the gaucho or

Indian habits and lifestyle, or celebrating them as the true souls of the nation, were grappling with what it was to be American.

## MODERNISMO

*Modernismo* was a late nineteenth- and early twentieth-century literary movement in Latin America closely identified with the beginnings of a true Latin American literature. Emerging out of European romanticism, it was a complicated movement whose goal was to revolutionize the form and content of both prose and poetry as a means to challenge naturalism and Western materialism and to raise culture to a higher level in Latin America. It was an intellectual awakening in Latin America with a profound political and economic impact. Its guru was Rubén Darío (author of "To Roosevelt," which opened this chapter), who not only coined the term "modernismo" but also inspired a generation across Latin America. Most modernists, including Darío, traveled to Europe and North America and borrowed modernist art forms from abroad, especially from France, but also from writers like Edgar Allan Poe and Walt Whitman. Yet, most found their themes and their inspiration at home, in the pampas of Argentina, in the islands of the Caribbean, in the backlands of Brazil—wherever their ideal views of art and life clashed with the reality of their homelands. While modernism was a wide-ranging global intellectual trend, modernismo was uniquely Latin American, and as a movement, it wrestled with the very real challenges facing the region.

The Cuban poet and revolutionary José Martí best personified the combination of artist and activist in the late nineteenth century. His poems inspired modernismo and his polemics fomented revolution. Martí was born in Havana in 1853 of Spanish parents. An eager learner, he was writing and publishing poems and essays as a teenager and was soon involved in anti-Spanish activities, espousing the liberation of his homeland from Spain, which still held Cuba as a colony. He dedicated his life to this cause, for which he would eventually die.

In 1871 he was arrested for revolutionary activities, among them founding a political newspaper, *The Free Fatherland.* He was imprisoned for six months and exiled to Spain. There he continued his education, receiving a degree in law and philosophy from the University of Zaragoza, but also keeping up his revolutionary polemics by publishing a pamphlet on the political prisons in Cuba. He left Spain in 1874, traveled through Europe, and met the elderly Victor Hugo, who was considered the apostle of French letters in the nineteenth century. Back in the Americas, he landed in Guatemala where he wrote his first book, *Guatemala,* dedicated to a girl he secretly loved. In 1878 he returned to Cuba but was soon forced into exile again. In 1881 he arrived in New York and passionately recommitted his life to Cuban independence. He traveled widely from his base in New York and wrote for prestigious Latin American newspapers, such as *La Nación* of Buenos Aires.

During his years in exile, Martí produced some of his most memorable poems, especially *Ismaelillo* (Little Ishmael, 1882), dedicated to his young son, and *Versos sencillos* (Simple Verses, 1891), which dealt with themes such as friendship, love, sincerity, justice, and freedom. His poetry revealed his ambivalence about his homeland and its Spanish heritage. He did not hate Spaniards; he hated the tyranny that they practiced in Cuba. In his poems, he expressed a love not only for things Cuban and American, but also for things Spanish. The following excerpt attests to this love.

> For Aragon in Spain, I hold
> A debt for values true
> With loyalty and courage bold
> She did my soul renew.
>
> And if a fool should ponder why
> This place so claims my soul.
> This Aragon, I would reply
> Made love and friendship whole.
>
> In Aragon the flowered vale
> Saw scenes of fierce defense
> A people's longing to prevail
> Though death be recompense.
>
> Should magistrate or king provoke
> The simple man's reply:
> Take up his musket and his cloak
> With willingness to die.
>
> That yellowed land I now recall
> The Ebro's muddy banks
> The Virgin's shrine—adored by all
> And noble heroes' ranks.
>
> I esteem the tyrant's foe
> If he be Cuban bold
> And if from Aragon, I know
> The same esteem I hold.
>
> I still recall the shady court
> Where beauty binds the stair
> Of silent naves I can report
> And somber convents, bare.
>
> That Moorish-Spanish land I love
> That flowered land so fair;
> The meager bloom of my life's trove
> Began to blossom there.[10]

Not just a writer, Martí is perhaps most remembered as a revolutionary, political commentator, and social observer. After his beloved island, the United

**Figure 10.2** José Martí was a Cuban writer who inspired his fellow citizens with his patriotism and poetry to fight for independence from Spain. He was killed in 1895 while participating in the movement that eventually led to the Cuban-Spanish-American War of 1898 and Cuban independence. Courtesy Library of Congress.

States most attracted his attention. Martí was ambivalent toward the United States. An ardent admirer of its political democracy, he was also appalled by its system of economic monopoly and big business. On the one hand, he saw political freedoms and individual rights guaranteed under a constitution that worked. On the other hand, he was disgusted by the economic exploitation of the poor, especially the masses of immigrants whom he saw arriving daily in New York. He wrote, "The Cubans admire this nation, the greatest ever built by freedom, but they distrust the evil conditions that, like worms in the blood, have begun their work of destruction in this mighty Republic. . . . They cannot honestly believe that excessive individualism and reverence for wealth are preparing the United States to be the typical nation of liberty."[11] As we will see in chapter 11, Martí merged his love of Cuba, his hatred of its subjugation to the Spanish, and his ambivalence toward the United States to build a movement to free Cuba in the 1890s, one that sought to unify all Cubans through its rejection of European culture and influences, for its celebration of the island's racial diversity, and for its commitment to full independence from all foreign powers.

In 1900 the Uruguayan José Enrique Rodó published an essay that embodied the movement of modernismo, entitled *Ariel*, which became extraordinarily popular throughout Latin America. Borrowing from the symbolism employed by Shakespeare in *The Tempest,* Rodó represented Latin America as Ariel and the United States as Caliban in his story. Ariel is the "noble and winged part of the spirit," whereas Caliban represents materialism and grossness.[12] At the simplest level, Rodó pictured Latin America as a land where spiritual harmony, ethics, and aesthetics still prevail, whereas the United States is not only given to materialism but also governed by the mundane priorities of the present, with little or no sense of the past or future.

In *Ariel,* which essentially was written in the form of a revered master distilling for his young disciples the essence of his wisdom, humanity is constantly being tugged apart by the opposite forces of spirituality and sensuality. *Ariel,* through which Rodó counseled the youth of Latin America, calls upon young people to live by a morality and for a beauty that transcends the moment. Art, science, religion, and other matters of the spirit should always be governed by a morality founded firmly in eternal principles. Contrasted with this view are those people who follow the utilitarian way of life, who put a premium on the present, on the accumulation of material goods, on the satisfaction of carnal and ephemeral needs. Basically, Rodó called upon Latin Americans to pursue unselfish ends and to cultivate an ideal that transcended material goals. Otherwise, they were condemned to embrace vulgar materialism, just as had occurred in North America, and people's spiritual needs would go begging.

Rodó left a mixed legacy. His views, as interpreted and perpetuated by others, encouraged the myth that Latin Americans possessed a spiritual superiority over North Americans. The lack of culture and the greedy materialism of these northerners crippled their civilization, in spite of its extraordinary economic and political accomplishments. In a more positive vein, Rodó encouraged a whole generation of Latin American intellectuals to embrace the notion that ideas and ideals *can* shape and reform societies. This notion gave rise in the twentieth century to important movements to use education to uplift the masses and to change the political and social life of Latin America.

Rodó had a vision of a unified Latin American culture, not one divided by nationalities and regions, each one distinct from the other. He, in effect, encouraged Latin Americans to think of themselves as being culturally unified. Although the pan-American movement was as old as Simón Bolívar, it was given a new impetus by Rodó and others. And it came at a time when Latin America's neighbor to the north, the United States, was extending its reach more forcefully in the region. The intermingled destinies of these parts of the Western Hemisphere are considered in the next chapter.

## CONCLUSIONS AND ISSUES

The search for Latin American culture and identity—for the soul of Latin America—preoccupied elites concerned with forging new nations and civilizations out of the ashes of colonialism. If Latin Americans were not simply Spanish, or Indian, nor African, who were they? Trying at once to shed their colonial past, to grapple with their largely impoverished and uneducated populations, and to distinguish themselves from an encroaching U.S., intellectuals worked to identify or invent the traditions, values, and habits that would define them as Argentines, Nicaraguans, or Peruvians. Latin Americans, such as Rodó in *Ariel,* Hernández in *Martín Fierro,* and Martí in his poems and essays, examined their reality and explained it with passion. Sarmiento's great work, *Facundo,* delved deeply, for example, into the very nature of Latin American civilization, which, according to Sarmiento, was a warring ground between the raw forces of nature and civilization. By the end of the century, they had created an entirely new literary movement—modernismo—which, while drawing from U.S. and European influences, challenged the foreign materialism and excess that seemed to threaten the very values, identity, and cultural autonomy of these new nations.

## Discussion Questions

How and why did intellectuals seek mental emancipation from their Hispanic past?

Why was the invention of traditions so important in nineteenth-century Latin America?

What role did the gaucho and Indian play in the invention of traditions?

What was modernismo?

How did *Ariel* embody the modernismo movement?

Why were many writers, including Rubén Darío and José Martí, so concerned with U.S. influence by the end of the 1800s? What types of ideas about Latin America did they foster in order to challenge the U.S.?

## Timeline

| | |
|---|---|
| 1816 | *The Mangy Parrot* (El periquillo sarniento) published |
| 1820s–1870s | Romantic movement in Latin America |
| 1838 and 1840 | *El matadero* (The Slaughter Yard) published |
| 1845 | *Facundo: Or, Civilization and Barbarism* published |
| 1872 and 1879 | *Martín Fierro* published |
| 1870s–1910 | *Tradiciones peruanas* (Peruvian Traditions) published |
| 1880s–1910s | Modernismo movement in Latin America |
| 1899 | *Aves sin nido* (Birds without a Nest) published |
| 1900 | *Ariel* published |
| 1902 | *Os Sertões* (Rebellion in the Backlands) published |

## Keywords

*Ariel*

*Aves sin nido*

*Facundo: Or, Civilization and Barbarism*

gaucho

modernismo

*Rebellion in the Backlands*

sertão

# Changing Worlds and New Empires

## Vindication of Cuba

On March 25, 1889, the *New York Evening Post* published a letter from José Martí, who worked tirelessly for Cuba's independence from Spain, but also warned of U.S. ambitions to deprive Cuba of liberty by annexing it. Six years after publishing this letter, Martí died in a fusillade of gunfire in Cuba while charging a Spanish military position. His passion burns through the controlled prose that he composed in English to vindicate Cuba.

We have suffered impatiently under tyranny; we have fought like men, sometimes like giants, to be freemen; we are passing that period of stormy repose, full of germs of revolt, that naturally follows a period of excessive and unsuccessful action; we have to fight like conquered men against an oppressor who denies us the means of living, and fosters—in the beautiful capital visited by the tourists, in the interior of the country, where the prey escapes his grasp—a reign of such corruption as may poison in our veins the strength to secure freedom; we deserve in our misfortune the respect of those who did not help us in our need. . . .

In New York, the Cubans are directors of prominent banks, substantial merchants, popular brokers, clerks of recognized ability, physicians with a large practice, engineers of world-wide repute, electricians, journalists, tradesmen, cigarmakers.

Absolute freedom from religious intolerance, the love of man for the work he creates by his industry, and theoretical and practical familiarity with the laws and processes of liberty, will enable the Cuban to rebuild his country from the ruins in which he will receive it from its oppressors. It is not to be expected, for the honor of mankind, that the nation [the U.S.] that was rocked in freedom, and received for three centuries the best blood of liberty-loving men, will employ the power thus acquired in depriving a less fortunate neighbor of his liberty. . . .

The [Ten Years'] war [1868–78] has been by foreign observers compared to an epic, the upheaval of a whole country, the voluntary abandonment of wealth, the abolition of slavery in our first moment of freedom, the burning of our cities by our own hands, the erection of villages and factories in the wild forests, the dressing of our ladies of rank in the textures of the woods, the keeping at bay, in ten years of such a life, a powerful enemy, with a loss to him of 200,000 men, at the hands of a small army of patriots. . . .

The Struggle has not ceased. . . . Hundreds of men have died in darkness since the war in the misery of prisons. With life only will this fight for liberty cease among us.

## THE EMERGING COLOSSUS TO THE NORTH

Today the United States is practically sovereign on this continent, and its fiat is law upon the subjects to which it confines its interposition. Why? It is not because of the pure friendship or good will felt for it. It is not simply by reason of its high character as a civilized state, nor because wisdom and justice and equity are the invariable characteristics of the dealings of the United States. It is because, in addition to all other grounds, its infinite resources combined with its isolated position render it master of the situation and practically invulnerable as against any or all other powers.[1]

Secretary of State Richard Olney's imperious proclamation in 1895 confirmed the worst suspicions that people such as Martí and Rodó held about the United States. It was an empire on the make in the late nineteenth century, and its principal target appeared to be Latin America. What had begun as a hemisphere of equal states during the heyday of Simón Bolívar and the period of independence had turned into a hemisphere of unequal nations where one—the United States—was determined to realize its destiny across the Americas.

The United States and Latin America made many points of contact during the nineteenth century. Even before the Wars of Independence, U.S. traders and whalers penetrated the old Spanish empire in search of markets and friendly ports. During the wars, the United States consistently supported the patriots in their revolution against Spain. Americans such as John Quincy Adams were motivated nearly as much by threads of a common ideology and political inheritance as by commercial motives, although the latter were never subordinated entirely to the former.

In the broad sweep of Latin America's international history in the century after independence, scholars have divided the period into two halves: the first, roughly to the 1860s; and the second, from about the 1860s to the turn of the century. During the first half, the new nations were particularly susceptible to direct interventions by European powers—principally Spain, England, and France. The United States also took advantage of the weakness of the new nations, such as Mexico, then in a state of political and economic chaos. During the second half, the growing stability and strength of the Latin American nations diminished the ability of foreign powers to brashly intervene in Latin American affairs.

Two other factors stemming from global imperial rivalries also shaped nineteenth-century intervention in Latin America. One, rivalry among European powers tended to restrain their ambitions in Latin America, since none wished to see the others gain advantages in Latin America. Instead, they turned their imperial ambitions toward Africa and Asia. And two, the United States itself checked European ambitions in Latin America because it was committed, according to the Monroe Doctrine of 1823, to preserving the territorial integrity and political independence of countries in the hemisphere.

As the nineteenth century progressed, a new sense of mission—one Americans called "manifest destiny"—gradually gained ascendancy in relations between the United States and Latin America. The Mexican-American War of 1846 to 1848, the many suggestions to annex Cuba, the William Walker invasion of Nicaragua in 1856, and other acts reflected the ambitions of Americans to extend the fruits of democracy and freedom, as well as U.S. power, not only across the North American continent, but also south into Latin America. Naturally enough, those neighbors closest to the United States—principally Mexico, Central America, and the Caribbean—bore the brunt of American expansionism.

Two factors impeded the flow of American power and influence into Latin America. One was the strength of England in Latin America. Throughout the nineteenth century, and up to the First World War (1914–1918), England was Latin America's principal trading partner, and English diplomats consistently opposed American encroachments. The Clayton-Bulwer Treaty, signed between the United States and the United Kingdom in 1850, for example, was the result of British efforts to keep the Americans from dominating the site of a possible transisthmian canal across Central America. Great Britain sought to protect its substantial territorial and commercial interests in Central America at the time. If a canal were built, whether in Nicaragua or Panama, the British wanted to guarantee that it would be a joint undertaking, thereby preventing either of them from gaining ascendancy over the other in the region. In the short term, however, it was the U.S. Civil War—which temporarily turned Americans inward, consumed by the passionate necessity of determining once and for all the great questions of national power and slavery—that opened the door to European meddling in Latin American affairs in the 1860s.

While France sought to reestablish its American empire through its Mexican venture with Emperor Maximilian, Spain was also in search of recreating lost empires. In 1861, it re-annexed the Dominican Republic, and in 1866 it seized the guano-rich Chincha Islands off the Peruvian coast, provoking a war

### A Latin American's View of Manifest Destiny

In 1856, the Chilean liberal writer Francisco Bilbao expressed sentiments shared by many fellow Latin Americans:

> The United States daily extends its claws in the hunting expedition that it has begun against the South. Already we see fragments of America falling into the jaws of the Saxon boa that hypnotizes its foes as it unfolds its tortuous coils. First it was Texas, then it was Northern Mexico and the Pacific that hailed a new master.
>
> Today the skirmishers of the North are awakening the Isthmus with their shots and we see Panama, that future Constantinople of America, doubtfully suspended over the abyss and asking itself: Shall I belong to the South or to the North? . . .
>
> Is there so little self-awareness among us, so little confidence in the intelligence of the Latin American race, that we must wait for an alien will and an alien intellect to organize us and decide our fate? Are we so poorly endowed with the gifts of personality that we must surrender our own initiative and believe only in the foreign, hostile, and even overbearing initiative of individualism?

In his essay, Bilbao then calls for Latin American unity, challenging his fellow Hispanics to emulate the best and most noble of North American virtues, while not neglecting the growing imperial power of both the United States and Russia. In a passage remarkable for its prescience, Bilbao concluded:

> United [writing of Latin American unity], Panama shall be the symbol of our strength, the sentinel of our future. Disunited, it will be the Gordian knot cut by the Yankee axe, and will give [it] the possession of empire, the dominion of the second focus of the ellipses described by Russia and the United States in the geography of the globe.

Francisco Bilbao, *La América en peligro,* 2nd ed. (Buenos Aires: Impr. de Bernheim y Boneo, 1862), pp. 144–54, in Robert Buffington and Lila Caimari, eds., *Keen's Latin American Civilization: History and Society, 1492 to the Present,* 9th ed. (Boulder: Westview Press, 2009), pp. 523–28.

not only with Peru, but also with Chile and Ecuador. Spain's efforts at remaking its empire proved as futile as France's.

Like French intervention in Mexico, Spanish reoccupation of the Dominican Republic seized upon instability in Latin America and the inability of the United States to invoke the Monroe Doctrine with force during the American Civil War. In the case of the Dominican Republic, its independence from Spain and Haiti (the first gained in 1821 and the second in 1844) was weakened by persistent elite infighting and economic problems. Invited by the Dominican Republic's then president Pedro Santana to reoccupy the country in 1861, Spain promised to restore security and prosperity to what had been its first major colony in the New World. But not everyone was eager to accept Spain's return, and rebellions soon broke out. Influenced by Spanish colonial administrators who told her of the folly of annexation and the futility of trying to defeat the rebels (and likely not wanting to tangle with the U.S. upon its exit from the Civil War), Queen Isabella II withdrew Spanish forces and annulled the annexation in 1865, much to the delight of the United States.

The Spanish were no less active in the Pacific in trying to remake their lost empire. In 1864 and 1865 a Spanish fleet under the command of a patriotic admiral named José Manuel Pareja provoked both Peru and Chile into war by seizing the Peruvian Chincha Islands and bombarding the Chilean port of Valparaíso. Ecuador and Bolivia joined their neighbors in this war against their former colonizer.

Spain had many pretexts for returning to the Pacific: Peru was not yet formally recognized by Spain as an independent nation; Spanish nationals employed on a Peruvian plantation had been mistreated and Spain took action to obtain the desired indemnification; and the Chileans had insulted Spanish honor and therefore had to be punished, among other reasons. What Spain ultimately hoped to accomplish with this small fleet of eight warships is questionable. In the end, Spain failed, forced to concede that its empire could never really be remade. The United States helped mediate the peace.

By 1870 the chapter on new or restored European empires in the Americas was closed. The French had failed in Mexico, and the Spanish in the Dominican Republic and the Pacific. The United States made it clear that further European efforts to remake empires were intolerable intrusions into American affairs. The Monroe Doctrine was now showing some teeth, especially in light of the massive military and naval power that the Civil War left in its wake. The warning to Maximilian's French troops to leave Mexico could easily have been backed up by the Union Army.

From the 1880s onward, the United States moved with even greater ambition in Latin America. By then, manifest destiny had been folded into a newer, more potent national drive: the drive for empire. Imperialism has both negative and positive aspects, depending on one's perspective. Some emphasize that the domination of one nation by another undermines the sovereignty of the subject nation and people and can bring serious negative consequences (such as political instability); thus, it is always intolerable. In the late nineteenth century, however, some saw empires as a reflection of a natural right of more powerful countries to dominate others; for these people, colonizers have both rights (to wealth and power, for example) and responsibilities (for instance, to bring development and "civilization" to the colonized country). At that time, many Americans were swept up by the notion that they possessed a God-given right to empire. In its simplest terms, that meant both acquiring new territories and expanding American commercial, political, military, and cultural influence.

Many expressed themselves on the need and justification for this new American empire, none perhaps so forcefully as the Reverend Josiah Strong in his 1885 book *Our Country.* An avowed social Darwinist, he felt that the Anglo-Saxon race was destined to rule the world. His rhetoric hammers home the theme of superiority and destiny.

> This race of unequaled energy, with all the majesty of numbers and the might of wealth behind it—the representative, let us hope, of the largest liberty, the purest Christianity, the highest civilization—having developed peculiarly aggressive traits calculated to impress its institutions upon mankind, will spread itself over the earth. *If I read not amiss, this powerful race will move down upon Mexico, down upon Central and South America,* out upon the islands of the sea, over upon Africa and beyond [italics added].[2]

Not all Americans agreed with the Reverend Strong or Secretary of State Olney. Some felt that democracy and empire were incompatible, and from this sentiment emerged an anti-imperialist movement at the end of the century. For the time being, they were in the minority.

## COMMERCE AND PAN-AMERICANISM

Political, military, religious, economic, and commercial motives all figured in the equation of growing U.S. interest in Latin America. Because both the United States and Latin America stressed the beneficial processes of industrialization and modernization in the latter half of the nineteenth century, their points of view often coincided. Both North Americans and Latin Americans agreed that increasing trade not only promoted economic prosperity but also increased understanding and harmony within the Western Hemisphere.

U.S. interest in Latin America was growing as early as the 1870s. In 1870, for example, the U.S. minister in Colombia signed a treaty for the construction of a canal across the isthmus of Panama (at that time, still a province of Colombia); the Dominican Republic was almost annexed to the United States; and the Ten Years' War (1868–1878) by Cuban insurgents against Spanish rule stirred nationwide sentiments to recognize the rebels as legitimate.

In this same spirit, the U.S. Senate passed a resolution in July 1870, asking the State Department for information on the status of commercial relations between the United States and Latin America. The resolution also requested recommendations on how to compete more effectively with Great Britain, which commanded the lion's share of Latin American trade. Secretary of State Hamilton Fish dispatched a circular letter to all ministers and consuls of the United States in Latin America asking them to report on trade and relations in their areas.

Replies soon began crossing the secretary's desk. Most generally, inattention or misjudgment by American manufacturers and merchants was cited as a distinct disadvantage. American prices tended to be higher at the point of shipping than those of their English counterparts. Insurance and commissions were apt to be higher as well; for example, they could be as high as 2.5 percent in New York versus 0.5 percent in European ports. Heavy American textiles lost out to English ones because most Latin American nations charged tariffs computed by weight. Europeans granted Latin American merchants longer credit terms than did Americans. English interest rates were frequently half of what Americans charged. Other suggestions by American consuls and ministers on how to best, or at least match, the English, included learning the language and customs of their customers, subsidizing American steamship companies, sponsoring an interoceanic canal, and encouraging reciprocity treaties to lower tariff barriers.

The firm of W. R. Grace & Co. was representative of U.S. commercial interests in Latin America. As early as 1870, the company was trading over much of South America out of its headquarters in New York, a city evolving rapidly into the premier center of commerce and trade along the Atlantic coast of the United States.

The Grace brothers and their partners were attuned to the different worlds of the United States and Latin America. They learned to speak Spanish well. They eventually established the first U.S. steamship service to the west coast of South America (1894), sponsored an interoceanic canal (through Nicaragua) at the end of the century, and actively sought in the 1880s and 1890s to improve hemispheric relations both politically and economically.

W. R. Grace & Co. developed rapidly in the last three decades of the nineteenth century, becoming the first American multinational company operating in Latin America. Founded in Peru in 1854 by an enterprising Irish immigrant, William Russell Grace, the company grew rapidly as a commercial enterprise based primarily on trade yet willing to expand in any direction that business took it. By the 1870s, the company was not only operating ships between the Americas but also was selling everything from locomotives to threading needles in South America.

W. R. Grace also imported new machinery for those interested in modernizing industries, acted as a banker by floating mortgages to local entrepreneurs, and constantly sought new opportunities. The company became actively involved in railroad building from Peru to Costa Rica, expanded into the growing rubber industry in Brazil in the 1880s, and promoted the first telegraph cable networks between the United States and Latin America. The Grace Company moved swiftly to the front of the tide of industrialization and modernization seen by elites as carrying both Latin Americans and North Americans toward progress.

The Grace enterprises grew at a time when the United States, in its search for resources and markets, actively promoted greater involvement in Latin American commercial affairs. President Chester A. Arthur declared in 1884: "The countries of the American continent and the adjacent islands are for the United States the natural marts of supply and demand. It is from them that we

**Figure 11.1** Clipper ships and downeasters (like this one, the *Jabez Howes* in 1920) helped bind the Americas more tightly together commercially in the nineteenth and early twentieth centuries and represented a sector of the growing modernization of Latin America, especially in tying Latin America more closely to the European and U. S. economies. Walter A. Scott. Courtesy Library of Congress.

should obtain what we do not produce or do not produce in sufficiency, and it is to them that the surplus productions of our fields, our mills, and our work-shops should flow, under conditions that will equalize or favor them in comparison with foreign competition."[3] The facts that the British still dominated trade and commerce with Latin America and that in the mid-1880s the United States possessed less than 20 percent of total Latin American trade spurred Americans even more in their determination to aggressively expand U.S. enterprises. American diplomats were especially aware of the relationship between close commercial ties and political and diplomatic influence. Secretary of State Frederick Frelinghuysen promoted this point of view before the Senate in 1884. "I am thoroughly convinced of the advisability of knitting closely our relations with the states of this continent, and no effort on my part shall be wanting to accomplish a result so consonant with the constant policy of this country, and in the spirit of the Monroe Doctrine, which, in excluding foreign political interference, recognizes the common interest of the states of North and South America. It is the history of all diplomacy that close political relations and friendships spring from unity of commercial interests. The merchant or trader

**Figure 11.2** From the 1860s on, rubber tappers like these in Guatemala in 1890 extracted millions of tons of latex for use in the factories of Europe and by the United States. Courtesy Library of Congress.

is the forerunner and aid to diplomatic intimacy and international harmony."[4] Throughout Latin America in the 1880s and 1890s, American entrepreneurs spread their influence not only through trade but also through direct investments—through the railroads and mines of Mexico and Central America, and through the sugar industry of Cuba, for example. The banana industry that grew to huge proportions in the twentieth century was established precisely in this period by ambitious American entrepreneurs.

While Minor Keith was building the railroads in Costa Rica in the 1870s and 1880s to connect the rich coffee-growing regions of the highlands with the Atlantic terminus of Puerto Limón, he found himself constantly facing financial crises. To create some momentum and to generate cash, Keith initiated a variety of businesses, such as exporting precious tropical woods. He also imported a few banana plants from Panama and planted them along parts of the railroad that were already completed near the warm and wet Caribbean coast of Costa Rica. He began shipping these bananas to the Boston market, which had developed a taste for the nutritious and delicious fruit a few years earlier when an enterprising Boston merchant imported some from

Jamaica. The market grew rapidly, and by the late 1890s, Keith had plenty of competition as banana production expanded with speed and profit in Costa Rica, Honduras, and Guatemala. The bananas were imported through the ports of Boston and New Orleans and rapidly made their way into the homes of North Americans. In 1899, Keith and his competitors formed the United Fruit Company, which came to dominate the industry for the next half-century.

The story of dynamic and creative American enterprise was replicated throughout Latin America at the end of the century. The Guggenheim family developed one of the most prosperous mining empires in Mexico. American syndicates channeled large amounts of capital and technical expertise into the silver mines of Peru, the tin mines of Bolivia, the copper mines of Chile, and into hundreds of other enterprises, from brewing beer in Peru to building canals in Nicaragua.

While the American development and exploitation of resources and opportunities in Latin America were largely the result of private enterprise, the governments of the North and South American states recognized the need to reach some sort of general accord in the promotion and encouragement of trade, industry, and diplomacy across the hemisphere. In 1889 a historic meeting convened in Washington to discuss hemispheric problems and opportunities. This meeting, called the First International American Congress, was largely the inspiration of Secretary of State James G. Blaine, a longtime promoter of the Pan-American movement. The goal of the congress, popularly called the Washington Conference, was to promote trade among the countries of the Americas and to provide mechanisms for solving inter-American disputes such as the War of the Pacific. Delegates from all of the Latin American nations (with the exception of the Dominican Republic, which already had a trade and commerce treaty with the United States) convened in Washington in October 1889. The delegates were promptly sent on a six-week train tour of the United States to impress them with the vastness and magnificence of the country. Instead, it left most of them exhausted and irritable with this flexing of muscle and pride by the Americans.

The conference met through the spring of 1890. In the end, it accomplished nothing of substance—no reciprocal trade treaties, no discounted tariffs or customs barriers, and no agreements on a mechanism for compulsory arbitration of international disputes. Many Latin Americans, especially the Argentinians and Uruguayans, were too committed to British and European interests to consider seriously altering those relationships in favor of the United States. And, bickering political factions within the United States itself prevented a unified American position.

When the conference adjourned, it left only one sure accomplishment: the establishment of a commercial information bureau in Washington. That bureau was the seed of the Pan-American Union, which in turn was the seed of the

Organization of American States, founded in 1948. Pan-Americanism embodied the concept that the nations of the Western Hemisphere have a great deal in common. Disciples of Pan-Americanism stressed shared political ideals, geographic unity, and membership within the mainstream of Western civilization. The ideal was as old as Thomas Jefferson and Simón Bolívar, who had expressed it in their own writings. The ideal took more definite form in the twentieth century, although it was most certainly born and nurtured in the nineteenth.

## THE CUBAN-SPANISH-AMERICAN WAR

Cuba and Puerto Rico continued as colonies of Spain in the late nineteenth century, long after the rest of Latin America had achieved independence. The principal reason for Cuba's ties to Spain was economic: the booming sugar industry, buttressed by rising demand for the island's tobacco leaf for cigars, made it too lucrative a possession for Spain to give up. In addition, the extremely wealthy landowners and merchants in Cuba feared that any change in governance would disrupt their political hegemony and threaten their possessions. Even the island's growing working class, mostly Spanish immigrants, felt bonds of loyalty to their homeland. Furthermore, the continued enslavement of masses of African and Afro-Cuban laborers until 1886 made elites fearful of social unrest should the political system be altered or overthrown. So the island continued under Spanish rule—fueled by slave labor and spectacular revenues from sugar and tobacco exports.

After midcentury, however, a growing number of Cubans embraced the cause of independence, motivated by desires for self-rule, economic freedom, slave emancipation, and modernization. They believed that Spaniards repressed and exploited Creoles (people of Spanish descent born on the island) and favored peninsulares. Creole rebels mounted a major challenge to Spanish sovereignty in the Ten Years' War, rising up in arms and capturing significant territory in the eastern provinces. Their grievances included slavery, unfair taxes, their lack of representation in decisions about the island, their lack of equality with peninsulares, and the desire to erase huge debts owed to Spanish capitalists.

The continuation of slavery was a particular sticking point in the war. By the mid-nineteenth century, slavery was still present on much of the island, but it was the wealthy western sugar plantations that most relied upon it for profits, and on the Spanish to maintain that way of life. It is no surprise then, that the Ten Years' War was sparked in the poorer eastern part of the island, where owners freed their slaves to create armies to fight Spain. It was there and in some urban areas where Afro-Cuban intellectuals were promoting a unified Cuban identity against Spain, where the seeds of abolition were sown, and where elites argued that slavery was an obstacle to the creation of a sense of

Cuban nationality. Slaves themselves joined the independence armies in large numbers, gaining their freedom and putting Cuba on the road to eventual abolition. But the freeing of slaves to fight also hurt the independence movement, as Spain used the specter of a race war and a breakdown of social order to convince rebels as well as sugar planters, fearful of a large free black population, to abandon any further thoughts of rebellion. Both abolition and independence would have to wait, though not for long, especially since the experience of emancipation during the Ten Years' War and their prominent role in fighting for the Cuban nation had mobilized slaves.

The Ten Years' War ended with a truce, but the patriots' ardor continued unabated, fired up by warriors in exile who dreamed of emancipating the island by invasion. A failed revolt in 1879 was followed by others in the 1880s. The patriots-in-exile simply did not have enough resources or organizational capacity to mount a successful attack. This changed once slavery was abolished in 1886, however, and the justification for Spanish rule waned. In these years, Cuba increasingly imported workers from places like China and the Yucatán peninsula in Mexico to supply a labor force drained by the end of the slave trade and the low reproduction rates of the slave population. Slaves, too, pursued their freedom through legal and financial means. Facing growing abolitionist pressure, Spain first passed the 1870 Moret Law, which granted free birth to all people born in Cuba from that point forward, though children of slave mothers would have to serve their masters for twenty-two years. With abolitionists pressing for more, and planters realizing how untenable slavery was becoming, in 1880 Spain passed the patronato law, which called for gradual abolition over eight years. Under even more intense pressure from slaves, Spain finally abolished slavery in Cuba in 1886. In these years, as well, U.S. investment took over much of Cuba's sugar industry, building even closer ties between the two countries. The turning point in the independence movement came in 1892, however, when poet-journalist José Martí founded the Cuban Revolutionary Party (PRC) in Tampa and Key West, Florida.

Martí provided the right mix of elements—money, followers, program, zeal, and mobilization—to finally challenge Spain's rule in Cuba. Traveling by train between New York City and Florida, Martí energized Cuban exiles and immigrants with fiery speeches and powerful rhetoric in his revolutionary newspaper, *La Patria*. He created an organization that recruited volunteers and raised money to buy arms and finance a major invasion. Most of the party's resources came from Cuban workers in New York and Florida whose production of clear Havana cigars (referring to their clear wrappers) created a boom industry and provided the money to attack Spanish rule.

Perhaps Martí's most important contribution was to shift the conversation about independence from a focus on challenging Spain's rule to promoting a positive image of the Cuban republic that would emerge from its overthrow.

### The Bronze Titan

Antonio Maceo Grajales (1845–1896) was one of the greatest military leaders of the Cuban independence movement. Beginning his military career in the Ten Years' War, he was given the nickname the "Bronze Titan" by fellow Cubans in reference to his skin color, large size, and status. A mulatto of mixed Afro-Cuban descent, he was born and raised in a rural area on the eastern part of the island. He was schooled in the Enlightenment and learned the values of order and virtue at home. Along with his father and brothers, he joined the Ten Years' War on the side of the rebels, quickly ascending the ranks due to his military skill and bravery. Yet, his racial background often was held against him by other elite rebel leaders wary of empowering blacks, especially since the rebel troops had many black soldiers who had flocked to the movement to gain their freedom from slavery through fighting for the cause of independence. Spanish officials succeeded in dividing the rebels with propaganda accusing Maceo and other black leaders of instigating a race war. Maceo nevertheless proved himself extremely valuable as a leader and worked his way up the ranks. It was in these early years that he received his nickname due to his bravery and seeming invincibility in the face of danger and injury. In 1878, he opposed the pact signed with Spanish officials that ended the fighting, arguing that there could be no peace until slavery was abolished and Cuba was independent. He spent the next years living outside of Cuba, largely in Costa Rica, until Martí's call to arms prompted his return. In the war begun in 1895, he proved himself once again to be an invaluable military leader, helping to spread the independence fight deep into the western part of the island, which, since the abolition of slavery, was much more willing to follow a black military commander representing the patriot cause. It was on his return from the western fighting that he was killed in a surprise run-in with Spanish troops in 1896.

This republic would be egalitarian, racially diverse, democratic, and authentically Cuban. His movement for Cuba Libre was a nationalist call for an end to Spanish domination and articulated the idea of a Cuban nation of equals that included all those born on the island, regardless of race. And in a new twist, Cuba Libre also called for freedom from the U.S., arguing that U.S. annexation and influence were as detrimental to the Cuban nation and independence as Spanish colonialism. This vision succeeded in uniting Cubans in exile with those on the island, including ex-slaves inspired by this call for equality and racial inclusiveness.

Between 1892 and 1895, Martí continued this campaign while bringing together former generals in the rebel armies. In early 1895, they believed that conditions were ripe for an invasion because the Cuban economy was in serious economic decline and discontent with Spanish rule was on the rise. They declared war on Spain and mounted several incursions into Cuba, mostly on the eastern end of the island because of its sympathy for independence. Martí himself died shortly after one of these landings, martyred in an assault on a Spanish bunker, but others took up the command and raised the flag of rebellion across the island. General Máximo Gómez took command of the forces in the east, while General Antonio Maceo led the forces in the west. Both were veterans of the Ten Years' War and enjoyed great prestige among the troops. Many other soldiers gained experience and assumed leadership positions, giving the movement a popular character that troubled Creole elites. By later the next year, the rebels numbered fifty thousand and controlled much of the Cuban countryside.

Spain did not give up easily. When the extent of rebel success became known, the government dispatched a veteran general, Valeriano Weyler, with orders to end the war by whatever means necessary. When he realized that the rebels had expanded their territory primarily by using peasant sympathizers for supplies and information, he ordered that the rural population be herded into camps in towns and cities where they could not aid the rebels. This policy, known as *reconcentración,* caused unspeakable hardships on the peasantry, due to the loss of property and poor conditions in the camps. Whole communities and plantations were destroyed, and tens of thousands perished before the policy was lifted. Weyler also ordered the sugar industry to raise production levels to help finance his campaign. Most sugar mills had curtailed harvests under threats from the independence generals that they would burn the fields and execute the managers as a way to disrupt production, gain followers, and punish opponents. Caught in the crossfire, many planters abandoned their fields and left the island for good.

By early 1898, the war had devastated the island. Spanish forces pulled back to urban garrisons, and revolutionary generals prepared to assault their positions in a final push to victory. Wealthy Cubans now faced the likelihood that Spain might abandon the island, in which case they would be at the mercy of the rebels and their Afro-Cuban forces. Some petitioned the U.S. government to step in as steward, or protector, for the island. Others lobbied for outright annexation to the U.S. The new president of the PRC, Tomás Estrada Palma, held talks with U.S. officials regarding military assistance and tutelage. The generals in the field, however, rejected any compromise short of total victory over Spain. Then, in April 1898, the U.S. intervened directly by declaring war on Spain.

The reasons for the intervention are complex. First, two popular New York newspapers waged a duel of sensationalist coverage of the struggle in Cuba and heavily favored intervention to support the independence forces. Second, the U.S. battleship *Maine*, sent to Havana to protect U.S. citizens and interests, blew up in the harbor in February, with heavy loss of life, leading to accusations

## Cuban Independence Movement

Too often the view of the Cuban independence movement, which culminated in 1898 with its separation from Spain, has been dominated by a North American perspective. It was, in fact, a long and often bloody struggle for independence led by patriotic Cubans such as Manuel Piedra Martel (1868–1942). Martel fought alongside some of the great heroes, such as Máximo Gómez, and served as an aide to Antonio Maceo. Martel remembered the battles and the heroism in graphic detail, and in this short extract catches some of the sacrifices Cubans themselves made on behalf of their independence from Spain. Notice the cordial behavior between the wounded Martel and a Spanish doctor. Despite the brutality of battle, codes of war still prevailed. Also notice the sound of triumph and pride as he summarizes the battle, perhaps exaggerated as to its significance in the annals of military history, but immensely significant for Cuban nationalism.

> The 29th [August 1897] dawned. Reveille sounded again over by the Priest's Hill [Loma del Cura]. How many who heard it yesterday [the battle was in its second day] were not around to hear it today? How many were about to hear it for the last time? Yesterday's combat had cost many lives on both sides; the one about to begin would cost no less. (p. 462)

> [Later in the day] I started on the road back. As I entered the portals of a house, right next to the door, I caught a bullet that fractured my left femur . . . my men, in rescuing me, put themselves in great danger.
> Taken inside the house, someone ordered two Spanish prisoners, who said they were part of the Military Health Service unit, to help me, no doubt thinking they knew something about surgery. These two poor guys were nothing more than stretcher bearers, but thinking they would be thought hostile if they didn't do something, they started to rub the wound vigorously and caused me such pain that I had to wave them off! Then one of the two, looking out onto the street, cried out: "Look, there goes our chief, Commander Benedic, of the Health Service."
> "Call him" I ordered.
> The Spanish doctor came in. . . . Finding himself in enemy hands didn't alter him a bit. I told him I had called him to do the favor of tending to my wound, and he told me that indeed was his duty. He administered some simple first aid because he had no other materials at hand. I thanked him and allowed him to go on his way. (pp. 464–65)

> Without a doubt this action at Victoria de las Tunas was one of the most important, best directed and executed in our war of independence. It's possible that such a case as this is not recorded in military history, in which a stronghold, such as this was, was attacked openly by force numerically the same as the defenders who were forced to surrender within forty-eight hours. (p. 468)

Manuel Piedra Martel, *Mis primeros treinta años: Memorias, infancia y adolescencia—La Guerra de Independencia,* 2nd ed. (Havana: Editorial Minerva, 1944).

**Figure 11.3** Cuban soldiers armed with carbines and swords during the Cuban-Spanish-American War of 1898. Although they were irregulars and guerrillas from the perspective of formal organized armies of the period, they proved effective in helping free their country from Spanish rule. W. Kilburn Co. Courtesy Library of Congress.

in the U.S. that Spanish agents had been responsible. Third, a group of pro-war Republicans, led by Assistant Secretary of the Navy Theodore Roosevelt, urged a reluctant President William McKinley to use the Cuban insurrection as an excuse to exercise the growing U.S. naval and military power at his disposal. Success in a war against Spain would raise the profile of the United States in the great powers club controlling world affairs. Finally, U.S. investors held several hundred million dollars of investment in Cuba that could be jeopardized by a radical rebel victory. During the U.S. occupation that followed the short war, these investments were protected, and the way was cleared for hundreds of millions more to flow into Cuba. The Cuban-Spanish-American War proved a pivotal event in both Cuban and U.S. history. The U.S. military intervention lasted a little more than four months and resulted in total victory for the United States. In defeat, Spain lost Cuba, Puerto Rico, Guam, and the Philippines, all of which the United States acquired except for Cuba, which U.S. forces occupied until 1902.

U.S. occupying forces refused to acknowledge the Cuban independence leaders who had fought so hard to expel Spain, many of whom had come from modest origins and were most excluded under Spanish rule. Instead, the U.S.

## The U.S. "Yellow Press" and the Cuban-Spanish-American War

The intense rivalry for circulation between two North American press moguls—William Randolph Hearst and Joseph Pulitzer—in the 1890s prompted them to focus intensely on Cuba and the alleged atrocities committed by Spanish authorities against the Cuban population. It made great copy, sold newspapers, and prompted popular support for U.S. intervention, but much of the reporting was gross exaggeration and patently false. Some excerpts, read with fascination by the U.S. public, follow:

[Spanish General] Weyler was a "fiendish despot . . . a brute, the devastator of haciendas . . . pitiless, cold, an exterminator of men . . . there is nothing to prevent his carnal, animal brain from running riot with itself in inventing tortures and infamies of bloody debauchery," opined the February 23, 1896, issue of the *New York Journal* (Thomas 331).

On May 17, 1896, a *New York World* correspondent in Havana wrote: "Blood on the roadsides, blood in the fields, blood on the doorsteps, blood, blood, blood. The old, the young, the weak, the crippled, all are butchered without mercy" (Thomas 336).

Perhaps the most famous of all the acts perpetrated by the inventors of the "yellow press," as Hearst and Pulitzer's tactics were labeled because of their flamboyant, colorful headlines, occurred in early 1897. One of Hearst's premier cartoonists, Frederick Remington, was holed up in the Hotel Inglaterra in Havana, barred from accompanying Spanish troops in the field. Remington cabled his boss, "Everything is quiet . . . There will be no war. I wish to return." Hearst fired back: "Please remain. You furnish the pictures and I'll furnish the war" (Thomas 340).

Hugh Thomas, *Cuba; or, The Pursuit of Freedom* (New York: Da Capo Press, 1998). On Remington, see also James Creelman, *On the Great Highway: The Wanderings and Adventures of a Special Correspondent* (Boston: Lothrop, 1901).

and white, wealthy Cubans tried to erase the presence of Afro-Cubans in the independence struggle and chose to recognize and promote moderate, upper-class Cubans to leadership positions on the island. This process found support among those of the Creole class who had long hoped the end of slavery would bring progress not through racial integration within a unified Cuban nation, but rather through a "whitening" like that witnessed in places like Argentina. Former rebel commanders and supporters found themselves ostracized and resented being denied their rightful victory as the U.S. appropriated their struggle and limited their sovereignty. When the occupation ended, most of the independence leaders, many of whom were black and had sacrificed for years, refused to cooperate with the new regime and formed a loose-knit opposition movement. Their opposition was hardened by the conditions imposed on Cuba in the 1901 Platt Amendment, which de facto turned the independent country into a U.S. protectorate. In exchange for the withdrawal of U.S. troops, the agreement gave the U.S. control over Cuba's foreign policy and loans, a naval base at Guantánamo Bay, and the right to intervene in the case that independence or social order were threatened. Many see in these events the seeds of the 1959 Cuban Revolution, led by Fidel Castro.

## CONCLUSIONS AND ISSUES

U.S. interests in Latin America were composed of many different elements. They included an altruistic or noble sentiment, manifest in efforts to spread U.S. culture and values, a baser desire to expand U.S. political and strategic influence in Latin America, and a commercial motive that viewed Latin America as a great marketplace where U.S. economic power should eventually prevail over European competitors such as the English. The experience of the Grace brothers as extraordinarily active and successful merchants and businessmen in Latin America is an example of the latter.

Latin Americans courted the United States as a political friend, trading partner, and important agent for modernizing and developing their countries. But they also eyed the United States with suspicion as a dominating and imperious neighbor whose might and arrogance could easily turn friend into foe. The trajectory of Mexico's history with the United States in the nineteenth century certainly was one example of this ambivalent relationship. So was the experience of Cuba.

As the twentieth century approached, new events, such as building a transisthmian canal and waging the Cuban-Spanish-American War of 1898, brought the United States and Latin America even closer together. The commercial relationship also deepened, with U.S. entrepreneurs drawn to Latin America to develop a host of industries and activities, from building railroads to exporting bananas. The Washington Conference of 1889 was the first major inter-American conference, and it gave official expression to the rapid development of relations between the American nations at the end of the nineteenth century. The Platt Amendment revealed the inequities in the relationships, and the U.S.'s intention to dominate them. These exceptional relationships would be severely tested as the twentieth century unfolded.

### Discussion Questions

What factors contributed to the rise of U.S. empire in Latin America by the late nineteenth century? What factors slowed its rise?

What was Pan-Americanism and why did it receive so little support in its early years?

Why did Cubans eventually seek independence from Spain beginning in the mid-nineteenth century?

How did race and slavery shape the Cuban independence movements?

How was José Martí's view of race and the Cuban nation different from the social Darwinism that was popular in other areas of Latin America at the time?

Why did the U.S. intervene in the Cuban war for independence in 1898 and what was the outcome?

## Timeline

| | |
|---|---|
| 1823 | Monroe Doctrine |
| 1846–48 | Mexican-American War |
| 1850 | Clayton-Bulwer Treaty |
| 1861–65 | Spanish annexation of the Dominican Republic |
| 1864–66 | Chincha Islands War |
| 1868–78 | Ten Years' War in Cuba |
| 1886 | Slavery in Cuba abolished |
| 1892 | Cuban Revolutionary Party formed |
| 1889–90 | First International American Conference/Washington Conference |
| 1895–98 | Cuban War of Independence/Cuban-Spanish-American War |
| 1901 | Platt Amendment |

## Keywords

Clayton-Bulwer Treaty
Cuba Libre
Cuban Revolutionary Party
Cuban-Spanish-American War
First International American Congress/
    Washington Conference
Guggenheim family
imperialism
manifest destiny

Organization of American States
Pan-Americanism
Platt Amendment
reconcentración
social Darwinism
Ten Years' War
U.S.S. *Maine*
W. R. Grace & Co.
yellow press

# REFORM AND REVOLUTION

## LATIN AMERICA IN GLOBAL PERSPECTIVE

During the first three decades of the twentieth century, Latin America became more and more engaged in world affairs. Europeans were caught up in full-scale imperial ventures in Asia and Africa. The United States may have avoided full-scale imperialist engagement, but nevertheless extended its investments and control over the Caribbean Basin and built an interoceanic canal in Panama. No place in the world remained entirely isolated, and Latin Americans often took part in developments that had global implications. The hemisphere became more tightly knitted into the fabric of world affairs.

Compared with the subjugation of Asia and Africa under European imperialism, Latin America enjoyed considerable freedom of action. Except for the Caribbean colonies, most of its peoples were politically sovereign and relatively independent in world affairs. Economically, too, Latin Americans enjoyed better standards of living and greater self-determination than did Asians and Africans. Their cultures drew on European, indigenous, and African sources, and their arts enjoyed some recognition abroad. By most measures, Latin America occupied an intermediate status between the imperial powers and colonized countries.

Nevertheless, most Caribbean islands still belonged to one or another European nation or, in the case of Puerto Rico and Cuba, lived under U.S. control. Moreover, U.S. influence grew during the First World War (1914–1918) as a function of U.S. security interests and its expanding economic reach. Even some of the more highly developed countries, like Mexico, Argentina, Brazil, and Chile, found themselves fending off foreign pressures and even occasional military incursions. Their leaders recognized that nation-building did not happen all at once—it was an ongoing, difficult struggle.

In general, the larger nations of Latin America charted their own destinies, though in some cases with significant foreign investment and influence. In most, these destinies included continued expansion of exports of minerals and agricultural goods. Prices mostly rose, so investors and workers kept on producing. Factories sprang up on the outskirts of major cities. New ports and rail lines stitched cities to far-off regions and foreign markets. Slowly but surely, political systems opened up to accommodate more voters and special interests, even those previously disenfranchised. Latin America's first populist movements, described in chapter 12, arose out of this growing participation.

The first decade of the new century, 1900 to 1910, saw greater prosperity in Latin America. Dictators promoted exports and industrial growth and suppressed labor unrest. Foreigners pumped money into new factories and infrastructure. The expanding economies achieved promising levels of profits and employment, although not everyone benefited equally. Few political upheavals shook the region, especially after the 1902 treaty that ended the Thousand Days' War in Colombia, though smaller rural rebellions and labor actions hinted at undercurrents of discontent.

**Map P3.1** The countries of modern Latin America.

The second decade, the 1910s, witnessed major disruptions and violence in the region. Foremost was the Mexican Revolution, which occupied the entire period. The First World War also brought submarine conflict, U.S. interventions and occupations, and substantial labor strikes. Many South American countries, cut off from imports during the war, saw accelerated industrialization during this era. The success of guerrilla actions in Mexico encouraged others to take up these new military tactics. And anarchist labor movements reached their peak from 1917 to 1919, producing a wave of general strikes and labor violence, as well as their often violent repression, that lingered in people's memories for years to come.

The 1920s saw the return of peace and business as usual to most of Latin America. In some countries, populists or revolutionaries managed to introduce more democratic procedures. In others, autocratic regimes went through the motions of governing by constitutional law. U.S. bankers and businessmen, meanwhile, elbowed out many German, French, Belgian, and even British investors, to assume leading roles in local markets. A number of countries joined the League of Nations in hope of furthering international norms and conduct. The U.S. Senate's refusal to join the League of Nations, however, meant that most substantial inter-American problems had to be addressed bilaterally or through the Pan-American Union (see chapter 11). The decade of peace and growing economies was shattered in late 1929, however, when the New York stock market collapsed and ushered in the Great Depression.

## HEMISPHERIC VISIONS IN 1900

When the year 1900 dawned in Latin America, observers found cause for much optimism. Pundits foresaw that, during the next century, the hemisphere would achieve the highest levels of prosperity and happiness of the entire second millennium. Most commentators were certain that the Latin nations, fast becoming modern and attractive, were catching up with Europe and the United States. Celebrations marking the arrival of the new century emphasized material progress, economic expansion, urban growth, and public order.

Mexico topped the list of modernizing countries, followed by Argentina, Brazil, and Chile. Europeans would soon call the latter the ABC countries, a shorthand way of saying "the more advanced nations" of the hemisphere. Underlying that judgment were the Eurocentric perceptions that Latin America was becoming racially whiter and more civilized. Neither assumption was entirely true or even welcome to all the peoples of the region.

Urban development provided a visual index of the so-called progress—virtually all the major cities had grown and been redesigned according to European models. Buenos Aires, whose facelift in the 1890s led it to be nicknamed the Paris of South America, boasted nearly a million people by the turn of the century. Rio de Janeiro, soon to be extensively remodeled as well, had about two-thirds of a million people in 1900. Mexico City was somewhat smaller, at 344,000, in part because the cities of Guadalajara, Puebla, and Monterrey attracted many urban-bound migrants. Santiago, Chile, had about three hundred thousand inhabitants by 1900, some of whom lived in Parisian-style apartments and flats. Prosperous residents in these and most other capitals enjoyed such amenities as running water, sewage systems, electricity, telephone, and gas. Moreover, they had railroads, streetcars, street lighting, telegraphy, and international cable connections. In fact, automobiles made their Latin American debut almost immediately after their invention. The wealthy few in the region lived as well as the upper middle classes of Europe and the United States.

Latin Americans of all social classes had mixed feelings about Europeanizing. Their schooling had taught admiration for and emulation of the Old World, yet their location in the New World suggested that they should be different. But how? Some argued that the Americas had a common heritage distinct from other world regions. This argument stressed newness (only four hundred years since Columbus), its openness to outsiders (they were nations of immigrants), an aversion to imperialism and its wars, and an affinity for democracy. This view, which undergirded the Pan-American system discussed earlier, lumped together Latin America and the United States as the American republics or the Western Hemisphere nations.

Another line of elite thinking, however, distinguished between U.S. and Latin American realities. Anyone traveling to the United States (and many well-off Latin Americans did) saw a nation devoted to achieving industrial wealth and military power far beyond the reach of its Latin neighbors. Indeed, the U.S. seizure of Cuba and Puerto Rico during the Cuban-Spanish-American War suggested that the United States was an imperial power in the making. Latin Americans also saw in the United States widespread poverty, racism, class antagonism, monopoly capitalism, and urban disorder worse than anything encountered in Europe. Rather than emphasize similarities north and south of the border, some intellectuals highlighted the contrasts. Out of this analysis arose a distinctively Latin American self-conception, or ideal.

Latin Americans' new philosophy in the early years of this century drew on diverse sources. One was nineteenth-century liberalism and positivism. These views suggested that humankind is perfectible, that evolution depends upon individual initiative by persons endowed with superior intelligence, and that scientific progress will eventually satisfy material needs and banish suffering. As seen in prior chapters, this view of the world often contained a social Darwinist component that recommended doing nothing for the poor and disadvantaged, in the spirit of survival of the fittest. These ideas convinced leaders in government and business that they were destined to rule over the hapless masses. They also believed that foreign investment would spur progress.

Finally, while some positivists, especially those in countries with large indigenous populations, began to look for ways to improve the racial makeup of the nation, including through education, most still doubted that anything that they could do would really help the masses. Only continued immigration of Europeans, with the prospect of "whitening" their populations, would improve their genetic stock.

A second source of Latin American thinking in these years was Spanish liberalism, sometimes called Hispanismo. Often overlooked by scholars, Hispanismo drew heavily on the writings of the German philosopher Karl Christian Friedrich Krause (1781–1832). Krausismo, as reinterpreted by Ibero-Americans, offered an antidote to positivism, arguing in favor of social unity and solidarity. It embraced Judeo-Christian values, including the need for uplifting the less fortunate. It also advocated for education at all levels, women's rights, labor unions, international law as the basis for peace, and correct living and personal virtues. According to Krausismo, social hierarchy was natural and necessary, sorting people into strata according to their abilities and intelligence. But everyone was part of the same whole, a concept called "social organicism." Finally, Krausismo valued ethical behavior and appreciation of culture over material success—the ideal was to live by moral and spiritual values, not merely ostentation and wealth.

Just as European liberalism prevailed among persons in the business and financial worlds, so Krausismo took root among teachers, intellectuals, and artists looking to challenge the exclusionary practices of positivists that had brought only more immiseration and inequality to their countries. Liberals approved of importing the latest technology and fashions from Europe, bringing progress at any cost. Krausistas feared that foreign influences would erode the moral qualities that they wished to promote. They denounced the materialism and vulgarity of foreigners, especially Americans, so Krausismo was especially influential among those challenging U.S. imperialism, like José Martí.

A new Latin American nationalism emerged by the time of World War I, drawing on the second line of elite thinking in the region. This nationalism mixed progressive ideas, like universal education, women's rights, collective bargaining, democracy, and social welfare, with traditional moral values. This nationalism favored solidarity, care for the downtrodden, and obligations to society. It evoked a spirit of harmony among citizens in the pursuit of good government and social justice, challenging the nineteenth-century liberal order and feeding new movements for social change. Krausismo was key in the thinking of early populists such as Hipólito Yrigoyen of Argentina and José Batlle y Ordóñez of Uruguay.

Those people promoting the nationalist program of the early 1900s had their work cut out for them. Nowhere had education achieved any degree of quality or penetration—few countries could boast even a 10 percent literacy rate. Universities, often run by religious orders, followed medieval curricula and avoided contact with the contemporary world. Women had fewer legal rights than men and scant access to education. Labor relations were desultory at best, punctuated by periodic uprisings of oppressed men and women against employers who called on police or army contingents to quell them with force. By the 1920s, however, some social change was afoot. Labor made minimal gains in a handful of places, and spectacular gains in Mexico. Race moved to the center of discussions about the nation, as urbanization, immigration, and expanding political participation transformed civil society; it shifted the discussion in many countries away from whitening to a celebration of mestizaje, racial democracy, and indigenismo. Anxieties about the growing presence of middle- and upper-class women in public settings and the professional workplace also became a topic of national debate, and both the state and the Catholic Church actively sought to manage and define the modern woman.

No Latin American country conducted fair elections, even by the minuscule proportion of citizens qualified to vote. Instead, autocratic or dictatorial regimes ruled on behalf of moneyed interests, old families, the Catholic Church, and foreign investors. So, from a sociopolitical standpoint, the progressiveness of Latin America remained an ideal of reformers and intellectuals with limited political influence. While much needed to be done, the elites had no intention of carrying out reforms that would reduce their own wealth and power.

Out of the tension between appearance and reality, the ideal and the practical, arose different movements and kinds of leaders in the Latin American countries. In some, modernizing autocrats like those of the nineteenth century continued to treat the masses as mere labor in need of a strict hand. In others, revolutionary currents erupted and challenged entire systems of government and society. In some cases, leadership reverted to dictators in the mold of nineteenth-century caudillos. One of the most remarkable developments in the region, however, was the rise of the populists, in many ways unique to Latin America.

# Early Populism in South America

## A Call to Arms

In 1925 Eliodoro Yáñez, publisher of Chile's most prominent newspaper, *La Nación,* wrote to a colleague after the military coup overthrowing President Arturo Alessandri, deploring the attempt to return the country to oligarchic rule. His sentiments very closely paralleled the rise of a strong strain of populism throughout South America. Yáñez called the new politics the "transcendent phenomenon of modern times . . . the admission of the popular classes into political life." Read this as a call to arms for change in governing Chile, as well as other Latin American countries. He would do away with elite rule and replace it with truly popular government that would respond to the great needs of the people.

> Like you, I believe that among the circles of Santiago there is a profound incomprehension of the universal movement toward democracy. . . . To advance today a presidential candidate who embodies the conservative, oligarchical tendencies, is to jeopardize the future tranquility of the country. . . . The transcendent phenomenon of modern times is the admission of the popular classes into political life. Throughout the world the defenders of classical liberalism have been learning this truth, and Chile will be no exception. The evolution that has been occurring has brought an end to castes, to special privileges, and to authoritarianism, and has raised attentiveness to the social problem, which is in large measure an economic problem, to the first level of state obligations.[1]

## THE POPULISTS

Beginning in the early twentieth century, principally in the Southern Cone, a new form of leadership appeared that was later dubbed "populism." Gradually it spread to other countries. After World War II, populism seemed to be the predominant form of politics in South America. By the 1960s, however, it had run its course, and a series of military coups brought an end to the era of classic populism.

We can distinguish two phases of populism: one that prevailed through the Great Depression of the 1930s and another that appeared after World War II. The first has been called the reformist phase of populism. Leaders generally addressed such issues as voting rights and elections, nationalism, and labor relations. They found broad agreement on these issues and built their movements around them. Members of most social classes voted for the populists, whose strategy was to reform society in order to protect it from destabilization either by the old guard or by radicals.

The second phase of populism began in the 1940s, when issues of political economy dominated national agendas. Urbanization and industrialization swelled the cities, creating a need for more government planning. Populist leaders reached out to working-class voters (who now outnumbered rural voters) through their unions, retirement institutes, and associations. They appealed to these new voters by offering larger shares of the national income and more factory jobs. Their programs were nationalistic as well, pledging to end the economic dependency that had prevailed since the previous century. This type of leadership can be called national developmentalist (see chapter 18 for more on this phase of populism).

All of the populists shared certain characteristics. First, they used election campaigns to get into office, worked to improve voting systems, and expanded suffrage and participation. Both altruistic and opportunistic motives drove them. They decried the oligarchical regimes inherited from the nineteenth century. Constitutions provided for democratic procedures, but citizens had little say, and bosses controlled elections under the oligarchs. Second, populists believed that material progress driven by exports could not be shared widely without enfranchisement of the masses. Of course, electoral reform would also permit the populists, who were not machine politicians, to win high office without the support of the traditional parties. So populism as a strategy required expanding suffrage and cleaning up voting procedures, as both a means and an end.

Third, the populists advocated other reforms as well, especially in education and labor relations. They argued that these areas, left to the private sphere by previous generations, were too important to be ignored by the state. Such issues had broad appeal to the electorate. Improved education, for example, would give children of immigrants and workers the opportunity to move up the social ladder. It would also create more jobs for the middle class. Even members of the elite could see the benefits of a literate, better-off citizenry, including social peace and a more productive workforce.

Regulation of labor relations also had wide popularity because it promised to eliminate some of the worst abuses by employers and to ameliorate conflict in the workplace. Akin to labor reforms were proposals to extend educational opportunities and equal rights to women, including the vote.

In contrast to nineteenth-century positivists, the populists generally favored increasing the role of the state in social and economic affairs, and some had mildly socialistic ideas. Still, they preferred evolutionary over radical change. The specific reforms depended upon time, place, and opportunity, and their significance lay in the promise to improve the general welfare. The origins of these reforms lay in Krausismo, imported from Spain in the late 1800s.

The populist parties were multiclass, attracting followers from many walks of life. The older, traditional parties of the late nineteenth-century liberal era, run by a small number of wealthy men, employed political hacks who herded obedient rural voters to the polls on election day. They were small and ineffectual. Populist parties, in contrast, appealed to such disparate groups as the urban poor, organized labor, students, artists, businesspeople, white-collar employees, professionals, feminists, and intellectuals. Moreover, these voters acted independently and displayed genuine loyalty to their candidates. The populist campaigns were more broadly representative, then, but they required astute maneuvering by leaders.

Populists possessed that elusive quality called "charisma"—that is, followers believed they had qualities that elevated them above the common people and warranted awe and reverence. These attributes might be superior communication skills, integrity, honesty, concern for the downtrodden, political prowess, energy, or dedication to a cause. Charismatic leadership made the populists more dynamic and attractive to the voters, accounting in part for their success and persistence.

The populists authenticated folk culture, insisting that native songs, dances, crafts, literature, and poetry were as legitimate as foreign imports. In this they broke ranks with the traditional elites, who looked down on anything except European art and culture. By embracing popular culture, these leaders were able to reach out to poor people, children of immigrants, and others who benefited from a more inclusive vision of the nation. The populists exalted the essential national spirit—*lo mexicano, lo argentino,* or *lo peruano.* Largely for this reason they were known as nationalists.

Dozens of politicians adopted at least some of these new electoral strategies in the first three decades of the century, and these were genuine populists. The style took hold first in the Southern Cone countries, probably due to their large cities, higher levels of literacy, intense contact with the outside world, and relative prosperity because of the export booms. These were areas where nineteenth-century paternalism exerted less influence, and where traditional rural forms of social control had lost some of their grip. Then it spread northward by emulation.

## THE REFORM POPULISTS

The most prominent reform populists were José Batlle y Ordóñez of Uruguay, Hipólito Yrigoyen of Argentina, and Arturo Alessandri of Chile. Born after the middle of the nineteenth century, they had relatively long apprenticeships before gaining the presidencies of their countries. Batlle and Alessandri were born into prominent families, whereas Yrigoyen's origins were middle class. Highly educated for the times, they were products of urban Latin America and were intensely aware of the contradictions between constitutional ideals and political realities. They had strong wills and personalities and avoided the usual paths to power. In particular, they avoided military service and family alliances. Their foreign experiences were limited to European visits and ideas—they resided abroad only after becoming famous. They set in motion changes that would affect the conduct of politics for the next half-century.

### José Batlle y Ordóñez

Batlle, or don Pepe, as he was known to the masses, was born in Montevideo in 1856. His father, an army general and prominent politician, served as president from 1868 to 1872. By the end of the 1870s, Uruguay's political life had stabilized around a two-party system (*colorados* and *blancos*), and Batlle was able to grow up in a culturally rich environment. He studied in the British School and later read law at the university in Montevideo. In 1880, he went to Paris for a year to round out his education.

Batlle seemed born to lead. Tall, burly, and gruff, he stood out in crowds. His exceptional intelligence pulled him into politics, usually on the side of civilian control and democratic procedures. In 1887 he founded *El Día*, a pioneer mass-circulation daily that became the conscience of the Colorado Party. Urbane, reform-minded, and self-assured, Batlle fashioned a high moral position for himself and his wing of the party. He stood for open, competitive politics that addressed issues, rather than traditional backroom dealings among a small clique of elites.

Ironically, Batlle managed to win the 1903 election in Congress by the very backroom dealings that he denounced. Once in office, though, he immediately set out to open up and modernize the system. When his arch-rival declared civil war in 1904, Batlle was forced to defend his office militarily, which he did

Jose Battle y Ordonez, Pres't Uruguay

**Figure 12.1** José Batlle y Ordóñez, the dominant figure in Uruguayan politics in the first quarter of the twentieth century, led his nation from a sleepy ranching backwater into one of the most admired and progressive countries in the hemisphere. His foremost biographer called Uruguay the "Model Country." Courtesy Library of Congress.

successfully. From then until his death, Batlle became the foremost figure in Uruguayan politics. His remarkable career boosted Uruguay into the forefront of progress in the entire region, making it a country envied and imitated by others. Batlle's Uruguay became known as the "Switzerland of South America," a "socialist utopia," and the "model country" because of his extensive reforms. Even today his name is revered.

Batlle's initiatives spanned education, governance, labor, women's rights, industry, technology, church-state relations, social welfare, and transportation. Because Uruguay was a compact country whose population lived within easy reach of Montevideo, Batlle's reforms could spread quickly. It was also among the most ethnically homogeneous, with few citizens of African or indigenous descent, so reform efforts did not have to grapple with the types of race-based inequality that plagued other countries. Moreover, with access to maritime shipping, he could finance the reforms with taxes from the booming export trade in cereals and livestock products. Most people approved of these changes and hailed them as progressive. Even foreign corporations appreciated his orderly government, if not necessarily his scrutiny of their profits.

### Abella de Ramírez, An Early Feminist Leader in Uruguay

Women in the Southern Cone led the drive to gain broader rights and equality before the law. Historian Asunción Lavrin provides a detailed account of these efforts and their eventual accomplishments. María Abella de Ramírez, an Uruguayan feminist and leader of the cause of equal rights, was born in 1863 on a cattle estancia. Abella gained an excellent education in local schools. She later moved to La Plata, Argentina, but returned to Montevideo, where she married into a politically active family. As an adult, Abella came to regard the Catholic Church as women's greatest enemy. She advocated separation of church and state, public education, and secular social services. Above all, however, she believed that Uruguayan women needed the right to divorce. By networking with leaders in neighboring countries, she developed a "minimum program" for women's rights, consisting of seventeen reforms. Her activism led to the formation of the Pan-American Feminine Federation, by which she maintained ties with leaders abroad. The minimum program covered full educational opportunities, equal access to and salaries in all professions, paternity laws, economic equality in marriage, suppression of the husband's legal tutelage over his wife's affairs, divorce, decriminalization of adultery, equality for all children, an end to government licensing and exploitation of prostitutes, political and citizenship rights, and criminal prosecution of wife batterers. These and other reforms would end the "enslavement of women" represented by marriage under existing laws.

Abella died in 1926, before the vote for women was achieved; however, suffrage was approved in 1932, and her minimum program was eventually enacted in the Women's Civil Rights Law of 1946.

Asunción Lavrin, *Women, Feminism, and Social Change in Argentina, Chile, and Uruguay, 1890–1940* (Lincoln: University of Nebraska Press, 1995).

Tens of thousands of voters registered during Batlle's first term (1903–1907), and they took part enthusiastically in the new direct elections. The Colorado Party reaped their loyalty and votes, and Batlle won renewed mandates in successive elections. Indeed, the terms "colorado" and "Batllista" became almost synonymous. In his second term (1911–1915), Batlle pressed ahead with his reforms and laid the groundwork for eventual approval of a new constitution in 1919. Uruguay also developed an active feminist movement in these years and in 1932 became one of the first countries in Latin America to grant women suffrage. By the 1920s, many saw Uruguay as the best-governed, most prosperous, and most admired country in Latin America.

Of all of Batlle's legacies, his populism needs emphasis here. He pioneered an approach to politics that others would imitate, consciously or otherwise. His devotion to Krausismo, his faith in popular sovereignty, his campaigns to expand electoral participation, and his efforts to create a modern nation mark him as the first genuine reform populist. That heritage belongs to Latin America, not just to Uruguay.

## Hipólito Yrigoyen

Only twenty miles from Montevideo, across the La Plata estuary, Hipólito Yrigoyen began his career in Argentine politics about the same time that Batlle rose to influence in Uruguay. The two men shared many similarities. They embraced the Krausismo that was popular in the late nineteenth century and thus focused on many of the same reform programs when they gained power. They fought for honest, competitive, issue-driven elections and worked hard to expand the franchise. They both remained down-to-earth in their personal lives yet were worshipped like saints by their followers. They strengthened the power of government, demanded respect from other countries, and fostered a spirit of nationalism among their citizens. And they both are considered innovators for creating an early form of populism.

Yrigoyen grew up in Buenos Aires and apprenticed in politics under the tutelage of his uncle, Leandro Alem. After a promising start, he dropped out in the 1880s, only to reenter politics advocating revolutionary action against Argentina's corrupt liberal oligarchy, which many increasingly saw as unable to meet the needs of a rapidly modernizing population. After several unsuccessful revolts, their party, the Unión Cívica, largely disbanded, and the despairing Alem committed suicide in 1896. Yrigoyen then inherited leadership of the group. He changed its name to Unión Cívica Radical (UCR, but generally known as the Radical Party) and shifted its strategy to nonviolent resistance. Called "*intransigencia*," the new strategy required abstention from voting and diligent assembly of an underground network of neighborhood and employee groups to keep alive the spirit of defiance. Yrigoyen proved brilliant in this conspiratorial activity, inspiring tens of thousands to work for eventual triumph of the radical program.

Yrigoyen, unlike Batlle, was not an effective, outgoing speaker who could rally outdoor crowds. Instead, he invited small numbers of collaborators into his parlor and inspired them with a mystical sense of their righteous crusade against evil and corruption. He vaguely promised a better world when they governed Argentina, and he called on all citizens to abstain from voting until they could win honest elections. This brilliant tactic allowed the radicals to claim as theirs all those disenchanted voters who stayed away from the polls or cast unmarked ballots. Each successive election became a further indictment of the oligarchy in power and its fraudulent elections.

By not making explicit his program, Yrigoyen became all things to all people; he also backed these vague promises with patronage. Ward heelers, neighborhood agents, regional bosses, and party whips all made promises as if they were sacred pledges from Yrigoyen himself. Meanwhile, his semi-conspiratorial party distributed food, jobs, and favors that further cemented followers' loyalties.

Yrigoyen's breakthrough came in 1912 when the president of Argentina, Roque Sáenz Peña, decided to extend the vote to all males over the age of eighteen. Sáenz Peña, who considered himself a friend of Yrigoyen and a liberal, hoped that this measure would ward off growing public cynicism and absenteeism. It did, but it also allowed the Radical Party to sweep the next congressional elections and to expand its following in the major cities of Argentina. Yrigoyen stood poised to win the presidency in 1916.

The radicals nominated and elected Yrigoyen, who after an entire career in the opposition could hardly believe that he had finally won. He was sixty-four years old. He stumbled many times in his first term (1916–1922), failed miserably in his second (1928–1930), and was ousted by a military coup. Yet, his impact on Argentine politics was huge. He oversaw the incorporation of hundreds of thousands of new voters and local representatives into the system. He carried out a university reform in Córdoba in 1918 that served as a model throughout Latin America. He established national monopolies over new railroad, shipping, and petroleum concessions. And he launched Argentine diplomacy into a trajectory of neutrality and international law that counteracted and rivaled the U.S. imperialism of the era.

But by the time he took office, Yrigoyen was ruling over a country that was very different from just a few years earlier. Waves of immigrants from Europe, especially Italy and Spain, poured into Argentina and by 1910, about 30 percent of its population was foreign-born. Some industrial cities had populations that were over 50 percent foreign-born. While immigrants were at first welcomed due to perceptions among some elites that they would whiten the population and bring skills and efficiency to Argentina's workforce, their sheer numbers and the fact that most were poor when they arrived soon soured elites on the migrants. But the immigrants continued to come, bringing with them not only new languages and habits, but also urban overcrowding, disorder, and radical ideas that had been nurtured in Europe's labor movements.

Yrigoyen tried to meet the demands of the growing working class by sponsoring legislation to extend recognition to more labor unions and to require decent working conditions, especially for women. These efforts came to little, however. His first term coincided with a surge of anarchist-led strikes across much of the country, especially between 1917 and 1921. Yrigoyen attempted concessions, but soon responded with brutal repression, culminating in the Tragic Week in 1919, during which hundreds of workers were killed and tens of thousands imprisoned. While labor activism waned in the 1920s, Argentina's elites nevertheless now viewed immigrants with a more skeptical eye. Their focus turned to nationalist education as a way to inculcate patriotism and

## Cultural Populism: Tango

Nothing captures the essence of populist reformism in South America as well as the music and dance of tango, born in late nineteenth-century Argentina and Uruguay. With African rhythms and European instruments and techniques, tango first emerged in lower-class areas of Buenos Aires and Montevideo, where it was danced in bars and brothels. To this day a popular local dance in working-class neighborhoods, it is heavily associated with the region's large immigrant population. Historians suggest that young middle- and upper-class men, in their search to transgress the constraints of upper-class society, often frequented the poorer areas, where they discovered tango and brought it back to wealthier areas, after which it came to embody the urban cosmopolitanism of the period.

By the early 1910s tango was being danced in theaters and salons in Argentina, though only after it had become a dance craze in Paris, London, and New York. Tango came to encompass many styles, from the sensual close-embrace and syncopated pace of the *milonguero* style to the more open embrace and elegant steps that characterized the dance in 1950s family clubs, to the *tango nuevo,* which blends tango music and electronica and is danced by youths in Argentina today.

The person most closely associated with tango in its heyday was Carlos Gardel (1890–1935). Born in Toulouse, France, to a single mother, he moved to Argentina when he was just a toddler. By his twenties, he was a well-known tango performer in both clubs and movies. His first tango song, *Mi noche triste* (My Sad Night), performed in 1917, was the first to feature lyrics. It told a story of tragic romance and confirmed tango's associations with nostalgia and melancholic love.

Gardel died in a plane crash in Colombia at the height of his career. While tango's popularity in Argentina has waxed and waned over the twentieth century, it still embodies Argentine culture and society, and in 2009, UNESCO added it to its Lists of Intangible Cultural Heritage.

Spanish heritage into the diverse Argentine population, while xenophobia found fertile ground among those blaming foreign-born anarchists and socialists, many of them Jewish, for Argentina's problems.

In some ways, Yrigoyen left a larger legacy than Batlle. Some see him as an heir of the caudillo Juan Manuel de Rosas and a model for Juan Perón, who soon would take the populist strategy to its limits. And many more Latin American politicians read about, witnessed, and emulated politics in Argentina, the spiritual leader of the Spanish-American world. For example, in the mid-twentieth century, populists like Velasco Ibarra of Ecuador and Arnulfo

Arias of Panama (see chapter 18) spent considerable time in exile in Buenos Aires. So Yrigoyen's innovations spread outward in space and time.

## Arturo Alessandri

The third early reform populist in Latin America was Arturo Alessandri of Chile. The son of an Italian diplomat who decided to stay in Chile, Alessandri grew up in upper-middle-class style and received a good education. Alert to the new ideas circulating in Europe, Alessandri surprised his college professors in 1892 by choosing a social law topic for his dissertation: urban tenements. He attempted to find the causes of the alcoholism, moral degradation, and short life spans of workers in Santiago and Valparaíso. He concluded that overcrowding in those cities' slums, called *conventillos,* was a major contributing factor. Alessandri proposed a series of incentives to encourage private builders to improve low-cost housing.

> In Santiago, the majority of the rooms are low, dark, humid, unventilated, even when cooking is carried on . . . [this crowding] is greatly detrimental to health and moral well-being. In Valparaíso there are 543 conventillos with 6,426 dwellings which house over 17,000 persons, which gives an average of three persons per room. Of the 543 conventillos, 203 are in reasonable repair; the rest are completely inadequate for occupation and lack the most basic conditions required for habitation.[2]

Alessandri moved into the world of politics and easily advanced up the ranks because of his talents and physical attributes. He was tall and handsome and had a robust voice that carried well in outdoor rallies. He emerged as a leading figure among the liberal splinter groups that had formed under Chile's parliamentary democracy, and he managed to forge a liberal alliance coalition for the congressional elections of 1916. His success placed Alessandri in position to run for president in 1920.

Alessandri had done a number of things to groom himself for the presidency. After launching his career in the central-south province of Concepción—an important shipping, coal-mining, and agricultural zone—he moved to the northern desert nitrate districts and ran for election there. Tarapacá, the main nitrate-processing port, was home to tens of thousands of Chile's rugged miners and dockworkers. Alessandri appealed to these laborers with a program calling for recognition of unions, protection against work accidents, limitations on work hours, and government neutrality in industrial disputes. He gained the nickname Lion of Tarapacá because of his billowing mane of hair and his forceful image while campaigning among the miners. By all accounts, he became committed to social reforms that would ameliorate the suffering of the working class and improve the representative character of the political system.

The year 1920 began catastrophically for Chile. The nitrate market plummeted due to the end of wartime purchases and the spread of air-reduction

## The Shift from Nitrate to Copper Exports in Chile

At the turn of the century, Chile supplied most of the world's demand for nitrates, used for fertilizer and explosive powder. Production took place in the Atacama Desert in northern Chile, one of the driest regions in the world. Great salt flats in the coastal mountains contained high-grade potassium nitrate, which miners broke up and delivered to the coast using narrow-gauge railroads. Huge refining plants ground up and purified the mineral, which was then shipped all over the world by freighter.

During the First World War, German scientists developed an industrial process for extracting nitrogen from the air and combining it with other elements. After the war, demand for mineral nitrates fell precipitously, throwing the Chilean economy into a depression.

Copper, which Chileans had long mined, made a dramatic comeback in the early twentieth century and by the 1920s had replaced nitrates as the leading export. El Teniente, the first industrial plant installed, was about 155 kilometers south of Santiago. It was financed and built by an American mining engineer, William Braden, who shortly afterward sold his interest to the Guggenheim Copper Company, which sold it to the Kennecott Company in 1915. El Teniente hauled coal from Concepción to smelt the ores, gaining efficiency from mass production.

During and after World War I, in response to demand for copper, U.S. firms invested in two huge open-pit mines, Chuquicamata and Potrerillos. These mines used the new Jackling process for smelting and easily surpassed El Teniente in production. The three mines, known as the Gran Minería (Big Mining), accounted for 80 percent of Chilean copper exports by the late 1920s. It was a classic enclave sector, highly automated and completely controlled by foreign management, with few links to the rest of the economy and with profits largely sent abroad.

nitrogen technology. Tens of thousands of miners were thrown out of work, and strikes erupted up and down the country. The rest of the economy went through postwar adjustments that exacerbated unemployment. The political elite, however, stood by idly waiting for the invisible hand of laissez-faire capitalism to sort things out. All of the social tensions relating to poverty, disease, alcoholism, and dislocation surfaced again, and the crisis deepened. Tired of waiting for the benevolent leadership of the elite to address the crisis, the masses seemed ready to take matters into their own hands.

Arturo Alessandri rose to the occasion, conducting Chile's first genuine presidential election campaign in history. He traveled up and down the country

**Figure 12.2** Nitrate miners in northern Chile in 1918, when the product was used for fertilizer and to manufacture explosives used in World War I. Courtesy Library of Congress.

making speeches and meeting with local leaders. He appealed especially to workers who had suffered the brunt of the depression. He argued that the country was on the verge of breaking up and needed serious reforms to mend class divisions. He advocated constitutional changes to allow government to intervene in social and economic matters. He would separate church and state, legislate rights for labor, allow the government to take over lands needed for public purposes, extend the vote to all men and women, create an income tax, and increase the power of the president vis-à-vis Congress. These changes would give the president the ability to pass social legislation that Congress would have difficulty blocking. In reality, he advocated a presidential system to replace the quasi-parliamentary system in force since the 1890s.

Conservative leaders banded together in 1920 behind the candidacy of one of their own, and they managed to get enough rural sharecroppers (*inquilinos*) to the polls to win the election by a tiny margin. Alessandri carried the mining and industrial regions, using traditional techniques shrewdly and energetically. This election marked the transition from elite parliamentarianism to mass politics, a harbinger of populism. Because the vote totals were so close, Congress had to decide the outcome. The house was deeply split, and for several weeks it delayed. Finally pro-Alessandri demonstrations and public outcry overcame the resistance of the elite, and they decided in favor of Alessandri. He took office in late 1920.

For the next two years Alessandri worked on his reform program and tried to help the unemployed miners who had voted for him. Tens of thousands were transferred to other parts of the country to lesser jobs, but the economy could not absorb all of them. Meanwhile, Alessandri could not get his bills passed by Congress, whose members refused to give up any of their elite privileges. Congress stymied him with its right of ministerial censure, whereby a simple vote of no confidence would force the resignation of a cabinet member. By 1924 Alessandri had dealt with eighteen cabinets turnovers, an average of more than four per year. He decided to campaign in the 1924 by-elections to gain majorities in both houses of Congress, in order to pass his program. He succeeded, furthering the transition to mass politics.

Even after the new, liberal-dominated Congress was seated, it would not pass Alessandri's reforms, because even liberal members wanted to protect their vested interests. Public outcry arose at the lack of progress, and in late 1924 agitation from his working- and middle-class supporters reached alarming levels. At this point, the Chilean army, long a model of the nonpolitical military, intervened. Army officers, enraged that their pay increases were sidetracked while legislators debated paying themselves salaries, marched to Congress to demand action. Intimidated, the legislators complied, and soon Alessandri signed his entire reform package into law. Then he resigned to protest the military violation of the constitution! Chile's early experiment with populism proved fateful in many ways. Alessandri resumed the presidency in 1925 and oversaw the constitutional revision that he had campaigned for five years earlier. Yet, he soon resigned again in a confrontation with his minister of war, Colonel Carlos Ibáñez, who aspired to the presidency himself. So Chilean affairs developed into a tense rivalry between reform electoral politics and military authoritarianism. Populism did not return to any degree, because party loyalty, class rivalry, and even military intervention prevented the kind of cohesive mass movements that characterized populism elsewhere.

## GENDER AND REFORM

The early populist movements in the Southern Cone coincided with and supported the rise of women's rights. Batlle and Irygoyen in particular spearheaded women's equality in civic life, in the workplace, and before the law. Women across the region, even in countries with leaders much less friendly to social reform, encountered a range of new opportunities, influences, and challenges in this period due to industrialization, immigration, urbanization, the spread of public education, and shifting land relations. The rise of mass consumption and the waning power of the Catholic Church, along with the emergence of new groups fueled by populist impulses and internationalist ideas—like the working class and the middle class—also brought great change and prompted elite concerns about development and national unity. In response, public officials, reformers, educators, and clergy sought to curb social disorder by debating the proper roles of men and women.

The working class, in particular, became a focus of reformers intent on limiting what they saw as the destabilizing influences of modern urban life and growing labor activism. The working-class family became their target, and reformers promoted the idea of a male breadwinner and his family living a modern consumerist life. While men were to earn a family wage, defined as enough to support a family with dignity, women were expected to be modern caretakers of the home, responsible for curbing their husbands' vices and raising healthy, moral children who would be the workers of the future. To support this, teachers, social workers, and medical professionals fanned out in both urban and rural areas, teaching women about modern standards of hygiene and nutrition, and modern consumer items. The growth of public education for women, too, was expected to foster this, turning women into modern wives and mothers as they gained new knowledge, responsibilities, and skills. Yet expanded state oversight reinforced the rights of men in the household and ideally served the goals of economic and social modernization, a transformation in women's condition that some scholars have termed the "modernization of patriarchy."

The difference between the ideals of modern domesticity and the reality of daily life was often great, however. Women were the heads of many households, and poverty contributed greatly to household instability. Moreover, urban life broke down the privacy of families as households gradually opened to local commerce, neighborhood groups, and social agents of all sorts. The rapid growth of public education meant that schools came to assume importance in the family as well. And finally, the cities themselves required more diverse jobs and skills than small towns did. Women filled many of these new positions.

Women's participation in the labor force varied in the late nineteenth and early twentieth centuries, when shifts in land ownership, the boom and bust of export-oriented production, and the import of European goods that upset traditional artisanal production brought instability to labor markets. One scholar estimated that women's participation in the labor force in Argentina declined from about 60 percent in 1867 to 22 percent by 1914.[3] These economic and social shifts meant that migration for labor became commonplace. Women predominated in cityward migration during this period, and increasingly passed from the informal, domestic economy to the formal wage force after the beginning of the twentieth century.

Nevertheless, by the 1920s, working women still clustered around the bottom rungs of the occupational ladder. Many women worked in informal settings producing the goods and services to supply daily life in the growing cities. As in the nineteenth century, the greatest numbers still provided domestic and personal services, working as maids, laundresses, retail workers, and prostitutes. Women in such service jobs could not easily organize for protection and advancement. The cult of domesticity influenced them as well, and they, too, were pressed to become housewives and mothers in their own households, rather than servants in the homes of others.

In contrast to the nineteenth century, poorer women were expected to seek the same type of privileged protection as wealthier ones, even if the reality of poverty and social instability often prevented it. In cities in Argentina and Chile, for example, where immigration and labor conflicts ran high, and where single motherhood could range up to 20 percent and the immigrant population as high as 50 percent, there was a general anxiety about poverty, anarchism, immorality, and crime. Middle-class reformers therefore targeted the many poor immigrant families with their charity and reform efforts. Believing that family stability and morality were the foundations for social peace and national unity, prostitution especially became a target of police and reform efforts. Prostitutes from Mexico City to Buenos Aires faced growing oversight, including periodic obligatory health exams, segregation into specified urban spaces, and regulations regarding their living arrangements.

The second-largest group of women worked in industry. Some produced goods at home, such as clothing, shoes, or bags, but factory production grew quickly in these years. Factory work was abysmal, paying miserly wages with few benefits and little stability. Men could barely support families on factory wages, and women in the factory workforce were paid even less. Factories were often all-male, or segregated by task, so that men were usually given jobs seen as more dangerous, difficult, or technologically advanced, and that were higher paid. Women were confined to jobs like sewing, washing, detail-work, and packaging, all tasks that were lower paid. Women did dominate in some industries; for example, in the 1910s and 1920s, women were the majority in Chile's textile, clothing, and tobacco factories. They were sometimes preferred because as labor organizing took on new energy in the 1910s and 1920s, some owners saw them as the ideal passive labor force. Many working women did join unions and form groups to press for better treatment and wages, and the Catholic Church took a special interest in organizing women workers. But in comparison to male workers, women were less frequently on the front lines of strikes.

Women's working conditions in the textile industry in Medellín, Colombia, in the first half of the century resembled those throughout the region. There, factories employed only single young women from nearby small towns. Many of the women had left the coffee-producing zone because their families could not support them. Their factory wages were so low that they often lived in

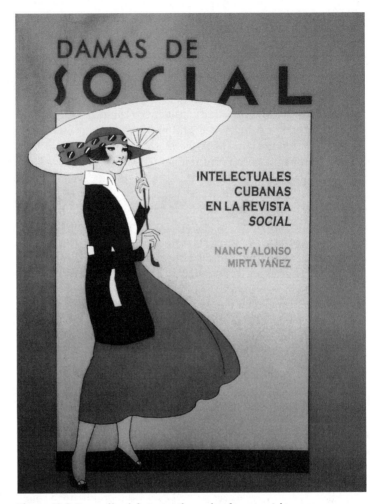

**Figure 12.3** Cover of book featuring the works of twenty-eight women intellectuals in Cuba between 1916 and 1938, whose voices were given audience in a leading Havana magazine. These activists addressed a broad array of feminist issues, from the vote to public art. Nancy Alonso and Mirta Yáñez, *Damas de Social: Intelectuales cubanas en la revista Social* (Havana: Ediciones Boloña, 2014), with permission.

dorms built by the managers and supervised by nuns. While work was onerous, urban life and living in a setting with other women also exposed women to new ideas, goods, and entertainment.

The process of economic modernization that had begun with the liberal reforms of the late nineteenth century presented women with a dilemma. On the one hand, opportunities for gaining money and skills outside the home exposed women to exploitation and sexism in the workplace. On the other hand, working-class women didn't have many choices for earning money, caring for their families, and seeking mobility.

The rise of mass politics in the first third of the twentieth century fostered the growth of feminist groups throughout Latin America. These groups varied, from the socialist feminists who argued for women's full civil and political rights and labor protections, to liberal feminists who pressed for reforms ranging from full political rights to legal protections for women in their roles as modern wives and mothers. Catholic reformers also organized, seeking improvements that would bring dignity to women as wives and mothers within the traditional family. These groups were fed by the expansion of public education that created a new cadre of educated middle-class women, some of whom now had professions as teachers, nurses, or social workers.

Women's suffrage was a key issue of feminist groups, though in almost every country, suffrage would not occur until midcentury. Feminist organizers pursued other goals as well, advocating for women's rights in the areas of family, labor, and education. Equality in marriage, divorce, parental rights, labor protections, and welfare all became important areas of activism. Supporters portrayed women's rights as essential to the creation of a modern republic, whereas opponents saw women's emancipation as a sign of disorder and immorality. In the end, while maternalism remained the focus of women's rights advocates, who rarely challenged the foundations of patriarchy, women achieved significant emancipation within their new roles as modern wives, mothers, workers, and consumers.

## CONCLUSIONS AND ISSUES

The early experiments in populism in Latin America ended in 1929, when the Great Depression struck the region and brought autocratic regimes to power virtually everywhere. The 1930s were not favorable for expansive electoral politics. Even Alessandri, who returned to office in 1932, abandoned his earlier style and ran an administration unresponsive to labor and the masses. Despite the disappearance of full-blown populist movements in the 1930s, certain broad trends favored their reappearance after World War II. Latin American industrialization spread due to wartime shortages. Meanwhile, agricultural and mining enterprises that had previously flourished due to lucrative export markets stagnated. Many laid-off workers decided to look for jobs and better lives in the cities. In most places, urban migration grew, and it accelerated after the war. Finally, new means of transportation and communication made it easier for politicians to create the kinds of bonds that fostered mass electoral movements. So the 1930s marked merely a hiatus in, not the demise of, populism.

## Discussion Questions

In what ways did Latin America become more integrated into global affairs in the early twentieth century?

What factors favored the rise of populism in the Southern Cone region of Uruguay, Argentina, and Chile?

How did populist politics differ from traditional ways of choosing governments? What characteristics stood out in the early populist leaders?

Where did the populists gain their ideas for new laws and programs? What obstacles did the populists encounter after winning presidential offices?

What social classes and sectors tended to support the populists and why?

How did urbanization and industrialization affect women's lives? Why did families become a focus of concern and reform in the early twentieth century?

## Timeline

| | |
|---|---|
| 1903–7 | First administration of President Batlle y Ordóñez |
| 1911–17 | Second administration of Batlle y Ordóñez |
| 1916–22 | First administration of President Hipólito Yrigoyen |
| 1928–30 | Second administration of Yrigoyen |
| 1920–25 | First two administrations of President Arturo Alessandri |
| 1932–38 | Third administration of Alessandri |

## Keywords

anarchism
blancos
charisma
colorados
copper
feminism

Krausismo
*La Nación*
nationalism
nitrates
populism
Radical Party

# Dictators of the Caribbean Basin

### How to Get Rid of a Caribbean Dictator

In 1929, Dr. José Rafael Wendehake, a member of the revolutionary junta seeking to overthrow the brutal Venezuelan dictator Juan Vicente Gómez, spoke with W. W. Waddell, commander of the U.S. cruiser *Asheville*, stationed in the port of Colón, Panama. Having lived in exile for over two decades, he appealed for support for their insurgent activities:

> Our people are suffering from a lack of education, from sickness, and hunger. Entire villages have been wiped off the map of Venezuela by malaria, because modern methods of sanitation have not been adopted. Our spiritual anemia is so great that the appropriation for education is ridiculous when compared with the expenses of the standing army that is maintained by General Gómez, entirely out of proportion to the small population.
>
> We want to found agricultural and industrial schools and divide the extensive lands of the country and open its ports to immigration for an injection of new blood . . .
>
> There are four hundred students in jails or working as laborers on the roads of the dictator, because of participation in political disturbances. . . . Our national poet, Máximo Andrés Eloy Blanco, decorated by the king of Spain, suffers for his patriotism in a cell of the Castillo of Puerto Cabello. . . . We want to reclaim our liberties lost for twenty-eight years under a tragic dictatorship that is an affront to civilization. We want to give our people education, bread and dignity with a democratic government under wise laws. All of our activities so far, both military and civil, have not been of the communistic order, nor are we pirates or filibusters; we are only patriots.[1]

During the 1910s and 1920s, as populism was expanding electorates in South America and promoting more open politics, an opposite trend was occurring in the Caribbean Basin—the region embracing the West Indies and Central America. A new generation of leaders, the Caribbean dictators, rose to power and imposed their rule on the poor and marginalized. As a group, the dictators were power hungry, ruthless, despotic, and vain. Their strong-willed methods fed many negative stereotypes in the minds of U.S. and European observers.

A common epithet used to describe the nations of the Caribbean Basin in this era was "banana republic," suggesting they were not genuine nation-states. And many in the United States held deeply negative attitudes toward Latin Americans. Some Americans stereotyped Latin Americans as racially inferior, childlike, violence prone, and untrustworthy. Others projected onto Latin Americans images of primitivism, anarchy, passion, and degeneracy, which in turn descended from European myths about nature and civilization. Many Americans used these stereotypes to justify intervening in the region, arguing that Latin Americans were incapable of orderly republican government and thus needed to be managed, pacified, or civilized. Such negative imagery reached its height in the early twentieth century, the age of the Caribbean dictators.[2]

Dictators chose to assume command of their countries for uncomplicated reasons. First, the legacy of the previous century had been caudillismo and arbitrary seizure of power. No tradition of democracy, shared power, constitutionalism, or governmental restraint limited potential dictators. Second, the economic rewards of becoming a dictator rose dramatically after 1900. Sugar, coffee, tobacco, cotton, petroleum, minerals, and other commodities earned lucrative prices in foreign markets. Once profit margins became known, U.S. banks were willing to lend large amounts of money for investment in various projects. Export prosperity, in turn, meant huge profits for those in control, usually dictators.

Third, the U.S. government sent naval and army contingents to occupy and govern several countries in the first third of the century, whether to collect debts, establish peace, or facilitate investment. Close relations between U.S. and local commanders tended to awaken ambitions of power in the latter. It became common for heads of armed forces to assume political control after U.S. troops withdrew. And protecting U.S. property headed the list of the dictators' responsibilities, ensuring the support of the colossus to the north.

U.S. policies were ambiguous. On the one hand, reform-minded, moralistic U.S. officials frequently attempted to modernize and democratize their southern neighbors, as if that were a simple chore. The American ambassador to England during the period of the Mexican Revolution, for example, told his British counterpart that his country's aim was to

"make 'em vote and live by their decisions."
"But suppose," the Briton asked, "they will not so live?"
"We'll go in again and make 'em vote again."
"And keep this up 200 years?" asked the Briton.
"Yes. The United States will be here two hundred years, and it can continue to shoot men for that little space until they learn to vote and to rule themselves."[3]

On the other hand, U.S. authorities often felt more confident leaving Latin American affairs in the hands of strong leaders with few democratic inclinations. As one apocryphal tale has it, a U.S. official, perhaps even Franklin Roosevelt himself, supposedly said of a Central American dictator, "He may be a son of a bitch, but he's our son of a bitch!"

## EVOLVING U.S. INFLUENCE

U.S. policy evolved significantly during the period known as the imperialist era (1898–1933). Military interventions multiplied during the early years, especially after Theodore Roosevelt's enunciation of his corollary to the Monroe Doctrine in 1904. This statement asserted that the United States would police the region and supervise regimes deemed irresponsible, which most often meant those unable to meet their debt obligations or those facing internal revolts. Under President Woodrow Wilson, the policy evolved further to include an emphasis on building the institutions to support, if not quite democracy, then the regular and peaceful transfer of power. The United States regularly interceded politically, economically, and militarily in the circum-Caribbean countries. Cuba, Panama, the Dominican Republic, Nicaragua, and Haiti were occupied by U.S. forces for extended periods and kept under control by naval threats, called "gunboat diplomacy." Even Mexico did not escape such demeaning treatment. The years 1901 to 1928 saw a total of fifty U.S. armed interventions in the region. Only the South American countries remained free of U.S. interference.

The Roosevelt Corollary to the Monroe Doctrine, included in his December 1904 address to Congress, stated: "Chronic wrongdoing [may] ultimately require intervention by some civilized nation, and in the Western Hemisphere the adherence of the United States to the Monroe Doctrine may force [us], however reluctantly, in flagrant cases of such wrongdoing or impotence, to the exercise of an international police power."[4] U.S. occupation often played into the hands of those who aspired to become dictators. The commanding officers of these U.S. occupying forces had little experience in diplomacy or Latin American politics, so their actions disrupted local governance. Traditional politicians found it increasingly difficult to retain control over their countries. U.S. commanders, meanwhile, in order to preserve law and order (their first priority), helped disarm existing armies and turn them into police forces. This further undermined the ability of the traditional elites to regain power, because the older armies had previously served their interests and frequently put them in power. Finally, the disruption and bungling that usually accompanied U.S. occupation stoked anti-American sentiment, which helped to inflame crowds and launch demonstrations. In the end, gunboat diplomacy actually led to greater instability and helped the dictators seize power.

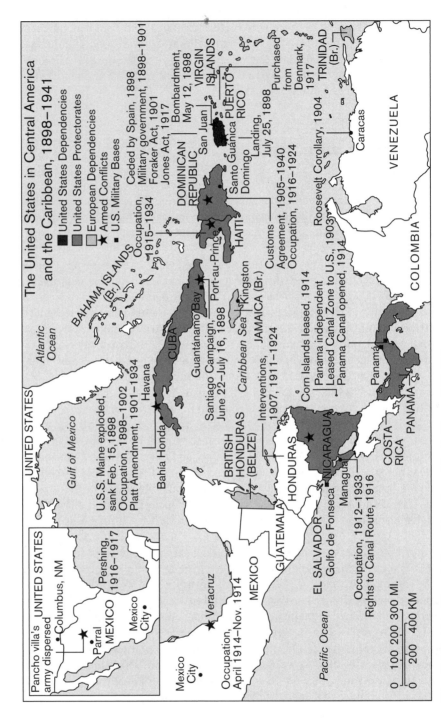

**Map 13.1** The United States in Central America and the Caribbean, 1898–1941.

The Caribbean dictators received a great deal of attention in the U.S. press because their countries lay near the United States, they received huge U.S. investments, and they operated within a U.S. defense zone during World War I. Some of these dictators became well known to ordinary U.S. citizens. Occasionally public opinion swayed U.S. policy, usually toward some intervention. That was the case of Cuba during the run-up to the Cuban-Spanish-American War. In most cases, however, neither the public nor the decision makers really understood the cultures and politics of the nations they attempted to control.

The dictators of the early twentieth century were born after the mid-1800s, making them mature or even elderly men when they took power. They usually belonged to old families that claimed descent from the conquistadors and monopolized the best lands and businesses. Most dictators had served as officers in their countries' armies until midcareer, when they felt called upon to assert themselves in government. In fact, the armies of these Caribbean countries were really just police forces for internal security, existing largely to protect the interests of the wealthy.

The dictators usually had advanced education from their countries' civilian schools, and some studied military science elsewhere. Those who were not military officers had usually completed college. Most had some personal experience with foreign countries through travel, study, work, or business dealings abroad. Spanish was, of course, their principal language, but several spoke English or French as well.

Once in office the dictators held onto power for a long time, using fraudulent elections or other deception backed by force. Their opponents were usually rival members of the Hispanic elite or occasionally mestizos trying to win support among the indigenous or black masses. In classic patronage style, the dictators typically favored their friends with lavish rewards and punished their enemies mercilessly. Some cultivated reputations of ruthless cruelty to discourage challenges to their power.

Non-elite rivals were dealt with especially harshly because they threatened the social preeminence of white elites over Indians and blacks. Most dictators ended up being overthrown by other dictators, usually at advanced ages. Their families could live comfortably for a long time off their accumulated wealth. Indeed, the dictators tried to create family dynasties, in which children and other relatives continued to enjoy the spoils of power.

## Estrada Cabrera in Guatemala

Manuel Estrada Cabrera provides a good example of the early twentieth-century dictator. Estrada ruled Guatemala for nearly a quarter of a century—the longest one-man rule in the region. During that time he preserved the archaic social system through brutal repression and violence. Still, as a man of his times, he also carried out a classically liberal program of economic change. In this he contin-

**Figure 13.1** Manuel Estrada Cabrera, seated in this 1909 photo, was a classic Caribbean dictator of the early twentieth century. His brutal rule helped to bring modernizing changes to Guatemala while also granting substantial rights to foreign companies, including the United Fruit Company. Courtesy Library of Congress.

ued the tradition of Justo Rufino Barrios of the 1870s and 1880s. Estrada in turn was followed by a dictator of legendary proportions, Jorge Ubico (1931–1944).

At the turn of the century Guatemalan society was fragmented into many subcultures. Over 80 percent of the population belonged to indigenous communities, most of which had little connection to the growing urban centers or global trade that was transforming Guatemalan politics and economy. They spoke over two dozen Maya-derived languages, cultivated New World crops with preindustrial methods, and had minimal contact with the white minority. Indigenous people worked communal lands, but they also worked for planters and agricultural corporations when required to do so. Forced labor, dating back to colonial times, continued.

The other 20 percent of Guatemala's population, sometimes called modern by outsiders, constituted an elite minority. A few families claimed direct descent from European roots, but the majority were mestizos and ladinos establishing their whiteness through their wealth, status, and habits. They governed the country, ran the money economy, controlled trade and production, made the laws, and supported a European-style society. Many looked down on the Indian majority, seeing them as a drag on the country's progress. The lives of Indians and ladinos (the term generally used for non-indigenous Guatemalans) rarely intersected, creating one of the most racially divided societies in Latin America.

Even so, the two Guatemalas did have one major point of contact: labor. Since the Conquest, elites needed indigenous labor to make their businesses profitable and their lives comfortable. Indians had traditionally worked the fields and plantations of elites and had worked in their homes as servants. They also transported goods to markets. Older forms of labor exploitation had evolved into standard debt peonage by the early years of the twentieth century. Under this system, indigenous people had to pay tribute taxes and religious tithes in cash, which was very scarce in their communities. Those who failed to pay could be jailed until they promised to work off their debts. Many thus had to find outside labor, often getting an advance that they then had to work to pay off.

Those who lived as peasants on lands owned by elites often found their debts to the hacienda stores impossible to pay off. They were trapped in debt servitude attempting to pay off their bills. The ultimate goal of these systems was exploitation of indigenous labor, without which the ladinos could not maintain the European lifestyles to which they aspired.

The antagonism of the two Guatemalas—indigenous and ladino—created deep tensions and hatreds. Rather than reforms that might have eased these conflicts, Guatemalan presidents usually devoted much of their time to suppressing uprisings and enforcing the labor and debt laws. They were supported by an elite who disdained the indigenous population as racially inferior.

Manuel Estrada Cabrera, who became president in 1898, ruled harshly. Estrada used his relations with military colleagues to preserve himself and his friends in power and to fend off rivals. He employed such brutal measures that other politicians labeled him a psychopath and attempted to impeach him. They failed. In the end, he was overthrown by his own army.

Estrada also carried out a program of economic investment that brought wealth to some but misery to the masses. This was the era when European and U.S. companies looked abroad for sources of raw materials, tropical commodities, and markets for their manufactures. The arrival of foreign investors in Latin America was generally hailed as progress because they brought capital, technology, skilled laborers, and permanent contacts with the outside world. Their advent in the Caribbean Basin—they had long since arrived in Mexico and South America—had been delayed by political turmoil and colonial restrictions. Now, it seemed, the smaller countries of the region could partake of imported progress and modernity.

**Figure 13.2** Late in the nineteenth century, bananas became a lucrative export crop from around the Caribbean Basin. National Photo Co., 1909. Courtesy Library of Congress.

For the most part, foreign companies did what they promised. They built railroads, streetcar systems, port facilities, processing plants, electric and gas utilities, telephone systems, and banks. They developed plantations, mines, ranches, and factories, mostly oriented toward foreign markets. They supplied capital and technology. And their managers, who circulated in the highest spheres of society, served as models for progressive Latin American citizens. In compensation, foreign companies reaped great earnings, often recovering their investments in a year or two and thereafter enjoying steady and secure profit flows.

Estrada and his counterparts welcomed these developers with open arms and lavish incentives—after all, they would allow the region to catch up with the rest of the world. Guatemala, because of its size, diverse resources, and huge labor supply, succeeded especially well in attracting investors. The United Fruit Company (UFCO), chartered in Boston in 1899, had already begun purchases of bananas along the Caribbean coast, and Guatemala became a prime supplier. UFCO received generous land concessions from the Guatemalan government to grow bananas, as well as subsidies to build a modern harbor at Puerto Barrios, on the Caribbean coast. In time it became the leading exporter of bananas to the United States and monopolized banana production in the region.

Along with plantations and the port, bananas brought a railroad, because the fruit had to be transported quickly to market. Estrada's government subsidized the construction of the rail line between the capital and Puerto Barrios and then authorized linkages with other Central American lines. By the 1920s this expanded system, known as the International Railways of Central America and owned by UFCO, transported 90 percent of Guatemala's rail freight. UFCO also owned a fleet of ships to move the bananas to markets.

Estrada also encouraged expanded cultivation of coffee, whose price had remained remarkably high over the decades. The rich volcanic soils of Guatemala's mountain regions were perfectly suited to the Arabica variety so prized in Europe and the United States. Planting, cultivating, harvesting, and processing were complex tasks, however, and Estrada looked outside Guatemala for the skills and labor to complete them. In order to set up the coffee industry, Estrada subsidized the immigration of thousands of German families and settled them on large tracts of choice land. The strategy paid off in terms of international earnings; by the 1920s, Guatemala was the third-largest coffee exporter in the world.

By the usual measures, Guatemala had made great progress during the Estrada reign. Capital investments, exports, railroad freight, urban growth, per capita income, and consumption all rose rapidly. Yet, only the small portion of white Guatemalans and the immigrants benefited from the prosperity. Indigenous people were forced to work more and harder under brutal labor regimes. Many lands that had belonged to their communities were confiscated for coffee and other crops. Taxes levied on their wages and purchases wiped out any chance that they might save money. The government, meanwhile, did not spend money on such things as education, housing, health, or literacy. The indigenous majority remained largely outside the system of rewards (but not of punishments), alienated from the so-called modern sector in the cities and ports.

Estrada kept up a fiction of democratic procedures. He had himself "reelected" several times. He also insisted on defending his nation's sovereignty by opposing U.S. pressure to declare war on Germany in World War I. Eventually, though, he did so and then expropriated German-owned property, including the electric power system and dozens of major coffee plantations.

Estrada was finally overthrown in 1920 by his army, backed by an alliance of neighboring countries with the approval of the United States, which disapproved of the excesses of Estrada's dictatorship. Many features of today's Guatemala may be traced back to the Estrada era: transport grids, cities, plantations, and wealthy families. Likewise, much of Guatemala's suffering also dates back to the Estrada era: disaffection of the indigenous masses, inadequate government services, a polarized society, illiteracy, and a highly unequal distribution of income. Yet, Estrada was not alone in following what he believed to be the path to progress. Most other dictators did virtually the same thing.

## García Menocal of Cuba

Cuba offers variations on the theme of Caribbean dictators. Mario García Menocal (1913–1921) and Gerardo Machado (1925–1933) both resembled

**Figure 13.3** President Mario García Menocal led Cuba during a sugar boom that brought Cuba into even closer relationships with U.S. investors. Bain News Service, 1910. Courtesy Library of Congress.

Estrada Cabrera in many ways, yet they governed a country more heavily influenced by foreign capital and very closely monitored by the U.S. government. Some background on Cuban independence is necessary before exploring their regimes.

Chapter 11 described how the United States declared war on Spain in order to end the Cuban independence war, protect Americans and their investments, and free the island from colonial oppression. Other Spanish islands—the Philippines, Guam, and Puerto Rico—were taken as spoils of war and became part of the emerging U.S. empire, but Cuba presented a dilemma to U.S. policymakers. They had intervened in Cuba in the name of freedom, yet they doubted that the Cubans could immediately become self-governing and guarantee U.S. investors' rights. Moreover, some U.S. leaders had long coveted Cuba as a territory for economic, strategic, and political benefits. Now that they had it, some reasoned, why give it up?

For nearly four years the U.S. Army administered Cuba as occupied territory; it cleaned up corruption, restored economic activity, and initiated the first successful campaign against yellow fever and malaria. Meanwhile, Cuban representatives promulgated a constitution and elected officials in expectation of becoming a sovereign country. Yet, self-government would not come easily. Under pressure from both Cubans and Americans, eventually the U.S. Congress reached a compromise that was embodied in the infamous 1901 Platt

## Massacre of Members of the Partido Independiente de Color in 1912

In 1908 Afro-Cubans, including many ex-slaves and veterans of the war for independence, organized the Partido Independiente de Color (Independent Party of Color, or PIC) to defend their interests, gain jobs and pensions from the government, and combat racism. Many felt betrayed after 1898, when they were denied full citizenship in the wake of achieving independence. They came from many walks of life but were mostly employed and owned property. Among other demands, they petitioned for clean government, better working conditions, and free higher education. They also rejected the idea promoted by whites that Cuba was a racial democracy, where the great promise of the independence-era Cuba Libre movement stated that all Cubans would be equals within the same nation. They argued that if they agreed that Cuba was a racial democracy, then black inequality would be seen as the fault of blacks themselves, rather than due to continued legal, social, and economic discrimination on the island. That creoles also promoted "whitening" through immigration and portrayed Afro-Cuban religious and cultural practices as "savage" supported their position. Below the surface, then, the PIC fought against discriminatory treatment by government officials and other forms of white supremacy that reemerged after independence.

The PIC grew quickly as Afro-Cubans from across the island flocked to its demands for full political equality. The government tolerated the party for a time, but in 1910, the president passed a law barring racially based parties, aimed at outlawing the PIC.

In mid-1912 leaders of the banned party organized a revolt in the eastern end of the island, where most lived. They hoped to force the government to compromise. Instead, the president ordered the army to attack without mercy. Invoking the Platt Amendment, the U.S. sent troops to join the Cubans in putting down the rebellion. Over the next several months, thousands of Afro-Cubans were killed in the fighting, a terrifying message to nonwhites. Some sought redress by joining with Marcus Garvey's back-to-Africa movement, but in 1921, the Cuban government repressed that movement as well, after which Afro-Cubans sought justice through other organizations such as unions, political parties, and reform movements.

For more on the repression of the Afro-Cuban rebellion, see Aline Helg, *Our Rightful Share: The Afro-Cuban Struggle for Equality, 1886–1912* (Chapel Hill: University of North Carolina Press, 1995).

Amendment. This amendment determined that the following year Cuba would become independent but would remain under the protection of the United States. As discussed in chapter 11, in exchange for withdrawing its troops, the amendment gave the U.S. control over Cuba's foreign policy and loans, a naval base at Guantánamo Bay, and the right to intervene if Cuba's independence or social order were threatened. In force until 1934, the amendment limited Cuban independence and reminded observers of the ultimate U.S. authority in the region. It also served as a template for U.S. rights in Panama under the 1903 treaty (see chapter 14).

Cuba, then, emerged from Spanish colonial rule only to fall under the supervision of the United States. The arrangement proved awkward and unpopular in both the United States and Cuba. Not only did it prevent full exercise of sovereign powers by Cuba's leaders, but it also made it possible to blame the United States for Cuba's failure to achieve stable government. Governments rose and fell, and marines landed and departed, in a desultory parade of humiliation for Cuba. The dictatorship of Mario García Menocal seemed at first to break this pattern.

García Menocal had fought heroically as a commander in the independence war and later served as police chief of Havana. He had also earned a fortune and valuable business experience by managing several U.S. firms. A conservative, he favored strong government, restricted suffrage, balanced budgets, and pro-business policies. He won election fairly in 1912, and when inaugurated the following year, he set about trying to restore the economy and the administration.

García Menocal attempted to enact his campaign promises, but corruption in his party and government soon overwhelmed his intentions. U.S. investment flowed into Cuba, especially after World War I broke out, and greed and personal ambition gripped his associates and relatives in office. Many former supporters (but not the U.S. government) gradually withdrew their approval, and his party seemed poised to lose the 1916 election. García Menocal decided to run again, however, and he used the considerable powers at his disposal to rig the results in his favor. His opponents protested and eventually revolted, but García Menocal carried the day, in part because the United States wanted to prevent further instability as it prepared to enter the war in 1917. García Menocal won his second term with fraud and police violence.

The usual suppression of protest following the election turned out to be unnecessary. Most people were distracted by a stupendous economic boom—called the Dance of the Millions—caused by immensely profitable sugar sales to the Allied countries during the final years of the war. More sugar lands were planted, mills installed, railroads built, ships commissioned, and workers imported than during any time in the past. The corruption and inefficiency of the government, and U.S. ownership of business, including much of the profitable sugar industry, did not seem to matter.

Gradually Cuba developed an addiction to sugar earnings that could be satisfied only by even greater exports to the industrial countries, the United States being the primary recipient. In the 1920s Cuba's relations with its richer customers epitomized the condition of dependency, or heavy reliance on industrialized countries to supply technology, machinery, capital, markets, and consumer goods. Cubans did only a few things on their own: cut and mill cane, refine sugar, and load cargo ships. And, of course, spend the profits. Dependency robbed Cuba of its sovereignty just as surely as did the foreign troops stationed on its shores.

Dependency brought ever-greater concentration of mill ownership and operations in foreign, mostly U.S., hands. Huge mill complexes, called *centrales,* mostly owned by U.S. corporations, gobbled up small and medium-sized plantations. Workers and even former operators found themselves permanently separated from capital ownership and forced to labor for others. One writer argued that the entire island had become proletarianized, citing Karl Marx's analysis of the conversion of craftsmen and tradesmen into a proletariat when they lost ownership of their tools. While the wealth kept sugar elites satisfied, the twin oppressions of proletarianization and dictatorship left many Cubans disenchanted, and Cuba faced revolts in 1906, 1912, 1917, and 1921. Each was met with U.S. military action.

Politics in the 1920s drifted because most major decisions were dictated by bankers, sugar barons, and industrialists. García Menocal did not run for a third term in 1920, perhaps so that he could enjoy the $40 million he was rumored to have stolen. Instead, he sponsored a former rival and rigged elections so that he won. In return, García Menocal's successor did nothing to disturb his golden retirement.

U.S. supervision of Cuban politics relaxed in the 1920s as part of a general retreat from direct intervention in the Caribbean. The last marines stationed in Cuba withdrew to Guantánamo in 1922. The Cuban government, meanwhile, became even more corrupt and tyrannical. García Menocal decided to run again in 1924 on the conservative ticket, but he was defeated in a genuine public rebuke of his previous record.

## Gerardo Machado

Cuba's next president, Gerardo Machado, seemed at first to defy categorization as a Caribbean dictator. He came from a modest family in the provinces and had worked his way up with little formal education or foreign experience. Though a military officer, he had won his commission fighting for independence. Later, Machado proved to be an effective administrator in several high public offices. He won the 1924 election fairly and promised an open, honest, and efficient government. And indeed the solid, reliable, efficient Machado prevailed during his first administration (1925–1929).

Machado not only constructed new railroads but also made them run on time. An indefatigable builder, he laid out highways, parks, utilities, public

**Figure 13.4** Worker harvesting sugarcane in 1940s Cuba. Amazingly, mechanized harvesters were only perfected late in the twentieth century. Courtesy Library of Congress.

buildings, ports, and other public works. Most of them were financed with easy bond money from Wall Street, authorized by an approving U.S. State Department. Progress also required training, so Machado expended much effort on schools, from elementary to university levels. He resisted challenges to his authority, however, and dealt harshly with unrest among laborers, students, women's groups, and the political opposition. In these respects, he resembled a number of other widely admired political leaders of the 1920s: Benito Mussolini of Italy, Carlos Ibáñez of Chile, and Augusto Leguía of Peru, for example.

---

**The Tourist Invasion**

Under Machado, Cuba began its transformation into a playground for wealthy and famous Americans. Machado took advantage of U.S. prohibition to promote a tourist industry that would attract both respectable and not-so-respectable Americans. He welcomed tourists by supporting U.S. investors who built hotels and restaurants in Cuba's most luxurious and cosmopolitan tropical locales. They also built sources of entertainment for these newfound tourists, including theaters and horseracing venues. This effort also included baseball stadiums, since the sport had been among Cuba's most popular since the 1870s, and the country had numerous amateur leagues, such as a sugar mill league made of teams of workers from the various mills. Tourists also provided a new market for gambling and prostitution, however, and by the 1930s and 1940s, the island had earned a reputation for its risqué nightlife. Bars, dance halls, casinos, and brothels brought together the wealthy and famous from across the U.S. and Latin America, creating a vibrant and dazzling cosmopolitan social scene at odds with the tyranny and inequality that marked the lives of most Cubans at the time.

---

As for Machado's economic policies, they departed little from those of his predecessors. American capital continued to flow in, further displacing Cuban businesses and facilitating ever-larger corporations that remitted profits to the United States. Sugar was king, as it had been throughout the nineteenth century.

Machado's career revealed signs of the typical dictator, however, which would be more visible after his unopposed reelection in 1929. Machado had amassed considerable wealth throughout his career, and he increasingly used force to deal with opponents. He had also learned that any successful president of Cuba must get along with Washington and Wall Street. So he spoke passable English and conducted himself with dignity and charm when around Americans. And most important, when seriously challenged, Machado lashed out at opponents with the powerful army he had assembled. Well-armed and loyal, the army ultimately guaranteed his regime.

The year 1929 proved fateful for Cuba, as it did for so many other countries. Machado won reelection virtually unopposed, and an amended constitution gave him a six-year term with more power than ever. As chief of both major parties, he monopolized politics and grew ever less tolerant of criticism. He began to imagine himself a benevolent and perpetual ruler of Cuba. Most Americans thought that would be best for Cuba, although the U.S. ambassador deplored Machado's autocratic tendencies.

In October 1929, however, the stock market crash sent sugar prices plunging to only a tenth of their previous levels, halved tax revenues, dried up bond money, and ended the prosperity that Cuba had enjoyed. When 1930 and 1931 proved even harder financially, Machado faced emboldened dissenters and dealt with them harshly. He invoked emergency powers to justify censorship, riot control, propaganda, school closures, exiles, and murders. The despot ceased to be benevolent.

Yet, the more violence he unleashed, the less control Machado had over politics. The heightened suppression led to conspiracies against Machado by students and military officers, including a network of secret cells created by middle-class professionals. As the Depression worsened, Cuba drifted toward civil war.

## NON-INTERVENTION POLICY IN THE 1920S

Cuban politicians and intellectuals were not the only ones concerned about the perilous developments in Havana. The U.S. ambassador and business community believed that the island could go up in flames if the violence escalated. By then, however, a subtle but profound change had taken place in U.S. policy toward the Caribbean region and its dictators. They would no longer enjoy unquestioned support from Washington merely because they protected U.S. property. The new approach—eventually called the Good Neighbor, or non-intervention policy—had in fact been evolving for several years in the State Department and White House. Among other things, it meant that the United States would abandon Machado and broker a transition to a new government.

The instability that erupted in Cuba in the early 1930s had already become widespread in other Caribbean nations during the 1920s. Dictators challenged dictators, and the ensuing bloodshed affected everyone, including U.S. residents. The usual gunboat patrols in the region did not always intimidate rivals, and often sparked even more instability. On numerous occasions U.S. Marines were landed to settle disputes and keep the peace. Such measures were only temporary, however, and often fueled deep anti-American sentiments. By the same token, diplomatic institutions designed to solve these problems without U.S. intervention, such as the World Court in The Hague and the Central American Court of Justice, failed utterly.

The mid-1920s shift in U.S. policy came about largely due to the influence of Henry L. Stimson, secretary of state under President Herbert Hoover (1929–1933). In 1927 Stimson had served as mediator in Nicaragua. A large contingent of marines landed there the year before, and Stimson hoped to find a way to remove them without becoming mired in a Nicaraguan civil war. Continual deployment of U.S. forces in Central America and the Caribbean seemed to do more harm than good. Nicaragua, it turned out, became a test case that was soon replicated in the Dominican Republic, Haiti, Panama, and Cuba.

GOODWILL

**Figure 13.5** "Goodwill," by Hugo Gellert, a 1928 cartoon of a U.S. Marine boot crushing the home of a Nicaraguan villager. In *New Masses*. Courtesy Library of Congress.

The basic scenario for withdrawal from Nicaragua was simple. A Marine contingent landed to protect a cooperative government. The local army, often politicized, demoralized, underpaid, and poorly armed, then was to be fashioned into a professional police force or national guard that could keep the peace and allow the marines to withdraw. In this case, the marines trained their own replacements. They chose levels of armament and training similar to U.S. National Guard units deployed during World War I. After these Central American constabulary forces, usually called the *guardias nacionales* (national guards), demonstrated the capacity to keep order, the marines departed.

The U.S. State Department issued an important revision of its policy toward the Caribbean region in 1928 when it circulated a brief written by its legal counsel, J. Reuben Clark. Known as the Clark Memorandum, it argued that the United States should not automatically send troops into civil conflicts in Latin America, even when U.S. citizens and property were endangered. The tendency to do so, under the authority of the 1904 Roosevelt Corollary, actually violated a much older policy toward Latin America—the 1823 Monroe Doctrine. Monroe had promised U.S. opposition to foreign interference only. U.S. intervention following the Roosevelt Corollary was entirely new and counterproductive, because it destabilized the republics and invited further intervention. Clark's message was clear: the United States should refrain from landing forces in the region unless a real extra-hemispheric threat arose, as was Monroe's original intent. The full meaning and ramifications of the new policy emerged in the years following the Wall Street crash, but continued political instability and rising anti-Americanism in Central America and Cuba in the 1920s certainly convinced U.S. decision makers that new approaches were necessary.

## CONCLUSIONS AND ISSUES

Caribbean dictators and U.S. political supervision seemed to go hand in hand during the early years of the last century. The dictators, strong willed, crude, yet effective in keeping power, governed their nations like despots. They took advantage of high prices for their countries' exports and amassed personal fortunes. Their cronies, often relatives and fellow military officers, likewise profited from the bounty of the new economic ventures. Much like Mexican dictator Porfirio Díaz, with his system of pan o palo (bread or stick), Caribbean dictators demanded obedience, adulation, and loyalty from their citizens, rewarding their closest allies handsomely. Those who refused could expect persecution at the hands of government officials and the dictators' thugs. These men employed crude but effective means to keep people in line.

U.S. officials sometimes decried brutality in their southern neighbors, yet they seldom took action against abusive dictators. Instead, compelling U.S. interests—security, profitable investment climate, and international cooperation—

seemed better served by stable, friendly autocrats. If these regimes could appear to be law-abiding and democratic, all the better. Many U.S. observers conde-scendingly believed that Latin Americans were incapable of orderly republican government anyway. Debating what to do with newly acquired tropical islands, a U.S. senator stated that bananas and self-government could not grow on the same section of land.[5] Many hoped, however, that U.S. guidance and example might someday overcome this basic failing.

Theodore Roosevelt put things even more bluntly in his 1904 corollary to the Monroe Doctrine: if the Latin Americans could not abide by his rules of conduct, they could expect a reprimanding visit and perhaps military occupation. Only during the 1920s did Washington policymakers recognize that they could not enforce, teach, or otherwise induce behaviors that they wished to encourage, such as social order, regular peaceful transitions in government, and debt repay-ment. Rather, frequent U.S. invasions and disciplinary operations often back-fired, creating more instability and undermining the very interests that drove U.S. diplomacy. Stimson and J. Reuben Clark pointed toward recognizing gov-ernments as they existed in the region. Events in Mexico, Brazil, Panama, and other places eventually proved these advocates of non-intervention to be correct.

## Discussion Questions

Did the rise of Caribbean dictators owe more to nineteenth-century traditions or to new demands as their nations confronted more global relations? Explain your answer.

Why did the United States assert itself in the Caribbean, as the "policeman of the hemi-sphere"? What effects did this have?

How did racism and exploitation shape Guatemala in the early twentieth century?

What role did U.S. capital play in Caribbean economies and societies after 1900? What effects did it have?

How did Cubans construct their newly independent nation in the 1900s? Consider political, economic, and social aspects.

How did the Platt Amendment shape Cubans' freedom to govern their nation? What did Cubans think of it?

When and why did U.S. policy toward the Caribbean Basin change from occupation to non-intervention?

## Timeline

| | |
|---|---|
| 1898 | Cuban-Spanish-American War |
| 1898–1920 | Rule by Manuel Estrada Cabrera in Guatemala |
| 1899 | United Fruit Company chartered in Boston |
| 1902 | Cuban independence, limited by Platt Amendment and annexation of Guantánamo naval base |
| 1904 | U.S. president Theodore Roosevelt's corollary to the Monroe Doctrine |
| 1912 | Suppression of revolt by Cuba's Partido Independeniente de Color |

1913–21          Presidencies of Mario García Menocal in Cuba
1925–33          Presidencies of Gerardo Machado in Cuba
1928             Clark Memorandum rescinding Roosevelt Corollary
1929             Wall Street crash ushering in Great Depression of the 1930s

## Keywords

banana republic
caudillismo
Clark Memorandum
Dance of the Millions
dependency
Good Neighbor policy (non-intervention)
guardias nacionales
gunboat diplomacy

imperialist era
International Railways of Central
   America
Platt Amendment
Roosevelt Corollary to the Monroe
   Doctrine
sugar centrales
United Fruit Company (UFCO)

# Divergent Paths to Modern Nationhood

## Panama, Brazil, and Peru

### The U.S. Canal Zone

The Panama Canal construction drew perhaps two hundred thousand laborers to Panama, mostly from the West Indian islands of Jamaica and Barbados. Many remained permanently in Panama, where they faced rejection by Panamanians and racial segregation by the Americans, but they managed to establish themselves in the country's middle class by the second generation. A fairly large number migrated again, often to the United States.

Eunice Mason, herself a descendant of West Indians in Panama, gathered a number of oral histories in the community, one of them from a Mrs. Taylor, who told this story:

> I was born in 1890, in the island of Antigua, a small island in the Caribbean. In 1904, at the age of 14, seven children, mother and father, left home and went to the island of St. Lucia, where my father was employed by the military government as a stone mason. Not long after that, it closed down, and my father decided to come to Panama. My father read of Panama and thought it a wonderful place to come to and because he saw progress in Panama. . . .
>
> In 1906 we joined my father in Panama. After coming here I continued my dressmaking. A great many of the West Indians were also coming to the Isthmus of Panama, and many of the parents with whom I dealt in St. Lucia were also here. They encouraged me to start a little private school. In my dressmaking class I taught girls. I did that until I got married in 1913.
>
> In those days, 1906–1907, there were no schools for us. The Panamanians were not willing to take in our children to school, because they said our children already had an education or gone half-way, and we would be blocking their children if they were to take in our children.
>
> My father didn't work for a very long time because he just could not take it—the life was so different. The understanding between colors was brought vividly to

the eye—that we were not accustomed to be so much about your color or to have such an [awareness of] your color, black and white. All of that he couldn't stand so he left the Canal Zone about 1912 and came to Panama, where he did mason work on buildings. . . .

When World War I broke and also World War II, ladies filled the spaces the men left. They went in on the commissary staff, teaching staff, in hospitals. There were more of them than previously. That gave the women a chance, which has helped a great deal of them until today. Because I remember when I was growing up it were mostly women working in the clubhouses, in the commissaries, laundry.[1]

The 1914 completion of the Panama Canal, one of the great engineering feats of the twentieth century, required a huge labor force for over a decade. The Caribbean islanders made up a human tidal wave that swept over Central America, first in Panama and later in neighboring countries.

The canal construction left a legacy of animosity among Panamanians, who resented not being able to profit from the canal's operation. It also left an underemployed workforce in Panama, made up largely of black, English-speaking, Protestant West Indians. Long ostracized but eventually accepted, the West Indians in Panama formed a tight-knit local community and fought for secure lives. Still, they suffered the same kind of discrimination and deprivation as blacks throughout the Americas.

After three generations, one of the West Indian descendants managed to run in the presidential election of 1994 and in April 2016 announced his intentions to run again in 2019: singer and actor Ruben Blades. Blades spent his early career in the United States, founded his own party, Papa Egoró, and ran a creditable campaign. He came in third, but his candidacy marked a breakthrough for Panamanians of West Indian descent; as elsewhere in Latin America, while skin color continues to be a key variable in determining difference, race is not rigidly defined, and Latin Americans of African and indigenous descent have moved into the highest circles of power.

## PANAMA, BRAZIL, AND PERU

While some Southern Cone nations developed under a new style of mass politics—and most Caribbean Basin countries languished under dictatorships—Panama, Brazil, and Peru each carried legacies from the nineteenth century that made them distinct from their neighbors: Panama was a part of Colombia until 1903; Brazil had only recently thrown off the shackles of slavery and monarchy; and Peru had experienced a devastating economic bust in the late nineteenth century that undermined elite unity. Because of their unique trajectories, each took a different path toward building sovereign nation-states in the early twentieth century. By the 1930s, each had a stable government, a more modern economy, and some semblance of mass politics. Yet they also remained segmented and fragile.

During the 1880s, before the United States attempted to build a canal in Panama, a French company formed by Ferdinand de Lesseps tried and failed to do so, foiled by tropical disease, poor design, and lack of resources. The failure was so devastating that the term "un Panamá" came to mean "debacle" in colloquial French. The reorganized company sold its canal rights to the United States in 1903. Simultaneously, Panamanians revolted and declared their independence from Colombia. The United States, deeply involved in this coup, quickly signed a treaty with the new nation granting the U.S. quasi-sovereign rights to build and operate a ship canal. Within months, the United States exercised dominion over the isthmus and began building a canal that still serves as a major maritime seaway.

Panamanian leaders responded to voracious U.S. claims on their nation by demanding larger shares of the jobs, revenues, and business generated by the canal. The United States refused to share the spoils for many decades, however, and Panama's history for much of the twentieth century revolved around struggles with the Colossus of the North. Eventually, however, the two countries negotiated and signed a treaty that promised the U.S. would hand over the canal to Panama and vacate its many military bases by the end of 1999.[2]

Brazil followed a different path in the first quarter of the twentieth century, a period known as the First Republic. Not dictatorial, populist, or nationalistic, Brazil's political system comprised a peculiar mix of patriarchal control at the state level and a detached, ineffectual federal government based in Rio de Janeiro. Although often portrayed as a period during which little of consequence occurred, the First Republic in fact gave birth to some of the most significant changes that Brazil had ever experienced, including rapid industrialization, the professionalization of its military, and its emergence as a South American leader in contemporary art, culture, and social relations. From a slave-plantation based monarchy in the late 1880s, by 1930 it had transformed into a modern nation-state that embodied both the cosmopolitanism and the extreme inequality that characterized the region.

Finally, in the early twentieth century, Peru managed to shrug off the defeatism and failures of the previous century and move toward a more national form of governance. Peru's segmented population, fragmented geography, and divided elite could not form a genuine nation-state. Yet the foundations were laid, especially during the eleven-year rule (*oncenio*) of President Augusto Leguía in the 1920s. The central government exploited high world prices for Peru's resources but failed to address the poverty and oppression of the largely indigenous masses. Instead, popular protests and discontent drew an extraordinary young leader, Víctor Raúl Haya de la Torre, onto the national stage.

Haya introduced mass campaigning and a progressive social agenda into politics, promising to incorporate Indians for the first time into the nation-state. Although he would never become president, his long career permanently changed the conduct of national affairs.

## PANAMA, THE U.S. CANAL, AND THE LIMITS OF SOVEREIGNTY

Events in the early 1900s ruptured the usually businesslike relations between Colombia and the United States. For one thing, Colombia's War of a Thousand Days disrupted rail traffic across Panama and led to several U.S. troop landings to restore order. The U.S. Navy kept part of its fleet in the vicinity to prevent depredations against the Panama Railroad. That railroad firm, operated by the New York corporation that had built it from 1850 to 1855, was now owned by the New French Canal Company, which emerged from bankruptcy in 1894. The Colombian civil war had ravaged Panama but ended in 1902, when the last liberal general gave in to U.S. pressure and signed an armistice aboard the U.S.S. *Wisconsin.* Although liberals believed that they had been robbed of victory by a partisan United States, both liberals and conservatives were exhausted by three years of warfare.

Rights to a canal crossing in Panama also bedeviled relations between Colombia and the United States. By 1900, the U.S. Congress had decided to build an interoceanic canal, favoring a route across Nicaragua. But the accession of Teddy Roosevelt to the presidency in 1901 changed that. He and his party favored the Panama route chosen by the French, as long as rights could be secured for a reasonable fee. His secretary of state negotiated a treaty to that effect with the Colombian minister in Washington. But there was little sentiment in Bogotá to accept the rather miserly terms offered by the Americans.

When the Colombian Senate rejected the draft treaty in early 1903, Panamanian leaders and Roosevelt alike decided on an alternative path. If Panamanians declared independence, they could write and approve a treaty without Colombia. The Panamanians conspired to revolt, helped by the railroad and French canal managers, and Roosevelt dispatched warships to both coasts to protect the fledgling nation. Independence came virtually as planned, on November 3, 1903, and within days the United States and other powers recognized Panama as sovereign. No one doubted that Panamanian aspirations and U.S. canal designs had coincided deliberately. Meanwhile, Colombians bitterly accepted the loss of their wayward province and future revenues that the canal would have provided.

In the thick of the plotting, Panamanians named a French engineer, Philippe Bunau-Varilla, as minister plenipotentiary in Washington. Bunau-Varilla had

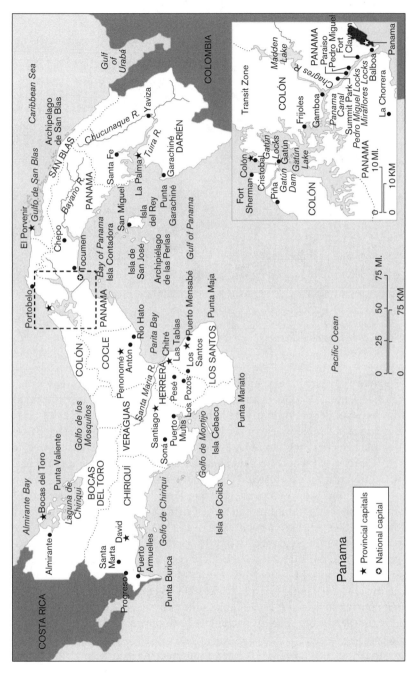

**Map 14.1** Panama.

**Figure 14.1** President Theodore Roosevelt at the controls of a huge Bucyrus steam shovel working on the Panama Canal in 1906, the first time a sitting president traveled outside the United States. By H. C. White. Courtesy Library of Congress.

given Panama's plotters money, intelligence, and supplies on the condition that he be named Panama's representative to the United States. In the first weeks following independence, Bunau-Varilla huddled with U.S. Secretary of State John Hay and signed a new treaty even more advantageous to the United States than the one rejected by Colombia. Furious, the Panamanians attempted to reject it, but relented when warned that the U.S. warships might leave and allow Colombian forces to return. The 1903 canal treaty was ratified, but it became the original sin in Panama-U.S. relations. It was signed by a Frenchman who felt no loyalty at all to Panama's future, and gave away virtually all canal rights and revenues to the United States.

After Panama's independence, two projects went on simultaneously: Panamanians worked to build a nation out of their colonial and provincial heritages, and Americans labored to construct a canal that would move ships between the Atlantic and the Pacific oceans. The canal was completed in 1914, and has operated continuously since 1920. Panamanians managed to create a genuine nation by the 1920s, but, like all nations, it has continued to evolve since its founding.

The canal was a marvel of American engineering and helped to project the United States into global affairs on the eve of World War I. Three sets of locks at either end raised ships to an eighty-five-foot-high artificial lake that, when connected to an excavated channel, made it possible for ships to steam from one ocean to the other. The locks operated by gravity flow, so that little energy was needed to run the canal. Ships no longer had to go around Cape Horn, saving thousands of miles and weeks at sea. It was the largest and costliest construction project ever undertaken by a government up to that time.

After the canal began operating in 1914, the U.S. government set up an efficient community in the Canal Zone (a ten-by-fifty-mile enclave) to administer it, under the Department of the Army. Panamanians were largely excluded and received few of the canal's benefits. In fact, Panama had two parallel governments: one for the republic and another for the U.S. zone. No one doubted which was more powerful. For the next twenty years or so the United States meddled in Panamanian affairs regularly, usually in the name of building and running the canal efficiently. Among the most damaging affronts to Panamanian sovereignty was the 1904 dissolution of its small army, which was replaced by a national police. Some years later, U.S. Marines even confiscated high-caliber rifles used by the police.

Panamanians swallowed their disappointment with the 1903 treaty and organized their affairs as quickly as possible. They wrote a constitution in 1904 and held elections in alternate years. They adopted a very controversial article, Number 136, giving the United States virtually the same rights that the Platt Amendment conceded in Cuba. Because the rights were already implied or spelled out in the 1903 treaty, it was largely redundant.

The United States exercised treaty authority to build, operate, maintain, and defend the canal and to import any people or machinery necessary for those tasks. The United States could take over any lands or waters deemed necessary for the canal, in addition to the five-hundred-square-mile zone. The United States could police and administer sanitation in the terminal cities of Panama City and Colón. And the right of military intervention meant that Panama could not adopt any policies deemed threatening to U.S. interests. Panama was not exactly a colony, but neither was it entirely independent. Perhaps "protectorate" is the best term.

Meanwhile, conservatives, who had spearheaded the independence movement, managed to win the first elections, using government favors and police interference. In 1908 and 1910 the U.S. government stepped in and supervised elections, giving the liberals a chance to win but also creating reliance on outside arbitration. The shortcomings of U.S. mediation became clear in 1910, when the incumbent president died, and U.S. authorities objected to the succession of the vice president. The latter, though an able and popular figure, was independent minded and a mulatto. The American minister convinced him to step down. From then on, the Panamanian elite nominated only white candidates from wealthy families. Candidates for president usually spoke

**U.S. Leaders Bar Liberal from Presidency Due To Race**

Longtime British minister in Panama Claude Mallet reported to the Foreign Office that U.S. authorities had blocked the succession of second vice president Carlos Alberto Mendoza to the presidency in 1910:

> It is really farcical to talk of Panama as an independent state. It is really simply an annex of the Canal Zone. . . . I am in a position to state positively that the attitude in Washington [against Mendoza's becoming president] was taken entirely on the initiative and recommendation of [Canal Chief] Colonel Goethals, who is prejudiced against Señor Mendoza on account of his color.

Claude Mallet to Foreign Office, August 22, 1910, FO 371/944/33140, Public Record Office, London.

English and had studied in the United States. Indeed, one president claimed that Washington was the stage upon which future presidents of Panama rehearsed.

National consolidation began in earnest in the early 1910s. A liberal, Belisario Porras, won the 1912 election and gave the country stability and a constructive administration. Porras had apprenticed in politics at an early age and gained broad experience—for example, he studied law in Paris, worked for the French canal company, and commanded a liberal army during the War of a Thousand Days.

In exile when the independence movement unfolded, Porras criticized its leaders for being subservient to the United States and especially for approving the 1903 treaty. In retaliation, the new government revoked his citizenship to block him from high political office. The measure did not work; with Porras's strengths and the liberals' numerical superiority, he was elected handily. The liberals remained in control for nearly twenty years, ten of them under Porras's leadership.

Porras made his peace with the American canal authorities and hosted an international exposition in 1915 to celebrate the completion of the canal. Panama, after all, would depend heavily on employment and business generated by the canal's operation. Hordes of laborers and clerks flowed into the zone each morning to work on the canal. Porras also set out to equip the country with institutions and infrastructure that had been neglected by the Colombians. He authorized the construction of hospitals, schools, roads, bridges, government offices, railroads, plantations, factories, and ports. Business prospered in Panama City and Colón, the two cities that bordered the Canal Zone.

Immigrants flocked in from all over the world looking for work and opportunities to get rich. By the end of World War I Panama had become a far more urban, cosmopolitan, trade-oriented nation than ever before. West Indian blacks from Jamaica, Barbados, and other Caribbean islands were the most numerous immigrant group. Although they suffered discrimination, most stayed and forged a cohesive subculture in Panama.

The small Jewish community in Panama swelled during the construction years and continued to receive newcomers in subsequent decades. Large numbers of Europeans, Asians, Middle Easterners, South and Central Americans, and, of course, Americans made their homes in Panama. They built their churches, schools, businesses, lodges, and civic clubs, creating a kaleidoscopic society in the tropical isthmus. For the most part, they got along well, especially when the economy prospered.

World War I led U.S. authorities to expand their military presence in Panama. They argued that submarine activity in the Caribbean and political instability in Central America made military bases in Panama necessary. They interpreted the 1903 treaty as authorizing conversion of the Canal Zone into a military fortress. The U.S. Army Corps of Engineers, which had taken responsibility during construction, continued to manage the canal itself, but the War Department set up a separate command in Panama that gradually eclipsed the canal itself in importance.

Then, during and after World War II, the U.S. Navy and Air Force set up more bases in the Canal Zone, joined by several intelligence agencies, including the well-known U.S. Army School of the Americas. Panamanians as well as other Latin Americans had little choice about having a major U.S. military presence in their midst.

Porras, a strong-willed autocrat who managed the country efficiently, did not integrate many non-elite figures into his circle of power. In the 1920s, many other groups emerged to seek their fortunes in the political arena. Occasionally Porras had to call in U.S. troops to keep order, because his own police were too weak. Tensions also broke out, often sparked by native citizens resentful of the many outsiders flooding the country.

Unable to succeed himself in the presidency in 1924, Porras selected Rodolfo Chiari, a sugar baron and grandson of an immigrant, to take over the government. A quiet man, Chiari was thought to be weak and easy to manipulate. He turned out to be his own person, however, and quickly gained control over the Liberal Party. The balanced approach of the Porras years ended, and an even more pro-business atmosphere prevailed in Panama's presidential palace.

Of the many dissident groups that arose in the 1920s, one would prove significant: the secret society called Acción Comunal (Communal Action). Like so many dissident groups in Latin America in the 1920s, it was made up of middle-class professionals, students, writers, and aspiring politicians who sought reforms and wanted to strengthen nationalistic sentiment in the country and to lessen the influence of the United States. It denounced concessions of new lands, questioned U.S. treaty rights, clamored for immigration controls, and advocated for a more forceful foreign policy. It claimed that Panama was merely a self-governing protectorate of the United States. Among other victories, the group claimed to have blocked congressional ratification of a new commercial treaty with the United States in 1926. The accession to power of its leaders in the early 1930s decisively affected Panama's quest for international status.

## BRAZIL'S FIRST REPUBLIC

After the overthrow of the monarchy in 1889, Brazil's 1890s elites attempted to give the country a modern system of republican government and allow maximum freedom for individuals and business. The 1891 constitution borrowed heavily from that of the United States, with a four-year presidential term, a bicameral legislature, states' rights, and separation of powers. The constitution weakened central government in Rio de Janeiro in several ways, however, compared to Washington. The president could not be reelected; states could levy export and interstate taxes and organize military forces; and states conducted all elections. On paper, Brazil adopted an advanced and efficient federal model, but it was never really implemented.

In a short time, this artificial structure gave way to a homegrown arrangement called the politics of the governors. Because under the federalist model the governors of the largest and wealthiest states were not restricted in their terms, revenues, and police powers, they became veritable dictators in their states. Coffee-growing São Paulo led the way, followed by Minas Gerais, Rio Grande do Sul, Rio de Janeiro, and Bahia. Other state governors played along with the powerful leaders.

The governors chose presidential successors and elected them through manipulation of state voting. Suffrage was heavily restricted during the First Republic, and elections were controlled through extensive patronage networks. If small states disagreed, the governors sent troops to skirmish until the proper decision was reached. Even the federal Congress came under the sway of the powerful governors. Thus, Brazil's government can be described as hyper-federalist during the First Republic (1889–1930).

The states of São Paulo and Minas Gerais, in particular, derived enough money from coffee export taxes to rival the federal government. For a time they actually agreed to alternate the presidency between outgoing governors of their two states, an arrangement called café com leite (coffee and milk), symbolic of the two states' economic strengths. So, despite the democratic and federal character of the constitution, the reality of politics rested firmly on money and military clout wielded by state governors.

At the regional and local levels, landowners and political bosses ruled like despots. These strongmen were called *coronéis* (colonels), after a system of national guard commissions held over from the nineteenth century. In fact, mere consti-

**Map 14.2** Brazil.

tutional provisions could not alter the authority of local paternalistic rule. Coronéis balanced patronage, violence, and intimidation to preserve their power, and there were frequent outbreaks of fighting between rivals in rural areas. Banditry and gunfights were endemic throughout rural Brazil until the 1940s.

Weak presidents who shared authority with Congress and the courts presided over national politics, yet their authority extended little beyond the capital city itself. Occasionally they gave subsidies to the states for railroads, immigrant labor recruitment, and economic development, but the states themselves also raised money from overseas banks. One remarkable subsidy, however, was begun by the states and later assumed by the federal government to support commodity export prices: coffee valorization.

In 1906 a bumper crop of coffee threatened to drive global prices down to ruinous levels. Brazil was the world's larger supplier of the beans. The states of São Paulo, Minas Gerais, and Rio de Janeiro vowed to buy up excess stocks to prevent a disastrous glut on the international market, but they could not convince the president to finance the stockpiling scheme. Ultimately, São Paulo, with the help of a shrewd broker in New York, managed to buy nearly half the 1906 and 1907 crop, thereby averting a major plunge in prices. In later years the coffee was gradually released in world markets without distorting prices. The federal government soon saw the benefit of the deal and assumed responsibility for buying up occasional surpluses. To this day, a federal agency buys and markets coffee in order to maximize foreign earnings.

The reluctant intervention of the federal government into the coffee industry signaled a retreat from the ideal of laissez-faire economics that had inspired the founders of the First Republic. Little by little, Congress voted more money for transportation, communications, and banking. Because of this pump priming, the country's economy grew rapidly, and some cities displayed signs of industrial progress. Factories, modern docks, high-rise buildings, streetcars, utility systems, and public offices sprang up in the early twentieth century. Behind the façade of commodities export prosperity, a solid foundation of industry emerged. By the early 1930s a half-dozen Brazilian cities were highly industrialized and provided for most domestic consumption. The growth of industry fostered the expansion of the middle class, working class, and industrial elite, many of whose interests were increasingly at odds with Brazil's powerful coffee-planter class.

Urban renewal and beautification transformed Rio de Janeiro, São Paulo, and other capitals into attractive places to live. Brazil's culture, a blend of African, indigenous, and Portuguese elements, became globally known, as movies shot in Rio glamorized its beaches and samba music invaded dance halls throughout the Western world. Rio's pre-Lenten Carnival, in particular, became a symbol of revelry that still equals New Orleans's Mardi Gras. Tourism further publicized Brazil's colorful attractions.

The nagging perception of Brazil's's racial and cultural backwardness seemed to evaporate with signs of urban progress. Universities opened, and a number of states upgraded their education systems. European immigrants flooded the cities of the southeast, adding a cosmopolitan, more European flavor to the region. The army was professionalized in the early twentieth century, and universal military service was justified as a way to raise levels of literacy, hygiene, physical fitness, and nutrition among the masses. Along with expanded education, universal conscription became an avenue to instruct Brazil's poor about what it meant to be a modern Brazilian citizen, including their responsibility to the new republic. Brazil seemed on the way to becoming Europeanized and modern, like the United States.

But the experience of progress was not evenly shared. Southeastern Brazil, the location of large, thriving cities like São Paulo and Rio and of the profitable industrial and coffee sectors, became associated with the most modern ideas and trends. The former sugar-growing areas of the northeast, however, where a large ex-slave population still lived, were increasingly portrayed as backward and poor. Southeastern elites emphasized regional difference and touted their own modernity, initiative, and even whiteness while decrying, in highly racialized terms, the blackness, traditionalism, and idleness of northeasterners. This racially nuanced regionalism exacerbated inequality in the country across the twentieth century.[3]

Indeed, nothing was done to uplift over a million former slaves or their dependents, who increasingly clustered in favelas, or the shantytowns and tenement districts of regional and state capitals. And Brazil's huge population of African descent—the largest outside of Africa—suffered systematic disadvantages that constituted an unwritten form of racial discrimination. In the 1930s, intellectuals such as Gilberto Freyre called the country a racial democracy and claimed that racism did not exist because of the history of racial mixing, which incorporated the best cultural elements from all of Brazil's races. Yet, in reality, immigrants moved swiftly upward in income and status, supported by elites who, infused with the scientific racism of the day, encouraged immigration from Europe as a way to whiten the population (branqueamento). Meanwhile, Afro-Brazilians remained at the bottom of the socioeconomic ladder.

Immigrant labor from Europe was most sought after in the early 1900s to work in the higher-paying jobs in the rapidly growing industrial sector. For example, in São Paulo in 1915, immigrants made up 85 percent of the industrial workforce.[4] While there was little legal discrimination against blacks in the aftermath of the First Republic, which fed the myth of racial democracy decades later, most were still excluded from higher education, political offices, and business opportunities. Artistic and sports careers were the best they could aspire to. For the rest, in rural areas, life entailed laboring on large estates in situations sometimes barely better than slavery, while in urban areas, most blacks made a living as day laborers and domestic servants.

**Figure 14.2** Brazil's carnival celebrations, which date back to the eighteenth century, were suppressed as vulgar and dangerous until the 1930s. Since then, however, Rio's samba schools, like the one pictured here in 1941, have become a symbol of national culture. Courtesy Library of Congress.

Brazil's indigenous population and tropical forests likewise felt the impact of European-style modernization. Coffee planters had already denuded vast regions of the southeast, and cattle ranches had replaced native forests in central Brazil. The Amazon had not suffered major depredations from rubber production only because its gathering depended on native stands of trees. Rubber tappers living in jungle huts daily drained off buckets of latex, cured the rubber over fires, and sent the product on to Manaus or Belém for export.

Native peoples of Amazonia were not so fortunate, however, because their labor was required to produce latex. European and American factories, producing electrical goods, tires, and rubber articles of all sorts, consumed latex voraciously. Traveling merchants and brokers in the Amazon, called *aviadores* (lenders), created a system of exploitation similar to debt peonage in Mexico and Guatemala. In addition, diseases from the outside world caused mini-epidemics among indigenous villagers. In some regions, such as the Putumayo, outright slavery was reintroduced as a way to gather rubber.[5] Population losses would certainly have been greater except that after 1910 cheaper rubber from Asian plantations drove Amazon rubber almost completely out of the market. Manaus's sumptuous opera house, a symbol of the region's once-extravagant wealth, fell into disrepair.

In many ways Brazil's hyper-federal political system failed to effectively govern a country that was undergoing rapid social and economic change. With an impractical constitution and archaic institutions, the government's leaders seemed increasingly out of touch with the nation's progress. By the 1920s the tensions caused by government ineffectiveness erupted into major challenges to the state. Far and away the biggest challenge came in a series of military rebellions called the Tenente Revolts (*tenente* means "lieutenant" in Portuguese). Civil-military relations had not been smooth since the early days of the First Republic, and became worse as the military became more professional. In 1922, several hundred officer cadets seized army installations to demand reforms, including more effective and open government. Their revolt was put down brutally, and those who survived were jailed or fled into exile. In 1924 the survivors and other cadets captured the capital of São Paulo and held it for nearly a month to protest their mistreatment and express their frustrations. When dislodged, they embarked on the Great March through the Brazilian backlands, which eventually covered twenty-four thousand kilometers and lasted over two years. The rebels disbanded in early 1927, but their cry for reforms left a powerful impression on educated Brazilians (see chapter 15).

Other sectors began to organize to change or overthrow the Brazilian government. The Communist Party, founded in 1922, managed to win some converts among intellectuals and labor leaders in Rio and São Paulo, and elected several representatives to city councils in 1928. Catholic leaders, dismayed at the general decline of religiosity since the separation of church and state in 1889, sought to resuscitate their moral and civil leadership through political means. Still other groups promoted nationalism, education, military defense, and public health. Building a stronger nation preoccupied concerned citizens.

A vigorous artistic revival, called modernismo, also arose in the 1920s. As seen in chapter 10, its proponents rejected the romantic and naturalistic aesthetics of Europe and tried to give expression to authentic Brazilian styles in painting, literature, music, sculpture, and even architecture. They chose the unlikely metaphor of cannibalism to convey their desire to eat and digest, not merely to copy, foreign artistic forms. Their leading journal, *Antropofagia* (Cannibalism), conveyed to readers the latest developments and experiments in modernist art.

Modernismo's defining moment came in 1922, when aesthetic rebels hosted the first Modern Art Week in São Paulo. There, for several days practitioners of the new styles showed off their paintings, read their writings, and held debates over the future of Brazil's culture. It was an artistic declaration of independence. By the 1950s, São Paulo's periodic exhibitions had become institutionalized in the *bienal*, a recurring event in even-numbered years that alternated with the Venice Biennale.

Visual artists in São Paulo made by far the most striking impressions. Paintings by Anita Malfatti, Victor Brecheret, and Di Cavalcanti blended European expressionism and cubism with scenes from Brazil and nativist themes. Later Cândido Portinari reflected Rio-based visions of the modernist aesthetic, with striking paintings of the *cidade maravilhosa* (the marvelous city), as Rio inhabitants referred to their city. Meanwhile, sculptors and architects wrought work that influenced global styles, including Oscar Niemeyer, one of the world's foremost figures in the development of modern architecture in the mid-twentieth century.

Novels, poems, plays, and musical performances enriched the offerings in São Paulo. Mario de Andrade emerged as something of a poet laureate of the decade. His famous *Macunaíma* became a best seller when it appeared in 1928 and later became a film. This rambling allegory of the Brazilian Everyman traces the history of the country through the experiences of its anti-hero, Macunaíma. Spiced with irony, wit, folklore, sex, and social criticism, this work strove to define a genuinely national genre.

Meanwhile, Heitor Villa-Lobos composed and conducted orchestral pieces based on folk music that used native instruments along with traditional ones. He sought to portray musically the lives of farmers, Indians, ranchers, and city dwellers. His lush arrangements evoked the sense of great jungles and savannas stretching across the continent. He remains Brazil's best-known composer of all time.

Accompanying these currents of artistic, intellectual, and political renewal came more forceful expressions of labor and peasant dissent. Unions, often under the leadership of anarchists and syndicalists, formed federations and called numerous general strikes between 1917 and 1919. Although these failed for the most part—in part due to state repression—and strike activity diminished in the 1920s, workers had taken important steps by asserting their rights. Politicians increasingly sought to address labor rights and to win workers' votes. By the late 1920s a kind of proto-populism arose in Rio de Janeiro to push for action. Amid the rapid rise of industry, which combined modern production with poor working conditions and urban poverty, many citizens believed that the government needed to address workers' rights and union representation, the so-called social question.

Brazil's peasants, on the other hand, had no clear means of organizing to improve their lives. Coronéis and their enforcers kept tight control over the rural masses, and they could always call in state and federal troops to back them up. Periodically the rural poor would erupt into violent confrontations with local authorities, only to be massacred by troops from the outside.

In addition, some regions fell under the grip of bandit gangs, like those of Lampião and Antônio Silvino. These two bandit leaders operated in arid northeastern Brazil, away from population centers and beyond the reach of authorities. For years they lived off the poor people and towns of the interior. Originally gunmen recruited by the great landowners, these two became freelance criminals. Their renown as outlaws along with their patronage toward their followers and occasional mercy for the poor turned them into folk heroes among some. They were finally hunted down and killed in the 1930s. In the end, the First Republic was overthrown not by the tenentes, the laborers, the peasants, the communists, or any other disgruntled sector of Brazilian society. Instead, a military revolt in the states of Rio Grande do Sul and Minas Gerais against the federal government and the state of São Paulo smashed the regime.

According to the café com leite agreement to alternate regional leaders in the presidential office, the outgoing governor of Minas Gerais should have been the sole candidate in 1930. The president reneged, however, and put his hand-picked successor, the governor of São Paulo, up for election. The governor of Minas Gerais, in turn, nominated his counterpart from Rio Grande do Sul, a little-known lawyer and former army private named Getúlio Vargas. He hoped to intimidate the president and force a compromise.

The president, however, stood firm and rigged the election in his candidate's favor. In mid-1930 the losers decided to mount a revolt to overthrow the government. They acted in October, and after several weeks the army high command stepped in. Fearing a bloodbath, the generals decided to remove the sitting president and usher in a rebel government, headed by Vargas. The rebels took over in October 1930, promptly labeling their victory the Revolution of 1930.

The rebels roundly denounced the First Republic elites for having done too little for the nation. Few of the presidents, mostly of European descent, had been memorable. Little social legislation had been written, let alone enacted. The educational system remained in the hands of state and local authorities, who, like their counterparts in the former empire, did not wish to tax themselves to educate the masses. The coffee protection programs largely defended the profits of planters and exporters in the state of São Paulo. Domestic industry gradually replaced imported goods, but consumers now paid more for inferior goods and workers had few rights.

The First Republic elites could certainly boast some accomplishments. Relative peace and plenty reigned; no foreign wars touched Brazil; the territory had been enlarged by 350,000 square miles without conflict; foreign investments had soared while the public debt remained modest; and Brazil had won new respect from foreigners impressed with its cities, resources, and energetic cultural and intellectual life.

Perhaps the strongest indictment of the First Republic was that it had not paid attention to electoral politics even as its neighbors in Argentina and Chile were engaged in some of the biggest experiments with mass politics of the day. Only a tiny fraction of the public voted, and their efforts were usually invalidated by fraud. No loyalty had been generated between an active and supportive electorate and an effective government, as patronage continued its hold on national and regional politics. As in 1889, the masses stood by idly in 1930 when soldiers overthrew the government and ushered in a new, more modern era. Brazil would never be the same again.

### The "Social Question" in Getúlio Vargas's 1929 Platform Speech in Rio de Janeiro

"We cannot ignore the social question in Brazil, one of the problems that must be taken up seriously by the authorities. The scant social legislation on the books is rarely applied, or is enforced only sporadically. This despite our obligations as signatories to the Versailles Treaty and as a member of the International Labor Organization, whose standards we do not uphold.

"If our government's protective tariffs give great profits to industrialists, then we should also give some protection to the workers, providing them with a comfortable and stable existence and help with sickness and old-age benefits.

"Women and children working in factories and stores receive special protection in civilized countries, yet such rules are unknown here.

"The federal and state governments must coordinate their efforts in order to produce a unified Labor Code. Urban as well as rural workers require legislation covering their labor rights, depending upon local circumstances. The Code should cover education, hygiene, nutrition, housing; protection of women, children, the infirm and the aged; and credit, salaries, and even recreation, such as sports and popular arts.

"We should create agricultural and vocational schools, inspect conditions in our factories and mills, clean up swamps, build workers' housing, and enforce laws on vacations, minimum wages, and consumer cooperatives.

"In the cities, where a large industrial proletariat exists, the situation can easily be improved. Workers should have access to telephones, electricity, and paved streets."

*A Revolução Nacional,* 1930, in authors' collections.

## NATION-STATE AND POPULISM IN PERU IN THE 1920S

Peru's history since independence has been more tumultuous, yet also more fascinating, than those of many other Latin American countries. The nation's trajectory rose and fell abruptly, shaken by heroes and scoundrels, earthquakes, booms and busts, and world events seemingly beyond Peruvians' control. During the 1920s, however, Peru looked as though it would break out of this pattern and achieve stability and progress. The reasons why it did not are both dramatic and suggestive of the causes for longer term volatility in Peru.

One person, Augusto Leguía, gave Peru its façade of stability and prosperity in the 1920s. In most ways an unremarkable politician, Leguía swept into and out of office in the early twentieth century without making many waves. A leader in the Civilista Party, he had won election and served most of the 1908 to

1912 presidential term. Although his party stood for reducing the role of military intervention in politics, it was often guilty of invoking it.

Leguía was also the beneficiary of a climate of unrest and renovation infusing the nation in the early twentieth century. A middle class had arisen in major cities and worked to modernize the society and gain access to political power. This meant, among other things, recognizing Peru's most marginalized peoples: the indigenous population and the workers. It also meant adopting new institutional forms, such as the separation of church and state, which was achieved in the Constitution of 1919. The spirit of the times combined hopeful expectation with a desire for steady leadership. Leguía satisfied both for more than a decade, from 1919 to 1930.

As a civilian, Leguía provided stable government punctuated with periodic elections (he himself was reelected twice). A well-traveled and educated man, he realized the need to cultivate public opinion. He dubbed his administration the Patria Nueva (New Fatherland), charged with implementing the new constitution. He devoted much attention to mingling with crowds while posing as a citizen president and to convincing newspapers to treat him favorably in their pages.

In fact, Leguía was an urbane dictator, along the lines of Benito Mussolini in Italy and Primo de Rivera in Spain during those years. He also recognized the importance of controlling the military, so he kept the army and navy loyal to him by providing them pay increases and expensive new armaments. Given the favorable circumstances of the 1920s, it was not difficult to keep most elite and middle-class Peruvians satisfied, and his elections were at least honest.

Leguía took in more state revenues than any other president before him and many since. The 1920s brought great prosperity to Peru, based on exports of minerals and agricultural products. Some of Peru's exports were traditional—for example, sugar, silver, cotton—whereas others responded to twentieth-century demands—for example, petroleum, rubber, and copper. In any event, jobs were plentiful, businesses profited, and many Peruvians found themselves moving into the middle or working class.

Leguía also borrowed enormous sums of money from the New York and London bond markets. He courted U.S. businesses and investments and initiated an ambitious program of public works. Construction of roads, railroads, ports, and public buildings went on throughout the 1920s. Thus, the modest social and economic reforms that he undertook met with public approval.

The changes that Leguía introduced in Peru had limited impact, both structurally and spatially. He gave in to worker and student protests and created a department to provide workers with disability insurance and to oversee industrial relations. But most Peruvians did not belong to unions and hence were ineligible for these benefits. He recognized indigenous rights in some parts of the Andes, an important step in a population that was in the majority indigenous. But he also revived the hated mita work system, which obliged Indians to provide free labor for public works. He guaranteed citizens basic civil rights yet routinely violated them when he felt threatened by criticism.

Many Peruvians, especially those whose precarious middle-class lives depended upon government jobs or contracts, believed that the country needed Leguía's firm, steady hand. They were definitely in the minority, however, because vast numbers of citizens had no say in government and did not feel represented by Leguía and his people. Even after the reforms of the independence period, which erased colonial-era legal distinctions regarding "Indians," Peru's indigenous population was treated unequally, and Indians were excluded from full citizenship. In the early 1900s, an indigenista movement emerged, led by middle-class intellectuals seeking to incorporate Peru's indigenous population into the nation materially and culturally. It foundered under Leguía, however, who himself promoted hispanismo, or a celebration of the Hispanic race, values, and culture as the basis of the Peruvian nation. Therefore, under Leguía, the highlands indigenous population remained excluded and continued to avoid contact with government in Lima, which intruded into their lives only to extract labor, taxes, military service, votes, or all of the above. They often limited contact to selling their potatoes and hand-woven textiles to urban merchants.

The rural workers along the coastal valleys, who toiled on estates producing sugar, cotton, vegetables, pisco (brandy), and fruit, labored under systems of exploitation hardly better than the days of slavery. Even the urban poor benefited little from the affluence of the 1920s. So the stability of the Leguía era was only a lull in the traditionally conflictive politics of Peru, masking for a time what remained a highly divided nation.

Another Peruvian leader, Víctor Raúl Haya de la Torre (1895–1979), had his finger on the pulse of the people. He emerged as a leader in the 1920s and played a prominent role in public affairs until his death. Haya, as he was known to his followers, grew up in the provincial capital of Trujillo in the north. His father had been a school principal and intellectual, so as a youth Haya had been exposed to a great variety of writers. This included Peruvian radicals like the self-taught José Carlos Mariátegui (1894–1930), a leading socialist thinker in Latin America and the founder of the Peruvian Communist Party, who saw Indians, not the urban proletariat, as Peru's primary oppressed class. It also included Manuel González Prada (1848–1918), who condemned elite exclusion and oppression of Peru's indigenous majority and called for it to rise up in rebellion against the ruling class.

Haya was more realistic about the ethnic, class, and regional differences dividing Peru—and also more passionate about reconciling his fellow Peruvians and leading them into a better future. He became, in fact, one of the great messianic populists of Latin America, calling for a multiclass alliance of workers, Indians, and the middle class to challenge imperialism.

**Figure 14.3** Haya de la Torre campaigning for president in 1931 election. Authors' collection.

In his early twenties, Haya moved to Lima for university study, and he soon became active in student politics. He vaulted into national affairs by helping to mediate the 1919 general strike in Lima. From there he founded a workers' university, like those that sprang up in Mexico and Russia after their revolutions. He was clearly a politician on the make, and he became known throughout Lima. He seemed equally at home in intellectual salons, union halls, and student gatherings.

In 1923, however, Haya played such a leading role opposing Leguía that he was jailed and deported. He wandered through the Americas and Europe for seven years; meanwhile, the Peruvian government shut down the schools and unions that he had helped create. In the long run, however, Haya converted his exile into martyrdom and a pilgrimage. He brilliantly turned adversity to his advantage.

Haya first visited Central America and Mexico. In Mexico City he founded a hemispheric movement called APRA—the Alianza Popular Revolucionaria Americana (American Popular Revolutionary Alliance)—a leftist (but not communist), anti-imperialist organization. His followers became known as Apristas. In fact, APRA never developed an international following, and most of its support came from Peruvians. In Central America Haya conferred with Panamanians who opposed U.S. canal policies and with the revolutionary

### Aprismo in Its Space and Time

This excerpt from the writing of Haya de la Torre in 1940 gives a flavor of his messianic thinking:

> Aprismo arises and acts in its Space (geographic, ethnic, and psychological) and its Time (era, economic state, moment of cultural and political development). With regard to Space, it appears on the Indoamerican Continent [Haya's term for heavily indigenous parts of Latin America] in a country such as Peru where problems of race, economics, education, production and communication are yet to be solved. On Time, Aprismo understands that it (historic time) is also relative. It is not chronological Time nor biological Time. It is a time marked by epochs of evolution, by levels of development, and by culture. So, the historic Time of the United States [for example] is not our Time in Peru, even though we both live chronologically in 1940. The United States, like European countries, has advanced in levels of civilization and culture, reaching an extraordinary level of development far from our own. This distance in culture and development between one people and another is (in historic Time), relative . . .
>
> For example: the Indoamerican nations [Ecuador, Peru, Bolivia, Guatemala, and Mexico] all live in the same (historic Time) on an analogous level of culture, of evolution, of civilization's advance. But that (historic time) of Indoamerican peoples is different from that experienced by the United States or Europe. Of course, that (historic time) can be similar to that of other peoples in the world, and even to some of the lesser developed peoples of Europe—such as New Zealand in Oceania, Egypt in Africa, and some of the Balkan countries in Europe. But that similarity in (historic time) is modified by the dissimilarity in (Space), which we have referred to above (geographic location, race, psychology, etc.) and so, as we consider differences in (Time), we have to consider, inseparably, differences in (Space) to achieve a unique and new principle, which we called (Historic Space Time).
>
> Now, Peru, as part of the Continent composed of twenty peoples which comprise the (historic Space Time of Indoamerica), possesses in Aprismo the genuine interpretation of its true politics.

Fragments of a June 1940 pamphlet, collected in Víctor Raúl Haya de la Torre, *Obras completas*, ed. Juan Mejía Baca (Lima: Librería Editorial, 1985), 1:174–90. Edited slightly for style.

Augusto Sandino, who fought U.S. imperialism in Nicaragua (see chapter 15). He also traveled in Europe for several years, where he observed and studied a variety of new doctrines and leadership styles. He felt energized by his travels, ready to return to his homeland to guide its destiny.

Haya was unable to put his ideas into effect until the overthrow of Leguía in 1930. In the eyes of many Peruvians, the president had become a dictator, serving the interests of business elites and foreigners and unable to sustain the economy after the Depression began in 1929. The dictator had to go; yet, it was just as wrong to blame him for the 1930s collapse as to credit him for the 1920s opulence—both were driven by outside forces. An ambitious army colonel,

Luis Sánchez Cerro, nevertheless led a revolt in the south that soon toppled and imprisoned Leguía. The deposed president perished in jail the following year.

The Sánchez Cerro junta promised a return to democracy and allowed exiles—including Haya—to return and participate in elections the following year. Haya's reputation had grown during his absence, and his party naturally nominated him for president. Sánchez Cerro also ran for president in 1931, setting the stage for one of the great populist contests of modern Latin America.

The 1931 Peruvian elections represented a sharp break with the past, promising democracy instead of dictatorship, youth instead of age. The APRA program that emerged during Haya's campaign combined remarkable vision with vague goals. Haya tried to incorporate too many philosophies and doctrines at once. He embraced mysticism, nationalism, socialism, and anti-imperialism. He claimed kinship with the ancient Incas. He championed the worker and the peasant farmer. Challenging the Hispanismo of Leguía and distinct from the cultural and racial emphases of indigenista movements elsewhere (see chapter 15), Haya viewed the exclusion of Indians from a communist perspective and focused on improving their economic condition as a way to incorporate them into the nation. His half-baked populism, delivered with such passion and sincerity, drew the masses to him spiritually.

Luis Sánchez Cerro also ran for president, and he, too, cut a flamboyant figure. Of mixed indigenous and Afro-Peruvian descent, he reveled in being a man of the people. He won the election by appealing to the same voters as Haya—the young, undereducated, poor, and mestizo population—and promptly jailed Haya, accusing APRA of plotting to overturn the election. His administration tried to aid the workers with more jobs and benefits, and it also attempted to transfer lands into the hands of peasants. But his meteoric career was cut short by an Aprista assassin's bullet in 1933, and the reform efforts languished.

For the next half-century, Haya moved in and out of the political limelight, and until the early 1960s he lived largely abroad. The army never forgave him for a massacre of soldiers and government officials by APRA followers during a 1932 uprising in Trujillo. The army effectively vetoed his ever serving as president, in one case after he had even won a slim electoral victory. The elite also feared that Haya would make good on his vague promises to restore the rights of the indigenous population and to provide decent wages for workers. Finally, the U.S. government found his nationalism too strident. So Haya never became president, even though he enjoyed massive popularity, and his party usually held a sizable share of seats in Congress.

Despite the fact that Haya never served as president, his program and popularity remained strong throughout the twentieth century. Never again would a leader like Augusto Leguía be able to govern the country while neglecting the interests of the masses.

## CONCLUSIONS AND ISSUES

A few common threads tie together the experiences of Panama, Brazil, and Peru in the first three decades of the twentieth century. Their economies grew in terms of technology, productivity, and output, and their engagement with world markets deepened. More and more citizens worked for salaries and belonged to the money economy. And increasing numbers of people took part in political campaigns, even though suffrage remained very restricted. The oligarchies that dominated governments in these countries were forced, however grudgingly, to take the interests of workers and peasant farmers more into account. Legislatures passed the first measures to protect the rights of the poor.

These countries exhibited the outward appearances of nation-states—they possessed stable governments, a monopoly on coercion, and territorial integrity—yet, their societies remained segmented and fragile. Large indigenous and immigrant sectors, in some regions a majority, did not fully identify with their nations' leaders. Rural and urban lifestyles were so different as to be almost irreconcilable. No easy ways existed for leaders to imbue their people with a sense of unity, and few tried more than a handful of half-hearted reforms aimed at reconciling the rural-urban divide and incorporating the masses into the life of the nation. During the tense era of the Great Depression and World War II, many societies grew even more polarized.

### Discussion Questions

What were the causes behind Panama's independence from Colombia and the construction of the canal there?

How did the United States inhibit the emergence of Panama as a sovereign nation-state?

How were Panama's civil-military relations different from those in most Latin American nations?

What political and social factors kept Brazil from becoming a democracy in the early twentieth century?

How did city life in Brazil differ from rural life?

What people and forces caused the overthrow of the First Republic in 1930?

What factors underpinned stability and order in Peru in the early twentieth century?

Was President Leguía a caudillo, a populist, or a democrat? How did he manage to govern the country for two terms without major opposition?

Describe Haya de la Torre's genius for inspiring the masses. How would you describe his political philosophy?

### Timeline

| | |
|---|---|
| 1889–1930 | Brazil's First Republic |
| 1903 | Panama's independence from Colombia, treaty with the United States |
| 1904–14 | U.S. construction of Panama Canal |

| 1908–12 | First administration of Augusto Leguía of Peru |
|---|---|
| 1912–24 | Administrations of President Belisario Porras of Panama |
| 1914–18 | World War I defense of Panama Canal |
| 1919–30 | Last administrations of Augusto Leguía in Peru |
| 1924 | Víctor Raúl Haya de la Torre founds APRA |
| 1930 | Brazilian revolt that brought Getúlio Vargas to power |
| 1931 | Haya de la Torre defeated by Luis Sánchez Cerro in national election |
| 1932 | APRA revolt, massacre of army officers |
| 1933 | President Luis Sánchez Cerro assassinated |

## Keywords

Acción Comunal
Alianza Popular Revolucionaria Americana (APRA)
aviadores
Carnival
coffee valorization
coronéis
favela
hispanismo
Panama Canal
Patria Nueva
politics of the governors
samba
Tenente Revolts

# Early Revolutionaries

## Mexico, Brazil, and Nicaragua

### Land and Liberty

In late 1911, agrarian leader Emiliano Zapata declared his manifesto against the Porfirio Díaz (1876–1911) and Francisco Madero (1911–1913) governments for failing to fulfill promises to the Mexican peasantry that date from the time of Juárez in the 1850s and 1860s. Named the Plan de Ayala, its slogan proclaimed Land and Liberty. It called for the peasants who tilled the soil to become the owners of the land, restoring to them the right to a decent and honorable life. Notice the strident use of fighting words: "oppressors," "traitors," "tyrants." This was a powerful call to arms in the name of agrarian reform and the righting of wrongs.

> We give notice: that [regarding] the fields, timber, and water which the landlords, científicos, or bosses have usurped, the pueblos or citizens who have the titles corresponding to those properties will immediately enter into possession of that real estate of which they have been despoiled by the bad faith of our oppressors, maintaining at any cost with arms in hand the mentioned possession.
>
> In virtue of the fact that the immense majority of Mexican pueblos and citizens are owners of no more than the land they walk on, suffering the horrors of poverty without being able to improve their social condition in any way or to dedicate themselves to Industry or Agriculture, because lands, timber, and water are monopolized in a few hands, for this cause there will be expropriated the third part of those monopolies from the powerful proprietors of them, with prior indemnification, in order that the pueblos and citizens of Mexico may obtain ejidos, colonies, and foundations for pueblos, or fields for sowing or laboring, and the Mexicans' lack of prosperity and well-being may improve in all and for all.
>
> [Regarding] landlords, científicos, or bosses who oppose the present plan directly or indirectly, their goods will be nationalized and the two third parts which [other-

wise would] belong to them will go for indemnification of war, pensions for widows and orphans of the victims who succumb in the struggle for the present plan.

The insurgent military chiefs of the Republic who rose up with arms in hand at the voice of Don Francisco I. Madero to defend the plan of San Luis Potosí, and who oppose with armed force the present plan, will be judged traitors to the cause which they defended and to the fatherland, since at present many of them, to humor the tyrants, for a fistful of coins, or for bribes or connivance, are shedding the blood of their brothers who claim the fulfillment of the promises which Don Francisco I. Madero made to the nation.[1]

## DEFINING REVOLUTION

Revolutions have occurred throughout history, yet scholars continue to debate what defines one. The concept is easily misused—for example, to speak of a Roosevelt or a Reagan revolution in the United States is inaccurate—so we should begin with a working definition:

> Revolutions in fact are political struggles of great intensity, initiated by political crises within particular historical societies and resolved . . . by the creation of a political capacity to confront the historical problems of these societies in ways that their pre-revolutionary regimes had proved wholly incapable of doing.[2]

By this definition, true revolutions are rare and cataclysmic events. Some of the best known in world history were those in France (1789), Russia (1917), and China (1949).

In describing the general patterns of revolution, historian Crane Brinton notes that after several years they lapse into a "reign of terror." He enumerates the causes of terror in this way:

> First, there is what we may call the habit of violence, the paradoxical situation of a people conditioned to expect the unexpected. The more violent and terroristic periods of our revolutions come only after a series of troubles have prepared the way.
>
> . . . a second and more important variable is the pressure of a foreign and civil war. War necessities help explain the rapid centralization of the government of the Terror. . . .
>
> Third, there is the newness of the machinery of this centralized government. The extremists are certainly not . . . altogether without experience in handling men, though they have dealt with revolutionists, not with all men.
>
> Fourth, this is also a time of acute economic crisis—not merely what we now call a depression, but a definite shortage of the necessities of life.
>
> . . . fifth variable, class struggles, clearly appears in the crisis . . . our sixth variable is . . . based on observation of the behavior of the relatively small group of leaders formed during the revolution and now in control of the government of the Terror.
>
> Finally, there is . . . the element of religious faith . . . heroic attempts to close once and for all the gap between human nature and human aspirations.[3]

Revolutionaries are even less understood than the upheavals they led. Over the centuries, they have been denounced as bandits, madmen, demons, and villains. Yet, they were often revered and idolized by their followers, sometimes rising into the hallowed pantheon of national heroes.

Latin America has experienced three genuine revolutions: those that began in Haiti in 1791, Mexico in 1910, and Cuba in 1959. Each continues to influence the course of its country's history. Latin America has also witnessed a large number of revolutionary movements, some of which succeeded partially, like that of Peru between 1968 and 1975 and that of the Sandinistas in Nicaragua between 1979 and 1990. Their impact, too, was often large. Beyond these, Latin America has had innumerable coups or insurrections over the past two hundred years, though their impact has been much narrower than the major revolutionary events. A key question among scholars is why some rebellions stop short of becoming major upheavals, while others grow into full-scale revolutions. Important factors that can encourage revolutions include an international context that fosters instability, problems of political legitimacy, intellectual movements, and mass involvement.

Proximity to the United States seemed to be important in Latin America because two of the biggest revolutions occurred in the neighboring countries of Mexico and Cuba. The United States had already played a major role in the independence movements, serving as inspiration and as supplier of arms. But U.S. influence in revolutionary upheavals has been more complicated than simply supplying arms and ideas. On one hand, the United States stood for the ideals that many revolutionaries evoked, like equality, justice, and democracy. On the other hand, the United States represented capitalist exploitation and imperialism, and anti-U.S. nationalism often fueled revolutionary fervor. U.S. involvement in the region also destabilized domestic politics, as seen in chapter 13.

Certainly the rise of communism as a rival model of state organization served as a catalyst for revolutionary forces in Latin America, helping to account for their antagonism toward the United States. The first communist state, the Union of Soviet Socialist Republics (USSR), was consolidated out of the ruins of imperial Russia in 1917. The United States and the USSR viewed each other as constant threats during the seventy-five years of their rivalry. Any Latin American nation that pursued major reforms or revolutionary changes that resembled the communism of the USSR automatically faced U.S. opposition. As we will see, however, the U.S. response to revolution in Latin America has usually been ambivalent.

In addition, revolutions occurred when times were getting better for most people and they had created rising expectations, but continued improvement was threatened by government, the ruling class, or some other actor. This moment of failed expectations, combined with corrupt elections that closed off the democratic path to change, often accounted for middle-class involvement in revolutionary movements. Indeed, members of the middle class tended to be the intellectual and military leaders of revolutions.

> ### The Revolutionary Process
>
> "The revolutionary process in these countries [Mexico (1910–1940), Bolivia (1943–1964), Guatemala (1944–1954), and Cuba (1956–1961)] can be divided into three stages. In the first stage, rebel movements organized and overthrew the old regime, usually dominated by military dictators. In the second stage, the rebels gained control of the governmental apparatus and, instead of revolutionizing society, established reformist governments; some of these governments were overthrown by force. After an interval, the revolutionaries returned to power and established revolutionary governments. At this point, the third stage and revolutionary change itself began: the revolutionaries gained control of and revolutionized the political and governmental systems, seized land and other properties, and introduced changes in foreign relations."
>
> Cole Blasier, *Hovering Giant: U.S. Responses to Revolutionary Change in Latin America, 1910–1985* (Pittsburgh: University of Pittsburgh Press, 1985), p. 4.

Extreme disparity in wealth and the cultural gap between elites and poor provided yet another reason for revolution in Latin America. The former tended to glorify European lifestyles, languages, and aesthetic norms, and took home the lion's share of national wealth, whereas the latter identified with indigenous and African cultures and often struggled not only with poverty but also economic insecurity. When middle-class intellectuals gave expression to their frustrations and sense of injustice, many poor eagerly joined in to fan the flames of revolution and carry the movements forward.

## THE MEXICAN REVOLUTION

Mexico, one of the most stable and advanced of the Latin American countries at the turn of the twentieth century, plunged into a devastating civil war in 1910 that became a genuine revolution. Some of the most colorful—and ruthless—people in its history played leading roles in that revolution, and the history of the hemisphere was permanently altered.

The revolution's causes were many. Relations with the United States figured prominently in the revolution, and anti-American sentiment characterized the period. Many Mexican elites in the north resented the outsize role of U.S. land and mineral investments, and northern workers resented bias against them by foreign owners and managers. The dominance of U.S. bankers and investors also stoked fears that Mexico's científicos had sold out to foreigners. Ultimately, however, internal factors proved equally decisive.

The long dictatorship of General Porfirio Díaz (called the Porfiriato), covered in chapter 8, came to an unexpected and humiliating end in 1911. By then, a vicious recession in 1907 and 1908 had bankrupted many businesses and left over a million workers unemployed, exacerbating the growing inequality that was a product of late nineteenth-century liberal policies.

Declining standards of living provoked huge workers' strikes, especially in the mining and textile industries. Most of these were put down brutally by rural police or occasionally by security forces from across the border, but not before they had radicalized workers. Class struggle reached alarming levels by 1910, but Díaz did not heed the words of anarchists, socialists, labor leaders, intellectuals, and even some government figures suggesting that revolt was imminent.

One of Díaz's severest critics was Ricardo Flores Magón, who was trained as a lawyer and long had been active in student organizing. In 1900, he and his two brothers founded the opposition newspaper *Regeneración.* The following year he helped organize a movement that later became the Liberal Party of Mexico. Harassed and jailed on numerous occasions, Ricardo and his brothers eventually fled to the United States and Canada, where they continued to publish their opposition paper.

While in exile, they were increasingly drawn to anarchists such as Mikhail Bakunin and Emma Goldman, and in 1907 they changed the paper's name to *Revolución.* In 1906 and 1908 they issued calls for revolt, but in both cases U.S. agents thwarted their actions. After his conversion to anarchism, Ricardo Flores Magón became vehemently anti-capitalist and anti-American, calling the United States a "nation of pigs." The Flores Magón brothers kept alive the radical wing of the opposition movement against Díaz, though their influence in Mexico was limited due to their exile.

Díaz, meanwhile, had grown old and careless, unmindful of the maneuvers by his ambitious associates to replace him. For a time he considered retiring, and in 1908 he even stated as much to U.S. reporter James Creelman, saying that he would not run for president in 1910 and that the elections would be free and fair. Yet, the man who took office in 1876 under the slogan of Effective Suffrage, No Reelection decided to run again. The 1910 election would definitely be his last, though, so he did not give it much attention. He expected it to be like the seven others he had rigged before: a mere formality. Instead, the Creelman interview set off a political firefight.

Francisco I. Madero, the young scion of an extremely wealthy family from the northern state of Coahuila, decided to challenge Díaz for the presidency in 1910. Like some other northern elites, he had become frustrated by the corrupt politics of Díaz and his científico cronies in Mexico City and sought a more inclusive regime. He announced his candidacy and developed a reformist platform, which he touted in several regional campaign trips. Something of a mystic, Madero believed he had a calling to rid the country of dictatorship, to provide honest democratic government, and to modernize the economy through education and better administration. Hardly in touch with the peasant masses and far from a social radical, Madero nonetheless addressed issues that mattered to millions of Mexicans. In short, he offered hope for a better future, including hope for Mexico's rapidly growing middle class, which felt increasingly frustrated by a political system that promised progress but seemed only to serve Díaz and his cronies. His candidacy took off in 1910.

Díaz decided to eliminate this unexpected threat by the usual methods, having Madero jailed and rigging the vote count in his own favor. Election officials announced a Díaz landslide, acknowledged a few opposition ballots, and then declared Díaz the winner. It looked like business as usual. Díaz soon after celebrated his eightieth birthday and even presided over a lavish celebration of the centennial of the Hidalgo revolt of 1810. He did not recognize the peril of his situation and the irony of the commemoration.

Madero escaped and made his way to Texas before unleashing a protest in the form of a "letter from jail." He called it the Plan de San Luis Potosí. Its main slogan was Effective Suffrage, No Reelection. He declared the end of the politics of patronage and corruption. He made vague reference to restoring lands stolen from indigenous villages. He decried the lack of schools, widespread illiteracy, and the enslavement and shipment of Yaqui Indians to labor in the henequen fields of Yucatán.

The Plan de San Luis Potosí was not a blueprint for radical socioeconomic reform—it neither endangered private property nor disrupted the evolutionary progress that Madero believed Mexico should make. Still, it offered hope of some change to millions of downtrodden Mexicans. Most importantly, it rallied an array of different groups to take up arms to overthrow the Díaz dictatorship on November 20, 1910.

To the surprise of many, including Díaz, in late 1910 a number of revolutionary movements sprang up throughout the country in answer to Madero's call. The mule driver/merchant Pascual Orozco led a powerful military contingent in the north, in league with the rebel governor Abraham González. Orozco was not particularly committed to Madero, but he used the allegiance to the Plan de San Luis Potosí to launch his movement. By January 1911 he had taken Mexicali and Chihuahua City in northwestern Mexico. His early successes attracted other local military bands, notably that of former bandit Francisco "Pancho" Villa. Their followers came from the northern ranch workers, who had long chafed at the enormous power of large landowners and who resented unequal treatment by foreign bosses and owners.

In the south, Emiliano Zapata also raised a revolutionary banner. Though the grievances of his followers were also rooted in agrarian causes, the reasons were distinct from those in the north. Zapata inherited lands that his family

**Figure 15.1** Colonel Pancho Villa in 1911; his military prowess at the Battle of Ciudad Juárez was widely known. Bain News Service. Courtesy Library of Congress.

had owned in the village of Anenecuilco, in the state of Morelos. For generations the Zapatas had served as its leaders. Therefore, it was natural for Zapata to be elected mayor and to take up the villagers' land claims against the encroachments of large sugar plantations. Unable to get satisfaction, Zapata recruited a band of armed followers to recover their lands, by force if necessary. The Zapatistas, as they came to be known, rose up against Díaz in early 1911 and then spent the next eight years fighting to get land reform onto the revolutionary agenda.

The breakthrough for Madero came in May 1911—ironically, in spite of his own orders. That month, Orozco and Villa wanted to take Ciudad Juárez, the large and strategic city on the Rio Grande, bordering El Paso, Texas. Madero feared a bloodbath and at the last minute attempted to call off the attack. Orozco defied him, however, and managed to take the city after several days of intense fighting. This victory turned the tide and persuaded Díaz, who by now had lost U.S. backing, to step down from the presidency. As he left for exile in Paris, he reportedly exclaimed, "Madero has unleashed a tiger, let's see if he can tame it." Díaz died in exile several years later.

Madero, heir apparent to the presidency, began a triumphal train journey to the capital. But with their common enemy now in exile, the revolutionaries found that they had little to unite them, and many quickly began to pursue their own paths. Zapata's peasants had begun seizing lands and had taken over many towns and garrisons. Villa and others in the north had stolen cattle and provisions, and they now began to seize large estates and to control factories and towns. And as yet, Madero had no proven revolutionary credentials, though all looked to him expectantly.

Great celebrations erupted upon Madero's arrival in Mexico City, but very quickly his popularity faded. He refused to be sworn in as president until a new election could be held late in 1911. Once sworn in, he insisted on governing with the consent of an unpopular Congress, elected during the Díaz period. He appointed conciliatory politicians from the upper class who would not accept the radical measures pushed by Zapata's peasants and Villa's rancheros. Finally, Madero lacked a strong sense of survival in politics. Raised in a wealthy family and educated at the Sorbonne and Berkeley, he was an idealist who trusted that good intentions and smart ideas would carry the day. That was a naive, and ultimately fatal, mistake.

Madero soon faced enemies and conspirators on all sides. Congress refused to pass even the mildest reform legislation that he proposed. Conservatives who had worked with the Díaz regime could not accept this newcomer and so started plotting a military coup. And the revolutionaries grew impatient with his lack of reforms and took matters into their own hands. When Madero sent envoys to coax them into line, they balked and prepared to fight once more. The uneasy peace of 1911 quickly dissolved into challenges and new fighting.

Zapata left the fold first. Madero had insisted that lands could not be taken without agrarian reform legislation; thus, the seizures by Zapata's followers were illegal. Because Zapata's sole aims were to take back lands stolen by the big sugar plantations and to regain village control over local politics, he refused to comply. Madero dispatched General Victoriano Huerta to assert federal authority in the south, and Zapata found that he and his followers were once again fighting against the federal government. Soon Orozco and others also parted ways with Madero. Mexico plunged deeper into conflict.

The regular army, meanwhile, virtually collapsed from incompetence, graft, and an unwillingness to fight. Within a year, five regional skirmishes were

**Figure 15.2** Emiliano Zapata, shown here in 1911, became a revolutionary hero for his steady defense of village land rights against the encroachment by large, wealthy landowners. His refusal to compromise with other revolutionary leaders on this issue brought him great popular support but also resulted in his 1919 assassination by Carranza's allies. Bain News Service. Courtesy Library of Congress.

under way, and Madero's army was incapable of controlling any of them. In office only sixteen months, and committed to the democratic process and gradual reform, Madero could not satisfy the many demands made upon him, whether it was to reward followers, to distribute land, or even to appoint loyal military officers. Madero's end came in the form of a coup by Díaz supporters and partly engineered by U.S. ambassador Henry Lane Wilson.

General Huerta, allied with a nephew of Díaz and supported by Henry Lane Wilson, conspired to overthrow Madero, setting off a period referred to as the counterrevolution, the last grasp for power by Díaz supporters. Worse, after the coup, they assassinated Madero and his vice president during a

**Figure 15.3**
Soldados and soldaderas. Young soldiers of the Mexican Revolution and their female companions, the famous soldaderas, or camp followers. Bain News Service. Courtesy Library of Congress.

fake escape attempt. The coup shattered the nation. Madero's reputation, however, soared. Having failed as a reformer, he became a martyr of the revolution.

After Madero's death, the crisis deepened, and fighting spread across the land. In an odd twist, the new U.S. president, Woodrow Wilson, refused to recognize Huerta's government, since he had come to power by overthrowing a democratically elected president and because President Wilson had little faith in Huerta's ability to quell the spreading civil war. Opposition to Huerta soon coalesced around a clever and ambitious man, Venustiano Carranza, an elderly rancher and politician from Coahuila who had supported Madero. Carranza mobilized opposition to Huerta and won some acceptance by the United States. Calling his forces the constitutionalists, he seemed to have the support of Villa and Zapata, who were fighting Huerta, too. These politico-military positions created a giant north-south pincer movement against the Mexico City regime. The country sank into generalized civil war.

Women soldiers and camp followers, called *soldaderas,* played a major role in the revolution. Most who joined the fight did so by following a husband, father, or brother, though some went simply because it was the only way to survive amid the devastating violence. Some took up arms alongside the men in the battlefield, though most found provisions, cooked, transported messages and arms, were prostitutes, ministered to the wounded, and comforted the dying. Several, disguised as men, even commanded troops. Their support and feats of bravery led them to be celebrated in the famous *corridos,* or troubadour ballads popular among the masses. One especially famous soldadera, Adelita, led to the soldaderas being nicknamed the *adelitas.*

Concerned about the widespread violence and with an eye toward trying to determine Huerta's successor, the United States intervened directly in the spring of 1914 to try to tip the balance away from Huerta. Using the pretext of protesting the arrest of some U.S. sailors and after hearing of German arms heading to Huerta, the U.S. invaded the port of Veracruz. The occupation halted the flow of arms and revenues to Huerta. Now fighting a foreign invasion in addition to multiple revolutionary fronts, after some months Huerta resigned and fled the country, leaving the way open for rivals to claim power.

But once again, the revolutionaries could find little common ground to unite them. Villa and Zapata both aspired to push the revolution forward, but neither had the national vision or skills to command the country. They chose a weak compromise figure who took over the presidential palace in Mexico City, and each retreated to his regional base to continue fighting. Carranza, meanwhile, wisely moved his headquarters to Veracruz after it had been evacuated in November 1914 by U.S. forces, who purportedly left behind a huge cache of weapons for Carranza's forces. Carranza unleashed his best general, Álvaro Obregón, against Villa, and in several spectacular battles, Obregón defeated Villa and neutralized him militarily. Obregón lost an arm during one battle but fought on, becoming a legend among his soldiers. Zapata, sensing the turning tide, retreated to his stronghold in Morelos. From mid-1915 on, the conflict continued, though it lost intensity.

Villa, however, could still inflict serious damage in the northern deserts of Chihuahua and Durango. He chose the desperate measure of provoking the United States in the hope that U.S. intervention would weaken Carranza's power. The first provocation occurred when Villa's troops ambushed and murdered over a dozen U.S. mining engineers. Then Villa crossed the border and raided the town of Columbus, New Mexico, seizing cash and arms and killing more than a dozen Americans.

In early 1916 President Wilson, under increasing pressure to do something about border violations, sent General John "Black Jack" Pershing with ten thousand troops (the Punitive Expedition) into Mexico to capture Villa. Pershing was unable to find Villa, though he fought with his forces, provoking a protest from Carranza, who in early 1917 had been elected president. After nearly a year, Pershing was called back and subsequently assumed command of the U.S. expeditionary army sent to fight in Europe when the United States entered World War I.

Revolutionary leaders who were committed to change, including victorious General Álvaro Obregón, forced Carranza to convoke a constitutional convention in 1916. The 1917 Constitution, still in force today, followed nationalistic, secular, and socially progressive lines. It declared that the state would confiscate landholdings in excess of certain sizes, depending on the region, and distribute them to peasants. It restored the ejido system of ownership in which villages managed production communally. It also nationalized all subsoil mineral, water, and hydrocarbon rights. Henceforth, mines and wells could be worked only under concessions from the government. It subjugated the church to the state by nationalizing all religious property and prohibiting public displays of faith, including the wearing of clerical garb. It decreed universal free education. And it contained a full bill of rights for labor.

One of the most contentious issues to emerge in the convention was women's rights. Women had played a prominent role on the battlefields, and feminists such as Hermila Galindo had joined political clubs in support of Carranza. Indeed, Galindo had become Carranza's personal secretary, and he let her promote feminist causes from that position. He also sent her as his representative to Cuba and Colombia. Carranza even allowed her to submit an item to the convention calling for full female equality, though it was rejected and women were denied citizenship rights. Nevertheless, the 1917 Constitution helped qualify the Mexican upheaval as an authentic revolution.

The Zimmerman telegram proved another memorable incident of 1917. In this secret telegram, the German government, anticipating U.S. entry into World War I, proposed that Mexico join in alliance with Germany to fight against the U.S. In exchange, after Germany won the war, Mexico would receive the northwestern territories that it had lost in the Treaty of Guadalupe Hidalgo (1848). Carranza wisely ignored this offer. British agents, however, intercepted the telegram and made its contents public, provoking an indignant response in the United States that helped push Congress into declaring war. It also pushed the United States to recognize the new government of President Carranza, effectively ensuring Mexico's neutrality during the war.

The last few years of the revolution were relatively quiet. General Obregón grew disenchanted with Carranza's unwillingness to carry out reforms and left Mexico City for his estate in the north. Villa and Zapata were marginalized and then murdered several years later by government agents, Zapata in 1919 and Villa in 1923. The United States, preoccupied with ending the war in Europe and negotiating a peace, paid little attention to Mexico after the worst of the violence seemed to have passed.

At the end of his term in 1920, Carranza tried to handpick his own successor. At that time, many saw Obregón as Carranza's natural successor, but Carranza had other ideas. Obregón and his supporters raised an army and rode to Mexico City to make sure it would happen, and they ousted Carranza from office. While Carranza was on his way to Veracruz, where he intended to regroup and fight back, he was captured and executed. The ranking generals of the revolution chose Álvaro Obregón for president and oversaw his election in 1920. That marked the close of the most violent phase of the revolution, though just the beginning of revolutionary change.

## Vasconcelos and la Raza Cósmica

Few changes produced as profound a shift after the revolution than the reinvention of race and nation, a process led by the extraordinary activist and intellectual José Vasconcelos. Vasconcelos pressed the revolutionary governments to put in place new educational and cultural policies that aimed to incorporate Mexico's indigenous population into the nation.

Vasconcelos became both minister of education and rector of the National Autonomous University of Mexico (UNAM) in 1920. From these two positions, he became an intellectual leader who tried to develop the ideological foundations for a more inclusive Mexican nation. His most well known explanation for this came in *The Cosmic Race,* an account of his travels through South America in 1922. In it, he explored the origins of human life, arguing that geographic distance had led separate races to evolve on each of the major continents, including the indigenous people in the Americas.

Columbus changed all that, however, by setting off great waves of European migrations to the New World. The Europeans also brought millions of Africans to labor in their plantations and mines. In the late nineteenth century, Asians flocked to the Americas as well, as indentured workers and merchants. So the Americas, according to Vasconcelos, became the site of a racial reunification of the earth's peoples.

This great racial and cultural mixing, which Vasconcelos referred to as a "racial synthesis of the world," had produced a fifth race that he called *la raza cósmica* (the cosmic race).

By arguing for the raza cósmica, Vasconcelos refuted commonly held ideas about the region's racial inferiority, which were held both by international observers as well as by nineteenth-century Mexican positivists, who saw their power wane after the revolution. First, Vasconcelos debunked the idea that mestizaje, or racial mixing, leads to genetic deterioration. He argued instead that it actually brings gradual improvement in characteristics, similar to hybridization of plants and selective breeding of animals. Second, he stated that the tropical climates of much of Latin America represent no obstacle to the emergence of advanced civilizations. Most of the ancient world developed in the tropics, including the Maya, Aztec, and Inca empires. History simply did not uphold the notion that the tropics stifle humans' creative energies. The cosmic race had not developed its full potential, Vasconcelos said, merely because it was still emerging. In time the mixed races of Latin America would realize their full potential.

This remarkable, optimistic, and ethnocentric theory helped Mexican intellectuals and artists re-create their nation's past in a more inclusive light, and most Mexicans today proudly claim themselves to be mestizo. Aided by Vasconcelos and other government officials, mural artists painted vast depictions of Mexico's history, idealizing the pre-Columbian era. In contrast to late nineteenth-century social Darwinism, which had heralded whiteness and Europe, these paintings portrayed Indians, mestizos, and mulattoes as strong, productive, peaceful, and noble. Europeans, on the other hand, were seen either as partners of the indigenous people or as corrupt and degenerate. Combining nativist themes with modern art influences from Europe, muralists produced spectacular arrays of mural paintings in the decades after the revolution. Muralists received public commissions from the new revolutionary government to depict the country's great traditions in an array of public venues. They chose government buildings and other public places in Mexico City, Guanajuato, and Guadalajara in particular, using murals to instruct the masses in the new revolutionary version of the nation. The most stunning, perhaps, are Diego Rivera's murals in the presidential palace, showing panoramic scenes from pre-Columbian times to the mid-twentieth century. In Guadalajara, Ministry of Interior murals by José Clemente Orozco recreated scenes of the Conquest and Father Hidalgo's uprising.

## THE REVOLUTIONARIES

The old guard—epitomized by Huerta and Carranza—were not revolutionaries in the usual sense. Though each very different in political views, they were mature men in their fifties by the time they took part in the revolution and did not fit the profile of angry young rebels. In some ways, they were opportunists, moving in on the heels of dramatic events and seizing the initiative. They did embrace some reforms, and Carranza even courted the radicals, but they never intended to carry out a total overhaul of Mexico's society and economy. Both Huerta and Carranza died shortly after being forced out of power, Huerta by natural causes and Carranza by an assassin's bullet.

The true revolutionaries, on the other hand, followed dangerous paths and perished young. They were born within a few years of one another—between 1872 and 1880—and mostly came from northern Mexico. Only Zapata and the Flores Magóns were from the south. With the exception of Madero, they came from poor or modest origins. Several were mestizos. Most were businessmen, but their chances of prospering evaporated when the revolution broke out. Rather than lose everything, they joined the war. They were ambitious and anxious to get ahead, so they enlisted while in their thirties.

None of the young revolutionaries had formal military training. Instead, they learned to fight on the job. They possessed combat cunning and excellent tactical skills, and they intuitively practiced guerrilla warfare before it became standard procedure in mid-twentieth-century revolutions. The revolutionaries who succeeded all became generals, and they maintained some capacity for military action even after the fighting ended. They understood, as a later revolutionary would say, that power comes from the barrel of a gun.

The revolutionaries were smart, reasonably well educated (except Villa and Zapata), and appreciated professional expertise. They surrounded themselves with university-trained aides, usually lawyers, who could transform their wishes into decrees, press releases, and laws. These lawyers, for example, dominated the proceedings of the 1916–1917 constitutional convention. Without these aides, many of the measures that the revolutionaries advocated would not have been codified.

Few of the revolutionaries traveled overseas before entering politics, yet foreign contacts and examples seem to have been important in shaping their ideas and careers. Madero certainly nurtured his visionary ideals while studying abroad. Flores Magón derived his anarchist philosophy from European writings and honed it on the stone of U.S. capitalism. The other norteños (Villa, Orozco, González, and Carranza) had acquired suspicious views of U.S. economic and ideological influence. Most opposed U.S. impositions and tried to uphold Mexican national sovereignty. They saw U.S. intervention as a national humiliation, and the científicos as sell-outs to foreign capital.

Most of the revolutionaries sympathized with some tenets of socialism without being doctrinaire Marxists. More importantly, their sense of injustice derived from experience, empathy with poor people, shared suffering, and a vague desire to lessen the inequality and exclusion that had prevailed under the Porfiriato. They were too busy with politics and warfare, however, to devote much time to reflective analysis of ideology.

## UNEASY TWENTIES

After the burst of revolutionary activity in Mexico in the 1910s, Latin American politics seemed to calm down in the 1920s. Economic recovery and modern weapons purchased after World War I helped this process. Throughout the region, autocratic regimes kept the peace and managed to defuse labor and political radicalism through a mix of mild reforms and repression. In Mexico, Presidents Álvaro Obregón and Plutarco Elías Calles stabilized affairs, with Obregón serving as president from 1920 to 1924 and Calles from 1924 to 1928. Calles even created an official party in 1929, after President-elect Obregón was assassinated. Elsewhere, too, enforced stability and growth seemed the order of the day, provided by such people as Leguía in Peru, Yrigoyen and Alvear in Argentina, the conservatives in Colombia, Gómez in Venezuela, and Alessandri and Ibáñez in Chile, though discontent burbled under the surface.

The Mexican elite still had major problems to contend with. A Catholic rebellion in the highlands, called the Cristero Revolt, mobilized conservatives, the faithful in major cities, and thousands of devout peasants in the countryside. It smoldered for years and left a bloody legacy of church-state antagonism. Triggered by the implementation of anti-clerical measures under the 1917 Constitution, this civil war was a major aftershock of the revolution itself.

Two other exceptions to the general peace occurred: the Prestes Column march in Brazil (1924–1927) and the civil war in Nicaragua led by Augusto Sandino (1927–1933). These actions by Prestes and Sandino cast revolutionary shadows far into the future.

## The Prestes Column

Luís Carlos Prestes enjoyed a long and wide-ranging career in Brazilian politics. Cast as heroic comandante of a revolutionary march in the 1920s, he later became the undisputed leader of the Brazilian Communist Party for a half-century. Until the advent of Fidel Castro, Prestes stood as Latin America's most renowned communist leader, and he was also the most ideological of the early revolutionaries.

Born in Porto Alegre, Brazil, Prestes grew up an only son with four sisters. His family moved to Rio de Janeiro when his father, an army officer, transferred there in the early 1900s. His father died when Prestes was only ten, so in his teen years he drew close to his mother and sisters, a surrogate for the missing father.

Because of his father's commission, Luís Carlos gained admission to the military academy, from which he graduated in 1919 with degrees in physical science and math. The next year he won a commission in a railroad engineering company. A quiet, serious man, he had trouble with both superiors and private contractors, whom he regarded as corrupt and unpatriotic. Prestes apparently sympathized with colleagues who carried out the first tenente revolt of 1922, but he was bedridden with typhoid and did not take part. That revolt occurred in Rio and mobilized young officers and cadets who protested the policies of the federal government (see chapter 14). The several hundred participants objected to President-elect Artur Bernardes's alleged statements about the army's senior officer, which the tenentes regarded as an affront to the army. Loyal units crushed the revolt, jailed hundreds of rebels, and stripped them of their ranks. The Rio government prosecuted the men with a severity unusual in Brazilian politics.

Two years later, some of the original rebels and hundreds of sympathetic young soldiers and state police took part in a second tenente revolt, this time in the capital of São Paulo. They captured and held the city for a month, showing that not even Brazil's main industrial center was safe from a military onslaught. Their aims remained vague: justice for workers, honest elections, reinstatement at rank for the 1922 revolutionaries, and respect for the armed services.

General Miguel Costa, a charismatic officer who commanded the São Paulo state police, led the 1924 revolt. After the city was surrounded by federal troops, he took his men north by railroad, and after several days they met up with Luís Carlos Prestes's unit, which had declared itself in rebellion. The latter had convinced about a hundred of his men to join the revolt, after which they

**Figure 15.4** Luís Carlos Prestes in the mid-1930s. Courtesy Hoover Institution Library and Archives, Stanford University.

commandeered a train and made their way to the rendezvous with Costa's forces. Together they continued their trek to the northeast, abandoning the train at its last station.

During the next two and a half years, the rebel forces made one of the most extraordinary marches in military history. They covered twenty-four thousand kilometers through some of the most forbidding terrain in the world, Brazil's sertão. Government forces, state police, and even bandit gangs harassed them. They had to drag their artillery and provision wagons, often by mule, over hills and deserts. They forded rivers even in periods of flood. All the while the tenente column lived off the land, buying or confiscating supplies as needed.

The very survival and continuation of the column depended to a great degree on the leadership of Luís Carlos Prestes. He took upon himself the tasks of upholding morale, discipline, hope, and forward movement. He proved a genius at tactical maneuvers to evade large pursuing forces and then ambushing them with lightning attacks. He intuitively developed a form of guerrilla warfare that was perfectly suited to his troops and the terrain. Within a few months the revolutionaries were called the Miguel Costa/Luís Carlos Prestes Column. Within a year they were known simply as the Prestes Column.

In the course of their marches, the revolutionaries developed a rationale and simple philosophy that became known as "tenentismo." It began with the original grievances of 1922 about political corruption, misuse of public office, and indifference toward the military. Expressed in hurried press encounters and sketched out in rural bivouacs, tenentismo gradually expanded into a broad call for social, economic, and political reform. Tenente spokesmen demanded that the government address rural poverty, illiteracy, malnutrition, boss politics, and violence. Many of the tenentes saw rural suffering for the first time in their lives during the march. And, of course, they demanded reinstatement in the army.

The government paid little heed to the revolutionaries' demands and continued to hound their dwindling ranks. Yet, in the cities middle-class Brazilians regarded the tenentes as young idealists who cared enough for their country to risk their lives. Their prescriptions struck many educated Brazilians as reasonable and indeed overdue. Some of the tenentes became celebrated for their exploits and for their passionate calls for reforms. In early 1927 the column abandoned its march, its troops having thinned to several hundred men. Its members crossed into eastern Bolivia, then dispersed to several countries in the region. Some tenentes sneaked back into Brazil and formed an underground revolutionary network. Prestes found employment as a mining engineer for a time, then made his way to Buenos Aires.

The tenente movement eventually had its greatest impact during the early years of the Getúlio Vargas regime and then quickly waned (see chapter 16). Prestes, however, continued to develop his ideas, and his prestige rose throughout Brazil. While in Argentina he became convinced that communism was the best form of government for Brazil, and he traveled to Moscow to study. Prestes became renowned in the 1930s due in part to Brazil's most famous modern novelist, Jorge Amado. Amado's sympathetic biography of Prestes, entitled *The Cavalier of Hope,* presented the handsome Prestes as both an idealistic revolutionary and an example of the finest elements of the Brazilian character. Amado contended that if Prestes ever came to power he would solve the problems of the poor. Meanwhile, intellectuals called Prestes the savior of the country. They were not even put off by his disastrous leadership of a communist putsch (coup) in 1935, which led to his arrest and imprisonment for ten years. His new image as martyr merely complemented that of revolutionary. At the end of World War II Prestes got out of prison and began his long career as head of the Brazilian Communist Party. He refused to take part in day-to-day politics after his party was outlawed in 1948, yet he enjoyed great prestige among subsequent generations of young radicals. Not until the early 1980s did a rival group oust him as general secretary of the party, by which time he was an octogenarian.

Unlike most other revolutionaries, Prestes lived to a ripe old age. Apart from his time in prison, Prestes lived for many years in Moscow and spoke fluent Russian. In the 1930s he had one daughter with a German agent, Olga Benaro, who was sent to help him. Olga later perished in a Nazi prison camp. Prestes remarried in the 1940s, reunited with his daughter, and raised a large family of daughters.

## Augusto Sandino

Nicaragua's most famous revolutionary, Augusto Sandino, grew up in a rural province a few years before Prestes's birth. Sandino's father, the teenage son of a wealthy hacienda owner, had an affair with an indigenous servant, and she bore him the child they named Augusto. The family recognized the baby and raised him on the hacienda, together though not always equal with the other children. Augusto grew up steeped in liberal politics, which basically meant hating the church for meddling in politics and hating the rival conservatives. Augusto also read extensively in the family library and developed a superficial grasp of general philosophy.

In 1920 Augusto fought with and killed another youth. He fled the province and made his way north to the Caribbean coast. There he got odd jobs with banana farmers and mining firms operating in the rainforests. Hounded by the police, he escaped to Honduras and continued on to Guatemala, Mexico, and even Texas. He learned some English and supported himself working as a mechanic and general laborer. While in Mexico, he gained respect for the revolutionary ideals of the 1917 Constitution and for Mexican defiance of the United States. He pledged that he himself would someday bring about the same kind of national renovation in Nicaragua. In 1926 Sandino returned to Nicaragua and found a job as supervisor in a gold mine. At nights, though, he met with the workers and taught them the rudiments of the revolutionary ideology he had learned in Mexico. Soon, many workers pledged their loyalty to Sandino and underwent military training.

The following year he and his twenty-nine followers joined the cause of General José María Moncada, who had declared war against the incumbent president. Sandino's band took to the hills, where they learned the basics of soldiering and guerrilla warfare. They balked, however, when General Moncada agreed to turn over his arms to a U.S. Marine occupation force in exchange for guarantees of a supervised election (which Moncada won). Sandino declared himself in rebellion, refusing to cooperate with any election held while U.S. forces still occupied the country, and his force became a guerrilla army. Many disgruntled soldiers from the liberal army also joined him. Sandinismo, as his credo became mythologized, emerged from these events, with Sandino as a national hero.

For several years Sandino's forces controlled thousands of square miles in northwestern Nicaragua. He perfected the techniques of guerrilla warfare, using it against the U.S. Marines and the new National Guard that the marines were training for peacekeeping duty (see chapter 13). Sandino mastered feint, illusion, and subterfuge. His success astonished many because the thousands of U.S. Marines chasing him represented the largest force that the United States deployed between the two world wars. Moreover, the marines used the latest weaponry, including airplanes. The echoes of Pershing's failed expedition to Mexico resonated in the volcanic valleys and rain forests of Nicaragua.

**Figure 15.5** Augusto Sandino in 1928, in guerrilla uniform. Underwood and Underwood. Courtesy Library of Congress.

Sandino had superb political abilities and a capacity to convince his own men and peasants that they would triumph and install a better form of government. He was able to articulate a spiritual vision—described by biographer Neill Macaulay as a "vague messianic mysticism"—that defied analysis yet appealed to poor peasants and farmers. Passionate in his love of Nicaragua, he hated the Americans for invading and imposing their will. His struggle was a crusade for national sovereignty.

Like any successful guerrilla campaign, Sandino's drew support from urban groups such as students, intellectuals, labor leaders, and disaffected politicians. Recruits from the cities took money, supplies, and intelligence to El Chipote, Sandino's mountain refuge.

An officer who served under Sandino in the 1927 campaign provided this description:

> Sandino is of medium height, very slender, weighs about 115 pounds; education limited to primary grades; an extreme optimist and possesses unusual ability in

### Sandino Warns a U.S. Mine Operator

"My dear sir: I have the honor to inform you that on this date your mine has been reduced to ashes . . . to protest against the warlike invasion your government has made of our territory . . . In the beginning I confided in the thought that the American people would not [condone] the abuses committed in Nicaragua by the Government of Calvin Coolidge, but I have been convinced that North Americans in general uphold the attitude of Coolidge . . . for that reason . . . everything North American which falls into our hands is sure to meet its end.

"The losses you have had in the mine you may collect from the Government of the United States . . .

"The pretext . . . Coolidge gives for his intervention . . . to protect the lives and interests of North Americans and other foreign residents . . . is a tremendous hypocrisy. We Nicaraguans are respectable men and never in our history have there been . . . events like those now taking place, . . . the fruit harvested by the stupid policy of your Government . . . You, the capitalists will be appreciated and respected by us as long as you treat us as equals and not . . . believing yourselves lords and masters of our lives and property.

"I am your affectionate servant, Fatherland and Liberty. A. C. Sandino"

Quoted in Neill Macaulay, *The Sandino Affair,* 2nd ed. (Durham: Duke University Press, 1985), pp. 119–20.

convincing others of the feasibility of his most fantastic schemes; extremely energetic; explains his plans in great detail to his lowest subordinates but often keeps his officers in doubt; is far from being coldblooded and was never known to commit an act of cruelty himself; very religious and believes that for every wrong committed adequate punishment will be meted out . . . little interest in acquiring money for personal use and rarely has a penny in his pocket; is very vain and sophisticated, fully believing that his wisdom is infallible . . . his one slogan is "The Welfare of Our Fatherland," always stressing an interest in the peasant class.[4]

Sandino's resistance became famous throughout the hemisphere, a David and Goliath contest that fascinated readers from New York to Buenos Aires. Young Haya de la Torre from Peru stopped and spoke with him, as did journalist Carlton Beals from the United States. News of his feats reached as far as China. Liberals in most places saw Sandino as a patriot who wished only to end the U.S. occupation of his country.

Sandino's fortunes rose and fell, and he spent from 1929 to 1931 in exile in Mexico, earning money and recruiting more followers. Mexican president Emilio Portes Gil promised moral and diplomatic support, though his assistance disappointed the revolutionary, and Sandino was confined largely to Yucatán while there, far from the center of power. When Sandino returned to

Nicaragua, he found the climate much less propitious for revolution. Presidential elections were prepared for 1932, with security for the balloting provided by the new National Guard. This time, liberal Juan Bautista Sacasa seemed destined to win. U.S. authorities, meanwhile, favored a convivial, outgoing fellow named Anastasio Somoza to command the National Guard. Somoza spoke good English, got along with Americans, managed politics well, and seemed content to be the leader of the guard, not president. Somoza's troops gradually replaced the U.S. Marines, as the latter withdrew from safeguarding cities, towns, and transport facilities. Sandino's operations, meanwhile, were effectively limited to the north coast banana regions.

After the election the marines completed their withdrawal, and the country seemed calm under the benign rule of President Sacasa. Sandino decided that he had no more reason to fight, so he sued for peace. He sent his pregnant wife to Managua to work out an agreement. Under it, he and his followers would retire to an agricultural colony in the north and still retain some of their weapons for self-defense and hunting.

After about a year at the colony, Sandino began to run into trouble with local authorities, so he flew to Managua to demand that Sacasa comply with their agreement. He had dinner with the president, and the two settled their problems. On the way out, however, Sandino and his aides were seized by Somoza agents, taken to the edge of town, and murdered. Shortly afterward, the National Guard invaded the agricultural colony and seized all of its men and weapons. Sandinismo came to an abrupt, although temporary, end.

The story of Anastasio Somoza's rise to power and his long dictatorship appears in subsequent chapters. Sandino's legacy, however, proved remarkably long. In the 1950s one of the old Nicaraguan revolutionaries spent considerable time briefing some Cuban exiles about the methods Sandino used to defy the Americans in the late 1920s. The Cubans included Fidel and Raúl Castro, who later became famous for leading their own revolution (see chapter 22).

Later, in the 1960s, young Nicaraguan patriots fighting against Somoza's son, the dictator Anastasio Somoza Debayle, named their clandestine guerrilla group the Frente Sandinista de Liberación Nacional (FSLN) after their hero from the 1920s and 1930s. Throughout the 1980s Sandinismo offered hope for a social-democratic alternative to both capitalism and communism in Central America.

## CONCLUSIONS AND ISSUES

Luís Carlos Prestes and Augusto Sandino were two more examples of early revolutionaries in Latin America who became heroes for later generations. They were born a few years later than their Mexican counterparts, whom they emulated to some extent. They came from respectable rural middle-class families that did not have roots in cities. They were outsiders who felt strong obligations to correct wrongs that they witnessed.

Moreover, they had certain advantages—family support, European heritage, and good educations for the period in which they lived—that carried them through the difficult years of warfare. Neither man was religious, but both had strong commitments to spiritual and moral values. Sandino traveled abroad and developed a revolutionary ethos while in Mexico. Prestes did not go abroad until after his leadership of the column, and then his travels definitely radicalized his philosophy. Both men took up revolutionary activities while still very young. Sandino, like most of the other early revolutionaries, died after a short career; Prestes defied the odds and died in 1990 at age ninety-two.

Revolutionary movements occurred in Latin America for a host of reasons, not the least being the challenge of building legitimate nation-states while under the close eye and economic influence of the United States. Other causes were the presence of a highly educated and ambitious middle-class seeking opportunity in the face of exclusionary politics, economic instability, and the marginalization of wide swaths of the population. In this climate, talented young men and women defied authority and used violent means to correct injustices in society. They were backed by millions of poor and disenfranchised people, who, in rising up in revolt against injustice, ensured that these would become genuine mass movements.

From the evidence presented in this chapter, we can see that the revolutionaries were from respected families, some of European and others of mixed background, who raised their children to lead moral lives. As youths, most future revolutionaries acquired good educations that made them aware of alternatives and later aided them in their struggles against the establishment. And many regarded these revolutionaries as visionaries, idealists, and eventually martyrs, so that younger generations came to revere their memories. As we will see, revolution continued to be an attractive option in the political life of the region.

### Discussion Questions

What conditions provoked revolutionary activities in Latin America? What sort of leaders gravitated to such movements?

What factors sparked the Mexican Revolution in 1910? Explain your answer.

Distinguish between the Mexican revolutionary "old guard" and the young rebels. How were their motives and methods different?

How did revolutionary movements arise in Brazil and Nicaragua despite the seemingly calm appearance of the region in the 1920s?

What roles did the United States play in early revolutionary movements?

Why did guerrilla tactics appeal to so many Latin American revolutionaries? Were they effective?

How did revolutions influence the role of race in the conception of nations?

## Timeline

| | |
|---|---|
| 1910–20 | Mexican Revolution |
| 1911–13 | Presidency of Francisco Madero |
| 1917–20 | Presidency of Venustiano Carranza |
| 1916–17 | Francisco "Pancho" Villa attacks Columbus, N.M., spurring the Punitive Expedition |
| 1922–27 | Military cadets and officers called *tenentes* revolt in Brazil |
| 1927–31 | Augusto Sandino revolt in Nicaragua |
| 1924 | Sandino murdered by National Guard commandant Anastasio Somoza |

## Keywords

Constitition of 1917 (Mexico)
Cristero Revolt
Mexican Revolution
Plan de Ayala
Plan de San Luis Potosí
Porfiriato

Prestes Column
Sandinismo
soldaderas
tenentismo
Zapatistas
Zimmerman telegram

# CONFRONTING GLOBAL CHALLENGES

From the 1930s to the 1960s, Latin America underwent abrupt and sometimes painful transitions of modernization. Global events impinged more forcefully than ever, especially in the form of the Great Depression (1929–1939), World War II (1939–1945), and the Cold War (1947–1989). In the 1930s, the larger nations found themselves unable to sell all their traditional exports while remaining dependent on the import of basic necessities. The loss of export earnings caused grave shortages of imports that spurred an increase in domestic manufacturing, eventually leading to a new economic nationalism throughout the region.

Together with these stressful adaptations came heightened ideological conflict, partly as the ripple effect of international struggles and partly as responses to internal dislocations. Hundreds of thousands of unemployed rural people moved into towns and then cities in search of jobs and opportunities for better lives. The Depression decade became a watershed in most countries in the hemisphere, when urbanization and industrialization transformed communities and lives. In countries like Chile and Mexico, discontent among mining and factory workers over their lack of rights spilled over into labor actions, and rural workers across the region chafed against the authority of large landowners. Both threatened the power of traditional elites.

Dictatorship seemed the régime du jour in the 1930s, probably as a response to these tumultuous events and adjustments and to the inability of the liberal oligarchies to manage them. One by one, governments fell to military or strongman regimes in the 1930s. Some leaders, influenced by communism, fascism, and Nazism, began to experiment with radical forms of leadership. Even the U.S. government, long a proponent of democratic procedures, swore off intervention and often gave its blessings to dictators who could maintain the peace and protect U.S. investors. Where the military did not rule outright, as in Brazil, it wielded great influence from behind the scenes.

World order deteriorated in the late 1930s and collapsed into all-out war. From Asia to Europe, Africa to America, conflict swept the world into a vortex of destruction and death. Most of Latin America experienced shortages of basic imported goods (consumer and machinery), intelligence breaches, political challenges, and even armed clashes. For a time, German submarine attacks converted the Caribbean Sea into a cemetery of Allied shipping. After the United States declared war on the Axis powers, Brazil attempted to lead Latin America into solidarity with the Allies. Mexico became a strong supporter of its northern neighbor. The record in other countries was mixed. No country, however, avoided all impacts from the war.

After the 1945 peace was signed and the world moved into a new era, Latin America seemed to bloom in a number of ways. For those countries that had supported the Allies, a glow of pride in victory shone through. In most places democratic forces arose and restored constitutional government. The urban economies that burgeoned with migrants and industrial growth now burst forth as world-class cities. Mexico City, Rio, Buenos Aires, Lima, Santiago, São Paulo, and Caracas joined the ranks of world metropolises. Their governments reached out to the masses of citizens with expanded suffrage, social programs, labor rights, and more inclusive nationalism. The arts, literature, and university life all blossomed in the postwar environment.

The biggest political change in postwar Latin America was the return of populism as the foremost expression of mass politics. The populists took up where their predecessors of the 1910s and 1920s left off, emboldened by huge new urban populations, radio, mass circulation dailies, and modern transportation. Brazil experienced such a surge in populist leadership that the period from 1945 to 1964 was called the Populist Republic. Juan Perón and his wife Evita, the quintessential populists, captured the hearts and minds of most Argentines after 1945. Elsewhere, too, charismatic, forceful, and dynamic figures rode waves of adulation into the presidential palaces of their nations. These were optimistic times, when citizens believed that their political influence and chances for attaining middle-class status and standards of living were never better.

By the mid-1960s, however, the optimism had evaporated, and more and more governments fell under military control. In large part, the populists fell prey to Cold War pressures from within and without—pressures that viewed economic nationalism and expanded political participation as communist threats. In a few cases, though, they also failed because of sheer incompetence. Populism seemed to disappear almost as quickly as it had emerged after World War II.

# The 1930s

## Years of Depression and Upheaval

### Panama Elections of 1932

In 1931, Panama's president was ousted by a brief armed coup led by a group called Acción Comunal (Communal Action). Two years later, the caretaker government they installed held elections for president. This election relied heavily on fraudulent votes, as did most other elections in the hemisphere. In the excerpt below, the British minister in Panama, J. Brosh, provides a rare description of the way in which candidates purchased votes and, in this case, how the voters thwarted the interests of the wealthier candidate. *Cédula* means "voter identification document."

Try to follow the electoral chicanery in the document below. It involved some deceit and the expectation that bribery would produce victory. In this instance, the bribers' opponents outwitted them! The Panchistas—representing candidate Francisco "Pancho" Arias—were the rivals of Dr. Harmodio Arias. The two men were not related.

> I have the honour to report that the National Electoral Jury has officially recognized Dr. Harmodio Arias as President elect of the Republic of Panamá . . . For the better understanding of the technique of electoral bribery in Panamá, I may explain that the price of a cédula usually runs from one dollar to a dollar and a half, though the value goes up as the date of the elections approaches. The person selling his cédula leaves it in the possession of the purchaser (i.e. the agent of one of the candidates), it being agreed that, on election day, he will come back for it, as without it he cannot cast his vote. In the ordinary way, if he does not keep his promise and reclaim the cédula, no irreparable harm is done, since the owner is at least prevented from transferring his allegiance to the rival candidate.
>
> In the case of the last elections, however, Señor Francisco Arias appears to have been undone by the adoption of a new and ingenious device, whereby the wily voter

procured the issue of two cédulas—one in his own name, which he ultimately used in the interest of Dr. Harmodio Arias, and another in a false name which he sold to the Panchistas but never utilized at all. . . .

It may be added that cédulas were given by the Jury to all and sundry, there being no test in respect of education or even language, but solely one of nationality. Thus it happened that hundreds of the semi-civilized Indians of the San Blas Archipelago, most of whom are illiterate and speak no Spanish, were placed upon the voting list and there was much competition for their suffrages.[1]

## IMPACT OF THE GREAT DEPRESSION

Many coups and attempted coups erupted in Latin America during the 1930s. At first, they were largely provoked by the economic crisis of 1929—the same crisis that triggered the Great Depression. In 1930 alone, six civilian governments were overthrown by their respective militaries. Soon more fell or simply collapsed from stagnation and ineffectiveness. The achievements of the populists and democrats during the first decades of the century seemed to evaporate like so much smoke in the air. Across the globe, the Depression created a sense of crisis, peril, and doom. In Latin America, many lost faith in republicanism, as the liberals who dominated the governments seemed too inept, self-interested, or corrupt to deal effectively with the unfolding crises. This crisis of political legitimacy led many to support the growing role of the military in public life, believing it could restore order amid chaos and collapse.

As the U.S. and Europe retreated to deal with their own crises, the Great Depression sparked a new sense of nationalism in Latin America, as well as a spirit of defensiveness and the determination to protect what each nation had. In country after country, writers, politicians, middle-class professionals, and economic elites harped on the need to create strength within their borders. They pledged to develop stronger governments, effective militaries, robust and independent economies, and more loyal citizens.

## ECONOMIC NATIONALISM AND SOCIAL REFORM

Along with the new nationalism came new economic ideas designed to foster independence or better insulate Latin America from the shock waves of international depression. In the larger countries especially, bureaucrats and intellectuals began to favor long-term industrialization as a solution to the cyclical booms and busts to which their economies were subjected in the global arena. Coffee faced prolonged market crises and had to be subsidized; world grain supplies often exceeded demand; beef prices were notoriously unstable, with exports subject to restrictions by importing countries; mining income fluctuated wildly with changing demand by refiners; and the sugar trade was controlled by importing countries. Each downturn in economic fortunes caused widespread unemployment and suffering in Latin America. Moreover, the loss of export earnings hurt public coffers, which relied heavily on trade taxes, and caused grave shortages of imports that crippled domestic life.

The solution, according to many, was to diversify and strengthen the economies by promoting domestic manufacturing. Argentina, Brazil, Chile, and Mexico were especially interested in this possibility. They, along with many other countries around the world, joined in the general debt moratorium of 1932 and considered the possibilities of bowing out of the international market altogether. This strategy, called "autarky," was a more elaborate form of protectionism that had always been present in one form or another in international trade. None actually sought full autarky, but with nationalist economic policies they began to reverse the effects of the Great Depression, gain some independence from global markets, and accelerate the transition from agricultural to industrial economies.

New international deals not requiring hard currency could revive trade; for example, Brazil exchanged coffee for German machinery without cash payments. In addition, high tariffs were part of a general plan to develop industries and broaden domestic markets. Multiyear plans would set production targets and direct public and private investment to national priorities. In addition, government and industry groups deployed mass propaganda campaigns to promote pride in domestically produced goods. The words "Hecho en México," "Indústria Brasileira," and "Producto Argentino" began to appear on goods and in advertising. Economic nationalism became a major feature of Latin America from the 1930s through the 1970s.

The 1930s also saw governments actively undertake programs to promote the general well-being of their citizens. All of a sudden, leading citizens and politicians began to speak of the "social question." The phrase had been coined in Europe in the 1890s to refer to working-class demands and actions to achieve decent standards of living for laborers and their families. Pope Leo XIII gave weight to these concerns in his 1891 encyclical *Rerum Novarum.* In general, the social question called for government and private initiatives on behalf of the poorest sectors of society, including the retired, disabled, infirm, handicapped, and chronically unemployed.

Until the widespread suffering of the Great Depression struck, labor-management relations had been left to the market, with very little involvement by government except when force was needed to quell a strike or demonstration. This contributed to a variety of glaring social problems: strikes, the proliferation of slums, periodic crises of unemployment, abandonment of laborers injured on the job or too old to work, child labor, and hostility toward the elites.

To be sure, the social question had been addressed by some constitutions, notably those of 1917 in Mexico, 1919 in Uruguay, and 1925 in Chile. Yet, actual programs and compliance were rare through the 1920s. The 1930s saw far more actual legislation passed and real institutions created to deal with labor and social problems. Labor codes became common, governments stepped in to mediate industrial conflict, social security systems were set up, public education expanded rapidly, and new programs began to provide food and medicine to the destitute. The social question was transformed from a charitable concern for the poor into a commitment by progressive governments.

## Race and Nationalism

When elites in Latin America took up the "social question" in the 1930s, they faced challenges distinct from those of their counterparts in Europe. The debate over race, in particular, took on renewed vigor as elites struggled to define more inclusive nations. As seen in chapter 15, in Mexico they invented the "raza cósmica," which united all Mexicans within a single nation.

In Brazil, where slavery had played such a prominent and divisive role in its recent history, race was particularly central to the social question, as seen in chapter 14. Like most other Latin Americans, white Brazilians held deeply racist views of human society, and during the early twentieth century promoted education and immigration as a path toward branqueamento, or whitening. But Brazil was also a country where, beginning in the 1920s, modernist artists and writers began to celebrate tropical and African themes in their work. Similarly, Brazilian intellectual and writer Gilberto Freyre invented a new racial past for his people. Having grown up in the sugar region of Pernambuco surrounded by large numbers of blacks and mestizos, Freyre objected to the widespread denigration of nonwhites. He sensed that Brazil had inherited a unique society, one that its ancestors had forged in the tropical plantations. They had fallen on hard times, to be sure, but current conditions were not due to the supposed racial inferiority of Brazil's mixed population.

Freyre's college studies in Texas (Baylor University) and New York (Columbia University) provided him with an opportunity to read broadly in history and anthropology. From his studies he devised an account of Brazil's past, which he published as *Casa grande e senzala* (1933), later translated as *The Masters and the Slaves*. *Casa grande* became an immediate best seller and was followed by sequels in the 1940s and 1950s. In this work, Freyre single-handedly rewrote his nation's past and constructed a new self-image for Brazil. His most innovative ideas had to do with racial mixing.

Freyre stated that three racial groups had come together in lowland Brazil during the colonial era: the Portuguese, indigenous people, and Africans. Each group brought physical and cultural characteristics especially suited for life on

**Figure 16.1** Gilberto Freyre synthesized Brazil's history using the lore of his plantation society upbringing and his advanced social science studies in the United States. Courtesy Escola Britannica.

the plantations. Africans and Indians, of course, were accustomed to the tropics and hence needed no special adaptation to the climate. The Portuguese brought a genius for organization and enterprise and founded cities. Native peoples contributed their knowledge of the land, flora, and fauna. Brazil became, then, a crucible for blending these populations and cultures into a new people especially fit for life in tropical America.

The blending, both physical and cultural, took place largely in the plantation big house, where members of all races commingled. Masters and their female slaves had many illegitimate children together over the long centuries of slavery, while slaves and Indians also had children. All of the children, regardless of race and class, played together in the big house and learned from their African and Afro-descendant nannies. Food recipes, children's games and stories, home medicine, folklore, hygiene, and all other aspects of daily life became fused into a peculiarly Brazilian synthesis. Meanwhile, according to Freyre, familial relations among all in the big house ameliorated the harsh aspects of slavery and plantation production. The upshot was the racially mixed and culturally blended Brazilians.

With distinctions of race blurred, people behaved as if they were members of one big family. Freyre wrote that Brazil's political culture, inherited from the days of masters and slaves, also obeyed the rules of patriarchalism. This included avoidance of confrontation and deference to powerholders. In all,

Brazilian society worked well because this unique history had produced what Freyre called a "racial democracy" in Brazil. Educated Brazilians applauded Freyre's theories and disseminated them in school books, magazine articles, poetry, and newspapers. His views on race relations, in particular, became a virtual consensus by the 1950s, allowing Brazilians to acknowledge their complicated racial past while ignoring its basis in exploitation and the continued injustices faced by Brazil's black majority.

Freyre's unique vision of Brazil found resonance among artists of the 1930s as well. The modernist movement (see chapter 14), which continued to thrive, increasingly portrayed blacks, indigenous people, and mulattoes as the body and soul of the nation. Cândido Portinari and Di Cavalcanti, in particular, chose to paint scenes of poor nonwhites in their work. Today we call this the "myth of racial democracy," because, contrary to Freyre's romantic ideas of the past, inequality and racism still exist in all facets of life in Brazil. But in the 1930s and 1940s, Freyre's ideas were heralded by elites seeking to define a more inclusive nation and deal with the social question without having to alter social divisions.

## Politics in Argentina and Brazil

In Argentina and Brazil, military coups toppled two governments within weeks of one another. On September 6, 1930, a contingent of army cadets marched on the Casa Rosada in Buenos Aires and deposed President Yrigoyen, whose senility had left him unfit to govern. On October 3 rebel forces in two of Brazil's most powerful states, Rio Grande do Sul and Minas Gerais, declared war and began maneuvers that led the army to overthrow President Washington Luís three weeks later. Although the underlying causes of these two movements were complex, the outcomes were relatively simple: strong regimes took power and imposed order in the face of growing instability brought on by the Great Depression.

In Argentina, General José F. Uriburu, leader of the coup, purged the government of top Yrigoyen collaborators and reined in public spending. He outlawed strikes, banned demonstrations, censored newspapers, and attempted to create a dictatorship. Within a short time, however, a more conservative coalition of landowners, businessmen, and political leaders formed behind the candidacy of General Juan P. Justo. The latter won an election and took office in 1932, inaugurating a term of limited and controlled response to the Depression.

A treaty with Great Britain, the Roca-Runciman Treaty, formed the centerpiece of the Justo years. To salvage the economy, it extended the favorable terms of trade that both had enjoyed since the previous century. Argentine meat and cereals would continue to be sold in England virtually duty free, while British goods would enter Argentina with low tariffs. These measures

## African Religion in Brazil: Candomblé

In 1938 and 1939, U.S. ethnographer Ruth Landes traveled to Bahia and Rio de Janeiro to study race relations and black Brazilian culture. Her account of this trip provides a wonderful portrait of the country under the dictablanda (weak dictatorship) of Getúlio Vargas. It also contains strikingly modern descriptions of Candomblé, a syncretic religion in Brazil with strong African roots. Founded in the early nineteenth century in the sugar and slave region of Bahia in northeastern Brazil, it blended different religious beliefs and practices from areas of West Africa with elements of Catholicism and indigenous practices. While Candomblé recognizes a Supreme Creator, it is also well known outside of Brazil for its orishás, who are lesser deities that act as protectors of each believer. During Candomblé ceremonies, believers are possessed by their orishá, as represented through dance, music, and ritual offerings. Candomblé was illegal in Brazil in the 1930s and virtually unknown in the United States.

In this excerpt, Landes asks a Brazilian colleague, Edison Carneiro, if Candomblé is

an "opiate for the masses?" I half jested.

"Call it that. But the real opiate is their ignorance and illiteracy—for which they are hardly to blame!" he protested impatiently. "Blame the landowners for that, and our whole inefficient economy. In my opinion, candomblé is a creative force. It gives the people courage and confidence, and they concentrate on solving the problems of this life, rather than on peace in the hereafter. I wonder, now, where the blacks would be without candomblé!"

"I notice that the priestesses are very close to the people."

"Very," he agreed. "The fathers and mothers are supposed to know all the answers, and also the few remaining diviners like Martiano. The daughters know certain answers, depending upon the length of their training and experience, and all the people have a general idea of what's to be done or of who can do it for them, because they all are related to somebody connected with candomblé.

"As in the popular Catholic belief, everything that happens has some mystery combined with it. I suppose nobody is believed to die a natural death, nobody gets married happily just as a matter of course, nobody is successful merely through luck or talent, nobody gets sick for natural reasons—but always there is some saint or god involved who is revenging himself or blessing his protégé, or some black magic is being practiced. The Catholic priests teach the people about the same thing as the mothers do—which is to rely on the saints and on obedience to commands rather than upon their own reason. God is a familiar idea here in this cathedral city."

Ruth Landes, *The City of Women,* 2nd ed. (Albuquerque: University of New Mexico Press, 1994), pp. 88–89.

kept goods flowing between Argentina and Great Britain. Argentina suffered fewer effects of the Depression as a result, though in the end it merely postponed the harsh choices forced on other governments in the region. Justo was succeeded by a civilian president in 1938. With conservative leaders focused almost exclusively on economic recovery, labor bosses and leftists exercised little influence under these autocratic regimes. Clearly, however, nationalistic sentiments and demands for better labor rights grew during the 1930s. Justo's regime, which strictly controlled politics for the benefit of the elite, failed to make any concessions to the middle and working classes. Because of this, historians later called it the "infamous decade."

To the north of Argentina, the Brazilian coup, grandly named the Revolution of 1930, ushered in the long regime of Getúlio Vargas, former governor of Rio Grande do Sul. Vargas and his aides had to deal with far more serious problems than Uriburu. Coffee prices plunged, loan payments depleted hard currency reserves, the number of unemployed swelled in the cities, and all over the country discontented politicians clamored for jobs and favors. Vargas responded by imposing a dictatorship, provoking a revolt in the state of São Paulo in 1932. After quashing this, he moved to restore democracy by holding elections and sponsoring a constitutional assembly. The resultant 1934 Constitution confirmed Vargas's 1932 enfranchisement of women and eighteen-year-olds, recognized the rights of labor, and mandated a system of balances between the executive and legislative branches. He soon became enormously popular, and the assembly chose Vargas as president for the 1934–1938 term.

Brazilians, like other Latin American citizens, began to consider different ideologies becoming prominent in Europe—notably fascism, Nazism, and communism—as replacements for the liberal capitalist models earlier in vogue. Movements arose to promote each of these, yet most politicians stuck close to Vargas because he controlled jobs and patronage. Clashes between the left and right became more vicious in 1935, culminating in a major communist-led revolt in November. Vargas used the failed uprising as an excuse to impose a dictatorship, and within two years he formalized it with a constitution (1937) and the name Estado Novo (New State), borrowed from Antônio Oliveira Salazar's autocratic Portugal.

Vargas ruled as an old-fashioned dictator, ignoring the constitution and the fascistic preferences of some collaborators. Some dubbed his regime a *dictablanda* (soft dictatorship). Vargas centralized power in Rio de Janeiro, signaling the end of loose federalism. To emphasize the change, he had state flags burned in a ceremony marking the end of the Old Republic. The federal bureaucracy grew quickly, though, as always, it functioned more through personal favors than administrative discipline. Finally, he strengthened the army and used it to secure his hold on power.

## How Bertha Lutz Won the Vote for Brazilian Women

Bertha Lutz was born into a prosperous Swiss-English immigrant family that settled in São Paulo in the nineteenth century. Her father, a public health specialist,
had carried out a sanitation program in the port of Santos in the 1890s. After the
turn of the century, the family moved to Rio de Janeiro, where the father joined
the staff at the Oswaldo Cruz Institute of Tropical Medicine. Bertha trained as a
botanist and zoologist, following her father's interest in science. She later con-
fessed that she found the usual women's careers, such as charity and education,
boring. She became a proponent of women's suffrage in the 1920s.

In 1922 her colleagues chose her to attend the first Pan-American Women's
Meeting in Washington, an event that changed her life. When she returned, she
founded the Brazilian Confederation for the Advancement of Women. For the
next several years she and her wealthy associates wrote articles on feminine
advances elsewhere. Their goals included making the elite Dom Pedro II Academy coeducational, putting women on the national councils on children and
labor policy, and shortening the workday for employed women.

In 1924, this time sponsored by the U.S. embassy, Lutz attended another
Inter-American women's meeting. There she won election as president of the
Inter-American Union of Women. By the late 1920s, inspired by a growing hemispheric movement promoting female suffrage, women decided to push for the
vote in Brazil. Because the constitution did not expressly forbid women from voting, they decided to push for a test case in the impoverished state of Rio Grande
do Norte. Women helped elect a sympathetic governor, who in 1928 sponsored
a law allowing women to vote in that state's election. When the Supreme Court
upheld their suffrage, other northern states followed suit.

Brazil's revolution of 1930, led by Getúlio Vargas, erased those gains, so the
feminist leaders decided to convoke a second National Congress of Women in
1932 to lobby for the vote. As president, Bertha Lutz took their petition to President Vargas. Vargas, desperate for support, promised to back their request but
counseled them to get into the mainstream to help him. He urged them to join
parties, run for office, and write newspaper articles.

True to his word, Vargas signed an electoral reform bill in 1932 that among
other things gave women the vote. Four women ran for seats in the constitutional assembly the following year, but only Bertha Lutz got enough votes to win.
She served on the São Paulo delegation for two years, then won reelection representing Rio de Janeiro.

In 1937 Vargas canceled all political activity and ushered in the dictatorial
Estado Novo, during which no elections were held. When the political system was
restored after World War II, however, no one questioned women's right to vote.

Based on author interview with Lutz (1972).

**Figure 16.2** Brazilian feminist leader Bertha Lutz during a 1925 visit to Buenos Aires. Courtesy Library of Congress.

Just as important, Vargas carried out policies of economic nationalism and social reform that transformed Brazil into an increasingly urban, industrial country by the end of World War II. He regulated mining and hydroelectric power, supervised foreign trade, intervened in export dealings, and further nationalized transport companies. In 1942 he struck a deal with the United States by which Brazil leased a naval base in its northeast in exchange for a steel mill. When operational in 1946, this mill—named Volta Redonda—formed the core of an integrated steel industry. Slowly government tutelage spread to many areas of the economy.

Vargas's progressive social policies, meanwhile, culminated in the Labor Code of 1943 as well as a system of social security that covered most urban workers and employees. New quotas on foreign hiring and minimum wage laws benefited poor Brazilians of all races, with many Afro-Brazilians migrating from the northeast to the south to work in industry or the public sector. Moreover, in 1940, legal restrictions on popular black cultural forms such as samba and Candomblé (an Afro-Brazilian syncretic religion) were ended.

And while women may not have had much chance to exercise the suffrage rights they received under Vargas, they, too, saw great change in these decades.

Since World War I, middle- and upper-class women had been seizing opportunities to move into public life, increasingly dissatisfied with traditional limits on their rights. A powerful Catholic and conservative reaction emerged against the appearance of the "modern woman." But Vargas's policies focusing on workers and the poor, including programs to create healthy families that could produce modern workers and citizens, provided new opportunities and status for women.

## The Popular Front in Chile

Chileans, who had experienced military coups in 1924 and 1925, were disinclined to resort to revolution in 1930, despite the virtual collapse of their economy. During the Great Depression, nitrate sales nearly stopped, and copper prices fell to only 15 percent of their former levels. President Ibáñez set up a public nitrates company, COSACH, to try to shore up prices, but it had little effect. Agricultural goods, meanwhile, rotted on docks and in warehouses for lack of customers. Perhaps half the employed lost their jobs. The government of General Ibáñez became so discredited by 1931 that he resigned in the face of student protests and a white-collar strike.

For nearly a year Chile had no real government, as the vice president and Congress fruitlessly attempted to solve the crisis. In one bizarre twist, a popular figure from the 1920s, air force colonel Marmaduke Grove, seized control and decreed a socialist government, but it too proved utterly ineffectual. Grove gave up after two weeks, and his successor resigned three months later. Eventually a conservative coalition emerged to support former president Arturo Alessandri and duly elected him in late 1932. By then the economy had bottomed out, and most Chileans had found ways to survive, if barely, by resorting to subsistence agriculture, migrating in search of work in the mines or cities, or scavenging.

In the presidency again, Alessandri decided not to undertake any reforms—as he had in the 1920s—because the treasury was empty and his government's survival was precarious at best. Besides, he had spent some time in Italy during the early years of Benito Mussolini and had come to believe in the benefits of autocratic government. He backed emergency industrialization efforts and repressed labor agitation in the interest of productivity. In 1936 he employed the army to intervene in a national rail strike and soon thereafter closed Congress. Toward the end of his term, he relented and expanded social security benefits (which included medical care) to a larger number of workers. Using such methods, he managed to hold on until his term ended in 1938.

Ideological conflict whipsawed the Chilean citizenry, however, and both Nazi and leftist movements became quite influential. The former backed Carlos Ibáñez in the 1938 presidential election, whereas several parties on the left, including the Communist and Socialist parties, formed the Popular Front, which nominated a wealthy businessman and former cabinet minister, Carlos Aguirre Cerda, for president. The election was disrupted by the Nazis' failed putsch, which discredited the party and helped to elect Aguirre Cerda.

Immediately Aguirre Cerda implemented some of the nationalistic economic policies that had appealed to leaders elsewhere in Latin America. For planning purposes, he created the National Development Corporation (CORFO), which received a large credit from the U.S. government. Soon this agency stimulated production in a wide range of industries: textiles, mining, fishing, ranching, and timber. Its investment in Chile's first large-scale steel mill, built in Concepción in 1941, proved especially important. All across the board, Chile experienced a remarkable economic recovery because of judicious government pump priming, plus rising demand caused by the onset of World War II.

Aguirre Cerda paid special attention to social needs overlooked by earlier administrations. He appointed Salvador Allende, a visionary physician, as minister of public health to oversee the social programs that he had promised in his election campaign. Allende, a committed socialist, expanded the hospital and clinic networks in poor communities to the point that Chile could boast of having the healthiest people in the hemisphere. The social security system expanded to embrace nearly the entire employed population. Finally, Aguirre Cerda invested heavily in schools and teachers' salaries, giving rise to his slogan, To Govern Is to Educate.

Aguirre Cerda supported the labor movement as well, backing their demands and, as was typical of many Popular Front governments, allowing them to retain independence in return for their loyalty. Chile had a very powerful labor movement, one born in the rough and isolated mining communities that sprang up around its coal, copper, and other mines. Workers had long been treated harshly by mine owners, who took advantage of weak labor laws, mining's importance to the national economy, and government backing to rule at will over their mines and nearby mining towns. Relations with labor thus were volatile, fed by the harsh and dangerous conditions of mining work and by anarchists, communists, and socialists, who made great inroads in organizing workers in these communities in the 1920s. Aguirre Cerda reached out to workers and gave them significant concessions, though like other pro-labor governments, rewards were granted only in return for worker loyalty and state oversight; protection went hand in hand with control. Indeed, though the Popular Front helped to expand worker organizing in the late 1930s and early 1940s, and workers made key gains in work and living conditions, Aguirre Cerda also outlawed independent unions and rural organizing.[2]

In 1941 Aguirre Cerda died and was succeeded by a member of his party, Juan Antonio Ríos, also a businessman committed to economic expansion. For the remainder of the war Chilean industry grew rapidly and drew more and more people to manufacturing jobs in the cities. Unlike his predecessor, however, Ríos was less tolerant of worker demands and especially their independence. Further, he did not cultivate the support or cooperation of the Socialist and Communist parties and instead used special wartime powers to suppress the left.

## Revolutionary Change in Mexico

Events in Mexico during the 1930s proved even more remarkable than those in South America. Relative peace had returned when General Álvaro Obregón gained power in 1920, created a stable government, and four years later stepped down for his successor, Plutarco Elías Calles. Like Obregón, Calles largely kept the generals in line through bribes, intimidation, and executions. Calles also managed to settle some lingering diplomatic problems with the United States.

The return to relative political stability seemed threatened by events after the 1928 election. A Catholic fanatic murdered President-elect Obregón. Calles quickly chose a new president, whom he controlled from behind the scenes. He convinced himself that in the absence of Obregón, he was indispensable for the well-being of the country. His aides gave him the title of Jefe Máximo (supreme chief) de la Revolución. By extension his new reign came to be known as the Maximato. Calles established his control to such an extent that he could withstand military revolts and a large rural rebellion, known as the Cristero War (1926–29), challenging his anti-clerical policies.

In order to broaden his support and end political unrest through managed elections, Calles created a party in December 1928. First named the National Revolutionary Party (PNR), it comprised three major sectors of the nation: the agraristas, labor unions, and the army. On paper this structure was designed to formalize these sectors' political activities and convey their wishes to the president. In fact, however, Calles used the party to centralize political rule and diminish the authority of regional powerholders by coopting their labor and agrarian bases. This left the party firmly in his hands.

When he formed the party, Calles asserted that his goal was to change Mexico from a country ruled by caudillos to one ruled by institutions and laws. But the PNR soon became a regimented, top-down party that managed highly controlled elections and used patronage to get votes. Government employees above a certain level had to belong to the party and contribute seven days' pay per year to its coffers. The party could also flush out potential contenders for the presidency and force them to declare their intentions. It moved Mexico slowly toward institutionalized presidential succession, though not toward democracy. Paradoxically, however, its very success in controlling the process allowed the president to postpone the federal agrarian and labor reform promised in the constitution.

Calles could not succeed himself in 1929, so he chose allies to occupy the presidency. They served as puppets, beholden to him and obliged to consult with him and his cronies on major decisions. After a few years, though, Calles's power began to slip because of his declining health and extended absences from the capital. Simultaneously, agrarian and labor groups became more assertive, especially as they became desperate in the depression-struck economy.

Behind the scenes, one of Calles's top officials, General Lázaro Cárdenas, former head of the PNR and now war minister, cultivated the support of unions and agrarian groups, carefully preparing the way for the presidential succession of 1934. A critical opportunity came in 1933, when a labor activist whom Cárdenas favored, Vicente Lombardo Toledano, put together a new labor organization, which became known in 1936 as the Confederation of Mexican Workers (CTM). It quickly became a main source of Cárdenas's support.

Calles, who intended to install another puppet president to extend the Maximato, disregarded Cárdenas's activities until too late. Cárdenas befriended junior military officers in the capital and won popularity among the enlisted men as well. Because no general had bothered to do that since 1920, a great chasm had arisen between the officers and the enlisted men. By the time the PNR convened in 1934, Cárdenas had sewn up the nomination. Calles bowed to the inevitable, confident that he could control Cárdenas in the way he had the previous three presidents. And indeed most expected Cárdenas to remain loyal to his political patron. They were deeply mistaken about this, however. Cárdenas not only gained full power but also began to implement the revolutionary program charted by the 1917 Constitution but still largely unfulfilled.

Lázaro Cárdenas, born in a small town in Michoacán in 1895, became the greatest president of Mexico since the revolution. His family was middle class and mestizo. Cárdenas, a smallish man with an active, versatile mind, finished primary school and worked at a number of odd jobs: artisan, pool-hall operator, and even a tax collector. His honesty and shrewdness proved critical attributes for a career in the army and politics.

Cárdenas had joined the revolution in 1913 at the age of eighteen, when he enlisted in Zapata's army. Later he switched to Obregón, to Villa, and finally to Calles. He served with unwavering loyalty to the latter throughout the 1920s. Then, as a progressive governor of his native state of Michoacán between 1928 and 1932 and simultaneously president of the PNR from 1930 to 1933, he began to aim for the presidency. In 1933 he became war minister—the second-most powerful post in government. He was clearly a rising power: a good general but a civilian at heart. Ideologically, he was inclined toward the left, whereas Calles and the rest were drifting in a conservative direction.

When the party convened in early 1934, Cárdenas was a shoo-in for the nomination. The party also worked up a platform for the next six-year term. Dubbed the Plan Sexenio, the platform stressed Cárdenas's key causes, including labor rights, land reform, and the expansion of public education for the masses. The tenor of the program proved too radical for Calles, but he accepted it as necessary for propaganda purposes.

Cárdenas then decided to make a real campaign out of the election, even though he was assured the support of the official party. He traveled almost 16,500 miles and visited all the states. His revolutionary slogan preceded him: "Workers of Mexico, unite!" On the road, he was careful to meet with local caciques and army garrison chiefs, but he also held audiences with common people. He often sat for hours in town plazas listening to peasants and workers who came to town to speak with him. They gave him the nickname Tata Lázaro (Father Lázaro) because he listened like a priest. His election in 1934 proved one of the smoothest in years. Even after his election, he continued to tour the country to meet with people. His popularity stood high at his inauguration in December 1934.

Cárdenas accepted Calles's suggestions for cabinet members and PNR president so that the Jefe Máximo would think he was in charge. By mid-1935, however, Cárdenas stood ready to make his move. With Calles away in Los Angeles for medical treatment, Cárdenas announced new and radical land and labor programs. He made it clear that he would lend official backing to agrarian and leftist union groups, and he even issued light arms to them. Cárdenas openly associated with such well-known leftists as Francisco Mújica (a principal author of the 1917 Constitution) and the CTM's Lombardo Toledano. Political tension reached a fever pitch, with right-wing fascist groups, the Gold Shirts, often clashing in the streets with their leftist rivals.

Calles returned to Mexico in May 1935 and denounced Cárdenas's initiatives as a "marathon of radicalism." But it soon became clear that Cárdenas could count on the backing of some generals, about half the politicians, most junior officers and troops, plus the recently armed agraristas and organized labor groups. Calles realized that he had been beaten and returned to Los Angeles. Calles and his followers sparred with the government until April 1936, when Cárdenas exiled them and asserted his full authority.

Cárdenas then proceeded to make good on his promises. During the rest of his term he distributed 50 million acres of land through the land reform agency—more than all of his predecessors combined. Much of Mexico's arable land changed hands. This signaled the virtual demise of the traditional hacienda and the influence of the hacendado class. An unfortunate side effect of the land redistribution, however, was a decline in productivity.

In the north, Cárdenas created one very large ejido, or communal landholding, meant to be a model for the others. Created from the former Terrazas estate on the Coahuila-Durango border, Ejido La Laguna provided collective title to the thirty thousand families who resided there. The families ran cattle and raised cotton and cereals, as before. La Laguna revealed the limitations of land reform: it was never a commercial success and results for peasants were mixed, but, like other ejidos, it improved opportunities for the formerly landless, who could gain access to lands, and it seemed to fulfill the revolution's promise of social justice. By providing land as a grant from the state, the government also drew peasants into its orbit, giving it a means of social control. Mexican land reform was a program with political and social goals rather than strictly economic ones.

Meanwhile, the CTM labor federation quickly grew to a million members, working so closely with the ministry of labor it was virtually an official agency. Lombardo Toledano, a strong-willed socialist as well as a pragmatic politician, became a major ally of Cárdenas. CTM-affiliated unions remained largely loyal to Cárdenas. In return for their support, Cárdenas most often supported union demands for better contracts.

Cárdenas also promoted educational expansion and reform. He embraced the concept of a socialist education that valued the general welfare over individualism and capitalism. He even passed a law including this brand of socialism in the official curriculum. Cárdenas was willing to put his money where his mouth was: education's share of the federal budget rose substantially, and during his term in office, Mexico built three thousand schools and trained one hundred thousand new teachers. Many of these teachers were recruited from the cities, often sent into rural areas to teach both literacy and the values of the revolution. Cárdenas challenged his teachers to be agents of change in their communities, spreading the word about the constitution and mobilizing adults to assert their rights under it. Under his leadership, public school enrollments ballooned, though they struggled to keep up with the rapidly growing population. Public school enrollment went from .8 million in 1907 to 2.2 million in 1940.

Feminists in Mexico were emboldened by the political opening provided by Cárdenas, as well as by Cárdenas's vocal support for women's suffrage; he pressed Congress to grant women the right to vote in 1937. Throughout the 1930s, suffragists made significant gains, even getting enough states to ratify a constitutional amendment to make it law. However, federal legislators ultimately exploited a loophole to prevent its final passage, denying women the vote for the time being.

But through the expansion of social programs, under Cárdenas women found new ways to participate in the political and social life of the nation. Some became emissaries of Cárdenas's mission to modernize rural households by teaching hygiene, habits, and nutrition. Others were educated to become teachers and fanned out into rural areas to bring education and the revolutionary message to the countryside. While rural communities embraced some of these

## Indigenous Rights

Most Latin American revolutionaries sought to bring social justice to the poor and downtrodden of their nations, and some singled out the achievement of indigenous rights as foremost among their aims. Their efforts coincided with and complemented a generalized defense of native peoples beginning in the early twentieth century. Led by writers, intellectuals, and social activists, this defense came to be known as indigenismo.

In some ways, indigenismo went back to the earliest defenders of Indians against European depredations. Over the centuries, a few intellectuals and clergy had sympathized with and defended indigenous people, perpetually at a disadvantage vis-à-vis the white establishment. (See chapter 10 discussion on earlier indigenista writers.) In the twentieth century such novels as Alcides Argüedas's *Raza de bronce* (1919), Jorge Icaza's *Huasipungo* (1934), and Ciro Alegría's *El mundo es ancho y ajeno* (1941) celebrated indigenous peoples and cultures. Artists, especially those in Mexico, depicted the indigenous past in positive, even heroic, terms.

The Mexican Revolution went far toward redeeming indigenous culture— indeed, the new official history claimed that the movement derived almost entirely from Indians and workers. But indigenistas did not simply want to celebrate Indians; they sought to improve them. Still, more rhetoric than action flowed from government agencies. The government now paid attention to the large and varied indigenous population, developing programs to promote local education and to revive or invent anew local economies centered on indigenous handicrafts. But, as mestizaje emerged as the foundation of national identity, Indians who retained their local languages, dress, and customs continued to be seen as culturally and even racially inferior. Moreover, though the Mexican Revolution had been fought in defense of indigenous land rights and social justice, villages struggled through the 1920s to reclaim stolen lands, and Indians remained politically marginalized. While indigenismo sought to redeem the masses, it also reinforced the idea that the indigenous population was somehow different, and needed to be reformed, subdued, or mestisized. Indigenismo, in this case as in earlier ones, remained a creole and mestizo project to deal with the persistent "Indian problem" and therefore fit well with the celebration of mestizaje.

From Mexico, indigenismo spread southward into Guatemala, where Miguel Ángel Asturias wrote the haunting *Hombres de maíz* (1949), about the modern Maya peoples. In Brazil, indigenismo did not take root as firmly as in Spanish America, perhaps because most of the native peoples along the coast had died or fled inland. Still, the remarkable explorer/soldier/ethnographer Cândido Rondon, himself half indigenous Bororó, established the Brazilian Indian Protection Service in 1910. Gradually its responsibilities expanded to management of vast reservations in the Amazon and far west.

Since the 1960s indigenismo has lost some of its urgency, and other issues have captured the attention of policymakers. The powerful literary voice of indigenismo was diluted by the hugely popular magical realism that came into vogue in the 1960s. Yet, in the late twentieth and early twenty-first centuries, a resurgence of political movements has occurred in both Central America and the Andes, one that seeks to unite indigenous groups around a shared identity to challenge authoritarian governments, exclusion, and inequality.

socialist teachers, others were attacked and even killed for challenging rural traditions. Other women were active in labor movements and land seizures. Still others, like Catholic activists, pushed back against revolutionary change. Catholic women challenged anti-secularism by managing to reopen churches and schools and by bringing religious content back into national celebrations.

Because his socialist program evoked open opposition from conservatives and the church, Cárdenas attempted to reach an agreement with the Catholic archbishop. He condemned Calles's prior persecution of the church but also urged the church to concern itself more with social problems and issues, in the spirit of the progressive 1931 papal encyclical known as *Quadragesimo Anno,* updating the 1891 predecessor. The prelate agreed, and church-state relations have remained mostly peaceful since then.

One of the most remarkable episodes of Cárdenas's presidency, the petroleum nationalization, came to a head in 1938. The episode began two years earlier, when petroleum workers' unions formed a federation and affiliated with Lombardo Toledano's CTM. These workers earned more than most laborers in Mexico, yet they endured special hardships connected with living in oil field camps, buying in company stores, and being away from their families for long periods. The oil companies, led by major British and American firms, refused to recognize the unions. The CTM backed the federation's call for a strike, which then brought on a mandatory six-month cooling-off period and eventual government mediation.

The labor ministry mediators ruled in favor of the laborers, thanks to Lombardo Toledano's influence with Cárdenas, but the companies still refused to settle. Instead, they appealed the case to the Supreme Court. Cárdenas and other high officials were already irritated with the oil companies because they had shifted their purchases away from Mexico in the 1920s and 1930s, largely to Venezuela. Exports had fallen from 193 million barrels in 1921 to 41 million in 1936.

When the Supreme Court also ruled in favor of the laborers in early 1938, seventeen of the biggest companies sent a joint message to Cárdenas refusing to comply with the judicial ruling. Cárdenas took this as defiance of Mexican

**Figure 16.3** Lázaro Cárdenas (front row, center), shown here with oil union leaders in 1938. He served as president from 1934 to 1940. His military career, 1934 presidential campaign, and widespread travels took him to the most remote corners of the country. His patient, receptive manner led many poor people to call him Tata (Father) Lázaro. Acme Newspictures. Courtesy Library of Congress.

sovereignty and immediately nationalized the companies. He put them under a government corporation, Petróleos Mexicanos (Pemex), created to administer public oil lands, contracts, and refining.

The foreign companies expected the U.S. State Department and White House to give them full backing, so they submitted huge claims to the Mexican government: $200 million for the U.S. properties and $250 million for the British. Cárdenas countered with an offer of $10 million, saying that he would pay only for actual capital investment, not untapped oil reserves. Besides, he stated, most oil firms had long since paid off their capital and equipment costs in the form of excessive profits.

The expropriation was enormously popular among Mexicans, who sensed in it a moment of nationalist pride in which Mexico had resisted the Goliath to the north. University students held parades in enthusiastic support and the Catholic Church had Sunday collections to help pay for the indemnity. As U.S. ambassador Josephus Daniels stated, Mexican women "poured out of their homes by the thousands to voice their ardent support of the leaders who had somehow made the people feel that the oil exploiters were the enemies of their country." In an almost "religious festival," they gathered together in front of the Palace of Fine Arts and sacrificed "wedding rings, bracelets, earrings, and put them, as it seemed to them, on a national altar." Crowds offered everything from "gold and silver to animals and corn."[3] While Mexican women would have to wait until the 1950s to gain suffrage, this was a key moment of mass nationalist political participation.

In the next two years the companies waged a vicious campaign to force Mexico to return their assets or pay their claims. President Franklin D. Roosevelt refused to intervene, however, because his ambassador there, Josephus Daniels, convinced him that the companies had erred in defying the Supreme Court decision and that they had gotten what they deserved. The coming of World War II and the need for good relations with this key supplier of oil and minerals also influenced Roosevelt's response. The two governments eventually set up an arbitration commission that awarded the U.S. companies $24 million in 1941.

Late in 1938 Cárdenas decided to restructure the official party. Renamed the Party of the Mexican Revolution (PRM), it now embraced four sectors: the existing ones of labor, agraristas, and the army, plus a new one, popular groups. These latter were in fact mostly public servants who could be manipulated by the bureaucracy and the president. By the late 1930s the CTM claimed 1.25 million members, the National Peasant Confederation (CNC) 2.5 million, the military its highest authorized strength at 55,000, and the popular groups 55,000. Significantly, in 1938 soldiers were given the right to vote, which enhanced the influence of junior officers, who could broker the votes of their troops.

The four PRM sectors were conceived as vertical pillars of the party, ostensibly to channel information and aspirations up. In fact, they were conduits for official patronage, where in return for support and jobs, the party demanded loyalty, payments, and controlled voting. The PRM's successor, the Institutional Revolutionary Party (PRI), would operate the same way after 1946.

By 1937 the top army generals were the only wild cards in the political deck capable of challenging Cárdenas's authority. However, one unsuccessful conspiracy and a failed revolt, seen by historians as the final gasps of the revolutionary struggle, helped strengthen the president's hold on power. By 1938 those who remained in the army were loyal to Cárdenas. He had succeeded in pacifying the army and reducing its share of the federal budget from 25 to 19 percent. Younger, academy-trained officers who had not fought in the revolution were by then reaching command positions.

In 1939 Cárdenas passed a military reorganization bill that attempted to eradicate the spirit of caste that had previously bound together officers against civil society. He hoped instead to implant a desire to be of service to the nation. Meanwhile, the 1939 Obligatory Service Law helped diminish the gap between officers, troops, and the civilian population. A final measure to subdue the army was the authorization of civilian armed forces, especially the CNC and CTM militias, to serve as counterweights against ambitious generals. The peasants, always armed and ready to intervene in civil wars, proclaimed their loyalty to Cárdenas. In 1938 Lombardo Toledano paraded one hundred thousand workers in Mexico City for Labor Day and bragged that he had thirty thousand arms. Tension became palpable between the army and the militias, but the maneuvers delivered a clear message.

The succession crisis of 1940 proved that Cárdenas had tamed his rivals. The atmosphere of crisis and ideological confrontation that year brought out radical candidates for the presidency. Yet ultimately, Cárdenas was able to name and elect a moderate as his successor: General Manuel Ávila Camacho. The latter was relatively unknown, a desk officer who had not fought in the revolution. His main advantage was possessing few enemies. He was the only candidate not opposed by at least two PRM sectors. He was also the last general ever elected president in twentieth-century Mexico. Cárdenas's pacification of the army became complete in 1943 when the army was dropped from the PRM.

Cárdenas won a place of honor among Mexican revolutionary leaders due to his successful reforms in the 1930s. His administration pushed the 1917 constitutional mandates further than they had ever gone before and, in some cases, ever would again. Most authors agree that the revolution turned conservative around 1940, after which it remained alive largely in the rhetoric of ruling party officials and in the demands that popular groups made of the PRI-dominated state. Cárdenas, in turn, became an unofficial conscience of the revolution, a reminder of why so many had fought.

## Dictatorship and Oil in Venezuela to World War II

The two countries that span the northern ridge of South America could hardly have had more unlike experiences during the Depression decade. Venezuela endured the classic dictatorship of Juan Vicente Gómez until his death in 1935 and then continued under military presidents until 1945. Colombia, on the other hand, not only held a peaceful election in 1930, but actually also transferred the executive branch from the Conservative to the Liberal Party without incident. Oddly, these developments reversed the nineteenth-century traditions of these two countries.

Venezuela gained some respite from petty caudillos and intermittent civil wars through the imposition of a dictatorship by General Cipriano Castro (1899–1908), who was replaced by his vice president, Juan Vicente Gómez, in 1908. The latter wielded power as an autocratic modernizer, much like Mexico's Porfirio Díaz and Argentina's Julio Roca. He provided maximum administration with a minimum of democratic procedure. He also became infamous as one of the most ruthless dictators in the region.

Gómez, a native of the western Andes state of Táchira, continued the tradition of government by army officers and strong-willed rulers. Rural in outlook and accustomed to obedience from underlings, the dictators from Táchira had a lock on the presidency, which they exercised through military domination.

Gómez's extraordinary twenty-seven-year rule coincided with the rise of Venezuelan oil exports. This development, made possible by Gómez's guarantee

**Figure 16.4** A workboat servicing an oil derrick on Lake Maracaibo, Venezuela. During the 1920s oil exports from this region surpassed those from the Mexican gulf coast, the leading producer before World War I. Since then, the Venezuelan economy has depended heavily on oil sales. John Vachon. Courtesy Library of Congress.

of order and progress, deeply altered the future of the country, setting in motion developments that few could have predicted.

Earthy, crude, and unconcerned with appearances, Gómez ran Venezuela as his personal realm. He tolerated a congress as long as it did what it was told and obediently reelected him. He supported a bureaucracy in Caracas, though he preferred to live on his cattle ranch sixty miles away. He had an unerring sense for holding and exercising power and cared little about the formalities of office. He promulgated four constitutions, none of which infringed on his absolute powers. He differed from his nineteenth-century predecessors mostly in the effectiveness of his administration, one that did not tolerate the kinds of revolts and strife that had plagued the country previously.

The oil deposits of Venezuela, centered around Lake Maracaibo on the northwestern coast, had long been known to exist. World War I spurred huge growth in war industries in Europe and North America, thereby awakening interest in the Venezuelan oil deposits. Furthermore, the unreliability of the Mexican oil fields during the revolution there led the big international oil companies (called the "majors" and later the "Seven Sisters") to invest in drilling around Maracaibo. The first well came in after the outbreak of the war, and by 1918 Venezuela had begun exporting crude. Gómez had Congress pass legislation favorable to the majors but also protective of the rights of the workers.

Soon European and U.S. companies built huge refineries offshore, on the Dutch islands of Curaçao and Aruba, where they would be immune from local instability. The companies did not want to repeat their experiences in Mexico, where revolutionaries had routinely collected money to refrain from blowing up refineries. These installations converted crude into bunker, heating, and fuel oil for export throughout the Atlantic Basin. As the global energy economy shifted from coal to oil, demand for crude burgeoned. In the course of the 1920s Venezuela became the world's largest petroleum exporter and enjoyed a bonanza.

Gómez's success was due to several initiatives. First, he professionalized the army by providing officers with training and modern weapons. He made absolutely certain that it remained loyal to him, sending to the firing squad anyone who challenged his authority. Second, Gómez created a secret police branch that spied on civilians and reported dissent. Anyone overheard criticizing the government ended up in jail, exile, or the grave. Press censorship was the accepted practice, softened by government subsidies to publishers. When students at the Central University protested his policies in 1912, he closed it indefinitely; it did not reopen until 1923. Third, he gave the country unprecedented income from petroleum, spreading around the benefits. This depended upon keeping the majors happy, which he achieved by giving them unusually favorable terms. The companies responded by shifting their purchases to Venezuela.

Although there was general social calm during the Gómez regime, a few nationalists became critical of the concessions given to the oil companies. In 1928 a group of student activists almost seized power with a lightning coup. The group was subdued, however, and 220 ended up in jail. Afterward, most were released on the condition that they leave the country. Later these exiles reemerged as an important force in politics, calling themselves the Generation of 1928.

The Depression barely affected Venezuela, so efficient was Gómez's rule and so profitable was the oil industry. Even when he died in 1935, at age seventy-eight, his regime continued without much change. The next two presidents, both generals who had served as ministers of war, did relax censorship and sentences of exile, so that by the late 1930s limited political activity had resumed. Moreover, the labor unions—led by the oil field workers—began to exert more influence in the political arena. Still, the military dictatorship remained in place until 1945.

## Democracy and Reform in Colombia

In Colombia, a transformation occurred in the early twentieth century, leading to the end of the vicious, bloody struggles for power of previous generations. This was attributed largely to the firm leadership of General Rafael Reyes (1904–1914), an autocratic modernizer in the mold of Porfirio Díaz or Guzmán Blanco. Reyes created an ingenious bipartisan system called the National Union. Basically, the liberals and conservatives each received half the appointive positions in the entire government, including cabinet posts, satisfying their parties' need for patronage. In exchange, the liberals accepted the seemingly permanent occupation of the presidency by the conservatives. This calmed partisan rancor and prevented the appearance of party rivalries for at least a generation.

The Colombian economy began to recover in the early years of the century, in part buoyed by Brazil's coffee price support program, which sustained the world price of coffee. U.S. and European consumers prized mild Colombian beans for their flavor, and used them to improve blends that included cheaper Brazilian beans. Bananas also made their debut along the north coast, and by the late 1920s Colombia was exporting more than any nation except Ecuador. Other crops also found lucrative overseas markets. The expanding economy complemented Reyes's successes in quelling political fighting.

In the 1920s the Colombian government signed two important treaties. In the first, with the United States, Colombia forgave the U.S. role in the 1903 secession of Panama and received an indemnity of $25 million. This normalized relations and allowed U.S. companies to begin exploring for petroleum, recently discovered on the north coast. Shortly afterward oil exports began from the port of Barranquilla. The second treaty, with Peru, provided Colombia with a corridor stretching down to the town of Leticia on the Amazon River. More generally, settling outstanding problems opened the way for foreign investment and bond sales, which expanded rapidly in the 1920s.

Colombia's alpine geography, dominated by three mountain chains and divided by major rivers, had long hampered regional transportation. The formation of the first South American airline, SCADTA, proved a major step toward overcoming this problem in 1920. In addition, new rail lines, riverboats, and roads helped integrate the country economically.

The long conservative reign, however, had allowed many social problems to fester, and discontent surfaced in manufacturing cities and plantation towns. One labor action became infamous—the Santa Marta banana strike. The U.S.-owned United Fruit Company called in Colombian troops, who opened fire on the strikers, leaving over a hundred casualties. This scene, which dramatized, if exaggerated, the injustices committed by foreign companies, became immortalized in Gabriel García Márquez's novel, *One Hundred Years of Solitude.* In many other parts of the country, moreover, poor people became upset over the

---

### Novelistic Account of Santa Marta Banana Strike of 1928

"The great strike broke out. Cultivation stopped halfway, the fruit rotted on the trees and the hundred-twenty-car trains remained on the sidings. The idle workers overflowed the towns . . . it was announced that the army had been assigned to reestablish public order. . . . There were three regiments, whose march in time to a galley drum made the earth tremble. Their snorting of a many-headed dragon filled the glow of noon with a pestilential vapor. They were short, stocky, and brutelike. They perspired with the sweat of a horse and had a smell of sun-tanned hide and the taciturn and impenetrable perseverance of men from the uplands. . . . Martial law enabled the army to assume the functions of arbitrator in the controversy, but no effort at conciliation was made. As soon as they appeared in Macondo, the soldiers put aside their rifles and cut and loaded the bananas and started the trains running. The workers, who had been content to wait until then, went into the woods with no other weapons but their working machetes and they began to sabotage the sabotage. They burned plantations and commissaries, tore up tracks to impede the passage of the trains that began to open their path with machine-gun fire, and they cut telegraph and telephone wires . . . the authorities called upon the workers to gather in Macondo. . . . Around twelve o'clock, waiting for a train that was not arriving . . . workers, women, and children, had spilled out of the open space in front of the station. . . . The captain gave the order to fire and fourteen machine guns answered at once. It was as if the machine guns had been loaded with caps, because their panting rattle could be heard and their incandescent spitting could be seen, but not the slightest reaction was perceived. . . . They were penned in, swirling about in a gigantic whirlwind that little by little was being reduced to its epicenter as the edges were systematically being cut off all around like an onion being peeled by the insatiable and methodical shears of the machine guns. . . . [Later] an extraordinary proclamation to the nation . . . said that the workers left the station and had returned home in peaceful groups. The proclamation also stated that the union leaders, with great patriotic spirit, had reduced their demands to two points: a reform of medical services and the building of latrines in the living quarters."

Gabriel García Márquez, *One Hundred Years of Solitude,* trans. Gregory Rabassa (New York: Harper and Row, 1970), pp. 307–15. In a later interview García Márquez admitted that he exaggerated these events to enhance their drama.

---

lack of roads, schools, hospitals, and welfare programs. The Depression exacerbated these shortcomings.

The presidential election of 1930 went ahead peacefully, and the liberal candidate, Alfonso López, defeated his conservative opponent, which had not happened for fifty years. López's success owed partly to the Colombian electorate's sense that change was overdue and partly to López's appealing platform, called the Revolution on the March. Arguing that the federal government had to address pressing social problems, he advocated far-reaching reforms that ultimately required constitutional amendments. He argued that without these reforms, Colombia might drift toward a violent revolution.

It took several years for the liberals to assemble their reform program, which was largely enacted in 1936. That year a package of constitutional amendments separated church and state, created universal male suffrage, gave labor the right to collective bargaining and strikes, and authorized government economic planning. In addition, Congress passed much larger budgets for education and social security than ever before. Finally, Congress passed a land reform bill committed to the principle of giving property to those who work it. In many ways, these reforms paralleled those of Lázaro Cárdenas in Mexico, and similarly provided the liberals with a mass base of popular, reformist-minded supporters who for the first time felt part of the political process

The liberal era that lasted until 1946 also expanded democratic processes. Individual civil rights were complemented by full freedom of the press, freedom of assembly, and honest elections. In these years Colombians bragged that their democracy had withstood dire threats, and they called Bogotá the Athens of South America, referring to the birthplace of democracy.

## Peru

The populist era launched by the election of 1931 was derailed a year and a half later by an assassin's bullet that took President Luis Miguel Sánchez Cerro's life. The country plunged into a dictatorship organized by the army and the oligarchy. Congress installed one of Peru's top generals, Oscar Benavides, in the presidency, where he remained until 1939. Even after passing the office on to a civilian successor, the army remained powerful behind the scenes. APRA, meanwhile, grew more popular even though its activities were proscribed by the government.

The Benavides regime weathered several years of economic depression and then began to enjoy expanding production and employment in the mid-1930s. In keeping with the times, Benavides introduced legislation creating new welfare and educational agencies to deal with the social question. These agencies included a ministry of health, labor, and welfare—which expanded public services to the working class—and a social security system. In addressing the social question, Peru merely followed the lead of many other governments in the hemisphere, and its reforms were milder than most. The benefits of these programs remained largely in the cities, thereby attracting a steady stream of migrants from the countryside. By the 1950s the influx of rural migrants would create huge shantytowns, called *barriadas*, in major cities.

Toward the end of the 1930s, the army felt secure enough to hold elections. APRA was disqualified from nominating candidates, however, because of its revolutionary past. The official candidate for president predictably won. Manuel Prado Ugarteche served a six-year term (1939–1945), guiding the country through World War II. At first he flirted with right-wing movements and Axis sympathizers, but after the United States joined the war, he threw his country behind the Allied effort. Peruvians did not fight in the war but instead supplied strategic materials for U.S. arms factories.

## EVOLVING U.S. POLICY IN THE CARIBBEAN BASIN

During the 1920s the U.S. State Department began to view military intervention and occupation in the region as counterproductive. Marine and army landings cost money, squandered goodwill, and often stirred up more trouble than they suppressed. The Clark Memorandum, made public in 1930, set out the new policy, which became known as non-interventionism and later the Good Neighbor policy (see chapter 13).

Franklin Roosevelt most fully enunciated the new policy regarding Latin America during his first year in office. The United States would no longer intervene militarily in the internal affairs of neighboring nations, regardless of whose interests were at stake. U.S. citizens had to obey the laws of the country in which they resided. U.S. investors with complaints had to exhaust local courts and other means to redress their grievances. The United States would no longer answer calls to support one or another party or even to supervise elections in the region. The U.S. foreign policy community achieved such a broad consensus on non-intervention that it held remarkably steady until the mid-1950s.

The pledge not to intervene militarily by no means meant that the United States would stop pursuing its national interests in the region. On the contrary, during the 1930s, as in other eras of U.S. isolationism, the hemisphere received even closer scrutiny. The U.S. government employed more active diplomacy, spying, judicious military presence, political intrigue, and economic persuasion to further its interests. In the case of several Caribbean nations, this meant working with dictators who promised to defend U.S. economic and security interests in exchange for various kinds of support, including military and police training and equipment, as well as investment to develop infrastructure. Thus the Good Neighbor policy consisted of shifting from military intervention to more subtle kinds of influence in Latin American affairs.

The Roosevelt administration made the most use of several innovative kinds of diplomatic persuasion in the 1930s. First, it created an economic aid program, administered by the Export-Import Bank and later by other agencies.

**FDR's Good Neighbor Policy**

"In the field of world policy, I would dedicate this nation to the policy of the good neighbor—the neighbor who resolutely respects himself and . . . respects the rights of others."—Franklin Roosevelt, inaugural address, March 4, 1933

"The essential qualities of a true Pan Americanism must be the same as those which constitute a good neighbor, namely, mutual understanding, and through such understanding, a sympathetic appreciation of the other's point of view."—Franklin Roosevelt, Pan American Day address, April 14, 1933

"That is a new approach that I am talking about to these South American things. Give them a share. They think they are just as good as we are, and many of them are."—Franklin Roosevelt, speech, January 1940

Bryce Wood, *The Making of the Good Neighbor Policy* (New York: Columbia University Press, 1961); Lenny Frank, ed., *FDR: Selected Speeches of President Franklin D. Roosevelt* (Los Gatos, Calif.: n.p., 2009).

Cuba and several other Latin American countries were among the first to receive such aid. Second, U.S. military presence continued to be projected throughout the region from several bases in the Caribbean and the Panama Canal Zone and by means of naval and air patrols. These actions were reinforced in the late 1930s by multilateral meetings and treaties to defend against possible European aggression in the hemisphere. Third, the president himself visited Latin America several times and made concerted efforts to win friends through a more responsive diplomacy.

Such measures, essentially public relations gestures, paid off handsomely in goodwill and cooperation. And finally, presidential emissaries and friends serving in the region used their authority to help install governments that were willing to work with the United States. Backroom deals, clandestine financing, shared intelligence, and subterfuge became standard operating procedures. It is fair to say that the U.S. presence was stronger despite the military restraint exercised.

## THE CLASSIC DICTATORS

Partly as a result of U.S. policy, a new generation of dictators took over Latin America during the 1930s. Most of them were military officers who had built police organizations with U.S. support to take over when American forces withdrew. They were, for the most part, chosen by U.S. officials to safeguard U.S. interests, and they received special treatment from the State Department.

They exercised absolute authority and wielded it arbitrarily, yet they always cooperated with the U.S. Roosevelt acknowledged this kind of arrangement once when referring to Nicaraguan dictator Anastasio Somoza: with people like Somoza protecting U.S. interests, marines did not need to be stationed in the region.

Who were these classic dictators? They were born in the 1890s and early 1900s, usually into poor or lower-middle-class families. They came from rural areas, with little access to the amenities of the capital cities. They lost contact with their fathers at an early age, through abandonment, death, or other causes. They were usually nonwhites in countries where the elites prided themselves on European lineage. Finally, they had only primary or secondary schooling, in countries where aspirants for power usually had university training, often abroad. For all these reasons, a few years earlier it would have been impossible to predict that they would become heads of state in their respective countries.

If the United States bore some responsibility for the rise of the dictators by encouraging the context for their growing power, local politics and society determined the kind of men who would prevail. Each local army or police force typically had a small number of elite officers who enjoyed privileged status and political power because of their upper-class family connections. Noncommissioned officers and soldiers, in contrast, were held in contempt by the wealthy, tolerated only because someone had to keep the lower classes in line, through violence if necessary. And occasionally these forces had to fight the armies of neighboring countries. These forces were not armies in the modern sense: their officers meddled in politics, fought among themselves, stole money and supplies, and cared little about the effectiveness or discipline of their troops.

The noncommissioned officers, on the other hand, usually came from the rural middle or lower classes, where loyalty to the white landowning elite was traditional. They held effective control over the rank and file and were only tenuously supervised by the elite officers. Thus a social gap opened up between noncoms and the upper brass that allowed the former to assume command of troops in moments of crisis. Once in command, such officers could then transform their positions into political leadership by appealing to the masses, assuming populist stances, or by eliminating rivals. This, in a general way, describes the rise of the dictators in the 1930s and 1940s.

These men had other, more personal characteristics that merit attention. They were quite intelligent despite their lack of regular schooling. They were politically astute and possessed the willpower to take advantage of opportunities that came their way. They displayed innate understanding of military tactics that, despite meager formal training, allowed them to prevail in actual combat. They distrusted colleagues, suspecting them of wishing to take power, so they never cultivated protégés who might become rivals. Instead, they groomed their sons for power in the hope of creating family dynasties. In many cases this succeeded: Somoza's sons Luis and Anastasio Jr. (Tachito) both wielded power in Nicaragua after their father's death. François Chevalier, Haiti's infamous Papa Doc, was succeeded by his son Claude, nicknamed Baby Doc. In the Dominican Republic, however, Rafael Trujillo failed in his efforts to shape his son Ramfis into an iron-fisted successor.

Most of the classic dictators managed to rise to the top as army officers, having been born into modest circumstances. They cleverly blended the skills of military command with political savvy. All were ruthless in getting power and holding onto it. They thought nothing of ordering the murder of a rival. They often enjoyed considerable popularity among the nonwhite lower classes, who admired their cunning, empathized with their successes, and responded to their more inclusive promises. They recruited middle- and upper-class collaborators using nationalistic rhetoric and appeals to Hispanic tradition. Finally, the dictators served as "cultural brokers" by mediating between and sometimes even translating for U.S. military occupation forces. Then during the transitions from armed forces under U.S. tutelage to national guards, they naturally emerged as future commanders.

## BATISTA AND TRUJILLO

Perhaps the most complex and long lived of the classic dictators, Fulgencio Batista ruled Cuba off and on from the mid-1930s until 1959. His background, talents, style, achievements, and failures make him almost a prototype of the classic dictator.

Both Batista's parents were poor mulattoes, and he was of mixed African, indigenous, Hispanic, and possibly even Chinese heritage. His father, Belisario, a sugarcane cutter in the northeast, claimed to have fought with Antonio Maceo during the independence struggle. Shortly before Fulgencio's birth, the family migrated to the sugar port of Veguita in Oriente province.

As a child Fulgencio cut sugarcane, but he also learned to read and write in a public school and a Quaker night school. His mother died when he was fourteen, and he wandered from town to town, doing odd jobs that he got using his good looks, charm, and speaking ability. At one point he worked as stable boy in an army barracks, where he earned the nickname *el mulato lindo* (pretty brown boy).

In 1921 Batista enlisted in the army, where he was assigned to the legal affairs office because of his ability to read, write, and speak well. His work as a law clerk taught him to type and take stenography. Later he taught these skills in the staff school. Another assignment required guarding President Zelaya's estate, for which he was given temporary army leave. In 1924 he married Elisa Godíñez and transferred back to regular service. There he became a trusted aide to his battalion commander, who promoted him to corporal and eventually first sergeant. Batista thus had a wide range of experiences and enjoyed an insider's view of the internal politics of the Cuban Army.

**Figure 16.5** Fulgencio Batista (right) meeting with the head of the CBS news bureau in Havana in 1935. Courtesy of Hoover Institution Library and Archives, Stanford University.

In 1933, during the depths of the Machado dictatorship, Batista served as stenographer in kangaroo courts impaneled to punish the dictator's enemies. His disgust with the abuses led him to join a subversive organization, the ABC. In that same year Machado was deposed amid terrible rioting, and a stand-in was installed as president. In September, however, Batista helped lead a sergeants' revolt against the commissioned officers, which toppled the government again.

Batista's success in 1933 derived in part from the breakdown in the chain of command in the army. The commissioned officers were mostly from the traditional elite and were white, unlike the noncoms and soldiers, who were mulattoes and blacks. The officers spent most of their time in leisure and political activities, centering on the aristocratic officers' club, far from the barracks. They had gradually lost the loyalty of the rank and file because of their isolation. This allowed Batista and his fellow conspirators to preempt command and overthrow the government.

The provisional government installed in September 1933 came under the leadership of Ramón Grau San Martín, a university professor of economics who had been prominent in anti-Machado activities. However, Sumner Welles, the

U.S. State Department emissary in Havana, refused to accept Grau San Martín because of his socialist ideas and inability to impose order. So in January 1934 Batista, by now a colonel and the most powerful person in Cuba, removed Grau San Martín, with the blessing of Welles. During the coming months the U.S. government supported Batista's de facto regime by extending to Cuba a $4 million Export-Import Bank loan, awarding Cuba the largest sugar quota of any Latin American country, and abrogating the Platt Amendment.

With Batista's close connection with the U.S. embassy, he at first exercised power from behind the throne. He moved to stage center in 1936, however, when he became chief of staff of the army. From then on he ruled Cuba more openly, using an informal alliance with labor, the Communist Party (legalized in 1938), and the army. Taking cues from the Roosevelt administration, Batista pushed for social and economic reforms, such as university autonomy, labor unions, women's suffrage, expanded primary and secondary education, and industrialization.

Eventually Batista called a constituent assembly that wrote the progressive 1940 Constitution. After its enactment he ran for president and won, partly due to his popular reforms and restraint as ruler. His four-year term saw great prosperity in Cuba, due to wartime spending by the United States. He became one of the United States's staunchest allies in the region over the next two decades, defending U.S. economic interests, opening the country up to U.S. culture and influence and, by the 1950s, ruthlessly repressing any opposition.

Another long-ruling classic dictator, Rafael Trujillo, was born in 1891, in San Cristóbal, Dominican Republic. He belonged to the small-town middle class of his region. He had eight brothers and two sisters. His scanty education and Haitian lineage barred him from white, aristocratic society. Shrewd and intelligent, he used his charm to move around in regional society. He gained a reputation for womanizing and rowdiness as a youth. At one point he worked as a security officer on a sugar plantation.

Trujillo's political career began during the U.S. military occupation of his country (1916–1924). In 1918 he signed on as an officer in the national guard police force organized by the U.S. Marines and won rapid promotion. When the United States pulled out, Trujillo became commander of the unit, which had been strengthened into a quasi-army. Although powerful now, Trujillo did not enjoy acceptance by the elite, which looked down on military officers.

Trujillo married a woman of the lower class in 1917, but he divorced her in 1924, partly because she held back his career. Three years later he remarried, this time to a high-society woman of good family. This marriage proved unhappy, too, because Trujillo consorted with a string of mistresses for the rest of his life. In 1927, for example, one of these women bore him his son Ramfis, whom he unsuccessfully tried to groom as successor.

Trujillo seized power in 1930, aided by the disorder caused by economic depression and a devastating hurricane. Though the old, monied elites never

---

### Massacre of Twenty-Five Thousand Haitians in the Dominican Republic in 1937

"For a century and a half Haiti and the Dominican Republic have shared the island of Hispaniola, located between Cuba and Puerto Rico. The arrangement has always been awkward, for the two nations differ sharply in language, ethnic tradition, racial heritage, religion, government, and family makeup. The border between the two nations was not fully delineated until the 1930s, and even then tens of thousands of Haitians remained on the Dominican side. The interpenetration of the two peoples grew during the annual sugar harvest, when thousands more Haitians crossed the border to cut cane.

"The Dominican dictator Rafael Trujillo, who inspected the border region in October 1937, expressed great irritation at the large number of Haitians living in Dominican territory. He was no doubt influenced by the Dominican tendency to view the largely Afro-descendant nation of Haitians as racially and culturally inferior to Dominicans, though settling the border also likely contributed to the massacre. He instructed the army to issue an ultimatum obliging Haitians to leave the country in four days; after that they would begin executing those who remained. One eyewitness reported that:

> the guards picked up a lot of people to help them with the raids on the Haitians and the killings . . . guards and the people who were helping them out dug big holes, then they brought the Haitians they had captured. They were tied one to another in groups, and they brought them to the edges of the holes. One by one they untied them before killing them. They were beaten to death. They were told to bend down and then they gave them a blow to the neck. They fell into the holes dead. Some of them were still alive when they fell, and still suffering. My cousin told me. He became sick when he saw what was happening and they threw him out of that place. . . . Practically without stopping, day and night, they spent many days killing Haitians. They used bonfires fueled with wood so they could see in the night.

"A U.S.-supervised investigation of the incident concluded that Trujillo should issue an apology and pay Haiti an indemnification of $750,000. This was done in 1938, on the eve of World War II. The case was never formally reopened."

Miguel Aquino, *Holocaust in the Caribbean* (Waterbury, Conn.: Emancipation Press, 1997), pp. 130, 140.

---

fully supported him, he garnered the backing of a new wealthy elite that had benefitted from his largesse and that for many years offered him their loyalty while overlooking his moral flaws and brutal tendencies. He also garnered some mass support with his challenges—in deed and in person—to the old guard white establishment.

In 1931, Trujillo created the Dominican Party, which became the country's sole political party, and through which he funneled patronage, controlled the population, and built a personality cult. From then until his assassination in 1961 he ruled the country like a despot. Until the late 1950s he was never seriously opposed by the United States, which indeed helped him remain in power by awarding the country a generous sugar quota in 1935.

Trujillo's personality defies easy description. Preoccupied with sex, he pursued women with all the means at his disposal, treating them with a jealous possessiveness. He was exceedingly vain and preened himself with hair grease, perfume, makeup, and powder. Later in life he used talcum to whiten his complexion. He always dressed formally and obliged his aides to do likewise. His vanity led him to rename the capital city after himself: Santo Domingo became Ciudad Trujillo.

Trujillo dominated the country and all its institutions. No one was beyond his influence. He used terror, secret police, spies, torture, propaganda, intrigue, graft, and subterfuge to manipulate and control others, leading to one of the bloodiest dictatorships of that time. One historian stated, "Trujillo's power was based as much on the consumption of women through sexual conquest as it was on the consumption of enemies of state through violence."[4] Yet, like others of his generation, he received support from the United States through the 1930s and 1940s due to his ability to protect U.S. economic and security interests.

## CONCLUSIONS AND ISSUES

The 1930s proved to be a complex, troubled, and dangerous time in Latin America. The Great Depression created severe hardships and suffering for the masses, and it bankrupted many governments. Partly as a result, rival parties and groups sought power, provoking a spate of revolts and coups in the region. The laissez-faire economic policies that had prevailed before 1929 had left governments open to indebtedness and financial shocks, and many wealthy families faced ruin. Disenchantment with the old liberal order led Latin American leaders and intellectuals to turn inward in search of national preservation. They sought strength in their own people and traditions, and they offered protection for native industry. At the same time, some of the radical experiments of the era, like communism in the USSR, fascism in Italy, and Nazism in Germany, appealed to young people. Radical movements arose and competed with the traditional parties, sometimes leading to violent clashes.

In most cases, the wealthy elite managed to retain control over their countries' governments. Many governments sought to soften the harsh effects of the Depression with enlightened social policies, like retirement benefits and free health care. Their response to labor assertiveness tended to be more unyielding: they used police to beat down strikers and created government-sanctioned unions that could be controlled from the top down. Most countries abandoned democratic procedures, if they existed, and relied on autocratic regimes and controlled elections to maintain stability.

In some areas, outright dictatorships emerged in the 1930s, sometimes with the blessing of the U.S. government, which had decided no longer to station military forces in the region (excepting in Panama, Puerto Rico, and Cuba). The leaders of these regimes became the classic dictators, portrayed in movies and novels about Latin America. Although not representative of the region as a whole, they do form a coherent group of leaders who reflected an important phase in circum-Caribbean leadership during the era of the Good Neighbor policy.

## Discussion Questions

How did the decade of the 1930s forcibly bring the world's nations into closer proximity, if not cooperation?

What economic, political, and social responses did Latin American leaders make to the Great Depression? How effective were they?

Were the coups that overthrew six governments the direct outcome of the Wall Street collapse of October 1929 or were deeper causes at their roots? Explain using three coups as examples.

Were the military governments that rose to power in the 1930s different from the dictatorships that preceded them? If so, how, and if not, why?

How did U.S. policy shift from the late 1920s to the 1930s with regard to relations with Latin America?

How were developments in Mexico under Lázaro Cárdenas the culmination of the policies launched during the 1910–1920 revolution? How were they the high point of revolutionary-era reforms?

What led to the rise of the classic dictators in the mid to late 1930s? Was it related to new U.S. policies toward the region?

## Timeline

| | |
|---|---|
| 1908–35 | General Juan Vicente Gómez of Venezuela wields dictatorial powers |
| 1928–34 | Maximato, when Mexico's Plutarco Elias Calles uses National Revolutionary Party to rule through puppet presidents |
| 1929–39 | Global Great Depression |
| 1930–45 | Military uprising in Brazil puts Getúlio Vargas in power |
| 1930–32 | Military coup in Argentina removes Hipólito Yrigoyen, installs military regime led by General José F. Uruburu |
| 1930 | Enrique Oyala Herrera in Colombia wins presidency, begins era of liberal dominance |
| 1930 | Military coup by Rafael Trujillo gives him control of the Dominican Republic |
| 1931 | Elections in Peru install President General Sánchez Cerro, who was assassinated two years later |
| 1932 | Elections in Panama install President Harmodio Arias |
| 1932 | Elections in Chile install President Arturo Alessandri |

| 1933 | Franklin D. Roosevelt launches Good Neighbor policy |
| 1934–40 | Fulgencio Batista assumes behind-the-scenes control of Cuba |
| 1934–40 | Lázaro Cárdenas serves as president of Mexico |
| 1938 | Cárdenas nationalizes the petroleum industry |
| 1938 | Trujillo orders massacre of Haitians |

## Keywords

APRA

Candomblé

Confederation of Mexican Workers (CTM)

dictablanda

Estado Novo (New State)

Good Neighbor policy

Great Depression

infamous decade

Institutional Revolutionary Party (PRI)

*The Masters and the Slaves*

Maximato

National Union

*One Hundred Years of Solitude*

Pemex

petroleum

racial democracy

*Rerum Novarum*

Revolution on the March

Roca-Runciman Treaty

World War II

# Latin America in World War II

## The Bonds of War

In 1944 the Brazilian Expeditionary Force (FEB), with over twenty-five thousand men and women, went to fight alongside the Americans and the Allied powers in Europe. They landed in Italy and played an important role in chasing the German Army north into Austria and securing the liberated territory. Friendships forged in battle during World War II between Brazilians and Americans proved deep and enduring. Many young officers rose to political prominence in Brazil in the 1960s and 1970s, and friendships with Americans dating from the battlefields enhanced U.S.-Brazilian relations for a generation.

In this oral history, Lt. Hugo Corrêa recounts events of April 1945 that led to the capture of a German Army division:

> The previous day, when we reconnoitered the area from which we would launch our attack, we saw a patrol from the 4th Company that had barely managed to return to base. It had been attacked with automatic rifles and grenades. To see those troops who could barely move because of the heavy fire they took was like a bucket of cold water thrown at us. We spent the night under a wall trying to sleep, so the next day we could advance on the enemy lines.
>
> Prior to marching, our artillery pounded the enemy positions with intense fire. Our orders were to set out as soon as the artillery fire began.
>
> I took up my position at the head of the squad and put Sergeant Andirás Nogueira de Abreu at the rear, to keep stragglers moving. When the artillery ended, we were on the crest of the hill. We surprised some German soldiers hiding in a bunker protected from artillery fire. They shot a few rounds at us and wounded Corporal Aldo. I had our machine guns put in position to fire on the bunker and ordered some grenades tossed in, the way you flush out cornered animals. Very soon a little white

flag appeared and fifteen Germans came out of the bunker pleading for us not to kill them. . . .

My next orders were to attack the city of Zocca at dawn, which we did without much trouble.

The Germans retreated but still patrolled and set up points of resistance, to harass our advancing troops. They also counterattacked. . . .

On the following day we crossed into a mountainous region, arriving at Levizzano, which was in the foothills of the Appennini, where we had an extraordinary view of the immense plain of the rich and developed Pó Valley.

In Levizzano we had a great surprise, in that the local inhabitants received us with shouts calling us "liberators," hugging and kissing us, and offering us wine. It was a welcome reception.[1]

Many Latin American nations contributed to the war effort. Mexico sent a squadron of fighter pilots into combat in the Philippines, and, even more important, hundreds of thousands of Mexican laborers, called *braceros*, crossed the border legally into the United States to take up jobs left vacant by Americans serving in the armed forces abroad. After the war ended, border crossings and trade remained heavy, reflecting the growing assimilation of the people along both banks of the Rio Grande. Throughout the border region, millions of business transactions and workers went back and forth every day. The border soon became not just a dividing line separating two nation-states, but a frontier that served as both a transition zone between the two countries and a place with its own unique culture and economy.

Beyond troops and workers sent by Mexico and Brazil, many countries from across Latin America participated in World War II. They enforced security measures aimed at protecting the Caribbean and the Panama Canal from German aggressions, repressed fascist parties and organizations, participated in multilateral security agreements, and made favorable trade deals that ensured a regular supply of primary products needed for U.S. wartime industry.

## INTER-AMERICAN DEFENSE

As the 1930s wore on, European diplomacy grew more tense and threatened to plunge the world into war again. Germany's chancellor, Adolf Hitler, flexed his nation's considerable muscle and promised to spread German influence throughout Europe and perhaps the world. Italy under Benito Mussolini grew aggressive, invading Libya and Ethiopia in northern Africa. The German and Italian regimes—Nazi and fascist, respectively—resembled each other in authoritarian structure, censorship, propaganda, militarism, and intolerance of minority populations. Meanwhile, Japan also began a decade of military expansion into China and Southeast Asia that would ally it militarily with the Nazi and fascist governments (forming the Axis powers) when war broke out in

September 1939. These events reverberated with threatening tones in the Americas.

In the spirit of multilateralism, cooperation, and good neighborliness that swept across the region, the nations of the Western Hemisphere participated in a series of inter-American meetings convoked to deal with security threats in the late 1930s. Because the level of hostilities increased with each year that passed, the meetings themselves took on increasingly ominous business, and the U.S. leadership role deepened. In 1936 the foreign ministers of the hemisphere convened in Buenos Aires and signed a treaty promising to submit hemispheric conflicts to mediation. Two years later, responding to Axis aggression in Europe, inter-American delegates in Lima, Peru, passed a more forceful declaration: the hemisphere pledged to defend itself against internal or external attacks.

When war actually broke out, the foreign ministers of the Americas hurriedly met in Panama in September 1939 to discuss ways to keep the war from spreading across the Atlantic. They declared a neutrality zone around the continents, extending three hundred miles out to sea. They also set up committees to coordinate economic responses to the war. These measures proved inadequate.

The fall of France to Nazi armies in June 1940 brought the war to the Americas. French and Dutch colonies in the Caribbean Basin, now under German control, could be used as platforms for aggression inside the neutrality zone. Martinique and the Guianas, in particular, could endanger oil tanker sea lanes, Panama Canal approaches, and air routes.

The United States called a meeting of foreign ministers in Havana that immediately put those territories under an inter-American protectorate. In effect, they were administered by the United States for defense purposes. The foreign ministers also beefed up counterespionage programs. The United States followed up by persuading Latin American governments to nationalize German and Italian airlines operating in their countries. In a short time, a network for inter-American defense planning began to take shape.

Between the Havana meeting and the December 1941 Japanese attack on Pearl Harbor—the same attack that plunged the United States into war—the U.S. government took a number of steps to improve its defense posture in the Americas. Several countries received financial aid in exchange for cooperation, and military assistance (under the Lend-Lease Act and military training programs) began to flow south. By the same token, Latin American countries gave the United States the right to operate bases and observation stations in their territories.

Meanwhile, Standard Oil heir and politician Nelson Rockefeller volunteered to set up an ambitious cultural exchange program to improve people-to-people relations. Under the awkward name "Office of the Coordinator of

Inter-American Affairs," Rockefeller's program sent U.S. celebrities like Will Rogers on tour to South America and brought performers like Brazil's Carmen Miranda, already well known in the United States, for return visits. It also sponsored feature films and news services favorable to the Allies. Under the program, Walt Disney traveled to Brazil and, in addition to producing multiple military training films, put out at least two feature films, including *The Three Caballeros*. By the mid-1940s, Disney had become a household name in much of Latin America.

The level of economic coordination also increased markedly to avoid short-ages caused by the war. The Roosevelt administration, whose first priority was to support Great Britain, the principal enemy of the Axis powers, simultane-ously strengthened the defense positions of its neighbors against the possibility of war. Several sites were especially critical to hemispheric defense. Panama was regarded as most exposed because of the canal's ability to move ships and supplies between the two oceans. A widening project on the canal brought prosperity to the Panamanians, and a friendly government after 1941 conceded lands for more defense bases. Scores of anti-aircraft sites sprang up around the canal.

U.S. military planners also regarded Brazil's northeastern hump as strategic because it extended into the south Atlantic and lay only 1,840 miles west of the African coast. With German general Erwin Rommel's rapid conquests across North Africa in 1941, it appeared that the German Air Force might be able to ferry planes to South America. From there they could reach Panama and even North America. To prevent that, Brazil leased a base in Natal to the United States for moving aircraft, troops, and supplies eastward to Africa and beyond.

Finally, Mexico's unguarded border and coastal waters left the United States vulnerable to Japanese attacks. The two governments negotiated a series of agreements that made Mexico a critical ally during the war. By the eve of the U.S. declaration of war, defense trouble spots in the hemisphere continued to preoccupy planners.

## Brazil in World War II

The most cooperative wartime ally in the hemisphere, Brazil strengthened what was already an unwritten alliance with the United States. After some haggling, President Getúlio Vargas concluded a deal with the Roosevelt admin-istration for the U.S. Army Air Corps to contract for a base at Natal, where Brazil bulges out into the south Atlantic.[2]

The U.S. base at Natal not only preempted a German air bridge but also made it possible to create a major Allied supply route to the European theater. In early 1944, Natal was the busiest U.S. air base in the world, the jumping-off point for tens of thousands of fighters, bombers, and cargo planes headed to

**Figure 17.1** President Franklin Roosevelt (left) visited the Natal air base in Brazil in 1943, returning from Casablanca. President Getúlio Vargas (seated behind him) had struck a good bargain in exchange for leasing the base. Courtesy Franklin Delano Roosevelt Library.

Europe. Female pilots flew some of these planes, freeing male aviators for combat duty.

The Natal base was also the site of a historic meeting between Presidents Vargas and Roosevelt in 1943, while the latter was returning from the Casablanca summit in North Africa. Later, well-known figures like Charles Lindbergh, Jack Benny, and Eleanor Roosevelt visited the base.

In exchange for the Natal base, Brazil received financing for an entire steel factory to be transplanted from Pennsylvania to a site near Rio de Janeiro. This plant, called Volta Redonda, formed the nucleus of what later became the largest steel industry in South America. In addition, the United States supplied the Brazilian military with a wide array of weaponry.

When German submarines sank several Brazilian freighters in November 1941, Vargas forged even closer links with the United States. After the Japanese attacked Pearl Harbor, Brazil agreed to host an inter-American meeting of foreign ministers to seek a united front against the Axis powers. Led by Brazil, most countries pledged their solidarity with the United States, severed ties with the Axis powers, signed the Declaration of the United Nations, and eventually declared war. The January 1942 Rio de Janeiro meeting presented a largely united front against the Axis powers. Brazil went well beyond that in the coming years.

---

### Rubber Supplies from Iquitos, Peru

Japanese occupation of virtually all Southeast Asian rubber plantations in 1939–1941 severely restricted U.S. supplies of this strategic material. Increased production of armaments, for shipment to England and for U.S. arsenals, added urgency to the search for new sources. The U.S. government created the Rubber Development Corporation (RDC) for buying Amazon rubber. To complement production in Brazil, the RDC encouraged shipments from Peru. The U.S. vice consul in Iquitos wrote about the effort in a memoir:

> I can remember the flurry of excitement . . . when, in May, 1943, the first token shipments of rubber, totaling about ten tons, were flown from Iquitos to Belem do Pará, at the mouth of the Amazon.
>
> The turning point came in 1944. The jungle monarch did not leap to his feet, but at least he began to stir. The pungent, smoke-stained balls gradually piled up in the RDC warehouse, a block from the Vice Consulate. In February, a record shipment of seventy-five gross tons of rubber slipped downstream aboard the RDC barge Manhattan. . . . When we read about the amount of natural rubber it took to manufacture one tire for a B-29, we hoped that the RDC Brazil was having more luck reviving the industry than was RDC Peru.

Quoted in Hank Kelly and Dot Kelly, *Dancing Diplomats* (Albuquerque: University of New Mexico Press, 1950), pp. 212–13.

---

The Amazon basin contained a big share of the native rubber trees in existence in the 1930s, and U.S. defense planners looked to them as a source for latex, a raw material critical for war industries. Japanese forces had already occupied the other major sources of rubber—Dutch, French, and British plantations in Southeast Asia. Therefore, the U.S. and Brazilian governments established a joint program designed to increase rubber production in the Amazon and earmark it for U.S. factories. Called the Battle for Rubber, the program cost millions of dollars and led to major migration into the rubber districts of the Amazon. In addition, scientists in Belém, near the mouth of the river, stepped up their research into better species and cultivation methods. Although they never achieved plantation cultivation, they made outsiders aware of the rich natural resources hidden in the rainforest.[3]

After the Rio meeting, President Vargas and his military advisors considered how to take full advantage of their wartime cooperation. Once the Allied powers controlled North Africa, U.S. attention shifted away from Brazil, now just a ferrying point for shipments to Africa. In order to achieve a higher standing after the war, Vargas decided that they had to make a blood sacrifice by sending troops to fight in Europe.

Two joint military commissions (one in Washington and one in Rio) worked out the myriad details of training, equipment, transport, maneuvers, command, and location. The division that went to Italy in 1944, called the Brazilian Expeditionary Force (FEB), numbered over twenty-five thousand men and women. The army also insisted on keeping up its strength at home, especially in the northeast around Natal and along the southern border with Argentina. By the end of the war, the effort had had a positive effect on the military and on nationalist sentiment in the country.

The FEB represented a level of training, logistics, coordination, and field combat far beyond the nation's previous experience. Still, U.S. navy transports took them to Italy and the U.S. Army supplied their weapons and uniforms. The Americans set the objectives for the division and supported them on the flanks. It was an important experience in international operations for both nations.

From its arrival in Italy in mid-1944 until its return to Brazil in 1945, the FEB performed very well as part of Lt. General Mark Clark's Fifth Army. It participated in the capture of a key mountain redoubt, Monte Castello, took the surrender of a German division, and helped clear the way for a spring offensive into northern Italy. U.S. Army planners tried to convince the Brazilians to remain in Europe after the war as part of an international force, but they were called home and demobilized.

Of all the Latin American countries, Brazil made the largest contribution to the Allied victory. This remains a point of nationalist pride for Brazilians, who commemorated their contribution with a Monument to the Dead of World War II in Rio de Janeiro, under which over 450 soldiers killed in battle are buried.

Almost as soon as the troop ships entered international waters, critics of Vargas began turning the FEB's participation in Europe into an appeal to end the dictatorship at home. How, they asked, could Brazil fight against dictatorship abroad while sustaining one at home? This and other attacks on Vargas had an effect, and many army officers returning home felt the need to help restore democracy. In October 1945, in fact, top army officers overthrew Vargas and held elections for a constitutional body that finished its work the following year.

In the long run, the FEB had important impacts on domestic affairs. After the war, the Brazilian Army renewed its commitment to joint planning and training with the United States, so the unwritten alliance continued. With U.S. participation, Brazil created the Superior War School in 1949, some of whose graduates later became prominent in the military takeover of the Brazilian government in 1964. Finally, much of what would later be called the National Security Doctrine among Latin American military thinkers derived from the writings of their Brazilian colleagues. Many of their ideas had been generated in consultation with American officers beginning in World War II.

**Figure 17.2** A 1944 photograph showing Italian residents of Massarosa, a small town north of Pisa, greeting Brazilian soldiers who had helped drive out the Germans. Courtesy Library of Congress.

## Mexico in World War II

President Cárdenas's choice for presidential candidate in the 1940 election proved one of the most important decisions in modern Mexican history. The nation faced three candidates offering divergent paths. On the right, former military officer Juan Andreu Almazán promised conservative policies, more church-oriented government, and an end to the revolution. He ran on the ticket of the National Action Party (PAN), identified with businessmen in the powerful northern industrial city of Monterrey, Nuevo León. On the left lay increased socialization under the more radical Francisco Múgica, an architect of the 1917 Constitution, a former governor and ministry secretary, and ideological heir of Cárdenas. Finally, in the center lay a moderate path of stability under the guidance of War Minister Manuel Ávila Camacho. This path would lead to the cooling of the revolution and to the abandonment of constitutional directives for change. Cárdenas sympathized with the leftist leaders but in the end chose the middle path. The onset of World War II, his recent confrontation with the Great Powers (United States and Great Britain) over oil nationalization, the German-Soviet pact, growing domestic opposition among elites to revolutionary radicalism, and the likelihood of U.S. hostility to a radical government in Mexico influenced his decision. Cárdenas expected the revolution to cool off naturally after he stepped down. Ávila Camacho echoed this sentiment in his inaugural address, which spoke of normalizing and consolidating existing social and economic advances. Since 1940, social progress has been gradual, evolutionary instead of revolutionary.

Ávila Camacho's leadership style differed sharply from that of his predecessor. He had served in Obregón's forces during the revolution but had not seen combat since 1920. As a desk officer and administrator in the 1920s and 1930s, he gained recognition as a negotiator and conciliator. Still, he was jokingly referred to as the unknown soldier because he had so little public recognition. He owed his appointment as minister of war partly to the fact that his brother was one of the "big five" military chieftains in 1939.

Even during the now-obligatory election campaign, change was under way. Ávila Camacho stated at one point that he was a *creyente* (believer), meaning that he was a Catholic and not anti-clerical. This signaled his desire to seek a friendly relationship with the church.

The pace of social and economic reforms slowed markedly under Ávila Camacho. He distributed only about 12 million acres of land, most of it awarded to individuals, not to ejidos. Private enterprise and individual initiative replaced socialist doctrine in public school curricula. Rather than train more teachers to carry the revolution into the countryside, Ávila Camacho and his minister of education devised a voluntary literacy campaign called "Each One Teach One." This avoided the tense confrontations between urban reformers and local village leaders that had arisen during earlier efforts. This campaign had limited success.

Leadership of the Confederation of Mexican Workers (CTM) shifted, too, at the new president's insistence. Fidel Velásquez, a moderate, replaced Lombardo Toledano, and labor actions became smaller, less political, and more focused on narrow economic demands. Wartime economic disruption generated stiff inflation—283 percent between 1939 and 1946. Only in the last year did the minimum wage increase, by 14 percent. Therefore, wages fell far behind cost-of-living hikes, and the CTM, which at times found itself outside of official favor during the war, was correspondingly weakened.

Partly to compensate for dwindling real wages, the Ávila Camacho administration created a social security system in 1942. The Mexican Social Security Institute (IMSS) selected a few well-organized labor sectors in Mexico City for early inclusion. In 1946 the coverage remained small—only 287,000 were covered in a nation of 25 million. It took another five years for its members to number 1 million. To this day, the Mexican social security system is among the least effective in the hemisphere for coverage and quality.

The Ávila Camacho administration vigorously promoted business growth. In 1940 the president expanded the role of the Nacional Financiera (created in

1934) into that of a national development bank. It was given a monopoly on incoming loans and investment capital, largely from the United States. All major projects had to be approved by the agency, and sometimes by U.S. officials as well. Moreover, domestic businesspeople could apply to it for venture capital, and during the war it became the equivalent of an industrial development agency. The new investments, wartime sales to the United States and Europe, and government encouragement, including a 1941 law granting tax exemptions to a wide range of new industries, gave a tremendous push to industrialization. Manufacturing grew at a fast clip during the war, and per capita income also rose rapidly.

The U.S. government made loans to the Nacional Financiera so that Mexico could continue to produce goods essential to Allied war industries. In addition to U.S. support, the two countries signed a reciprocal trade agreement in 1942, wherein Mexico guaranteed to supply the U.S. with an array of goods needed for the war effort at fixed prices, including its entire production of silver. Tariffs and trade barriers virtually disappeared. The United States also made considerable loans to Mexico through the Export-Import Bank. Finally, a U.S. technical team went to Mexico to recommend improvements for the decrepit rail system.

U.S. business was encouraged to invest in Mexico and to stimulate exports. It also sought closer ties to the Mexican business community, joining with national manufacturers in the National Chamber of Industry, formed in 1941. All of the trade that these programs generated turned Mexico into the raw materials arsenal of the United States, and by extension, of the Allied powers. At home, Mexican industry expanded rapidly to meet domestic demand left unfilled by the drop in imports from the U.S. during the war. Older industries such as beer, textiles, and steel made gains during the war, as did newer ones such as pharmaceuticals and automobiles.

Finally, in order to counteract claims that foreign business was becoming too powerful, the government passed a law in 1944 to require 51 percent Mexican ownership of key sectors, including the motion picture, fishing, broadcasting, carbonated beverages, transportation, and publishing industries. Still, President Ávila Camacho doubtless ran a pro-business and pro-American administration.

World War II brought greater cooperation between the United States and Mexico than ever before. Desires for a common defense posture had led to successful arbitration in 1941 of the old oil and land claims against Mexico. In addition, the U.S. government supplied Mexico with Coast Guard cutters for patrol purposes. When German subs sank two Mexican tankers in the Gulf of Mexico in May 1942, Mexico declared war on the Axis powers. Several months later, six former presidents of Mexico issued a joint communiqué endorsing the declaration of war.

Mexico had always been a haven for spies because of lax surveillance and easy access to the United States. This had been especially true in the late 1930s, when German spies operated quite openly. Accordingly, Mexico had already begun to crack down on some fascist groups in the country. After Mexico declared war, however, government repression grew, now in cooperation with the FBI. Minister of Interior Miguel Alemán assumed counterespionage duties. And in 1941, President Ávila Camacho passed the law of social dissolution, which allowed the government to arrest and punish any foreigner or Mexican citizen seen as a threat to public order or national safety. A visible symbol of the new policy of cooperation with the United States came in 1943 when Presidents Ávila Camacho and Roosevelt met in Monterrey and later toured the United States. From that time on all U.S. and Mexican presidents have exchanged visits at least once.

Mexico sent an air squadron to the Philippines in late 1944, which allowed Mexico to qualify for Lend-Lease war material and gave the country a strong sense of national pride. The decision to send combat forces came in early 1944, when the U.S. and Mexican presidents agreed that Mexican aviators would participate in the occupation of Manila. That spring the Mexican Air Force conducted maneuvers and carefully selected the participants of the group, known as Escuadrón 201. The final group, which included 38 pilots and 254 ground and support personnel, traveled to the United States for several months of training and indoctrination. They checked out in P-47s, which were among the largest fighter planes used in the war.

Escuadrón 201 arrived in the Philippines in May 1945 and fought beside the U.S. Fifth Air Force. In the following months, the squadron flew fifty-nine missions in support of U.S. ground forces and acquitted itself well. When the war ended, members of the squadron returned to a hero's welcome in Mexico, and almost immediately their service became mythologized. The veterans of Manila monopolized the command of the Mexican Air Force for the next thirty years.

A final Mexican-U.S. collaboration concerned labor. The two neighbors agreed to allow three hundred thousand Mexican workers, called *braceros,* to enter the United States to work in factories and take the places of Americans who had joined the armed forces. The largest number employed at any one time was about seventy-five thousand, but several times that number streamed into the United States without legal authorization. An additional agreement allowed Mexicans and Americans to serve in the armed forces of the other country without jeopardizing their citizenship. Under this agreement, 250,000 Mexicans enlisted in the United States, and about 14,000 saw combat duty.

Recognizing the important roles that Mexico had played in the war effort, hemispheric leaders decided to meet there in early 1945 to plan for the first United Nations (UN) conference, scheduled for San Francisco in April. Dubbed the Chapultepec Conference after the historic palace where it was held, the inter-American summit dealt with such issues as representation on the future UN Security Council, continuation of the Pan-American Union, and UN mem-

**Figure 17.3** Mexican braceros at work for the Acheson, Topeka, and Santa Fe Railroad in 1943. British Combine. Courtesy Library of Congress.

bership for Argentina, which had not severed relations with the Axis powers during the war. The Chapultepec Conference delegates agreed to lobby for two permanent seats for Latin America on the Security Council and to authorize the Pan-American Union to continue under UN aegis. In order to accommodate Argentina, they allowed Buenos Aires to join the UN as a charter member if it broke ties with the Axis powers.

By the end of the war, Mexican society and politics had changed significantly. A middle class had emerged in larger Mexican cities—a class supported by employment in industry, government, banking, and commerce. This middle class increasingly voiced its desires through the ruling party, especially its popular section, made up largely of public employees. The ruling party likewise changed, dropping the army as an institutional member and drawing its rank and file increasingly from government employees. Technicians, bureaucrats, economists, and engineers replaced the labor and peasant leaders. It became a middle-class party whose revolutionary rhetoric was the principal reminder of its rural and violent origins.

President Ávila Camacho completed the transition from military to civilian rule begun by President Cárdenas. At the end of the war, with prosperity returning and Mexico beginning to exercise a role in world affairs again, he reached out to the newest constituency in the party, government bureaucrats, for his successor. The presidential candidate, Miguel Alemán, came from within the party itself, having served as finance manager for Ávila Camacho's election and minister of interior (gobernación) during the war. He was also Mexico's first civilian president since the revolution.

## The Americas during World War II

Throughout the Americas, countries responded differently to the war. From the U.S. point of view, the most important responses were those of Brazil and Mexico, which proved highly cooperative. Panama's response was deemed critical also because of possible German attacks on the canal or on ships that used it. The canal itself was highly vulnerable to sabotage. Moreover, merchant vessels carrying strategic supplies and even U.S. warships were vulnerable to attack while approaching or leaving the canal. So early defense planning focused on the canal and its surroundings.

When U.S. authorities presented a long list of security measures for Panama to take, the new president, Arnulfo Arias Madrid, demurred, saying he would keep his country strictly neutral in the war. Arias's nationalism played well among Panama's masses but angered elites, who usually identified with the United States. When Arias left the country secretly in mid-1941, U.S. observers alerted government officials, who promptly overthrew him. Arias's successor cooperated fully with U.S. defense planners, and the canal remained secure for the rest of the war. While officials in Brazil, Mexico, and Panama worked most closely with their U.S. counterparts, leaders in the Caribbean archipelago, running from Cuba southeast to Aruba, also cooperated to improve U.S. security.

Early in the war German submarines scouted the waters of the Caribbean and the Gulf of Mexico, finding U.S. coastal defenses virtually nonexistent. After the fall of France in June 1940, a far more dangerous situation arose for inter-American security. French and Dutch territories in the Western Hemisphere that came under German control could be used for submarine bases and even to mount air attacks. Therefore, at a special diplomatic gathering in Havana the governments of the hemisphere assumed jurisdiction over these territories until the end of the war.

The French island of Martinique and the Dutch islands of Aruba and Curaçao proved to be especially troublesome. The former had formidable naval defenses under the command of a pro-German officer. The large proportion of north-south shipping that passed close by could fall victim to torpedo or air attacks. Allied officials worked hard to neutralize the ships stationed there and to prevent Martinique from becoming a center for Axis espionage. Aruba and Curaçao, meanwhile, contained the Dutch Shell Oil Company refineries, which supplied much of the East Coast of the United States with heating fuel. An

---

### A Dominican Admiral Recalls 1942 Submarine Threat

"On the morning of the 18th of February, [German] Kapitan Leutnant Achilles took [submarine] U-161 into Trinidad's Port-of-Spain harbor, which he knew well as a former merchant ship officer, to sink two ships. A month later he replicated the operation at Port Castries, St. Lucia.

"Little was known of the many exploits and actions of the German submarine service in the Caribbean and the West Indies during World War II. . . . Ships travelled unescorted, with their navigational marks and lights displayed. . . . In February 1942 as a result of Operation Neuland, 28 ships totaling 160,000 tons, were sunk in the Caribbean. . . . The most important oil supply bases in the Caribbean were the target of this mission. . . . Each of the U-boats operating there sank 6 to 10 ships. . . . During the first six months of 1942, Axis submarines sank 585 ships in the Atlantic. . . . Between February 1942 and December 1943 they sank 400 ships in the Caribbean Sea . . . U-516 made the most sensational raid on the isthmus of Panama since the days of Drake."

Rear Admiral Cesar de Windt Lavandier, Dominican Republic Navy, retired, unpublished manuscript.

---

early submarine attack at Aruba nearly blew up the refineries and prompted Allied planners to station U.S. forces there permanently.

Argentina was the major exception to general hemispheric cooperation with the Allies during World War II. Just as the Buenos Aires government was about to declare its solidarity with Great Britain in 1943, a group of pro-German army officers, some of whom had trained in Germany and Italy in the 1930s, seized power and declared absolute neutrality. They continued to sell beef and cereal to England but, despite enormous pressure from the United States, refused to break ties with Germany. Juan Perón, a leader of the coup who would dominate Argentine politics for a generation, believed as late as 1944 that Hitler might fight the Allies to a draw and remain powerful in world affairs. As a result of this belief, Argentina severed ties with the Axis powers only in March 1945, when German defeat was imminent, in order to join the United Nations.

Even so, thousands of German veterans and officials managed to escape to Argentina during 1945 and to establish new identities for themselves. Perón also employed German scientists to start a nuclear research agency. Remarkably, Perón's actions during 1944 and 1945 did not prevent him from winning the presidential election in 1946. U.S. opposition to him actually backfired and increased his popularity among a population that was inspired by his nationalist stance against the U.S. As seen in chapter 18, by 1947 the U.S. State Department was obliged to mend fences with him.

## NEW ECONOMIC PARADIGMS: FROM ECLAC TO NEOLIBERALISM

During and after World War II, Latin American governments, businesses, and workers suffered great difficulties due to weak markets for primary products and shortages of imports, both consumer and capital goods. A striking new theory began to take hold in the postwar era, one that proposed industrialization and state intervention to encourage growth.

Witnessing the devastation of the Great Depression, the economists proposing these changes had lost faith in laissez-faire capitalism in the 1930s and increasingly advocated that their governments take an expanded role in decision making—and even ownership. Such intervention in the economy was to include multiyear planning, arbitration of labor disputes, investment in infrastructure, joint ownership of basic utilities, and close monitoring and regulation of money and credit markets. This hands-on style of government eventually gave politicians much more influence than in earlier capitalist systems.

In 1948 a group of Latin American economists, led by Chilean Raúl Prebisch, formed a United Nations think tank to study development problems in the region and to propose integrated planning approaches. Called the Economic Commission for Latin America (ECLAC—the Caribbean was added to the name in the 1980s), it conducted a number of in-depth analyses of why Latin America kept falling farther behind the industrialized countries. They found that continuing to depend on exports of raw materials and food had actually impoverished their countries, because over the long run these commodities fell in price relative to manufactures, which were largely imported. The only solution, they suggested, was to industrialize.[4]

Because Latin America began to industrialize long after the north Atlantic World had done so, it needed to create special conditions in order to succeed. First, market protection would be necessary until domestic "infant industries" could compete with more established ones abroad. Second, nations with small populations should band together into common markets to help one another industrialize. Third, governments should promote manufacturing, through subsidies, infrastructure investment, tariff protection, easy loans, and other means.

Finally, ECLAC economists said, governments should tolerate inflation as an unavoidable by-product of development during the early stages of protected industrialization. Strict monetary controls to eliminate inflation would strangle these economic efforts. In all, these prescriptions, often labeled "structuralism" because they promised to change basic economic structures, became ECLAC doctrine, and they were widely adopted throughout the region.

ECLAC policies also favored the working classes by advocating education and training, nutrition, housing, better wages, collective bargaining, and expansion of the domestic market for consumer goods. These social policies later came to be called populist because they could be used by politicians to garner support among the masses. At their core, however, the ECLAC approach addressed overall objectives of economic development, not political advantage.

The results of following ECLAC doctrine, although promising at first, were damaging in the long run. Protected industries used inefficient machinery and invested in capital-intensive production methods in countries where unemployment ran high. Members of urban unions formed labor aristocracies that were often closely allied with government officials and whose leaders became fabulously wealthy. Investors likewise reaped profits far out of proportion to their economic contribution. The costs were transferred to consumers in the form of high-priced, low-quality goods. By the 1960s Latin America's industry could not compete globally yet wielded enough power to protect itself from competition. Latin America fell further behind the advanced economies of Europe, North America, and increasingly Asia.

Because they had followed ECLAC prescriptions, most Latin American countries of the 1960s and 1970s were referred to as having mixed economies, or state capitalism. The governments exercised powerful tools of planning, regulation, and investment. Even the most right-wing governments often exercised some command over the private sector. Therefore, some regimes' economic policies contradicted their laissez-faire philosophies, which they justified by stating that the policies were a temporary measure until their economies could catch up.

By the 1980s the economies of the major Latin American countries had been through decades of turmoil and inconsistent leadership by government economists. The ECLAC approach could no longer be defended. Meanwhile, dictators gave way to populists, who were succeeded by the military, which then faced severe crises and eventually decided to restore power to civilians. In light of the confusing array of institutions, regulations, controls, and laws inherited from preceding regimes, many people began to favor a return to the simpler rules of laissez-faire capitalism. This approach, also supported by the Republican administrations and international banks in Washington, came to be known as neoliberalism or the Washington Consensus. The coincidence of *apertura* (democratization) and the rise of neoliberalism in much of the region meant that most emerging democracies in the 1980s attempted to adopt the new economics. This put them on common ground with the international banking community, the major industrial powers, and one another.

A renewed interest in regional common markets proved an especially promising outcome of the new economics—they had been attempted in the 1950s and 1960s but were abandoned in the 1970s. In the late 1980s several new regional organizations moved ahead: Mercosur, including Brazil, Argentina, Paraguay, Uruguay, and Venezuela; NAFTA, comprising the United States, Canada, and Mexico; and the Andean Group of Colombia, Ecuador, Bolivia, and Peru. At the first-ever Summit of the Americas in 1994 in Miami, the hemisphere's presidents pledged to move beyond regional markets to free trade by the year 2005.

## CONCLUSIONS AND ISSUES

The cataclysmic events of 1939 to 1945 left the world, including Latin America, deeply altered. Brazil's cooperation with the Allied powers gave it a huge boost in prestige and international projection. Brazil came close to gaining a permanent seat on the UN Security Council, and it definitely surpassed its rival, Argentina, in military and economic power. Ties with the United States remained close for decades afterward, especially linking the two countries' armed forces. Mexico also forged a new and positive relationship with its neighbor to the north, ending the tension and antagonism of the previous generation. The economic and migratory flows caused by the war gradually erased the frontier as a barrier and created an intermediate land where Mexicans and Americans lived and worked together. The war economy unquestionably improved the lives of people on both sides of the border and bound them closely together.

Fifty years later, in 1994, the North American Free Trade Agreement (NAFTA) would take that process another step forward, integrating the two economies, as well as Canada's. It was never true that Latin America stopped at the Rio Grande. From the seventeenth century on, Mexico had encompassed most of what eventually became the U.S. Southwest. After the 1848 peace, the United States only partially succeeded in Americanizing the region. Moreover, from the time of the Mexican Revolution on, intensifying trade and migration turned the tide back toward Latin Americanization of the Southwest. World War II accelerated the process. Soon after the year 2000, people of Hispanic descent became the largest minority in the United States.

Meanwhile, the U.S. occupation of bases and territories in the Caribbean Basin returned many of those areas to the status of protectorates, as they had been early in the century. Panama would have to live with the highly unequal 1903 canal treaty for another generation, and military bases in the region bristled with armaments. Regardless of the flags that flew over the Caribbean islands, no one doubted that the United States could exercise any de facto powers it wished there.

As a direct outcome of the war and the Chapultepec Conference, the governments of the hemisphere agreed to overhaul the diplomatic arrangements that had evolved since the late nineteenth century, today known as inter-American law. First, they approved a multilateral agreement (the 1947 Rio Treaty) that created procedures for mutual defense. It was the most advanced agreement of its kind and served as a model for the later western European and Asian treaties of the North Atlantic Treaty Organization (NATO) and Southeast Asia Treaty Organization (SEATO). Second, they converted the Pan-American Union (established in 1890) into the Organization of American States (OAS) in 1948. This organization fit within the larger framework of the United Nations and exercised prior jurisdiction over regional disputes. The Latin American republics emerged from the war without major losses, except for the greater power that the United States now wielded in the world as a result of the Allied victory over the Axis powers. In the postwar era the hemisphere leaders very soon found that world affairs continued to impinge on their lives.

### Discussion Questions

How did the nations of the Americas view the increased threat of war in Europe in the late 1930s?

What were the various types of hemispheric collaboration with the Allied war effort?

What geographic locations were regarded as especially vulnerable in the event that the war should spread to the Americas, and why were they so critical to hemispheric defense?

How did Brazil come to play a major role in World War II? What were its main elements?

Why did Mexico, at odds with the United States in 1938, agree to settle outstanding problems and become a wartime ally? What was the impact within Mexico of this alliance?

Was Mexico's military contribution as large as its economic one? Why or why not?

What role did Panama play in World War II? Was it rewarded for this cooperation?

How did Latin Americans change their thinking about macroeconomic policy during and after the Great Depression?

### Timeline

| | |
|---|---|
| 1939–45 | World War II |
| 1936 | Buenos Aires Conference |
| 1938 | Lima Conference |
| 1939 | Panama Conference |
| 1940 | Havana Conference |
| 1940–46 | Manuel Ávila Camacho serves as Mexico's wartime president |
| 1942 | Rio de Janeiro Conference |
| 1942–45 | Brazil cedes Natal air base to U.S. forces |
| 1942–64 | Bracero Program sends Mexicans to work in the U.S. and enlist in armed services |
| 1944–45 | Brazilian Expeditionary Force serves in Italian front during World War II |
| 1945 | Mexico's Air Force Squadron 201 serves in the Philippines during World War II |
| 1945 | Chapultepec Conference |

### Keywords

Allied powers
Amazon rubber
Axis powers
braceros
Brazilian Expeditionary Force (FEB)
Economic Commission for Latin America (ECLAC)
fascism

Lend-Lease Act
Nacional Financiera
Natal air base
Nazism
neoliberalism
North American Free Trade Agreement (NAFTA)
submarine warfare

# The Classic Populists

## The Sayings of don Pepe

At mid-twentieth century, José "Pepe" Figueres Ferrer led Costa Rica toward the consolidation of a remarkable and lasting democracy. He was not only one of the leading social democrats in the mid-twentieth century—espousing social reforms, economic opportunities, and democratic values—but his appealing philosophy was preserved in sayings that could be readily understood by all. Savor the "Sayings of don Pepe" for their pithy wisdom and down-home exhortations, used to instruct and rally his followers.

> There can be no liberty without social justice, nor social justice without liberty.
>
> Our movement must be built on the strong shoulders of the young.
>
> Military victories by themselves mean little. What matters is what is built upon them.
>
> We wish to eliminate poverty, yet at the same time we should look after the cultural development of the country; we should not be a society of abundance without cultivating the spirit as well.
>
> Why tractors without violins?
>
> Those of us who inherited a valuable past ought to enrich our present with ideas which will make the future even better.
>
> The revolution has not ended. A constructive revolution cannot be based on rigid statements nor ideologies. It is made with ideas that bring about plans for real progress, no matter how modest; with a book under our arm, a tool in our hand, and mystical inspiration in our heart.
>
> If one does not live as he thinks, he will think as he lives.[1]

## CLASSIC POPULISM

From the late 1930s until the late 1960s, the populist style of voter recruitment and leadership swept Latin America, affecting the region far more than did similar movements in the United States. Elections proliferated and voter rolls burgeoned. For the first time ever, Latin Americans had the opportunity to freely choose their next leaders. Radio, television, mass circulation dailies, and huge outdoor rallies became common ways to win voter loyalty. Women's suffrage became the norm across the region, as one country after another granted women the right to vote. The leaders themselves became known all over the world for their flamboyant images and bold initiatives. It was an exciting time, when cities boomed and factories hummed, when women had access to new professions and children crowded into newly funded public schools, when the middle class moved into new homes and neighborhoods and the working class experienced their first shot at getting ahead. In short, it seemed like the promises of modernization were finally going to be fulfilled. Latin American politics seemed to finally escape from the grip of dictatorship and was coming of age. An American journalist captured this transition in the title of his book on this era, *Twilight of the Tyrants*.[2]

The populist era was optimistic yet unsettling because no one knew how the entrenched power holders—the Catholic Church, the army, the landed elite, the bankers, the foreign investors, and the traditional parties—would respond to these changes. For a time the populists and the establishment managed to cooperate. Most populists, to be sure, welcomed the support of any and all backers, and many power brokers believed that they could benefit by allying with popular leaders. These broad populist coalitions drew from all classes and walks of life, and their appeal reached into neighborhoods, small towns, cafes, and factories. They were the first nonviolent mass movements in the region's history. As long as the populists did not threaten existing power holders, they prospered and gave Latin America a more modern face. By the mid-1950s, however, populist leaders were beginning to upset the older elites. Confrontations became frequent. Sometimes the army reacted to mass mobilization, the church opposed liberalizing laws, and industrialists objected to political recruitment of their workers. For their part, the populists could get along without elite supporters and appealed more openly to the masses. Political tensions rose.

Eventually the horizon for populists clouded up and turned stormy. In Argentina, Brazil, and Peru, military coups removed leading populists on the grounds that they endangered public order. Populists were accused of subverting the military, attacking the establishment, breaking the law, overspending their budgets, and encouraging communism. Unspoken was the complaint that the populists were successful enough at the ballot box to ignore the interests of the rich and powerful.

Classic populism had its roots in the 1930s. No full-blown populist movements arose then, due to hard economic times. Yet, a new mix of economic and social factors began to favor this innovative style of leadership. Virtually all the classic populist figures of the 1950s and 1960s got their start in the 1930s.

As discussed in chapter 16, the Great Depression struck the countries of Latin America with crippling force, destroying businesses and throwing hundreds of thousands of people out of work. Trade fell sharply, and prices for the region's products plummeted. Hundreds of thousands of rural workers and poor farmers made their way to the cities, hoping to find jobs and homes. They were desperate and ready to follow leaders who would promise them a better life. These leaders became the classic populists, who gained power and exercised it boldly—willful rulers determined to guide their countries through the hard times at hand.

Born in the 1880s and 1890s, the later populists were much younger when they came to power than the reformers portrayed in chapter 12. Three of them—Víctor Raúl Haya de la Torre, Lázaro Cárdenas, and Juan Perón—were born the same year, 1895. Some spent time in the military before switching to politics, a fact that may account for their occasional autocratic tendencies. They pushed voter recruitment and built more modern parties with which to mobilize their followers. They learned to use the newly available medium of radio, and a few experimented with public relations techniques.

These classic populists were born into provincial families whose status ranged from lower middle to upper class. Although raised in relative comfort and security, they were forced to leave their homes in order to get ahead. Their origins outside the national capitals meant that they had to learn the ways of the national elite. This gave them an edge over traditional leaders because they could manipulate elite values and symbols better than persons socialized to wealth and power from birth. Little interested in foreign travel, the later populists studied in their national universities or military academies and often got their start in politics as student leaders. A few ventured abroad and brought back fresh ideas, especially from Europe. Loners almost as a rule, they had neither mentors nor protégés, with few exceptions.

The populists who gained power after 1930 were dedicated politicians whose personalities drove them to run for public office. They spoke well, projected appealing images, balanced diverse coalitions expertly, maintained composure in crises, and accomplished much of what they set out to do. Because the later populists evoked controversy as well as hero worship, historians have a difficult time taking their measure. They do, however, deserve a prominent position in twentieth-century history.

## Getúlio Vargas

Getúlio Vargas was born in the little town of São Borja in the southern province of Rio Grande do Sul, Brazil. His father was a rancher, an army general, and a prominent politician in a region where those professions often went together. The family cattle business produced a comfortable income, but life in the pampas was often harsh and fraught with danger. From an early age, Getúlio aspired to be a soldier like his father, and he enlisted in the army when only eleven. Physically unimpressive, bookish, guarded with others, and a loner, he was probably not cut out for a military career.

After several discouraging incidents in officer training school, Getúlio soured on the military and enrolled in law school. He finished up in 1907 and began practice in Porto Alegre, the state capital. He also began to dabble in politics, a common sideline for lawyers in Latin America. Once engaged in politics, Vargas steadily climbed the ladder, rising to governor of his state in the 1928–1932 term. From that office he led a revolution in 1930 and seized the presidency for what turned out to be a fifteen-year stint. In these years, Vargas metamorphosed from a traditional leader to a dictator to a populist. Called a chameleon because of these alterations, he probably changed style to keep pace with world events—the Depression, the rise of fascism and Nazism, the world war, and the return of democracy after 1945.

Even before he became a full-fledged populist in the late 1940s, Vargas pursued policies that would enhance his success later. He issued decrees that protected Brazilian industry, jobs, resources, and trade in its relations with the outside world. This gave him a reputation as a nationalist. He centralized authority in federal agencies, curbing the traditional powers of state governments. In particular, he built up the army at the expense of state militias. He extended government control over labor relations, offering job protection and fringe benefits for workers while making strikes illegal. He extended the vote to women and eighteen-year-olds, though he later canceled all elections. Finally, he experimented with new communications media, using radio and the press far more effectively than had any of his predecessors.

Vargas's reputation for leadership grew during the dictatorial Estado Novo period (1937–1945). He instituted a civil service system that made government more effective. He skillfully bargained with the United States for an integrated steel mill, called Volta Redonda, which the United States donated in exchange for military cooperation during World War II. The mill later became the centerpiece of a bold industrialization program. And he decided to send troops to fight with the Allies in 1944 and 1945 to enhance Brazil's international standing. This infantry division, named the Brazilian Expeditionary Force, performed impressively in the Italian campaign (see chapter 17).

When the war was over and censorship ended, however, many people protested Vargas's autocratic methods. He tried to transform himself into a democrat by promising elections and by founding two new groups, the Social Democratic Party (PSD) and the Brazilian Labor Party (PTB). He was unable to carry out the transformation smoothly, however, and was overthrown by top army

**Figure 18.1** Getúlio Vargas (waving), far and away Brazil's dominant figure in twentieth-century politics, governed the country from 1930 to 1945 and from 1951 until his suicide in 1954. He is shown here campaigning during the 1950 presidential election. Authors' collection.

generals in August 1945. Already sixty-two years old, he might have left politics and enjoyed a quiet retirement.

After attempting to defend his record in Congress, Vargas moved to his family ranch in Rio Grande do Sul and withdrew from the Rio de Janeiro political scene. When the 1950 election approached, however, numerous collaborators urged him to run again. The country and political system had changed profoundly since his last campaign—in 1930—so he relied on his daughter, Alzira Vargas do Amaral Peixoto, in Rio to manage his candidacy. It was largely on the basis of this election that Vargas gained renown as a populist.

Vargas's supporters worked around the clock in 1950 to give their leader an appealing image and to get out the vote for him. They built his reputation as the "father of the poor," won earlier by his sponsorship of the 1943 Labor Code. They also portrayed him as a nationalist who would protect and expand the country's industry, providing jobs and infrastructure for the urban masses. His image, that of a paternalistic grandfather figure smiling and smoking a cigar, familiar to everyone, was plastered all over the country. Toward the end of the campaign, Alzira organized a grueling airplane tour of the country that touched down in eighty-four cities and towns. At each stop, Vargas gave a tailor-made speech drafted by staff members that he himself revised. His

48 percent victory in a three-man race was a veritable landslide, and he took office amid great popular acclaim.

Vargas tried very hard to carry out his promises to the masses, especially regarding the protection of natural resources, economic planning, and the fair distribution of wealth. He created a national development bank to channel public loans to basic and critical industries. He proposed nationalizing all petroleum development and refining—a sector notorious for high profits and excessive remittances abroad. This proposal passed in 1953 and gave rise to Petrobras, today one of the world's largest state-owned companies. Vargas also submitted to Congress a bill that would have nationalized electric utilities so that they could push service into poor and rural areas. This bill failed due to heavy lobbying from the industry. Finally, Vargas continued to give special attention to labor laws, social security, unemployment, and welfare services.

Yet Vargas's efforts to carry out his promises to the masses often fell short. Employers enforced the labor code at their discretion, and social programs to benefit the poor were unevenly implemented and rarely reached into rural areas. Even in urban areas, social security, medical care, welfare, and even basic housing and food were in short supply among the poorest. Brazil's urban favelas, or shantytowns, which sprang up amid the urban and industrial growth of the late nineteenth century, grew quickly as industry took off in the mid-twentieth century and people poured into the cities in search of jobs. The favelas were seen by populists as a site of disease, immorality, and crime, and mid-century politicians proposed to replace them with public housing projects, but these too rarely came to fruition. Many favelas were eradicated, especially in wealthy urban enclaves in cities like Rio, pushing the city's poorest into the nearby hills to rebuild their favelas, still without running water, sewage, or other services.

In all, Vargas's second administration produced some major social progress, yet it did so in a climate of heightened political and economic conflict. Vargas's PSD-PTB coalition in Congress began to unravel. The military became restive over advances made by labor unions. The economy plunged into a recession after 1952. And Vargas lost some of the deft touch he had shown in earlier times. His administration began to founder in early 1954. Faced with multiple crises and removal by the military in mid-1954, Vargas decided to take his life rather than surrender. His suicide heightened people's sympathy for him and turned him into a martyr. His suicide note became a testament to his populist legacy.

> Once more the forces and interests against the people are newly coordinated and raised against me. . . . I follow the destiny that is imposed on me. After years of domination and plunder by international economic and financial groups, I made myself chief of an unconquerable revolution. I began the work of liberation and I instituted a regime of social liberty. . . . I returned to govern on the arms of the people.

A subterranean campaign of international groups joined with national groups, revolting against the regime of workers' guarantees. . . . I have fought month after month, day after day, hour after hour, resisting constant, incessant pressures. . . . I cannot give you more than my blood. . . . I gave you my life. Now I offer you my death. Nothing remains. Serenely, I take my first step on the road to eternity and leave life to enter history.[3]

After Vargas's death, many politicians tried to don his mantle, even some who had opposed him. By the same token, others widely adopted the methods that he had used to forge a majority in 1950. In effect, Brazil in the 1950s became a populist republic, with at least eight major figures vying for national power.

## Juscelino Kubitschek

One of Vargas's imitators attempted to outperform his mentor. Juscelino Kubitschek, born into a modest family, lost his father when only one year old. He had only his mother to push him forward in life. He strove to overcome these handicaps, and after earning a degree in medicine he entered politics in his native state of Minas Gerais. He prospered in the tumultuous scene of urban politics and joined Vargas's PSD in 1945. By 1954, the year of Vargas's suicide, he had his sights set on the presidency.

Juscelino, or JK, as his followers called him, played two sides with his considerable personal skills and all the expertise he could muster. On the one hand, he had to move deftly among the parties, factions, and other candidates in order to avoid being eliminated in backroom dealings. On the other hand, he hit the campaign trail in early 1955, emulating Vargas's historic 1950 campaign. He presented himself as a modernizer and promised to achieve "50 years' progress" in his five-year term. He broke the sound barrier in a jet fighter. He barnstormed tens of thousands of miles in a leased DC-3 to visit hundreds of cities and towns. He used the radio with skill and recorded television spots for that new medium. He seemed to be everywhere at once.

Even though he won just a plurality of the votes (two other candidates ran), he completed the process, begun by Vargas, of modernizing Brazil's electoral system. As president, he even signed into law a bill creating the secret, uniform ballot for national elections. Kubitschek accomplished an amazing amount during his five years as president. Many observers believe that if he had been allowed to run for a second term he might have surpassed Vargas's record. He invited foreign manufacturers, especially automakers, to build plants in Brazil. By the end of his term, Volkswagen, Ford, and General Motors had begun production, and within a few years Brazilian cars were being manufactured with 99 percent domestic components. Automobiles, in turn, spurred expansion in other areas, like petroleum and rubber products, highways, and repair shops. Soon cars became status symbols for the middle class and provided markets for a wide spectrum of goods and services. Under Kubitschek, electric power

### Kubitschek's Brasília

Kubitschek held a national competition to find the best team to design the new capital. Three outstanding modernist planners and architects, Lúcio Costa, Oscar Niemeyer, and Burle Marx, won the competition. Their plan laid out the city in the shape of a jet airplane. At the eastern tip, where the cockpit would be, they located the president's office, Congress, and the Supreme Court. Behind them, in the "navigators' seats," were arrayed the twenty ministry buildings that headed up the executive branch. The two wings stretching north and south contained housing compounds, called super-quadras, each with its own school, shopping center, playground, and church. The symbolism carried through to the city's orientation: it faces east, flying into the sunrise and the future.

projects, capital goods industries, mining, steel, and petrochemicals also received strong support from the government. Kubitschek skillfully blended selective foreign investment with nationalist protective policies. Industrialists, in particular, enjoyed huge profits during his term.

A new capital city at Brasília became the centerpiece of Kubitschek's administration. Conceived as a whim, the project grew into an obsession for him, and with customary energy he made sure that enough of the city was finished to inaugurate it before his term ended. In January 1961 he handed over his office to his successor, Jânio Quadros, in Brasília.

Kubitschek inspired his administration with a quest for *grandeza,* that is, enthusiasm for Brazil's future bordering on the grandiose. He believed that by sheer will power and astute planning, he would be able to accomplish everything he dreamed. He and many others expected Brazil to join the First World and to become a major power within a short time. Brazil's rapidly growing population of urban poor represented the flip side of grandeza, however. Some truly benefited, especially unionized workers in the new auto and steel factories, who, as key allies of the populist government, received steady income and benefits, including medical care and access to housing. Yet many others failed to find work in the formal sector and settled instead in the favelas, making their living with domestic service, itinerant jobs, or scavenging. They too heard the populist promises, but by the mid-1950s they had grown increasingly disenchanted with its limits, including the pledges of improvement and shows of patronage that appeared before elections but that quickly evaporated once a politician was elected. And while racial lines were not strictly drawn in Brazil, the populations of favelas were disproportionately Afro-descendant.

**Figure 18.2** Photo of women's section of Adhemar de Barros's Social Progressive Party, at a 1953 meeting in São Paulo. Courtesy Museu Adhemar de Barros. Authors' collection.

Nevertheless, wealthy and educated Brazilians and the international community continued to celebrate Freyre's idea of a racial democracy in these decades, buoyed by the apparent social mobility of blacks at midcentury, including the emergence of a small black middle class. In the 1950s, UNESCO even funded a series of studies of Brazil to try to understand why, especially in comparison to the U.S., it had been able to create a "racial paradise." When the studies came out in the 1960s, however, the results surprised many, showing continued discrimination that, while described in terms of class by Brazilians, was determined largely by skin color.[4]

Meanwhile, other populists came forward after Vargas's death to vie for his followers. One, longtime populist Adhemar de Barros, squared off against newcomer Jânio Quadros for the state governorship of São Paulo, a stepping-stone to the presidency. Surprising most observers, Jânio defeated Adhemar and went on to win the presidency in 1960, a stunning display of prowess and audacity. Ironically, his fall was just as fast; he resigned after just eight months in office, blaming conspiracies and opposition to his programs. Two years later he even lost a gubernatorial election to his arch-rival, Adhemar de Barros.

**Figure 18.3** João Goulart in parade in New York, 1962, as he attempted unsuccessfully to gain support from major banks and the U.S. government for development financing. United Press International. Courtesy Library of Congress.

Two other powerful populists were among Vargas's closest heirs, arising from state politics in Rio Grande: João Goulart and Leonel Brizola. Goulart had been a friend and collaborator of Vargas and became labor minister and Labor Party chief in the 1950s. He served as vice president from 1955 to 1961 and then succeeded to the presidency when Jânio Quadros resigned.

Brizola worked his way up in Vargas's Labor Party, married Goulart's sister, and became part of the inner circle after Vargas's death. He was able to use those connections to vault into the important role of governor of Rio Grande do Sul from 1959 to 1963. Both men used populist methods to win over voters and to build large followings. In other regions of the country, too, politicians stepped forward to claim the leadership that Vargas had pioneered. Brazilian politics gave the false impression of being permanently enthralled by populism.

### Juan and Eva Perón

In 1943, as Vargas began his shift toward electoral politics and his metamorphosis into a populist, the extraordinary Juan Perón organized a coup against the Castillo administration in Argentina. Although it had the trappings of a fascist putsch, Perón deftly steered it toward a populist government in 1944 and 1945. By then he had managed to become frontrunner in the campaign for the presidency, which he won the following February. His phenomenal rise was just the beginning of a dramatic change in Argentine public life.

Perón was born in a small town on the pampas of Argentina into a family with only modest chances of mobility. Perón entered military school as a teen and virtually lost contact with his family. After his commissioning, he rose slowly through the ranks, with few opportunities for promotion. He took part in the bloodless coup of 1930 that overthrew Hipólito Yrigoyen, but he did not take any civilian post afterward. In the late 1930s, in recognition of his growing stature as a leader among mid-ranking officers, he won a tour in Europe and witnessed Italy's preparations for war and the rearmament of Germany.

On his return to Argentina, Perón organized a secret officers' clique, called the United Officers' Group (GOU). Its role was to strengthen the nation's military readiness, block communist advances, thwart an alliance with England, and promote its members' careers. In June 1943 the GOU took over the government in order to carry out its agenda. Perón expanded the circle of members and improved their positions, thereby winning their loyalty. As ringleader of the coup, he reserved key positions for himself: minister of war and vice president. Surprisingly, he also took over the Department of Labor, which for years had languished in neglect.

As labor chief, Perón called in union officials and convinced many to work with him. Using classic patronage, he offered them contract enforcement, higher wages, benefits, and relief from anti-union actions by employers in exchange for following his lead. Under his direction, unions grew in membership and power, even though their leaders did not fully trust Perón. The labor movement did, however, provide a base of support for his future presidential bid.

Perón's physical appearance—tall, handsome, and commanding—and his politico-romantic liaison with a well-known female radio personality boosted his growing recognition among voters. Eva Duarte, a star of radio and stage, handled public announcements for him, and they began living together. Beautiful, willful, and outspoken in her support for Perón, she became his most effective spokesperson. Their romance scandalized some, but it also kept the couple in the public eye.

Perón's rise faltered in October 1945, when the army high command stripped him of his offices and jailed him to derail his presidential bid. At that point, major Buenos Aires unions mobilized their members in a huge protest in the downtown Plaza de Mayo to protest the arrest of *el líder,* Juan Perón. Although uncertain about Perón's loyalty to labor, the union leaders had no doubt that his opponents would end the privileges that Perón had given them. Their protest, the largest in decades, convinced the generals to release Perón and allow him to run for president. Often viewed as the moment of the birth of Peronismo, his campaign signaled that mass politics had truly arrived in Argentina. Perón and Eva quickly married and went on the campaign trail. It was an uphill battle, against the traditional parties, the U.S. ambassador, and the government itself, but they pushed ahead, touting the gains that labor had made and his plans to nationalize basic utilities and services. Eva Duarte Perón, now known as "Evita" to her admirers, gave powerful speeches that persuaded voters to support her husband. She helped turn a October 1945 rally into a creation myth for Peronismo, as his movement was called. When the election was held in February, Perón won an impressive majority of the nearly 3 million votes cast.

Once in office, Perón launched an energetic program to take control of transportation infrastructure and promote industrialization in order to break Argentina's dependence on foreign markets and investment. Because prices for Argentina's main exports, cereal grains and beef, were high, he created an agency, the IAPI, to market them abroad. By controlling exchange rates, Perón skimmed off nearly half the export revenues for reinvestment in manufacturing. For a time, industrialists profited enormously from his subsidies and tariff protection.

Meanwhile, Perón also boosted wages to the highest levels in decades to broaden domestic markets for manufactures. Migrants streamed into Buenos Aires and other cities in search of the good life. Most were rewarded with union-protected jobs and low-cost government services. Evita was especially effective in addressing these migrants from the pampas, whom, along with the urban workers, she endearingly called the *descamisados* (the shirtless ones). In doing so, she inverted the meaning of a word that in the early 1940s had been used by Perón's opponents to insult his supporters.

Peronism, like classic populism more broadly, was a transformative experience in many countries in Latin America. Both men and women participated in politics and society in unprecedented ways under populist leaders. Emboldened by reforms and rhetoric that heralded the role of the working class in the industrializing nation, unions became increasingly active under Perón. This activism grew in opposition to the decades of exclusion and repression by traditional elites and exploded into a new language that put the male worker at the center of national development. It captured the working class's sense of exploitation and abuse, and allowed unionized workers to assert themselves with newfound pride as full citizens in the more socially inclusive nation. As one of his working-class supporters stated, "Well, with Perón we were all machos."[5]

Women, too, participated in new ways in public life, though populism left an ambivalent legacy for women across Latin America. It brought them important rights, for example, suffrage and greater access to social services, but it also continued to portray women largely as wives and mothers. For example, many countries implemented special laws for women workers based on assumptions about their weaker, more vulnerable nature and a desire to protect the family. Women's participation in public life, whether as workers or voters, was to be an extension of their role in the domestic sphere. Nevertheless,

**Figure 18.4** Juan and Evita Perón, center, with labor federation leader, right.
Courtesy of Hoover Institution Library and Archives, Stanford University.

women did find new freedoms in the city and factory. Modern consumer culture in the cities brought new fashions and entertainment, and access to education continued to grow. The modern woman now had her own earnings for the first time, which provided her with a dangerous degree of freedom according to conservative and Catholic opposition. In the factories, too, women were a growing presence. In Argentina, they took jobs in the venerable meatpacking industry and worked for companies like Armour and Swift, though usually in tasks different from their male counterparts. Some even became union activists, such as Doña María Roldán. As portrayed by historian Daniel James, Roldán embodied the ambivalent experience of women workers under populism. She was both a dedicated wife and an ardent Peronist. She worked hard alongside the other women and men in the factory, led union activities, struck, and spoke at rallies on behalf of Perón, yet she always maintained that her Catholic faith, and duty to her husband and children were her priority.[6]

Perón's economic program, called import substitution industrialization (ISI), fared well for several years without causing undue difficulties. Ranchers and farmers, to be sure, protested their forced contributions to government coffers, but everyone else seemed to benefit, especially the masses. Wages as a share of national income rose from 46 to 57 percent, helping to drive domestic demand and factory expansion.

Only in 1949 did the boom falter, due to a number of factors. A drought cut Argentine production about the same time that European grain harvests began to satisfy domestic demand. Wartime foreign currency reserves finally gave out, forcing Perón to pay for imports with cash. And rural producers refused to send cattle to slaughter and left farmland fallow to protest the IAPI's confiscatory policies. For the first time since Perón won election, Argentina experienced food shortages.

Evita played a critical part in buoying Perón's popularity. She became his personal representative in the labor department (now a secretariat) and managed liaison with union officials. She also presided over a sprawling welfare organization called the Eva Perón Foundation, which operated as a charitable slush fund. During regular hours the ill and destitute could meet with Evita and receive favors, jobs, cash, or simply attention. As time went by, her compassion and largess became legendary among the masses and she was enormously popular among the nation's poorest. Parents started naming their daughters Eva and women copied her hairstyles. Much of Perón's appeal among the poor was due to Evita's work in the foundation and the Labor Secretariat.

After women won the right to vote in 1947, Evita targeted them as voters by organizing the Peronist Women's Party. As a separate section of the Peronist government, the party was on par with other branches of Perón's government and had about five hundred thousand members by the early 1950s.[7] As with men, the franchise was granted not to empower women but rather to bring them under the umbrella of the Peronist state. Women voted in the 1948 congressional elections and then in the 1951 presidential race. In the latter, they overwhelmingly supported Perón, whom they credited with the franchise and other feminist gains.

Perón also undertook some remarkable foreign policy initiatives. Seeing that the United States and the USSR were drifting into the Cold War, he proposed that countries without a vested interest in the nuclear standoff and partition of Europe remain neutral. He termed this the Third Way, equidistant between capitalism and communism, and an inspiration for the global nonaligned movement that would follow later in the 1950s. He sent top diplomats abroad to advocate for Argentina's case, and a number of Third World leaders gave him their support. This stance gave Perón considerable flexibility and influence among the non-aligned nations. In addition, he created an inter-American confederation of labor, called ATLAS, which also remained apart from the U.S. and Soviet-aligned confederations. In the early 1950s, a half-dozen national federations affiliated with ATLAS, increasing Perón's prestige.

Perón lobbied to have Evita run as his vice-presidential candidate in 1951, but the army high command vetoed her. Never happy with a first lady of dubious social background, the generals balked at the possibility of Evita succeeding to the presidency and assuming command of the armed forces in the event of Perón's death. Perón backed down, but conspiracies began to surface within the officer corps from that time on. He could no longer count on the total loyalty of his comrades-in-arms.

In public, Evita played the firebrand to Perón's moderate, stable presence. Speaking as one from humble origins, she could condemn the wealthy and the powerful in colorful, vivid terms. She demanded lower prices, rent controls, more charity, jobs, and respect for the downtrodden. Paradoxically, when she wore expensive furs, gowns, and jewelry, often purchased with foundation money, the public loved it, vicariously participating in the elite baiting. Evita and Juan spoke to opposite ends of the social spectrum. She would stand up for the poor and oppressed while Perón hobnobbed with industrialists and bankers. Theirs was a unique case among the populists of shared charisma, when two leaders enjoyed separate yet related adoration by their followers.

Perón won reelection in 1951 by a landslide, but soon afterward the Peróns' success began to fade. The economy continued to shrink, in part due to government policies that shifted national income away from workers toward owners. Inflation started to eat into the gains that workers had made in preceding years. Agricultural production and hence exports dropped far below their 1940s peaks. In his zeal to turn the economy around, Perón began to oppose labor strikes and wage increases, arguing instead for belt-tightening by workers. He invited large foreign firms to exploit natural resources and start up heavy industry, thus betraying in the eyes of workers his earlier nationalist stance.

The death of Evita, a victim of cancer at the age of thirty-three, proved the blow from which Perón never fully recovered. Inoperable, the disease quickly took away her life in 1952. She attempted to transfer her charisma to Perón with appeals to the masses and a biography, *The Reason for My Life*, but it did not succeed. Her passing left a painful gap in Argentine leadership.

By 1953 the burdens of governing without Evita were evident. Perón grew testy and combative. He took over the leading newspaper, *La Nación,* because it criticized him. He picked a fight with the formerly supportive Catholic Church over its refusal to declare Evita a saint. He quarreled with labor over contracts with foreign oil and auto companies. Regime supporters, calling themselves *mazorcas* (harking back to Rosas's thugs in the 1830s), beat up opponents and brawled in the streets. The steady, calm leadership that he had provided earlier disappeared.

The end came in July and August 1955, amid signs of rapid deterioration in public order. Mazorcas attacked priests and damaged churches. Perón distributed arms to those unions that still supported him in order to counteract the threat of a military coup. He threw down the gauntlet to elite groups that had deserted him, threatening to kill one elite for every Peronista killed. His desperation was obvious. The army finally acted by arresting and sending Perón into exile in Paraguay. A junta of generals chose one of its own to preside over dismantling the entire Peronist movement. It seemed that Perón and populism were about to be eradicated from Argentine politics.

## ANDEAN POPULISTS

After World War II, the countries along the west coast of South America experienced intense recruitment of the masses into politics, and a number of populist leaders rose to power. The distinctive peoples, history, and geography of the Andean nations gave populism characteristics different from those of Brazil and the Southern Cone. In particular, the strong indigenous traditions of Ecuador, Peru, and Bolivia gave rise to appeals to their ancient civilizations and their hostility toward Spaniards. In societies divided by race and ethnicity, Andean populists stressed cooperation and consensus while promising to raise depressed standards of living.

In Colombia and Venezuela, greater Spanish immigration and mixing with Indians had produced mestizo majorities who constituted an ethnic as well as social middle class. Issues of equity, development, and nationalism proved especially powerful in attracting them to populism. Likewise, the incorporation of lower-class citizens into politics became the driving force of populism.

Chile was exceptional in this regard because its well-organized parties, constitutional tradition, and advanced social legislation prevented an upsurge in populism. Only one more president (after Alessandri) emerged as a populist: Carlos Ibáñez during his 1952 to 1958 term, and when he stepped down, politics resumed its march toward socialism.

### Víctor Raúl Haya de la Torre

Peru's leading populist was Víctor Raúl Haya de la Torre, whose active career spanned six decades, from 1920 until his death in 1979. Haya, as he was known to followers, grew up in Trujillo, a city on the north coast of Peru. His father was a schoolmaster, so Haya enjoyed a comfortable upbringing and strong academic formation.

After graduating from high school, Haya attended the venerable University of San Marcos in Lima, where, someone joked, he majored in student politics. His initiation and first success occurred in 1919, when he joined a general strike among Lima workers and became their spokesman. From then on, he served as go-between for university students and Lima's fledgling labor movement.

In 1921 Haya founded the Popular University, inspired by comparable socialist schools in Europe. There, his colleagues from San Marcos taught basic skills and life classes while gaining an acquaintance with how the other half lived and worked. He deepened his commitment to student activism in 1922, when he visited the University of Córdoba, Argentina, site of momentous reforms in governance in 1917. Haya's biggest campaign came in 1923, when he led street protests against President Leguía's proposal to ally Peru formally with the Vatican. The protests turned violent, and the government shut down the Popular University and sent Haya into exile.

Haya spent the next seven years traveling, meeting distinguished figures, and preparing for his eventual reentry into politics. He drank deeply of European culture and politics in the 1920s, connected with other dissident leaders in Latin America, and shaped the ideas that he would disseminate for the rest of his career. In 1924, while in exile in Mexico, he founded the APRA Party (American Popular Revolutionary Alliance). The party continued to bear this hemispheric name even though it never spread much outside Peru.

Haya's biographers have devoted a great deal of attention to his mystical and inspirational philosophy, which sought to harmonize Inca civilization with Hispanic traditions and ultimately to forge a nationalist synthesis of the two in contemporary Peru. In fact, Haya's success owed much more to his ability to appeal to people's emotions and his mesmerizing rhetoric than to a coherent doctrine. Followers believed in him because of his charismatic authority, which he exuded in all settings. U.S. writer John Gunther wrote of him in 1941, "I saw Haya three times, and each time I felt that I was meeting one of the greatest personages of America."

After the army overthrew Leguía in 1930, Haya returned to Peru and won great acclaim from his followers, who had remained faithful in his absence. His party now blossomed, and he toured the country campaigning for the presidency. His opponent was Colonel Sánchez Cerro, the army officer who had led the coup against Leguía. Sánchez Cerro was himself something of a populist, a man of the people with mixed racial heritage and the ability to make credible promises to many constituencies.

Sánchez Cerro won the election of 1931 and assumed the presidency, only to be stymied by the Depression. Then in 1933 an APRA zealot assassinated him. This ended Peru's brief flirtation with democracy and populism. The army and representatives of Peru's wealthy classes assumed power and instituted a dictatorship, banning all electoral politics.

In 1932, APRA staged a revolt in Trujillo, and in the thick of the fighting it executed some sixty captive army officers and public officials. The army retaliated. Hundreds, perhaps as many as two thousand, Apristas taken prisoner when Trujillo was recaptured were executed near the ancient ruins of Chan Chan. The bitterness and distrust engendered by these events poisoned relations between APRA and the army for decades. Haya and his lieutenants were jailed and the movement outlawed for many years. For the next generation, the army and oligarchy barred Haya as a presidential candidate. He spent much of his time abroad or under house arrest, and he never occupied the presidency. Yet, especially after the party was once again legalized in 1945, APRA continued to grow and became the country's largest and most successful mass-based party. No one doubted that Haya could have won the presidency had he been allowed to run. (For Haya's unsuccessful presidential campaign, see chapter 14).

APRA owed its success to many factors. Haya's charisma grew over the years, enhanced by his political persecution. In exile, censored, and barred from elections, he symbolized the struggle against elitist policies that kept most Peruvians from exercising their democratic rights. He also had the freedom to make opportunistic deals. In 1956, for example, he supported his rival, conservative candidate Manuel Odría, in exchange for special considerations in Congress. For long periods of time APRA managed to elect a large congressional delegation, one that kept its program and promises before the public even during times when conservative governments turned dictatorial and repressed the left.

In fact, APRA became a loyal opposition, able to criticize and denounce government misconduct while never having to shoulder much responsibility itself. Its message was simple: the oligarchy monopolized government positions and exploited the workers and peasants while mortgaging the country to foreign capitalists. Haya and APRA promised to restore national control over resources, to raise the standard of living, and to protect the interests of the downtrodden. The oligarchy, however, stole some of APRA's thunder when, in order to undermine support for APRA, it enacted the very reforms that APRA advocated, bringing about the gradual modernization of government structures. Yet popular support for APRA's opponents remained thin, as the social distance between the wealthier, more modern coastal areas and the rural highlands grew. Left out of Peru's midcentury growth were its many indigenous highlanders, those living in the more mountainous areas of Peru, where land tenure patterns remained among the most unequal in the Americas.

Peruvian intellectuals in the 1930s and after promoted a new Peruvian identity that synthesized indigenous and Hispanic elements, yet this version of mestizaje continued to portray the Catholic and Hispanic parts as superior to the rural indigenous ones. Mestizaje, which came to be taught positively in public schools, may have included everyone, but not as equals. It implied that Peru's Indians needed to be "de-Indianized" or "mestisized" into modern culture and markets, seen as most possible through rural-to-urban migration. And indeed, between 1940 and about 1960, the size of the population identified as indigenous dropped from over 50 percent to less than 37 percent.[8] At the same time, living standards for most indigenous people actually dropped after 1950, fostering rural discontent that would explode in the 1960s.

In the 1962 presidential election, the elite divided over whom to support and did not ban Haya from running. Haya, as candidate of the largest party, seemed destined to win. In fact, he received a plurality yet not the requisite one-third of the votes. According to the constitution, Congress had to decide the election outcome. Recognizing that he could never get enough votes in Congress, he struck a deal for rival candidate Odría to assume the presidency if APRA could control the cabinet, that is to say, the executive branch of government.

The military became incensed at this crass deal and stepped in to annul the election. It held a new election in 1963, in which Haya could not run. This time a Christian Democrat, Fernando Belaúnde Terry, won with promises to carry out social and economic reforms to benefit the masses. The United States backed Belaúnde, as did the moderate middle class, and he took office with a mandate for change. Haya remained sidelined for the next twenty years, watching as Peru descended into conflict and dictatorship.

## José María Velasco Ibarra

A middle-class law professor from Ecuador's Sierra (highlands region), José María Velasco Ibarra first occupied the presidency in 1934 as a result of Depression-era instability. He held office for only a year before being overthrown. At that time he did not display signs of his later populist qualities, only his ambitions.

During several years in exile, he began to cultivate a personal following by posing as a defender of the laws and people's interest. In fact, he used his absences to enhance his popularity, claiming that the oligarchy exiled him to keep the people from electing their true representative, *el gran ausente* (the great absent one).

In 1944 Velasco forced the resignation of the incumbent president, using his growing organization to mobilize huge protests and strikes. While serving as provisional president he oversaw a constitutional convention and then won election as president. He had no party or ideological platform, appealing instead to the masses of poor people, whom he called the *chusma* (rabble). He employed superb speaking skills, especially when addressing crowds of his followers. He criticized others' shortcomings mercilessly. A tempestuous and changeable leader, Velasco began to lose support as soon as he was elected, and he came to rely increasingly on the conservatives. By 1947 he had alienated many powerful collaborators, and the military removed him from office.

In 1952 Velasco returned from his exile in Argentina to run again for president, and this time he won a huge victory, drawing most of his votes from the lowland provinces along the coast. In 1952, 358,000 persons voted, or just over 10 percent of the total population. Campaign managers had now adopted public address systems, radio, mass leafleting, and other modern election techniques. Velasco was quite astute in making promises that the masses wanted to hear, while assuring his wealthy backers that nothing would change.

Velasco both caused and benefited from growing electoral participation. Velasco's style had become famous by the 1950s, conveyed most often by his boast, "Give me a balcony, and I will be president!" Velasco perfected a populist style and attracted massive numbers of loyal voters. Meanwhile, he had a knack for choosing issues that elicited widespread support. He denounced a 1942 treaty by which Peru had gained a huge tract of the Amazon basin belonging to Ecuador, and he convinced the people to back a campaign to reclaim it. Occasional border skirmishes with Peru punctuated his terms in office. He also claimed two hundred miles of territorial waters to protect Ecuador's rich

**Figure 18.5** José María Velasco Ibarra campaigning in the early 1950s, courtesy Banco Nacional del Ecuador. Authors' collection.

fishing grounds. When he returned to power in the 1960s he actually impounded U.S. tuna trawlers that had not paid a special license, an incident known as the Tuna Wars.

Velasco won elections again in 1960 and 1968. Both times the military deposed him, even though by 1970 he had created a dictatorship with the backing of the army. He was nothing if not unpredictable. Meanwhile, in the 1950s another populist movement, called the Concentration of Popular Forces (CFP), arose in the coastal city of Guayaquil. Its two main leaders, Carlos Guevara Moreno and Assad Bucaram, became the populist arch-rivals of Velasco. Guevara Moreno, a skilled speaker and charismatic figure, created the CFP. He enjoyed a strong following and expected to run for the presidency. In 1959, however, he surprised observers by withdrawing from politics.

In the early 1960s Assad Bucaram, the self-educated and energetic son of Lebanese immigrants, managed to take over the CFP and expanded its following among the multitudes of rural migrants streaming into Guayaquil's *barriadas* (slums). An imposing figure with a booming voice, Bucaram soon became the boss of Guayaquil politics. In the course of the 1960s his popularity spread throughout the lowland provinces, reflecting the basic coast-highland division in Ecuador's political geography. Traditional families viewed him with extreme displeasure, incensed at the idea of a rude and boisterous figure like Bucaram becoming president.

The elite eventually found a way to block the presidential ambitions of don Buca, as he was nicknamed, using his parents' immigrant status as an excuse. The old master managed to skirt this obstacle in two ways. First, he helped his close aide and relative Jaime Roldós win the presidency in 1979, giving Bucaram access to the highest level. Then he himself won election to Congress and muscled his way into the head of that body. Ironically, though, don Buca and Roldós began fighting almost immediately, and the latter asserted his independence by pulling out of the CFP. The military, meanwhile, seemed disinclined to get involved.

In 1981, however, Ecuadorian populism virtually ended. Roldós perished in a plane crash, and Bucaram died a few months later. Since then, nonpopulist figures have held the presidency. The only serious populist rebirth, the 1996 election of Bucaram's nephew, Abdalá (nicknamed El Loco—the Crazy One), ended in his impeachment less than a year later.

## Rómulo Betancourt

Like so many other populists, Rómulo Betancourt got his political start in a university. Born into a wealthy family near Caracas, Venezuela, Betancourt showed great aptitude for school and moved to the capital for preparatory study. At the Central University in Caracas, he fell in with student activists and studied law on the side. In 1928 he and his colleagues staged protests and strikes against the seemingly perpetual dictatorship of Juan Vicente Gómez.

In response, the government shut down the school and jailed the protesters. Many, including Betancourt, managed to escape from the country and live in exile.[9] This group, later known as the Generation of 1928, became the legendary founders of the Democratic Action (AD) Party. Years later Betancourt would usher this generation into the government.

During his exile Betancourt traveled in the Caribbean and settled for a time in Costa Rica, where he associated with leftist intellectuals and edited a newspaper. There his ideas began to take shape, forming a vision for Venezuela to become a democratic, quasi-socialist country. He imagined that workers and campesino farmers could be mobilized and that his generation would lead them. After a few ill-fated attempts at armed invasions, the exiles gave up trying to organize guerrilla movements and stuck to propaganda.

Gómez died in 1935, and his successor allowed the exiles to return and form political parties. Betancourt and others of the Generation of 1928 recruited teachers, rural leaders, and labor union officials. Their most important coalition, Movement for Venezuelan Organization (ORVE), eventually evolved into the AD. They paid special attention to the petroleum unions because during the 1930s Venezuela had become the world's largest oil exporter.

The two generals who governed Venezuela after Gómez both attempted to liberalize politics gradually, but only for groups willing to recognize their authority. Betancourt kept his party separate and underground to avoid associating too closely with the military regime. Finally, however, the party emerged formally in 1941 as AD, and it immediately began national recruitment.

For several years AD built its following and prestige as an independent party, Betancourt serving as its coordinator and ideological inspiration. He moved gradually away from his socialist beginnings and came to advocate a strong central government that would regulate but not take over the nation's businesses. In particular, he planned to overhaul the contracts enjoyed by the biggest international oil companies so that Venezuelans would benefit more from their profits.

In 1945 the incumbent government attempted to steer elections toward a handpicked successor, while AD and other groups fought against them. After a great deal of maneuvering, AD joined with some middle-ranking army officers to overthrow the regime and install a provisional government, in which Betancourt was the chief authority. The military collaborators quickly melted back into the barracks, leaving AD in charge of reforming the entire system of government.

Betancourt and the AD enjoyed three years of relative freedom to enact a modernization program. Betancourt's reputation largely stems from these halcyon years. First they overhauled the electoral system, giving the vote to women and eighteen-year-olds while also providing for secret ballots and widespread voter enlistment. AD went out of its way to create committees in rural towns and villages to complement its original urban constituency. Venezuela held its first modern elections ever under the AD, in 1946 and 1947, each of which drew over a million voters and established a model for future elections.

Betancourt then renegotiated the law covering oil production, providing for a fifty-fifty split of net profits from petroleum exports and refining. The leading companies, called "the majors," agreed to this in exchange for guarantees of labor cooperation and no expropriation. Betancourt spoke of using the oil profits to build basic industry and diversify the economy, so that one day the country would not have to depend on hydrocarbon exports. One of his supporters, novelist Arturo Uslar Pietri, called this policy *sembrando petróleo* (sowing the oil). AD also invested in schools, clinics, rural roads, light manufacturing, and electrification. Finally, AD announced an agrarian reform program that not only made land available to the landless but also provided credit, training, access to markets, and extension services. This, too, won much support from both urban and rural citizens, who feared the instability brought on by a landless campesino class.

Betancourt, who served as provisional president in the early years, declined to run in 1947. Instead, the famous novelist Rómulo Gallegos, author of the classic novel *Doña Bárbara,* ran and won with 74 percent of the votes. AD seemed to be a juggernaut in these years. Expectations ran high that Gallegos would continue to implement the program that Betancourt had initiated.

Military commanders, however, urged on by wealthy businessmen and landowners, became uneasy with AD's rapid reforms. The AD leadership failed to take other party bosses into their planning, and within months after the election, plotting began against Gallegos. Overconfident after its massive election victory, AD did not take precautions, and it was easily overthrown by a military coup in December 1948. Betancourt and his colleagues again went into exile, and the populist experiment ended temporarily.

For the next decade, Venezuela was ruled by General Marcos Pérez Jiménez, the last in a long line of dictators from the ranching state of Táchira. Pérez Jiménez rolled back many reforms, installed politicians who supported the army, and reassured foreign and domestic businessmen that their interests would be protected. The military diverted the oil revenues from education and health to major construction projects like a superhighway from the inland capital of Caracas to the coast and a steel-producing center on the Orinoco River.

In 1958 disgruntled army officers, egged on by civilian forces, overthrew Pérez Jiménez and brought back constitutional government. The following year Betancourt won election as president, and he restored the policies of the late 1940s. Somewhat chastened now, Betancourt followed a more moderate course and worked closely with rival party leaders. He also took a strong stand against the guerrilla groups that had sprung up around the Caribbean Basin following the Cuban revolution. In 1959 Venezuela took the lead in creating an oil cartel that would later become quite powerful—the Organization of Petroleum Exporting Countries (OPEC). Through OPEC, member countries coordinated policies and controlled global prices in an effort to lessen the economic vulnerability caused by their oil export dependency.

After 1960 Betancourt and the AD alternated in office with a more conservative party, the COPEI, which had been organized in the 1940s. Representing a Christian Democratic philosophy, COPEI stressed honesty in office, protection of the family, and pro-business economic policies.

By the 1970s Venezuela had consolidated a strong democratic tradition and avoided the military takeovers that swept most of the region. Analysts credited the populist era forged by Betancourt's AD for this transition to democracy. Yet, in this same decade, Venezuela also began to experience the dramatic economic fluctuations caused by its continued oil dependence, as well as facing a renewed debate about oil nationalization whose resolution would set its course for decades after.

## Jorge Eliécer Gaitán

Colombia forged deeper democratic traditions than the rest of Latin America. Conservative Party presidents had dominated elections from the 1880s on with few interruptions. The country earned reasonable returns on its exports and enjoyed a good reputation among foreign investors. With a few exceptions (the War of a Thousand Days in particular) Liberal Party leaders remained in their role of loyal opposition. Virtually every citizen and civic organization identified strongly with one party or the other.

In 1930, the liberals managed to win the presidency because the conservatives split and ran two candidates. The liberals took advantage to pioneer social and labor legislation that soon turned them into the majority party. They not only guided the country peacefully through the Great Depression but also initiated what would become a sixteen-year liberal era (see chapter 16).

After a stabilizing term led by President Enrique Oyala Herrera, Alfonso López Pumarejo won the presidency in 1934. Calling his administration the Revolution on the March, he carried out social and economic reforms that were remarkably innovative for Colombia. He separated church and state, created universal male suffrage, legalized labor unions and collective bargaining, and gave the government the power to regulate and even to expropriate private property in the public interest. Successors went even further with social and economic change, instituting land reform, expanding social security, and increasing federal funds for education.

Following World War II, however, social tensions erupted in Colombia, causing critics to charge that these reforms either had gone too far or had come too late. Only a small proportion of the eligible population voted, and voters always elected representatives of the traditional parties. Politicians were trapped in the liberal-conservative debates from the last century, while masses of poor and unemployed people streamed into the cities in search of better lives. The time was ripe for a bold leader capable of grappling with modern problems.

That leader was Jorge Eliécer Gaitán, a young and ambitious lawyer from Bogotá. Gaitán and his dissident liberals decried the old-fashioned ways of the party wing dominated by Alfonso López (elected to a second term in 1942) and called for a thorough renewal of its ranks and policies. Gaitán insisted on running for president in 1946, thereby splitting the party vote and allowing the conservatives to win.

Gaitán was not only a rebel within liberal ranks but also within the elite that traditionally governed Colombia. Born in Bogotá into a lower-middle-class family, he was of mestizo heritage. He worked his way through law school and then made a name for himself as a criminal lawyer. Outspoken and articulate in public settings, he gravitated toward politics and his father's party, the liberals. In 1928 he leapt to national attention by denouncing a massacre of banana workers by the army, which had been called in to break a strike against the United Fruit Company in Santa Marta. His investigation and speeches in Congress (to which he had won election in 1928) became a cause célèbre. He was clearly a young man on the rise.

During the liberal period, Gaitán served in a wide range of public offices. He finished out a term as congressman and was reelected. He served as a city councilman in Bogotá. In these jobs he represented well the people who elected him, gaining notice as time went on. The liberal bosses decided to test his mettle by appointing him mayor of Bogotá in 1936. He served only a year before alienating some labor leaders and oligarchs, who convinced President López to have him removed.

Later, party chiefs tested him in the positions of minister of education and of labor. Faced with major policy choices that went against the liberal grain, he invariably went with his instincts. This repeatedly alienated powerful liberals who felt their own oligarchical privilege threatened by Gaitán. These same liberals forced Gaitán to step down before long. Still, these national positions gave him the opportunity to display his considerable administrative talents and to travel throughout the country. Combative, eloquent, ambitious, and devoted to attending to the needs of the rural and urban masses, Gaitán's popular support continued to grow among a middle-, working-, and lower-class population, fired up by promises of economic reform and political inclusion.

In 1945 the Liberal Party split badly, and Gaitán decided that he would run for president the following year. No longer even nominally tied to Liberal Party rules, he mounted a modern political campaign, complete with a convention, radio coverage, newspapers, and a punishing travel schedule. He remained the boss, however, as all populists did, and seemed to have limitless energy for every last detail of the campaign. This personal touch translated into the name of his movement: Gaitanismo. Even people who opposed his candidacy admitted that he possessed charisma and the power to arouse the masses.

As expected, the liberals split their votes in the 1946 election, and Gaitán came in third. Analysis of the returns, however, indicated that he would be the man to beat in 1950. Even without major party backing or deep pockets, he took virtually all the major cities, plus the coastal provinces. His liberal rival, Gabriel Turbay, bowed out of politics and died a short time later. So many people expressed their preferences for Gaitán in the 1946 election that the Liberal Party leaders realized that they would have to nominate him in 1950 or face serious repercussions from their base.

Gaitán had a complex mixture of progressive ideas, a visceral drive to lead, and an innate ability to connect with the masses of poor people. Taken in isolation, his slogans sounded arrogant and overwrought, yet in the heat of a speech, on the radio, and in meetings with aides, they inspired faith and elevated him above the ranks of ordinary politicians. Perhaps his most famous statement best sums up his complexity: "I am not a man! I am a people!" Already he was compared with Juan Perón, whose inexorable drive to the presidency paralleled Gaitán's.

In 1947 and 1948 Gaitán recovered from the recent grueling campaign, built up his law practice, and got ready to run for the presidency. He kept his name and picture in the press and attended party meetings, but he did not have a particularly high profile. He managed to forge an alliance between Gaitanismo and the Liberal Party, though not without a great deal of argument and opposition from liberals who did not support his more progressive ideas and who likely resented his widespread popularity.

Meanwhile, the general mood of the country grew harsh, with rising rates of crime and violence, an uncompromising attitude on the part of the conservative government, and increasing antagonism between liberals and conservatives. Thus began what was later known as La Violencia, the decades-long fighting that claimed 350,000 lives. In all likelihood, Gaitán himself fell victim to this trend toward brutality and killing.

In April 1948, with diplomatic delegations from around the Americas present for the founding of the Organization of American States, including a young Fidel Castro, Gaitán was fatally shot by a lone assailant. Gaitán had just emerged from his office, accompanied by several colleagues, when a deranged, shoddily dressed man stepped in front of the group and shot him dead.

Gaitán's death caused an immediate outpouring of grief and anger from Bogotá's poor, who rioted and looted for days. Their last, best hope of electing someone who cared about them had now vanished. The Bogotazo, as the rioting became known, in turn fanned the violence in the countryside, so that by the 1950s Colombia had descended into endemic civil war.

Other Colombian leaders attempted to reach out to the masses the way Gaitán had, but they failed. After a five-year military dictatorship in the 1950s, Colombia returned to the previous two-party system, with power alternating between the conservatives and the liberals. Populism in Colombia died along with Gaitán.

### Víctor Paz Estenssoro

The last Andean leader considered here, Víctor Paz Estenssoro, of Bolivia, enjoyed a reputation both as a revolutionary and a populist. As the events of his rise to power in 1952 fade into history, his party (the Nationalist Revolutionary Movement, or MNR) increasingly looks like many others in the populist mainstream. But Bolivia is a special case in that the MNR sought change in a country that was largely indigenous, with some of the worst inequality and racism in the hemisphere, and where a small Creole elite had dominated indigenous workers for centuries.

 Paz grew up in the southern district of Tarija, where he completed high school. He then attended the National University, graduating in economics. In 1932 he volunteered for duty in the Chaco War (1932–1935), a brutal assault on Paraguay over a disputed scrubland territory that held key river transport and possibly oil. Many of Bolivia's poorly equipped, conscripted soldiers died of thirst in this inhospitable place. Other casualties mounted as Bolivia's military leaders led troops from one blunder to another. As South America's deadliest international conflict in the twentieth century, it was a crushing defeat for Bolivians, who lost more territory in the war than Paraguay had demanded at its outset. It also led to the creation of the Chaco Generation, which blamed traditional elites for the disastrous war and turned to more radical politics after its end.

After Bolivia lost, Paz joined a "young Turks" group of officers who were disillusioned with traditional elites and concerned about the government's inability to deal with rising indigenous and labor unrest, especially in the critical tin-mining industry. At that time, the tin industry provided about 80 percent of national exports, and by World War II it was producing about half of the world's tin. These officers participated in the 1936 coup led by David Toro and Germán Busch. Paz served in several capacities, making economic policy and helping fashion a more modern constitution.

The reformers lost power in 1939, and, outraged at the military's massacre of striking miners and their families at Cataví in 1942, they founded a party, the MNR, to pursue their goals. Since the Chaco War, these reformers had been able to count on the sympathetic support of soldiers from the war, many of whom were indigenous, and, like the largely indigenous mineworkers, had been drafted into a dangerous situation by Creole elites, who seemed to view them as mere cannon fodder. The following year the reformers seized power again and held it until 1946. Paz served as finance minister in this government.

Conservative military forces removed the reformers again, and Paz went into exile in nearby Argentina, staying for the next six years. He kept the party alive through clandestine networks, and he broadcast opposition radio messages to Bolivia. Paz also forged an alliance between his group, comprised of veteran officers, and organized labor. By then, labor opposition to Creole politicians included not just miners but also indigenous plantation workers, whose demands were met with brutal repression in the late 1940s. Women workers played a particularly important role. They formed the Barzolas, a group named after a woman miner who had died at Cataví and that organized strikes, protests, and demonstrations during the late 1940s. By then, the experience of conscription for the Chaco War and labor organizing had mobilized Bolivia's indigenous population into an active, potentially revolutionary political force.

In 1951 Paz ran for president in absentia and won 53 percent of the vote. Before he could return, however, reactionary forces induced the military to take power again, claiming that they were reversing communist advances. At this point, the MNR carried out a coup in which the powerful tin miners' union played a crucial role. Paz returned to take charge of a revolution.

One writer described the MNR government that emerged as a "many-headed monster" because of the disparate and competing forces it contained, from the miners to the urban middle class to the communists. Paz gave three cabinet posts to the tin miners and quickly carried out his campaign promises. He nationalized the tin mines on the grounds that as private entities, they had not contributed to national development. In fact, Paz turned control of the mines over to the unions, a remarkable feat considering that tin still comprised close to three-quarters of government tax revenue, the industry was dominated by just three families before its nationalization, and the largely indigenous workforce had few labor protections prior to this. He then raised wages across the board and subsidized basic necessities to stimulate the economy. He also extended social security to virtually all urban workers. Finally, he carried out the most complete agrarian reform since the Mexican program of the 1930s; as in Mexico, it marked the first time that the indigenous people were key beneficiaries of government reforms.

Paz enacted several other reforms in order to bolster his political position. He extended the vote to all adults, regardless of literacy, hoping to reap support from the poorest strata of society. He weeded out enemies from the army officer corps and kept the troop strength low in order to discourage army involvement in politics. He also allowed the miners and peasant leagues to keep weapons that they had obtained during and after the revolution. The government could use these irregular militias to counterbalance the army.

By the 1960s, the MNR had become more moderate. This in part reflected its closer ties to the U.S., which in the 1950s pumped aid and loans into the country in an effort to curb radicalism, making Bolivia the largest recipient of U.S. foreign aid in Latin America at the time. Because the MNR did not carry out widespread dismantlement of existing socioeconomic structures, some writers refer to it as populist rather than revolutionary. Paz certainly fit the definition: charismatic, chosen by election, reformist, and devoted to improving the lives of the poor. Revolution was cut short as well by a military coup in 1964, the first in a series of military interventions that would dominate political life until the end of the 1990s. But Paz's later career—a productive term in the early 1960s and a successful administration in the late 1980s—continued to fit the populist definition.

## CENTRAL AMERICAN POPULISTS

Few populist leaders arose in Central America, largely because of the oligarchical character of these nations' governments. When challengers seemed capable of capturing power, they were simply suppressed by the military. The exceptional cases of Costa Rica and Panama confirm this general rule.

Costa Rica did not have an army capable of defeating an insurgency, so when a clever and popular landowner, José "Pepe" Figueres, organized a revolt, the army resisted and then surrendered to Figueres's "revolution" in 1948. A revolutionary and a populist, Figueres quickly held elections, convoked a constitutional convention to restore democracy, and then ran successfully for president. Costa Rica returned to its democratic traditions, an exception in the troubled lands of Central America.

Panama also lacked an army, mostly due to the presence of the U.S. canal administration and many military bases in the Canal Zone. Until 1930 U.S. authorities monitored politics and stepped in to maintain law and order so that the canal could function efficiently. In 1931, however, the United States decided to stand on the sidelines while a group of middle-class reformers calling their movement Communal Action took power and deposed a corrupt and ineffectual president.

Communal Action was led by Harmodio Arias, a gifted forty-five-year-old lawyer who arose from modest beginnings to become one of the country's most effective leaders. Though not a populist himself, Harmodio paved the way for the appearance of populism in his country. After the group's seizure of power in 1931, he went to Washington to serve as ambassador and to win changes in the hated 1903 canal treaty. He ran for president in 1932 and won in Panama's first free and honest election. He served as president for a four-year term, then wielded great influence during the early years of his handpicked successor's administration.

Harmodio accomplished a great deal while in public life, much of it intended to turn his country into a genuine nation-state rather than a mere client of the United States. He oversaw negotiations with the United States that in 1936 resulted in a treaty that gave Panama more benefits from the canal. He founded the University of Panama, the country's first postsecondary institution. He strengthened the police force so that it could play a larger role in maintaining law and order. He established the Popular Savings Bank and attempted to deal with the lack of housing in Panama City and Colón. Most of all, Harmodio guided the country through the hardships of the Depression and served notice to the United States that Panama wished to be treated as a partner in operating the canal.

Harmodio's brother, Arnulfo Arias, groomed himself for the presidency during the 1930s, and in 1939 he launched his campaign with the full backing of the government and the police. Overzealous and tempestuous, Arnulfo hounded his opponent into resigning and then won the 1940 election unopposed. Panamanian politics would never be the same again. Born into a poor rural family in 1901, Arnulfo Arias managed to get a good education in Panama and eventually graduated from Harvard Medical School. Following in his brother Harmodio's footsteps, he entered politics in the late 1920s and did not abandon it until his death in 1988. An American observer said of him, "Politics is in his blood." He ran for president five times, was elected three times, and was deposed by the military three times. He served two and a half years as president, spent two years in jail, and lived fifteen years in exile.

The most successful vote-getter ever to campaign in Panama, Arnulfo was a populist in the mold of Perón, Haya de la Torre, and Velasco Ibarra. His party, called the Panameñistas, was little more than a personal vehicle for its leader's career. Yet, his credo of Panameñismo (Panamanianism) struck sympathetic chords in the hearts and minds of a majority of the citizens. Arnulfo Arias's accession to the presidency in October 1940 began a short and tumultuous term. Critics called him a Creole führer, a petty tyrant, a megalomaniac, a gringo baiter, and worse. He lasted barely a year before being ousted by his own minister of justice, with the blessing of U.S. authorities.

Arnulfo returned to office in 1949 and presided over an administration characterized as one of "irresponsibility, pillage, and privilege." Many citizens were happy to see him overthrown in less than two years. For the next decade, Arnulfo instructed his followers not to vote at all, like Yrigoyen's campaign of intransigencia earlier in the century. In 1968 Arnulfo won the election with ample margin, only to be overthrown by a military coup after eleven days in office. Finally, he competed well in the 1984 election, but the official vote count gave the election to his opponent, Nicolás Ardito Barletta, effectively ending his career.

## CONCLUSIONS AND ISSUES

In the two decades following World War II, Latin America saw the rise of an expansive, quasi-democratic politics known as populism. This style of politics consisted of electioneering by dark horse candidates, often with scant party backing, who mobilized masses of voters. These candidates were charismatic, spellbinding, ambitious, and colorful. They did not always prove to be effective as presidents, but they won and held the loyalty of huge numbers of people, sometimes even after their deaths. A few movements identified with these populists—even using their names—are still powerful in the region today.

Political scientists note that the populists did not foster town hall–style democracy or empower their followers by consulting them on major decisions. Many of the populists were autocratic and willful egotists uninterested in what the masses thought. But they did promote the use of elections and expanded suffrage into rural areas and into the ranks of the poor, female, and disenfranchised—an irreversible process. The populists also managed—through a kind of mystical union with the people—to implement reformist policies acknowledged to be the will of the people. Whether they really perceived popular will or used their powers to create the illusion that they did, we may never know. The populists were, however, extraordinarily successful in generating mass enthusiasm, framing broad national issues, taking bold stands, and mobilizing people to achieve their ends. For better or worse, Latin American politics have never been the same since.

### Discussion Questions

What characteristics and policies distinguished the classic populists from their predecessors in the 1900–1930 period?

What conditions favored the rise of the populist style of politics in the 1930s and 1940s?

How did the experience of women, men, indigenous people, and the working class change under the classic populists?

How and why did populists like Vargas and Perón change from autocrats and dictators into champions of democracy?

How did the militaries of the various countries react to the rise of populist presidents and why?

Was populism a revolutionary or evolutionary reformist force in Latin America? Explain the difference and reasons for your choice.

## Timeline

| | |
|---|---|
| 1930–45 | Getúlio Vargas seizes power in Brazil and serves as autocratic president |
| 1934 | José María Velasco Ibarra chosen as president of Ecuador, the first of five terms |
| 1940 | Arnulfo Arias of Panama wins presidential election, the first of three terms |
| 1945 | Rómulo Betancourt wins Venezuelan presidential election at the head of the Democratic Action Party |
| 1946–55 | Juan Perón serves as elected president of Argentina |
| 1948 | Revolt led by José Figueres gives Costa Rica a new constitution; Figueres elected president in 1953 |
| 1948 | Jorge Eliécer Gaitán, leading contender for Colombian presidency, assassinated, sparking La Violencia |
| 1951–54 | Getúlio Vargas serves as elected president of Brazil, the height of his populist career |
| 1952 | Víctor Paz Estenssoro leads revolt that installs him as president of Bolivia |
| 1952 | Perón's wife, Evita, dies of cancer |
| 1956–61 | Juscelino Kubitschek serves as president of Brazil |
| 1960 | Rómulo Betancourt returns to the presidency of Venezuela, alternating terms thereafter with Christian Democrats |

## Keywords

American Popular Revolutionary Alliance (APRA)

Bogotazo

Brasília

Chaco War

Communal Action

Concentration of Popular Forces (CFP)

Democratic Action (AD) Party

Generation of 1928

import substitution industrialization (ISI)

Nationalist Revolutionary Movement (MNR)

Organization of Petroleum Exporting Countries (OPEC)

Peronism

Peronist Women's Party

Petrobras

populism

United Officers' Group (GOU)

Volta Redonda steel complex

# DICTATORSHIP, DEVELOPMENT, AND DEMOCRACY

The global conflict known as the Cold War (1947–1989) dominated most of the second half of the twentieth century, pitting the U.S.-led Western bloc against the USSR-led Eastern bloc. Latin Americans took sides reluctantly, viewing the conflict as peripheral to their interests. Many, in fact, remained neutral or followed Juan Perón's Third Way of non-alignment in Cold War struggles. A few, impressed with Fidel Castro's 1959 revolution in Cuba, actually defied the Colossus of the North and instituted socialist governments. Still, no nation escaped the pressures brought to bear by the superpowers.

The geopolitical riptides created by the Cold War brought dramatic and even tragic outcomes in the hemisphere. Part V deals with some of the coups, assassinations, espionage operations, secret atomic weapons programs, guerrilla conflict, counterinsurgency campaigns, human rights abuses, and economic warfare that resulted from the confrontation between the United States and the Soviet Union. Even after its end, the Cold War cast long shadows throughout the region.

The economic experience of Latin America proved mixed. After World War II a boom in global markets for Latin America's exports raised hopes that the gap between rich and poor countries might gradually close. Then suddenly commodities prices collapsed in the early 1950s, to the detriment of Latin America. Most leaders reverted to the policies of import substitution industrialization (ISI) and protectionism designed in the 1930s. As a result, light industry increased as countries promoted consumer goods production, while traditional exports and foreign trade diminished in importance to national income. Heavy reliance on imported capital goods and foreign direct investment, however, soon undermined the ISI strategy of building more independent economies. A few countries managed to build up their heavy-industry sectors—Brazil and Mexico in particular—but the rest turned to common markets, directed economies, international loans, and other measures to keep their production expanding in pace with population growth. Nowhere did they succeed fully.

In the 1970s two sharp hikes in oil prices caused widespread disruption in regional economies, even in Mexico and Venezuela, both of which exported oil. Most countries had to curb imports to maintain balance in their foreign payments. In the late 1970s, huge sums from oil-producing countries flowed into Latin America in the form of direct and indirect loans. This volatile situation could not last, and the Latin American economies nearly collapsed during the global recession of 1981 and 1982. Several countries defaulted on loans of "petrodollars" and took drastic measures to survive. The so-called Lost Decade in Latin America in the 1980s ravaged labor relations, infrastructure, financial institutions, social welfare and education programs, and even governments. Inflation soared as even basic goods became out of reach for the majority.

As these disruptions occurred, a radical shift in economic thinking took place in the industrialized countries and international banks. During the 1980s economic managers embraced neoliberal theories harking back to Adam

Smith's and David Ricardo's eighteenth-century classic works. These revived theories gradually displaced the Keynesian economics advocating government intervention that had prevailed since the 1930s. The new theories required privatizing government enterprises, reducing public spending, ending regulation, and promoting freer international trade. New loans to the region were often conditional upon the adoption of these neoliberal policies and austerity measures, and huge, painful adjustments affecting hundreds of millions of people resulted in the 1980s and 1990s.

Politically, the Cold War pressured hemisphere leaders to ally with the United States. After the governments of Cuba, Chile, and Nicaragua became communist or socialist, with support from guerrilla forces, the United States toughened its stance and supported military dictatorships in Latin America. Virtually all of South America fell under such regimes, which differed from the traditional dictatorships in important ways. Chapter 23 relates how this occurred.

The countries of the Caribbean Basin responded to global events in quite distinctive ways. The Cuban Revolution, covered in chapter 22, led some leaders to veer to the left, especially in places still under neocolonial influence. Revolution seemed a viable option for societies trapped in economic backwardness and repression. Leftist parties and guerrilla movements sprang up across the region to challenge the conservative, authoritarian forces in power. Where dictators could resist the left, they became even more entrenched, usually with help from the United States. The region had not seen such intense turmoil since the era of independence and emancipation in the previous century.

Across Latin America, economic development, educational opportunities, and better social welfare programs fostered demographic growth, migration, and urbanization. Many countries for the first time became more urban than rural, and more working and middle class than lower class. Although race still played an important role in determining social status, it was less an outright barrier to mobilization than ever before. Indigenous and Afro-descendant rights groups emerged in areas like the Andean region, the Caribbean, Brazil, and Mexico, demanding lands, political rights, and an end to discrimination. Labor unions, too, grew even larger after the populist era. Like indigenous rights groups, they often became targets of right-wing repression in the 1970s and 1980s.

Women, too, experienced new opportunities in the second half of the twentieth century. Suffrage was just the beginning of their formal political participation, as many joined parties and ran for office. While the Catholic Church still had great influence in limiting access to divorce, abortion, and birth control, the sexual revolution and access to their own wages battered the forces of patriarchy. Economic changes that spurred migration to cities or to the United States and authoritarian violence disrupted households, breaking down traditional social relationships and forcing men and women to forge new ones.

Perhaps the brightest facet of Latin America's recent history has been the recognition of its cultural achievements. Long dismissed as derivative or underdeveloped, the arts in Latin America thrived and won global recognition after midcentury. Painters whose careers peaked in the 1930s—David Siqueiros, Frida Kahlo, José Clemente Orozco, and Diego Rivera in Mexico, joined by Cândido Portinari, Anita Malfatti, and Di Cavalcanti in Brazil—became internationally famous. Soon Latin American artists representing many styles were featured in European and North American galleries. Music like Cuban son, Brazilian bossa nova, Andean waltzes, and Mexican rancheras enjoyed international appreciation. Films from Latin America began to win awards at festivals. A growing number of Latin American actors, writers, composers, and directors made fortunes in Hollywood. International critics came to recognize that Latin American arts drew upon a rich and diverse culture that combined elements of indigenous, African, and European traditions.

The popularity of Latin American culture shone most, however, in literature. Latin American works of fiction dated back to the early nineteenth century, but none won much attention until the twentieth. All of a sudden, in the 1960s the world discovered Jorge Amado, Gabriel García Márquez, Mario Vargas Llosa, Julio Cortázar, Alejo Carpentier, and Carlos Fuentes. Their styles, often called "magical realism" because of the fanciful events narrated within a realistic setting, became a sensation in the United States and Europe. Later Clarice Lispector, Isabel Allende, and Elena Poniatowska won international acclaim for their novels, which emphasized feminist themes and critiqued authoritarianism in the region. Translated editions of these authors' books sold by the millions, generating a publishing boom. Latin America gained renown for world-class writers in the realm of fiction.

Poetry and essays from the region also gained recognition. Octavio Paz, Pablo Neruda, and Jorge Luis Borges captivated readers everywhere. They often traveled abroad to lecture or teach. By 2015 six Latin American writers had won Nobel Prizes for literature. The so-called Latin American boom in fiction led publishers to resurrect writers of the nineteenth and early twentieth centuries, and many of them also rode the wave of popularity.

During the last seventy years, two Latin American countries followed paths substantially different from those of their neighbors. Mexico came out of World War II economically strengthened and stable under the one-party regime that Calles and Cárdenas had built in the 1930s. The official party, or PRI, won all presidential elections from the 1930s until 2000, when it lost to opposition candidate Vicente Fox. By 2012, the PRI had retaken the presidency. Despite fairly steady leadership at the top, Mexico experienced considerable upheaval over economic and social issues; state violence, and in recent years drug war violence, have been persistent. Chapter 19 traces these events.

Colombia, although subject to the same global forces as the rest of the hemisphere, also pursued developments quite distinct from those of its neighbors.

The populism so prevalent in South America disappeared with the death of Jorge Eliécer Gaitán in 1948. The two-party liberal and conservative system then dissolved into a dictatorship in the mid-1950s, accompanied by the horrific warfare known as La Violencia. In 1957 party leaders managed to restore their legitimacy with an agreement to share government between them. From then to the present, elected civilian presidents have governed Colombia. The violence abated in the 1960s, and the economy recovered. Even so, violent struggles between the government, paramilitary forces, guerrillas, and drug cartels have since wracked the country despite recent peace accords, as seen in chapter 20.

Since the beginning of the twenty-first century, the prospects for Latin America have looked quite positive. Politically, most nations have democracies guided by constitutions. Socially, most indices of well-being have crept up from their low points in the 1980s: income, literacy, life expectancy, school enrollment, and access to water, electricity, and housing. The Latin American middle class grew.

Economically, most countries accommodated to the global policies of neoliberalism and improved their performances, even if the gains were shared unevenly. Internationally, the end of the Cold War brought respite from the battles and intrigues of previous generations, though the War on Terror has reshaped security concerns in the hemisphere. If not free of ideological biases, most leaders and movements at least were able to formulate positions and programs that addressed the needs of their constituents. Communism nearly disappeared, often replaced by social democratic movements inspired by European parties.

Chapter 25 analyzes the most significant developments throughout Latin America in the twenty-first century. Three trends stand out. One is the increasing globalization of the economy, resulting in a growing involvement by Latin Americans in global trends; the second is the return to power of leftist governments and, subsequently, the reassertion of conservative forces by the middle of the second decade; the third is the rapidly increasing Hispanic population in the United States, bringing the United States and Latin America even closer together, especially economically and culturally. The 2016 election of Donald Trump as president of the United States has brought both immigration and trade agreements into question, however. The Trump administration appears to champion a new nationalism that stresses the primacy of U.S. interests at the expense of globalism. What impact this will have on hemispheric relations remains to be seen.

# Mexico since World War II

## The Zapatista Revolt of 1994

The Zapatista Army of National Liberation (EZLN), a group named after Emiliano Zapata fighting for the rights of the dispossessed indigenous in Mexico, launched its revolutionary crusade against oppression with a ringing call to arms, published on January 1, 1994. But, though launched in the highlands in southern Mexico, from the start it signaled a new era of rebellion, having its own website and using the Internet in savvy ways to build a global following. Read the call to arms for the passion and conviction—and frustration—that it carries in its message of war against the rulers of Mexico, some of whom are named specifically for crimes against the people in the full document.

First Declaration of the Lacandon Jungle

Today We Say: Enough Is Enough!

To the People of Mexico: Mexican Brothers and Sisters:

We are a product of 500 years of struggle: We have been denied the most elemental preparation so they can use us as cannon fodder and pillage the wealth of our country. They don't care that we have nothing, absolutely nothing, not even a roof over our heads, no land, no work, no health care, no food nor education. Nor are we able to freely and democratically elect our political representatives, nor is there independence from foreigners, nor is there peace nor justice for ourselves and our children.

But today, we say ENOUGH IS ENOUGH. We are the inheritors of the true builders of our nation. The dispossessed, we are millions and we thereby call upon our brothers and sisters to join this struggle as the only path, so that we will not die of hunger due to the insatiable ambition of a 70-year dictatorship led by a clique of traitors that represent the most conservative and sell-out groups. They are the same ones that opposed Hidalgo and Morelos, the same ones that betrayed Vicente

Guerrero, the same ones that sold half our country to the foreign invader, the same ones that imported a European prince to rule our country, the same ones that formed the "scientific" Porfirista dictatorship, the same ones that opposed the Petroleum Expropriation, the same ones that massacred the railroad workers in 1958 and the students in 1968, the same ones that today take everything from us, absolutely everything.

To the People of Mexico: We, the men and women, full and free, are conscious that the war that we have declared is our last resort, but also a just one. The dictators are applying an undeclared genocidal war against our people for many years. Therefore we ask for your participation, your decision to support this plan that struggles for work, land, housing, food, health care, education, independence, freedom, democracy, justice, and peace. We declare that we will not stop fighting until the basic demands of our people have been met by forming a government of our country that is free and democratic.

JOIN THE INSURGENT FORCES OF THE ZAPATISTA ARMY OF NATIONAL LIBERATION.

General Command of the EZLN, 1993[1]

The revolt that broke out in the state of Chiapas on January 1, 1994, formed part of a broader protest against abusive government and deteriorating economic conditions in the south of Mexico. Long a region of poverty and unrest because of ethnic tensions and economic insecurity, Chiapas quickly became a symbol to observers all over the world of the failings of Mexico's most recent development programs. Neoliberal economics had won the endorsement of the international banking community, to be sure, but Mexican labor leaders, priests, intellectuals, and grassroots activists decried the policies' impact on peasants and poor people. Once again, they argued, the interests of the masses were being sacrificed to benefit the super-rich of Mexico. The time had come, they said, to put an end to the crushing poverty of the working and farming people of Mexico.

Mexico, the only country in the hemisphere to undergo a thorough revolution early in the twentieth century, has an exceptional history. It has endured almost constant meddling and powerful influences of all sorts from the United States, its colossal neighbor to the north. As the largest Spanish-speaking nation in the world, Mexico is a trend-setter for other countries in the Caribbean Basin. And, except for the era of Cárdenas in the 1930s, Mexico has not been governed by a genuine populist.

In addition, compared with its own past and with other Latin American experiences, Mexico has been politically stable and economically prosperous for most of the period since 1940. The official party, reorganized by Cárdenas in 1938 and renamed the Institutional Revolutionary Party (PRI) in 1946, elected every president until 2000, and all served out their six-year terms. About 90 percent of the PRI candidates for state governorships and Congress have also been successful, though most often patronage, electoral manipulation, and outright violence have been needed to guarantee these results. Since 2000, increased party competition and more honest elections have meant the

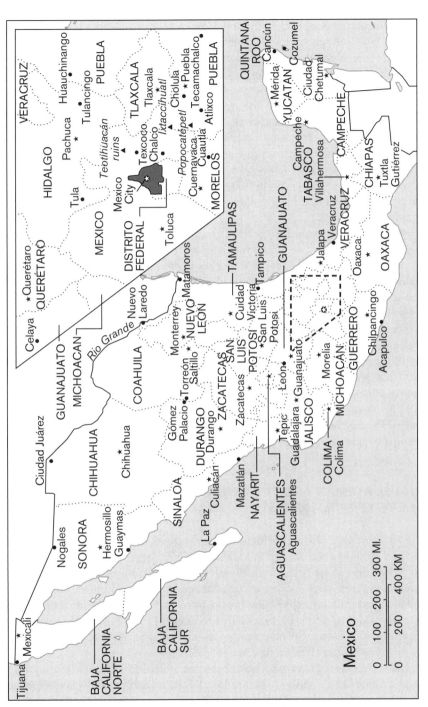

**Map 19.1** Mexico.

PRI no longer holds a political monopoly. Still, Mexico has been exceptional in its political steadiness over several generations.

The Mexican economy received massive injections of capital and technology from abroad right after World War II, and it performed above average for decades after. Some analysts even spoke of the "Mexican Miracle," referring to its notable political stability and economic growth through the 1950s and 1960s. More recently, and despite the Lost Decade of the 1980s, a period when Mexico experienced a devastating economic crisis, Mexico's economic integration with the United States and Canada in the 1994 North American Free Trade Agreement (NAFTA) seemed to confirm its destiny to join the ranks of developed nations. Since then, however, the economy has undergone major structural reforms that have shaken it to its roots and raised doubts about its long-term prospects.

Mexico's early revolution, political stability, and economic success do not mean, however, that it is somehow divorced from Latin America, or that it is immune to the problems faced by other countries pursuing development in the region. Recent scholarship has exposed a much darker side to Mexican growth and stability, revealing the violence that was needed to guarantee the conditions for economic growth and electoral victories. With an infamous student massacre in Tlatelolco in 1968 and then the economic crises of the 1970s and 1980s, the legitimacy of the PRI came under serious attack. By the mid-1980s, the PRI was experiencing serious defections and finally lost the presidency in 2000. Mexico also trembled in 1994 with the peasant rebellion in the southern state of Chiapas, which brought back memories of the great revolution of 1910 to 1920. Nevertheless, Mexico remains the heart of northern Latin America, playing the role of big brother for Central America, trade partner in the Caribbean, and regional spokesperson in international organizations.

## MIGUEL ALEMÁN AND THE GENERATION OF LAWYER PRESIDENTS

The 1946 passage of the presidency from Manuel Ávila Camacho to Miguel Alemán brought a sea change in Mexican politics. Until then, presidents came from the ranks of army generals, mostly those who commanded troops in the revolution. Afterward, a string of presidents with no revolutionary credentials, and even less military experience, moved into Los Pinos, the name of the presidential residence since the 1930s. This midcentury generation of presidents, spanning from 1946 to 1976, trained in law and entered the bureaucracy young; for that reason, we call them the "lawyer presidents."

The lawyer presidents were born between 1900 and 1922, exclusively into lower-middle- and middle-class families. Educated and urban—except for the rural-born Gustavo Díaz Ordaz—they all entered politics before they turned forty. They had very little foreign experience, having graduated from Mexican schools, mostly the National Autonomous University of Mexico (UNAM). Their vocation, the law, prepared them to be negotiators, mediators, and, when necessary, enforcers.[2] These lawyer presidents embodied the Mexican Miracle, with their urban origins, education, and focus on stabilizing growth. But they could not hide that this Miracle had come at great cost, including endemic corruption and fraud, poverty, and violence.

The 1946 presidential succession raised a basic question about the future of Mexican government: Would the new president return to the revolutionary program of the 1917 Constitution and thereby complete Cárdenas's task? Or would he follow the moderate path taken by Ávila Camacho, essentially cooling down the revolution to little more than rhetoric? The leading political figures of the day (known as the Revolutionary Family) decided on the latter course. In May 1945 they secretly chose Miguel Alemán, minister of interior (gobernación), as the official nominee of the PRI and almost certain victor in the election.

Alemán, a civilian, a bureaucrat, and a nonrevolutionary, had been a mere eighteen years old when the fighting ended in 1920. The choice of Alemán proved decisive. For the rest of the century, all presidents have been civilian, all have come up through the ranks of the party, and all have shown little interest in revolutionary social justice. Miguel Alemán was the first of a long line of presidents whose style may be described as "managerial."

Along with this shift, government and financial planners changed their priorities after World War II. They deemphasized social goals (higher wages, education, welfare, health, nutrition, and so forth) and focused on promoting economic growth. This resulted in a concentration of ownership and wealth in the hands of a business elite (with its foreign partners) and the state. After 1945, the Mexican rich got much richer, the government expanded its role in the formal economy, and the poor benefited only somewhat. Rural populations gained the protection of government crop supports, while urban residents enrolled in welfare and food subsidy programs. The choice of Miguel Alemán confirmed this shift in policy and signaled the end of the revolution.

Alemán, born into a wealthy family in Sayula, Veracruz, attended college and then chose a career in law and public service. During the 1930s he rose through the political ranks in his state to become governor in 1936. He remained steadfastly loyal to the official party, and in 1940 he became treasurer of Ávila Camacho's presidential campaign, a sensitive position. As a reward, he was appointed minister of interior, with powers roughly equivalent to those of the U.S. president's chief of staff and attorney general combined.

A close personal friend of Ávila Camacho, Alemán handled such delicate jobs as strike prevention, surveillance of Axis agents, and repression of the fascist Sinarquista movement. Essentially, Alemán managed the executive branch of government like a chief of staff. This experience planted the seeds for the growth of Mexico's intelligence service, which Alemán would formally create once he became president and which was an important source of political repression in the twentieth century.

Alemán's 1945 nomination established a model for later successions and shows the dominant role of the president in the political life of the country. Invariably the top party leaders gathered fourteen months ahead of the election and secretly decided on the president-designate. Sitting presidents were called the "great electors" because of the influence they wielded in this process, so much so that the procedure became known as the "*dedazo*" (tap of the finger), suggesting that they in essence chose their successors. In most cases, they chose the minister of interior because he had been in charge of political coordination for the previous administration and knew the country inside and out. While the tightly controlled succession process expanded the PRI's control of the state, the party often chose candidates who would swing the party's policies and rhetoric to the left or right in response to pressure from the opposition.

The man chosen was called the *tapado* (hidden one)—so named because only a few powerful men knew who he was. Knowing the identity of the tapado was like money in the bank because it allowed access to the future president ahead of other favor seekers. Persons in the know could negotiate deals, appointments, contracts, and the like without public scrutiny. Insiders typically got appointed to the official campaign staff. Together, this built the foundations for patronage that cemented the PRI's power in the country. Once the nominee became widely known, he became the candidate and began to campaign.

The election campaign, obligatory since Cárdenas's 1934 candidacy, played an essential part in establishing the nominee's authority. It was a public relations exercise to let the country know something about the candidate and his ideas. It also allowed the nominee to develop contacts and fund-raise throughout the country. Perhaps most important, the campaign exposed the nominee personally to millions of people and allowed the PRI to build his image as the next president.

Miguel Alemán promised to continue Ávila Camacho's programs and largely lived up to that promise. His was a business administration that emphasized economic growth and stability. Indeed, government officials spoke of a planning strategy called "Stabilizing Development." This was nothing more than Ávila Camacho's deemphasis of social reforms in favor of private enterprise. Alemán's approach also contained the seeds of authoritarianism in that the government became more repressive of popular protests that might endanger economic growth.

Stabilizing Development delivered what it promised: orderly economic expansion. The Mexican gross national product (GNP) grew at an average annual rate of 6 percent from 1946 until the late 1970s, a truly remarkable record that doubled the size of the economy every dozen years. By the same token, the high population growth rate (3.5 percent per year) doubled the number of mouths to feed every twenty years. So real per capita growth did occur, but more slowly than GNP.

Political leadership style changed markedly after 1940. Presidents were managers and party bosses, not revolutionaries. They avoided ideological discussions and pursued material growth at all costs. This strategy also required the government to participate in the economy as owner, manager, and regulator, producing what is commonly called state capitalism, or a directed economy. The state, through the development bank Nacional Financiera, became Mexico's leading investor.

In foreign policy, the presidents aligned Mexico with the United States because it was the best source of trade, tourism, technology, and investment capital. Even Daniel Cosío Villegas, a leading Mexican historian and critic of the United States, admitted that because it was Mexico's destiny to be a U.S. neighbor, Mexico should make the most of any opportunities that geography presented. At the same time, Mexico occasionally chose a different path than the U.S., especially in diplomatic matters, asserting its independence as a sovereign nation.

One of Alemán's first acts upon taking office in 1946 was to call an official party convention. He devised a moderate program and changed the party's name to the Institutional Revolutionary Party, a seeming contradiction in terms that points to the party's success at using revolutionary mythology to cement its legitimacy. He completed the removal of the army from politics, begun by Cárdenas, when he dropped the military from formal party representation. The party's symbolic circle changed from four sections (workers, peasants, popular groups, and military) to three. This change reflected both the aging of the revolutionary generation and the rise of university-trained professionals to leadership roles.

From Alemán's administration onward, the revolution became a great myth to which government officials paid lip service but that had scant policy impact. In addition, the party became virtually identical with the government because all public jobs required party membership and contributions to its coffers. Public employees, in turn, used their positions to make money on the side through graft. Corruption and patronage, funneled through the party, thus became entrenched features of twentieth-century politics.

Miguel Alemán may also be credited with starting the Green Revolution in Mexico. Instead of land redistribution, he promoted commercial agriculture on a large scale. He began three major river valley projects that provided irrigation water for lowlands growers: the Rio Fuerte north of Mazatlán, the Tepalcatepec in Chiapas, and the Papaloapan in Veracruz and surrounding states. He also financed irrigation works on the Colorado River in Baja California that made the desert flower along the border. These huge projects not only encouraged commercial-scale agriculture but also provided cheap hydroelectric energy for industry. With these innovations came others that aided agriculture. Scientists introduced hybrid corn varieties adapted to the semiarid highlands, and in the course of the 1950s, corn yields soared.

The most remarkable growth in agriculture came in the north. From Nuevo León to Baja California, agribusiness for export flourished. Many of the crops

---

**Death of the Revolution**

As early as 1947 Mexican historian Daniel Cosío Villegas pronounced the revolution dead. His postmortem analysis was both nostalgic and pessimistic. He sympathized with the quest by the great reformers, the 1917 Constitution, and Lázaro Cárdenas to remake Mexican society along socialist, communitarian lines. He saw, however, that those goals had been abandoned by the post-Cárdenas presidents. Many of the social conquests of the 1930s were now lost as the revolutionary family enriched themselves at the expense of social change. Since Cosío Villegas's statement, many writers have agreed that the revolution died after World War II.

For more on Cosío Villegas's critique of the PRI, see Daniel Cosío Villegas, "Mexico's Crisis," in *American Extremes* (Austin: University of Texas Press, 1964). Originally published as "La crisis de México," *Cuadernos Americanos* 6, no. 2 (March–April 1947): 29–51.

---

were the same as had been grown during the Porfiriato—cotton, cereals, sugar, and winter vegetables—but some new ones, like rice and sorghum, were introduced. Much of the prosperity of the north derived from this activity. In addition, commercial farms located near major cities profited by selling food to local markets.

Abundant farm production and the price support system encouraged better nutrition and, along with better health care, led Mexico's population to grow faster than almost any other nation in the hemisphere. This put severe strains on education, health, and welfare agencies and required sustained economic expansion. Many rural areas could not offer enough land, jobs, or opportunities to support the growing population, and their young people led the migratory tides that flowed into urban areas like Mexico City, Guadalajara, and Monterrey from the 1940s to the 1960s.

On the debit side of the Green Revolution ledger, the ejidos received scant support from the government. Well-organized ejidos thrived and their residents had access to water and other community resources. Others struggled, however, and often they either rented their lands to large agroproducers, turned inward, or fell into disuse.

Infrastructure projects helped private enterprise immeasurably during Alemán's term. His administration completed the Pan-American Highway, built an all-weather road across the Isthmus of Tehuantepec, and quadrupled the number of miles of paved highway in the country. In addition, he completed the reorganization of the National Railway Company. He also carried out a thorough restructuring of the oil company, managing to double its production and turn a profit besides. These and other projects helped Mexican industry keep up with foreign competitors.

Nacional Financiera attracted more and more foreign capital, which it channeled into industrialization. Foreign firms that produced automobiles, tires, electrical appliances, and other consumer durables moved into Mexico, usually finding ways to evade the 51 percent ownership rule, such as partnering with local capital or incorporating abroad. Sears Roebuck de México was a major innovator, encouraging sales of Mexican-made goods in its stores.

This import substitution industrialization (ISI) evoked a degree of national pride in the slogan Hecho en México, but it also created a trade dependence on the United States and Europe. Mexican manufacturers had to import their machinery, capital, technical employees, and sometimes even raw materials from abroad. By the late 1950s, Mexico was producing most of its own consumer items, though at the cost of new types of dependency.[3]

The growth model adopted by the Alemán administration did not provide for increased wages or benefits. Labor leaders were bought off by the PRI, ensuring worker loyalty even as real wages declined throughout the years following World War II. Indeed, the government stated openly that it would continue to hold down wages in order to promote economic growth. When that growth was threatened by strikes, Alemán cracked down, using Cold War anticommunist rhetoric to justify the repression. In a case involving Pemex workers, for example, he sent in federal troops to break up their strike. Moreover, he reined in major unions by forcing out leaders sympathetic to worker demands and replacing them with PRI cronies, who often stayed in place for decades.

Finally, Alemán cultivated that old friend of the Mexican politician: graft. During his last year and a half as president, and continuing into the next administration, Alemán amassed a fortune, as did his close associates, known affectionately as "the gang." He and his "gang" profited from the development of Acapulco as a tourist destination and enjoyed hobnobbing with international celebrities there. He also institutionalized electoral fraud, intervening in state elections so that the PRI would win close races. The blatant manner in which he did this alienated the middle class—a group of people who had otherwise benefited considerably during his term. Indeed, Alemán's term saw the middle class grow large and prosperous.

Corruption remained endemic in the Mexican political system, a fuel for elections and bait for winning converts. In fact, the PRI managed vast amounts of graft that flowed up and down the governmental hierarchy, constituting a system of finance parallel to the public treasury. It began with the president, who received huge payoffs for approving deals for his powerful associates. Ministers, heads of agencies, bureau chiefs, supervisors, union leaders, and inspectors also took in large sums on the side and typically enjoyed a wealthy retirement. Many lucrative jobs—for example, in the federal police, customs administration, bureau of taxation, and contracting authorities—were bought and sold for large sums of money. Virtually all public servants, all the way down to the street cleaners and traffic cops, took payoffs to supplement their wages.

**Figure 19.1** UNAM's library, begun during the Alemán administration, features indigenous designs in mosaic tile. It towers over the sprawling campus on the southern edge of Mexico City. Authors' collection.

The media was bought as well, and reporters regularly took payments for favorable press coverage.

Alemán's pro-business bias did not please all Mexican leaders in the late 1940s. Lombardo Toledano, for one, denounced the end of traditional worker and peasant policies after World War II. He and other leftists founded the Popular Socialist Party (PPS) in 1947 to revive the spirit of the revolution. By that time he had become one of the most influential leftists in the hemisphere and founding president of the Confederation of Latin American Workers (CTAL).

Foreign policy under Alemán kept to the course charted by Ávila Camacho. He maintained unusually close relations with the United States. Alemán and U.S. president Harry S. Truman exchanged formal state visits in 1947. The two made agreements for foreign aid, loans, technical assistance, investment, and freer trade to flow across the border, and in many ways the frontiers began to fade away as a barrier to the movement of goods, people, and capital. Alemán also built a new campus for the UNAM to train future technocrats and professionals. By the 1970s, the UNAM had become the largest university in the hemisphere, with a quarter of a million students.

The army found itself increasingly marginalized from politics and national affairs in general. Its share of the federal budget was cut to 8 percent by the end of Alemán's term and averaged 7 percent for the rest of the twentieth century. The military establishment still has authority in its area and holds veto power over military alliances. For example, in 1947 the military accepted the U.S.-sponsored Rio Treaty for mutual defense, but the following year it vetoed a military role for the newly organized OAS and even prevented Mexico from signing a military assistance agreement with the United States in 1952.

In the end, the Alemán presidency represented much that would come to characterize Mexico in the next two decades. On the one side were solid economic accomplishments and political stability headed by bland technocratic leaders that indicated to the world, and to Mexicans, that the country was on the cusp of achieving true development and modernity. On the other side, however, limited social reforms, labor control, occasional repression, and a rapidly growing and urbanizing population that was often forced to find work in the informal sector hinted at cracks in the plan.

## Adolfo Ruiz Cortines

The next administration, that of Adolfo Ruiz Cortines, has been called old wine in a new bottle. The new president continued the policies and administrative style of his predecessor. When elected, Ruiz Cortines was a sixty-two-year-old bureaucrat from Veracruz. Born poor and orphaned at an early age, he had sought his fortune in politics. At age twenty-two he moved to Mexico City and did odd jobs for various revolutionary leaders. In these years he earned a reputation as a solid administrator. He became a close friend and associate of Miguel Alemán and served with him as treasurer in Ávila Camacho's 1940 campaign. Later he was appointed minister of interior by Alemán, which almost assured him of the official nomination.

Under Ruiz Cortines the economy achieved the structure that it retained for the next four decades. It contained nearly equal parts of private and public assets, with massive infusions of capital provided by investors in the United States and Europe. U.S. investment alone doubled from 1950 to 1958, and in the latter year made up some 65 percent of the foreign total. Most U.S. capital was invested in manufacturing, so U.S. investors could benefit from Mexico's protection of industry.

Tourism became a major component of the economy, contributing on average 5 percent to GNP between the 1950s and the 1970s. Acapulco continued its ascent as an exotic destination for the international jet set, and welcomed stars like Elizabeth Taylor, Rock Hudson, Ronald Reagan, and Rita Hayworth. The state also promoted Mexico's cultural sites, like Chichén Itzá and Teotihuacán, drawing national and international travelers seeking to experience Mexico's indigenous past. The pattern of low wages and concentration of income continued virtually unchanged. Due to the high level of foreign involvement, Mexico's economy remained sensitive to fluctuations in the U.S. and global economies.

Ruiz Cortines did manage to improve the social security system somewhat, expanding its coverage in some isolated northern states and rural areas. Still, the system mostly served formally employed people and their families in major cities. The government's welfare strategy was to allow the high rate of urbanization and industrialization to bring clients to the social agencies, rather than to reach out to them in rural areas or on the streets.

Ruiz Cortines pushed Congress to extend suffrage to women, which was done in 1953. Two years later, women voted for the first time in federal elections. Women had fought hard for the vote in the 1930s. But when it finally came in the 1950s, it was largely a gesture from the top at a time when electoral control ensured that women's votes could not disrupt planned electoral outcomes.

The Alemán and Ruiz Cortines administrations confirmed the analyses of critics who claimed that the revolution was dead. These two presidents did, however, set important precedents for the future: the method of presidential selection, identification of modernization with private enterprise, close association with the United States, and institutionalization of graft and fraud.

### Adolfo López Mateos

Born in 1911 in the central highlands state of Mexico, Mexico's next president, Adolfo López Mateos, was the son of a small-town dentist. He received a good education, and while in college he became a student political leader and activist in the Socialist Labor Party. In the early 1930s he switched to the official party, drawn by Cárdenas's bold leftist policies. He eventually earned his law degree at the UNAM, after which he became a professional administrator.

López Mateos served as minister of labor under Ruiz Cortines, and he earned a reputation as being sympathetic to labor yet also a party loyalist. He proved especially good at averting strikes through official mediation. He won the presidential nomination in 1957 with solid backing from Cárdenas, Alemán, and Ruiz Cortines.

After years of lackluster and conservative-style rule, the revolutionary sheen that had early on bolstered the PRI's legitimacy seemed to be tarnished by the mid-1950s. The PRI chose López Mateos in part so that he could move the party in a leftward direction and appeal more directly to the Mexican people. López Mateos gave more attention than his predecessors to foreign affairs, in which he guided Mexico into the group of non-aligned, Third World nations. Though friendly toward the United States, López Mateos nonetheless felt obliged to keep his distance from the colossus, revealing once again the nationalist independence that has often marked Mexico's relationship with its more powerful neighbor.

López Mateos's major decision was to befriend Cuba after the 1961 Bay of Pigs invasion. He maintained good relations and trade with Cuba when the rest of the nations in the hemisphere broke relations with Fidel Castro (see chapter 22). He based his position on the belief that other countries, in order to achieve national respect and sovereignty, might need to undergo a nationalist revolution like Mexico did in the 1910s. For example, in the 1980s Mexico upheld the rights of Central Americans to determine their own forms of government, even if communistic, and refused to endorse the U.S. Contra war there. The official

Mexican position held that "Mexico neither imports nor exports revolutions" but respects its neighbors' right to self-determination.

López Mateos claimed credit for settling the Chamizal dispute with the United States. In 1864 the Rio Grande (which established the border) shifted its course, giving El Paso, Texas, six hundred acres of land formerly in Ciudad Juárez, Chihuahua. Negotiations begun by U.S. presidents Kennedy and Johnson restored the land to Mexico. López Mateos also reached an agreement that obliged Arizona agribusiness to stop dumping highly contaminated water into the Colorado River before it entered Mexico.

In an attempt to redress rural problems that had become glaring during the 1950s, López Mateos instructed government agents to award 30 million acres to small farmers. By the end of his term they had transferred less than a third of that, mostly as colonization grants in the south. Indeed, while earning a reputation as a reformer in comparison with presidents who came before and after, López Mateos was different only in degree. For example, repression of rural and working-class protests remained common.

López Mateos did pay more attention to social welfare than his predecessors. Although he was not a practicing Catholic, he sympathized with the more progressive stance contained in the message of the Second Vatican Council (or Vatican II) and encouraged Mexicans to support social programs undertaken by the church. He expanded the social security system markedly and pushed a public health program that included pest control. He also created a special social security institute for government employees, called ISSTE. It soon became the best in the nation, providing excellent benefits, including old-age pensions, disability coverage, health care, maternity care, life insurance, funerals, layoff indemnization, vacation spas, housing, low-interest loans, sports complexes, day-care centers, scholarships, and discount stores.

López Mateos reformed the party system, partly in response to the leading opposition parties, the PAN and the PPS, which were becoming frustrated with repeated electoral defeats. The PAN, dating back to 1939, represented urban, middle-class, largely Catholic voters and consistently polled about 10 percent of the votes, with stronger followings in its core states of Guadalajara and Michoacán and among female voters. Lombardo Toledano's PPS suffered from endemic fighting among its leftist constituents and rarely elected more than a few candidates.

To put a better face on what was obviously one-party autocracy, López Mateos asked Congress to create a minority representation system to help small parties. The system provided five congressional seats for every 2.5 percent of the national vote received and additional seats for every 0.5 percent above that. The PAN and the PPS thus won several dozen seats between them and began to act more like a loyal, if largely powerless, opposition in Congress.

López Mateos also pushed education with new, prefabricated schools built with self-help techniques. He funded teachers' quarters to make rural schools

## Violence and the PRI

For many decades, scholars touted Mexico's unique democracy, which blended a stable single-party state with modernizing growth in ways that seemed exceptional in Latin America. They added that not until the 1968 Tlatelolco Massacre did the PRI engage in widespread repression. More recently, however, scholars have begun to reexamine that belief in light of newly opened security archives and increasing evidence of widespread repression and violence by the PRI dating back decades.

In the 1950s, state-sponsored repression was directed at agrarian activists and labor unionists seen as threatening the PRI's project for growth. Among the more notorious was the government crackdown on railway labor leader Demetrio Vallejo, who led a series of strikes in 1958 and 1959, calling for increased wages. The strike grew to include electrical workers, oil workers, and teachers. When the workers voted overwhelmingly for Vallejo to lead the union, the PRI stepped in to try to force a government-backed leader on them, which workers refused. The government was forced to let Vallejo become secretary general of the union. In March 1959, the union declared a strike, and this time the government hit back. It seized the railway industry and attacked the strikers, killing a handful, arresting thousands more, and firing close to ten thousand. Vallejo was among the arrested, and spent the next eleven years in jail on charges of sedition.

Repression of rural movements was equally harsh. Among the more well known was the assassination of agrarian leader Rubén Jaramillo. During the 1940s and 1950s, Jaramillo became known for repeatedly defending land and labor rights in his home state of Morelos. Due to his vocal and occasionally violent defense of local workers and peasants, he earned a great deal of support but also repeated death threats. In the early 1960s, despite promises from President López Mateos to protect ejidos in the area, a group of ranchers seized ejido lands. When the small farmers retook their lands, the federal army forcibly removed them. But for the federal government, Jaramillo remained a problem. In May 1962, federal police and soldiers seized him, his pregnant wife, and three relatives and killed them.

These cases are discussed more fully in Robert F. Alegre, *Railroad Radicals in Cold War Mexico: Gender, Class, and Memory* (Lincoln: University of Nebraska Press, 2013), and Gladys I. McCormick, *The Logic of Compromise in Mexico: How the Countryside Was Key to the Emergence of Authoritarianism* (Chapel Hill: University of North Carolina Press, 2016).

more attractive to urbanites. New textbooks distributed during his term had a leftist bias, harking back to the 1930s, and aroused opposition in some local communities.

López Mateos tried to keep labor unions reined in, and in 1959 he decided to use federal troops to break up a national railroad strike. Soon afterward, to compensate for this harsh treatment, he devised a profit-sharing arrangement, mandated by the 1917 Constitution but never instituted. This benefit, eventually paid by all large enterprises, became the first such program in the Americas.

Mexico moved further toward state capitalism under López Mateos. Previously the government had merely directed the economy with tariffs and trade controls and with targeted investments made by Nacional Financiera. López Mateos decided to make the state an active participant in economic decisions. He used government funds to buy majority ownership in a number of industries, even foreign ones, and then used public proxy votes to assure that socially desirable goals were pursued in addition to profits. For example, he took over the motion picture distribution system, owned by an American expatriate, and used it for public education and entertainment, though also propaganda. He also nationalized the foreign-owned electrical power industry so that rates could be held down. PRI leaders hoped that this progressive presidency would help to quell undercurrents of opposition and reinforce popular loyalty to the party.

### Gustavo Díaz Ordaz

The next president, Gustavo Díaz Ordaz, took power in 1964 and quickly moved the presidency in a more conservative direction. He came from the conservative and heavily Catholic state of Puebla. While serving as minister of government under López Mateos, Díaz Ordaz had proven to be an autocrat. As a signal that his administration would not tolerate liberal ideas, he fired the president of the PRI for advocating modernization of the party—including primary elections—to make it responsive to popular sentiment. Díaz Ordaz strengthened the PRI's authoritarian side.

The 1960s were a heady time across the globe. Student protests and workers' strikes erupted all over the world, including in Mexico, to challenge the power of elites and the constraints of the traditional social order. Those born at the start of the Mexican Miracle were coming of age at that time, and they absorbed global ideas and culture with enthusiasm. Historian Eric Zolov argues that they embraced U.S. and British rock; some even began their own rock bands, such as Los Rebeldes del Rock, singing *refritos*, or covers of English-language songs by musicians like the Rolling Stones or Janis Joplin, before developing Mexican rock sounds and songs in Spanish.[4]

The 1960s Mexican counterculture movement known as La Onda defended freedom and justice in the face of decades of corruption, fraud, and state violence. Students focused their protests against the lack of democracy and endemic poverty that pervaded the country. Under Díaz Ordaz, the government applied especially heavy repression to control them, but in the end they revealed the weakening legitimacy of the PRI's rule.

The most famous protest, the Tlatelolco Massacre, occurred in Mexico City in 1968. The government had won the bid to host the Summer Olympic Games—the first time they were held in the developing world. Hoping to use the games to win greater prestige for Mexico, Díaz Ordaz spent $200 million in preparation. Beginning in the spring of 1968, high school students decided to use the games as a forum to reveal the corruption of the government, arguing that the money should have been spent to alleviate poverty. They initiated a series of demonstrations that soon spread to other high schools and universities, and even began to draw support from their middle-class parents, teachers, and university professors and leaders. Riot police, called the *granaderos,* skirmished frequently with the student protesters, especially as the summer wore on, and they threatened to disrupt the games. Unwilling to meet the students' demands for more political transparency and help for the poor, and with the games nearing, Minister of Interior Luis Echeverría decided to crack down on the protesters to assure Olympic officials that Mexico City security would be tight. The army even occupied the UNAM, violating the school's long-standing tradition of autonomy.

On the eve of the Olympic Games, some five thousand students and others gathered to demonstrate peacefully in the Plaza de las Tres Culturas, also known as Tlatelolco Plaza. Sniper fire from unknown sources broke out, and the police opened fire on the crowds. Official figures indicate that three to four hundred people died in the melee that ensued, but some observers claimed that thousands were killed. Army units, meanwhile, machine-gunned El Colegio de México, a prestigious and independent college in downtown Mexico City. Although no one was hurt there, the attack appeared to be a warning to Colegio professors not to criticize the government.

The games went on largely as planned, but the massacre sent a chill throughout the population. While official violence against peasants and laborers was not unheard of, never before had it targeted middle-class students—and in such a public way. The PRI never recovered the prestige that it lost in Tlatelolco. The intellectual and artistic communities, in particular, rarely lent their support to the state afterward.

Díaz Ordaz's term ended in 1970, and with it the stable period of economic expansion over which previous administrations had presided. He had managed to maintain high growth rates only at the expense of overvaluing the peso, increasing foreign debt, and giving protection and costly subsidies to inefficient industries. As one critic noted, the state and the industrialists had joined together in an "alliance for profits," a pun on the name of the U.S. aid program Alliance for Progress. The economic model kept alive by Díaz Ordaz could not continue indefinitely, and external shocks would end it sooner than expected.

## Origins of the Maquiladora Industry under Díaz Ordaz

Women workers predominated in the so-called maquiladoras—factories located along the Mexican side of the border with the United States. These were sometimes referred to as "in bond" or "twin plants" because they imported duty-free raw materials and components that were assembled on the Mexican side of the border into consumer products that were then exported exclusively to U.S. markets. Mexican workers, mostly female, provided virtually all the assembly and packaging labor.

Begun in the 1960s, maquiladoras became a major source of jobs in northern Mexico and an important part of the country's industrial economy. About a half-million people worked in over two thousand plants making electronic goods, apparel, furniture, automobile parts, and other consumer products. Nicknamed maquilas, they were criticized for low pay, exploitative labor practices (especially of women), pollution, and a failure to contribute to Mexico's development. Defenders pointed out that they created jobs and transferred technology into Mexico.

The 1994 North American Free Trade Agreement (NAFTA) extended the duty-free zone farther into Mexico and opened domestic markets to maquiladora goods. Eventually they became integrated into the global market.

## Luis Echeverría

As minister of government in 1968, Luis Echeverría had authorized the attack on the Tlatelolco protesters. When he was nominated to be the next president, then, he had a major public relations deficit to overcome. Perhaps because of this, Echeverría went out of his way to pose as a leftist and a reformer. In the words of one analyst, he tried to become a populist and out-reform Lázaro Cárdenas (1934–1940), whose administration was still considered the high point of the revolution. He shifted uneasily from centrist to leftist positions during the campaign, hoping to rebuild the labor-peasant-party coalition of the 1930s and to reestablish the legitimacy of the PRI. Like Cárdenas, he campaigned at the grassroots, meeting thousands of constituents face to face in an attempt to generate enthusiasm. He wore tropical *guayaberas* rather than suits, to seem like a man of the people. Most observers believed that he failed.

The year after he took office, to atone for the Tlatelolco Massacre, Echeverría released the students imprisoned in 1968. He also lowered the voting age to eighteen to win support from young people. He used media and public relations consultants more than any of his predecessors, projecting an image of himself as the restorer of the revolution. Echeverría's attempts to gain public support slowed but did not stop the gradual erosion of regime acceptance by the masses. He may also have won some respite from the criticism by intellectuals and newspapers. In the long run, however, the PRI paid a price for the years of autocracy and abuse of power. Public approval in polls among voters plummeted, and the PRI relied more and more on fraud to ensure electoral victories. The PAN, the opposition party, began to win more elections.

Echeverría shifted the focus of economic policy toward the countryside, where the PRI had long counted on substantial backing. He funded rural highway and electrification programs and spoke of reviving the ejidos with massive new transfers of land. He completed the improvement and consolidation of the national railroad system, which opened to great fanfare. While supervising these projects, Echeverría traveled more than any other president since Cárdenas.

In addition to reestablishing political support among peasants, he hoped that his rural development program would prevent the spread of guerrilla warfare and terrorism, then on the rise throughout Latin America. Despite his efforts, however, several organizations emerged in the south of Mexico, and urban kidnappings occurred frequently. Echeverría unleashed counterinsurgency measures similar to those of the Dirty Wars in South America, then pitting generally right-wing dictatorships against communist, socialist, and reformist movements bent on revolutions.

In order to improve his image as a populist reformer among middle-class voters, Echeverría closed some tax loopholes that benefited the rich while imposing price controls to help the rest of the population deal with inflation. He nationalized the tobacco industry and telegraph systems in order to reduce prices. In 1972 he lifted Mexico's long-standing ban on birth control programs and launched a family-planning campaign to bring down the birthrate. He did so with the acquiescence of the Catholic Bishops' Council. This policy was popular with the middle class and won acclaim abroad, especially when the population growth rate fell from 3.4 percent in the 1960s to 3.2 percent in the 1970s. Mexico's program became a model for other developing nations.

The economy, however, began to falter during Echeverría's term because of a number of factors. His piecemeal, politically motivated actions exacerbated, rather than ameliorated, the socioeconomic problems inherited from Díaz Ordaz. Meanwhile, the oil crisis of 1973 had an equivocal impact on Mexico. Even though Mexico did not join OPEC, as an exporter nation it received greater revenues from rising world prices. Yet, the general inflation and higher interest rates that accompanied the oil shock hurt Mexico, too. The government, buoyed by increased oil revenues, increased expenditures on a variety of social programs while selling petroleum-derived products at below cost in domestic markets. This move was popular, but poor planning led to economic imbalances and inflation. During his last year in office Echeverría was forced to devalue the currency, the first change in the dollar-peso exchange rate since 1953. Devaluation immediately doubled prices for imported goods and generally raised all costs for consumers. Devaluation was a major defeat for the president. A lawyer by training, Echeverría did not have a firm grasp of financial matters. His spending programs, subsidies, and trade policies all cost much more than Mexico could afford.

## Mexico City Today

By 2015, Mexico City was the fifth largest city in the world, with over 20 million people living in the greater metropolitan area. Across much of the twentieth century, migrants flowed into the city from the countryside, drawn by its schools, jobs, and the excitement of an urban culture. The sheer size of the city challenges its leaders every day. Even minor problems—like traffic jams, power failures, and subway accidents—turn the city into a concrete jungle.

Worse problems arise from long-term neglect. While elites live tucked away in walled mansions and high-rise apartments, about a quarter of the population lives in shantytowns located in a dry lake bed northeast of the city and other outlying areas that have only limited electricity and scarce water. Nearby factories recruit there for cheap labor but often do not provide basic residential services. In addition, the bowl-shaped Valley of Mexico, where the city is located, traps pollution and turns the air toxic during much of the year. Since 2000, the city has developed new forms of modern transportation—metrobuses, new subway lines, and bike sharing, for example—to alleviate the crowding and pollution, though the results are uneven.

Natural conditions also can wreak havoc on daily life in a city built on both a lake and volcanic rock. The terrible earthquake of 1985 leveled huge swaths of the city and left thousands dead and hundreds of thousands homeless. In addition, depletion of underground water reserves has caused sections of the city to sink steadily into the ground—a total of thirty-three feet in the past eighty years! The very survival of the city depends on finding new sources of water outside the Federal District.

In recent years, Mexico City has become less of a draw as Mexicans have sought opportunities elsewhere, in the maquilas of the north or in the U.S., for example. Nevertheless, Mexico City remains a cultural and financial center and its middle class has grown substantially since 2000. Global and domestic businesses and excellent universities, publishing houses, museums, theaters, and research institutes sustain one of Latin America's most vibrant cultural and business atmospheres.

He finally acknowledged the end of the Mexican Miracle when he replaced the long-term strategy followed since World War II. In place of Stabilizing Development, he unveiled Shared Development, implying a redistribution of income in favor of the masses of poor Mexicans. His policies lacked coherence, however, and responded to political needs more than to economic logic. Thus the boom in oil revenues did not end up putting Mexico on firm economic footing. Instead, it helped to set off a series of economic and political crises that would ultimately contribute to the ouster of the PRI in 2000.

## ECONOMIC CRISES AND THE TECHNOCRATIC TURN

Before the oil-driven boom of the 1970s turned into bust by the 1980s, PRI leaders pursued a shift in political strategy they hoped would enable it to weather the turbulent economic times. After decades of rule by lawyer-politicians, the party sought experts in economics and public administration who they felt could introduce technical expertise into running the government. With this technocratic turn, they wanted not only to better manage the economy but also, by claiming that technical knowledge and experience were shaping policy, to undercut growing accusations that favoritism, corruption, and political survival were deciding factors in PRI policy making.

With this in mind, party leaders nominated José López Portillo to be their candidate for the 1976 presidential election. Trained as a lawyer and a lifelong friend of President Echeverría, López Portillo had served as finance minister under Echeverría and seemed capable of implementing the political transition to technocracy while managing the fallout of global instability in oil markets. He initiated this strategic turn, which was more fully implemented by his successors. Beginning with Miguel de la Madrid (1982–1988), every president in Mexico between 1982 and 2012 had a degree in public administration, business, or economics from Harvard or Yale.

The technocrat presidents ended up managing the nation through decades of instability. From the oil boom of the 1970s to the Lost Decade of the 1980s, followed by neoliberalism and economic opening in the 1990s, they forged policies in a global environment over which they had limited control. Most maintained satisfactory levels of growth interspersed with wrenching disasters, including those in 1982 and 1994. The disasters were partly of their own making, since some purposely delayed making difficult decisions until the end of their terms, leaving the crises for their successors to clean up. For example, López Portillo defaulted on the foreign debt in 1982. Likewise, Carlos Salinas de Gortari (1988–1994) devalued the peso in December 1994 just before leaving office, setting off a crisis that spread across Latin America and became known as the "tequila effect."

The technocrats were closely associated with the PRI's decision to abandon the reforms promised in the Constitution of 1917. Instead, their training in neoliberal theory led them to put private capitalists' interests ahead of public welfare on the assumption that what was good for business was good for Mexico. Economic growth above all else became the dominant principle in public finance, globally as well as in Mexico, especially after the end of the Cold War in the early 1990s reinforced neoliberal criticisms of socialist economics.

Reversing Echeverría's redistributive policies and populist approach, the technocrats rolled back the revolution by dismantling public programs and institutions, privatizing public enterprises, ending subsidies, lowering tariffs, and shifting income even more toward capitalists and investors. If Alemán's generation had allowed the revolution to die, López Portillo's disposed of the body. Little in the Constitution of 1917 was sacred anymore.

The technocrat presidents rarely needed the army to enforce this radical shift in policy, using the PRI's extensive bureaucracy and system of patronage to smooth over opposition. The army served as a silent partner of the civilian elite. Despite suffering on the part of the masses in the 1980s and 1990s due to stagnant standards of living, uprisings were few and manageable. The Mexican army's loyalty to the government since the end of the revolution was unique in Latin America.

A key factor that threw a wrench into the PRI's plans for a smooth transition to technocracy, however, was the one that many in the PRI thought would underpin the process and save the party: the discovery of vast new oil reserves in the Gulf of Mexico. Since the late nineteenth century, Mexico's politicians had exploited the country's abundant petroleum. In the early decades of the twentieth, Mexico relied on foreign oil companies to develop and profit from oil, though the Constitution of 1917 called for limiting foreigners to operate by government concession. After Cárdenas nationalized the industry in 1938, incorporating production, refining, and distribution into Pemex, the major foreign oil companies left Mexico. While it was a political victory for Cárdenas and his allies, nationalization left Mexico unable to sell much oil abroad. Most Mexicans approved of the move, believing that this resource should be preserved for development purposes and for future generations. Even today, eighty years later, as the government debates welcoming foreign investment or selling off some of the industry, it remains a controversial issue and has prompted many Mexicans to demand continued public ownership.

Under López Portillo, between 1976 and 1980, exploration confirmed the existence of immense new reserves of petroleum. These offered the opportunity to raise new investment capital through sales abroad. The timing of the discovery could not have been better. OPEC had limited global oil supplies between 1974 and 1979, driving up prices. López Portillo believed that Mexico, by exporting oil, could now have its cake and eat it too. All this was possible without even joining OPEC.

The government began huge investment programs financed in part with loans borrowed against anticipated new revenues from oil exports. It invested in manufacturing, farming, transportation, and infrastructure. It also expanded subsidies for consumer goods. López Portillo called this "sowing the petroleum," just as Venezuelan president Rómulo Betancourt had done. And for a time the strategy worked: the economy grew at prodigious rates between 1978 and 1981, buoyed by petroleum investments, continued state economic intervention, and deficit spending.

With the influx of oil profits and investment, domestic consumption grew rapidly. Because López Portillo did not carefully regulate demand in the economy, inflation surged. By 1982, prices had nearly doubled. Government spending under López Portillo also outstripped revenues, leading to heavy borrowing abroad. In addition, the demand for imports soared, and López Portillo met balance-of-payments shortfalls with more borrowed money. After all, the global banking system was awash in petrodollars, or the huge revenues earned by petroleum-exporting countries, and international banks could offer loans virtually interest free. Mexico borrowed liberally, guaranteeing the loans would be paid back based on projected oil earnings.

However, in 1981 global oil prices fell and Mexican export revenues plummeted. Interest rates for borrowing shot up as well, and investment capital began to flee the country. Suddenly, the bubble of prosperity burst, and devaluation became inevitable. By early 1982, López Portillo had to suspend his government's policy of a fixed exchange rate for the peso, and the peso lost almost half its value. As the value continued to drop, López Portillo realized that he might not be able to service the foreign debt, which had to be paid in dollars. In an extraordinary move, he announced that Mexico would suspend payment on the debt and take measures to prevent further capital flight. He decreed the nationalization of the banking industry. The world looked on, shocked as Mexico's economic miracle morphed into a financial debacle from which the country would take years to recover. That same year, when López Portillo's successor, Miguel de la Madrid, took office, he confronted an economy in freefall.

De la Madrid, a lawyer with a postgraduate degree in public administration from Harvard, had gained experience as budget director under López Portillo. Despite his expertise, however, he could do little as global oil prices continued their slide. Mexico's economy slowed further, and for much of the 1980s, the growth rate was stagnant or even negative. The country's problems were compounded by a massive earthquake in Mexico City in 1985, which registered a magnitude of 8.0 on the Richter scale. It killed close to ten thousand people and left hundreds of thousands homeless. At any time, this would have been a devastating event, especially amid an economic slump. The blow turned even worse when the PRI did little to aid the victims in the aftermath of the earthquake. Rather, authorities initially rejected international aid and funneled resources to party members while denying them to political opponents. In the face of this lackluster government response, citizens' brigades formed to dig out the bodies and to provide basic supplies like water, food, and shelter.

In this context, and in an effort to turn around the economy, de la Madrid declared an end to the state capitalism model that had prevailed since the 1930s. Under severe pressure from international lenders, who made new loans contingent on neoliberal policies, de la Madrid accelerated reforms: balanced budgets, privatization of public enterprise, lower taxes and tariffs on trade, limits on wage increases, the end of price controls on consumer goods, and the elimination of most subsidies and other social programs for consumers. International Monetary Fund (IMF) loans that demanded these neoliberal policies

**Figure 19.2** Cuauhtémoc Cárdenas, son of President Lázaro Cárdenas, pictured here in 2013 announcing his confidence in a PRI decision regarding Pemex. He lost the presidential election of 1988 but won the mayor's race in Mexico City nine years later. Courtesy Eneas De Troya, Wiki Commons.

brought austerity to Mexico and reversed most of the revolutionary gains of previous decades. The 1980s became known as the Lost Decade in Mexico.

Public criticism of how the PRI had managed the economic crises led to a weakening of PRI power in the 1980s and 1990s. As the PRI abandoned revolutionary reform and increasingly committed to preserving its own power above serving the citizenry, public acceptance of one-party rule declined. Calls for democracy grew louder and opposition appeared from several directions. Most surprising, opposition arose within the PRI itself. In 1986, the PRI splintered, with a reformist wing called the Democratic Current challenging the party's *dinosaurios,* as the old guard were called. The reformers demanded internal changes in candidate selection. When that failed to materialize, and the PRI chose Carlos Salinas de Gortari as its candidate, the Democratic Current broke from the PRI, and in the 1988 presidential election ran its own candidate, Cuauhtémoc Cárdenas, son of the 1930s president. Like his father, he promised populist policies and an end to corruption. Cárdenas and other members of the Democratic Current later created an opposition party, the Party of the Democratic Revolution (PRD), in 1989.

Amid the economic crisis and return to democracy that spread across the region during the Lost Decade, world attention focused on the Mexican elections. Lending countries, international monetary institutions, and trade partners all watched closely, as did a population disenchanted after six years of economic devastation. News media, opinion polls, and election monitoring by the opposition made it difficult to steal elections without further weakening the PRI's legitimacy. Indeed, when the PRI carried the 1988 race by a thin margin, Salinas took office under a cloud of suspicion about the blatant fraud attending his election. Many observers believed that Cárdenas likely won the election. Two years later Peruvian novelist/politician Mario Vargas Llosa declared on Mexican TV that Mexico was a "perfect dictatorship."

Salinas, an economist with advanced degrees in both public administration and government from Harvard, dedicated himself to maintaining the orthodox policies implemented in the 1980s. He held the peso at an artificially high rate throughout his term, using speculative capital from abroad to cover budget deficits. Salinas also prepared Mexicans for NAFTA by continuing to sell off state-owned enterprises, encouraging freer trade, and ruthlessly squelching labor demands. His presidency promised to mark Mexico's reentry into the world of responsible governance and global economics, as recognized when it became the first country from the developing world to join the Organization for Economic Cooperation and Development. Instead, his policies ushered in a domestic debacle.

Still reeling from the losses of the 1980s, Mexico's population remained disenchanted with the fraud that had clouded Salinas's 1988 election. The state sell-off of industries, including airlines, steel mills, and banks, ended up as a grab by elite insiders. By 1994, the country had twenty-four billionaires, just a few less than the United States and Germany. Most notoriously, presidential insider Carlos Slim bought Mexico's telecommunications industry, known as Telmex, and turned it into a private monopoly that both underserved the Mexican people and made Slim the richest man in the world by 2015.

Salinas's legacy is most closely associated with three issues: the implementation of NAFTA, the EZLN uprising, and party corruption. NAFTA arrived with great promise on January 1, 1994. Salinas and his allies argued that the agreement with the United States and Canada would integrate Mexico into the global economy while bringing jobs, opportunity, and economic growth. His predecessor had already begun reducing tariffs and eliminating import quotas when he led Mexico into the General Agreement on Tariffs and Trade. NAFTA went much further by stipulating a ten-year period during which most tariffs would be phased out among the three countries. But while it brought growth in trade and investment, it also meant an influx of foreign goods that undercut small businesses and led to widespread layoffs in traditional sectors. It also rapidly expanded the presence of foreign-owned maquilas producing for export. Labor unions became one of the biggest casualties of NAFTA, as employers ignored labor laws with the consent of the Mexican government.

On that same day—January 1, 1994—the world awoke to news of the EZLN peasant rebellion in the southern state of Chiapas. The region had always suffered more poverty, government inattention, and landowner abuse than the rest of the country. Most of the people of Chiapas were indigenous, and many still spoke indigenous languages and lived in communal villages. Over the centuries, outsiders had despoiled their lands and rights, and public officials had paid little heed to their protests, causing a legacy of bitterness and anger. The Zapatista movement sought to redress these grievances through an armed uprising and a negotiated peace.

The EZLN timed its revolt to begin with the start of NAFTA. They were especially critical of some of the land policies that Salinas had implemented to prepare Mexico for NAFTA. For example, he amended Mexico's Constitution of 1917 to allow communal lands, which were to be held in perpetuity by the communities, to be privatized. EZLN analysts blamed NAFTA, and neoliberal policies in general, for further eroding their rights and standard of living. When they rose up, the revolutionaries captured several towns and demanded that the government meet certain conditions before they were liberated, as seen in the opening of this chapter.

President Salinas feared that a weak answer to the EZLN would frighten foreign investors, and so the government overreacted by sending a large contingent of soldiers into the region to suppress the revolt. He did not anticipate that this overzealous response would alienate the international community. The government's campaign against the Zapatistas dragged on for several months, exposing Salinas to accusations of both incompetence and brutality. Finally, he agreed to negotiate with the rebels, using Catholic leaders in the region to mediate. The talks dragged on for many years without reaching a satisfactory conclusion.

With the PRI's legitimacy at an all-time low and facing an internal revolt and popular discontent with Mexico's lack of democracy, Salinas had to pick his successor. He chose a reform-minded politician, Luis Donaldo Colosio, who the PRI hoped would rehabilitate the party's image. Before the election, however, an assassin killed Colosio while he was campaigning in Tijuana. Faced with a succession crisis that Mexico had not seen since the 1920s, the president quickly chose Ernesto Zedillo as the candidate. Like Salinas, Zedillo was among the youngest men (age forty-two) ever to head up the PRI ticket. He was a trained economist with a PhD from Yale. With little popular support, he campaigned on the merits of the country's stability. He implied that a vote for any other candidate would plunge the country into further fighting and lead to economic chaos. Little did he know that at least one of these outcomes was virtually certain anyway. Zedillo won the 1994 election in what some in the government believed was the fairest election ever held in Mexico to that point. But in September 1994, just over a month after Zedillo was elected, the secretary-general of the PRI and brother-in-law of Salinas, José Francisco Ruiz Massieu, was assassinated, another blow to the party's legitimacy and stability.

In this climate of uncertainty, Salinas's term in office ended. He chose to flee Mexico for Ireland rather than face accusations of corruption at home. Moreover, by then, suspicions of graft had begun to swirl around Salinas's brother Raúl, also suspected of ordering the murder of Ruiz Massieu. By the time Salinas left the country, his critics blamed him for the economic fallout of the Lost Decade, the wrenching neoliberal reforms, and his doubtful election victory. He embodied the decades of corruption and favoritism that marked the PRI's rule. Some began referring to him as *chupacabra*, a horrific bloodsucking goat demon in rural legend.

For many, then, Zedillo offered a welcome change, even as he dealt with huge challenges. When he took office in December 1994, he immediately devalued the peso in the hopes of moving toward a freer market exchange of the currency. This move, which Salinas had long delayed, touched off one of the worst financial crises in the second half of the twentieth century. Exchange speculators drove the peso down to less than a third of its former value, while the government spent all of its reserves trying to prevent the peso's fall. The short-term funds that had kept the economy afloat evaporated overnight. The government's response to the crisis was to take more of the neoliberal measures favored by the IMF: limits on government spending, 20 to 35 percent higher utilities fees, and a 50 percent increase in the value-added tax. These neoliberal measures were designed to avoid inflation, public debt, and higher interest rates (which in mid-1995 ran about 100 percent per year). But most Mexicans were hit hard by the crisis. By early 1995, most found their real incomes reduced by up to half and bank credit unattainable. Bankruptcies multiplied, tens of thousands of workers were laid off, and major construction projects were canceled.

To help Zedillo, U.S. president Bill Clinton put up a treasury loan guarantee that, matched with IMF and World Bank credits, totaled $50 billion. This helped to cover Mexico's immediate debt obligations and restored confidence in the peso. By the time the two presidents met personally, in October 1995, Mexico's economy had stabilized and had begun a slow recovery from the crash. Both men hoped that sustained employment and development would also vindicate the decision to enact NAFTA.

The two presidents met again, this time in Mexico City, in May 1997, the first time in almost twenty years that a U.S. president had traveled to Mexico. Zedillo and Clinton could now point to solid economic gains in the previous eighteen months. For one thing, Mexico had paid off the 1995 loan ahead of schedule. The GNP was growing at nearly 5 percent, and inflation (previously in triple digits) was at about 18 percent. Unemployment stood at low levels, reflecting new jobs created by considerable foreign investment but also by the exodus of workers to the United States. For the time being, Mexico benefited from its partnership with the booming U.S. economy.

The recovery did not, however, raise the standard of living of all Mexican workers. It was not until 1999 that Mexico returned to its 1994 annual per capita income levels. Yet neoliberal policies meant that disparities between rich and poor Mexicans continued to grow. In that respect, the promises of the technocrat presidents still had not been kept, and tens of millions of Mexicans remained in what the UN termed "extreme poverty."

**Figure 19.3** Mexican children standing in front of a corrugated tin-roof shack alongside railway tracks in 1964. Railways drew both goods and rural migrants to urban areas, where the newly arrived often settled on unclaimed lands on the outskirts of cities and beside railways and other transportation routes. United Press International. Courtesy Library of Congress.

With formal sector jobs unable to meet employment demand, many Mexicans made their way into the informal economy, creating opportunity where they could find it but without the benefit of state laws and protection. It included any work that did not fall within the purview of the state, from unregistered small businesses and casual laborers to street musicians, domestic servants, and wandering taco vendors. With the economic disruptions since the 1980s, the informal economy thrived. By 2013, 60 percent of the population labored in the informal economy, which accounted for over 25 percent of Mexico's GDP.

During the 1990s, migration exploded as Mexicans moved north to the border maquilas and then to the United States in search of work. Changes in the U.S. economy as well as tougher border enforcement led many to stay, not wanting to risk leaving and being unable to return. By 2014, about 12 million Mexican immigrants, many of them unauthorized, lived in the United States, over half of them in California and Texas.

On the political scene, Zedillo reached an accommodation with the Zapatista guerrillas and gradually improved the electoral system at the expense of the PRI. Partly due to this, in July 1997 opposition leader Cuauhtémoc Cárdenas won the mayoralty of Mexico City, the second-most powerful job in the nation. Cárdenas's PRD, meanwhile, attracted many progressive voters and politicians from the PRI. In addition, rival parties won more seats than the PRI in the lower house of Congress. The PRI still held the presidency, at least until the elections in 2000.

## THE OUSTER OF THE PRI

The July 2000 election became a historic divide, when the little-known PAN governor from Guanajuato, Vicente Fox (2000–2006), won the presidency and ended seventy-one years of single-party rule by the PRI. A number of factors contributed to his victory: public repudiation of the official party; high vigilance of the electoral process by national and international observers; unwillingness of Zedillo to intervene in the election; and an appealing candidate who promised to fight corruption, crime, and PRI bossism.

Fox was a middle-aged businessman who grew up on a ranch and yet earned degrees at the Inter-American University in Mexico City and at Harvard. He learned English and U.S. business methods and spent much of his career managing the Coca-Cola corporation in Mexico. Drawn into politics in middle age, Fox chose the conservative PAN and rose to prominence in Guanajuato. Tall and ruggedly handsome, in his usual cowboy boots and hats, he presented a fresh alternative to the PRI technocrats: a highly educated, economically experienced conservative with popular and political appeal.

Fox seized the initiative by striking up a friendship with recently elected George W. Bush. Their meeting, the first for each, promised a special relationship between the two neighbors. Fox proposed a dramatic change in U.S. policy, granting Mexicans virtually free access to U.S. residency and dual citizenship. Under his plan, NAFTA would be transformed from a tariff-lowering customs union to a virtual common market, much like the European Union (EU). This plan met only tepid reception in the United States.

The new administration promised transparency, even initiating a series of laws intended to open up the government to public scrutiny. Fox also cracked down on drug trafficking and corruption, and unveiled a major development effort, the Plan Puebla-Panama, that would spur trade, investment, and new employment in southern Mexico and Central America. Fox made other efforts to stamp his government as innovative: he visited the Vatican, spoke to the U.S. Congress, and pushed through a free-trade treaty with the EU that had been negotiated by Zedillo.

Fox's honeymoon proved short-lived. The terrorist attack on New York's World Trade Center on September 11, 2001, put U.S. borders on alert and temporarily brought trade and migration to a halt. The recession that followed spread quickly to Mexico, which depended heavily on exports to the United States and on international tourism. On the domestic front, some of his cabinet officials proved to be inept, and he lost precious time extinguishing factional disputes. He did not have a majority in either branch of Congress, and he failed to establish a working relationship with the PRI and the PRD. Even his marriage to a TV newscaster did not spark much interest or rescue his falling approval ratings. By mid-2002 Fox had disappointed many former supporters.

The congressional elections held in July 2003 revealed just how far Fox had fallen in the public's esteem. The PAN lost scores of seats in the lower house, most of which were picked up by the PRI. The PRD also increased its representation in that house. As a result, Fox lost any chance of forming a working majority in Congress and of passing major legislation in his last three years. In many ways, he became a lame duck president.

Since the early 2000s, Mexico has functioned as a multiparty state. Though the PAN won the 2006 election, under the new president Felipe Calderón (2006–2012), it struggled to recapture the energy it had in 2000. Once again, the 2006 elections were clouded with suspicion, this time in the form of a wildly popular leftist candidate running for the PRD, Andrés Manuel López Obrador, who claimed the elections had been fraudulent. AMLO, as he is also known, was an avid advocate of the poor while mayor of Mexico City from 2000 to 2005, and has a long career defending indigenous rights.

When it became clear that AMLO's immense popularity would make him a frontrunner in the 2006 elections, his political opponents attempted to have him arrested, though that failed in the face of the millions who came out to support him. When he lost the 2006 election by a razor-thin margin, his supporters once again took to the streets to protest fraud. When he lost again by a wider margin in 2012, he stepped back from politics. However, he continues to have widespread support, representing popular discontent with the politics now dominated by the PAN and the PRI.

Calderón, as well as his successor, PRI party member Enrique Peña Nieto (2012–), have ushered Mexico through a turbulent period. The economy has been relatively stable and continues to grow, and the explosion of stores and restaurants in upper-middle-class neighborhoods suggests the growth of Mexico's middle class in recent years. But smooth political transitions and economic rebound have been complicated by a devastating war against the country's drug cartels. Calderón launched the war in 2006 by mobilizing the Mexican military to fight the cartels, pledging an end to the drug trade and to drug-related violence. By capturing or killing cartel leaders, they set off a territorial war among remaining cartels. Roughly 70 percent of the drugs coming to the U.S. from South America and Asia come through Mexico.

Corruption in the government, military, and police has facilitated the drug trade. As the power of the military and police in the country has grown, human rights have suffered, with murder, rape, and kidnapping endemic in some areas of the country. Violence against women has been particularly pervasive. Politicians and journalists who are critical of the cartels are themselves victims of the violence. Between 2007 and 2014, about 164,000 people were murdered or disappeared in Mexico.

## CONCLUSIONS AND ISSUES

From the lawyer presidents of the midcentury period through the technocrats in its final decades, Mexico has seen enormous economic growth and relative political stability. By the 1970s, the majority of Mexicans were urban and literate, and working in either industrial or service sector jobs rather than agriculture. The revolutionary policies of the 1920s and 1930s, which had promised agrarian reform and socialist education, are in the distant past as Mexico is now a global center of trade, production, and culture. But Mexico remains a country where a sizable minority in the south speak indigenous languages, where northern ranchers still run cattle, and where throngs of city dwellers eke out a living in the informal economy. The revolution may be dead, but Mexico's diversity remains a vivid reminder of the complex possibilities and challenges that lie ahead.

### Discussion Questions

How did Mexico pass from a presidency dominated by army generals to one occupied by lawyer-politicians? Did ordinary Mexicans find their lives improved? Why or why not?

What was the Mexican Miracle and how did it impact Mexican politics, economy, and society?

What were the causes for the loss of PRI legitimacy from the 1960s to the 1980s? What were the causes of rebellions such as the student demonstrations of 1968 and the 1994 Zapatista rebellion?

Why did the PRI turn to technocrats as leaders beginning in the 1980s? What were their goals?

Why did the PRI allow reforms in the 1980s and 1990s that eroded its monopoly on power? What motivated the PRD and then the PAN to challenge the dominant party?

Did Mexicans trade greater democracy for less economic and social well-being in the twenty-first century? What have been the biggest challenges that Mexico has faced since the 1990s and how have they reshaped Mexico?

How much does Porfirio Díaz's lament, "Poor Mexico, so far from God and so close to the United States," apply to the post–World War II experience of the two nations?

### Timeline

| | |
|---|---|
| 1946–52 | Miguel Alemán serves as president |
| 1953 | Women achieve full suffrage |
| 1952–58 | Adolfo Ruiz Cortines serves as president |
| 1958–64 | Preident Adolfo López Mateos serves as president |
| 1964–70 | Gustavo Díaz Ordaz serves as president |

| | |
|---|---|
| 1968 | Tlatelolco Massacre |
| 1970–76 | Luis Echeverría serves as president |
| 1973 | First OPEC oil embargo |
| 1976–82 | José López Portillo serves as president |
| 1982 | Mexico defaults on its debt, nationalizes banks |
| 1982–88 | The Lost Decade |
| 1985 | Devastating earthquake in Mexico City |
| 1982–88 | Miguel de la Madrid serves as president |
| 1988–94 | Carlos Salinas de Gortari serves as president |
| 1994 | NAFTA implemented; Zapatista revolt in Chiapas |
| 1994–2000 | Ernesto Zedillo serves as president |
| 2000 | End of PRI's single-party control of the presidency |
| 2000–2006 | Vicente Fox serves as president |
| 2006–12 | Felipe Calderón serves as president |
| 2012–present | Enrique de la Peña serves as president |

## Keywords

Confederation of Latin American
   Workers (CTAL)
Green Revolution
import substitution industrialization (ISI)
Institutional Revolutionary Party (PRI)
La Onda
maquiladora
Nacional Financiera
National Action Party (PAN)
National Autonomous University of
   Mexico (UNAM)
North American Free Trade Agreement
   (NAFTA)

Pan-American Highway
Party of the Democratic Revolution
   (PRD)
Pemex
Plan Puebla-Panama
Popular Socialist Party (PPS)
Stabilizing Development
technocrat
Tlatelolco Massacre
Zapatista Army of National Liberation
   (EZLN)

# Colombian Conundrum 20

## The Assassination of Gaitán

The assassination of liberal leader Jorge Eliécer Gaitán on a sidewalk in Bogotá on April 9, 1948, set off a wave of violence that engulfed Colombia for a generation. The following accounts of this event capture the sense of immediacy and urgency of the moment.

> Mendoza Neira and Gaitán walked ahead through the short and narrow passageway from the elevator to the street. The other three followed close behind. Mendoza Neira, on Gaitán's right had taken the leader's arm and was talking as they approached the street. It was 1:05 p.m. They had reached the street and had taken no more than a few steps when Mendoza Neira felt the caudillo [Gaitán] wheel, as if to turn back. Three shots rang out, then a fourth. Mendoza Neira saw a man holding a gun in front of them. Vallejo saw him too: "He was perfectly in control of himself . . ., in his eyes there was a look of hatred."
>
> Gaitán fell heavily to the ground. His friends were momentarily paralyzed. Cruz was the first to kneel beside the fallen leader. He lay on his back. Blood trickled from a hole in the side of his head. He was breathing with difficulty, and Cruz could not find a pulse. As the doctor raised his leader's head, gastric juices flowed from his mouth. Cruz felt a cold hand. "All is lost," he muttered. Gaitán had been hit in the back by two other bullets, which tore through his lungs, always the source of his power. A third lodged in the back of his head.[1]

The Ambassador in Colombia (Beaulac) to the Acting Secretary of State

Bogotá, April 9, 1948—3 p. m.

Confidential 190. Liberal Party chief Jorge Gaitan was shot and killed about 1:15 p.m. today on Carrera Septima and Jimenez de Quesada in central Bogotá. Mob seized and killed assassin, dragged corpse to front Presidential Palace, then hanged it on public street. Mob invaded Capitolio, seat of Pan American Conference, ransacking building and attempting set fire at least one wing. Within one hour after Gaitan's assassination, armed individuals and bands began looting shops, with determined attacks on hardware shops to obtain weapons, including machetes, iron pipes, guns, etc. Bomb was thrown into ground floor Edificio Americano where offices U.S. delegation housed on seventh floor.[2]

The Ambassador in Colombia (Beaulac) to the Acting Secretary of State

Bogotá, April 11, 1948

Priest in parish church Santa Ana in Teusaquilla district sermon mass to faithful carry arms and shoot anyone seen looting or arsoning. "If you kill looter don't come [to] me [to] confess it. It not sin." Priest made clear any action parishioners take should be cooperation organized authority. Government urged people stay inside and moved curfew up to 1900 to give army chance clean up snipers.

Gaitan's funeral reported scheduled Thursday. Gaitan's embalmed body at home and police allowing three to five in at time view it. Large crowds outside home but order maintained. Radio announced no papers published but all four Liberal Party papers had asked radio appeal readers help restore order. Government announced 1445 EST over radio group who attempted foment revolution last Friday after seizing radio stations had been arrested including two Russian agents and other foreigners.[3]

## LA VIOLENCIA

The assassination of Jorge Eliécer Gaitán on April 9, 1948, echoed like a curse through the corridors of modern Colombian history. The masses believed that some hidden conspirators, most likely the conservatives, had taken away their leader. The Liberal Party bosses, not wholly supportive of Gaitán while he lived, found themselves without a credible candidate for the upcoming presidential elections and unable to build a consensus. For years afterward, politicians would be measured against Gaitán to gauge their ability to generate enthusiasm, to attract lower-middle-class voters, and to rise above the level of patronage deals and partisan bickering. Few compared favorably to the slain leader.

The country's elite, both liberal and conservative, may have felt relief that the populist champion of the people had been eliminated from the scene, but they and all Colombians soon paid a high price for his death. The partisan violence that had begun to seep out onto the streets of villages, small towns, and cities now flooded the nation. Self-defense and guerrilla groups allied with both the Liberal and Conservative parties grew quickly and fought a vicious war against each other and against communist guerrilla groups, mostly in the countryside. It engulfed the country in the 1950s, smothering its tranquility and claiming over a quarter of a million lives.

The conservative-led government clamped down in an attempt to control the rioting and killing. Censorship, summary arrests, and a permanent state of siege went into effect. After Gaitán's death, liberals agreed to accept appointments by President Mariano Ospina Pérez, hoping that a show of cooperation with the conservatives might lessen the partisan fighting in the countryside.

**Figure 20.1** The Plaza de Bolívar in downtown Bogotá witnessed much of the rioting and looting that became known as the Bogotazo, following the 1948 assassination of Jorge Eliécer Gaitán. Courtesy Jorge Láscar, Wiki Commons.

This sharing harkened back to the administration of Carlos E. Restrepo (1910–1914), when the reformist Republican Union got minority party representation and other power-sharing measures included in the constitutional reforms of 1910. Those earlier reformers believed that this would help end the bloody wars that had wracked the country during the nineteenth century, culminating in the War of a Thousand Days (1899–1902; see chapter 9).

In 1948 Ospina attempted to keep liberals in his cabinet, but conservatives were not united behind his efforts at power sharing. Thus Ospina also used the army to harass liberals. Under these circumstances, liberal appointees broke with the president and resigned from their offices. Faced with hostility from conservatives, they even refused to run a candidate for president in the 1950 elections and abstained from voting. They alleged that government partiality and police abuse made fair elections impossible. The death of Gaitán threw them into disarray.

The new conservative president who took office in 1950, the fascistic Laureano Gómez, had been a primary opponent of Ospina's power sharing. He extended the state of siege and deployed the army and police against liberals. Most of the subsequent killings were mutual acts of revenge committed by liberals and conservatives, especially in rural villages and towns, where federal authorities had little power. Local chiefs tied to political parties and driven by historical disagreements over land and rural power commanded large personal followings that targeted their opposition. Politics at the local level often had a family feud dimension, and rivalries were entrenched and deeply personal. In the supercharged partisan atmosphere of rural Colombia, killings begat more killings, and the violence continued to escalate. Local authorities who attempted to arrest perpetrators were targeted for reprisals. Protestants—in this largely Catholic country—also suffered attacks because they were associated with the liberals. In the end, nothing served to end the killing. After a slowdown in the mid-1950s, violence resurged in the 1960s and 1970s, taking new forms and justifications.

Colombians have long argued that their country is distinct from the rest of Latin America, in part because of their long tradition of two-party political rule. Since 1910 they have enjoyed almost uninterrupted civilian, constitutional government. The military has remained in the barracks, with only one exception—when the army followed General Gustavo Rojas Pinilla into power between 1953 and 1957. Moreover, except for Gaitán, Colombia had few populist leaders, none of whom created regimes like those of the Peróns in Argentina, Getúlio Vargas in Brazil, or Rómulo Betancourt in Venezuela.

Colombians proudly called Bogotá the Athens of South America because of the democratic commitments of the leaders as well as the cultural sophistication of the country's elite. Educated Colombians enjoyed debating republicanism, or what one historian called "the ideals of public life." They even claimed that their Spanish diction and pronunciation were purer than any other in the hemisphere. Colombians believed that their system of federal government was among the most effective in the world. Finally, they believed that the moderation that they practiced in public affairs had helped avert the civil wars and strife that plagued many neighboring countries.

Colombia is decidedly not like its small Caribbean neighbors to the north, nor did it follow the path of populism and dictatorship of many other countries of South America. Yet it is not as atypical as the myth of exceptionalism suggests. During the nineteenth century it was one of the most strife-ridden countries in the hemisphere. And although it did not experience full-blown populism, Colombia witnessed truly terrifying episodes of insurgency in the twentieth century. Finally, while it did not have authoritarian state-led Dirty Wars such as in Southern Cone countries like Chile, Argentina, and Brazil at the end of the twentieth century, the level of violence in political society revealed deep social divisions.

## THE CONSERVATIVE ERA

The post–World War II conservative administrations of Mariano Ospina Pérez and Laureano Gómez managed the economy reasonably well, overseeing solid growth in industry and agriculture. In the spirit of the nationalist era, they supported public ownership of key industries as a way to complement private enterprise. Ospina inaugurated a government-owned steel mill at Paz del Rio, Boyacá, and Gómez created a state petroleum industry, the Empresa Colombiana de Petróleos (ECOPETROL). They balanced their budgets, promoted exports, opposed strong unions, and welcomed foreign investors. Overall, government policy favored the continued growth of import substitution industrialization (ISI).

On the international front, President Gómez accepted a U.S. invitation to send troops to fight in Korea, in the first military action of the United Nations. No other Latin American country did so. The Colombian armed forces supported the decision as a way to build morale, purchase new weaponry, gain combat experience, and broaden the scope of their mission. Also, Gómez wished to show his solidarity with the United States in the Cold War.

Yet while the economy and international relations were going well, the conservatives struggled to resolve social and political problems and reestablish social peace. For example, the conservatives instituted several social programs, but the results were limited. In 1948 they created a profit-sharing scheme like that in Argentina, and shortly afterward they organized a rudimentary social security system. These social programs came too late, however, to win the president much support from the working class. In this respect Colombia was far behind most countries in the hemisphere, where social security began to be instituted in the 1920s.

Moreover, Gómez's traditionalism became apparent when he proposed amendments to the constitution to expand presidential powers, centralize authority in Bogotá, and permit corporatist representation in the Senate, even by the church. These reactionary politics alienated all but a few hardcore ideologues.

Furthermore, rural areas continued their descent into conflict, especially in areas like Cundinamarca, Tolima, and Cauca, where since the 1930s clashes over land inequality remained common. During the "Revolution on the March" in the 1930s, peasants emboldened by liberal promises had seized lands, asserting that it belonged to those who work it. In an effort by the liberal government to quell the growing squatters' movement, some received titles to the lands, angering the opposition. Conservative governments after World War II therefore sought to roll back policies favoring landless peasants, and landowners retook formerly seized areas, feeding the partisan violence of the period. In alliance with Communist Party activists, peasants organized self-defense groups to fight back, exacerbating the brutality of La Violencia and contributing to the rise of rebel activity in its aftermath.

Because of the state of siege, the opposition of liberals, and the growing defections in his own party, Laureano Gómez presided over what amounted to a civilian, quasi-clerical dictatorship. Despite pressure from moderates within his party, he clung to power tenaciously and refused to step down. He closed Congress to end the attacks on himself, and he appointed an assembly to adopt his autocratic constitutional reforms. His opponents went on a virtual war footing.

The turmoil and bitterness that Gómez evoked, against the backdrop of rural violence, probably contributed to the heart attack that partly incapacitated him in mid-1953. Still clinging to power, Gómez tried to dismiss his chief of the armed forces, General Gustavo Rojas Pinilla, for allegedly conspiring against him. Rojas refused to step down, however, and instead deposed Gómez. It was Colombia's first military coup since the turn of the century and one that many Colombians—including moderate conservatives and virtually all liberals—supported in the hopes of ending the partisan strife that fueled La Violencia.

General Rojas had not actively plotted to take the presidency; he merely led a junta into power. In the absence of anyone obviously better suited to take the office, however, Rojas decided to take charge. He quickly came to relish the exercise of power and to view himself as Colombia's savior in the dark days of political dissolution and violence.

The constitutional assembly that Gómez had impaneled now legalized Rojas's mandate, appointing him to serve as president until the end of Gómez's term in 1954. A year later, it extended the term until 1958. The public responded positively at first, hoping that his Government of the Armed Forces would end partisan fighting and restore order in the countryside. Rojas moved quickly to lift the most oppressive aspects of the state of siege and allowed liberals in exile to return home. The Liberal Party recovered and soon collaborated partially with the government.

Rojas created a government staffed largely by conservatives, but he welcomed the cooperation of liberals and buttressed his authority with church sponsorship. The optimism that followed the departure of Gómez brought temporary respite from the violence. He offered amnesty to fighters who agreed to lay down their arms, and thousands took him up on the offer.

Rojas apparently saw himself as a Colombian version of Spain's Generalissimo Francisco Franco, a firm, authoritative figure who would pacify the nation from above. He exhibited mildly populist qualities as well, promising to spread the benefits of progress to all classes of people. For example, Rojas authorized women's suffrage in 1954. As it turned out, he did not hold elections during this period, and hence women did not vote until after his overthrow. He also carried out other initiatives designed to win popularity. He created a rival labor federation affiliated with Juan Perón's ATLAS in Argentina. He offered credit to small farmers. He established a charity like Eva Perón's foundation and appointed his daughter, María Eugenia Rojas, to administer it. This foundation largely helped resettle refugees from violent rural areas into urban centers.

These programs ostensibly would shift power and income from the traditional oligarchy to the masses of Colombians.

In the end, Rojas presided over a dictablanda (soft dictatorship), as Brazilians referred to Vargas's Estado Novo. But his social programs and political reforms never paid off fully because Colombian politics and sensibilities were so different from Argentina's and Brazil's. When he failed to win adulation through his actions, Rojas created a propaganda agency to foster his glory with pictures, busts, news clips, and admiring stories.

The economy seemed to boom at first, with high coffee prices, new investment by foreign firms, and deficit spending. One author called the general prosperity a "dance of the millions." It turned out to be a hollow boom fueled by temporary conditions that soon gave way to inflation. Moreover, the general relaxation of economic controls induced many public officials to enrich themselves.

In 1956 the violence surged again from those who had not accepted the offer of amnesty, and Rojas responded like an army officer, with raw force. This probably provoked only greater resistance on the part of rebels, including Manuel Marulanda, nicknamed Tirofijo (Sureshot), who switched from Liberal to Communist party ally in this period. In 1964, he created the Revolutionary Armed Forces of Colombia (FARC). Meanwhile, the world market price for coffee, Colombia's major export, plummeted after 1955, causing major economic hardships. Rojas apparently decided that he needed to remain in office longer to impose the pacification and reconciliation he had promised. He began seeking support for another term and even convinced the constitutional assembly to extend his term to 1962.

At that point, liberals and most conservatives balked. Party leaders Alberto Lleras Camargo and Laureano Gómez met in Spain in 1957 to negotiate an agreement under which liberals and conservatives shared power in a restored civilian government. They then mobilized a general business strike to protest Rojas's attempt to continue in office, and they were joined by students and some unions. At the same time, they conspired with the army high command to remove Rojas. Rather than watch the country deteriorate politically and economically, the army sent Rojas into exile in May 1957.

## NATIONAL FRONT, 1958–1974

The bipartisan National Front, designed to replace Rojas, required full sharing of power between the two parties. The agreement was signed in the spirit of peaceful coexistence and initiated a period of "controlled democracy" in which liberals and conservatives monopolized politics. In addition to dividing public offices between the parties (as had been done before), the new agreement provided for alternation of the liberals and conservatives in the presidency for four terms of four years each, from 1958 to 1974. As the majority party and due to divisions within the Conservative Party that prevented them from agreeing on a candidate, the liberals occupied the presidency in the first and third terms. For the second and fourth terms, only conservatives ran for president.

All high-level government posts, elective or appointive, including those of cabinet ministers and legislative and judicial agencies, were scrupulously apportioned between the two parties. Lower-echelon jobs, meanwhile, were converted to merit civil service appointments. This minimized the partisan conflict that fueled electoral competition and violence. Legislation in Congress required two-thirds majority to carry. Finally, third-party candidates were barred from elections, so communists and other parties were excluded from formal political participation.

The National Front largely accomplished what it set out to do: restore civilian government to leaders from the traditional elites, diminish political conflict, encourage economic development programs, and defuse La Violencia. Alberto Lleras Camargo, a veteran liberal who had served as president in 1945 and enjoyed a good reputation, served as the first National Front president. He had proposed the National Front to conservative leader Laureano Gómez. Lleras Camargo's 1958–1962 administration sought to restore peace and achieve some economic growth.

Lleras Camargo set the policy agenda for the rest of the National Front presidents, if not exactly the tone of government. Studiously neutral, almost bland, he cultivated the image of a healer. He took to heart the goals of the U.S.-supported Alliance for Progress, articulated in 1961, and positioned Colombia to become a showcase for democratic development. The army, while still patrolling the countryside, began carrying out civic action projects to help towns and villages. Lleras Camargo also took up the old liberal banner of agrarian reform and created an agency, INCORA, to make land and agricultural extension available to poverty-stricken rural families. Many believed that improved living conditions in the countryside would mitigate La Violencia, since much of it had been fueled by tensions over land conflicts. Yet by the end of the decade, INCORA had distributed only a small amount of land.

The next three administrations continued programs launched by Lleras Camargo. In the late 1960s the government undertook a more vigorous program of economic development, entrusting planning to university-trained economists, engineers, and technicians. Government agencies and mixed public-private enterprises borrowed heavily to build up the infrastructure and expand national productivity. They also pushed to diversify exports, favoring flowers, bananas, coal, and nickel to lessen dependence on coffee. Industrial associations and producers' organizations played more active roles in policy formulation, too. After years of stagnation, the economy responded, producing something of an economic boom that lasted into the 1970s.

Under the National Front, violence abated, at least for a time. In response, the government eased the state-of-siege measures and eventually ended them. Yet, peasant alienation over their exclusion from politics as elites closed ranks in the National Front, as well as the unfulfilled promise of land reform, kept rural discontent alive. Peasants were backed by communist and other leftist organizations that had also been excluded under the National Front arrangement.

The National Front government also faced a serious challenge from an old adversary, General Rojas Pinilla. Rojas had returned soon after his exile and managed to win acquittal of charges of corruption filed against him. Rather than fade into obscurity, he founded a party, ANAPO, devoted to the principles and initiatives of his earlier administration. To the chagrin of traditional party bosses, ANAPO proved quite popular among urban lower-class and campesino voters.

As a candidate in the 1970 election, Rojas became a genuine populist, traveling around the country shaking hands and promising to redress the grievances of poor people. He criticized the oligarchy for monopolizing power and wealth for generations, and he promised to use government for the benefit of the masses. Because third parties could not participate, Rojas ran as a conservative. Recalling the "dance of the millions" prosperity of his 1950s regime, many voters believed that he could deliver again and decided to vote for him.

Rojas stunned the traditional party leaders by coming within 1.6 percent of taking the 1970 election. The victor, conservative Misael Pastrana (1970–1974), won by only a slim margin, so he made sure that ANAPO did not share in the spoils. ANAPO soon began to decline in popularity. Many followers were disappointed that Rojas did not fight the election outcome, which most believed was the result of government fraud. The M-19 guerrilla movement emerged, declared itself to be the armed wing of Anapismo, and struck out on its own.

Four years later, Rojas's daughter, María Eugenia Rojas, ran for president on the ANAPO slate, after the National Front agreement lapsed. She received just under 10 percent of the votes, an indication that the party would not be able to mount a credible campaign for president again. Rojas himself died the following year. ANAPO gradually shifted toward the left, began espousing a socialist philosophy, and cooperated closely with the Communist Party. It suffered a thorough defeat in the 1976 by-elections and was reduced to insignificance. In 1978 it supported the conservative Belisario Betancur for president. The M-19 lived on, however.

## BEYOND THE NATIONAL FRONT

The late 1960s and 1970s was a deceptive period in Colombia, where the stability of the National Front arrangement masked deep, underlying problems, including a burgeoning drug trade and growing rebel activity. Liberal and conservative leaders saw these problems and decided in 1968 that the political climate was still too unsettled to return to fully competitive elections in 1974. They thus amended the constitution to phase out the bipartisan arrangements gradually. The presidential contest of 1974 was open to all parties, but the winner was obliged to share executive appointments equitably with other parties for one more term. Liberal president Alfonso López Michelsen decided to split cabinet posts evenly between liberals and conservatives and designated the defense minister as a neutral. Other practices of the National Front lingered as well. The Liberal Party, seemingly assured of winning elections for president by its larger voter base, continued the office sharing until 1986, at which point it reverted to appointing exclusively liberals. It returned to bipartisanism again in 1990. However they divided appointments, by the 1970s, philosophical differences among presidents had become less important than personal styles. Contentious issues of the past, like church-state relations, economic intervention, state and local autonomy, and property rights, no longer caused fights between the parties.

What did increasingly preoccupy liberals and conservatives was a different struggle, one not between each other but rather against new, powerful forces. Drug cartels were turning Colombia into the narcotics clearinghouse of the world. Violence at higher levels than anywhere else in the hemisphere had become endemic. And guerrilla bands continued to grow, emboldened by Maoist and other extremist ideologies. They were nurtured by discontent among the country's peasantry and working class, both of which saw demands for land and labor reforms go largely unfulfilled in the closed political system. These forces brought unsettled times to Colombia.

While violence had abated in the 1960s, it did not disappear; instead, it persisted at lower levels in several regions. In many places banditry and street crime overlapped with politically motivated offenses. The violence did not threaten the government, so it did not trigger permanent state-of-siege measures. Yet, there was a sense that society was ill and that civil conflict lay just beneath the surface tranquility. It also hampered the full suspension of state-of-siege measures. People began to barricade their homes and planned their lives around security measures. Private security became a booming business, as tens of thousands of men were employed as private guards for homes and businesses.

In short, the remnants of La Violencia kept the administrations of the 1970s on the defensive, made life insecure for most citizens, and plagued state and local government in affected regions. The sense of disquiet and despair was heightened by the sheer ideological diversity of the movements opposing the government.

Many citizens sympathized with the Cuban Revolution and regarded the United States as an imperialist nation; these citizens provided fertile ground for various guerrilla groups that grew to prominence by the end of the 1970s. Others took inspiration from the rise of liberation theology, which took on even more resonance in Colombia because it was identified with radical priest Camilo Torres Restrepo. After years of political activism, in 1965, Torres joined the National Liberation Army, an urban-based guerrilla band that emerged out of discontent with traditional party politics. When police captured and executed him in 1966, he became a martyr to the leftist cause, adding fuel to the flame of rebellion. The ferment and diversity of these movements made their total suppression impossible, especially once the drug trade had penetrated politics, the economy, and society.

### The Drug Trade

The narcotics industry destabilized Colombia after the 1960s. At first, farmers raised marijuana (Colombian gold) for export to the United States, shipping from La Guajira on the Caribbean coast. This did not remain profitable, so some traffickers began to refine and export cocaine from semiprocessed material (yellow cake) imported from Peru and Bolivia, where coca leaf was grown. In the 1980s, cocaine became popular in the United States and Europe, driving up the price and defying efforts to control it. Entrepreneurs in Colombia formed organizations called cartels by which they managed and financed the central and most lucrative parts of the cocaine business. In particular, they took over and expanded existing distribution networks in the United States, especially in New York and Miami.

Cartel agents operated refining laboratories in South America, where cocaine was purified for re-export. They also set up elaborate smuggling routes to the United States and Europe, corrupting officials throughout the Caribbean Basin. They supervised overseas distribution networks. Finally, they oversaw money-laundering operations to hide the sources of their profits. It became a multi-billion-dollar industry.

The major drug cartels operated in Medellín, Cali, and Cartagena—industrial and agribusiness centers where they did not attract too much attention at first. Medellín, for example, had 1.3 million inhabitants in 1975, of whom 200,000 were unemployed. In addition, 32,000 women worked as prostitutes, and 40,000 families lived in shantytowns. Accordingly, the cartels found it easy to hire all the operatives they needed.

Gradually, the cartels assembled cadres of buyers, shippers, bankers, accountants, pilots, gunmen, chemists, and assorted underworld characters. The profit margins were so phenomenal that no expense was too great for the cartels. They corrupted Colombian officials with bribes and threats, assuring themselves of secure places to run their businesses. The cartel chiefs, many still young men, became legendary and notorious figures. Some, like Pablo Escobar and Carlos Lehder, even nurtured political aspirations and ran for Congress.

In 1978 presidential candidate Julio César Turbay Alaya's campaign promised a "moral crusade to stamp out corruption." Indeed, many public officials faced the terrible choice—cooperate or die—forced upon them by cartel traffickers. When they chose the former, often getting wealthy in the process, the public's respect for civil servants began to decline. Those who would not accept bribes were murdered by the cartels to intimidate others into cooperating. The cartels' favorite targets were prosecuting attorneys, judges, and police officials.

A dramatic turning point came when Pablo Escobar and his associates in the Medellín cartel assassinated the crusading attorney general Rodrigo Lara Bonilla in 1984. By then, the cartels were so entrenched it seemed that only full-scale warfare could defeat them. Indeed, many cartels, flush with U.S. dollars, employed small armies of gunmen as guards and enforcers. After first resisting it, President Belisario Betancur (1982–1986) approved an extradition law that would send drug traffickers to the United States for prosecution and launched a war on drug crime.

The sheer volume and profitability of the drug trade, and the corruption it spread, convinced hemispheric leaders to organize a coordinated attack against the cartels. The U.S. government took the lead, convoking inter-American meetings and financing programs designed to slow the drug trade. The multifaceted program, dubbed the War on Drugs, itself consumed billions of dollars each year. It entailed the eradication of coca fields in Peru and Bolivia (where the raw material was grown), the destruction of processing labs, the interdiction of shipments, aerial surveillance in the Caribbean Basin, espionage, suppression of money laundering, and the prosecution of distributors in consuming countries. These enormous forces at times seemed to rival the forces marshaled against the Soviet Union during the Cold War.

Colombian cooperation proved essential for success in the War on Drugs. To be sure, many Colombians as well as some U.S. agents in the country took bribes from the drug cartels, undermining attempts to eradicate the business. Yet, for those public officials who fought the drug trade, the cartels unleashed terrible attacks. In the 1980s and early 1990s, thousands of federal judges, political candidates, district attorneys, police detectives, and prison officials were murdered in retaliation for operations against the cartels.

Colombia's leaders also paid for the war with their own and their families' blood. For example, liberal presidential candidate Luis Carlos Galán was murdered in 1989 on Escobar's orders for threatening to crack down on the drug industry. It was a terrible price to pay, because Colombians did not even consume narcotics heavily. Government leaders recognized, however, the corrosive effects that the cartels had on society, public honesty, and politics, and many made immense sacrifices.

The struggle in Colombia became even more vicious when the cartels entered into deals with guerrilla groups. These arrangements developed after leftists began kidnapping and ransoming children of cartel bosses to raise money. The cartels responded by sending hit teams against the guerrillas in retaliation. Eventually, some cartels struck agreements whereby the guerrillas stopped kidnapping and served as mercenaries for the cartels. With plenty of cash and freedom of movement, the drug lords could offer attractive terms.

Some cartels bankrolled guerrilla forces in exchange for providing protection services. Cartel planes that before had been returning empty from the United States began carrying automatic weapons, grenade launchers, explosives, and sophisticated detonating mechanisms that they turned over to the guerrillas. From the standpoint of those fighting drugs, this development could not have been worse.

### The Guerrillas

Rural guerrilla warfare that had surfaced in the late 1950s in Colombia spread rapidly during the early years of the Cuban Revolution. Militant leaders, drawing on university students, disgruntled intellectuals, bandits, alienated peasant leaders, and the disaffected in general, could attract hundreds of men and women to their ranks. The FARC, working with the Communist Party, became the most powerful guerrilla group. For much of the 1960s and early 1970s, however, the FARC was relatively small and marginal. Urban guerrillas appeared in the late 1960s and were even more difficult to detect and suppress. The M-19, begun in the wake of the 1970 elections, combined rural and urban guerrilla tactics.

Many leftist intellectuals and reformers sympathized with and helped the guerrillas. The revolutionaries' underground support units offered safe houses, weapons caches, medical aid, legal services, and escape routes. With their origins in protest against traditional elites, the guerrillas frequently carried out acts of social justice in order to build a wider base of support.

With little opportunity for political participation or other forms of legal opposition, and with over half the population living below the poverty line in the mid-1970s, the FARC continued to attract support. The government battled the FARC and other guerrilla forces without much success. Guerrillas targeted elites with bank robberies, kidnappings, and hit-and-run attacks on military posts. The army and security services responded by cooperating with their U.S., Brazilian, Argentine, and Chilean counterparts, constituting an informal counterinsurgency alliance (see chapter 23). Right-wing generals at times threatened democracy in Colombia. Repression grew, and authorities invoked state-of-siege powers repeatedly. Student-police strife occurred regularly. Critics spoke of a partial militarization of the country.

In 1979 and 1980, President Julio César Turbay Alaya's (1978–1982) government seemingly engaged in battles everywhere against urban guerrillas. In January 1980 the feared M-19 group raided an army arsenal, much to the embarrassment of the government. In the subsequent crackdown, authorities claimed that they captured fifty-six hundred weapons, fifteen vehicles, and one thousand uniforms. The danger was real.

By the 1980s everyone recognized that crime, drugs, and guerrilla activity were self-reinforcing, but they constituted a Gordian knot impossible to untie. The drug cartels threatened or killed politicians who attempted to shut them down, while the guerrillas continued to hit government targets. The 1985 capture of the Justice Palace showed the extreme power and daring of these groups. M-19 staged the raid to force the president to negotiate, and the army responded with a massive counterattack. Scores of people died, including half of the Supreme Court justices. By then, M-19 was the second largest guerrilla group in the country with somewhere between fifteen hundred and two thousand members. The world looked on appalled, and the Colombian government, already crippled by accusations of drug-fueled corruption, lost even more credibility in its fight against violence and crime.

In order to quell the violence, President Betancur offered the guerrillas amnesty and access to the political system. The FARC, which by that time had between three and four thousand members and close to three dozen fronts operating under its command, accepted and in 1985 transformed itself into a party, the Patriotic Union (UP). As a legal entity, it received considerable support from across the spectrum, from disaffected citizens to communists. Its leadership suffered, however, from systematic attacks by right-wing paramilitary groups, and many UP members and candidates were assassinated. Then in 1990 President Virgilio Barco (1986–1990) struck a similar deal with the M-19, which renounced violence and fielded candidates for virtually all offices in that year's election. For a time, it seemed like Colombians had found a path out of the violence.

President-elect César Augusto Gaviria (1990–1994), political heir to the assassinated Luis Carlos Galán, seemed to find a partial solution to the cartel problem in 1990. A pragmatic hard-liner determined to eliminate the drug industry, Gaviria offered a deal to the cartel bosses. On the one hand, he would continue to raid, arrest, prosecute, and punish narcotics traffickers to the full extent of his powers. He would also extradite persons wanted on drug charges in the United States. On the other hand, he offered more lenient treatment to drug bosses who turned themselves in—no extradition, lighter sentences, and better prison accommodations.

Gaviria's gamble paid off. Cartel leaders began to surrender, including the notorious head of the Medellín cartel, Pablo Escobar. His enemies, however, were numerous and Escobar had to go into hiding. Aided by special U.S. forces and equipment, a Search Bloc was created by the Colombian military to find Escobar. They did, hiding in Medellin, and the most infamous of the drug lords died in a firefight in December 1993. The drug trade continued, but it became increasingly tied to, and increasingly difficult to distinguish from, guerrilla and paramilitary activity.

## ECONOMY AND SOCIETY

Despite the terrible battles that Colombian presidents had to wage against the drug industry and the guerrillas, the economy performed well; on average, the GNP rose about 4 percent a year in the period 1974 to 1995. This growth, moreover, occurred across the board, in mining, manufacturing, and agriculture. For a variety of reasons, the government had never intervened as fully in the economy as had other Latin American governments, and the private sector managed to adapt well to changing global trends and markets.

Business associations have been especially powerful in Colombia's economy. The Colombian National Federation of Coffee Growers, formed in 1927, managed to uphold quality and price levels for its product and to preserve its foreign markets. The National Association of Industrialists likewise has played a major role in expanding manufacturing. These and other groups negotiate with presidents from positions of authority.

Much of the economic growth of the last half-century was financed by capital owned by a small number of families. Colombia witnessed a growing concentration of wealth, as had the rest of the hemisphere, even as the appearance of new manufacturers, export businesses, and service industries spread the wealth beyond the traditional elite families. The fact that Colombian enterprises are distributed throughout a number of cities—Medellín, Cali, Barranquilla, Bucaramanga, and Cartagena, in addition to Bogotá—meant that a broader business class emerged as the economy diversified. As in the rest of Latin America, a sizable middle class emerged as well.

The drug trade also contributed significantly, dumping billions of dollars into the economy and providing jobs for many. While a destabilizing force politically, it nevertheless continued to bring capital into the country during years when other Latin American countries were being battered by economic crises. In the 1980s, it contributed about 6 percent of Colombia's GDP.

With all of these changes, the labor movement grew. By the 1960s, several union federations had become more independent and assertive. The high point of collective action came in 1977, when general protest strikes broke out in response to inflation and wage policies. But amid the violence and repression by actors on all sides, Colombia's labor movement has remained among the weakest in the region. Despite rates of economic growth that appeared favorable by comparison with its Latin American neighbors, Colombia's poverty rate remained high, at over 40 percent, through the 1990s and into the first decade of the new century.

The 1991 Constitution, which replaced that of 1886, responded to growing popular pressures for reform and solutions to the nation's problems. It incorporated into basic law many of the sociopolitical trends evident since the 1950s. Largely the work of President Gaviria, the new constitution made senatorial elections at large (popular vote), rather than by departments (states) nationwide,

### Indigenous Rights in the 1991 Constitution

"Art. 10 That the native tongues and dialects of the country's ethnic [indigenous] groups are official languages—along with Spanish—within the territories occupied by these groups. That education in those territories will be, henceforth, bilingual.

"Art. 96 That the definition of Colombian nationals includes members of Indian groups who share the country's borderlands; this being done in accordance with the principle of reciprocity as applied in official treaties.

"Art. 171 That the Colombian Senate will contain an additional two senators [beyond the one hundred elected nationally] elected by the country's indigenous communities.

"Art. 246 Indigenous authorities may exercise jurisdiction within their territories, in conformity with their own norms and procedures as long as these do not conflict with the Constitution and the laws of the Colombian Republic

"Art. 329 The formation of indigenous territorial units will be undertaken in line with the provisions of the Organic Law of Territorial Organization; territorial limits are to be set by the National Government and with the participation of representatives of the indigenous groups. Also, the reservations (resguardos) remain collective and inalienable property.

"Art. 330 The indigenous territories will be governed by councils organized and regulated in accordance with the customs and practices of their own communities. These councils will exercise a variety of functions including: enforcing laws pertaining to use of the soil and settlement; designing policies and programs for economic and social development of their respective territories and in line with the National Development Plan; promoting and supervising state investment; keeping track of and distributing their resources; conserving natural resources; coordinating programs and projects developed by the different communities within the territory; collaborating [with the national government] in maintaining public order; representing the territories before the national government; fulfilling all other obligations stipulated by the Constitution and the laws.

"Moreover, the exploitation of natural resources within these territories must not threaten the cultural, social, or economic integrity of the indigenous communities. In all decisions concerning such exploitation, the national government will facilitate the involvement of representatives of the affected communities."

The full text of the Colombian Constitution of 1991 can be found at http://confinder.richmond.edu/admin/docs/colombia_const2.pdf.

allowing grassroots organizations greater access to candidates. It also decentralized authority by changing governorships from appointive to elective offices. Mayors have been popularly elected since 1988. The constitution also protected the rights of indigenous people, Afro-Colombians, and women.

The new constitution barred extradition of citizens who surrendered to Colombian authorities—a measure that induced more drug lords to turn themselves in. Attempts were made to improve the shattered judicial system. The constitution also confirmed the civil nature of marriage and freedom to divorce. Finally, it declared the state to be neutral among the various religions, thereby ending official ties to Roman Catholicism. The overall outcome of these changes was a more open, decentralized, and democratic system of government.

## Narcoguerrillas, Paramilitaries, and Peace

The government's truce with guerrillas fell apart during the administration of Ernesto Samper (1994–1998). Assassinations and threats against the UP closed out the political option to former guerrillas, who returned to violence once again. By this time, closer ties between guerrillas and cocaine traffickers fed a new, more vicious violence. Booming cocaine consumption in the United States and Europe proved too lucrative a business to resist, despite international efforts to contain it. The cartels grew into virtual nation-states within Colombia's borders. Moreover, the cartel money flowing to politicians and the judiciary corrupted large segments of the civil service. When the U.S. government learned that Samper's presidential campaign had benefited from drug money, it withdrew its support and barred him from visiting the United States.

During the 1990s pressure from the United States gradually reduced coca cultivation in Bolivia and Peru, and production increasingly migrated north to Colombia, where coca growing, manufacturing, and distribution were protected by the guerillas. By the late 1990s, Colombia had become the world's largest producer of both coca leaf and cocaine. Moreover, the drug lords introduced poppies for making heroin, which was gaining popularity in the United States. The enormous power of drug profits and the private armies they could support pushed Colombia to the brink of collapse.

An explosion of paramilitary groups in the 1990s complicated peace efforts, as the government began a clandestine war against the guerrillas and traffickers. These soldiers, at first drawn from the ranks of disgruntled regular troops, grew into a rival army no longer answerable to the military commanders who had spawned them. Though they were formed to fight against the drug cartels, they soon expanded their mission to target guerrillas as well. And they too prospered from the drug and weapons trades and became vicious in prosecuting the war. Like the guerrillas, they found that taxing civilians directly could be lucrative.

During these years, violence against Colombian citizens by both paramilitary organizations and guerrillas grew quickly. One of the largest paramilitary organizations was the United Self-Defense Forces of Colombia (AUC), which joined together numerous smaller paramilitary groups into a single organization. By 1997, they had identified key areas where they would target guerrillas, and they soon became as feared. They targeted not just rebels, but leftist activists of all stripes, including students, leftist politicians, and human rights workers. In their attempts to control various areas of the country, both the guerrillas and the paramilitaries forced citizens to choose sides or face execution. Some were killed simply for living in an area controlled by the other side. Internal displacements surged as Colombians fled in search of safer locations.

Under the administration of Andrés Pastrana (1998–2002), Colombia instituted a policy of negotiations with the guerrillas in the hope that a deal might slow the kidnappings, threats, and assassinations and weaken their ties to drug trafficking. Pastrana allowed the guerrillas to carve out a demilitarized region in the southeast where the army and police would not enter. Creating a state within a state, the FARC took over many state functions, including performing civil ceremonies, levying taxes, and maintaining order. Pastrana hoped that by lifting pressure on the guerrillas, they might be more willing to negotiate an end to the decades-long civil war.

Simultaneously, Pastrana reached out to Washington to propose a program called Plan Colombia. His proposal included both economic development and military aid. Since a primary goal was to eradicate coca production, loans and aid would go to coca leaf farmers on the condition that they raise an alternative crop. President Clinton also expanded trade conditional upon Colombia's acceptance of neoliberal conditions, including austerity measures such as a sell-off of state-owned businesses and cuts to social spending.

Yet by far the largest amount of the aid, roughly 80 percent, went to expand the military and police to build up the Colombian armed forces to battle the guerrillas. The United States poured several billion dollars into the plan, sold to Congress as an anti-drug effort. This was to be a final solution to the drugs and guerrilla crisis in Colombia, though its impact was weakened because it failed to deal directly with the drug traffickers and paramilitaries.

Pastrana negotiated with the rebel leaders for several years without making progress, and although the number of casualties from warfare declined, he got no closer to diminishing the power of the drug interests and their guerrilla allies. Indeed, the FARC was stronger than ever at the advent of the new century, with estimates suggesting it had close to sixteen thousand members. The National Liberation Army had perhaps five thousand members. The middle class eventually lost patience with Pastrana's failure and, in a move that distinguished Colombia from the leftist trend in politics in the region after 2000, elected the Conservative Party's Álvaro Uribe (2002–2006). The new president announced an end to negotiations with the guerrillas and a full-scale war against them. The public responded with support, as did the U.S. government. By this time, Colombia was receiving the third-largest flow of U.S. foreign aid in the world, after Israel and Egypt.

Controversially, Uribe managed to push through a constitutional amendment that allowed for his reelection, keeping him in office until 2010. Corruption and electoral fraud continued to plague elite politics in the country, voter abstention remained high, and controversial coca leaf eradication efforts left peasants as discontented as ever with the agrarian politics in the country. But Uribe encouraged a new phase in the civil war between guerrillas, paramilitaries, and drug traffickers. He increased military pressure on the guerrillas and drug lords. This was with full support from the United States, which after September 11, 2001, saw the guerrillas in a new, more threatening light amid the War on Terror. In what seemed a paradox, Uribe also pushed for an end to the paramilitary forces, realizing that they had to be brought back from the jungles before he could make a lasting peace with the guerrillas. By the late 1990s, the AUC had grown to eight thousand members and was functioning as an autonomous military force in the country. Its membership grew even more rapidly during the early 2000s, reaching sixteen thousand members. But, after a series of talks beginning in 2003, Uribe reached an agreement with the organization, which called for its members to lay down their arms by 2006 in exchange for amnesty.

While some paramilitaries continued their activities, the peace negotiations opened up the space for Uribe to move more concertedly against the guerrillas. By 2010, continued pressure from Uribe, backed by U.S. aid, had reduced the FARC to seven thousand members. Under Uribe, Colombia also experienced a 40 percent drop in its murder rate, though coca leaf production and the drug trade continued to grow.

Uribe was followed in office by his close ally, Juan Manuel Santos. As minister of defense under Uribe, he had led efforts against the guerrillas, including a high-profile rescue in 2008 of former presidential candidate Ingrid Betancourt and three Americans who had been held by guerrilla kidnappers for years. His election indicated a continuation of Uribe's security policies. Santos will likely be remembered most for initiating peace talks with the FARC that began in November 2012. His government and the rebels negotiated terms that included land reform, wider political participation, the end of illegal drug production, and amnesty for most rebels. By August 2016, they had reached a final deal that also included a cease-fire, the laying down of arms by the rebels, and a plan for their reentry into civilian life. It was ratified by the Colombian Congress in December 2016. While many welcomed peace, many others opposed the deal, including former president Uribe, who stated the agreement allowed the rebels to get away with murder. Moreover, guerrilla groups, including the National Liberation Front, and paramilitary organizations continued to operate in Colombia and drug trafficking remained robust. Thus, despite a deal to end the fifty-two-year war that left had 220,000 dead, the future of peace remained uncertain.

## Gender and War in Colombia

The 1991 Constitution was to usher in a new era for women in Colombia. It recognized women's full political and legal rights, rights to property and labor equality, rights within the family, and rights to "bodily integrity and autonomy." The constitution recognized that women in the 1990s in Latin America were no longer bound so fully by the patriarchal expectations that had limited their mothers and grandmothers. Rather, women now were professionals, politicians, social workers, students, wives, and mothers—even guerrillas. The government even instituted a quota for women in politics; women had to make up 30 percent of electoral candidates and high-level public service positions.

Ironically, given these gains, patriarchy remains entrenched and feminist movements have been relatively weak in Colombia. Women still earn less than men for the same work, and abortion is nearly impossible to obtain, even in the cases of rape or the health of the mother. For a country known for its beauty queens, women's beauty remains a priority and plastic surgery is pervasive. Beginning in the 1970s, it became common for drug traffickers to compete for the affections of beauty queens, and many became human trophies in the war over territory. According to the UN Gender Inequality Index, Colombia ranks below the Latin American average for gender equity, and below places like Libya and Myanmar.

Gender-based violence during the years of worst violence was particularly acute. Reported cases of sexual assault grew by 50 percent in the ten years after 2003, and domestic violence grew by 30 percent. Many more cases of both went unreported amid the civil war. In a new twist on the violence, acid attacks on women grew substantially in that same time, making it one of the world centers of this particular type of gender violence and unique in the region. Few attackers faced any prison time for these offenses. The fact that, according to the negotiated peace settlement with Santos, most guerrillas will not face prosecution for their crimes was particularly troubling to women's groups.

Displacement and war have had a devastating effect on families. Since 1985, there have been close to 6 million Colombians displaced at one time or another by the fighting. Indigenous people and Afro-Colombians have been disproportionately affected, as have women. Some statistics suggest that while two-thirds of babies in the 1970s were born to married parents, that figure had dropped to less than one-quarter by the early 2000s. A 2011 victims law, which promised compensation and land restitution for victims of the civil war, was promising, though by 2017, few had benefited.

Women's groups were on the frontlines to press for an end to the violence. They have formed an array of new alliances since the 1990s, including groups like the Women's Network of the Caribbean, formed in 1994, Ruta Pacífica de Mujeres, founded in 1996, and the Social Movement of Women against War and for Peace, a network of women's organizations that joined together in 2000. While feminist groups historically were not strong in Colombia, they have grown in importance in recent decades due to the extremes of violence, displacement, and war. Through demonstrations, meetings, and other protests, they compelled the Santos administration to acknowledge the unique impact of the violence on women and to compel the government to take action to protect them.[4]

## COLOMBIA IN THE WORLD

While the drug trade was the most visible connection between Colombia and the world, the nation has also been a leader in hemispheric politics, security, and culture since World War II. Colombia hosted several important international meetings, such as the 1948 founding of the Organization of American States (OAS), the 1966 formation of the Andean Common Market, and the historic 1968 Conference of Latin American Bishops in Medellín, which launched a wave of left-leaning Catholic reforms and activism. During the 1980s Colombia pressed hard for peace negotiations in Central America, giving rise to the Contadora talks in Panama. In this light, the 1994 election of former president Gaviria as secretary general of the OAS recognized and reconfirmed Colombia's vital role in hemispheric affairs.

In the world of literature, Colombia produced one of Latin America's most well known writers, recognized in 1982, when Gabriel García Márquez won the Nobel Prize in literature. His works, beginning with *One Hundred Years of Solitude* (1967), sold millions of copies in dozens of translated editions. Probably no other Latin American writer did as much as García Márquez to ignite the region's literary boom.

Except for García Márquez's work, however, Colombian culture was little known to the outside world. Rather, bad news swamped outsiders' impressions of Colombia. Images of drug lords and guerrilla warriors crowded out more favorable images of the country. For example, in Tom Clancy's best-selling 1990 novel *Clear and Present Danger,* the United States mounts an illegal invasion of Colombia to wipe out a cocaine-producing operation. It was hardly an advertisement for Colombian tourism.

In recent years, however, Colombia has become more well known for cultural contributions. Colombian pop star Shakira exploded onto the global music scene in 2002, later performing the 2010 World Cup official song. And Colombian telenovelas have reached worldwide viewing, even spawning popular shows abroad such as *Ugly Betty.* Even a much more nuanced portrait of Colombian drugs and violence emerged with Netflix's 2015 release of its

**Figure 20.2** Gabriel García Márquez, Colombian author who won the Nobel Prize in literature, was one of Latin America's most revered writers. Courtesy *PBS News Hour.*

popular drama *Narcos,* which traces the rise of Pablo Escobar and the role of the U.S. Drug Enforcement Agency there.

## CONCLUSIONS AND ISSUES

Colombia straddles two subregions of the hemisphere, the Caribbean Basin and the Andean republics. Colombian diplomats, intellectuals, politicians, businesspeople, and clerics provide leadership for many nations in both regions. Known to be profoundly conservative, Colombians have seldom been innovators in social or political policy. Many features of the last century seem to be preserved in today's society, as portrayed by Colombia's most famous novelist, Gabriel García Márquez. Colombia's society is stratified, its status system rigidly controlled, and its local affairs deeply familial. Physical geography, including its prominent mountain ranges and vast eastern plains, also kept Colombians more apart than together, reinforcing the power of regional leaders and social relations.

The severe challenges faced by post–World War II administrations, in the form of endemic violence, guerrilla movements, paramilitary groups, and the narcotics industry, strengthened the Colombian elite's tendency to retrench and protect inherited values and relationships. This tendency was most pronounced during the period of the National Front, explicitly designed to preserve order. After 1974, however, the Liberal Party, always more open to change, dominated the presidency and managed a gradual democratization process. A return to conservative rule after the turn of the century has fostered more sustained economic growth, and, in recent years, a lessening of violence. Most importantly, it has continued to foster a more national outlook on the part of most Colombians.

## Discussion Questions

What initiated the fighting known as La Violencia? What was its impact on state and society?

Why did the nation's celebrated democratic traditions fail in the 1950s and usher in the autocratic regime of Rojas Pinilla?

Why was the drug business so difficult to eradicate?

What caused the rise of the guerrilla movements and what was their influence on Colombian politics and society?

How has the Colombian state tried to deal with the guerrillas and drug traffickers over the years, and why have its solutions largely failed?

What are paramilitary forces and how did their rise affect the civil war?

What factors predisposed Colombia to exercise leadership in Latin America?

How has Colombia's relationship with the United States evolved since World War II?

## Timeline

| | |
|---|---|
| 1930 | Beginning of liberal dominance |
| 1946 | Beginning of conservative dominance |
| 1948 | Assassination of Jorge Eliécer Gaitán, followed by Bogotazo |
| 1950s–1960s | La Violencia |
| 1953–1958 | Military coup and regime of General Rojas Pinilla |
| 1958 | Restoration of democracy under National Front |
| 1991 | New constitution replaces that of 1886 |
| 1998 | President Pastrana convinces President Clinton to support Plan Colombia, a huge anti-drug and counterinsurgency program |

## Keywords

Alliance for Progress
Empresa Colombiana de Petróleos (ECOPETROL)
import substitution industrialization (ISI)
La Violencia
M-19
Medellín cartel
narcotraffickers

National Front
National Liberation Army
Patriotic Union (UP)
Plan Colombia
Revolutionary Armed Forces of Colombia (FARC)
United Self-Defense Forces of Colombia (AUC)
War on Drugs

# Caribbean Basin Countercurrents

## A Slave's Story

Jean-Robert Cadet was raised as a child slave in Haiti in the 1960s, a century and a half after slavery had been abolished on the island. His autobiography recounts how he escaped from that life, made his way to the United States, and through education managed to become a middle-class American. He has since created a foundation in the United States that works to end child slavery in Haiti. The story is movingly and vividly told, beginning with his first memories of being a slave:

> Florence . . . was a beautiful Negress with a dark-brown complexion and a majestic presence. I came into Florence's life one day when Philippe, her white former lover, paid her a surprise visit. He was a successful exporter of coffee and chocolate to the United States and Europe. Philippe lived in Port-au-Prince, Haiti, with his parents, two brothers, and a niece. He arrived in his Jeep at Florence's two-story French country-style house in an upper-class section of the city. A bright-eyed, fat-cheeked, light-skinned black baby boy was in the back seat. Philippe parked the car, reached in the back seat, and took the baby out. He stood him on the ground and the baby toddled off. I was that toddler.
>
> Philippe greeted Florence with a kiss on each cheek while she stared at the toddler. "Whose baby is this?" she asked, knowing the answer to her question. "His mother died and I can't take him home to my parents. I'd like you to have him," said Philippe, handing Florence an envelope containing money.
>
> "I understand," she said, taking the envelope. He embraced her again and drove off, leaving me behind. Philippe's problem was solved.
>
> My mother had been a worker in one of Philippe's coffee factories below the Cahos Mountains of the Artibonite Valley. Like the grands blancs of the distant past who acknowledged their blood in the veins of their slave children by emancipating and educating them, Philippe was following tradition. Perhaps he thought that Florence would give me a better life. . . .

> Every night I slept on a pile of rags in a corner of Florence's bedroom, like a house cat, until I was six years old. Then she made me sleep under the kitchen table. . . .
>
> As I got older, I learned what kind of day I was going to have based on Florence's mood and tone of voice. When she was cheerful, the four-strip leather whip, called a martinet, would stay hung on its hook against the kitchen wall.
>
> I knew three groups of children in Port-au-Prince: the elite, the very poor, and the restavecs, or slave children.[1]

Restavecs are slave children who belong to well-to-do families. They receive no pay and are kept out of school. Since the emancipation and independence of 1804, affluent blacks and mulattoes have reintroduced slavery by using children of the very poor as house servants.


## STORM WARNINGS OFFSHORE

The Caribbean Basin—embracing the Greater and Lesser Antilles plus Central America—has a distinctive history, quite unlike that of North and South America. Of the island colonies, only Haiti and its neighbor on the island of Hispaniola, the Dominican Republic, achieved their full liberty before the beginning of the twentieth century, the former in 1804 and the latter in 1865. So the history of the Caribbean since 1900 must begin with the struggles for independence.

However, the major powers continued to interfere in the new Caribbean nations even after they won their independence. This informal imperialism, as experienced by the recently liberated island nations, was especially degrading. One critic of U.S. foreign policy, a former diplomat in the region, referred to this imperialism as "jungle diplomacy." As chapter 13 made clear, this region was especially prone to government by dictatorship and U.S. intervention. The epithet "banana republic," in fact, was a U.S. invention.

Central America received much the same treatment from the rest of the outside world, which valued its people mostly for their ability to produce bananas and coffee and perhaps host a ship canal. For these reasons, the Caribbean Basin experienced more instability, corruption, violence, and outside meddling than did virtually any other region in the world. These factors also made the area fertile ground for revolution. Some major episodes—such as the Mexican Revolution, Sandino's movement, and the Cuban upheaval of 1933—have already been discussed in earlier chapters. The Caribbean Basin was also fractured by social fault lines and surrounded by political instability.

After World War II, some reformers in the region decided to eliminate dictatorships by means of military coups. Some merely excluded tyrants hoping to return to power. Many movements, however, recruited the young, idealistic, and university educated, and they often came from middle-class families.

These latter revolutionaries coalesced into a movement called the Caribbean Legion. They tried to bring reform to the region but often failed in the face of grave inequalities, elite opposition, and U.S. Cold War pressures.

## THE FIGUERES REBELLION

In December 1947 José Figueres of Costa Rica, angry at the intention of ex-president Rafael Calderón Guardia (1940–1944) to run for office again, traveled to Guatemala, where President Juan José Arévalo (1945–1951) had recently won election and set up a deeply reformist government. Figueres, known to all as "don Pepe," negotiated an agreement called the Caribbean Pact that created the Caribbean Legion for the purpose of promoting democracy in the region. Arévalo promised arms and military assistance so that don Pepe could overthrow the Costa Rican government dominated by Calderón. In exchange, don Pepe promised that he would help other opposition groups overthrow dictators in nearby Nicaragua, Honduras, and the Dominican Republic.

When the 1948 elections, which were won by an opponent of Calderón's, were annulled by Calderón's allies in Congress, don Pepe organized a rebel force at his farm in the southeast of Costa Rica and activated his military alliance. Immediately advisors and arms arrived from Guatemala, and Figueres advanced toward the capital. Because Costa Rica had a small army, the rebels fought mostly against Calderón's communist supporters in the banana workers' union. The action, a civil war rather than a coup or revolution, lasted over a month and sacrificed about two thousand lives. Figueres's forces prevailed. When they captured the capital, they exiled the incumbent leaders.

Don Pepe insisted that his rebellion aimed only to restore democracy, but once victorious he and his reformist allies called a convention to write a new constitution. They named their regime the Second Republic, signaling the start of a new era. Adopted in 1949, the constitution established a decentralized state with stronger democratic safeguards than before. It created a number of autonomous agencies, outside of executive control, that carried out broader social and economic policies than the previous state. Thus government became more engaged in citizens' lives yet less centralized. Women gained the vote, and elections came under the supervision of the Supreme Electoral Tribunal. Most surprisingly, the constitution abolished the army and assigned law enforcement to a police agency. To a large degree, it legalized some reformist trends already under way during the previous administrations.

Far more dramatic than the new constitution was the advent of a generation of young leaders in Costa Rica. The forceful and charismatic don Pepe amazingly declined to run for president and supported an ally and the victor in the annulled 1948 elections, Otilio Ulate, for the first term. Then don Pepe ran for office in 1953 and won a stunning victory. Calling his movement the National Liberation Party (PLN), he ended the era of oligarchic control of the government and brought in a new generation of principled, educated, and determined young officials. They continued to run Costa Rica for decades. Don Pepe served his first term from 1953 to 1958 and another from 1970 to 1974, and his collaborators served for several other terms. In fact, his son, also named José Figueres, won election as president in 1994 on the PLN ticket.

Figueres's collaborators did not hesitate to impose programs on the private sector if they benefited the majority of the population. Entirely democratic in ethic, they believed in government providing a decent living for all citizens. Costa Rica came to rival Uruguay as the foremost welfare state in the hemisphere. The country had so little foreign investment, however, that this democratic socialization caused no adverse reaction from abroad. Instead, the modest profits from exports of coffee, cattle, timber, and bananas were spread more equitably and, by Latin American standards, the country achieved a level of social welfare that stood out in the region.

A number of exiles from other Caribbean states had aided Figueres's 1948 rebellion. After their success, they called on don Pepe to help them, as promised in the 1947 Caribbean Pact. Figueres did allow them to assemble and train in Costa Rican territory, and he provided money and arms. He also founded the Institute for Political Education in San José, which published the pro-democracy journal *Combate*.

The Caribbean Legion's most dangerous enemy was Anastasio Somoza, the dictator of neighboring Nicaragua. The fact that anti-Somoza exiles were preparing to invade from Costa Rica provoked Somoza to make a preemptive strike, forcing Figueres to call a truce and bring the Nicaraguan exiles under control.

Next, Costa Rican–sponsored exiles invaded the Dominican Republic, then under the dictatorship of Rafael Trujillo. This invasion failed, as did operations against Cuba's Batista and Venezuela's Pérez Jiménez. Soon the Caribbean Legion languished. The regimes that it opposed were too entrenched and well armed to be easily overthrown, and the United States pressured Figueres and others to stop promoting invasions, even though Figueres was ardently anticommunist. The U.S. government had begun fighting the Cold War and insisted on tight security in what it considered its private lake, the Caribbean Sea.

Despite calling off the Caribbean Legion, Figueres continued to promote democracy in the region, supporting exiles and speaking out against tyrants. He harbored Rómulo Betancourt after his ouster from Venezuela in 1948. He helped Nicaraguans planning to assassinate Somoza. And he supported the production of print and broadcast material favoring democracy. For a time, Figueres was the anchor for pro-democracy movements in the region. He received good press from most outside observers.

## GUATEMALAN REVOLUTION OF 1954

For over a decade, the people of Guatemala had been under one of the most oppressive dictatorships in the region, that of General Jorge Ubico (1931–1944). But, as World War II was about to end, Ubico faced growing opposition from reformists in the middle class, especially university students and segments of the military, and he stepped down and was replaced by an equally unpopular general. The new leader attempted to calm the reformist wave with minor concessions, but the politically active middle class clamored for democracy. When the general rigged elections and declared himself the winner, two army officers formed civilian militias and removed him in a bloodless coup. They quickly established a junta and scheduled new elections.

The surprise victor in the 1945 elections was a mild-mannered professor, Juan José Arévalo, who until then had been living in Argentina for over a decade, in exile from the Ubico regime. The junta nominated him because he had no ties to existing parties. He also had a strong following among students, who had emerged as the heroes of the movement against Ubico. His election was the fairest in Guatemalan history to that point and initiated a ten-year period that later became known as the Democratic Spring.

Followers hailed Arévalo's return as a national redemption; thousands flocked to the airport to welcome him. A tall, handsome, imposing figure, he spoke forcefully about his plans for reforming the nation. Most of all he promised to educate, promote culture, and improve the lives of the poor and oppressed. He won the election by a landslide, in an outpouring of relief that the dictatorship had finally ended.

Juan José Arévalo's ideas, which he referred to as "spiritual socialism," or Arevalismo, came from several sources. He had been deeply impressed by the U.S. administration of Franklin Roosevelt during the 1930s, especially his forceful intervention in the economy and efforts to protect common citizens from economic harm. Arévalo also embraced progressive aspects of Argentine society that he observed while in exile. Finally, he and other leaders were inspired by the Mexican Revolution—an appealing model to many.

Arévalo quickly drafted legislation to benefit ordinary people. His social security law of 1946 instituted workers' disability insurance and maternity leave. Soon, the new Social Security Institute began enrolling employed persons for medical care and eventual retirement benefits. The 1947 Labor Law enacted new benefits and protections for Guatemala's workers in a country that prior to this had had few, if any, protections.

Arévalo also experimented with land reform to help peasant farmers and peons become independent producers, though the scale of reform paled in comparison to what followed under his successor. In the 1940s, the majority of Guatemala's population was Mayan and lived in highland towns and villages. Most were illiterate and impoverished, and few had access to things like regular electricity or water. Because of the country's strict vagrancy laws, many worked as peons on the large coffee and banana plantations of whites and ladinos, feeding the national economy. Some also owned tiny plots on which they grew some subsistence crops. In many ways, they lived a world apart from the urban reality of Arévalo and his supporters. And while Arévalo pursued some land, labor, and social reforms that touched the rural highlands, his reforms were more often oriented to modernizing urban areas.

Arévalo's reforms, which were viewed by some in the context of the Cold War as socialist, did not sit well with landowners, industrialists, and foreign investors, especially the powerful United Fruit Company (UFCO). Still, his spiritual socialism explicitly criticized communism, he refused to legalize the Communist Party, and he sent some communists into exile. His tolerance of communist leadership in key labor and university sectors, and his appointment of the controversial Colonel Jacobo Arbenz as defense minister, however, caused considerable opposition and provoked a number of attempted coups. Arévalo survived largely due to the army's obedience to Arbenz. When Arbenz was elected president with 65 percent of the vote in 1950, democratic reformism received renewed stimulus. Although just an army officer, Arbenz had married a wealthy Salvadoran and together they acquired large landholdings. He also aspired to lead his country, participating in the 1944 coups and serving as defense minister under Arévalo.

The most questionable act in his climb to power was the alleged 1949 assassination of General Francisco J. Araña, his principal rival for the presidency. As the elections neared and it became clear that Araña would lose, Araña told President Arévalo to arrange for transfer of power to him or Araña would overthrow the president and seize power for himself. To prevent this and ensure a democratic transition to a reformist, Arévalo conspired with Arbenz and others to remove Araña from the picture.[2] Arbenz won the election by an overwhelming majority in late 1950, but these questionable acts tarnished his record.

Arbenz's National Unity Party contained labor unions, public employee associations, peasant organizations, many military units, and a variety of splinter groups from across the ideological spectrum. Arbenz himself was a populist and a nationalist whose inspirations came from a variety of sources. Notably, he and his wife read Marxist ideas and by the end of his time in office, Arbenz had become increasingly receptive to communism. While communists never held more than a small minority of seats in his government, they were a highly disciplined group whom he counted among his closest advisors while in office.

With support from international banks and local capital, Arbenz promoted major economic projects while also attempting to reduce Guatemala's depend-

**Figure 21.1** President Jacobo Arbenz speaking to supporters in 1954. Associated Press. Courtesy Library of Congress.

ence on the United States. His most daring undertaking, however, was the 1952 agrarian reform act. This act nationalized large uncultivated landholdings, which the government planned to distribute to small farmers. Former owners received compensation in twenty-five-year government bonds. The new owners, mostly peasants, paid for the land in small installments. While in office, Arbenz distributed land to over one hundred thousand poor highland families.

UFCO stood among the major landowners who lost property under the law. Holding a near-monopoly on banana exports, rail service, and shipping throughout Central America, UFCO claimed to be mortally threatened by the new land and labor reforms. Since the late 1940s, it had engaged in a campaign to portray Arévalo and Arbenz as ardent communists bringing the Cold War threat of Soviet invasion to the heart of the hemisphere. UFCO encouraged the U.S. State Department to cooperate in a campaign to discredit and perhaps replace the Arbenz government. United Fruit's former legal counsel, John Foster Dulles, now served as secretary of state, and Dulles's brother Alan, who sat on the UFCO Board of Directors, was director of the Central Intelligence Agency (CIA).

**Figure 21.2** During the CIA-directed coup of 1954, foreign pilots dropped leaflets on Guatemala City to frighten the populace, gathered to hear a speech by Col. Carlos Castillo Armas, who took over as president after the army overthrew Jacobo Arbenz. Courtesy Library of Congress.

The White House authorized the CIA to destabilize the Guatemalan government by conducting a campaign of propaganda and conspiracies. Eventually these efforts paid off in a coup orchestrated by the CIA. A rival army officer, Carlos Castillo Armas, staged a small, poorly armed invasion from Honduras. Meanwhile, a propaganda blitz by the CIA made Castillo Armas's forces appear more numerous and popular than they actually were. The army high command panicked, knowing that if they did defeat Castillo Armas they might face a U.S. invasion.[3] They soon withdrew military support from Arbenz who resigned and fled into exile. Castillo Armas became president, and Guatemala's Democratic Spring ended with the onset of a brutal winter.

This blatant U.S. intervention and the restitution of UFCO properties opened the way for a counterrevolution in Guatemala. The new regime canceled all the programs and electoral reforms instituted since 1945, and the country fell under full dictatorial control of the army. Among its first acts was to outlaw communism and repress Guatemalans tainted by a connection with leftist groups. For the next three decades, few elections were held, and no elected president served out his term. Brutal repression, censorship, assassinations, ethnic warfare, and flagrant profiteering by high officials characterized Guatemala. During this time, the U.S. government provided tens of millions of

**Figure 21.3** Rigoberta Menchú, human rights leader from Guatemala who championed the cause of her fellow Maya and won a Nobel Peace Prize for her work. Shown here at a 2015 meeting in Costa Rica. Courtesy Government of Costa Rica.

dollars in developmental and especially military aid to assist the Guatemalan military and police forces develop counterinsurgency techniques and arms. U.S. technical advisors, including Green Berets, were stationed in Guatemala to assist in developing counterinsurgency forces.

From the 1960s to the 1980s, the government was in a civil war with leftist guerrilla groups challenging its brutal rule and demanding more democracy and social equality. A range of regime opponents formed these groups, including discontented military officers, university students, and labor and peasant leaders. The most well known, the Guerrilla Army of the Poor, emerged in the 1970s, linked to both labor unions and peasant organizations. By the 1980s, it had joined together with other guerrilla groups as well as with communists to create a united front against the military and paramilitaries. Violence escalated dramatically in the 1980s. Many of the guerrilla groups were based in the rural highlands—areas that were largely populated by Mayans—feeding the distrust that elites already felt toward Guatemala's indigenous majority. Tragically, the army targeted indigenous villagers as its enemies.

The attacks against Maya peoples became so intense that as many as a million fled across the border into Mexico to survive. The plight of these refugees was dramatized in the feature film *El Norte,* made in 1983. Countless nonmilitant opposition groups emerged in the 1970s and 1980s as well, organizing peasants, labor, and Catholics in defense of democracy. The ethnic war gained worldwide attention when thirty-three-year-old Rigoberta Menchú won the Nobel Peace Prize in 1992 for her courageous work on behalf of her fellow Maya.

The only other Guatemalan ever to receive a Nobel Prize (1967, for literature) was Miguel Angel Asturias, who wrote for much of the mid-twentieth century about Guatemala's repressive and unequal political and economic systems. His major novels include *El Señor Presidente* (1946; a trilogy loosely depicting General Ubico's dictatorship), *Strong Wind* (1950; about the abuses by the United Fruit Company), and *The Mulatta and Mr. Fly* (1963; a story about the mix of indigenous and imported cultures).

From the mid-1980s, when President Marco Vinicio Cerezo began his term (1986–1991), Guatemala lived under uneasy democratic governments. Sporadic guerrilla attacks, army coups, general strikes, and adverse international publicity plagued the country. Efforts to stimulate dialogue among the country's deeply divided peoples—the Maya majority, the European minority, the mixed groups (called *ladinos*)—brought some respite from war but did not guarantee peace.

A dramatic breakthrough occurred on December 29, 1996, when the government and the guerrillas signed a peace treaty. The latter were represented by the Guatemalan National Revolutionary Unity (URNG). A UN military observer team arrived in 1997 to help with the demobilization of the rebel forces, which officially numbered about six thousand at that point; women made up about 18 percent of that total and served in both combat and support roles.[4] Later that year thousands of Guatemalan refugees who had fled to Mexico began to return. Guatemala's thirty-five-year civil war finally came to an end. Experts estimated that over 150,000 people perished in that brutal war, with as many as 50,000 more unaccounted for. Hundreds of villages were entirely wiped out. Sporadic violence still punctuated the next several years. Some have characterized the brutal assault on Mayan culture and people as genocide.

In the late 1980s, the Catholic Church assigned Bishop Juan José Gerardi Conedera, who for decades had defended indigenous rights and condemned the violence by the military, to serve on the government's National Reconciliation Commission. In April 1998, he announced the release of the commission's report, which stated that the army and its allies were responsible for 80 percent of the wartime atrocities. Two days after the release of the report, Gerardi was bludgeoned to death with a cinder block, a crime for which three army officers were later convicted, with a fourth person, a priest, convicted as an accomplice. One year after the release of the report, its conclusions were upheld by a UN Truth Commission report.

Since then, Guatemala has had regular democratic transitions in government, though it has continued to face high levels of violence, electoral fraud, corruption, and social exclusion. Communities have struggled to come to terms with the factionalism and divisiveness that tore them apart. For example, Guatemala today has a much higher rate of widowhood than it did before the 1970s. Yet new types of organizations, such as the National Coalition of Guatemalan Widows, have emerged to try to rebuild communities, compel a national discussion about the violence, and demand change.

Only recently has more light been shed on the impact of the decades of brutality, especially after the 2005 discovery of a vast archive of documents from the Guatemalan National Police that had been abandoned in a warehouse in Guatemala City and that covered the period of the civil war. But justice for those killed remains elusive, and the overwhelming majority of those who perpetrated the violence have not been punished.

## DUVALIER DYNASTY IN HAITI

Haiti, which occupies the western third of the island of Hispaniola, lived through an era even more tumultuous than did its neighbor, the Dominican Republic. Subjected to humiliating interventions in the 1910s and international ostracism throughout the 1920s and 1930s, Haitians had great difficulty forming stable governments. Moreover, their nation usually ranked near the bottom of the Latin American indices for political, economic, and social development. Few visitors realized the illustrious history of Haiti's people, who had overthrown a slave regime and European colonialism in the 1790s and early 1800s.

A populist government came to power in Haiti in 1946, one devoted to giving blacks a larger voice in government (previously dominated by upper-middle-class mulattoes). The new president, Dumarsais Estimé, sought to provide modern services for poor Haitians, especially in labor relations, public hygiene, and education. He introduced black Haitian culture into his public ceremonies instead of following traditional Catholic rites. When in 1950 Estimé tried to rig elections to continue in power, however, the general who had installed him stepped in and took control. Things remained largely unchanged until 1956, when the army withdrew support from the president, and a heated succession campaign ensued.

François Duvalier, a public health doctor and intellectual long active in politics, was instrumental in the collapse of government in 1956. Duvalier's populism and background in fighting tropical diseases among Haiti's poorest patients, for which he earned the nickname Papa Doc, brought him great popular support. For decades before he took office, he promoted Pan-Africanism and sympathized with the plight of the black majority, who suffered at the hands of mulatto elites. In the early 1950s, he was forced into hiding for opposing the 1950 coup. When the government began to waver in 1956, he announced his candidacy. He ran for president in 1957 with the backing of the army and a wide swath of the rural population, promising to bring calm and prosperity. His campaign called for the political triumph of Negritude. This was a pro-black literary and intellectual movement that emerged in the colonized world to reject assimilation to white imperial cultures as a way to end black inequality. He concurrently organized paramilitary forces to intimidate opponents and assure his victory. Thus his election in 1957 in reality meant a return to dictatorship.

Inaugurated as president at the age of fifty, Duvalier had lost the idealism of his youth and ruled instead by terror and coercion. He did not allow organized groups to oppose him, and he declined to call elections. He exalted and manipulated popular culture, including the black Haitian syncretic religion Vodou, which he used to win broad acceptance and to intimidate rivals. He also professed sympathies with black nationalism and African liberation movements.

In his consolidation of totalitarian powers, Duvalier cleverly pitted groups against one another, so that in the end he was the final arbiter. No one doubted, moreover, that death could result from disagreeing with Papa Doc. Indeed, a macabre cult of death attached to the thugs known as the Tontons Macoutes (mythical bogeymen in Haiti), a paramilitary group he created in 1959 and which by 1961 was twice the size of the army. Under Papa Doc's direction, the Tontons Macoutes created a reign of terror, bringing torture, rape, and imprisonment to his opponents. People widely believed that, through black Haitian religious leaders loyal to Duvalier, the Tontons Macoutes had turned thousands of persons into zombies, suspended in a state of death-in-life. Myths like these enhanced the power and awe that Papa Doc exercised over most Haitians. The Tontons Macoutes, meanwhile, persisted well into the 1990s. During their reign of terror, they assassinated between thirty and sixty thousand Haitians.

Sadly, Duvalier's campaign promises to improve health and education evaporated after he gained power, and the Haitian people suffered terrible deprivations at the hands of labor brokers, sugar planters, corrupt police, and tax collectors. He seized peasant lands and gave them to his closest allies and secret police members. As a result, Haiti's urban slums grew substantially, and people there were forced to scratch out a living from nothing. He converted the army into an ineffectual bureaucracy while forming a fearsome palace guard loyal to himself. He attacked and demeaned the Catholic Church, allowing it to operate only as an adjunct of the state. The U.S. looked on with dislike at his graft and corruption but accepted his brutal regime as a way to prevent the spread of communism in the region. Through all of this, his support among rural black citizens remained strong.

Papa Doc cast himself in the tradition of Haiti's black heroes. A 1964 publication proclaimed, "Dessalines, Toussaint, Petion, Christophe, and Estimé are five distinct Chiefs of State who are substantiated in and form only one and the same President, in the person of François Duvalier." In fact, he represented the worst features of the Caribbean dictator. He wasted his tremendous authority and charisma on vain and petty adulation, combined with brutal repression.

In 1971. Duvalier died in office, and his son Jean-Claude (nicknamed Baby Doc) succeeded him. Jean-Claude had never taken his leadership role seriously, instead dabbling in university studies and living well in France. Papa Doc created the Council of State in the late 1960s to provide continuity after his death. While Baby Doc allowed the council to run Haiti for a time, he soon asserted his influence by firing the chief advisors.

**Figure 21.4** François "Papa Doc" Duvalier, president and then dictator of Haiti from the 1950s until his death in 1971, shown here introducing his son, Jean-Claude "Baby Doc" Duvalier, as the country's next ruler. Courtesy of Hoover Institution Library and Archives, Stanford University.

Baby Doc's major interest lay in economic expansion through trade. He courted the U.S. government and won approval to bring in more investors looking for cheap labor. Haiti's elite prospered under the new regime, but wages remained the lowest in the hemisphere and its people the poorest. This trend continued under the Caribbean Basin Initiative (CBI) launched by U.S. president Ronald Reagan in 1983 (see chapter 24). Baby Doc married a wealthy socialite (significantly, from the mulatto elite) who spent lavish sums on entertaining and travel. Cronyism, careless fiscal management, and tolerance of criminal activity all characterized his reign. He had no interest in the intellectual pursuit of Negritude or African solidarity.

Government services and the economy stagnated under the Duvalier dynasty, and many things changed, largely for the worse. Population growth soared, taxing the infrastructure and natural resources of the country. Poor people took any jobs that opened, regardless of the pay, and those who could not find jobs cleared small plots of land to farm in the hills. Slash-and-burn cultivation devastated the environment, stripping the country of forest and eroding the fragile mountainous soils. Infectious diseases like tuberculosis remained common, and Haiti had the highest HIV/AIDs infection rates in the Americas by 2000. The industrial growth induced by the CBI did not begin to lift the country out of poverty.

Eventually public disgust with Baby Doc erupted in rioting and demonstrations, abetted quietly by the Catholic Church and political activists. In early 1986, Baby Doc decided that his position was untenable and accepted a U.S. offer to escape into exile. He took up residence in a Paris mansion and lived with his wife and retainers in opulence for the next decade.

Haiti reverted to military government, which in fact consisted of an uneasy coalition of armed units, secret police, powerful businessmen, drug traffickers, and corrupt bureaucrats. Pressured by international opinion and rocked by their own instability, the military finally allowed free elections in late 1990. A leftist Roman Catholic priest, Jean-Bertrand Aristide, won and took office in February 1991.

Aristide's first term was cut short by another military coup in late September, led by General Raoul Cédras. This brazen usurpation of power in turn triggered a robust international reaction led by the United States, which imposed a strict economic embargo on Haiti. Thousands of Haitians fled on small, fragile boats bound for the United States, provoking a crisis. U.S. authorities returned most of these impoverished exiles back to Haiti. For a time the "boat people" became the focus of a national debate on immigrants in the American press.

Meanwhile the United States, along with the UN and the OAS, pressured the military to allow Aristide to return. Faced with a possible U.S. military invasion, the Haitian generals yielded in late 1994 and fled the country. Ex-president Jimmy Carter went to Haiti to assist in making this important transition. Aristide returned to his homeland in October 1994, accompanied by over twenty thousand U.S. troops. They, along with soldiers from other member UN countries such as Canada, were there to ensure security and help in the transition to democracy by training an apolitical police force; helping rebuild rural roads, hospitals, and schools; and overseeing fair elections. Aristide himself ended his term in 1996 and was replaced in the presidency by René Préval, a close associate who won the election in December 1995.

President Préval fought valiantly to improve Haiti's economy and to attract foreign companies and investments, while complying with international lending agencies' requirements that he end deficit spending and privatize public enterprises. For nearly his entire five-year term, Préval found himself blocked by opposition politicians (increasingly drawn from Aristide's followers) and public employees fearful of losing their jobs. Political violence continued, putting pressure on the small UN peacekeeping force that remained on the island.

The presidential election of 2000 drew several unknown candidates into the contest, but they soon withdrew when former president Aristide's name went on the ballot. His Famni Lavalas Party seemed to be a juggernaut no one wished to oppose. Aristide, duly elected in November amid protests and claims of fraud, took power in February 2001. The new president faced the same difficulties as his predecessor, and in his second administration Aristide displayed less concern for fiscal rigor, honesty, and social improvement. All across the country, people suffered through water and electric shortages, unemployment, protests, and civil servant strikes. In 2003 gangs of regime opponents began seizing towns and cities to force the overthrow of Aristide, and the president seemed unable to contain the outbreaks of violence. He appealed unsuccessfully for international assistance, then abruptly resigned in February 2004, by which time rebels controlled most of the country.

The United Nations immediately sent a peacekeeping force to restore order on the island and broker a regime change. Diplomats chose Boniface Alexandre as provisional president and quickly arranged for foreign aid to restore electricity, water, health care, and food deliveries to the chronically poor. He was followed in 2006 by René Préval (2006–2011) again, who oversaw an economic expansion and initially saw strong support from many of Haiti's urban poor. But his government will likely most be remembered for the 2010 earthquake, which devastated the capital, Port-au-Prince. Numbers remain in dispute, but between fifty thousand and two hundred thousand people were killed and millions more were left homeless. Roads, hospitals, government buildings, schools, and businesses were destroyed, and even the main seaport and airport in Port-au-Prince sustained extensive damage. When Michel Martelly took over as elected president in 2011, he faced the task of rebuilding, a job made more difficult by the country's history of poverty, bureaucratic delay, corruption, and foreign debt. Disease also hampered recovery, and UN peacekeepers later accepted blame for inadvertently setting off a cholera epidemic in 2010 that killed over eight thousand more people. By 2016, foreign aid agencies such as the American Red Cross were implicated in the problems for having siphoned off hundreds of millions in funds while showing little in return. The country continues to rebuild.

## PANAMA IN THE SPOTLIGHT

No issue so focused Panamanian attention as the U.S.-run Panama Canal. Leased permanently to the United States in 1903 in exchange for protection when Panama separated from Colombia, the Panama Canal Zone became the major bone of contention between the two nations. The canal was, in the words of one observer, "a body of water entirely surrounded by trouble." Twice the two countries altered the terms of the original concession to benefit Panama (1936 and 1955 treaties), but these did not assuage Panamanian nationalist sentiment. Most Panamanians wanted the United States to provide them with more benefits and eventually turn the canal over to them. They regarded the canal as their national patrimony.

In 1964 students from Panama clashed with their American counterparts in the Canal Zone, and the incident blossomed into full-blown riots that lasted

**Figure 21.5** The January 1964 flag riots in Panama, triggered by U.S. Canal Zone students' objection to raising a Panamanian flag, touched off days of fighting that left more than two dozen dead and prompted the United States to begin negotiating the end of its canal ownership. Courtesy Hoover Institution Library and Archives, Stanford University.

several days. Twenty-six people died in the fighting, and Panama suspended relations. The following year, the presidents of the two countries appointed negotiating teams to completely rewrite the terms of the canal concession, with an eye to eventually turning the canal over to Panama. They worked out a treaty package but had to shelve it due to political difficulties in both countries.

Panama held elections in mid-1968, leading to the inauguration of the populist veteran Arnulfo Arias on October 1, 1968. Arias had served twice before as president (in 1940–1941 and 1949–1951) and had been deposed by the military both times. His return to the presidency reflected a broad desire among the electorate for change, as well as a reluctance of the military to falsify the ballots. Arias quickly disappointed and angered powerful forces, however, and he was again overthrown, this time after only eleven days in office. A military junta took control of the nation.

After some jockeying for power among the top officers, Colonel Omar Torrijos emerged as head of state, a position he held until his death in a plane accident in 1981. Like the Arias brothers in the 1930s, Torrijos ushered in new political players and reached out to unrepresented groups, especially small farm owners and workers. Over the long term his politics weakened the hold of the oligarchic families on the reins of government and made the National Guard (renamed the Panama Defense Force from 1983 to 1989) the arbiter of power. Torrijos decreed a constitution, a new labor code, offshore banking reg-

**Figure 21.6** President Jimmy Carter (left) and Panama's strongman Omar Torrijos signing the historic Carter-Torrijos Treaties of 1977, which would transfer the canal to Panama in 1999. Courtesy Carter Center.

ulations, replacement of the legislature with a council of municipal representatives, and greater government supervision of the economy. In many ways his regime paralleled those described in chapter 24.

Torrijos did not believe that the United States had the will to intervene in the Caribbean region unless threatened directly, so he played power politics boldly. He secured Soviet aid, befriended Fidel Castro, helped the Sandinistas, and permitted increased drug traffic through the country. He also courted literary celebrities like Graham Greene and Gabriel García Márquez. It was an impressive show of independence.

Torrijos's major accomplishment, however, was obtaining new treaties to replace the 1903 Panama Canal Convention. In brief, he badgered U.S. presidents and diplomats long enough and persistently enough to cause them to take up the canal issue seriously. Torrijos and President Jimmy Carter signed the Carter-Torrijos Treaties in 1977. They pledged the two countries to a gradual transfer of operations until December 31, 1999, when Panama would take full possession of the canal. The United States has exercised a residual protective role since that date, under an umbrella neutrality treaty.

While the two countries bargained, the United States poured aid and loans into Panama, buoying the economy and allowing Torrijos to triple the government payroll. The country soon topped the ranks of nations in per capita debt, and the economy became distorted by easy money and graft. Drug traffickers paid officials in Panama for the right to land and refuel their planes, and banks profited from laundering their illegal money. Meanwhile, international money flowed into Panama to take advantage of low taxes and banking secrecy. This so-called offshore banking sector boasted assets of over $30 billion by 1980. Critics pointed out that the apparent prosperity of the Torrijos years was an illusion, built on loans, drugs, and a bloated bureaucracy. After the treaties were signed, Torrijos stepped back from active leadership and chose a civilian ally to become president and to found the Revolutionary Democratic Party (PRD). The party gradually emerged from a shadowy existence to become a major force in the 1990s.

## CONCLUSIONS AND ISSUES

The Caribbean Basin underwent great turmoil during the decades following World War II. In some regions, the struggles for independence spilled over into internal conflict after the countries gained nationhood. In others, campaigns for modernization of the economies created social tensions and pressures for reforms. Even Central America, long independent and relatively mature in its political evolution, experienced unusually intense fighting over a variety of issues. Postcolonial and anti-imperial struggles continued for generations.

The countries that defied the United States—Guatemala, Cuba, Nicaragua, and Panama—found themselves under great pressure and often the targets of military intervention. The defiance did produce stronger national solidarity, but often at tremendous costs in economic and human terms. For better or worse, the United States continued to regard the Caribbean Basin as a private preserve and defense zone.

### Discussion Questions

How did Costa Rica become the most peaceful and successful democracy in the Western Hemisphere?

Did the Arévalo and Arbenz governments in Guatemala carry out a revolution or merely reforms? Explain.

What role did the United States play in the demise of democracy in Guatemala, and why would it choose to overthrow a democratic regime in the 1950s?

How did the Duvalier dictators draw on Haitian culture and tradition to consolidate their hold on power?

What convinced the U.S. government to negotiate a new Panama Canal treaty in the 1960s, to replace the original from 1903?

Should we characterize as revolutionary or dictatorial the nationalist actions of Omar Torrijos, which led the United States to agree to give Panama the U.S. Canal there? Why?

### Timeline

| | |
|---|---|
| 1945–51 | Juan José Arévalo president of Guatemala |
| 1947 | Caribbean Pact and creation of the Caribbean Legion |

| | |
|---|---|
| 1948 | José "don Pepe" Figueres revolution in Costa Rica |
| 1949 | New constitution in Costa Rica |
| 1951–54 | Jacobo Arbenz president of Guatemala |
| 1954 | CIA-orchestrated coup overthrows Arbenz |
| 1953–58 | President Figueres's first administration |
| 1957–71 | François "Papa Doc" Duvalier elected president of Haiti, extends his rule indefinitely |
| 1964 | Flag demonstrations in Panama Canal Zone lead to negotiations for new treaty |
| 1968–89 | Coup deposes just-elected president Arnulfo Arias, replaced by a military regime |
| 1971 | Jean-Claude "Baby Doc" Duvalier succeeds to presidency upon death of his father |
| 1977 | General Omar Torrijos of Panama and U.S. president Jimmy Carter sign treaty for joint operation of the canal and its turnover to Panama in 1999 |
| 1986 | Baby Doc driven from power by demonstrations and riots |
| 1991 | President Jean-Bertrand Aristide of Haiti overthrown; later returns to complete his term |
| 1996–2001 | René Préval president in Haiti |
| 2001–4 | President Aristide returned as president of Haiti |
| 2011 | Michel Martelly elected president in Haiti |

## Keywords

Caribbean Basin Initiative (CBI)
Caribbean Legion
Carter-Torrijos Treaties
Central Intelligence Agency (CIA)
Costa Rican Revolution of 1948
Democratic Spring
*El Norte*
Guatemalan coup of 1954
Guatemalan National Revolutionary Unity (URNG)

Guerrilla Army of the Poor
National Liberation Party (PLN)
Negritude
Panama Canal
Revolutionary Democratic Party (PRD)
spiritual socialism
Tontons Macoutes
United Fruit Company (UFCO)
Vodou

# The Cuban Revolution and Its Aftermath

## The Voice of the Revolution

On July 28, 1959, Fidel Castro addressed a half-million Havana residents plus peasants (*guajiros*) trucked into the city from the countryside about the ongoing revolution. Only six months had passed since Fidel's forces had triumphed, and Cuba still pulsed with excitement and expectation. Listen to the voice of the revolution, Fidel Castro. This charismatic leader wrapped himself in the desires of his people. Not all agreed with him, and many fled when he became a Marxist dictator. But no one doubted the power of his rhetoric and his ability to inspire.

> Peoples never support a government without reason. Peoples never support their leaders without reason. And for those abroad who slander us, those abroad who are our detractors, those who slander us, while talking of democracy, there is no better argument than the million and some Cubans who have met here this evening. (Applause).
>
> To those who in the name of, or hypocritically invoking the word democracy, slander us, we can say that this is a democracy, democracy is the fulfillment of the will of the peoples, democracy is as Lincoln said, government of the people, for the people and by the people. (Extended applause)
>
> A government which is not of the people is not democratic. A government which is not for the people is not democratic. And what has the government of the Cuban revolution been since the first of January 1959 if not the government of the people, by the people and for the people? (Applause).
>
> Government of the people, not for a privileged group of the people. Government of the people, not an oligarchy which subjects the people to exploitation. Government of the people, not for a military caste or politicians, as we have always had in Cuba. (Applause).

Government of the people for all the people, this indeed is democracy. Government not for the landholders, as it has been in the past, nor for the great interests, as it has been in the past, but government of the people, by the people and for the peasants, first of all (applause), for the peasant, first of all, because no one can deny that the peasants constitute the most forgotten and suffering part of our people. (Applause).

Government of the people, by the people and for the humble, first of all, because the humble constitute the majority of our people and the most suffering and forgotten part of our people. (Applause).

And for those who do not understand or who do not want to understand, this is the secret of the tremendous strength of the Cuban revolution, and not the fact that it overthrew the bloody tyranny which oppressed us, because it could have overthrown the tyranny but maintained in the country the conditions which made this tyranny possible. It could have overthrown the tyranny and brought about a simple change of men in the government. It could have overthrown the tyranny and perpetuated, in the public life of our country, the same vices from which we had suffered since the beginning of the republic. It could have overthrown the tyranny to continue with petty politicking, but it was not thus. It overthrew the tyranny to bring about a revolution. It overthrew the tyranny not only to free the people from crime and murder and torture and oppression, but also to free the people from a misery as criminal and as cruel as the overthrown tyranny. (Applause).[1]

## PRELUDE TO REVOLUTION

No hemispheric event in the latter half of the twentieth century rivaled the Cuban Revolution in terms of its impact on Latin American history and international relations. When Fidel Castro led his army into Havana on January 7, 1959, he inaugurated a new age in regional affairs. As the Cuban Revolution turned toward the left and became a Marxist movement, it undermined U.S. hegemony in the hemisphere and inspired the creation of scores of similar guerrilla forces. Castro himself became a hero and a model for millions of admirers around the world. To his enemies, by the same token, he represented a sinister, even devilish force. Latin America would not be the same after his accession to power.

Cuba had enjoyed considerable prosperity under the early Batista administrations (strongman 1933–1940, president 1940–1944), but after World War II a malaise settled over the island. To be sure, the economy grew rapidly from tourism and exports, and political freedoms led to intense competition for public office. Cuban disquiet arose because of massive fraud in the public sector, control of the economy from abroad (mostly the United States), and the growing power of gangsters and criminal bosses in the drug, smuggling, gambling, and prostitution businesses. The disparity between the liberal, egalitarian republic promised in the 1940 Constitution and real events caused major dissatisfaction on the part of the middle class, intellectuals, and students.

---

**History as Images**

The engravings by Antonio Canet (see figs. 22.1 and 22.2) present some events surrounding Fidel Castro's capture and subsequent trial for the aborted attack on the Moncada Barracks in Santiago de Cuba, on July 26, 1953. That day is revered in Cuba as the beginning of the revolution. The images shown here reflect the heroic dimension that Castro cultivated among Cuba's people. And notice how closely Canet identifies Castro with the great Cuban patriot of independence, José Martí. The captions are from the originals written in Cuba. Antonio Canet, one of Cuba's most prolific painters and engravers, worked for decades capturing the revolution. These images came from his last work, a graphic essay on the course of the revolution.

---

Such was the turmoil in 1952 that Fulgencio Batista came out of his retirement in Florida to run for president and, according to him and his cronies, rescue the nation. He promised to clean up politics and restore good government. When the prospects of his winning seemed questionable, he activated his contacts among army generals and simply seized power by force. He then settled in for another long turn at the helm of state.

Rather than pursuing reform, his rule became more repressive than before, and he allowed Cuba to continue to grow as a playground and source of profits for wealthy foreigners. By that time, Cuba had fairly high standards of living by comparison with the rest of Latin America, yet also some of the highest rates of inequality. While the wealthy lived in cosmopolitan glamour, the rural poor continued to labor in the impoverished countryside, where the rhythms of sugar production and the absence of things like schools, running water, and electricity determined their daily lives.

Batista's coup evoked widespread criticism and protest. University students expressed particular rage, pointing out that the dictator had violated his own constitution. A lawyer and former activist at the University of Havana, Fidel Castro emerged as the leader of a conspiracy to overthrow Batista. Born in 1926 in Oriente province, Fidel had been raised on his father's sugar plantation. His father had emigrated from Spain after having served in the Spanish Army during Cuba's war of independence. Fidel's mother had been the family cook.

In 1945 Fidel entered the University of Havana, where he eventually earned a degree in law and gained a large following among student activists. He was tall, handsome, well spoken, and charismatic. In 1947 he launched his revolutionary career by participating in an unsuccessful invasion of the Dominican Republic. While in college he also joined the opposition Ortodoxo Party. In the course of

**Figure 22.1** In the second trial held in the chambers of the Judicial Building, Fidel invoked the 1890s independence hero José Martí (right) as the intellectual inspiration for the attack. Courtesy Antonio Canet.

his travels in the region with other students, Castro met with the Caribbean Legion group in Costa Rica and with other pro-democracy leaders. He was in Bogotá in April 1948 when Jorge Gaitán was assassinated. The violence and looting that followed left a deep impression on him. He was also deeply affected by the suicide of Ortodoxo Party founder and Senator Eduardo Chibás in 1951, who killed himself during his weekly radio show to protest government corruption. In the aftermath, Castro decided to run for the House of Representatives, but the elections were canceled when Batista seized power in 1952.

When Batista took over the Cuban government, and when legal and electoral paths to challenging Batista closed, Fidel and his younger brother Raúl decided to mount an armed movement. With smuggled arms and underground contacts with labor unions and disgruntled politicians, Castro's band of 167 rebels, including 2 women, assaulted the army's headquarters in Santiago, the Moncada Barracks. The attack, carried out on July 26, 1953, failed utterly. About half of the revolutionaries died, and the rest were imprisoned, including Fidel.

Castro used his subsequent trial as a forum to speak out against Batista and to claim the high ground of a heroic revolutionary. His reformist, nationalist philosophy came out in a famous five-hour speech, "History Will Absolve Me," made from the defendant's docket. He called for an end to imperialism, dictatorship, oppression, and corruption, as well as the reinstatement of the 1940 Constitution. The trial proved so popular that the government suspended the

**Figure 22.2** Coming from Tuxpán, in the province of Veracruz, Mexico, after a long crossing, Fidel Castro and his compañeros disembarked from the yacht *Granma* on the Las Coloradas Beach in Cuba, in the province of Oriente. Courtesy Antonio Canet.

proceedings and sent Castro and the other defendants to the Isle of Pines penal colony. By then, written copies of his speech had begun to circulate widely, and he soon became a hero to the opposition.

Upon his release in 1955, Fidel and Raúl Castro were exiled to Mexico, where they teamed up with other leftists and guerrillas. Ernesto "Che" Guevara, an Argentine physician and revolutionary sympathizer, joined what would become the core of a new insurgent force. They gathered weapons and money and studied guerrilla tactics with veterans of the Sandino movement in Nicaragua. Back in Cuba, allies were distributing propaganda that aimed to build popular opposition to the Batista regime.

By the following year Castro had assembled a force of eighty-two rebels, and they set out for Cuba from Tuxpán, Mexico, aboard a cabin cruiser named the *Granma.* They landed near Niquero on the southeastern coast. Castro expected simultaneous uprisings all over the island to support his invasion. The broader revolt never materialized, and Batista's army easily overcame Castro's small force, sending Castro, Raúl, Che Guevara, and nine others fleeing into the Sierra Maestra mountains. Many of Castro's companions were killed or wounded in this inauspicious start.

During the next two years the revolution took root and the 26th of July Movement grew, flourished, and finally triumphed. Castro's forces remained mobile at first, in classic guerrilla fashion, then became strong enough to create permanent camps. The local peasants lent support and intelligence and then began to enlist, while sympathizers from other countries joined as well. Castro

## Revolutionary Goals

Fidel Castro enumerated the five revolutionary laws he and his followers would have broadcast by radio had they succeeded in capturing Moncada Barracks:

"The First Revolutionary Law would have returned power to the people and proclaimed the Constitution of 1940 the supreme Law of the land, until such time as the people should decide to modify or change it. And, in order to effect its implementation and punish those who had violated it . . . the revolutionary movement, as the momentous incarnation of this sovereignty, the only source of legitimate power, would have assumed . . . the legislative, executive, and judicial powers. . . .

"The Second Revolutionary Law would have granted property, not mortgageable and not transferable, to all planters, sub-planters, lessees, partners and squatters who hold parcels of [160 acres] or less . . . and the state would indemnify the former owners on the basis of the rental which they would have received for these parcels over a period of ten years.

"The Third Revolutionary Law would have granted workers and employees the right to share 30 percent of the profits of all the large industrial, mercantile and mining enterprises, including the sugar mills.

"The Fourth Revolutionary Law would have granted all planters the right to share 55 percent of the sugar production and a minimum quota of forty thousand arrobas [bushels] for all small planters who have been established for three or more years.

"The Fifth Revolutionary Law would have ordered the confiscation of all holdings and ill-gotten gains of those who had committed frauds during previous regimes. . . . Half of the property recovered would be used to subsidize retirement funds for workers and the other half would be used for hospitals, asylums and charitable organizations.

"Furthermore, it was to be declared that the Cuban policy in the Americas would be one of close solidarity with the democratic people of this continent, and that those politically persecuted by bloody tyrants oppressing our sister nations would find asylum, brotherhood, and bread in the land of Martí. Not the persecution, hunger and treason that they find today. Cuba should be the bulwark of liberty and not a shameful link in the chain of despotism."

Fidel Castro, *History Will Absolve Me* (New York: Lyle Stuart, 1961).

set up a portable transmitter with which to broadcast his Radio Rebelde, calling for insurrection. Foreign observers—visiting to assess the strength and nature of the movement—came away impressed with the ardor and progressive ideas of the youthful leader. The *New York Times* even sent a reporter to interview him, leading to a series of well-publicized articles.

**Figure 22.3** Fidel Castro taking control of Cuba in January 1959. He was an appealing figure in his battle to overthrow the Batista dictatorship, and elicited sympathy from the U.S. public after being interviewed by U.S. reporters. He turned out to be the longest-lasting dictator of modern Latin America, only relinquishing power to his brother Raúl in 2008. United Press International. Courtesy Library of Congress.

Much of Castro's success depended on the readiness of many Cubans to support a change of government. Disgruntled employees, students, enlisted men, union members, teachers, and aspiring politicians jumped on the bandwagon and conspired with the guerrilleros, making it a truly mass-based movement. In addition, foreign sympathies favored Castro, who was seen as a fresh, honest, devoted reformer pitted against a corrupt dictator.

Castro's growing international reputation led the U.S. government to embargo arms shipments to Batista in early 1958, signaling a shift in U.S. Cold War strategy away from supporting petty dictators, who sparked opposition movements they could not contain. So, although the sides were somewhat lopsided in terms of troop strength, Castro's seven thousand soldiers had the advantages of public support, esprit de corps, battle readiness, and sheer momentum.

In December 1958 Batista ordered an all-out assault on Castro's mountain strongholds. Meanwhile, he promised to raise wages and hold new elections. Both efforts failed miserably. He did not fool the public, and government forces melted away when confronted with withering guerrilla attacks. When it became clear that the war was lost, Batista and his high command fled the island with as much cash as they could scrape together.

Castro took seven days to march into Havana, consolidating his hold on power by appointing trusted lieutenants as military commanders in the provinces. He ordered the executions, arrest, or even torture of thousands of Batista collaborators, especially those with military or police service. When he arrived in the capital, Castro disarmed the population and put the irregular forces under the command of his revolutionary army, which his brother Raúl commanded. There was no doubt, then, that Fidel alone controlled the destiny of the nation.

Besides eliminating the old regime through executions, exile, and expropriation, Castro sought to build a new society, one guided by nationalist and socialist principles. He spoke of the "new Cuban man," motivated by love of country and solidarity with fellow citizens, instead of by greed and self-interest. He set out to spread the wealth that had been noticeably concentrated in the hands of rich Cubans and foreigners. By early 1959, he had enacted rent reduction laws and lowered utility rates, seized property from Batista-era government officials, and increased wages. Castro also spent heavily on school construction, nutrition programs, clinics, public health campaigns, housing, and literacy classes.

In May 1959, Castro introduced an agrarian reform law that aimed to end rural unemployment and radically redistribute wealth. He called his approach "humanism," which meant "government by the people . . . liberty with bread and without terror." Many wealthy people, former supporters of Batista, fled into exile. Castro also viciously cracked down on any opposition, and tens of thousands of dissidents were jailed in the early years after his takeover.

Castro pledged to end gender and racial inequality as well, though the Cuban revolutionary government was much more active in challenging the former than the latter. Women had been critical in Castro's success in overthrowing Batista, ferrying arms, supplies, and information to the Sierra Maestra mountains and even occasionally taking up arms themselves. Haydée Santamaría was among the most notable. She fought in the assault on the Moncada Barracks in 1953, and along with fellow rebel Melba Hernández was imprisoned in its aftermath. She trained with the guerrillas in the Sierra Maestras and fought in the women's batallion in the rebel army. She remained a prominent cultural leader after 1959, while Hernández became a prominent politician in Cuba, even rising to be a member of the Central Committee of the Communist Party.

In August 1960, Castro also created the Federation of Cuban Women, which aimed to incorporate women into the political and social life of the country by challenging traditional gender roles. It was led by Sierra Maestra rebel and wife of Raúl Castro, Vilma Espín. The federation was a key player in the end of illiteracy on the island in the 1960s. It also facilitated the expansion of women's work opportunities, and women received education and training that gave them access to jobs outside of domestic service.

In 1966, Castro proclaimed a "revolution within the revolution" to erase gender stereotypes that kept women confined to the home and family, and that treated women unfairly in the workplace. With the support of the federation, he enacted laws to protect pregnant women and working mothers. The 1975 Family Code, which brought full legal equality to women, mandated that men and women share family burdens and even hinted at men's domestic duties. He initiated programs to bring appliances into homes to ease the domestic burdens of women and created many day-care centers. His goal was to free women from the home in order to allow them to join the workforce more fully, which was necessary to meet production goals, build support for the party, and enable women to achieve a socialist consciousness.

Though women's political and professional roles grew substantially in the 1970s and 1980s, legal emancipation did not erase traditional ideas and practices about male privilege. In the end, the Cuban Revolution was a profoundly masculine event—what some called *machismo-leninismo*—even as women saw substantial improvements in their quality of life, professional opportunities, and economic independence. Moreover, despite the creation of the federation, women's incorporation and transformation was to be a top-down affair directed by Castro himself.

Castro also set out to end Cuba's subservience to the United States. His foreign policy broadened to include interaction with all countries, not just the pro-U.S. allies. In all, he took a strikingly radical approach. Castro had welcomed help from all sides during the revolution—he even received CIA money channeled through Costa Rica. The core of his coalition, however, remained center-leftist in orientation. Some close associates, especially his brother Raúl and Che Guevara, were Marxists who pushed to make Cuba into a communist state. They urged Fidel to join with the Soviet Union and oppose the United States on many fronts. They traveled to Moscow to confer with Premier Nikita Khrushchev, who defied U.S. world leadership and sought to spread Soviet influence. Castro did not claim to be a communist himself until nearly two years later, but his regime had a distinctly leftist quality from the beginning. He played a dangerous game in the Cold War environment.

By cutting off arms shipments to Batista, the Eisenhower administration had indirectly helped Castro come to power. Early in 1959, however, the United States began trying to rein in Castro. Exuberant in his role as leader and nationalist to the core, Castro refused to offer assurances to the U.S. that he would protect its interests. Instead, he spoke of nationalizing the sugar industry, the most obvious remnant of imperialism and obstacle to socializing the economy. He also spoke of diversifying Cuba's trade connections to lessen its dependence on the U.S.

Soon, an international game of tit-for-tat flared up: Castro defied the United States and the latter responded with ever-sharper sanctions. When he made a deal to buy Soviet crude oil, U.S.-owned refineries refused to refine it, leading Castro to nationalize them in June 1960. By July 1960, the U.S. had cut Cuba's sugar quotas drastically, an especially harsh measure since the U.S. had been

## A Rebel in Cuba

Before his career as a Latin American historian, Neill Macaulay (1935–2007) served as a soldier, first in Korea in the mid-1950s and later as a revolutionary in Cuba in 1958–1959. Like many young people at the time, he supported the cause of overthrowing corrupt dictators like Fulgencio Batista in Cuba and of restoring democracy in the hemisphere. Taking up arms for the cause, however, showed unusual daring, and his memoir about that experience, *A Rebel in Cuba,* shows us how good intentions can lead to unintended consequences. Macaulay soon abandoned the island and opposed the Castro regime, but late in life he reached out again to his former comrades-in-arms. January 1959 was a heady time to be in Havana, and Macaulay captured the excitement:

> We arrived in Havana on the afternoon of January 6. Our first stop was to Camp Columbia where Escalona hoped to talk with Comandante Camilo Cienfuegos. . . . Barbudos [bearded men] and militiamen wearing a highly individual assortment of green uniforms and armed with a variety of weapons lounged about. A few unarmed civilians and men dressed in the khaki of Batista's army wandered around.
>
> Fidel had yet to arrive in Havana. The Maximum Leader was slowly making his way along the Central Highway from Oriente, stopping at all the towns and cities on the way. He was preparing for a showdown with the rival revolutionaries in Havana by rallying the people of the provinces behind him, making sure that the military posts along his route were in the hands of barbudos. The guerrillas of the Directorio Revolucionario, three or four hundred in all, had abandoned Las Villas and were now camped out at the University of Havana. . . .
>
> In the (Cabaña) headquarters building, we found Comandante Che Guevara. El Che was receiving visitors. A line about a block long and composed mostly of upper-class Cuban ladies and their teen-age daughters led into Che's jefatura. We politely pushed our way through these elegant, ecstatic females and into the building. Che was alone in a little office, sitting behind a big desk that was pushed up against the doorway to keep the visiting women at a distance. The famous guerrillero stood up and motioned to us to come in. Escalona climbed over the desk to embrace his old comrade from the Sierra Maestra. Then he introduced Manolo, Cienfueguero, and me. I was presented to Che as un Americano que es un revolucionario de carajo. Che smile pleasantly, nodding to each of us. He was reserved but not cold. He wore a loose-fitting fatigue uniform and had a black sling around his neck; he said that his arm had been hurt in Las Villas but that it was better now and he really didn't need the sling. . . .
>
> "We have just left the University," Escalona said. They have some little tanks there. Do you think [they're] going to create any problems?"
>
> "Bueno, chico," Che replied, "I do not know. They are probably angry about last night when Camilo made them give up the Presidential Palace."

Neill Macaulay, *A Rebel in Cuba* (Micanopy, Fla.: Wacahoota Press, 1970), pp. 152–57. Reprinted by permission.

buying over three-quarters of Cuban sugar at the time. Castro soon expropriated United Fruit, IT&T, Standard Oil, and other U.S. corporations, causing losses totaling billions of dollars. In October 1960, in an attempt to try to isolate and undermine the regime, the U.S. declared a partial trade embargo on Cuba, which it expanded to a full embargo in February 1962. In April 1960 Eisenhower also authorized the CIA to begin training a secret counterrevolutionary exile force in Central America.

These years witnessed many bitter confrontations between Cuba and the United States, confrontations that undermined U.S. leadership in international affairs and, in one instance, brought the world to the brink of nuclear war. The standoff with the United States strengthened Castro's hand and enhanced his fame. Young people and leftists all over the world emulated him by growing beards, wearing army fatigues, planning guerrilla movements, and denouncing the United States. Among sympathizers around the world, Castro and revolution represented the future and the possibility of change against seemingly impossible odds.

The failed Bay of Pigs (Playa Girón) invasion by Cuban exiles in April 1961 severely embarrassed the new president, John F. Kennedy. The CIA, with Eisenhower's authorization, had recruited, trained, financed, and readied an assault force to overthrow Castro. Ostensibly an initiative of Cuban exiles, the landing was in fact a full-blown covert operation by the United States, which foolishly believed its success in overthrowing Arbenz in Guatemala in 1954 would translate to Cuba in 1961. With the launch on hold until after Kennedy's inauguration, the force awaited its orders.

Kennedy, not wishing to appear soft on communism, allowed the operation to go forward. After some preliminary bombing attacks, however, he withdrew air support; thus the invaders landed virtually unprotected on the south side of the island. Castro's army, forewarned by spies in Miami, captured the entire force and exposed its sponsorship by the CIA. Kennedy suffered a major humiliation in this incident and sought other ways to overthrow Castro. Castro, by contrast, became more popular than ever by having defeated the hemisphere's most powerful force.

Another flash point occurred the following year, when Kennedy blockaded Cuba in order to force the Soviets to stop installing intermediate-range nuclear missiles on the island. In an effort to prevent another U.S.-backed invasion of Cuba and in response to U.S. nuclear missiles in Turkey able to reach the Soviet Union, Khruschev and Castro reached an agreement in mid-1961 to place Soviet missiles on the island. When Kennedy learned of the missiles, he issued an ultimatum to Khruschev and blockaded the island. For two weeks a U.S.-Soviet confrontation seemed imminent, until Khrushchev agreed to withdraw the missiles in exchange for a U.S. pledge not to invade Cuba. The U.S. also secretly agreed to remove the missiles from Turkey.

In the end, the crisis lessened U.S.-Soviet tensions as they increasingly sought to open up clear lines of communication in order to prevent global nuclear war. Castro dug in and fortified his position in the aftermath of the missile crisis. For the remainder of the 1960s, Castro retained close ties to the Soviet Union and also allied himself more closely with communist leaders in Beijing and eastern Europe, seeking to spread guerrilla war throughout the Third World.

## ERNESTO "CHE" GUEVARA

Che Guevara, who for a time served as a roving ambassador of revolution, coined a famous phrase in that era: "One, two, many Vietnams!" As the U. S. became bogged down in Vietnam, Che called for more resistance to U.S. interventions abroad. An Argentine born in Rosario in 1928, Che grew up in a family with aristocratic lineage but little wealth. The eldest of six siblings, he suffered from asthma from the age of two. Like Teddy Roosevelt, Che fought to overcome his asthma with outdoor living, exercise, and a strong will.

When he was sixteen, the family moved to Buenos Aires, where Che studied at a leading high school, going on to earn his degree in medicine in 1953. He was an excellent student throughout these years. But he also began to travel by motorcycle in South America to gain a deeper knowledge of the world. He developed a deep empathy for the poor and sick of the region.

After his graduation, Che set out for even more distant lands, visiting Mexico and Central America. He met a number of leaders in exile who would eventually come to power in their respective countries. Of foremost importance were Fidel and Raúl Castro, who recruited him into their invasion force on the *Granma.* One of the few survivors, Che made his way into the mountains to serve as medic and eventually commander. He, Fidel, and Raúl became close over these months. He earned everyone's respect by learning to cope with his asthma in the difficult terrain.

After the triumph of the revolution, Che became a Cuban citizen and headed Fidel's industrialization program. He remarried and had four children in Cuba. Along the way he served as president of the national bank, minister of industry, and roving ambassador in search of foreign aid. Moreover, he served as a theorist of the revolution, especially regarding socialist economics and guerrilla warfare. His book on the latter became an instant best seller all over the world.

In 1965, Che disappeared from public view and spent months in the Congo in Africa, applying his theories and training guerrilla leaders. The following year he returned to Cuba to launch another campaign, his most famous (and disastrous). He began to place guerrilla soldiers in eastern Bolivia in order to

**Figure 22.4** Despite his fragile health, Che Guevara played a critical leadership role in early revolutionary Cuba. He commanded a division during 1958 and then served in the cabinet under Fidel Castro. Seen here in 1964 smoking a Cuban cigar, a signature act by the revolutionaries. United Press International. Courtesy Library of Congress.

spark a revolutionary movement among peasants and workers, as a prelude for a continent-wide insurrection. In 1967, he took personal command of the unit. However, U.S.-trained Bolivian rangers detected his force, tracking him down with sophisticated counterinsurgency equipment. They captured Che and most of the guerrilleros and executed Che. The cycle of rural uprisings in Latin America contracted noticeably afterward.

## GLOBAL IMPACT OF THE CUBAN REVOLUTION

Castro's new role as a leader of anti-imperialist movements in the Third World paid off handsomely. However, the reality of building his revolution once Cuba was cut off from aid and trade with the U.S. soon set in. The Soviet Union found itself obliged to subsidize the Cuban economy and supply all of the arms required by Castro's growing army. The cost was estimated at over $300 million a year. Meanwhile, Cuban defiance of the United States induced some Latin American leaders to distance themselves from the United States and follow independent directions in foreign policy.

The traditional U.S. political forum in the region, the Organization of American States (OAS), lost much influence. In the early 1970s rival leaders

### Che on Guerrilla Warfare

"We consider that the Cuban Revolution contributed three fundamental lessons to the conduct of revolutionary movements in America. They are: (1) Popular forces can win a war against the army; (2) it is not necessary to wait until all conditions for making revolution exist—the insurrection can create them; (3) in underdeveloped America the countryside is the basic area for armed fighting. . . .

"The part that the woman can play in the development of a revolutionary process is of extraordinary importance. . . . The woman is capable of performing the most difficult tasks, of fighting beside the men; and despite current belief, she does not create conflicts of a sexual type in the troops. In the rigorous combatant life the woman is a companion who brings the qualities appropriate to her sex, but she can work the same as a man and she can fight; she is weaker, but no less resistant than he. She can perform every class of combat task that a man can at a given moment, and on certain occasions in the Cuban struggle she performed a relief role. . . .

"'Know yourself and your adversary and you will be able to fight a hundred battles without a single disaster.' This Chinese aphorism is as valuable for guerrilla warfare as a biblical psalm. Nothing gives more help to combatant forces than correct information. This arrives spontaneously from the local inhabitants, who will come to tell its friendly army, its allies, what is happening in various places; but in addition it should be completely systematized. . . . An intelligence service also should be in direct contact with enemy fronts. Men and women, especially women, should infiltrate; they should be in permanent contact with soldiers and gradually discover what there is to be discovered."

Che Guevara, *Che Guevara's Guerrilla Warfare,* trans. I. F. Stone (New York: Vintage, 1968), pp. 1, 86, 101.

almost took control of the OAS in the name of ideological pluralism. Castro was definitely the inspiration for this rebellion against U.S. influence.

The United States attempted to win back hemispheric sway in the 1960s through a carrot-and-stick combination of foreign assistance and military repression. In 1961, President Kennedy launched an ambitious, wide-ranging, and sometimes confusing program called the Alliance for Progress, designed to strengthen cooperation and mutual security among the republics of the Americas. The Alliance for Progress responded directly and obviously to Castro's revolution. It especially appealed to progressive leaders in Latin America who sought social and economic reforms within a democratic framework.

Latin American countries and the U.S. pledged tens of billions of dollars in developmental aid to help improve standards of living and lessen the appeal of revolutionary movements. Kennedy's program won widespread praise—naively, in retrospect—as a new beginning for Latin American-U.S. cooperation. For a time, it gave the United States an opportunity to refresh its leadership.

The military side of the alliance focused on the Caribbean Basin, thought to be especially vulnerable to communist insurgencies. Working with military governments in Guatemala, Honduras, El Salvador, Nicaragua, and the Dominican Republic, the United States sponsored training and rearmament programs to combat guerrilla movements. It sent U.S. military personnel to train Latin American soldiers and police forces, and trained thousands more at the U.S. Army's School of the Americas in Panama. They pursued various strategies, including civic action, counterinsurgency, jungle warfare, and police training. The goal was to train modern, professional armies that would maintain social order while combating communist subversion. In fact, most regimes became more efficient dictatorships.

The struggle between military and insurgent forces escalated in the late 1960s, with the appearance of urban guerrilla movements in major cities. These may have been inspired by Castro's revolution, but they took entirely different approaches, relying on subterfuge, publicity, clandestine organization, and terrorism. Brazil's Carlos Marighella literally wrote the book on this style of warfare, which he pioneered. Called *The Minimanual of the Urban Guerrilla* (1969), Marighella's work stressed organizing a network of secret, independent cells that could survive attacks by government agents. Each cell was given missions, often from leaders whom they never met, to help prepare for revolution. These included hiding rebels, producing or amassing weapons, distributing propaganda, raising funds, or even carrying out acts of terror aimed at undermining government legitimacy and creating a sense of social disorder.

Through terrorist acts and other forms of resistance, urban guerrillas sought to provoke authorities into wholesale repression and brutality against the citizenry. They argued that people would soon tire of government abuses and support a revolution by the guerrillas. This new challenge to established authorities, impossible without the lead of Cuba, induced a wave of military takeovers in South America, to be discussed in chapter 23.

By 1970 Castro's revolution had begun to falter and required a renewal. For one thing, the promise of a high-income, independent, industrial economy and agricultural diversification had failed, and the country reverted to its dependence on exports of primary goods, including tobacco, nickel, and especially sugar in exchange for petroleum and manufactures. The Soviet Union subsidized Cuba heavily, causing accusations that Castro had merely traded one imperial sponsor (the United States) for another (the Soviet Union). To be sure, the general welfare of the population had improved measurably: Cuba's literacy, nutrition, schooling, housing, and health were among the best in the hemisphere by 1970.

Yet, in some respects little had changed. No elections were held, old-fashioned machinery held down productivity, imported technology worked poorly in the tropical environment, and political control was tightly centralized. Castro tried to raise morale (and deflect criticism) with a crusade to harvest 10 million tons of sugarcane in 1970, a feat he felt would prove Cuba's independence and revolutionary commitment. All Cubans were called on to contribute to the nationalist effort, and Castro himself could be seen cutting cane. The effort failed, and some Cubans began to lose faith in the regenerative power of the revolution.

Between the 1970s and the collapse of the USSR, Castro continued to react to external stimuli while making small adjustments domestically. He often found himself having to realign the economic policies and bureaucracy of the revolution to meet popular sentiment, and socialism occasionally was accompanied by small-scale privatization in order to meet Cuba's needs and refresh popular commitment to the revolution. He maintained an active foreign presence in Africa during the period of decolonization (1970s–1980s) but pulled back in the 1990s, with the end of the Cold War. He promulgated a constitution that set up a system of regional councils to spread power more broadly than the Communist Party had done. Yet, all high-level decisions and appointments continued to flow from Castro himself.

## DOMINICAN INTERVENTION

In April 1965, twenty-four thousand U.S. armed troops landed outside of Santo Domingo, the capital of the Dominican Republic. They put down a rebellion and settled in for a yearlong occupation. Some observers believed that the invasion prevented a revolution like Fidel Castro's from occurring. Others saw it as an unjust intervention that revealed the bankruptcy of U.S. calls for democracy and reform. For better or worse, the United States would not allow a second communist government in the region, even if it risked their self-proclaimed mission to promote democracy and social equity through the Alliance for Progress.

The background of the invasion involves the regime of Rafael Trujillo, which lasted from 1930 until his assassination in 1961 (see chapter 16). By the late 1950s, there were multiple opposition movements forming against Trujillo's brutal and venal dictatorship, including those in the middle class and the political left who wanted him removed from power. Some had taken to planning armed insurrection, including the Mirabal sisters. Four sisters, three of whom were assassinated by Trujillo in 1960, became martyrs to the cause and galvanized opposition on the island. The United Nations recognized their critical role in challenging repression and serving as an example to other women's groups across Latin America by naming November 25, the anniversary of their assassination, as the International Day for Elimination of Violence against Women.

By the late 1950s, Trujillo had become increasingly erratic, corrupt, and unreliable as a Cold War ally. In the end, he was assassinated by members of the Dominican armed forces. After decades of backing him, the U.S. CIA also favored bringing down Trujillo because policymakers feared that if he continued in power, a broader movement like Castro's would emerge to challenge yet another classic Caribbean dictatorship. With financial aid and assistance from the State Department in arranging democratic elections, the Dominican political elite created a democratic government in 1962. The winner was Juan Bosch, a fifty-one-year-old novelist and longtime enemy of Trujillo. Bosch had founded an opposition party, the Dominican Revolutionary Party (PRD) in 1939, while in exile. For almost half of his life—twenty-three years—Bosch had lived abroad, waiting, planning, and plotting against the dictator.

Juan Bosch, who took office in February 1963, was an intellectual out of touch with local politics after decades of living in exile and overly sanguine about reforming the country. He changed the name of the capital from Ciudad Trujillo back to its original Santo Domingo, then set to work on a constitution. The new constitution, ratified in July, separated church and state, legalized divorce, and set maximum expenditures for the armed forces. Another measure transformed the massive Trujillo family holdings into state enterprises, a kind of instant state capitalism. Many businessmen and old families, hoping to buy the holdings cheaply, were angered by the move. As it was, bribery and influence peddling, rampant under Trujillo, continued under Bosch.

The U.S. ambassador strongly supported Bosch, despite the latter's initial stumbles, but U.S. military attachés in the embassy did not, thinking that the leftists and communists in the PRD constituted a security threat. Only seven months into the new government, the top army general, Elías Wessin y Wessin, decided to remove Bosch. A staunch Catholic and anticommunist, Wessin y Wessin believed that Bosch would lead the country down the road to Marxism and dissolution. So Bosch went into exile again—not an unfamiliar move for the old battler—and the military assumed control.

The army installed a mild-mannered civilian, Donald Reid Cabral, to reverse course and sell off the former Trujillo properties. He reinstated the church-state alliance and ordered communists jailed again. Liberal aid from the U.S. and a bigger quota of U.S. sugar imports helped wealthy families gain control over the economy. Meanwhile, exiled opponents rallied to the PRD and plotted their return to power.

In November 1963 Lyndon Johnson succeeded to the U.S. presidency and devoted much more attention than his predecessor, John Kennedy, to U.S. business. His advisor for Latin America policy, Texan Thomas Mann, made it clear that U.S. business interests and national security would be his chief concerns.

In the aftermath of the Cuban Revolution and facing a troubling situation in Vietnam, he would not automatically deny recognition to military governments and might in fact welcome them if they followed pro-U.S. policies. The stick approach in the Alliance for Progress would definitely prevail over the carrot.

In the Dominican Republic, opposition to Reid Cabral was widespread, involving some army units, exiles, politicians, and leftist groups of many sorts. In April 1965 a pro-Bosch revolt broke out among junior officers and quickly spread to slum districts in Santo Domingo. The bulk of the army remained loyal, under Wessin y Wessin's command, but street fighting threatened order in the city. When the U.S. ambassador could not give Reid Cabral any assurances about bringing in U.S. troops, the latter abandoned the country, and the rebels took the palace. A desultory artillery duel between Cabral's forces and the rebels broke out on the outskirts of Santo Domingo. At this point the U.S. ambassador called President Johnson and requested troops, which were ordered in almost immediately.

Johnson did not know if a communist takeover was imminent, but he believed that even the slightest hint of Marxism might undermine his position at home and his growing commitment to the Vietnam War. Therefore, he decided to intervene and freeze events in the Dominican Republic. On television he said, "The American nation cannot, must not, and will not permit the establishment of another communist government in the Western Hemisphere." Later it became clear that no communist threat existed and that the OAS had not given its prior authorization for the action. The troop total reached twenty-four thousand, and the fighting soon ended. As in Guatemala in 1954, the United States quashed a reformist government in favor of one that promised stability, support for U.S. business interests, and loyalty during the Cold War.

After several months of negotiations, a civilian caretaker government was set up, and elections were scheduled for mid-1966. By then, U.S. troops had left the island. When the ballots were counted, a veteran of the Trujillo regime, Joaquín Balaguer, emerged the clear victor over candidate Bosch. A canny fifty-nine-year-old lawyer and statesman, Balaguer promised peace, stability, and jobs, and he managed to deliver, with generous help from the United States. Having lived in exile since 1963, he was seen as untainted by the revolt and invasion.

Balaguer's first three terms, lasting twelve years, proved successful, in part due to U.S. assistance, and the rancor of the past faded. Very gradual reforms modernized the capital, and high sugar profits trickled down among the people. The old part of the capital was restored for tourism, which peaked during the 1992 commemoration of Columbus's first voyage to the New World.

Balaguer stepped down from the presidency for two terms but left the PRD (which he had taken over from Bosch) in control of the country. Party rivals were unable to transfer Balaguer's popularity to themselves, so the former president exercised power from behind the scenes. He stood for reelection in 1986 and managed to hang on through the mid-1990s, a remarkable case of political longevity. Bosch also remained active at the head of a new party but did not win any elections.

Balaguer's principal opponent in 1994, former Santo Domingo mayor José Francisco Peña Gómez, accused Balaguer of rigging the election. International observers there confirmed widespread irregularities. In the resultant crisis, Balaguer agreed to hold new elections with outside monitoring. The 1996 election pitted Peña Gómez, who was ailing from prostate cancer, against Leonel Fernández, the young protegé of Bosch who had helped the latter form his new party in the 1980s, the Dominican Liberation Party (PLD). Surprisingly, Balaguer turned on his own party and backed Fernández, who swept the election. Peña Gómez died two years later.

Fernández, a law graduate, professor, and ideologue of the PLD, took full advantage of the economic opportunities available in the late 1990s and brought about extraordinary economic growth. The Dominican Republic also participated more energetically in hemispheric organizations like the OAS under his leadership. He governed with humanity and good judgment and only stepped down because the constitution did not permit reelection. He sustained warm relations with other leaders in the region and took special interest in improving relations with Haiti.

Hipólito Mejía of the PRD won the 2000 election and seemed to revert to the old and discredited ways of Balaguer. He promptly stopped all initiatives begun by his predecessor and appointed PRD party loyalists throughout the government. The economy pitched into recession, as did most of the region's, and public discontent began to rise. Rather than build relations with Leonel Fernández, Mejía attacked him viciously and denounced everything he had done. Fernández almost immediately began preparing for the 2004 election.

Partisan tensions grew fierce, as citizens and opinion makers lined up behind Fernández or Mejía. Bickering and backstabbing ensued. Adding insult to injury, Mejía managed to amend the constitution so that he could run for reelection. It was to no avail, for Fernández, benefiting from the widespread discontent with Mejía amid an economic collapse in the early 2000s that many blamed on Mejía's policies, won a massive victory in the 2004 election. He then won reelection and served until 2012. During those eight years in office, he chalked up an extraordinary record of financial stability and economic growth, investment in infrastructure and development, reform, and prosperity.

When Mejía ran for reelection in 2012, he once again lost to the PLD candidate, Danilo Medina, who served out his term and won reelection in 2016. Medina became a popular leader with close ties to the Dominican people and invested in social programs such as education while keeping the economy strong. His approval ratings topped 90 percent at times. Beyond the Dominican Republic, however, he became better known for his policies against Haitians and their descendants born on Dominican soil. In 2013, Dominican courts stripped citizenship from about half a million Haitian-descendant Dominicans, forcing them to try to register as immigrants or be deported to Haiti. In the aftermath, a patchwork of policies was put in place that led some Haitian-descendant Dominicans to leave the country voluntarily, some to register as immigrants, and others to be deported. While some saw this as an attempt to tighten Dominican borders and improve the economy, others viewed it is as a new phase of race-based discrimination against Haitians that goes back to the nineteenth century and that saw its worst expression in the 1937 massacre under Trujillo (see chapter 16).

## SANDINO'S REVENGE IN NICARAGUA

The longest family dynasty in modern Latin American history, that of the Somozas, came to an end in 1979, felled by a guerrilla movement. The revolution, led by the Sandinista Front for National Liberation (FSLN), founded in 1961, took its name from Augusto Sandino, whose guerrilla forces in the early 1930s stymied both the Nicaraguan and U.S. Marines. Sandino was eventually betrayed and murdered (see chapter 15), but some of his followers survived. Several Nicaraguan youths, inspired by these tales, named their liberation movement after Sandino. Unfortunately for them, Cold War tensions in the Caribbean Basin made such movements targets for suppression.

Shortly after forming the FSLN, about twenty would-be-revolutionaries established a base camp in the mountains of northwest Nicaragua. A Sandino veteran, Santos López, introduced them to the terrain and taught them guerrilla strategy and tactics. For years the FSLN led a precarious existence, losing battles and soldiers but learning the skills of survival warfare. In 1963, for example, the FSLN recruited a peasant force that was devastated by the National Guard. In 1966 it launched an urban guerrilla campaign and was again smashed by government forces. After each defeat the FSLN retreated into the mountains of the north to plan its next actions.

But the FSLN grew in strength as it challenged a regime that excluded the majority. By the 1960s, land concentration, the breakup of villages and households, and urbanization had led to significant social unrest under Somoza. The FSLN by that time was a diverse group, including workers, landless peasants, women, and university students. Encouraged by liberation theology, rank-and-file clergy broke with the church hierarchy and its backing of the regime to support the FSLN as well. They criticized the centuries of inequality and exclusion that had characterized the country and were particularly critical of the Somozas, whom they accused of dictatorship and repression. Priests began to participate in demonstrations, hunger strikes, and speeches. They aimed special criticism at the abuses and torture of those arrested by the Somozas and helped to publicize it beyond Nicaragua.

Since the church had traditionally been a bastion of female participation, religion became critical in drawing women into the FSLN. As in Guatemala, Christian grassroots communities helped to keep the movement alive amid terrible repression.

In the early 1970s the FSLN began to split into factions. One faction favored political action to raise money and arms for its rural colleagues. Another followed the pure route of the *foco* (small guerrilla operation), favored by Che Guevara. A third sought out workers and students for urban guerrilla activities. This split produced rivalries but also created a flexibility and resourcefulness not available before.

The FSLN also benefited indirectly from the 1972 earthquake, which devastated the capital, Managua. The regime of Anastasio (Tachito) Somoza so bungled the rescue and relief efforts that it alienated most Nicaraguans. For example, it withheld Red Cross blood from clinics and later resold it to foreign countries for profit. Moreover, high-level officials refused to move the capital—located in the most intense fault zone in Central America—because they owned most of the land there. The rubble where downtown Managua had stood, therefore, became a constant reminder of the profiteering that Somoza and his henchmen had indulged in.

From 1975 the struggle intensified on both sides, and the FSLN suffered major defeats and demoralization. Yet, the years of fighting, plus declining support for the corrupt regime, gradually led the international community to condemn Somoza and to call for a negotiated settlement. The United States, long a major backer of the Somoza dynasty, withdrew aid in 1978 and pressured him to leave office.

Other countries, including Cuba, Venezuela, and Panama, sent arms and aid to the Sandinistas. Somoza refused to budge, however, and unleashed more terror against the guerrillas. When Somoza had his longtime political rival and a member of one of Nicaragua's most prominent families, Pedro Joaquín Chamorro, assassinated in 1978, he completed the alienation of international observers and Nicaraguan elites. The end approached.

In the spring of 1979 even the OAS voted to urge Somoza to step down, and several countries severed relations with him. The FSLN, having reached an agreement to coordinate its separate commands, then launched an all-out offensive. Its forces encroached on the suburbs of Managua and threatened Somoza's infamous bunker headquarters downtown. At this point the United States sent an emissary to convince Somoza to resign, and he finally agreed in July. He fled the country and took up exile in Paraguay, the guest of another dictator, General Alfredo Stroessner. The following year Uruguayan guerrillas assassinated Somoza.

The Sandinistas quickly consolidated their hold on the country and began to restore order. Some forty to fifty thousand people had died in the fighting. Strikes and battles had knocked out a large share of the nation's industry. Perhaps 150,000 people crowded into refugee camps, and another 120,000 had fled into neighboring countries. Farms stood abandoned and roads destroyed. The cleanup alone loomed as a formidable job.

The provisional government, composed of a nine-person board, had representatives of all the major revolutionary factions. The Sandinistas held a majority of the seats and dominated its decision making. Their program reflected the coalition nature of the junta: they called for good government and democratic procedures, land reform, nationalization of Somoza-owned properties, higher pay and benefits to workers, support for unionization, broader access to basic services, rent control, more schools, equality for women, non-aligned foreign policy, and an overhaul of the army. The program stood left of center but was not wholly Marxist.

Nationalization of the Somoza holdings sounded like a simple way to spread the benefits of the economy, yet it also proved divisive. The government immediately became a major landlord and employer, controlling 41 percent of the nation's business. Meanwhile, foreign and domestic businesspeople decided not to reinvest profits until the long-term plans of the Sandinistas were clear. Thus their machinery and buildings gradually deteriorated in value, while the owners pushed production to the maximum to extract profits from their plants. As the value of private investment declined, the government share of ownership increased.

Revolutions do not succeed overnight, and the government continued to favor men over women when doling out the rewards of victory. Observers and scholars remain uncertain about the extent of women's participation in the front lines of the Sandinista struggle, with estimates of women's participation ranging from 7 to 30 percent of the combatants. Regardless of the number, some women played prominent roles in FSLN forces from the beginning, even as they struggled against sexism. Many more served in support functions, drawn to the FSLN by the great disruptions to family and village life caused by the economic policies of the Somoza regime.

In 1977, reformist women created the Association of Women Confronting the National Problem (AMPRONAC), which promoted women's and human rights in the face of the repressive Somoza regime. The goal was to make women central actors in the social and political reform of the country. When the FSLN overthrew Somoza in 1979, it incorporated women's rights into its platform. The FSLN supported feminism and enacted a series of laws aimed at women's emancipation. The Association of Nicaraguan Women Luisa Amanda Espinoza (AMNLAE), created soon after the FSLN took over, challenged sexist policies, thinking, and practices. A number of government agencies began to encourage compliance with the laws enacted in the 1980s to give women legal equality in the home.

In power just a bit over ten years, and operating in a relatively impoverished and underdeveloped context, the FSLN saw only limited results. Women did gain new government roles, especially in areas seen as an extension of their domestic duties. But women never participated in the political and social life of the nation at the levels claimed by the FSLN, even though in Nicaragua, where women had long been excluded due to the twin oppressions of patriarchy and dictatorship, the growing awareness of gender-based inequality was notable.[2]

The Sandinistas immediately adopted a foreign policy featuring broader ties with communist bloc nations, especially Cuba and the USSR. They called this "ideological pluralism" and vowed to respect the rights of all political groups. In their zeal, however, they exercised some censorship and stifled critics. This shift in policy raised Cold War concerns in Washington.

In 1979, the United States quickly recognized the Sandinista government and pledged $75 million to help rebuild the country. Very soon, however, relations cooled as the new government began returning favors by aiding guerrilla organizations in neighboring countries and forging stronger ties with Cuba. The election of Ronald Reagan to the U.S. presidency in November 1980 further undermined U.S.-Nicaraguan cooperation. Reagan and Congress, pointing to Sandinista gunrunning to Salvadoran guerrillas, canceled the aid program and vetoed loans from international banks. They cut the sugar quota and enacted economic sanctions.

A more direct threat to the Sandinistas soon emerged. The CIA began training counterrevolutionary forces, called the Contras. Many Contras, referred to by the CIA as "freedom commandos," were former National Guard officers. Ronald Reagan supported this and other assaults, in what became a fixation for him. By that time regime leadership had largely devolved onto Daniel Ortega, a Sandinista who had won democratic elections in 1984, and the young leader took up the challenge with vigor. A clandestine war broke out in Central America that for years defied mediation.

The Contra War sapped the vigor of the Sandinista revolution and slowed the nation's recovery from the struggles of the 1970s. It kept the populace on constant alert and robbed the economy of labor and investment. In the end the Contra War also undermined the second Reagan administration, because presidential advisors carried out illegal activities against the Nicaraguan government, the so-called Iran-Contra scandal. The sorry spectacle ended only when President Oscar Arias Sánchez of Costa Rica negotiated a peace agreement in 1987, for which he received the Nobel Peace Prize.

In1990 the Sandinistas lost the presidential election to opposition candidate Violeta Barrios de Chamorro, widow of Pedro Joaquín Chamorro. FSLN leader Doris Tijerino laid the blame on the short time they were in power and the failure of the revolution to change people's consciousness. Others cited the fear of

**Figure 22.5** President Oscar Arias Sánchez of Costa Rica won the Nobel Peace Prize in 1987 for leading his neighboring countries into a regional peace treaty that ended the Central American wars. Authors' collection.

a U.S. invasion, especially after witnessing the invasions of Granada in 1983 and Panama in 1989. Concern about the Sandinista leadership was compounded by the regional economic crisis and the ongoing war with the Contras, which plagued some regions of the country throughout the 1980s (see chapter 24).[3]

## CONCLUSIONS AND ISSUES

Throughout the Caribbean region, long-festering disputes among elites, grinding poverty, and anti-American nationalism produced tensions of volcanic proportions. Cubans felt these tensions deeply and heeded the call to revolution in the 1950s. Fidel Castro proved a brilliant leader, able to elicit loyalty from followers while broadcasting an appealing message to the world. His guerrilla campaign in the Sierra Maestra mountains in 1957 and 1958 served as inspiration to tens of thousands of young people who desired change.

Once in power, Castro learned that he could not achieve as much as he promised, partly because the U.S. government and private investors exercised broad control over the island. He set about to free the island, angering the United States. He then struck a deal with the Soviet Union for economic and strategic aid. By 1960, Cuba had become the hottest spot in the Cold War.

Two confrontations—the Bay of Pigs invasion in 1961 and the Cuban Missile Crisis in 1962—nearly caused a war between the superpowers. When the crises subsided, Castro and Che turned their attention to spreading guerrilla warfare throughout Latin America and Africa. A number of governments, and many would-be revolutionaries, took seriously the possibility of broad-based insurgencies led by communists. Established regimes and their military backers feared such an outcome, and revolutionaries welcomed it.

When instability in the Dominican Republic led to a civil conflict in April 1965, the U.S. government sent a large force to the island to quell the fighting. Although not a full-scale revolution, the fighting might have allowed more progressive elements to come to power. Instead, the United States stabilized politics there and backed a figure from the Trujillo dictatorship, Joaquín Balaguer. The new regime remained in control of the country until the 1990s, usually with Balaguer as president. The knee-jerk invasion by the United States served warning to other leaders that limits existed as to what the U.S. would tolerate in terms of reformism during the Cold War. The gunboats were back under a new flag: the Truman Doctrine (containment of communism) instead of the Roosevelt Corollary (Caribbean stability).

Yet another insurgency arose in the region—this one in the mountains and cities of Nicaragua. Invoking the cause of Augusto Sandino from the 1920s and 1930s, young revolutionaries of the FSLN challenged the long dynasty of the Somoza family. For fifteen years the FSLN fought sporadically, unable to make progress against the U.S.-backed regime. Finally, however, in the mid-1970s the tide turned, and Somoza went on the defensive. A strategic alliance among several guerrilla movements made it possible for the FSLN to surround and capture the capital of Managua in 1979. The last Somoza president fled into exile and was assassinated shortly afterward. The socialist Sandinista government faced opposition from the United States, which launched the counterinsurgency Contra force against it. The conflict finally ended in 1987, leaving the country more bankrupt than ever. The 1990s brought peace but continued political instability.

## Discussion Questions

What factors allowed a small revolutionary force in Cuba, without serious foreign backing, to overthrow an entrenched and well-armed dictator?

To what degree was the Cuban revolution a conflict between modernizing forces and the remnants of the U.S.-owned economy?

Can revolution be "contagious," spreading among nations or over time like a virus? How might this happen?

Were the Dominican people attempting to instigate revolution in 1965? Why did the U.S. respond so aggressively?

What factors allowed the Sandinista insurgents to finally topple the dictator Somoza?

To what extent did socialist revolutions in Cuba and Nicaragua change traditional ideas about gender and women's roles in society?

What impact did U.S. interventions have on its worldwide reputation? Why was it willing to put that reputation at risk?

## Timeline

| | |
|---|---|
| 1940 | Constitution promulgated in Cuba; strongman Fulgencio Batista elected president |
| 1952 | Batista returns to Cuba, runs for president, and then overthrows the elected government |
| 1953 | Fidel and Raúl Castro lead failed attack on Moncada Barracks in Santiago |
| 1956 | Castro brothers lead failed invasion of Cuba on yacht *Granma;* survivors flee to Sierra Maestra mountains, where they build a guerrilla force |
| 1959 | Castro's armies defeat Cuban forces, expel Batista, take control of the island |
| 1960 | Castro creates the Federation of Cuban Women |
| 1961 | United States suspends diplomatic relations with Cuba and later mounts failed invasion at Bay of Pigs (Playa Girón) |
| 1961 | Dictator Rafael Trujillo assassinated in Dominican Republic |
| 1962 | United States pressures USSR to remove missiles from Cuba, risking nuclear war |
| 1963 | Juan Bosch elected president in Dominican Republic |
| 1965 | Coup attempt and fighting prompt U.S. president Lyndon Johnson to send military force to "prevent another Cuba" in the Dominican Republic |
| 1965 | Caretaker government led by Joaquín Balaguer elected in Dominican Republic; dominates politics until the 1990s |
| 1967 | Ernesto "Che" Guevara captured and killed while attempting to promote revolution in Bolivia |
| 1979 | Sandinista guerrillas overthrow dictator Anastasio Somoza of Nicaragua, install reformist, left-oriented regime |
| 1981–87 | U.S. government–backed former Somoza officers, called Contras, fight subversive war against the Sandinistas |

**Keywords**

26th of July Movement

Alliance for Progress

Association of Nicaraguan Women Luisa
  Amanda Espinoza (AMNLAE)

Association of Women Confronting the
  National Problem (AMPRONAC)

Bay of Pigs invasion

Contras

Cuban Missile Crisis

Dominican Liberation Party (PLD)

Dominican Revolutionary Party (PRD)

Federation of Cuban Women

*Granma*

machismo-leninismo

Organization of American States (OAS)

revolutionary foco (small guerrilla band)

Sandinista Front for National Liberation
  (FSLN)

# The National Security States

# 23

## A Call for Peruvian Reform

On June 24, 1969, less than a year after taking power in a coup, the president of Peru, General Juan Velasco Alvarado, announced a sweeping agrarian reform law that effectively disenfranchised many landed oligarchs and began a deep transformation of Peru's distribution of wealth. Read parts of President Velasco's speech and hear the voice of reform, the call to arms to vindicate Peru's Indians, the commitment to a radical restructuring of Peru's social, economic, and political structures. Some listeners heard freedom and equality; others heard the voice of a demagogue and destroyer of traditions. What do you hear?

Compatriots:

Today the Revolutionary Government decreed the Agrarian Reform Law, and in doing so has returned to the country the most vital instrument for its transformation and development. History will mark this 24th of June as the beginning of an irreversible process which lays the basis for an authentic national greatness, [one] founded on social justice and the true participation of the people in the richness and destiny of the country.

Today, on the Day of the Indian, the day of the peasant farmer, the Revolutionary Government returns the best of all tributes to the entire nation by promulgating a law which forever puts an end to an unjust social system, a system which held those who work the land in poverty and in injustice, who worked a land that belonged to others, a land always denied to millions of peasants.

The Revolutionary Government has lifted the national aspiration for justice and forged it into an ironclad instrument for justice. From now on, the peasant farmers of Peru will no more be disinherited pariahs, who lived in poverty from womb to tomb, and who looked on impotently at the same future for his children. From this day, the Peruvian peasant farmer will in truth be a free citizen whose rights to the yield of the land is finally recognized by the country, and whose just place in society is acknowledged, no longer the second class citizen, the man to be exploited by other men.

We [Armed Forces] assumed political power to turn it into an instrument to transform our nation. No other motive moved us. We wished to give Peru a government able to initiate with resolution and courage the saving work of our true national development. We were conscious from the beginning that such an effort would demand sacrifices and efforts on the part of all Peruvians, because we knew that in a country like Peru, characterized by abysmal social and economic inequalities, the work of development had necessarily to be a work of transformation. To overcome our national underdevelopment means reordering Peruvian society and altering the economic, political, and social structures of our country.[1]

Beginning in the 1960s, a new type of military regime appeared in South America. These regimes had much in common with one another, yet they bore little resemblance to traditional dictatorships in the region. Instead, the generals who led them were middle-aged career officers who preferred to remain aloof from politics. In the words of some analysts, they were antipolitical. They tended to avoid the limelight and often remained anonymous. They all came from white, middle-class families and graduated from military academies. Virtually all of them had studied overseas, and a few had seen active duty abroad. The Argentines were in their early fifties when they took power, the Brazilians in their early sixties. While most were army men, several navy admirals took part as well. The few who stood out in public memory had frightening images and evoked fear in the citizenry. This generation of officers left a dreadful legacy of repression, torture, and death. They spawned the Dirty Wars of South America.

## NEW MILITARY MISSIONS

Historians disagree over whether guerrilla movements arose in opposition to the military or vice versa. On the one hand, the 1950s witnessed several insurgencies in Latin America, so military planners in the United States and abroad devoted increasing attention to counterinsurgency strategies and jungle warfare training. On the other hand, many military dictatorships existed before serious guerrilla activity began, so some historians argue that tyrannical governments sparked the rise of armed opposition movements. Regardless of which came first, all analysts agree that the 1960s Cold War context moved the struggle between these two forces toward a climax. In most cases, the military pushed civilian politicians out and established powerful conservative dictatorships that repressed leftist forces. By the 1990s Cuba remained the only country in the hemisphere under revolutionary or Marxist leadership.

Historians call the new military regimes "national security states" because of their dedication to domestic order above all other goals. During the 1950s and 1960s, military planners, especially in the Southern Cone countries, began developing new missions for their armed forces. The Cold War standoff between the United States and the USSR and the advent of nuclear weapons meant that the Latin American militaries would probably never become engaged in major international armed conflicts. Instead, they saw armed domestic insurgencies such as those taking place in eastern Europe, Asia, and Africa as the most likely challenges to their institutions. Rather than face external enemies, in other words, they would face internal threats to security. Therefore, they reorganized their defenses to ward off communist takeovers from within.

The new military doctrine, taught in the general staff colleges of Argentina, Brazil, Chile, and elsewhere, drew in part from U.S. training programs. Tens of thousands of Latin American officers received training in the School of the Americas, located in the Panama Canal Zone, until 1984. Gradually, not only the doctrine but also a solidarity spread among officers throughout the hemisphere, and a kind of inter-American military brotherhood developed. The armed forces invited one another to training programs, joint maneuvers, defense planning, weapons plants, and intelligence sessions. The common enemies of the new military were rural or urban-based Marxist insurgencies. This sense of shared endeavor reached its pinnacle in Operation Condor, a collaboration among right-wing dictatorships in the Southern Cone to fight insurgency through shared intelligence and targeted assassinations.

The National Security Doctrine stipulated that the armed services had to go beyond military preparedness in their fight against communism. The best defense against communism, it held, was a well-run, prosperous nation, in which every citizen had a job, a home, and a decent standard of living. Military leaders therefore placed a premium on economic growth and social order. They often viewed civilian leaders as corrupt and incompetent and blamed them for their countries' economic ills or rising leftist movements.

Even worse, some of these civilians had allowed leftists, including occasionally communists, to infiltrate public agencies. In the Cold War context, the inclusion of leftists, whether they called themselves socialists, populists, or liberals, was seen as a serious threat to stability, according to the generals. It took only a short step in logic for officers to conclude that in many cases the armed services themselves could run their countries more efficiently than civilian politicians. They had professional training, discipline, and a dedication to the national well-being. Once in power, the new military worked with technocrats who staffed the bureaucracy to boost economic development and pursue counterinsurgency programs without interference from civilians or democratic politics. They believed, rightly so at first, that many citizens would welcome the cool, competent management of their nations by a new political culture and structure known as "bureaucratic authoritarianism." Thus the Cold War scenario had a very peculiar impact on the missions of the Latin American military, broadening them to include nation-building. What many supporters did not realize at the outset was that bureaucratic authoritarian governments, impelled by U.S. funding and infused with Cold War paranoia, would ultimately wage vicious wars against their own citizens.

## Argentina

Argentina had the dubious distinction of developing the first national security state. From the mid-1950s, that country's armed forces viewed civilian leadership and leftist politics as dangerous to national welfare. In 1955, they overthrew the elected government of Juan Perón and installed a military regime that lasted three years. In 1962 they substituted a general for the duly elected president, Arturo Frondizi. After another flirtation with democracy, they replaced the civilian president with General Juan Carlos Onganía in 1966. He served four years, followed by two other generals, Roberto Levingston (1970–1971) and Alejandro Lanusse (1971–1973). No one doubted that the generals ruled Argentina throughout this period.

Each intervention by the army ratcheted up the level of confrontation between civilian groups and military elements. Students always protested takeovers, and the army responded by shutting down the universities. Unions struck against economic austerity measures that cut the income of workers, and the military outlawed strikes. The confrontations escalated in severity as the 1960s wore on. For example, the Cordobazo of 1969, a forty-eight-hour general strike in the industrial city of Córdoba, left a bloody toll of dead and wounded among protesters and police alike.

Meanwhile, writers, journalists, and artists denounced censorship, and they suffered more repression and limits on expression. The military increasingly divided the citizenry into friends—usually middle- and upper- class Argentines fearful of the growing political polarization and social disorder—and foes. They saw the latter as threats to the security of the state, a means through which communism could infiltrate the nation. By 1973 the level of confrontation between the government and the opposition reached alarming levels. Labor federations routinely shut down the economy with general strikes. Several powerful guerrilla movements, operating in the major cities and some rural areas, sought to undermine public confidence in the government and create a sense of social disorder by kidnapping and ransoming foreign businessmen, robbing banks, and committing other acts of terrorism. The tension between the government and its citizens began to resemble a civil war.

Part of the reason for the impasse in Argentine politics was the persistence of a strong Peronist movement, representing about 25 percent of the electorate. The military had exiled Perón and prevented his party from running in elections, but it could not erase the loyalty of his followers. No other party could win a working majority in Congress or govern the country effectively without Peronist support. Peronists were strong within the labor movement as well, using unions to organize against the military. Yet the generals who had exiled Perón could not imagine allowing him to return. Perón represented the worst aspects of civilian politicians, those that the generals had vowed to purge. They could not work with him, yet they could not govern without him.

For his part, Perón behaved as something of a spoiler from his exile in Madrid. He encouraged his followers to resist the military and did not allow them to form coalitions, and he did not let any other national leader emerge from the Peronist ranks. He did nothing to discourage the rebel groups who operated in his name, especially the Montoneros, known as the armed wing of Peronismo. The Montoneros soon became known for spectacular terrorist maneuvers, including bombings, kidnappings of high-profile domestic and foreign executives, and even the assassination of the military leader who had helped engineer the overthrow of Perón in 1955. The 1973 merger of the Montoneros with another guerrilla group, the Revolutionary Armed Forces, proved especially ominous: it created the single largest clandestine army in the hemisphere. The more chaotic Argentina became, the more likely it was that the army would have to call Perón back to save the country.

In 1972 General Alejandro Lanusse decided to deal with the Peronist dilemma once and for all. He opened negotiations with Perón to let him return and run for president, if he would commit to ending the guerrilla warfare being waged in his name. Perón agreed, and a hastily called election allowed one of his aides to assume the presidency. El Líder's return to Argentina, after an eighteen-year exile, was greeted with battles among the various armed groups operating in his name. His plane had to be rerouted to another airport for security. It was an inauspicious sign.

Lanusse's gamble with Perón operated on two levels. On the one hand, if the aging populist could really end the guerrilla struggle, the Argentine army would be rid of its most formidable challenge in 170 years of national history. On the other hand, if he failed (he was showing all of his seventy-eight years) he would be discredited among his followers and no longer able to prevent other Peronists from taking strong positions in national politics. Either way, it seemed, the military would benefit.

Unfortunately for Lanusse, neither scenario played out. Instead, Perón enjoyed a measure of success during the year he served as president before abruptly dying of natural causes. He reduced inflation by browbeating unions and employers into signing a social pact that stabilized wages and prices and restored labor's share of national income to 1950 levels. Yet while he had considerable support, the radical left was no longer willing to bend to traditional party politics, and university students and guerrillas refused to back his reforms. He attenuated the guerrilla struggle, partly by stepping up counterterrorist operations, many of them illegal and brutal. The federal police seemed to be coordinating these efforts and led a paramilitary group of the Peronist right called the Argentine Anticommunist Alliance (Triple A). His attacks on radical Peronist supporters soon drove the Montoneros underground. Meanwhile, Perón spent his last months basking in the adulation he so craved.

Perón's third wife, María Estela "Isabelita" Martínez de Perón, elected vice president in 1973, succeeded her husband upon his death. In 1951 the army had vetoed Perón's attempt to have his wife Evita run as vice president, but this time the army had acquiesced as a condition of getting him to return to the country. Isabelita Perón became president in July 1974.

The army now faced what it saw as the worst of all worlds: a female commander-in-chief with little experience and less authority, the intensification of guerrilla warfare, the collapse of the development program and the social pact with workers and employers, and constitutional limitations on the army's counterterrorist operations. The generals pressured Isabelita to allow them to respond vigorously, and she put her close advisor and confidant José López Rega in charge of antisubversive activities. Officially minister of social welfare, López Rega actually coordinated the Triple A campaign of surveillance, torture, kidnapping, rape, and murder of leftists, initiating what later became known as the Dirty War. Government death squads unleashed horrors against the civilian population in order to crush the guerrillas.

For more than a year and a half the military tolerated the awkward situation that Isabelita Perón created for them. Because Juan Perón had died while enjoying the full sway of his popularity, the military had to wait until Isabelita proved herself incapable of governing the country. By March 1976 Isabelita presided over a collapsed state, so the army removed her and took power in the name of national security. The evolution of the national security state was nearly complete. The generals who assumed power in 1976, men in their midfifties, had no intention of returning government to civilians until they had purged the country of communists, guerrillas, and leftist sympathizers. Their goal of purifying the country became a sacred mission, more profound than mere doctrine.

General Jorge Videla served for five years as head of the military government. He pulled out all the stops in the Dirty War against the guerrillas. Although barbaric beyond all reckoning, it nonetheless succeeded after about three years. By then virtually no guerrilla group could resist the army's power, and few even attempted to do so. However, in the process, many leftists with no guerrilla ties were also targeted, including students, intellectuals, union lead-

**Figure 23.1** General Jorge Videla (in uniform in car), who had just seized power in Argentina, seen escorting the president of the Sociedad Rural to the association's 1976 Exposición Rural. Courtesy Edgardo E. Carbajal, Wiki Commons.

ers, and even social workers. Their families, too, became targets of military violence.

The legacy of the Dirty War, in suffering, psychic torment, broken families, and death, haunted Argentina through the 2000s. Estimates of the number of persons "disappeared" by the military alone run to thirteen thousand, though some human rights organizations put the number closer to thirty thousand. Tens of thousands more were imprisoned and tortured. No accounting can ever be made of the other human losses suffered in the Dirty War.

For many years, *las madres* (the mothers) of missing persons paraded weekly in Buenos Aires's Plaza de Mayo demanding news of their loved ones. They came together spontaneously as they discovered each other outside a government ministry trying to gather information about their missing children. Called "*las locas*," or the madwomen of Plaza de Mayo, by the military, with their demands for more information, they helped to undermine the regime's legitimacy. Always emphasizing that they were simply mothers, they were a powerful indictment of the military regime and helped bring international condemnation down on it. The regime saw them as enough of a threat that it disappeared three of the mothers in an attempt to silence them.

Since then, the Madres have been joined by the Grandmothers of the Plaza de Mayo, a group of women whose pregnant daughters and daughters-in-law were kidnapped by the regime and who gave birth before they were killed. The babies were adopted clandestinely, and the Grandmothers have worked tirelessly since then to find them, including by pressing for faster and more easily available DNA testing. By mid-2016, they had located 120 of an estimated 500 missing grandchildren.

---

### Description of Las Madres by U.S. Journalist in Buenos Aires

"They would not go away, those pushy women circling the Plaza de Mayo silently, as if under water, photographs of their sons, daughters and husbands swinging on chains from their necks like good-luck charms. Sometimes the women would bear the photographs on placards; sometimes they would hold a snapshot delicately out in front of them between the index finger and the thumb, presenting unassailable proof to anyone who cared to look that the subject of the picture did, at one time, exist. Every Thursday the Mothers of Plaza de Mayo performed their half-hour ritual across the street from the presidential Pink House, and then dispersed for a week. But they would not go away. In many of the photographs the children posed formally, in dresses and coats and ties. In several, they looked saucy before the camera. That was in better days, before the subjects came to be counted among the desaparecidos: thousands, possibly tens of thousands of men, women and children who, as alleged enemies of the state, disappeared under the military government of Argentina in the late 1970s."

Roger Rosenblatt, "Things That Do Not Disappear," *Time,* 123, no. 74 (January 23, 1984), p. 74.

---

The story of the Mothers has been retold countless times in documentaries, feature movies, novels, and biographies. American audiences saw the worst aspects of the Dirty War dramatized in films like *Only the Emptiness Remains* (1984), about the Madres, and *The Official Story* (1986), about elite attempts to cover up complicity in the reign of terror.

The military did not succeed in its attempts to revive the economy. Inflation continued at high levels, unemployment soared, and the GNP actually shrank several years in a row. The principal reason for poor economic performance was the austerity measures imposed to wring inflation out of the currency before beginning privatization and expansion. Unfortunately, just when the Argentine economy showed signs of growing again, the 1980 to 1982 world recession hit and plunged the country into deeper trouble. The army had nothing to show for the previous four years of economic hardships except more of the same. By then, the civilian support the military had received when it first seized power had dissipated, as Argentines turned away from a regime it now blamed for repression and continued economic malaise.

By 1982, the one best hope for the army to remain in power and regain legitimacy seemed to be a successful foreign conflict. General Leopoldo Galtieri, both army commander and president, decided to invade the Malvinas (Falkland) Islands. These islands had been occupied by Argentina in the 1820s after independence, but were seized by a U.S. naval vessel and then turned over to

British forces in 1833. From then on, Great Britain administered them as a crown colony. For a century and a half, Argentina protested the occupation, but the British refused to cede the islands. They had little economic or strategic importance by the 1980s, but held a huge symbolic value to Argentines.

In April 1982 Galtieri's forces invaded the islands and managed to capture most of the land. Soon, however, the British counterattacked and waged a successful war on land, sea, and air. By early June, the Argentines had surrendered. Galtieri resigned as commander-in-chief and president. The armed forces were discredited and defeated, and faced emboldened opposition movements that engaged in national strikes and widespread public demonstrations to protest military rule. While the military initially tried to repress them, the debacle in the Malvinas led it to step aside and hold elections soon afterward.

In 1983 Radical Party leader Raúl Alfonsín took office. He soon after created the National Commission on the Disappearance of Persons, which produced a lengthy report about the disappearances called *Nunca más* (Never Again). While Alfonsín's government dabbled with prosecuting those who had led the repression, the military threatened another coup in 1987 if they were not shown lenience. By later that year, the government had issued extensive pardons, foreclosing the possibility of the prosecution of human rights abuses in the courts for the time being.

## Brazil

The Argentine army spent twenty-one years (1955–1976) intervening in politics before it took over the government completely and instituted the national security state; the Brazilian army did so much more decisively. It seized power in March 1964 and relinquished it only twenty-one years later, in 1985. In that long period of dictatorship, the army created the quintessential national security state.

The formulation of National Security Doctrine in Brazil began in the 1950s, at the Superior War College in Rio de Janeiro. There, intellectuals, planners, strategists, and generals mulled over the likely threats to Brazil's peaceful development. They decided that internal forces, including not just leftist ideologues but also the problems of poverty and inequality, would menace the state more than external ones. They concluded that a strong central state, with safeguards against subversion, and a solid economy would be the best way to stop the growth of leftist opposition.

As the 1960s began, however, two presidents, Jânio Quadros (1961) and João Goulart (1961–1964), seemed to challenge these plans. While Quadros was elected with broad popular support, he tended toward authoritarianism in domestic issues until he resigned unexpectedly (and to this day without a full explanation) just seven months into his term on August 25, 1961. Goulart, his more radical vice president, took office and, despite limitations the army imposed on his powers, allowed more popular participation in governance. Unions in particular grew under his rule, and the military interpreted this development as evidence that communism was invading Brazil. Goulart also publicly criticized the U.S. and implemented nationalist economic reforms that brought more wealth and opportunities to workers and peasants, even as they drove up inflation. At the same time, a balance of payments problem and the U.S. cutoff of all aid to Brazil meant the economy took a nosedive. With U.S. support, Goulart's civilian and military opponents organized to remove him from office.

Army Chief of Staff General Humberto Castelo Branco led the army coup against Goulart on March 31, 1964. A veteran officer with ample experience in many lines of military work, Castelo proceeded with little problem. He expected to govern as provisional president for a year or so, long enough to purge leftist leaders from high positions. He thought that the 1965 presidential election could possibly be held on schedule. With this plan in mind, Castelo and his team removed about three hundred politicians and leftists from sensitive positions, taking away their political rights (a unique Brazilian process known as *cassação*) for ten years. Particularly visible figures were urged to leave the country. A number of people vehemently opposed to the coup went into exile in order to continue the fight against the army. Meanwhile, Castelo turned the economy over to a team of fiscally orthodox managers who instituted a painful austerity program to bring down the triple-digit inflation. Congress continued to operate through this period, and a majority of its members accepted the coup as necessary to fix the economy and reestablish social order.

Castelo's relatively benign plan unraveled quickly, however, and the temporary regime became permanent. First, the doctrine of the national security state held that a long, recuperative period was needed to immunize the nation against Marxism and instability. Moreover, the economy did not respond to austerity as expected. Finally, the global scene took on more ominous tones as the Vietnam War deepened, Che Guevara stirred up revolution, and the United States invaded the Dominican Republic to keep out communists. Castelo found himself leading a military regime estranged from its early civilian allies.

Many ranking generals decided that they could not return control to the politicians without a thorough housecleaning and reconstruction of the nation. They had plans for foreign investment, infrastructure projects, social reforms, constitutional amendments, and more. It would take a long time, and those who advocated permanent military government called themselves the hardliners. They represented a majority of the active generals.

Castelo found himself outvoted among the generals. A broad purge of civilians was begun. Elections were postponed, politicians sidelined, and universities shut down. As this occurred, civilian opposition, especially from students

**Figure 23.2** General Humberto Castelo Branco led the 1964 coup in Brazil and served as president for three years. A moderate, he hoped to restore civilian government. Instead, hard-liners extended the military regime until 1985. Courtesy Government of Brazil.

and labor groups, escalated. For decades, students in Brazil had been organizing to press for the democratization of student life and more access to higher education, as well as participating in campaigns for literacy and rural sanitation. When the military took over in 1964, students faced severe repression and their organizations were outlawed. Through the mid-1960s, as students around the world launched protests, Brazil's university students protested against military rule, U.S. involvement in Brazil's educational system, and repression. Their actions culminated in an explosive set of student demonstrations in 1968, including one that reached one hundred thousand students in Rio, which severely tested the military's leadership. Urban guerrilla groups arose as well to disrupt the military governments and linked up with foreign revolutionaries, including those from Cuba.

For the next two decades five-star generals succeeded one another in power and presided over Brazil's destiny. The presidents were all in their sixties, most came from Rio Grande do Sul on Brazil's border with Argentina and Uruguay, and all had spent some time in the Superior War College, a strategic think tank. Most had some foreign training or duty tours. None was charismatic, and only Emílio Garrastazu Médici attempted to become popular. None tried to extend his own term beyond the five years provided by the constitution. Even more surprisingly, all of the presidents made a point of holding regular elections for local, state, and federal offices, and they worked more or less cooperatively with Congress. In fact, the number of persons who voted in elections rose more rapidly under military rule than during the preceding populist era.

Each army president had his own style, agenda, and coterie of supporters, which gave him a distinctive administration. Artur da Costa e Silva (1967–1969), a model hard-liner, ruled by decree and responded to opposition with harsh measures. Guerrilla warfare and terrorism mounted, and repression reached into all corners of society. For example, in 1969, the communist student guerrilla group known as the Revolutionary Movement 8th October, or MR-8, kidnapped the U.S. ambassador, portrayed by Alan Arkin in the 1997 Brazilian film *Four Days in September,* in order to protest the military regime. Summary arrests and torture became common, and Costa e Silva closed Congress more than once due to so-called insubordination. He judged this internal war to be necessary in order to purge the nation of undesirable elements, including the student protesters.

Costa e Silva suffered a stroke and was replaced by Médici (1969–1974), former director of the National Intelligence Service, a spy and repression agency. His selection signaled the desire of hard-line generals to root out and destroy subversives. Médici did so, cooperating with state police and the armed services' intelligence branches. A wide array of paramilitary forces carried out a terrifying campaign against anyone suspected of subversive activity.

The latest counterinsurgency methods were imported from the United States, but in Brazil they were applied with little regard for human or civil rights. Thousands of people were seized and interrogated, many were tortured, and hundreds died in police or military custody. The worst of Brazil's Dirty War, from 1969 to 1972, actually preceded Argentina's, although repression against leftists continued in Brazil until the end of the military government in 1985.

Médici did attempt to improve his image using public relations advisors. He tried to project a pleasant image on television. He pushed soccer and tried to take credit when Brazil won the World Cup in 1970, saying it was evidence that Brazil was on the path to Grandeza. He expanded television service throughout the country with satellite relays. Finally, he took undeserved credit for a surge in economic activity after 1968, sometimes called the Brazilian Miracle. In fact, the rapid growth in production occurred after three years of shrinkage and was due to massive investments by foreign corporations. Profits from the surge benefited mostly foreign investors, Brazilian businesspeople, and middle-class managers. While middle-class consumers had access to more goods than ever before, wage freezes meant that poorer Brazilians actually had less. During this period, Brazil's distribution of income became the most inequitable in

---

### Tropicalismo

The global counterculture movement of the 1960s reached Brazil just as the military regime was trying to repress political leftists, though at first the military saw no problems with allowing them to thrive. Brazilian music was already well known due to the worldwide popularity of the musical style bossa nova, identified with songs such as "The Girl from Ipanema," by Astrud Gilberto. By the mid-to late 1960s, Brazil had one of the world's most vibrant music scenes, drawing on both domestic and international influences. Composers such as Caetano Veloso and Gilberto Gil created a new musical style, dubbed Tropicalismo, which blended traditional Afro-Brazilian music with electric instruments and "foreign musical styles such as rock, soul, bolero, and rumba." They wrote clever lyrics that "juxtapos[ed] images of violence and poverty with familiar national mythologies associated with the idea of Brazil as a tropical paradise." By the late 1960s, the military government finally realized the subversive nature of Tropicalia, and in late 1968, both Veloso and Gil were arrested and sent into exile for two years. Both later returned to Brazil and continued composing and performing, achieving international acclaim.

Based on Christopher Dunn, "Tropicalism and Brazilian Popular Music under Military Rule," in Robert M. Levine and John J. Crocitti, eds., *The Brazil Reader: History, Culture, Politics* (Durham: Duke University Press, 1999), pp. 241–47. Quotes from p. 243.

---

the world among industrialized countries. Elites justified this inequity by saying that "the cake must grow before it can be divided."

During these years, statistics began to show the concentration of Afro-Brazilians at the economic bottom, and Freyre's theory of racial democracy began to be referred to as a myth. This was hastened by the emergence of new black rights groups, including the Unified Black Movement, which condemned the military leaders for focusing on poverty while ignoring continued racism.

Médici did succeed in stamping out terrorism and guerrilla activity, though at a terrible cost to civil society, political freedom, and individual rights. Increasing numbers of voters cast blank or marred ballots to protest the lack of true representation. In fact, the disqualified ballots rose to 25 percent of the total and served as an indictment of his regime. During these years, Brazil also became a continental leader of the National Security Doctrine, spreading right-wing ideology and military training and assistance to other countries in the region in an attempt to stamp out insurgency.

In 1974 Ernesto Geisel won the vote among the generals and became president. An administrative officer formerly in charge of the state petroleum corporation, Petrobras, Geisel belonged to the group called Castelistas,

**Figure 23.3** Edson Arantes do Nascimento, known the world over by his nickname, Pelé, took Brazilian soccer to its greatest heights, including its first World Cup in 1958. By 2015 Brazil had won five World Cup titles. Courtesy Brazilian Postal Service.

followers of Castelo Branco's moderate line. Determined to turn over power to civilians by the end of his five-year term, he took steps to democratize the country in preparation. He had to grapple with increasing public criticism of the military government and with challenges from Congress. He found himself most beset, however, by army hard-liners, who opposed any loosening of their control. He walked a difficult line, vigorously opposed by generals and civilians alike.

The greatest economic challenge that Geisel faced was the 1973–1974 oil crisis, under way when he took office, because Brazil's economy depended almost exclusively on energy generated from imported petroleum. The balance of payments tilted massively against Brazil, and Geisel took emergency measures to cope. He expanded oil exploration and authorized foreign companies to participate. He ordered three nuclear generators from Westinghouse. He pushed construction of the Itaipú dam, the world's largest hydroelectric plant at the time. The economy, meanwhile, entered a period of jagged ups and downs as it adjusted to expensive energy, rising inflation, shifting employment, and irregular consumer demand.

Geisel found himself criticized from an unexpected quarter in 1977 when U.S. president Jimmy Carter decried violations of human rights in Brazil. Irked by this censure and by a refusal by the U.S. Atomic Energy Commission to ship test fuel for the Westinghouse reactors, Geisel broke the twenty-five-year military alliance with the United States and signed a $10 billion deal with Germany for the transfer of advanced nuclear technology. Brazilian-U.S. relations later recovered, but never were as close as in the late 1960s.

Geisel was unable to round up enough support among military leaders to facilitate the transition to a civilian successor, so he chose a colleague willing to commit himself to continuing the democratization process, by then called *abertura,* or opening. General João Figueiredo governed from 1979 until 1985, when he turned the office over to civilians. Like his predecessors, Figueiredo avoided the limelight and served as caretaker. He disliked politics and public appearances, yet he never wavered from his commitment to abertura. This opening allowed for a surge of labor and student activism in the late 1970s. Brazil's industrial workers organized en masse for the first time to demand higher pay after years of stagnant wages and high inflation. In 1979, over 170,000 metalworkers staged a protest in São Paulo, forcing the government to intervene. Violence ensued and arrests followed, though protests continued throughout the year until the government finally agreed to a new law that legalized direct union-management negotiations and called for regular wage adjustments. During the protest, the metalworkers had been led by a then little-known leader, Luiz Inacio da Silva, or Lula. Though he faced arrest in the aftermath, the movement led to the creation of the Workers' Party in Brazil, which soon would be one of the country's most powerful parties.

When his term expired, Figueiredo allowed Congress to select a civilian president. Protests calling for direct elections (*diretas já*) swept the nation but foundered on an army veto. Instead, through indirect elections in early 1985, Congress chose a veteran politician from the center of the ideological spectrum, Tancredo Neves. The last votes necessary to give Neves a majority came from the tiny Liberal Party, led by the little-known José Sarney. Sarney won the vice-presidential nod in exchange for his support.

The final transition from military to civilian rule contained both high drama and pathos. On the eve of his inauguration, Tancredo Neves fell ill and was operated on for an intestinal disorder. For ten days he fought off fevers and infections while Brazilians prayed for his recovery. Ultimately, he lapsed into a coma from which he never recovered. He was buried amid tremendous honors, regarded as a hero for having steered the country from military to civilian rule. The tragedy lay in his being denied a chance to preside over the restored democracy. Instead, Sarney donned the presidential sash in 1985.

## Chile

Chile's military planners and policymakers had long been worried about the leftward drift of Chilean politics. Since 1958 a socialist doctor-politician, Salvador Allende, had enjoyed a growing reputation for leadership and coalition building among center-left parties and factions. He came close to winning the 1964 election and was thwarted only by a last-minute deal between moderates and conservatives and by U.S. aid to his opponents. Allende himself may not have been a threat, but the communists, socialists, Maoists, and others in his camp were certainly anathema to Chile's conservatives and military authorities.

To the army, the salvation of Chile seemed to ride on the shoulders of the capable and popular leader of the Christian Democrats, Eduardo Frei (1964–1970). After winning the presidency with a campaign called Revolution in Liberty, Frei pursued a set of policies in line with the goals of the U.S. Alliance for Progress that brought major reforms in the economy, government, political system, and social institutions. He claimed that he could check the leftward trend of voter preferences by instituting progressive reforms. He enacted a land reform program and legalized rural cooperatives and unions. He "Chileanized" the foreign copper-mining giants by making the government the principal shareholder in these enterprises. He brought down inflation rates and attracted substantial new foreign investment. Health and educational programs expanded substantially. In short, Frei accomplished a remarkable array of reforms that benefited the lower classes. This was especially important during the Cold War, since Chile's combination of strong mining and industrial unions and a poverty rate around 50 percent could make Marxism especially appealing. In some senses, in the 1960s, Chile stood apart from its neighbors in the Southern Cone, where guerrilla groups and military rule increasingly consumed public life: its democracy seemed secure, economic stability and reform were in place, its revolutionary left seemed tamed by its inclusion in broader political coalitions, and its military remained in the barracks.

Many analysts believe that Frei's success led to his undoing because increased services and benefits only whetted people's appetites and fueled rising expectations for more. By the same token, the rapid pace of change frightened conservative voters, who shifted their support from Frei's Christian Democratic Party to the National Party ticket, headed by former president Jorge Alessandri, son of former president Arturo.

In the 1970 election, voters split three ways but gave a plurality (36.5 percent) to Salvador Allende, who was backed by a broad coalition of center and leftist parties that joined in the Popular Unity (UP). This important election attracted clandestine monies from foreign governments, including the United States and to a lesser extent Cuba.

The Chilean military had a strong tradition of professionalism and disengagement from politics. Its last full interventions had taken place in 1924 and

1925, when the army took power, instituted social and constitutional reforms, and handed the presidency to Arturo Alessandri. Since that time, Chile had enjoyed a reputation for authentic democracy, though recent research has revealed the sporadic repression of labor movements in the twentieth century. After the 1970 election, however, the military became increasingly involved in politics, culminating in its coup d'etat of September 1973. This usurpation of constitutional authority was one of the central and tragic moments of modern Chilean history, although it seemed not entirely unpredictable, given Allende's record between 1970 and 1973 and concerted U.S. efforts to unseat him.

Even before Allende's inauguration, the U.S. tried to keep him from taking office with a two-pronged strategy: on one side it unsuccessfully tried to manipulate Chile's Congress to prevent it from confirming Allende's election to office, and on the other, it encouraged and backed middle-ranking military officers to stage a coup that would prevent him from taking office. The plot went awry, though, and resulted in the death of a high-ranking general. The plotters failed to derail Allende's inauguration and later revealed that the U.S. CIA had encouraged them.

The U.S. government, meanwhile, continued to work against Allende, alleging that he constituted a threat to Western Hemisphere security. Even before Allende took office, U.S. president Richard Nixon, in an effort to destabilize Allende, ordered the CIA to do all it could to "make the economy scream."[2]

Allende had not misled the voters during the campaign: he promised that if elected he would nationalize major banks and insurance companies, the copper giants, and the telephone and electric power industries. These involved two hundred of the largest firms in the nation, including most U.S.-owned companies. He also pledged to extend the vote to illiterates and to carry out a much bolder land distribution program. Finally, in perhaps his greatest defiance of the U.S., he would recognize Cuba and carry on friendly relations with all nations, including communist and socialist ones. Once in office, he began to effect these changes, using the constitutional means at his disposal as president. He also raised the minimum wage so that workers received a 50 percent increase in real income.

At first, the citizenry and economy responded warmly to Allende's program, and it appeared that his "peaceful road to socialism" would succeed. Factory output rose when workers spent their larger share of national income on consumer goods. Congress approved the measures necessary to nationalize major sectors of the economy. In the April 1971 municipal elections, pro-Allende candidates won 50 percent of the votes. In the second year, however, the scene changed considerably, and Allende had to struggle to keep his government on track. Opposition parties cooperated to block his measures, U.S. vetoes cut off international loans, U.S. trade embargoes cut off replacement parts, large landowners and industrialists slowed production to sabotage the economy, and the economy began to contract. Worse, organizations of workers, employers, housewives, peasants, and other groups began to protest policies unfavorable to their interests.

Some, like conservative housewife groups, protested shortages that arose due to production shortfalls, higher demand by the working class, and the emergence of a thriving black market. Indeed, women became important opponents of Allende. With his focus on a predominantly male working class and peasant labor force, he largely excluded women. Facing rationing and price controls, and surrounded by U.S.-backed propaganda that portrayed Allende's socialism as the first step toward the destruction of the Chilean family, they came out strongly against him.

In one well-known demonstration in December 1971, tens of thousands of middle- and upper-class women demonstrated in the streets in what became known as the March of the Empty Pots. Center-right women's groups also worked to stop the state takeover of grocery stores, staged numerous public demonstrations, and even took over pro-Allende radio stations. Always drawing on their roles as wives and mothers, they tried to provoke and even ridicule the military into taking action to save the Chilean family and nation.[3]

Even Allende's strongest supporters were a source of disruption, however. Unions and peasant groups challenged the pace of Allende's reforms and demanded faster change. Some branched out on their own, invading lands and factories before given approval by Allende, thereby radicalizing his socialist experiment and leading to increasingly unwise economic policies. Public order dropped precipitously and the political center disappeared as middle-class moderates turned away from Allende. Moreover, while Allende faced the meddling of the U.S. and increasingly Brazil, he refused to ally fully with Castro, insisting that Chile was on its own democratic path to socialism, La Vía Chilena.

Leftist groups also began to chafe under the limits of La Vía Chilena. The Revolutionary Left Movement (MIR) was a political and guerrilla organization that had offered some support to Allende at his election but increasingly found itself at odds with the reformist nature of his government. By 1973, it had grown to about ten thousand members and backers and had become a concern to the Chilean military and conservatives. Beyond the MIR, other more radical leftist groups engaged in well-publicized terrorist acts against the military and conservatives, prompting counterinsurgency operations by the military.

Allende, meanwhile, carried on with his reforms, and Popular Unity won support from 44 percent of the voters in the March 1973 congressional elections. Society had become increasingly polarized between those who supported Allende and those who did not. At best, the country faced government gridlock; at worst, it would plunge into civil war.

In mid-1973 army chief of staff general Augusto Pinochet began to organize a coup against Allende. He chose his allies carefully and sidelined those he did not trust. When the time came, on September 11, 1973, Pinochet mobilized his forces and surrounded the presidential palace. After nearly a day of skirmish-

**Figure 23.4** Following the Pinochet coup, Isabel Allende took up exile in Venezuela with her family. Her 1982 novel, *The House of the Spirits*, an international best seller, established her as a leading feminist voice in Spanish-American fiction. Today she is Latin America's most widely read author, with over 65 million copies sold. She has lived in California since 1988. Courtesy Isabel Allende.

ing and aerial bombardment, the army stormed the palace. Amid the attack, Allende died, likely by committing suicide, after giving a final radio address to the nation earlier in the day.

Pinochet took power with the support of the majority of Chileans, who thought the military's rule would be temporary. Pinochet ruled with a three-man junta for months before assuming power as sole head of state in June 1974. Throughout 1973 and 1974, the army and police carried out a drastic campaign to eradicate leftists. DINA, the National Intelligence Directorate, proved the most brutal and feared agency of repression. Pinochet formed DINA in November 1973 and it served as a sort of secret police under his rule. Tens of thousands of Allende sympathizers fled the country into exile. Thousands who stayed perished at the hands of the police, in torture chambers and in jails. The army pursued guerrilla groups in the mountains and soon eliminated or drove them into exile. Political freedoms and civil rights, long the pride of Chile, virtually disappeared. The 1982 movie *Missing*, starring Jack Lemmon, dramatized some of these events for American audiences, as did later films like Isabel Allende's *Love in the Shadows* (1996).

Some of the most virulent repression targeted leftist intellectuals, writers, and performers. Within days of the coup, the military had rounded up and imprisoned thousands of professors, students, and other members of the cultural left. One of the most notorious cases was the abduction, torture, and murder of folk singer, composer, and university teacher Víctor Jara. As a leader of the Chilean New Song movement in the late 1960s, Jara and others transformed the sound of popular music, introducing socially committed themes that, like other global folk movements, focused on love, peace, and justice while challenging poverty, imperialism, and human rights abuses. Jara had supported Allende and even composed the Popular Unity theme song "We Will Triumph," used when Allende ran for office. Arrested on September 12, 1973,

---

### Torture at Villa Grimaldi

In 1975, a young Chilean, Pedro Alejandro Matta, then in his third year of law school, was dragged into a living nightmare, the Pinochet regime's torture chamber at the Villa Grimaldi. This villa outside Santiago became a horror chamber, filled with cruelty, suffering, and death. The chilling account of survivor Pedro Alejandro Matta reminds us of how deep political differences can dissolve the fabric of civility and democracy:

> I felt them take me by the ankles and drag me out by the legs from the auto in which they brought me. Afterwards, they threw me on a blanket and picked it up by the ends to carry me. . . . A few moments later, they shoved me into what I thought was a crypt of some sort, cold floor, very cold, and dark, and I calmly awaited my death, my eyes blindfolded, the way they brought me in. . . . I thought that after the last two days, of indescribable torture, they finally heard my pleas to kill me once and for all, and so they put me in this crypt. . . . I could, finally, die in peace. . . . However, it was not to be, they had taken me to the Villa Grimaldi, as I later learned, and the crypt I thought I was in was the bunk in a cell two meters high, two meters long, and a little over a meter wide, without light or ventilation, big enough only to hold the bunk on which I lay. I was alone. Later, when I recovered a bit physically, I learned that the Villa Grimaldi was kind of like an assembly line of torture instruments. They were applied in sequence, gradually increasing in severity and intensity. As another survivor described it once: to start with an area of possible death—blows and electric torture, "the grill"—then, one arrived at an area of probable death—isolation rooms, "the dry submarine," "the wet submarine," burns, "the telephone," hangings by the arms folded backwards; and, finally, one arrived at an area of near certain death—trucks crushing one's legs, death by immersion, and lashes with chains.
>
> The final product of this macabre assembly line was a human being destroyed . . ., or dead.

Pedro Alejandro Matta, presentation at a School of the Americas military training session, May 1975; included by permission.

---

he was brutally beaten, shot multiple times, and dumped on the street by military forces on September 15.

Like the other national security states, Pinochet's Chile instituted censorship, citizen surveillance, and martial law. The army closed universities and suspended political activity. A cloud descended over Chile. In fact, by 1976 all of the Southern Cone was under military rule. Coordinated efforts throughout the region, code-named Operation Condor, encouraged military leaders in Brazil, Argentina, Chile, Bolivia, Paraguay, and Uruguay to share intelligence and to return fleeing leftists to face punishment at home. They also carried out assassinations and disappearances of leftists from their own and other Southern Cone countries in order to suppress leftist activism.

Backed by technical support and military aid from the U.S., they targeted not just guerrillas but also leftist students and teachers, union and peasant activists, and sympathetic priests and nuns. Indigenous Chileans suffered as well. Efforts by Mapuche Indians in the south of Chile to keep their lands and sell their wares was met with sharp opposition from conservative landowners. Backed by the Pinochet regime, which saw the Mapuche people as under communist influence, the landowners and military harassed the Mapuche using intimidation and repression, forcing them into even harsher lands further south. Others experienced repression due to their membership in unions or political parties. More than one hundred Mapuche Indians were killed or disappeared. Chile's truth and reconciliation commission, formed after the end of military rule in the early 1990s, concluded that the Mapuche Indians had faced "extreme cruelty," and the Inter-Church Committee on Human Rights in Latin America stated that they had been "pursued . . . simply because they were Indians."[4] In the context of the Cold War, indigenous identities and practices were often recast as subversive.

Pinochet claimed that economic disorder had been a major reason for his coup, and he quickly set out to reorganize and reprivatize the economy. As in the rest of the region, Chile received a strong dose of austerity medicine to bring down inflation, break strikes, shrink government payrolls, eliminate subsidies, and raise taxes and fees for government services. To accomplish these goals, Pinochet put the economy in the hands of people trained in orthodox, free-market economics, many of whom held Ph.D. degrees from the University of Chicago. They attempted not only to revive free enterprise capitalism but also to prove that laissez-faire economics work in the real world. Critics came to call them the Chicago Boys because of their doctrinal zeal.

Chile experienced severe economic contraction from 1973 until about 1978, as credit dried up, companies large and small went bankrupt, and nationalized firms (except copper) were returned to their former owners. Income again became concentrated, and high unemployment was tolerated as a necessary by-product of the recovery process. Of note, many seized agricultural lands were not returned to former landowners but rather were converted into profitable agro-export ventures, most notably grapes.

For many poor and working-class Chileans, the dictatorship was a period of want; while Pinochet promoted mass consumption of items like appliances and cars, many Chileans continued to struggle to provide food and shelter for their families.[5] In the early years after Pinochet took power, and when political parties and unions were shut down and men were more often targeted for repression if they were publicly active, women's groups stepped into the void to meet society's needs. As in many women's movements of both the left and the right during the years of dictatorship in the Southern Cone, they used maternalism to forge movements that worked for change. They formed communal kitchens, sewing workshops, and shopping collectives, and joined forces to help other families build homes, provide food and shelter, and care for their children. While presenting themselves as apolitical mothers and wives, these maternalist activities nevertheless pointed to the failure of the military state to provide for many Chileans. From 1978 to 1980, the economy grew at robust rates, seemingly vindicating the Chicago Boys' approach. Then the 1980 recession struck and brought the economy to a standstill again. Finally, from the mid-1980s on the Chilean economy performed very well, fueled by strong capital flows from abroad, aggressive export promotion, a well-managed fiscal system, and investments in infrastructure. Yet the growth left many behind.

In terms of repression, Dirty War tactics, economic orthodoxy, anticommunist foreign policies, and conservative social policy, Chile's military regime resembled the other national security states. It differed in one respect, however: Pinochet stayed in power for the entire seventeen years of military rule. He assumed the role of exalted leader and savior of the country, unlike his Brazilian and Argentine counterparts. He gave his regime the sacred task of purifying the citizenry and political system. He allied with the Catholic Church (a staunch foe of Allende) and proclaimed divine sanction for his actions. Pinochet ran a one-man dictatorship.

According to his own constitution, Pinochet was to step down in 1989. Because of his success in bringing about economic growth, however, he believed that the citizenry wanted him to remain in power. Therefore, he ordered a plebiscite in 1988: Should he step down or continue in power another eight years? What he did not realize was how widespread opposition to him had become. In a unique reversal, in May 1983, Chile's copper miners union called for a national protest and staged its own empty pots protest to draw attention to the regime's continued failure to provide enough jobs, income, housing, and food for many Chileans. And, although conservative women continued to be a backbone of Pinochet's rule, other women's groups were among the most vocal in opposing him by the 1980s. They faced the repression, fear, and economic crisis that had plagued his regime with protests, meetings, and hunger strikes throughout the 1980s. Chile also witnessed a blossoming feminist movement at this time, demanding democracy and women's full political inclusion.

When the votes were cast, a solid 55 percent opposed Pinochet's continuing in power, so he stepped aside and allowed elections for a civilian successor. A 2012 movie, *No,* starring Gael García Bernal, tells the exciting story of how young people mounted the successful plebiscite, which amounted to a recall. In 1989 Christian Democratic leader Patricio Aylwin won a four-year term. Thus ended Chile's national security state—with an election.

Pinochet retained his post as commander-in-chief of the armed forces, however, and continued to monitor politics from his army headquarters until 1998. Then he took up a seat he had designated for himself in the national Senate, despite protests from his opponents. He was eventually indicted in a Spanish court on genocide charges and detained in England to be extradited. He was later arraigned in Chilean courts on human rights abuses and other crimes, but died before his trial.

## Uruguay

From early in the twentieth century, Uruguay gained an enviable reputation for the most democratic politics and progressive social policies in the hemisphere. It was known as the Switzerland of South America. Even when partisan strife and economic difficulties beset the country in the 1960s, few observers believed that Uruguay could succumb to military dictatorship. The democratic tradition was simply too strong.

But three factors undermined democracy and plunged Uruguay into a military regime that was as repressive as those of the national security states of neighboring Argentina and Brazil. First, the stable, state-subsidized, egalitarian society—forged during the 1910s and 1920s under the leadership of don Pepe Batlle—had become unaffordable given Uruguay's tiny economy. By the 1960s politics had degenerated into a fight for spoils in a quasi-socialist economy. This widespread insecurity fostered a vicious scramble for public office to control government patronage for one or another special interest group. The entire focus of politics was on distribution, not production. Uruguay bankrupted itself and poisoned its civic culture in the process.

Second, in response to the escalating partisan conflict in Uruguay, dissidents formed guerrilla groups, and for the first time in generations terrorism surfaced on the streets of Montevideo. The foremost guerrilla group, the Tupamaros, first appeared in 1963 and by 1967 enjoyed extraordinary success. The Tupamaros, named after an eighteenth-century Inca revolutionary, Túpac Amaru II (see chapter 1), combined well-planned military strikes with brilliant publicity stressing their activism supporting the working class. The already crumbling government put up an ineffectual resistance, while the army increasingly assumed authority. The resultant power vacuum in Montevideo worried the military leadership, especially at a time when rebel forces in many parts of the world were gaining the upper hand.

Third, Uruguay fell under military rule because of outside pressure. Brazil and Argentina, governed by army generals who campaigned to strengthen national security in the region, encouraged their Uruguayan counterparts to join them in exercising power. Uruguay's civilian leaders simply could not resist the pressure from within and without. A spate of assassinations by guerrilla forces in April 1972 led the military to assert its control over civilian authorities. The army pressured the new president, Juan Bordaberry, and Congress to declare a state of internal war so that it could carry out a full-scale counterinsurgency operation. Civilians acquiesced, and the army soon achieved a number of important victories against the guerrillas.

President Bordaberry, meanwhile, became a virtual captive of the army, unable to tamp down the growing struggle. A year later, when congressional leaders tried to rein in the military, the latter closed Congress, and the government became a military dictatorship. Bordaberry went along with the fiction that he governed. When his term was about to end in 1976, the military simply removed him.

The military established a regime in which its terrorism replaced that of the Tupamaros without any pretense of benefiting the working classes. In a little over a year, the military rooted out the principal leaders of the guerrilla organizations and murdered them. The military arrested, tortured, and killed large numbers of citizens in the process. The army used the same methods that had proven successful in Argentina and Brazil. By 1979 political prisoners made up 1 percent of the population (the highest ratio in the world), and another 17 percent lived in exile.

Uruguay's military regime did not produce a single leader like Pinochet of Chile. Its generals remained anonymous and unforgiving in their purge of leftists and opponents. They adopted neoliberal economic policies designed to prune government payrolls and reduce spending, and the economy sank deeper into stagflation. The general standard of living fell to pre–World War II levels.

In order to update the constitution in 1980, the army conducted a referendum on a proposed constitution that allowed strong military participation in most aspects of government. Despite heavy spending by proponents of the proposed constitution, citizens voted it down by a wide margin, signaling their repudiation of army rule. Rebuffed by the vote, the army began a process of gradual democratization that culminated in the 1984 election of a civilian president, Julio Sanguinetti (1985–1990, 1995–2000).

## Peru

Peru's government had wavered from right to center, and from dictators to populists, since the 1930s. The elite preferred autocratic regimes, elected or not, that could keep the indigenous and mestizo masses under control. By most social and economic indices, Peru trailed far behind the rest of the continent. Political leaders, however, had little interest in reforms, much less in revolution.

Beginning in 1963, however, newly elected president Fernando Belaúnde Terry devoted more than just lip service to reforms in the Peruvian economy and society. An architect by training and pro–United States by temperament, Belaúnde set out to achieve some of the goals of the Alliance for Progress. The platform of his party, Popular Action, included land reform, improved tax collection, more housing, better farming methods, industrialization, schools, and so forth. Leading Peruvian analysts and foreign observers alike hailed Belaúnde's program as progressive.

The land distribution program was narrow, however, and focused mostly on the Amazon region, where colonists were supposed to start profitable farms. But virtually none was successful because of the lack of knowledge and investment by the colonists. Meanwhile, huge plantations and ranches in the populated regions went untouched.

In the capital of Lima, Belaúnde, who was a U.S.-trained architect and had a long history in urban planning and public housing, undertook a public housing program to alleviate the suffering of hundreds of thousands of squatters who lived in shantytowns, or barriadas, on the outskirts. But as elsewhere in Latin America, population growth and urbanization outstripped the expansion of public services in cities in this period. Shantytowns therefore became permanent fixtures in Lima, where rural poor and highland indigenous people resettled as they sought opportunities in the city.

Had Belaúnde succeeded with these and other initiatives, Peru would have been a different place. His plans were ambitious but ran head-on into the unwillingness of the elite to give up its wealth and privileges. Congress, meanwhile, watered down or blocked much of his legislation, and the economy stagnated, leading to higher unemployment. The enthusiasm that had greeted Belaúnde at first now turned to disaffection.

Peru's military leaders had given some thought to the changing nature of their national defense requirements in the Cold War. An army think tank, CAEM, had come up with a blueprint for a stronger economy and reinforced institutions, called Plan Inca. Still, the army had little stomach for meddling in politics. Its long history, studded with defeats at the hands of foreigners, contrasted with periods in which the army ruled the nation poorly.

The army found itself drawn into politics, however, by a dispute over petroleum rights in 1968. The International Petroleum Corporation (IPC), a medium-sized production and refining operation owned by Standard Oil of New Jersey, negotiated a contract with Belaúnde that allowed for nationalization of an installation in return for a payment. High-handed tactics by the company had long offended Peruvian nationalists, however, and Congress refused to ratify the contract when it learned of the payment. Scandalized by Belaúnde's inept negotiations and the company's attitudes, a high-ranking officer, Juan Velasco Alvarado (1968–1975), mobilized his troops and seized power. He immediately nationalized the IPC and renamed it Petroperu amid great public rejoicing.

Counter to the conservative policies of military governments in other areas of South America, military strategists in Peru reasoned that they might counterbalance their poor historical record and reduce popular discontent by presiding over a positive, constructive period at the helm of government. Because civilians had proven themselves unable to reform society and the economy, the army would do it for them.

**Figure 23.5** General Juan Velasco Alvarado, president of Peru from 1968 to 1975, led the Peruvian Institutional Revolution, which ousted president Fernando Belaúnde Terry and started Peru on a nationalistic course. This included nationalization of major foreign-owned properties and widespread reform programs, such as the expropriation and redistribution of land. Courtesy Dutch National Archives, Wiki Commons.

General Velasco showed a certain flair for leadership when he assumed the role of president. No aspect of the country's life escaped his attention. Widespread land reform proved one of his most popular undertakings. He created a new agency to confiscate 350,000 acres owned by the U.S. firm operating the Cerro de Pasco copper mine. The miners themselves were invited to take up farming there to raise their standard of living.

The next phase of land reform targeted the coastal plantations of the north, where sugar and cotton estates had operated since colonial times. These were converted into communal farms operated by and for the workers. Union leaders assumed the lead in converting these businesses into cooperatives. In a short time they adjusted and produced solid profits for the unions. They were hailed as a great success.

The land reform agency then turned to other extensive highland estates, the backbone of the old landed elite. Expropriation followed a different path here. In some cases, expropriated lands were turned into state-run farms, frustrating expectations and leading to conflicts and even land seizures. In other cases, after lands were expropriated, they were subdivided into self-sufficient small-holds, termed *minifundias* by the new peasant owners. This withdrew crops and animals from the market and resulted in food shortages in the cities. In all, land reform redistributed 13 million acres, a creditable if uneven record.

Velasco then turned his attention to other sectors of the economy. He created an industrial development agency, Induperu, to stimulate greater production and self-sufficiency. Fishing fleets and fishmeal processing plants were converted to cooperative ownership under Pescaperu and continued to prosper for several years. Domestic banks and insurance companies were partially nationalized. Some of the mines, meanwhile, were consolidated into a public enterprise called Mineroperu. It enjoyed strong profits because of high world prices for minerals. The military also nationalized railroads, telecommunications, coastal navigation, and electric power.

In order to make his administration a true revolution rather than a mere stewardship of the economy, Velasco sponsored a program called SINAMOS to build grassroots participation and support for the army's objectives. Neither a party nor a publicity campaign, SINAMOS sought to create a new sense of citizenship among the common people. It envisioned self-help programs, literacy, voter registration drives, small-scale cooperatives, and public debate on the destiny of the nation. Government representatives formed community groups, which then federated into local, state, and national associations. SINAMOS intended to give Peruvians a sense of pride in their nation and of participation in the revolutionary process. Parallel institutions provided radio and press communications among local and regional groups.

The regime tried to change elite prejudices against the indigenous population by using new, more inclusive language in government publications. It stipulated that the term *indio*, traditionally pejorative in Peru, would henceforth be changed to *campesino*, meaning peasant. The shantytowns were to be renamed *pueblos jóvenes* (new townships). For a time the terminology seemed to catch on. The traditional monetary unit, the *sol*, was renamed *inti*, a native word. Even traditional street names were altered to emphasize Peruvian themes. For example, Avenida Woodrow Wilson became Avenida Garcilaso de la Vega after a famous Inca chronicler. In 1976, after Velasco left office, Quechua was recognized as an official language in heavily indigenous areas. This effort to foster a more inclusive vision of the nation was especially important, since indigenous people made up close to one-half of the population.

To stress the innovative character of his government, Velasco forged an independent foreign policy as well. Eschewing the traditional Cold War alliance with the United States, he struck up relations with Cuba, Chile, and China. He purchased a wing of MiG fighters from the USSR and another of Mirages from France. He declared that Peru would no longer abide by the orthodox rules of the World Bank and the International Monetary Fund. He also took belligerent stances toward Peru's traditional enemies, Ecuador and Chile, by stationing troops and aircraft on their common borders. The United

States, meanwhile, went along with Velasco, reasoning that he was not as hostile as Fidel Castro or Salvador Allende and served as a counterpoise to communist expansion.

For nearly five years General Velasco could do no wrong. His nationalized companies reported profits, inflation was down, export earnings were up, his popularity was high, and no one put up much opposition to the government. Foreign observers were fascinated with what Velasco called the Peruvian Institutional Revolution. Fidel Castro reportedly said that for the military to carry out socialist reforms was like firefighters starting a blaze in their own firehouse. The military regime was not Marxist, not repressive, and not bankrupt. It did not commit the terrible excesses of the other military regimes in the region at that time. Many began to tout this unique experiment as a model for other modernizing countries. To be sure, the army administered top-down change, but it seemed to work.

But in 1974 things began to go sour for Velasco. His own health faltered, and doctors amputated his leg. He became irritable with aides and colleagues. The SINAMOS program did not move Peru any closer to real participatory democracy, and some politicians now dared to criticize him for not holding elections. Even worse, the economic success stories of preceding years turned into debacles. In a short time, the rich fishing grounds off Peru's coast turned barren due to long-term climatic shifts, and the fishing fleet had to be put into mothballs. World prices for minerals plummeted when the Vietnam War wound down, and Mineroperu began to post serious losses. Adjustments to wages and dividends angered workers, who began to protest. Layoffs provoked demonstrations. Meanwhile, Petroperu had run short of crude oil to refine and issued contracts for international companies to explore for new fields. This seemed to violate the nationalist stance that the government had taken with IPC and caused considerable opposition. On the positive side of the ledger, though, companies found high-quality crude on the eastern slopes of the Andes.

Velasco, who had reveled in his early successes, proved inept in dealing with his failures. Poor health made it impossible for him to carry on the duties of president. An associate, General Francisco Morales Bermúdez, deposed him in 1975. Morales could see the ship of state, heavily indebted (US$5 billion), sinking, so he announced his intention of allowing more political participation. Implicitly admitting that SINAMOS had failed to generate public support, he began to govern more by decree and repression. With the economy shrinking, Morales fired his leftist advisors and instituted a program of austerity to appease international bankers. Peru began to resemble the other national security states.

Just as Morales executed this turn to the right in 1976, however, Velasco died. During the state funeral, hundreds of thousands of people paid homage to him and used the occasion to demonstrate against recent policy shifts. Protesters actually stole the coffin and proclaimed that the government did not deserve to possess his remains. Morales then changed direction again, hoping to win back support, but it was too late. By 1977 he announced that the military would remove itself from power as soon as a constitution could be adopted and elections held. Morales did not have Velasco's flair for leadership nor his faith in the destiny of the Peruvian revolution. His administration proved to be a major disappointment and only added to the army's reputation for mismanagement.

The Peruvian regime differed from the other national security states. First, Velasco played a leading role, like Pinochet, but he did not have the staying power of his Chilean counterpart. Second, the nationalizations seemed to be largely opportunistic moves driven by whim and public opinion polls, not guided by doctrine or carefully laid-out plans. Likewise, no sustained effort transformed popularity into lasting support for the regime, much less for the army. When Velasco exited, the whole experiment collapsed around him. Despite attempts at popular reforms and a more inclusive vision of the nation, Peru still remained divided socially and politically.

The army's retreat from power smacks of irony. The army's bête noire, Haya de la Torre, won the job of presiding over a constitutional convention in 1978 for the purpose of restoring civilian rule. Fernando Belaúnde Terry won the election held in 1980, to replace the military that had ousted him in 1968. He won by promising to undo the harm and distortions introduced by military rule. Although no strong guerrilla movement existed prior to military rule, during Velasco's administration one of the most treacherous and powerful insurgencies of all time arose in Peru—Sendero Luminoso (Shining Path). In the end, like the Argentine army, Peru's was discredited by its mismanagement and exited office largely in disgrace, leaving it to Belaúnde to deal with the rise of one of the most challenging rebellions in Peru's history.

## CONCLUSIONS AND ISSUES

The national security states outlined in this chapter differed from earlier military dictatorships. They arose out of a tidal shift in defense missions brought on by the Cold War. They pursued programs and ideologies developed in army think tanks. They reflected the professionalization of militaries across the regions and created formal structures of power and recruited many officers into public service. They sought to clean up corruption and inefficiencies that had plagued civilian governments. They also tried to purge society of leftist activists seen as dangerous to their mission of conservative order and economic growth. In fact, the wave of terror against the citizenry dominates our memory of that era. Even the relatively benign Peruvian regime did not escape accusations of abuse.

The national security states arose out of domestic politics in each country, but they also fit into regional and global trends. The Cold War set the stage for military intrusions into government, while the Cuban Revolution and the Vietnam War hoisted warning flags against guerrilla movements. Internal rebellion certainly heightened the sense of peril among army officers and convinced them to act in concert to eliminate the danger.

After the officers were in control, other demands kept them from renouncing power until they had worn out their welcomes. Finally, most were institutional governments, not the work of a single leader or a small group. Armies as organizations took power and later relinquished it, usually hounded out by civilians.

## Discussion Questions

How did the national security regimes of the 1960s–1980s differ from the dictatorships of earlier times?

Were military regimes somehow "contagious" in the 1960s, spreading from country to country? How might that have happened?

What were 1960s and 1970s leftists pursuing as they challenged political authorities? What were their demands and why?

Why and how did women's movements become important political and social actors during the military regimes of the 1960s–1980s?

What restraints kept the Brazilian military from closing democratic government and committing atrocities at the level of their colleagues in Argentina and Chile?

Why and how did the United States play a larger role in the military coming to power in Chile than in neighboring countries? What outcomes did that have?

What accounts for the different ways the militaries exited from power in South America? How similar were the causes of their exits?

How could Uruguay, the Switzerland of South America, succumb to military government in the 1970s?

Which came first, the guerrilla movements or the military regimes? Support your position with reference to at least three national histories.

## Timeline

| | |
|---|---|
| 1947–89 | Cold War between the United States and the USSR |
| 1955 | Argentine military overthrows President Juan Perón |
| 1962 | Argentine military overthrows President Arturo Frondizi |
| 1964–85 | Brazilian military overthrows President João Goulart, setting up permanent regime |
| 1968–79 | Peruvian government mishandles nationalization of foreign oil company; military establishes permanent regime under General Juan Velasco Alvarado |
| 1972 | Uruguayan military exercises control over President Juan Bordaberry |
| 1972 | Uruguayan military disbands Congress, asserting authority over president from behind the scenes, to extricate revolutionaries |
| 1973–89 | Chilean military overthrows President Salvador Allende, setting up permanent regime |

| 1974 | General Ernesto Geisel begins process of returning power to civilians in Brazil |
| --- | --- |
| 1975 | General Francisco Morales Bermúdez deposes Alvarado in Peru, convoking constitutional assembly elections two years later for transition to civilian government |
| 1975–89 | Operation Condor in Southern Cone |
| 1976–83 | Argentine military regime; Dirty War against leftists |
| 1976–84 | Uruguayan military presides over the nation without restraints |
| 1977 | Mothers of Plaza de Mayo formed in Argentina |
| 1980 | Fernando Belaúnde Terry elected president for four-year term in Peru |
| 1982 | Argentine military invades the Malvinas/Falkland Islands; defeated by British |
| 1983 | Raúl Alfonsín elected president of Argentina, replacing military rule |
| 1984 | Uruguayan elections lead to civilian government under Julio Sanguinetti |
| 1985 | General João Figueiredo restores power to civilian government in Brazil |
| 1988 | Plebiscite in Chile ousts Pinochet, leading to elections following year |

## Keywords

bureaucratic authoritarianism
Dirty War
Islas Malvinas, or Falkland Islands
La Vía Chilena
Mothers of Plaza de Mayo
National Intelligence Directorate (DINA)
National Security Doctrine

nationalization
Operation Condor
Peruvian Institutional Revolution
Popular Action
Popular Unity (UP)
Shining Path
Workers' Party

# Democratization and Conflict in the Late Twentieth Century

CHAPTER

24

### A New Religious Passion

Beginning in the 1980s, membership in evangelical Protestant churches exploded in Latin America, growing so fast that in many regions they now have more followers than the Catholic Church. The process was not so much conversion as spiritualization, for most new adherents were practicing religion for the first time. They tended to be poorer, of mixed racial and cultural heritage, and with little formal education. Yet their fervor astonished observers and spurred many to study this outburst of religiosity in a region where Catholicism was long thought to hold a monopoly. One such study recorded the words of a man in Belém, Brazil, telling of his conversion and a healing in the Assembly of God:

> The doors began to close; things were bad. My wife got sick and couldn't do anything at home. She suffered a lot with that swelling of her face. The swelling just got worse and worse. It was then that I had a revelation, when I was working at the hospital for minimum wage. And the Lord spoke to me saying this: "Your wife's cure depends on you." I said, "What do you mean, Lord?" It was a Sunday, the second Sunday of April, 1981. . . . I said, "Is that really you, Lord, speaking to me? If it is you, and you are the master of truth, if you are the savior of the world like people say you are, and you heal, I want you to take me to the place where your truth exists, and there I will accept you as my savior." . . . And He went ahead, with me following.
>
> I arrived home, and my wife was lying in the hammock. That was when I told her I was going to church to accept Jesus Christ as my savior, and she said, "I'll go with you." I said, "You're sick; you can't," and she said, "No, I'm going."
>
> So I arrived here (in the church), and when I went in they were singing that Hymn Number 15. Then the whole congregation stood up, and I said, "I want to accept Jesus as my savior." They all knew that I was a very hardened man when it

came to the gospel. I had a bad reputation. And so the whole church stood up and the pastor said, "Let us pray for this citizen who wants to accept Jesus as savior." At that moment great power filled the church, but I didn't recognize it. . . . A week later my wife's face had returned to normal.[1]

The powerful strains of Pentecostal Protestantism promoted stability in family life, encouraged personal responsibility, and spawned self-help organizations across Latin America. Notwithstanding this force for improving morality and duty within society, the rise of self-help groups and other types of civic organizations reflected much larger changes occurring in Latin America as the century came to a close. The year 1980 marked a watershed in Latin America's modern history, the beginning of two difficult and tumultuous decades.

The national security states of South America were on the defensive, with some tracking toward restoration of power to civilians. Most guerrilla operations had been shut down, and public opinion ran solidly against military government. Oil prices slumped, hurting producers Venezuela, Mexico, and Ecuador, but doing little to help the oil-importing nations. Generalized inflation in the 1970s had pushed interest rates into double digits, making it difficult for Latin American nations to keep up payments on their burgeoning debts. Meanwhile, the GDP slipped in the United States and Europe, signaling the onset of the worst global recession in fifty years.

The global economic crisis of the 1980s spawned what became known as the Lost Decade in Latin America, a period when one authoritarian government after another fell in the face of rising popular discontent with economic crisis and repression. In the wake, a wave of democratization flooded over the region, often accompanied by a turn to neoliberalism and a virtual abandonment of public welfare programs by the 1990s.

While many of the new presidents tried to harness mass sentiment with neopopulist platforms and promises, they were often stymied by economic limits, the ideological sway of anti-statist economists, the continued looming presence of conservative military forces, and an increasingly aware and disenchanted populace. As civilian politicians sought a return to constitutionalism and economic growth, they also faced new or continuing leftist uprisings, such as the FARC in Colombia, the Zapatistas in Mexico, or Sendero Luminoso (Shining Path) in Peru, that would prove even more intractable than their guerrilla forebears.

## RECESSION AND NEOLIBERALISM

In the Southern Cone in the 1960s and 1970s, the military's ability to make their economies run smoothly and equitably underlay their justification of the national security states. The Brazilian Miracle, the surge of growth in Chile, and sporadic good times in Argentina were supposed to make the loss of civil liberties palatable. And in some cases they did, at least for a while.

Yet the military's economic performance turned out to be mediocre, generally accompanied by a sharp concentration of income in the hands of the wealthy. In addition, military governments welcomed foreign investors and acquiesced to the demands of international bankers. Then, with the severe downturn of the early 1980s, the military governments lost much of their remaining civilian support, and criticisms of their economic mismanagement grew. The hard times of the 1980s hastened their retreat from power.

Economists called the 1980s the "Lost Decade" because the region's economies stagnated and sometimes shrank painfully. The average 1.2 percent annual rise in GDP did not keep up with population growth. In the 1980s, the region experienced its worst recession in a half-century. Little new investment took place from either public or private sources. Industries failed to compete with more aggressive companies in Asia and at first withdrew further behind protectionist barriers. Meanwhile, the international debts contracted in the 1970s continued to drain the economies of working capital. No wonder that development planners in Latin America could not overcome obstacles to growth. Theirs seemed a dismal science indeed, as an economist once called his discipline.

The economic crisis began with the 1980 recession in the United States and then spread to major trade partners, especially Mexico, Brazil, Venezuela, Peru, Colombia, and Chile. The Reagan administration took office in January 1981 and, seeking to drive down inflation at home and improve the long-term competitiveness of the U.S. economy, took drastic measures that reverberated through the debt-ridden economies of Latin America. This position led to further declines in global trade, bank credit, employment, and international loans and investment. Interest rates, meanwhile, remained high. For Latin America, it was the worst of all worlds.

A generalized debt crisis swept the region in 1982, causing Mexico to default (see chapter 19) and Brazil, Argentina, and Chile to experience severe hard currency shortages. These in turn caused grave social and political problems. In Argentina, the military invaded the Malvinas (Falkland) Islands in hopes of diverting attention from hardships at home. After losing the war with Great Britain, they were obliged to relinquish power to civilian leaders.

The fiscal emergency in Brazil nearly derailed the Figueiredo government's timetable for the return to civilian rule. In Chile, activists organized protests, strikes, and press campaigns to try to force Pinochet out of office. And in Mexico the economic crisis led to a debt moratorium, devaluations, the nationalization of domestic banks, and a thorough overhaul of national policy. Other countries in the region shared the hard times and troubles. Across the region, the UN estimated that poverty levels surged to over 40 percent of the population.

The severity of the early 1980s economic crisis forced Latin American leaders to reevaluate their economic theories. Economic nationalism had dominated the region since midcentury, with states playing a prominent role in trying to foster production, investment, and trade. (For the postwar rise of structuralist economic theories, see chapter 17.) Yet the crisis of the 1980s compelled leaders to abandon protectionist policies—policies that many blamed for the recession—in search of an alternative path out of the crisis.

Neoliberal economics swept the region in the 1980s, brought to Latin America both by foreign-trained economists and by international banks. Neoliberalism appealed to people of all walks of life in Latin America. It would extricate politicians from private-sector intervention and oversight, and thereby free the state from having responsibility over the economy. It would allow large businesses to move more aggressively into global markets. Gradually the notion of free-market economics spread, gaining favor among a majority of policymakers, and it became the new orthodoxy.

Some of the biggest players promoting neoliberalism were the International Monetary Fund and other international lenders. As countries in Latin America struggled to pay back their loans during the Lost Decade, international banks allowed for new loans or the renegotiation of old loans based upon a set of conditions aimed at establishing financial austerity domestically while opening up the economies of Latin American to foreign investment and trade.

The neoliberal doctrine consisted of several key principles, many of them in line with liberalism's celebration of individualism and private property rights. First, privatization would put government-owned enterprises up for sale to domestic or international investors. Second, labor unions would negotiate contracts directly with employers, rather than through state mediators. Third, the maze of regulatory laws and rules would be stripped away to allow entrepreneurs room to operate. Fourth, the free market would require the reduction or elimination of tariffs and quotas on foreign trade, floating rates for currency, relaxation of controls on capital transfers, free sale of land and other resources, balanced budgets, and alleviation of debt repayment. In short, neoliberalism prescribed running the economy with an emphasis on individualism and growth rather than nationalism and collective social welfare. International lenders encouraged the turn to individualism by issuing new loans with conditions attached, such as government budget austerity and reduced spending on public welfare.

The Lost Decade and subsequent turn to neoliberalism had an important impact on the labor force in Latin America. With its assault on unions and wages, it often placed workers in a more precarious position vis-à-vis owners.

This was exacerbated by free-trade agreements that encouraged investment with legal and regulatory changes that weakened workers' rights. But it also opened up more opportunities for women in the formal economy, especially in key export sectors such as the manufacturing of clothing from Honduras, electronics from Mexico, or agro-industrial production of foods such as grapes from Chile.

With the diminished power of male-dominated unions and patronage networks over hiring, owners often turned to female labor, seen as more flexible and apolitical—and whom they could pay less. The informal economy grew as well in this period, increasingly dominated by women, as families tried to grapple with the impact of repression, migration, and economic recession and austerity. With fewer labor and union protections in the formal workplace, and the informal economy growing quickly, the workforce saw growing casualization at the end of the twentieth century.

Having defaulted on its loans in 1982, Mexico soon became a key target of neoliberal reforms. The state sold off state-owned enterprises in banking and telecommunications, among others, and dropped its tariffs and quotas in order to open up the economy to more trade. It also attacked unions, modified the constitution to allow the privatization of communal lands, and abandoned many of its welfare programs, all in order to attract new loans and investment and to lay the groundwork for NAFTA (see chapter 19).

## Chile

Chile took a different path to democracy and neoliberalism than other countries in the Southern Cone, with the military leader Augusto Pinochet pursuing economic neoliberalism before he was voted out, leaving office in 1990. Heavily advised by University of Chicago–educated economists and technocrats, as early as the mid-1970s, Pinochet pursued market-oriented reforms. He cut tariffs, curbed unions, sold off state-owned industries except for copper, and trimmed welfare programs. He also privatized both education and the pension system in an effort to expand global trade and to entice foreign investment. And in many ways it paid off, with Chile's economy under his elected successors Patricio Aylwin (1990–1994) and Eduardo Frei Ruiz-Tagle (1994–2000) performing among the best in Latin America.

Aylwin had been the leader of the Christian Democrats under Allende and had led the democratic opposition to the socialist president. He had also been a leader of the democratic opposition under Pinochet and a key figure in the plebiscite vote that set the stage for Pinochet to be voted out of office. In some ways, his presidency proved transitional, since he slowly eroded military power during his four years in office.

Once he took office in 1990, Aylwin continued with Pinochet's liberalizing schemes, though by then it was clear that the Chilean neoliberal "miracle," as it was sometimes called, had come with great social costs. As businesses boomed and the economy grew, federal spending on housing, education, and health care dropped precipitously, and wages trended lower. By the early 1990s, the wealth gap had grown substantially by comparison with two decades earlier, and close to one-half the population still lived below the poverty line. Aylwin tried to alleviate this poverty by expanding both taxes and federal spending in the areas of housing, education, and health care. The incomes of the poor and working class, which had dropped during the 1970s and 1980s, now began to rebound, and the number of people living below the poverty line dropped to about one-third of the population.

Frei took office with a great deal of support. Like Aylwin, he had been backed by a center-left coalition of parties known as the Concertación, which held power from 1990 to 2010. As the son of the former president and a prominent Christian Democrat who had also led the movement to return Chile to democratic governance, he appealed to a wide swath of voters. He continued with Aylwin's reforms in the fields of education and social welfare, while also remaining a stalwart supporter of policies that had turned Chile into the model case for neoliberal reforms.

The economy continued to grow for most of the 1990s. Significantly, Frei led efforts to transform economic liberalization into more formal economic integration in the region by pursuing policies and agreements with other countries that promoted market-led interdependence and fostered closer ties to and competitiveness in the international economy. He signed multiple free-trade agreements with countries in the Western Hemisphere, and negotiated Chile's entry as an associate member into Mercosur, a common market of countries in South America.

Under Frei, Chile finally began to deal with some of the legacies of the Pinochet-era repression. Many in Chile had opposed prosecuting the members of the military who had taken part in the torture and disappearances, partly out of a desire to move forward as a nation and partly due to the enormous power that the military still wielded in the country. In fact, Pinochet remained as head of the armed forces until 1998, during which time he stopped human rights investigations and prosecutions.

In 1998, however, Pinochet was detained in London, where he had traveled to receive medical treatment. While there, a Spanish judge issued an order for his extradition for the torture of Spanish citizens in Chile during the dictatorship. The British government debated whether to send him to Spain to face prosecution. This reopened the conversation in Chile about prosecution for the crimes. Some officials argued that since the crimes occurred in Chile, they could only be prosecuted there, whereas leftist politicians supported his detention in England. The matter was only resolved when a British official declared that due to his advanced age and poor physical and mental health, Pinochet should not face prosecution.

After close to a year and a half in England, Pinochet finally returned to Chile. There authorities stripped away his immunity (which he had since he was a senator-for-life) and charged him with human rights violations. In the end he was deemed mentally unfit to stand trial, and though Chileans continued to try to prosecute him, he died in 2006 before the trial ever took place. But the episode reinvigorated a debate in Chile about national reconciliation that would only grow in the years to come.

## DEMOCRACY AND NEOPOPULISM

The failure of authoritarian governments to deal with the mounting economic crises in the 1980s and growing middle-class discontent with their brutal repression caused a crisis of legitimacy for authoritarian regimes that swept most of them out of power in the 1980s and 1990s. The region witnessed a democratic opening, a return to constitutionalism, and a renewal of civic life. Political parties, labor unions, and civic organizations once again flourished, and religious and self-help organizations sprang up around the region both to demand more government support for the region's poorest and to fill in for the deterioration of public services that resulted from neoliberal austerity measures.

As civilian leaders forged ahead with a return to constitutionalism, many experimented with new forms of populism, though the process varied widely and success proved uneven. This development was also limited by the ominous influence of conservative militaries that occasionally threatened to leave the barracks and return to politics if popular forces and calls for prosecution of former military leaders for human rights abuses became too vocal.

Among the many rationales for the national security states had been a frankly political motive: to eradicate populism. Since midcentury, military leaders believed that populists stirred up the masses, destabilized governments, awakened appetites they could not satisfy, fostered social disorder, and fomented crises so that they could solve them and become popular heroes. Army officers in their respective nations disliked Juan Perón, Getúlio Vargas, Juscelino Kubitschek, João Goulart, Arnulfo Arias, Haya de la Torre, José Velasco Ibarra, Rómulo Betancourt, and other populists. In most cases the dislike was mutual. The national security states therefore sought to discipline their citizens so that they would not succumb to the deceptive appeals of populism. And in most cases, during the long years of authoritarian rule, the populists either died or grew too old to run for office once the military governments fell.

When the Brazilian military allowed exiles to return and run for office in 1979, however, three of their "most unwanted" populists campaigned and won major victories. Leonel Brizola, Goulart's brother-in-law and the most audacious foe of the army in the 1960s, formed a new party and ran successfully for the governorship of Rio de Janeiro state in November 1982. Miguel Arraes, also a trenchant opponent of the 1964 coup, won a seat in Congress and then won the governor's race in Pernambuco in 1986. In São Paulo state, meanwhile, Jânio Quadros lost a bid for governor in 1982 but then won the mayoralty of São Paulo city in 1985, a position more powerful than most governorships. So the old populist magic still worked with many voters.

Other factors favored the return of populism. Electorates had grown rapidly since the 1960s, and hundreds of millions of voters were now eligible to vote and eager to participate. Many new voters had no direct memories of the classic populists yet were attracted by their legends. Vargas, Perón, Evita, Kubitschek, and others became even more celebrated in death than in life. Also, the electoral laws in most countries now extended the vote to illiterates and teens, who after growing up knowing only the harsh undemocratic rule of military governments could be recruited by populist methods.

Old-style populism, however, fell short in the redemocratizing nations of Latin America. None of the pre-military-era populists managed to capture the presidency in Brazil. In Panama, Arnulfo Arias's 1984 campaign failed, and he died four years later. Assad Bucaram in Ecuador, thwarted in his bid for the presidency, ended up supporting a relative, Jaime Roldós, for president in 1979. For two years, Bucaram and Roldós sparred for control, but then both died, and populism in Ecuador largely disappeared.

Instead, a new kind of populism arose in the mid-1980s, practiced by younger leaders. This neopopulism had many of the characteristics of the earlier version—appeals to nationalist sentiment, charismatic leadership, mass media blitzes, promises of reforms, and evocation of the common people's interests—but it differed in some key ways. Most important, in the context of rising neoliberalism by the end of the century, neopopulists abandoned state economic intervention. Instead, some cobbled together so-called heterodox approaches, while others embraced neoliberalism as salvation for their countries.

The neopopulists were mostly young, white, middle class, university educated, and well spoken. They had traveled abroad and were conversant in global issues. Like the classic populists (except Perón), none had pursued a military career. In addition, whereas the earlier populists had avoided existing parties and instead formed their own personal organizations, a few neopopulists remodeled the old parties to fit their needs.

Still, neopopulists addressed their appeals directly to the masses, usually on television, without acknowledging any intervening organizations. They posed as outsiders untainted by the corrupt politics of the previous generation, and they attacked the incumbent regimes mercilessly. Finally, the neopopulists were up to date in the latest media techniques, especially television and polling.

The neopopulists' pursuit of market-oriented, private enterprise programs alienated some of their institutional support. Unions, business associations, and others repudiated the neopopulist leaders when they learned that they would no longer enjoy special access to patronage. These groups had given only lukewarm support anyway and quickly withdrew from the coalitions. Many protested vigorously at the first signs of austerity programs.

The unorganized masses, on the other hand, saw the bold new policies as innovative and daring solutions to long-festering problems. In fact, the dramatic policy shifts enhanced the neopopulists' charisma and reputation for leadership. Polls showed that neopopulists received the most support from among the poor who worked in the informal sectors—those outside the mainstream economies and most vulnerable to downturns. To be sure, some neoliberal measures caused widespread suffering among the masses, and poverty rates at first soared. Still, the poor approved of the radical measures, believing them to be the harsh medicine needed for healing.

Neopopulists faced other challenges, however, that would lead some of them to moderate their more reformist programs by the 1990s. Some struggled to translate their popular appeal into enduring governing coalitions, especially when economic crises limited their ability to meet both popular needs and the neoliberal calls for lower taxes and policies to promote growth at all costs. Others had to deal with internal uprisings that led them to implement authoritarian measures to crack down on opposition. Through it all, they had to manage the calls for social justice for the disappeared of the 1970s and 1980s and rebuild nations torn apart by decades of military rule.

## Peru

Peru underwent a transition to civilian rule in 1980 after the discredited army returned to its barracks in disgrace. The victor in the elections held that year, Fernando Belaúnde, had been unceremoniously removed by the army twelve years before. His Popular Action Party won a 45 percent plurality. Now sixty-eight years old and chastened by his failures in the 1960s, Belaúnde no longer posed as a populist nor even an advocate of the common people's interests. He avoided attacking the military and instead took office promising to continue the political cleanup begun by his predecessor, General Morales Bermúdez, though now complemented by free-market economics.

Belaúnde emphasized economic recovery led by exports. This meant increased production for foreign markets so that Peru could earn hard currency and resume paying off the huge debt incurred by the military. It also meant austerity measures at home, which Peruvian workers were not expecting. Protests and strikes spread, in part because the world recession dried up markets for Peru's goods. Although not Belaúnde's fault, the recession could not be overcome by free-market policies, which merely punished workers and consumers. Wealthy Peruvians moved their capital abroad for protection. Economic indices, meanwhile, went from bad to worse.

Privatizing land, or returning it to private owners, brought opposition from peasant leaders, members of rural cooperatives, and unions on big collective farms. Other state enterprises put up for sale languished on the auction block when no one stepped forward to buy them. Production slipped, and shortages grew unbearable, especially in the cities. Belaúnde eventually appointed another government agency to deal with the economic crisis, but he himself increasingly ignored the country's problems and spent his time hobnobbing with the Lima elite in private clubs and restaurants. Meanwhile, in the mountains, a new guerrilla organization had begun to operate—the dreaded Sendero Luminoso.

Sendero had been founded by a university professor from Ayacucho, Abimael Guzmán, who had become disaffected by Peru's unequal society and been inspired by travels in Mao Zedong's China. Upon his return, Guzmán began to gather converts to his revolutionary philosophy and to organize them into clandestine cells that would spark an uprising that would overthrow the bourgeoisie and achieve a communist revolution. He found fertile ground in Ayacucho, a region that had seen little benefit from Velasco's reforms, and where rural peasants and romantic university students found themselves disenchanted with the corruption of bourgeois democracy. By the late 1970s Sendero had perfected a mission and modus operandi that seemed invincible.

Like other guerrilla bands, Sendero built its command structure out of almost totally isolated cells, each one composed of leadership cadres, battle orders, weapons caches, and regional assignments. Guzmán trained the first cell leaders and sent them out, and gradually these trained hundreds more, until every part of the country had Sendero representatives. Some cells operated in the cities, others in rural areas, always in isolation from one another. They communicated with controllers infrequently and only through highly secret channels. It was almost impossible for police to break into their command structure.

Members of Sendero had all been trained in operations and doctrine, and their faith in Guzmán bordered on absolute. Hundreds perished in suicide missions, and hundreds more died at the hands of police interrogators. Theirs was a faith as total as that of any religious fanatic. Women as well as men staffed the cells, and they penetrated all walks of Peruvian life. Their devotion to the cause and success in winning new recruits increased with the deteriorating political and economic situation in the country. Gradually Sendero spread across the valleys and hamlets of highland Peru, clashing with and eventually displacing many local authorities. By the mid-1980s two-thirds of the highlands had fallen under Sendero control, and their area expanded with each passing year.

President Belaúnde, who had dealt forcefully with guerrilla groups in his first administration, dispatched the army to defeat Sendero in the early 1980s. To his dismay, the army could not prevail against Sendero's superior tactics, nor could it gain the cooperation of peasants in areas under Sendero influence. Even more disturbing, Sendero offered protection to farmers who produced coca leaves, the raw material from which traffickers refined cocaine. Because

## Women and Rebellion at the Turn of the Twenty-First Century

Women held prominent positions of authority in two of the best-known uprisings in Latin America in the 1990s, the Zapatistas (EZLN) in Mexico and Sendero Luminoso in Peru. Women in both countries had long been active in political struggles, such as the independence movements and the Mexican Revolution. But, as in many other guerrilla movements of prior generations, women were typically relegated to secondary positions other than the occasional exemplary leader. However, in both the EZLN and Sendero Luminoso, women played an active role in leading political and military actions.

Both organizations reflected a regionwide critique by indigenous activists of the especially harsh impact of neoliberalism on indigenous communities. They were also influenced by women's rights organizations of the 1960s and included calls for women's rights as part of their platforms. But they differed from the 1960s second-wave feminist groups, which tended to focus on issues specific to middle-class women; both the EZLN and Sendero identified peasant women as suffering the worst forms of oppression because they faced discrimination based on their class, race, and gender. Both groups protested the conditions that made rural life for women so hard, such as the lack of basic health care, schools, and even food for their families, and they mobilized these women by condemning patriarchy alongside their message of class struggle. The EZLN even included the Women's Revolutionary Law as part of its platform, which it developed in consultation with indigenous women and which included a list of demands that blended individual freedoms and political rights.

coca production generated a lot of cash from the narcotics trade, fees and taxes collected by Sendero financed its arms and training programs. Sendero gradually became a state within the Peruvian state.

During his last two years in office, Belaúnde lost all the public support that he had enjoyed in 1980, and he left the dwindling powers of government in the hands of subordinates. The most that could be said is that he managed an election and a peaceful transition to his successor, Alan García. As Peru's first neopopulist, García fizzled before he could test the full possibilities of this approach. At age thirty-six—the youngest president ever to serve in Peru—García was handsome and well spoken. Haya de la Torre had been his mentor, helping to groom him for power. García seized the reins of the Aprista Party after Haya's death and ran an effective campaign in 1985. Through him, APRA won its first presidential victory.

Essentially improvising, García mixed interventionist, Keynesian initiatives developed by ECLAC with neoliberalism. Oddly, this unorthodox approach succeeded at first, pulling the economy out of the deep slump of the Belaúnde years and sparking Peru's first two years of economic growth in a decade. Inflation, meanwhile, went down, giving hope that the economy had finally turned a corner.

García's policies included an anti-inflation package and higher wages and blocked transfers of capital out of the country. He famously refused to pay interest on foreign debt in excess of 10 percent of export earnings. This unusual measure pleased the public but alienated international bankers, who cut off further credit until Peru agreed to adhere to the new, stricter lending guidelines of the neoliberal era.

García also announced an independent foreign policy, as had Haya and other classic populists. He recognized Cuba and worked to reduce U.S. influence in Central America. This played well with the public yet did not challenge major power strategists unduly. Nevertheless, a suspicious United States government suspended nonmilitary aid. With his nationalist foreign policy and focus on rebuilding the Peruvian economy, García enjoyed great support at first.

But García's program faltered in 1987 as his mixed policies began to generate opposition from a range of groups, including manufacturers, farmers, bankers, retailers, and workers. Shortages appeared as production in factories and on farms diminished. A serious trade deficit and shrinking currency reserves led García to announce that he would nationalize the banking system. This act sparked an explosion of protests and induced the opposition to coalesce into a single force. At the head of the opposition stood Peru's foremost novelist, Mario Vargas Llosa, an advocate of neoliberalism and leader of a conservative and centrist-liberal party alliance that eventually took the name FREDEMO (Frente Democrático, or Democratic Front).

By the late 1980s, economic stalemate gripped the nation. García froze, incapable of initiating any new policy or making the earlier ones work. He tried to regain support with *balconazos,* his famous impromptu speeches from the balcony of the presidential palace, but they lost their appeal. As with other populists before him, his speeches could only accomplish so much when accompanied by economic hardship. In an effort to reenergize the economy, he tried austerity measures, but they only worsened his declining approval rating. The economy groaned to a halt and then shrank for two years. García lapsed into emotional burnout from overwork and tension, disappearing into the palace for days at a time.

The decline in public authority emboldened Sendero Luminoso to take total control of huge areas in the Andes and Peru's Amazon region. It had very strong cells in the cities as well. In areas Sendero controlled, its leaders performed most government functions, from collecting taxes to running the schools. In some Sendero towns, peasants noted a marked improvement in public services and safety. In other regions, however, peasants armed themselves or furiously resisted Sendero, which just as often employed outright terrorism and brute force to intimidate the inhabitants.

Like peasants in Colombia, they often found themselves caught between rebels who offered them little other than violence and a distant state that did little to alleviate grinding poverty and exclusion—and which often viewed all highland peasants as suspected rebels. Given the remarkable spread of Sendero, some observers questioned whether the army could even win an all-out war against it. The army tried, but in the process, by suspecting highland peasants of being rebels, they ended up killing tens of thousands of indigenous people in the 1980s. Years later, Peru's Truth and Reconciliation Commission concluded that of the seventy thousand fatalities produced by the armed conflict between 1980 and 2000, 75 percent were of indigenous descent.

Alberto Fujimori, one of Latin America's most colorful and strong-willed presidents of recent times, succeeded García. A middle-aged engineer of Japanese descent, Fujimori had never before dabbled in politics. But he became so disgusted with García's collapsing administration that he formed a new party in late 1989, Cambio 1990 (Change 1990). Made up of other professionals, small-business owners, Pentecostal and evangelical Protestants, and discontented members of the middle class, Cambio 1990 entered the 1990 presidential race. Fujimori posed as the friend of the downtrodden and mixed-race majority (the Cholitos) and promised to end rule by the white oligarchs (the Blanquitos). Amazingly, his 25 percent put him in second place.

The runoff pitted Fujimori against novelist and establishment favorite Mario Vargas Llosa, thought by most to be the favorite to win the election. The well-financed Vargas Llosa preached doom and gloom, however, and the need to institute draconian austerity measures. Vargas Llosa also held negative views of Peru's indigenous population. While he opposed the oppression of Indians, he nevertheless saw Peru's modernization as lying not in a celebration of Indian practices and culture but rather in their disappearance through mestizaje. Voters turned away from the frightening rhetoric of Vargas Llosa to the more upbeat message of Fujimori.

Fujimori campaigned on the need to protect the citizenry against the ravages of more economic shocks. He spoke vaguely of dealing with the country's problems in a professional manner without citing specific measures. To everyone's surprise, Fujimori received over 56 percent of the runoff vote and took office in July 1990.

Fujimori quickly enacted austerity measures, called Fuji-shocks by critics—the sort that he had denounced during his campaign. One observer termed his reversal of policy a "bait and switch," though it was a turn to neoliberalism that was all too common among neopopulists once they took office. He put virtually all state enterprises up for privatization. He ended subsidies for staple foods, provoking a spike in price levels. He did, however, create a special aid program for needy people, and he gained a lot of media coverage giving out aid personally. Meanwhile, Fujimori seemed imperturbable and immune to pressures of all sorts.

**Figure 24.1** Campaign poster for Peru's presidential candidate Alberto Fujimori in 1990. He posed as an outsider who would defend the interests of common people. A practical and articulate man, he convinced a majority that he could bring growth and equity to the nation. Authors' collection.

Remarkably, the shock treatment began to produce dividends by 1991, when inflation fell to a tolerable range and the recession abated. By 1993 the country began its first sustained growth in over two decades. Foreign credit returned, new jobs appeared, business invested in new plants and equipment, and Fujimori's approval rating stayed surprisingly high. He also instituted health programs to alleviate epidemic diseases and improve the productivity of Peru's workers.

Encountering adamant opposition from Congress in 1992, Fujimori mobilized the army and simply closed Congress until further notice. He accused it of obstructionism and corruption and began to rule by decree. He purged the judiciary of judges who blocked his reforms. He also proclaimed a state of siege so that he could carry on the war against Sendero, which still controlled a sizable portion of the country. The public did not protest these emergency measures because it believed that the president needed special powers to solve the nation's economic and security crises.

Sendero stepped up its attacks on the government after Fujimori closed Congress. Guzmán may have believed that Fujimori was more vulnerable because of his closure of Congress, or he may have acted because Sendero had lost its base in much of the highlands. Many peasant leaders had originally cooperated with Sendero merely because it was a lesser evil than the Lima government. Fujimori's successes in reviving the economy and reforming the administrative system, however, convinced many local officials to shift their allegiance back to the government. As they did so, they turned their arms against Sendero and drove it out of region after region. This reversal in the highlands may have motivated Guzmán's decision to attack the regime.

Fujimori met Sendero's 1993 offensive with a concerted military and publicity campaign, and at a critical moment his people captured Guzmán. This proved a major breakthrough because it decapitated the centralized command structure that Guzmán had built. For months Sendero drifted leaderless and by 1995 was clearly on the retreat. Guzmán, meanwhile, languished under heavy guard in a prison island offshore. The 2002 movie *The Dancer Upstairs*, directed by John Malkovich and starring Javier Bardem, portrays the seeming spell the movement cast over the nation until Guzmán's arrest.

Fujimori believed that he needed more than five years to complete the reorganization and stabilization of the country, so he held elections to choose a new Congress. The new body dutifully changed the constitution to allow Fujimori to be reelected immediately. In 1995 Fujimori ran and won handily, beginning his second term with a fresh mandate.

Fujimori represented neopopulism at its most effective. A convincing speaker on television (where he hosted a talk show) and so unorthodox as to be appealing, he overcame voters' mistrust and became their savior. His reforms were neoliberal in inspiration yet required strong leadership reminiscent of the classic populists. Although he used military force to close Congress, he claimed that his mandate came from the people and was exercised in their name.

Fujimori had less success in solving the oldest border dispute in Latin America. Peru and Ecuador had squabbled over their border along the upper reaches of the Amazon River since independence. Various border conflicts marked the dispute, and in 1941 they finally erupted into a short but intense war between the two nations that threatened to break the united front that the United States desired from Latin America during World War II. The United States, along with Chile, Argentina, and Brazil, mediated a truce that resulted in the Rio Treaty of 1942. Peru not only won the border conflict in the field but also gained the lion's share of territory in the treaty. But Ecuador eventually renounced the treaty, and another round of border conflicts began in the 1960s, culminating in Ecuador's armed occupation of parts of the disputed territory in January 1995. It couldn't have come at a worse time for Fujimori.

A 1998 treaty finally settled the long border conflict with Ecuador, giving Ecuador key land use rights in Peru. And in 1999 three agreements between Peru and Chile updated the 1929 treaty, bringing remaining disputes from the

**Figure 24.2** Ecuador mobilized for war with Peru in 1939. Photo shows the Sucre unit installing anti-aircraft guns outside Quito to intercept attackers. The United States and other countries prevailed on Ecuador to accept territorial losses in the Amazon in order to prepare for World War II. Courtesy Library of Congress.

War of the Pacific (1879–1883) between those two countries to a close. Fujimori visited Chile in December 1999, the first ever by a Peruvian head of state.

In December 1996 Fujimori faced another challenge from an unexpected quarter. A small guerrilla group, the Túpac Amaru Revolutionary Movement, seized the Japanese ambassador's residence during a reception, capturing scores of prominent foreigners and Peruvian authorities, including the president's brother. The hostage crisis lasted for four months, during which Fujimori seemed paralyzed. Finally, in April 1997 he ordered an infiltration assault in which one hostage and all of the guerrillas perished. The president received congratulations for the operation, which seemed to prove Peru capable of managing terrorist threats.

**Figure 24.3** Alejandro Toledo in 2015, at
his alma mater, Stanford University.
Authors' collection.

This was evident in Peru's management of the drug wars as well. By early 2000, and in cooperation with the U.S., the Peruvian government had reduced the total acreage of illegal coca leaf under cultivation by almost two-thirds. Even after the Peruvian Air Force shot down a small, unarmed aircraft carrying U.S. missionaries in the Amazon region in 2001, the U.S. and Peru continued to cooperate in the War on Drugs.

But the War on Drugs eventually contributed to Fujimori's downfall. By 2000, one of his principal advisors and the head of Peru's intelligence service, the corrupt and autocratic Vladimiro Montesinos, was caught in a major scandal. Nationally televised videos showed him bribing politicians, media moguls, and scores of other powerful Peruvians to back the Fujimori regime. The public already abhorred his secretive, high-handed techniques, and they applauded seeing Montesinos caught on his own tapes manipulating power and influence in the regime. By then, Montesinos, who had at one time been a paid collaborator with the CIA, had become a pariah with that agency as well. During the 1990s it had come out that he was selling arms to Colombian narcotraffickers and taking payments from them as well so they could operate freely along the jungle borders. Fujimori found himself unable to divorce himself from the actions of Montesinos. Moreover, in that same year, Fujimori encountered problems when despite some controversy surrounding its constitutionality, he ran for and won a third term in office, amid claims of fraud, beating out his opponent, Alejandro Toledo.

Toledo appealed to an array of voters because he began as an impoverished shoe-shine boy of indigenous parents, but went on to become a Stanford-educated economist. He pledged to maintain market reforms while promoting investment in social programs, infrastructure, and wages, giving Peru's poorest hope that he would help them. He also promised to investigate government corruption.

Though Fujimori won the election, by November he was forced out amid popular backlash against his corrupt governing style. He fled into exile in Japan, and years later he was convicted in Peru of embezzlement and human rights abuses for his use of death squads against Sendero Luminoso and other rebels. As of 2016, he remained in jail in Peru. An interim government served until 2001, when Alejandro Toledo won a close election and became Peru's first indigenous president. Since then, powerful indigenous rights organizations have impelled national discussions about inequality, discrimination, and the political rights of Peru's indigenous population.

## Argentina

Civilian rule returned to Argentina in 1983, following the country's defeat in the Malvinas (Falklands) War. Army-supervised elections gave Raúl Alfonsín (1983–1989), leader of the Radical Party, 52 percent of the votes, compared to the Peronistas' 40 percent. In returning power to civilians, the army had insisted that they not pursue judicial charges against officers for their actions in the Dirty War or the Malvinas debacle. In fact, once in office Alfonsín did indict those who served in juntas after 1976 or held command posts during the war. To avoid prosecution, most of the country's highest-ranking officers retired or resigned, and the army shrank to its smallest size in generations. Argentines were relieved to be rid of military rule but many were deeply disappointed at the time by the light sentences received by officers known to have committed atrocities.

Alfonsín took over a country devastated by economic mismanagement, internal repression, and a failed war. Citizen morale stood at an all-time low. The new president had to make his way through a political minefield, and he did not emerge unharmed. To salvage the economy, Alfonsín reached agreement with the Peronistas and international lenders to carry out a general restructuring program with austerity measures, but also with some protection for the working class. Called the Plan Austral after the new unit of currency that it created, the program applied neoliberal prescriptions. Alfonsín's finance minister began dismantling myriad controls and regulations inherited from past regimes. He also cut wages, began privatizing public enterprises, and scaled back government spending on subsidies and salaries. The program succeeded in bringing down inflation and restoring the nation's credit rating, but it did not stimulate general growth, as planners had expected. Meanwhile, social disorder further threatened his legitimacy. Members of a new generation of army officers began to abuse their power, kidnapping leftists and threatening politicians who were hostile to the armed forces. Alfonsín's public authority plunged, and his party lost a critical midterm election in 1987.

Alfonsín's last major initiative, a second economic plan called Austral II, attempted to deepen the neoliberal policies recommended by his advisors. This plan, plus major capital investments and petroleum discoveries, got the economy growing again, but it was too late to save Alfonsín's presidency. His party lost the 1989 election to the Peronist Carlos Menem, and Alfonsín actually stepped down in disrepute before the end of his term. Neoliberal prescriptions alone could not overcome the economic and social malaise that plagued the country.

Like García in Peru and Fernando Collor de Mello in Brazil, Carlos Menem (1989–1999) used neopopulist strategies to win office and govern his nation. He so thoroughly dominated the political field that analysts began to compare his reign with that of Juan Perón nearly a half-century earlier. Born in the province of La Rioja in 1930, Menem rose through the ranks of the Peronista party and achieved national prominence in the late 1980s as an outspoken critic of Raúl Alfonsín's policies.

In May 1989 Menem won an overwhelming victory on the Peronista party ticket, taking office five months early to try to contain the economic crisis. Inflation had made the peso worthless, and only dollars or other foreign currencies could be used for purchases. The GNP was one-sixth lower than it had been at the beginning of the decade, and unemployment had soared. Goods disappeared from supermarkets, crowds milled in the streets as people discussed and protested the shortages, and the economy virtually stopped altogether. As a candidate, Menem had promised to carry out a classically Peronista program of raising wages, stimulating production with loans and subsidies, starting construction work to revive the economy, and postponing repayments on the foreign loan. These pledges appealed to the masses just as much as they had in the 1940s.

Once in office, however, and like other neopopulists, Menem reversed his course and carried out a neoliberal stabilization program. Protests arose from the unions, public employee groups, and other sectors that had supported his election, but he ignored them. To cushion his program's impact on the very poor, he created the Federal Solidarity Program, which provided direct assistance to the unemployed. He did everything possible to sustain his support from the unorganized masses who had voted for him.

Privatization of major state enterprises topped Menem's list of priorities. Most of these enterprises lost money, saddled the government with debt, and

**Figure 24.4** Carlos Menem as president in 1999. He first ran for office in 1989, then won a second term until 1999. He excelled as a neopopulist who manipulated public opinion and dominated national affairs. Courtesy U.S. government, Wiki Commons.

were political liabilities. By late 1993 virtually all of the public companies were at least partially owned by private interests, including the oil monopoly, YPF. In 1993 the economy began to grow at a brisk rate, just in time to reinforce the Peronista bloc in Congress and to elect delegates to a constitutional convention that would authorize a second term for Menem. The president kept up a vigorous schedule of travel throughout the country, especially in the western region, where he grew up. His direct outreach and programs for the poor drew significant support from the rural working class.

Perhaps Menem's most important innovations were a national monetary board to oversee the money supply and his decision to peg the peso to the U.S. dollar. The public's ability to open dollar-denominated bank accounts and exchange pesos for dollars proved critical to his success. Almost overnight, inflation halted and the savings rate went up. Even more important, concessions to foreign investors, who could move money into and out of the country freely, convinced them that Argentina was a good risk. Menem, in an amazing about-face, embraced most of the neoliberal policies being promoted by the International Monetary Fund, the World Bank, and the United States—the so-called Washington Consensus.

Argentina prospered for the remainder of the 1990s, receiving high prices for its exports and foreign capital to expand the economy. Brazil became a major investor, because Mercosur reduced tariffs on goods traded within the region, and it became advantageous to build joint plants for the larger market. In addition, Argentina grew closer to the European Union and experienced much immigration from there. Menem enjoyed ample support from the public and maintained a working coalition in Congress. His flamboyant private life, however, erupted in several scandals, and he eventually divorced his wife and remarried. Moreover, he was heavily criticized for pardoning the military officials convicted of human rights abuses during the Dirty War.

Menem had to stand aside for the 1999 presidential succession, and several Peronista candidates battled for the nomination. The Radical Party chose Fernando de le Rúa, former mayor of Buenos Aires, and elected him, but his mandate foundered due to a growing economic malaise similar to that which struck in Brazil. The peso had become overvalued, as had the Brazilian real, because of growing public debt and deficit spending by the federal and state governments. Unemployment had remained about 15 percent for years and tax revenues languished. Argentina became vulnerable to an attack by international currency traders.

The first few years of the new century were a turning point for Argentina, when the country seemed to be on the brink of economic and political collapse. De la Rúa fought to rein in the budget and discipline the unions, but the global recession of 2001 proved fatal for him and the dollar-pegged peso. He went through several finance ministers before being forced to allow the peso to float on currency markets, which in turn led worried investors to flee with their capital. Emergency measures he instituted, such as conversion of dollar accounts to pesos and freezing assets above a certain amount, coupled with even higher unemployment, led to massive demonstrations against the government.

By the end of the year de la Rúa resigned in favor of his vice president, who also resigned amid growing chaos. Finally, the presidency went to a Peronista, the former governor of Buenos Aires province, Eduardo Duhalde. In a series of tense negotiations, Duhalde brought an end to the demonstrations and order to the economy, but at the expense of his own term. He agreed to hold elections in early 2003 so the public could participate in the selection of a new president. In a few months, the peso sank to about a quarter of its previous value and seemed to stabilize. Yet bankruptcies, capital flight, emigration, and widespread poverty descended upon the once-prosperous country, setting the stage for a turn to center-left politics for the next ten years.

## Brazil

Brazilians welcomed José Sarney as president in 1985 and even anointed him with some of the sainthood that they had conferred on the deceased Tancredo

Neves. Sarney's accession was met with optimism and goodwill after twenty-one years of military dictatorship. Although little known and representing the poor northern state of Maranhão, Sarney nonetheless enjoyed a long honeymoon. He undertook the building of a working coalition in Congress around his tiny and unknown Liberal Front Party.

Sarney also continued the abertura process by freeing unions and employers to pursue collective bargaining and by allowing communists to operate legally for the first time in thirty-eight years. Electoral system reform gave illiterates the vote, lowered the voting age to sixteen, and selected the president by direct ballot. Finally, in November 1985 Sarney oversaw municipal elections and the next year congressional elections, in which record numbers cast ballots and exercised their civic rights. The return to democracy was in full swing.

As in Argentina and Chile, however, the postdictatorship presidents faced demands from some corners that they arrest military leaders for human rights abuses. For many, it was not just about justice, but also about how to rebuild a nation torn apart by the deep suspicions and polarization that marked the Cold War years. They argued that only through national recognition and punishment of the crimes could the nation truly heal. Yet the army had exacted from Tancredo Neves the promise of a decree of amnesty for military officers accused of crimes while serving in their official capacity. Sarney did not try to reverse this decree, and carried out no reprisals. Those who fought the dictatorship disagreed with the amnesty and kept alive the memory of the military atrocities through books, memoirs, movies, and public testimony. A chronicle of the tortures and deaths, kept secretly by the archdiocese of São Paulo, appeared later as *Nunca mais* (Never Again) and was soon translated into several languages.

Sarney inherited an economy in disarray, and he made reorganization a high priority. To be sure, the GNP had begun to grow again, and export earnings were strong, but the foreign debt, totaling over $80 billion, cast a pall over capital markets. In addition, a huge internal debt fed triple- and quadruple-digit inflation rates, which threatened to become hyperinflation—an uncontrollable upward spiral.

Moreover, economic ministers in the 1970s had devised baffling and counterproductive controls and mechanisms. One economist euphemistically called the system "heterodoxy" because it combined elements of classically liberal, Keynesian, and socialist approaches. In fact, it was an insoluble maze that choked off business initiative and foreign investment. Unsure of how to proceed, Sarney kept advocates of both ECLAC and neoliberal doctrine in his cabinet. Meanwhile, inflation soared.

In 1986 Sarney unveiled the Cruzado Plan, a heterodox scheme inspired by the Argentine Austral experiment. The president decreed the creation of a new currency, the *cruzado*, to replace the *cruzeiro*, which had circulated since 1942. To protect the cruzado from inflation, he ordered a price and wage freeze,

## Benedita da Silva and the Political Opening

By the time military rule ended after two decades in Brazil, society and politics had changed dramatically. During the dictatorship, popular organizations arose to address the problems caused by Brazil's massive urban growth; rural migrants streamed into the cities in search of jobs and education. They most often ended up living in favelas, where basic services like water, electricity, or police forces were absent. Millions of Brazilians lived in these cramped, disease-ridden, impoverished areas, and the military regime suppressed any discussion of the problem.

In this climate, neighborhood organizations developed to address the problems, and their leaders became natural contenders for political office once democracy returned. Benedita da Silva was one such organizer. The daughter of poor, Afro-descended rural migrants to the city of Rio de Janeiro, da Silva fully understood the poverty and despair that often marked favela life in urban Brazil. She became a member of the Workers' Party, which had formed in 1980. The Workers' Party tended to represent grassroots interests and needed candidates to run for office once elections returned. It also was more open and diverse than many traditional parties, and this appealed to progressives, women, and evangelicals.

Indeed, the Workers' Party instituted quotas for women as its candidates to ensure they would gain a foothold in the party. By 1986, da Silva had become one of only 26 women out of 599 deputies in the National Assembly, and she was one of its only seven black deputies. In 1994, she became the first woman ever to win a Senate seat in Brazil, and during the presidency of Lula, she became a government minister.

while he went through the motions of reducing government deficits and making other adjustments. The government printed the new currency and then launched it with a major publicity campaign against inflation.

The Cruzado Plan proved enormously popular because it provided for a stable currency that would bring economic development and growth. Sarney went on television to exhort citizens to cooperate by reporting any illegal price or wages increases. The feeling of empowerment that swept the nation stunned observers. One government economist believed that it was economic democracy at work. Soon tens of thousands of people donned badges calling themselves Sarney's *fiscais* (watchdogs) and began monitoring price tags in stores and businesses. For several months, prices remained stable, and the country enjoyed genuine euphoria.

Gradually, however, inflation began to creep back, and the government proved powerless to prevent it. By early 1987 Sarney was obliged to launch another package of reforms, the so-called Cruzado II, which included a suspension of interest payments on foreign commercial loans. This effort met with more skepticism, and the resultant price stability lasted only a few months. Toward the end of his term, Sarney launched a third, desperate plan, introducing the cruzado novo currency (worth 1,000 old cruzados) and a new list of economic measures. This plan barely slowed inflation at all. Sarney's once-brilliant image as a leader was tarnished beyond recognition. His approval ratings sank into single digits by the end of his term, setting the stage for the emergence of neopopulism in Brazil.

The Brazilian electorate had grown so disenchanted with President Sarney and the major parties that it voted wholesale for nontraditional candidates. Out of more than a dozen who ran for president in the first-round election of 1989, they voted for Fernando Collor de Mello, a virtually unknown figure from the small northeastern state of Alagoas, and Luiz Inácio Lula da Silva, a metalworkers' union manager and candidate of the Workers' Party, setting the stage for a runoff.

In the second round in November 1989, with better financing and strong media support, Collor won a slight majority. He was a handsome, polished, well-spoken, young man (forty years old when elected) who emphasized his distance from regular politicians by running almost without a party. Instead, he used a highly professional campaign staff to flood the media with his image, his shallow promises of national renewal, and his claims to be an outsider who cared about the common people. In fact, Collor came from a rich and well-connected family. He had grown up in Rio and Brasília, where his father served several terms as senator. The family owned a chain of newspapers and radio and television stations in the northeast.

Collor stressed several points in his speeches. First, he promised to moralize public life and eliminate corrupt politicians, whom he denounced as "maharajahs" who controlled regional politics and lived in opulence. Second, he pledged to carry out neoliberal policies, including privatization, freer trade, and smaller government. Third, he guaranteed to end inflation with a shock treatment. Yet, Collor's victory probably gained most from his appeal to youth over age, the modern over the old, and the fresh over the stale. It was largely a television-driven campaign during which Collor spent hundreds of millions of dollars to project an appealing image of himself.

The labor candidate, Lula, made a phenomenal showing in view of the fact that his Workers' Party (PT) was new and that he had not run for national office before. A plain-looking, bearded young man, Lula spoke directly and honestly about his years in union organizing (see chapter 23), his program to increase workers' incomes and benefits, and his opposition to excessive foreign control of the economy. He advocated greater public regulation of the economy and a shift in income to working-class families. Many of his campaign aides were leftists and intellectuals who had suffered during the military regime. Lula himself had been jailed for a month under the military regime for his union activities.

When Collor took office in January 1990 he declared a bank holiday and initiated drastic reforms designed to bolster the currency. He ordered banks to transfer funds in excess of about $1,000 into accounts that would remain frozen for eighteen months. This would "wring out" excess demand from the economy, he said, and thus dampen inflation. He launched another currency, the cruzeiro, worth the same as the previous year's new cruzado, which would cease to circulate. Because of the sharp contraction in money available to consumers, the new unit quickly rose in value domestically and abroad. The shock could not have been greater, and it took months for the economy to return to normal.

Collor also instituted price and wage controls in the name of the free market, saying that prices had to be pegged at the previous year's levels. A government team carried out a veritable blitz of reform measures, led by the thirty-six-year-old minister of economy, Zélia Cardoso de Mello (not a relative). The team closed down agencies and ministries, laid off public employees, deregulated whole sectors of the economy, cut back spending, and overhauled the rules governing banks.

The public not only accepted but also applauded these initiatives in the desperate hope that the new president would truly eradicate inflation. The public believed that spiraling prices caused the greatest hardships to the greatest number and that only drastic, painful measures could stabilize prices. Congress followed suit and approved most of his program in the following months.

Collor's brash and daring assault on inflation suffered two major flaws. It was far too complex to be implemented quickly by fiscal authorities at all levels, and it required drastic curbs on spending that the president simply would not carry out. Soon inflation began to creep back, and it ate into Collor's approval ratings and effectiveness. Arrogant to a fault, however, he believed that he could prevail by sheer willpower and personal energy.

Collor also took a calculated risk by inviting the United Nations to hold its second Earth Summit on the global environment in Rio de Janeiro. Scheduled for 1992, the summit attracted delegates from most countries of the world, plus tens of thousands of observers representing public interest groups. Brazil had been heavily criticized in recent years for deforestation of the Amazon rainforest and for abuse of indigenous people. The criticism had reached a high point after the assassination of indigenous activist Chico Mendes in 1988. Mendes had been active in the rubber tappers' union in the Amazon, which since the late 1970s had been pressuring the government to set up reserves to protect both the livelihood of local residents as well as the region from environmental destruction. Local rubber tappers had taken to blocking outsiders from coming in to log and ranch in the region. The global environmental movement took notice of Mendes's work, and in 1987 the National Wildlife Federation and the Environmental Defense Fund flew him to Washington to lobby the U.S. and the global banking community to support sustainable economic activities that would not destroy the rainforest. In 1988, Mendes was killed by a large rancher whose claim to lands formerly used by rubber tappers he had challenged. Mendes was one of close to two dozen rural activists killed that year for opposing the encroachment of wealthy landowners, and his death generated global outrage and awareness about the destruction of the Amazon. In his case, the landowner and his accomplices received prison sentences of nineteen years.

After Collor took office, he decreed an end to fiscal incentives for forest clearing and set up huge indigenous reserves, yet many environmentalists were skeptical. Collor hoped that by sponsoring the summit he could improve his and the country's image, which he did. By then the pace of deforestation had slowed, and indigenous groups continued to speak up about their rights. Not all of the country's ecological problems were improving, to be sure, but Brazil's sponsorship of the summit strengthened the position of those committed to better policies.

Apart from the whirlwind economic program and environmental grandstanding, Collor's administration did little else of substance. He kept up an incredible flow of publicity from press conferences, media leaks, and impromptu appearances. He and his beauty queen wife seemed to appear at every gala function in the country. He jogged, drove fast cars, flew a supersonic fighter plane, and traveled abroad. On the sly, investigators later revealed, administration officials were salting away tens of millions of dollars from bribes taken in exchange for favors and concessions to contractors. The administration's glitter concealed crooked backroom deals.

Collor was certainly a neopopulist, albeit a short-lived one. His image gained him charismatic authority with the masses, especially among young and poor voters, who wanted desperately to believe in someone. He ran without party ties or obligations to major political factions. He made expert use of media specialists and pollsters to portray himself as the embodiment of a better future for Brazil. He promised reforms that would benefit the masses and break the power of the oligarchy. He polled especially well among new voters: the sixteen- to eighteen-year-olds, illiterates, and rural poor.

Collor's term ended by impeachment in 1992, an unprecedented event anywhere in the Americas. Congress, spurred on by the press and growing public demonstrations, gathered evidence of bribe-taking by Collor's personal secretary and opened a formal investigation. Congress had its share of scandals and was not known for political bravery, but when polls and citizen complaints began to flood Brasília, members of Congress saw their duty. Collor resisted until the end and refused to resign, so he was impeached.

Like other populists, Collor had chosen a virtual unknown for his vice-presidential running mate, Itamar Franco, from the interior state of Minas Gerais. An elderly bachelor who expected to coast through the administration with little to do, Franco was suddenly thrust into the limelight by Collor's impeachment. Itamar Franco assumed caretaker responsibilities and avoided major initiatives or disasters. Congress emerged from the impeachment with a great deal more authority, so the president worked closely with legislative leaders. The economy lapsed back into its triple-digit inflationary mode, but performed reasonably well. The country marked time until the next election.

The 1994 election marked a turning point in modern Brazilian history. It put clear choices before the voters and resulted in decisive changes. A wide range of candidates ran in the first round, including the perennial populist Leonel Brizola. Lula again represented the Workers' Party, offering much the same platform as he had in 1989. He had solid backing from unions, students, the intelligentsia, and a portion of the middle class. A centrist candidate, however, Fernando Henrique Cardoso—a sixty-three-year-old sociologist, former senator, and world-renowned Marxist scholar—took an early lead in the polls. By then, however, he had long since abandoned his Marxist principles and instead promised neoliberal economics, concern for the poor, and a balanced approach to the foreign debt. Cardoso won over 45 percent of the first-round votes and was proclaimed the winner.

In fact, Cardoso won the election largely on the basis of his economic stabilization program, implemented in July 1994 while he was serving as finance minister. By far the most carefully planned and executed effort of its sort, it created yet another currency, the real, loosely pegged to the U.S. dollar. For months before the money circulated, businesses were obliged to record all of their transactions and accounts in a dollar-equivalent unit, as preparation for shifting to the real. The government saved up $40 billion in hard-currency reserves to withstand any run on the exchange rate. Finally, a huge publicity campaign preceded and accompanied the new currency, essentially working to convince the population as to the steady value of the real.

The Plano Real worked even better than its creators hoped. Officials used all manner of coercion to prevent businesses and unions from increasing prices or wages before the plan went into effect, and afterward they remained vigilant against clandestine price hikes. In some cases, the government authorized the importation of cheaper foreign goods to drive down prices. The value of the real held relatively steady for more than a year after it began trading in July 1994. Inflation during the first year, moreover, stood at less than 10 percent. It seemed nothing short of a miracle, the lowest price increases in decades. The public credited Fernando Henrique Cardoso with this success and accordingly elected him in October 1994 in the first round of voting.

The new administration took office on January 1, 1995, and pursued neoliberal policies while keeping a wary eye on sources of inflation. One by one, public enterprises were offered for sale to private consortia, resuming privatization begun under Collor and Franco. Brazil's economy performed remarkably, posting growth rates consistently above 4 percent a year through the mid-1990s. The foreign debt, meanwhile, had been reduced through rescheduling with commercial banks. Moreover, although still large, it receded in importance due to the overall expansion of the GNP.

**Figure 24.5** Former president of Brazil Fernando Henrique Cardoso at the Earth Day meeting in 2012. Due to its territorial size and economic strength, Brazil plays an important role in mitigating global climate change. Courtesy Fabio Rodrigues Pozzebom/Agência Brasil, Wiki Commons.

Cardoso began making trips abroad during his first six months in office. He met with Southern Cone presidents to advance negotiations on Mercosur, the common market embracing Brazil, Argentina, Uruguay, and Paraguay. He met with President Bill Clinton to discuss Latin America. He visited Europe, finally, where he conferred with business and finance leaders. He enjoyed a remarkable honeymoon.

President Cardoso began to meet resistance to his program in his second year, the result, ironically, of the 1988 Constitution, whose writing he had presided over. That charter gave Congress more power than the executive branch, and lobbyists soon tied up many of his legislative initiatives. Moreover, corruption remained common, also hampering administration. It proved particularly difficult to rein in expenditures when the bureaucracy, higher education, entrenched business interests, and organized labor opposed any cuts in spending. Without cuts, the president could not initiate any programs for the poor and uneducated.

Cardoso therefore oversaw an administration devoted to the status quo in which the rich continued to get richer and the poor poorer, therefore failing to address what remained one of the world's worst records for inequality. Economic performance depended on inflows of short-term foreign investment, which the president could not curtail for fear of halting job growth.

Imbalance in the federal budget also put pressure on prices, which rose gradually and called for an adjustment in the exchange rate. Yet the president remained adamant that the real should remain stable, so it became overvalued vis-à-vis the dollar. Finally, the president, facing the end of his five-year term without much progress, made a deal with the devil. He negotiated a constitutional amendment that allowed him to run for reelection yet reduced the presidential term to four years. He cut so many deals with congressional leaders, making so many concessions and giving away so much patronage, that it undermined his own authority and ability to pass his programs.

Cardoso won outright reelection in fall 1998 by gaining over 50 percent of the popular vote. Unfortunately, the economy had become vulnerable by then, and when in early 1999 the governor of Minas Gerais, Itamar Franco, announced that his state would default on debts to Brasília, international traders mounted a successful campaign to force devaluation.

Still, Brazil entered the twenty-first century as a middle-ranked nation in economic terms, politically stable and socially complex. With the fifth largest land area, the sixth largest population, and at the time the seventh largest economy in the world, Brazil had influence in global affairs. Brazil led its Southern Cone neighbors Argentina, Uruguay, and Paraguay in Mercosur, and its diplomats played leading roles in international organizations. Any major developments in the Western Hemisphere necessarily included Brazil. Yet Cardoso began his second term as practically a lame-duck president.

By the time the parties were gearing up for the September 2002 elections, Cardoso had lost most of the public approval that he had earned in his first term. His party nominated José Serra, an economist who had served competently as health minister, to run for president. Lula da Silva, who had run for president in the previous three elections, won the nomination of the Workers' Party again. This time, however, Lula captured first place in the election and then nearly two-thirds of the runoff vote. His victory marked a dramatic change in the course of Brazilian politics.

## RESULTS OF DEMOCRATIZATION

The presidencies of Belaúnde, Alfonsín, and Sarney, along with several others, shared several common features. For one thing, all three men were veteran politicians in their fifties and sixties. None had military experience, but they had survived army regimes. Once in office, they reestablished constitutional procedures. They held free, direct elections and pluralistic, party-based decision making. They also began to apply neoliberal economic policies, although inconsistently. The plans that their advisors assembled had standard as well as unorthodox elements. They struggled with massive foreign debts, high inflation, pent-up labor demands, social inequality, demands for justice after years of repression, and overregulated financial systems.

These transitional presidents enjoyed one major advantage, however: the relaxation of international tensions that accompanied the waning of the Cold

War. Internal and external military threats gradually disappeared (except for Sendero Luminoso in Peru). As a result, the armed forces retreated into the background. Still, civilian politicians had difficulty making army officers accountable for their actions. Only Alfonsín managed to bring the worst offenders to trial, and as a result he suffered three unsuccessful coup attempts. In Brazil, Peru, and later Chile, the army enjoyed immunity from prosecution.

The problems these transitional democratic governments faced—problems that stemmed from the legacies of military rule, the crises of the Lost Decade, and a changing electorate—set the stage for the turn to neopopulists in each of these places. Neopopulism shared many of the characteristics of earlier populism, including the leaders' appeal to the masses, the promise of reform, and a reliance on mass media to build a following.

Yet Latin America had changed a great deal since midcentury, and the economic crises had fostered a turn to neoliberalism that often was at odds with populist programs. Moreover, the population now making demands on these presidents was much larger, more diverse, and less organized, and thus was no longer so easily constrained and disciplined by unions or other mass organizations.

As a result, the heterodox prescriptions of neopopulists, which mixed Keynesian and liberal economic policy and attempted populist programs amid high inflation and demands from international and domestic elites for austerity, often fell short of either fixing the economy or substantially improving the standards of living of the majority. As a result, neopopulism would soon give way to a leftist turn in politics across the region, as a pink tide swept over much of South America in the first decade of the new century.

## PEACE, DEMOCRACY, AND NEOLIBERALISM IN CENTRAL AMERICA AND THE CARIBBEAN

To many observers, leftist forces seemed more threatening than ever in Central America in the early to mid-1980s. Guerrilla activity in places like Guatemala and El Salvador remained high, and military regimes there launched into what would become one of the most vicious phases of repression as they sought to stamp out any traces of possible communist support. At the same time, as in South America, Central America and the Caribbean experienced a wave of democratization and a neoliberal economic opening beginning in the 1980s. Unlike in South America, however, the U.S. continued to intervene aggressively in the region, especially since the Sandinistas posed a threat to Washington's preeminence there. Indeed, Central America became home to one of the earliest efforts to tie market-driven growth to curbing leftist forces in Latin America. To contain the Sandinistas, who had won control in Nicaragua in 1979, and thereby to keep Marxism from spreading, the Reagan administration unveiled the Caribbean Basin Initiative (CBI), a development program that offered low tariffs and investment money in exchange for cooperation with U.S. policy aims in the region.

Nevertheless, the fighting that centered on Nicaragua undermined peace to such a degree that neighboring countries, and indeed nations from around the globe, tried to convince the United States to end its sponsorship of the Contras. From these efforts, a new sense of solidarity swept the region, prompting plans for political and economic cooperation. By the end of the century, the leftist threat seemed to have waned, as democracy, neoliberalism, and peace and reconciliation efforts dominated across the region.

As the civil war between the Sandinistas and the U.S.-trained and funded Contras grew, it spread to nearby countries. For example, President Reagan bribed the Honduran government to allow construction of a Contra base on the Nicaraguan border. U.S. forces landed in Honduras and helped prepare the terrain for Contra attacks, and U.S. advisors accompanied many Contra operations.

Reagan received a great deal of criticism for his Nicaragua policy, at home and abroad, so in 1982 he announced the CBI. Countries that qualified (by supporting U.S. policies, lowering tariffs, and allowing imports of machinery and raw materials) became eligible to receive aid plus investments from U.S. corporations. These projects were mostly factories where local workers assembled final products, like the maquiladoras in Mexico. The most common industries begun under CBI auspices produced finished clothing, usually located in free-trade zones. Of the almost two dozen participating countries, the Dominican Republic, Haiti, and Guatemala received the largest amount of CBI investment. Congress excluded Nicaragua for political reasons.

Rising trade with island nations under the CBI also encouraged other enterprises. Tourism, always a mainstay of the Caribbean, bounced back, becoming a major factor in its recovery from the 1980s recession. U.S., Canadian, and European tourists visited by the millions, traveling mostly by plane and cruise ship. Offshore banking and data input services also grew in importance in the late 1980s.

Despite the CBI, the Reagan administration's policies in the Caribbean echoed the era of gunboat diplomacy. In 1983, Reagan ordered the Pentagon to invade the tiny island nation of Grenada. This invasion, justified on the grounds that a Marxist coup put U.S. citizens in jeopardy, was analogous to Lyndon Johnson's invasion of the Dominican Republic eighteen years earlier, on a much smaller scale. Grenada, tiny in comparison, did not pose any real security threat to the United States. But the U.S. State Department elicited an invitation from several governments in the region to intervene in Grenada to stop the revolutionary government. The occupation accomplished its objective, though only after serious communications and logistical errors had greatly embarrassed U.S. military officials.

Moreover, aid to the Contras violated international law, and a clandestine CIA attack on Nicaraguan port facilities even brought a World Court judgment against the United States. In 1984 Congress attached an amendment to the federal budget banning military aid to the Contras. Nevertheless, the administration continued to channel supplies and cash to the area through surreptitious means coordinated by the staff of the National Security Council. By the time the ban was lifted in 1986, information had leaked out about the illegal aid. These leaks led to the Iran-Contra scandal, indictments of high officials, and later pardons by President George H. W. Bush.

As the decade came to a close, moves toward peace and democratic elections spread across the region, including Nicaragua, El Salvador, and Guatemala. They were presaged by a series of meetings aimed at ending the Contra War and other regional hostilities, including continued guerrilla fighting and counterinsurgency actions. At first these were called the Contadora Talks, named after the Panamanian island resort where they began in 1983. Representatives of Central American nations and several others took part in these talks over the next few years, while the United States dragged its feet, not wishing to abandon the Contras in Nicaragua.

Coming out of the Contadora Group, Esquipulas I took place in May 1986, attended by the five Central American presidents and resulting in an agreement to end the fighting and seek peace and economic cooperation in the region. By 1987, the Central American talks had led to an agreement that included a cease-fire and the bases for permanent peace, such as a return to democracy and free elections. President Óscar Arias of Costa Rica (1986–1990, 2006–2010) came up with an acceptable plan, called Esquipulas II, after the Guatemalan town where it was initialed. Arias subsequently received the Nobel Peace Prize for his efforts.

In the following years, democratic elections became the norm in the region. In 1990, the Nicaraguan government held elections for virtually all executive and legislative offices in the country. The campaigns, very intense and competitive, attracted thousands of observers because they tested the ability of the Sandinistas to transform their government into a democracy. It would be a plebiscite on the revolution. Opposition candidate Violeta Chamorro won the election, and the parties that supported her gained a majority in the legislature. Daniel Ortega, head of the Sandinista government, passed the presidential sash to her peacefully late that year.

Regional cooperation extended to the economic sphere as well. Several cultural and economic blocs coalesced or reemerged to seek better ways to promote economic development. The Central American Common Market, for example, which had lapsed into inactivity in the 1980s, took on new life in the 1990s. Moreover, the five participating countries plus Panama created the Central American Parliament, designed to resolve border and economic disputes and perhaps develop more uniform immigration and social policies.

**Figure 24.6** Violeta Chamorro cartoon figure wielding Bush and Contra boxing gloves to take on Daniel Ortega in Nicaragua's 1990 presidential election. Courtesy Library of Congress.

Integration proceeded in the Caribbean as well. The Caricom economic group, for example, which was formed in 1975, expanded its trade in the 1990s.

## DRUGS AND THE CHALLENGE TO DEMOCRACY IN CENTRAL AMERICA

Just as the presidents of Central America were joining forces economically and many countries were returning to democracy and relative peace, a new threat emerged that tied together the region in new and increasingly violent ways. The amount of drugs—mostly from Colombia—being shipped to the United States increased rapidly in the 1980s (see chapter 20). The multi-billion-dollar industry had complex roots. Colombian producers already dominated shipments of marijuana grown along the Caribbean coast. The rise of cocaine consumption, however, required other sources. The raw material for cocaine was coca leaves, which grew in Bolivia and Peru, as well as Colombia. Local processors reduced the leaves to a paste and sent it north to Colombia by airplane. Elaborate factories in Colombia completed the refining, after which the pure cocaine was put onto airplanes for dispatch to the United States and other markets. U.S. criminal organizations handled most of the distribution of drugs in the United States. Their payments to Colombian suppliers, however, required special handling to evade detection and taxes. This process, called money laundering, took place mostly in banks around the Caribbean region.

The ratio between the price of coca leaves, a staple product in Bolivia, and the value of the refined product on U.S. streets was on the order of 1 to 10,000, creating a huge potential for profits all along the supply chain that linked the Andes through Central America to the United States. As cocaine became more popular during the 1980s, the price rose even more, fueling the largest illegal industry in the world. This prompted President Alan García of Peru to state, partly in jest, that the cocaine trade was the only successful multinational industry ever created by Latin Americans.

Mafia-like organizations called cartels sprang up in Colombian cities to oversee production, transport, refining, and financial arrangements. For a time, the cartel in Medellín dominated the drug trade, but soon the Cali and Cartagena cartels joined in. They employed veritable armies of professionals to carry on the business. Their operations stretched down into Peru and Bolivia for raw materials, through Central America, the Caribbean, and Mexico for transport and money laundering, and finally to the United States and Europe for markets.

The narcotics trade proved terribly destructive to many Latin American nations. The cartels controlled significant shares of the GNP in Bolivia, Peru, and Colombia, where they wielded enormous power in all branches of government. At least a dozen other nations were drawn into the narco-trafficking business, including places like Nicaragua, Honduras, and Mexico; Peru, Colombia, and El Salvador actually witnessed more violence in the 1990s in part because of the expanding drug trade. The cartel bosses bribed and intimidated officials, murdered rivals, bought and sold front companies, and introduced drug consumption everywhere they operated. They made alliances with guerrilla organizations, often trading weapons for raw materials or security services.

The United States invested considerable effort in curbing the supply of narcotics in its so-called War on Drugs. U.S. officials financed programs designed to end the growing of coca plants, for example. This sometimes went against the grain of local customs and economy in Peru and Bolivia, where chewing coca leaves was as common as smoking tobacco in the United States. And U.S. policy goals were often confusing and even contradictory. For example, the CIA actually sanctioned some drug trade in Central America in order to raise money for the Contras and has since been shown to have had direct links to the explosion of crack cocaine consumption in the United States in the 1980s.

In the 1990s, U.S. officials and elites in Latin America began to claim some victories in the War on Drugs. They pointed to arrests of prominent cartel leaders like Pablo Escobar, and flat demand for cocaine in the U.S., as evidence of their success. Not until the explosion of drug-fueled violence in Central America and Mexico after 2006 would these leaders realize that the drug trade was far from ended, and that it had merely changed its shape.

## DICTATORSHIP, INVASION, AND THE U.S. CANAL

During the 1980s drug trafficking increased substantially in Panama. Drugs had been smuggled through Panama at least since the 1940s, but in the 1980s both logistics and money laundering became major businesses there. The National Guard (renamed the Panama Defense Force in 1983) usually had a hand in various illegal activities, especially drugs.

When Colonel Manuel Antonio Noriega became head of the Defense Force in 1983, he oversaw arrangements by which the cartels sent drugs and money through the country. Many lawyers, politicians, and bankers profited along with Defense Force officers. With all this activity came increasing scrutiny by the U.S. government.

Noriega ruled Panama from behind a facade of constitutional government. He installed and removed several presidents during the time he served as commander of the Defense Force. He also ran something of an intelligence brokerage in the Caribbean region. He maintained contacts with the Cuban and Nicaraguan regimes while also exchanging information with the U.S., Honduran, and El Salvadoran governments. The fact that he also permitted a number of other illegal activities in Panama eventually gave him an unsavory reputation.

Noriega put the United States in an awkward position. George H. W. Bush, vice president under Reagan and then president from 1989 to 1993, had dealt with Noriega on an official basis since the 1970s and presumably found him acceptable. By 1987, however, Noriega had become an embarrassment to the Reagan-Bush administration. Noriega had profited from drugs, helped furnish illegal weapons to the Contras, shared intelligence information, and now ruled Panama as a dictator.

In December 1989 President Bush authorized Operation Just Cause, a full-scale military invasion of Panama. The alleged purpose was to arrest Noriega for prosecution in Florida on drug charges. In fact, the invasion boosted Bush's popularity by making him appear decisive, and it also diverted attention from the fact that the United States had been complicit in Noriega's rise to power. It also allowed U.S. authorities to put the Panama Canal treaty implementation back on track. The invaders captured Noriega, and U.S. courts eventually tried and sentenced him to forty years in jail. In the meantime, the United States installed a caretaker government and launched a major aid program to revive the ailing economy.

The aftermath of the 1989 invasion left the United States with sufficient power to dictate the terms of peace. State Department and military officials encouraged reforms and disbursement of aid in ways that stimulated the economy. Democratic procedures led to revising the constitution, replacing the military with a national police, and adopting neoliberal economic policies. An interim government assumed authority in 1990 and held a plebiscite, allowing it to test brand-new election procedures. U.S. presence diminished in the early 1990s as peace resumed and the nation approached normalcy again. The free press revived and party politics ramped up. Behind the scenes, meanwhile, plans went forward for Panama to take over the canal in 1999.

The 1994 presidential election saw a former ally of General Torrijos win by a narrow plurality of votes—the constitution did not allow for runoffs. Ernesto Pérez Balladares, a U.S.-trained businessman, led the PRD into the presidency and enjoyed a substantial block of votes in the legislature. He undertook an economic program of privatization and greater integration into world markets. He worked with a new agency to administer lands and buildings turned over by the Panama Canal. Corruption and drug trafficking continued, but Pérez Balladares managed to avoid too much scandal. Unemployment remained high. Preparing the country to assume ownership of the canal proved to be his most positive legacy.

In 1999 the PRD's candidate lost to the country's first female president, Mireya Moscoso. Widow of former president Arnulfo Arias, Moscoso had long dabbled in politics. Yet she had little administrative experience and adopted the oppositionist style of her late husband. Campaigning to represent poor and rural constituents, she mobilized the discontented. Once in office, Moscoso presided over the transfer of the canal to Panamanian ownership, promising to maintain the waterway and provide the same services as the United States had. To her credit, the canal continued to operate efficiently throughout her administration.

Few other initiatives proved as fruitful, however, because the world recession caused Panama's economy to grow very slowly. Moscoso was not eligible for reelection at the end of her term in 2004. Instead, voters chose Martín Torrijos, son of the former dictator, to lead the country in the 2004–2009 term. Under his leadership, Panama once again surged in importance as the U.S. expanded the War on Terror after 9/11 to include areas of vital strategic interest, such as the Panama Canal.

## CUBA AND THE END OF THE COLD WAR

The 1980s had been particularly difficult in Cuba, due not only to the world recession but also to the decline and dissolution of the Soviet bloc. Cuba's economy had long since reverted to dependence on sugar and tobacco exports, sold at subsidized prices in communist countries. The economy stayed afloat by reexporting cheap petroleum from the USSR, as well as by Soviet credit to cover Cuba's imports.

Economists calculated that Cuba cost the Soviets several billion dollars a year in the mid-1980s. Fidel Castro partially repaid the aid with a vigorous pro-USSR foreign policy and an active role in furthering the socialist cause in Africa. At one point, Cuba maintained thirty thousand troops in Africa.

Throughout the early years of the Cuban Revolution, Castro resisted all pressure to democratize the country. He argued that the great advances that Cubans had achieved in health, education, housing, and nutrition far offset losses in political participation. He stated that Cubans enjoyed more civil liberties than under Batista and that true democracy required a decent standard of living, not an artificial system of politics. Finally, he said, the Cuban people were quite happy with his leadership, which in effect gave him legitimacy.

But after his failure to achieve a symbolically important 10-million-ton sugar harvest in 1970, Castro began to alter the political system. Without relinquishing personal control, he spread responsibilities more widely among persons who had worked with him throughout the 1960s. In 1975 he held the first Communist Party congress, which wrote a constitution, ratified the following year in a plebiscite. The new system boasted the National Assembly of people's representatives, called Poder del Pueblo. The National Assembly elected a council of state, headed by Castro himself. The degree of participation, however, barely increased because party members ran the elections.

Cuba's 1980s economic experience was, if anything, worse than the rest of Latin America's. The USSR capped aid to Cuba and intimated that Castro should find a way to earn his living by trading with the noncommunist world. By the time the USSR began its twin processes of perestroika and glasnost (economic and political liberalization) in the 1980s, Cuba was seriously out of step with its long-term ally.

Cuban leaders faced major political dilemmas around 1990. First, Castro, now sixty-four years old, was unable to repudiate communism and formulate a new regime, as the Russians had done, because of his history of opposing the United States. Second, the huge and prosperous Cuban exile community in Florida stood on the sidelines waiting for Castro to die or be overthrown. If that happened, Cubans feared, the island would be swamped by exiles bent on reclaiming their lands and businesses. Exiles might cause a bloodbath or undo thirty years of revolutionary reform, or both. Unable to resolve these predicaments, Cuba's leaders remained committed to the communist path, though the 1990s would witness the transformation of Cuba's relationship with the United States and Western Europe.

When the Soviet Union dissolved and its bloc of allies collapsed, Castro found himself cut off and isolated from most of the world. In the early 1990s only Cuba, Albania, Laos, and North Korea maintained the kind of closed, Soviet-style economy that had once prevailed among communist countries. Cuban economists, desperate to adjust to the end of Soviet aid, took steps toward allowing private initiative and foreign currency transactions. Fortunately, tourism began to expand as growing numbers of European and Canadian tourists took advantage of cheap prices and unpolluted beaches, providing some hard-currency income.

Still, despite robust efforts to wean the nation from Soviet aid, Cuba's economy shrank drastically, to only about 70 percent of its previous size. The government put a brave face on the situation, calling this the "special period," but the shortages and suffering proved horrendous. Food disappeared, electricity went out, transport ground to a halt, and health indices plummeted.

Meanwhile, large numbers of refugees continued to cross the Florida Strait each year. Since the days of the Mariel boatlift, which led at least 125,000 to flee to Florida in late 1980, people had been driven out of Cuba by economic problems and political control on the island. This continued influx of refugees contributed to social and political problems in Florida. Washington instituted naval patrols to restrict flows of exiles and reached an agreement to return most to Cuba.

In 1995 the Clinton administration made plans to normalize relations with Cuba by lifting the trade embargo and travel restrictions. But in February 1996, progress halted when three small aircraft flown by Miami-based exiles were shot down by Cuban fighters while dropping leaflets over Havana. The pilots' deaths caused a furor in Washington, leading to further trade restrictions. The incident also strengthened the Cuban exile community's power. Congress did, however, pass a law authorizing academics, athletes, and artists to travel to and from Cuba.

The United States came under international pressure to end the restrictions, even enduring a suit by the European Union over retaliatory economic measures. Pope John Paul II visited Cuba in 1998 to call for ending the island's isolation and to press Castro to allow religious and civic freedoms. Perhaps most important, hundreds of thousands of European and Canadian tourists voted with their vacations by traveling to Cuba for sun and relaxation. As tourism on the island continued to grow, it pulled Cuba's economy out of the depression caused by the withdrawal of Russian subsidies. In 2000 tourism produced more money than sugar and tobacco combined. Tens of thousands of U.S. citizens also traveled to Cuba, most illegally. Amid this opening, a robust lobby arose in the United States to normalize relations, and relaxation of the trade ban permitted shipments of food and medicine after 2001.

By 2002 Cuba had established a new place in world affairs, despite domestic problems. For example, tourism forced acceptance of the dollar as an official currency, and prostitution returned. Worse, a gap in standards of living opened between those in the dollar economy and ordinary Cubans left outside it,

### The Mass Exodus of El Mariel

"The family reunification visits of 1979 had some unforeseen and explosive ramifications. . . . in 1979 and 1980 Cubans made a number of attempts to seek asylum in foreign embassies, and seagoing vessels and aircraft were hijacked by those seeking to flee.

"The most dramatic and far-reaching asylum-seeking attempt occurred on April 1, 1980, when a driver crashed his bus through the gates of the Peruvian embassy in Havana. Peru's ambassador immediately granted asylum to the driver and his five passengers. Angered, Castro responded by withdrawing police protection for the embassy and declaring it open. This action led another 10,850 asylum seekers to pack into the embassy grounds . . .

"Within a few days, Peru, Costa Rica, the United States, and Spain agreed to take in a few thousand of the asylum seekers. In the meantime in South Florida, hundreds of individuals prepared a ragtag flotilla to pick up relatives and friends. . . .

"The government denigrated and systematically harassed the crowd gathered inside the embassy. On April 19, through the coordination of the [Committees for Defense of the Revolution], it mobilized nearly one million people to march in repudiation of the crowd. 'Que se vayan! Que se vayan!' . . . The next day Castro announced that those wishing to leave could do so and opened the port of El Mariel so vessels could come to fetch them. The government used the opportunity to deport thousands of so-called 'undesirables.' They are 'the scum of the country,' Castro blasted in his May Day speech . . .

"During the first fifteen days of the Mariel exodus, 16,000 refugees arrived in Key West. . . . When the last vessel reached Key West, over 125,266 refugees had crossed the Florida Straits.

"While the Mariel exodus served as an escape valve to release mounting frustration and rising anti-government feelings, it backfired because it hurt Cuba's international reputation . . .

"While the U.S. media sensationally exaggerated the proportion of so-called undesirables, the actual number of Mariel entrants who were criminals and mental patients was small. . . . According to official immigration records, the total number of actual criminals and mental patients was lower than in the general U.S. population.

"Artists and intellectuals were overrepresented among Mariel exiles. . . . [one of them] author Reynaldo Arenas, perhaps the best known of all Mariel exiles, wrote bitterly about his experiences in Cuban Miami. . . . 'If Cuba is Hell, Miami is Purgatory.'"

Luis Martínez-Fernández, *Revolutionary Cuba: A History* (Gainesville: University Press of Florida, 2014), pp. 157–62.

highlighting the limits of Castro's socialist path. And while health and education levels returned to previous levels, standards of nutrition and physical well-being were not acceptable to the Cuban people. Moreover, there was an ever-growing sentiment among the young, who had never known anything other than Castro's Cuba, that they wished they had better access to the world, including its news, goods, travel, and the Internet.

## CONCLUSIONS AND ISSUES

The 1980s brought turmoil, poverty, and suffering to much of Latin America. Wars, low-intensity conflicts, economic recession, and dislocations of people ravaged many nations. The Dirty Wars in the Southern Cone countries left tens of thousands dead, maimed, or missing, as they did in Central America as well.

The economic collapse of the early 1980s proved so severe that it induced a major shift by policymakers. They abandoned the nationalist approaches devised by ECLAC in the 1950s and 1960s and turned to market mechanisms to drive economic decisions. A new orthodoxy emerged, called neoliberalism, which prescribed freer trade, privatization, and less government employment and spending, and which dismantled decades-old intervention and regulation by public agencies. Neoliberalism often brought gains in productivity from workers, businesspeople, and professionals. While economic growth returned to most countries by the 1990s, however, this growth came with costs.

After surging in the 1980s, poverty levels once again dropped back, but unemployment remained high and economic growth ultimately benefited the wealthy much more than the poor. This exacerbated already high rates of inequality in the region, not the least through the sell-off of state industries to the wealthy. Economic disruption meant more people migrated in search of work, swelling cities and free-trade zones as well as expanding illegal migration into the U.S.

In some countries, such as Mexico, small domestic industry lost out as free-trade agreements brought foreign investment, multinational corporations, and foreign goods with which they could not compete. Austerity measures imposed by the IMF and other international lenders meant that public spending on education, health, and social security dropped precipitously. Civic organizations and Protestant churches often burst onto the scene to fill the gap, facilitated by the end of military governments and the dire needs of the region's poorest.

The economic hardships of the early 1980s helped drive the military to withdraw from government and allowed civilians to restore democratic administrations. Democratization occurred fitfully, hampered by continued meddling by army officers, an inexperienced generation of leaders, and millions of new voters. Several patterns emerged in South America. For a time, populists who survived from the 1960s made comebacks. Then, managerial governments devoted to economic stabilization and democracy predominated. By the 1990s, several countries had chosen neopopulist leaders—people who used the old methods of vote gathering while insisting on neoliberal economic programs. Their inability in most cases to fulfill their promises helped to spur the leftist turn in the region in the early 2000s.

The Caribbean Basin, meanwhile, at first endured an escalation of political violence sponsored by the United States. But the decade ended in relative calm. The Contra War wound down in 1987, when belligerent and neighboring countries signed a peace accord. A new economic approach based on freer trade and offshore manufacturing boosted some Caribbean economies, and most pledged to honor democracy and free elections as they moved toward national reconciliation. Peace accords with guerrilla groups by the 1990s, which often transitioned into political parties amid the return to democracy, introduced a new era of political competition to the region.

Only in Panama and Cuba did the situation worsen during the 1980s. In the former, an impasse between Washington and the dictator Manuel Noriega led to an armed invasion that returned Panama to U.S. tutelage. And in the latter, Castro found himself isolated by the dramatic end of the Soviet Union and the breakup of its eastern bloc of allies. Willing to pursue only small internal reforms and unable to deflect hostility from the exile community in Florida, Castro rode out the uneven 1990s in the hopes of finding some longer-term solution to the island nation's economic and diplomatic dilemmas.

## Discussion Questions

What factors caused the economic difficulties of the 1980s and how did the leaders understand the problems and attempt to solve them?

The transition of Latin American nations back to democratic government in the 1980s contained similar elements. What were these elements and how did they come about?

What was the legacy of decades of military government in the Southern Cone? The legacy of democratization?

How did neopopulism differ from the classic movements of the mid-twentieth century in terms of its style of governance, its followers, and its policies? What challenges did it face and what was the impact on its programs?

What explains the hard line taken by U.S. presidents in the Caribbean Basin, and what results can be attributed to their actions? What impact did free markets and democracy have in that region?

How did the rise of the drug trade from Latin America to the United States and Europe shape how these regions were tied together, and how did the connections between producers and their markets change?

How did Manuel Noriega rise to power in Panama, despite the U.S. presence there? What was his impact in Panama?

How did the end of the Cold War impact Cuba? Why were Cuba and the United States unable to set aside decades of hostility in order to normalize diplomatic relations in the 1990s?

**Timeline**

| | |
|---|---|
| 1980–84 | Return to democracy under Patricio Aylwin (Chile), Fernando Belaúnde (Peru), Raúl Alfonsín (Argentina), and José Sarney (Brazil) |
| 1980s | Lost Decade in Latin America |
| 1980s | Ronald Reagan reinstitutes "gunboat diplomacy," invades Grenada, and sponsors the Contra War against the Sandinistas in Nicaragua |
| 1985–2000 | Rise of neopopulists Alan García (Peru), Alberto Fujimori (Peru), Carlos Menem (Argentina) and Fernando Collor de Mello (Brazil) |
| 1989 | George H. W. Bush orders an invasion of Panama to arrest Manuel Noriega and carry out canal treaty |
| 1990s | Cuba's ailing economy devastated by withdrawal of Soviet assistance after fall of USSR, initiating island's "special period" |
| 1990s–2000s | Economic and political stability under Itamar Franco (Brazil), Fernando Henrique Cardoso (Brazil), and Alejandro Toledo (Peru) |

**Keywords**

austerity
Caribbean Basin Initiative (CBI)
cartels
Central American Parliament
constitutionalism
Contra War
Esquipulas I and II
International Monetary Fund (IMF)
Iran-Contra scandal
Lost Decade
Mariel boatlift

Mercosur
neoliberalism
neopopulism
*Nunca mais*
Operation Just Cause
privatization
Sendero Luminoso
War on Drugs
War on Terror
Washington Consensus
World Bank

# Latin America in the Twenty-First Century

### Berta's Ulcer

Cuba's "special period," a euphemism for the nearly one-third drop in its economy in the mid-1990s, caused enormous hardships for most citizens, especially those who had little to fall back on. The economic collapse was largely due to the fall of the Soviet Union, which had subsidized much of the Cuban economy since Castro's turn to communism in the early 1960s. Its impact was deep and widespread, as the following short piece indicates. It is about a woman who finds a surprising way to use the island's famed health-care system to ameliorate the shortages.

Cuban writer Nancy Alonso, well known in Cuba and abroad, captures these difficulties and reveals the creative ways in which Cubans dealt with the crisis. Alonso grew up with the revolution and continues to believe in its goals. She graduated from the University of Havana with a degree in biological sciences and for 25 years was a professor and researcher there. She also taught physiology at the University of Jimma's Institute of Health Sciences in Ethiopia for two years, as part of Cuba's medical and educational outreach and service overseas. Alonso's literary voice provides human insight into the ironies of Cuban society.

Berta arrived at Central Havana Emergency Hospital before eight o'clock in the morning, although her appointment was for nine. She was so nervous that she hadn't been able to stay at home. She preferred to be waiting close to the place where they would do the test, the same one that last year had resulted in the diagnosis of her illness. She felt anxious not only about all the things they would do to her body but also about the results of the examination.

Two months before, Berta had begun to smoke, something she never did, not even when she was an adolescent and wanted to put on grownup airs. At first she felt nausea when she inhaled, but after a week she could go through a pack of cigarettes in twenty-four hours as if she'd been a chain-smoker her entire life. She needed to breathe in all the smoke she could. And coffee, a swig of coffee, before every cigarette.

While she waited her turn, she went out to the street to smoke a few more times. If the test turned out well, she wouldn't be doing that again for another ten months, as the date for the repeat examination began to draw near.

When she entered the laboratory, she was helped to swallow the slender tube that would examine the condition of the walls of her stomach. She listened as the doctors evaluated what they observed, and most important of all, the conclusion: her gastric ulcer had not healed.

Berta tried to hide her euphoria. Her efforts with cigarettes and coffee had produced the desired effect. There was the ulcer, live and latent. This would give her the medical certification guaranteeing a dietary supplement to her ration book of basic food items. Now she could have another year of breakfasts with milk. Problem solved.

She tucked the valuable paper with the positive lab result inside her purse and spied the cigarette pack that she had kept hidden from the doctors. She would give it to someone with a nicotine habit because she—that's for sure—wasn't somebody who liked to smoke.[1]


## DEMOCRACY AND THE TURN TO THE LEFT

Democratic politics deepened across much of Latin America in the first part of the new century. It was accompanied by relatively buoyant economic growth that pointed, many thought, to the end of dictatorship and economic recession. Other currents were at work as well. Many were frustrated by neopopulism, economic malaise amid growth, political corruption, and traditionalism. Seemingly endemic poverty and inequality further fueled new social and political movements. People took to the streets and made new demands. Across the region, but especially in South America, leftist governments won democratic elections as a "pink tide" swept across the region. Polemical, outspoken leftists like Hugo Chávez in Venezuela, Evo Morales in Bolivia, Daniel Ortega in Nicaragua, and Rafael Correa in Ecuador pushed to the forefront of politics. They were accompanied by more mainstream leftists like Lula da Silva in Brazil, Michelle Bachelet in Chile, and the Kirchners in Argentina. In general, voters rejected U.S.-backed conservative and neopopulist politics and instead turned to radical and leftist options.

New leaders faced challenges like growing drug-fueled violence, continuing corruption, massive migration and urbanization, environmental degradation, and, always it seemed, intractable poverty. In foreign affairs, two of the biggest changes the new leaders faced were the unfolding global War on Terror after 9/11 and the growing role of China in the region.

After decades of neoliberal policies, Latin America is now experiencing the full force of globalization. To compete in this new economy, Latin American

**Figure 25.1** Daniel Ortega, former Sandinista leader and president of Nicaragua, speaking in Santiago on the thirtieth anniversary of the death of Salvador Allende. Ortega won reelection as president in 2006, 2011, and 2016. Photo courtesy of Alejandro Stuart, Stanford University Libraries Special Collections.

countries have forged new trade agreements with each other and lessened dependence on the U.S. through policies like new investment and trade relations with countries like China, Russia, and Australia.

To address a mixture of traditional and new concerns, many leftist leaders have supported socialist policies. They have used the state to encourage some redistribution of resources and power, as well as to satisfy demands in the areas of social and economic justice while continuing their countries' integration into global markets. Even the most appealing leftists—leaders like Evo Morales, Lula da Silva, and Michelle Bachelet—have had to moderate their calls for reform in order to foster economic growth and limit the potential for conservative backlash.

Conservatives nevertheless remain vital in the region, even winning the presidency in the early 2000s in countries like Mexico, El Salvador, and Colombia and returning to power in the middle of the second decade in places like Argentina and Brazil. The armies in most countries have stayed out of politics, except for a few cases, like Honduras in 2009. Most officers active during the period of military regimes in the late twentieth century have retired voluntarily or been removed from duty, and truth commissions were established in countries like Chile, Argentina, Guatemala, and Brazil to investigate human rights' crimes during the military era. Only sporadic conflicts, such as a border skirmish between Peru and Ecuador, guerrilla attacks in northern Colombia, the drug wars in Mexico and Central America, and conflicts between miners and indigenous Yanomamis in the northern Amazon have provoked military mobilizations.

The investigation of human rights abuses during the Dirty War years led to some deep and often painful probes into the past of countries like Guatemala, Argentina, Chile, and Brazil. Religious and judicial authorities published accounts, called *Never Again,* of persons who had disappeared in the repression to ensure that the wars and their victims were not forgotten. Since 2000, numerous, often very prominent, former military officers and their supporters in Guatemala, Argentina, Chile, and Brazil have faced prosecution for their crimes, as leftist presidents annulled pardons and opened up avenues to punishment and reconciliation. In a landmark case in Argentina, in August 2016, thirty-eight military officials were convicted for their crimes; twenty-eight of them, including a former general, received life sentences. That some of the new leftist presidents, including Presidents Lula da Silva and Dilma Rousseff of Brazil and Michelle Bachelet of Chile, had themselves been jailed or tortured by the military during the Dirty Wars helped push forward the justice-seeking agenda. The truth commissions represented a dramatic shift in how Latin Americans dealt with their past—honestly, and, equally important, openly, without fears of retribution.

Since 2010, more conservatives have been elected, such as in Chile and Argentina, and conservatives impeached leftist Dilma Rousseff in Brazil. But economic sluggishness has hampered the right's ability to pursue its platforms, especially in Argentina, Venezuela, and more recently Brazil. Overall, left, right, or centrist, Latin America remains committed in principle and practice to democratic transitions, constitutional government, and civilian control.

## Venezuela

No country saw the pink tide sweep over it more forcefully than Venezuela under the leadership of Colonel Hugo Chávez (1999–2013). Middle-aged, fairly short, and compact in build, Chávez came from a small town and enlisted in the military at an early age. He chose the paratroopers and rose in rank during his career. He had a good natural intelligence and better-than-average memory, but was largely unschooled. Nevertheless, he proved to be a disciplined, uncompromising, and forceful leader. In 1992, he attempted a military coup against the corrupt president Carlos Andrés Pérez. The coup failed and Chávez spent two years in jail before being released. By then, he had won over many sympathizers among the Venezuelan middle class.

In the mid-1990s, Chávez assembled a team of collaborators who believed, as he did, that the traditional parties had entirely sold out to big business, especially foreign companies. Vast amounts of money flowed to politicians' foreign bank accounts, with no accountability to the voters. Neither the Acción Democrática (AD) nor COPEI, which had alternated in power since 1958, had clean hands, with each taking advantage of its power to strip the treasury of

**Figure 25.2** President Hugo
Chávez speaking to crowds in
Caracas. Authors' collection.

vast amounts of state money. The people had become estranged from government, and their interests were largely forgotten by those in office.

To bolster his image, Chávez invoked the memory of his hero—the Liberator, Simón Bolívar—as the person whose career he admired most and sought to emulate. Native son Bolívar has evoked a near divine reverence among Venezuelans over the years, and Chávez often referred to his movement as the "Bolivarian Revolution." These references sometimes took on a messianic character. Chávez even had Bolívar's bones disinterred in 2010 in an effort to show that his enemies had poisoned him. When that failed, he commissioned a grand, new mausoleum in which Bolívar's remains were reinterred.

Chávez's first election in 1998, followed by his reelection in 2000 under a new constitution that his supporters wrote, showed his enormous popularity with middle- and working-class voters. Chávez's favorite pastime became vilifying the elite, especially politicians from previous administrations.

Chávez built up loyalty among his political allies by distributing lavish patronage. Shooting from the hip, holding long-winded discussions on nightly television appearances, and hosting a call-in show, Chávez seemed to be everywhere and all-knowing. His folksy speaking style entertained his listeners, many of them poor, who viewed Chávez as their deliverer. He glibly told his opponents that they were wrong-headed and doomed to fail.

Domestically, Chávez shook up the business community by ending their favorable treatment. Consequently, many companies stopped expanding and shifted assets offshore. Tens of thousands of professionals also left the country, fearing that the regime might make a radical shift to the left and press for confiscations and nationalizations, as did the Cuban Revolution of 1959. The inflow of foreign capital also halted, due to uncertainty about the future. These and other economic developments caused a major recession and unemployment—both of which Chávez blamed on his opponents and foreign enemies.

For Chávez, the path to achieving his leftist revolution lay in gaining control of the nation's oil industry, but this jeopardized his support from both workers and the middle class. When Chávez tried to take control of the state-owned oil monopoly, PDVSA, by firing its president in 2002, an outpouring of opposition and a workers' strike stymied him. Moreover, this occurred just as Chávez was losing support from the middle class, who increasingly viewed him as overly divisive and disruptive in both style and policies.

Many cheered when a military group seized power in April 2002 amid the oil demonstrations and strikes. But support for Chávez was too strong. Chavistas poured into the streets in opposition. Within days, Chávez was back in power, though now a loose coalition of unions, business federations, media firms, and students began to form in opposition, culminating in a general strike in December that lasted into February 2003. Chávez managed, however, to break the back of the strike.

Even after a visit in January 2003 by ex-president Jimmy Carter, who recommended—with OAS support—an early referendum on Chávez, or an early election, he clung to power. Venezuelans were unwilling to abandon their long and deep commitment to the democratic process, even in the face of such a controversial leader.

Amid the lengthy strike, Chávez fired seventeen thousand workers and took over PDVSA. But a rapid drop in oil output soon after the takeover delayed his dream of using oil profits to fund a social revolution. Chávez nevertheless used some oil earnings to fund social programs. In part, he emulated Cuba's health and other social policies, and poverty levels had dropped some by 2006. His support from the lower classes remained strong, and he was reelected in 2006.

Chávez openly defied the United States and pushed for Latin Americans to work together to offset U.S. influence. He criticized U.S. policy on a number of fronts and made a controversial visit to Iraq when that nation's leader, President Saddam Hussein, was regarded as a U.S. enemy. He worked closely with OPEC countries to boost global oil prices. He made several trips to Cuba to meet with Fidel Castro, whom he saw as a mentor. On one such trip, he concluded a deal to sell petroleum to Cuba on very favorable terms.

President George W. Bush attacked Chávez, who opposed the U.S. invasion of Afghanistan in the global War on Terror. Yet throughout this period, the U.S. and Venezuela maintained diplomatic and trade ties, likely due to the fact that the U.S. remained Venezuela's primary market for oil. Signaling a new era in hemispheric politics, Chávez formed strong ties with other Latin American presidents and succeeded in gaining their support for his government—all despite U.S. opposition. Venezuela was even allowed to join Mercosur in 2012.

As Chávez grew more dictatorial, democracy suffered. His opposition, drained by the middle-class exodus, remained weak and dispersed; state institutions were largely powerless to challenge him due to his widespread support among the poor. By 2008, he managed to win voter approval for a constitutional change allowing him to seek a third term in office.

While Chávez touted increased spending on health care, social security, and education, as well as a drop in indicators like infant mortality and the poverty rate, his opponents argued that too few oil profits made their way to the broader masses. Instead, they contended that the standard of living remained unchanged, while corruption and the mishandling of public funds burgeoned.

The global downturn in 2008 only exacerbated Venezuela's problems, due largely to a precipitous decline in oil prices. A rebound soon came, but in 2014 the economy was still in a recession and oil prices continued to be very low. For a country where over 90 percent of its foreign income is from oil, the results were devastating. Inflation rose quickly to 100 percent or more, shortages of basic household items became common, and the value of Venezuela's currency fell. While the long-term effects remain uncertain, it is a crisis that Venezuela had not seen since Chávez took power.

Chávez won reelection in October 2012, but died of cancer in March 2013. His successor was longtime Chavista Nicolás Maduro (2013–), whom Chávez had chosen for vice president when he was reelected in 2012. Although Maduro was officially elected to office in April 2013, it was by a slim margin, and he has struggled to reign in opposition both inside and outside his party. As the sheen of Chávez has worn off, Maduro's support has plummeted, made worse by Venezuela's dire economic situation. In 2015, he faced protests and demonstrations over corruption, inflation, and violence, much of it a legacy of Chávez's economic and fiscal policies. His government's crackdown on the protests only exacerbated the deteriorating social and political situation. Finally, in January 2016, Chávez's Socialist Party lost control of Congress. As the year progressed, a continued slump in global oil prices and a drop in production left the economy in tatters, even though it sits on the world's largest known oil reserves. The IMF declared it the world's worst-performing economy in 2016, shrinking a projected 10 percent. By midyear, many Venezuelans were facing daily food shortages, electricity rationing, and a lack of other goods and services. Riots and looting had broken out, and those who could were crossing the border into neighboring Colombia to buy food. The future of the left in Venezuela remained uncertain.

## Bolivia

As part of the return to democracy in the 1990s, more nations than ever before began to recognize the racial and ethnic identities and rights of Afro-descendant and indigenous people. Rather than the language of difference inherent in indigenismo or of assimilation in mestizaje, countries have declared themselves to be multicultural, and have revised laws and policies accordingly. Respect for ethnic and racial diversity is now part of the law in many places.[2]

Since the 1960s, indigenous and Afro-rights groups have become better organized and more powerful across the region as well. In the 1990s, they met more regularly at large international meetings in places like Ecuador, Mexico, and Guatemala, where thousands of representatives from two dozen countries in the region voiced their demands, which ranged from legal and resource rights to calls for justice for groups targeted during the Dirty Wars due to their race or ethnicity. By the early 2000s, indigenous groups had taken explicit aim at neoliberalism as the cause of continued discrimination and injustice. They argued that the focus on privatization impinged on ancestral land rights. They demanded autonomy and land, and, embracing the global waves of multiculturalism, challenged mainstream national efforts to assimilate them and erode their traditional sources of income and well-being. They also condemned environmental devastation and the adoption of genetically modified crops. They argued that private companies were exploiting them without leaving behind any wealth. Nowhere have these protests been sharper than in Bolivia, where indigenous people protesting the privatization of natural resources launched a "Water War" and later a "Gas War" in the early 2000s.

Evo Morales Ayma's election as president of Bolivia in 2005 set a new stage for indigenous rights in the region. Morales emerged as a leader of the coca growers' union and gained an international reputation for refusing to comply with U.S.-led coca eradication efforts. He later transformed that into national political prominence as a representative of the Movement toward Socialism (MAS), which he helped found and of which he was a member when elected to the legislature. By the early 2000s, he was a highly respected leader of Bolivia's indigenous masses, becoming the first self-identified indigenous person to preside over the heavily indigenous nation. His presidency was especially welcomed among the masses of indigenous people suffering some of the worst poverty, infant mortality, illiteracy, and life expectancy in the hemisphere.

Evo's election was a remarkable confirmation of his popularity among Bolivians. His broad appeal garnered him over 50 percent of the vote. Soon after taking office, he raised the minimum wage and cut his own salary, as well as those of the cabinet and Congress. He also nationalized the gas and oil industries, using the extra revenue to fund social programs to improve health care and reduce illiteracy and poverty. He encouraged the nation's indigenous citizens to participate in local and national politics. In 2009, voters approved a new constitution that defined Bolivia as a plurinational state and declared natural resources to be the patrimony of the nation. Voters also approved a limit on the size of private landholdings.

But like others who supported socialism in Latin America in the early twenty-first century, Evo has been more reformist than radical. He has pursued gradual change to represent the diverse groups in Bolivia and avoided confrontation with the conservative opposition. Rather than outright expropriation of the energy industry, for example, he renegotiated contracts more favorably for Bolivia. As he stated in a 2006 interview, Bolivia sought "partners, but not bosses." Some of Evo's greatest successes have come through demobilizing social movements and channeling indigenous demands through the state. Evo also moved away from the United States to forge closer ties with Chávez in Venezuela and Castro in Cuba. Perhaps the best-known rejection of the U.S. leadership came during his defense of coca growers in the face of eradication efforts.

In spite of his popularity, Evo's policies and actions have provoked some stiff opposition. Radical ethnic separatist movements continue to challenge him. Wealthy agribusiness interests in the Santa Cruz region, a region also rich in gas and oil, have led to calls there for secession. Some of this opposition has been distinctly racial, as largely mestizo and white lowlanders in Santa Cruz have been accused by indigenous highlanders of stealing Bolivia's wealth. Those very Santa Cruz communities see the indigenous population as unjustly seeking to seize their regional wealth. But when the opposition tried to recall him in 2008, Evo won a two-thirds majority. Even after he was reelected the following year, numerous indigenous rights groups argued that he had not done enough for Bolivia's poorest.

Evo won reelection in 2014, and Bolivia remains deeply dependent on oil and gas exports. Its economic dependence ties it into a global economy that is fearful of investing too much there due to the threat of nationalization. The energy industry, in the meantime, has drawn charges of mismanagement, inefficiency, and corruption.

Yet Evo's popularity remains strong, though not strong enough to pass a 2016 referendum that would have allowed him to run for a fourth consecutive term. The ruling MAS party nevertheless nominated him in December 2016 to be their candidate in the 2019 elections, stating that they would seek legal avenues to allow for his election. Conservative opposition has accused him of authoritarian radicalism. But his supporters continue to credit him with reducing poverty and illiteracy, as well as steadfastly challenging both U.S. imperialism and environmental degradation caused by foreign companies. His continued defense of the right of Bolivians to produce coca leaf for domestic consumption has put him in the crosshairs of U.S. anti-drug policies. Finally, his promotion of indigenous rights and communal well-being over neoliberal doctrines has kept him at the forefront of the pink tide in the region.

## Brazil

Lula da Silva, born in the poor northeast of Brazil, migrated with his abandoned mother to São Paulo. While still a teen, he went to work in a metal fabrication shop. After an accident idled him, he worked as a union leader in the auto industry. In the late 1970s, his union led a series of strikes that defied the military regime's ban on walkouts, and their success prompted leaders, including Lula, to found the Workers' Party in 1980.

In his first three bids for the presidency, Lula ran unsuccessfully as a labor leader and a socialist, promising to bring about major socioeconomic reforms. In 2002, however, Lula moderated his pitch and reassured the business community that he would respect the interests of capital and international lenders. Middle-class voters found his makeover genuine, and he won. Afterward, he reiterated his business-friendly statements and appointed moderate economic cabinet members. This stance stabilized the real and brought warm responses from financial leaders.

In office, Lula stuck with moderation, accepting neoliberalism and its requirements for debt repayment, export-oriented growth, and balanced budgets. Yet he also raised the minimum wage, lowered some taxes, and expanded aid to students. He initiated programs to reduce poverty and hunger, such as Bolsa Família, which gave subsidies to poor families.

Lula and the Workers' Party were not immune to the corruption so endemic to Brazilian politics. Accusations of voter fraud by Workers' Party leaders went all the way to Lula's inner circle, though Lula himself escaped blame. He won reelection in 2006 with 60 percent of the vote. He still had the support of the poor, and the booming economy and his rejection of his conservative opponent's neoliberalism secured his victory.

During his second term, Lula expanded social programs and pursued development in transportation, energy, and social services. He supported affirmative action programs that targeted Brazil's race-based inequality and championed laws against domestic violence. Racial and gender equality became cornerstones of his administration.

Lula also expanded Brazil's role in hemispheric affairs and laid out an ambitious project to widen Brazil's leadership in regional and international affairs. He strengthened trade and diplomatic ties with other South American countries and challenged U.S. financial and trade influence in the region. He also sought to counter economic dependence on the industrial countries through closer ties with China. For example, in 2011 Brazil signed a $7 billion agreement with China to increase soybean and raw materials exports to China. Chinese investment in Brazil and other Latin American nations has expanded at the same time.

Lula's protégé and chief of staff, Dilma Rousseff, succeeded him after winning the 2010 election. A former urban guerrilla who suffered at the hands of the military years earlier, Dilma continued Lula's policies while staffing the government with her own people. She protected state infrastructure projects and social services and even expanded Bolsa Família. Rousseff still faced the challenges that have confounded generations of Brazilian politicians before her, including massive urbanization, high rates of illiteracy and poverty, some of the highest inequality in the region, and widespread crime. Yet she garnered widespread support and handily won reelection in 2014.

Her second term in office was mired in controversy, including corruption charges that tore at the heart of her government. Government spending to host the 2014 soccer World Cup and the 2016 summer Olympics generated an outpouring of protest against the diversion of funds to host the events instead of alleviating poverty. By 2015, Rousseff's popularity had plunged amid a wave of demonstrations sweeping urban areas. The crisis expanded to a wider critique of mass corruption among Workers' Party officials under investigation for receiving billions of dollars in bribes through contracts with Petrobras, the state-owned oil and gas monopoly. A continuing economic recession meant that the economy had shrunk since 2014, and GDP per capita continued a descent that began early in her tenure. In 2016, Rousseff's conservative opposition finally succeeded, managing to impeach her for improper budget manipulations, after which they took over the presidency and replaced the cabinet with conservative allies.

## Argentina

The start of the twenty-first century was not promising for Argentina. In 2001, its economic boom collapsed. Economic growth slowed and unemployment exploded. A poverty rate that had grown only slowly in the early to mid-1990s suddenly jumped from 19 percent in the mid-1990s to close to half the population by 2002. National condemnation focused on continued corruption and weak leadership under Menem. Riots, demonstrations, and looting soon followed, and scholars began to ponder how one of the region's historically wealthiest countries had, by the early 2000s, become one of its economic disasters. Making things worse, the IMF and the United States refused a bailout, and the Argentine government faced the hard decision of whether to meet loan repayment conditions or to relieve the suffering of its people. Argentina slashed public spending, inciting more revolts. Between 2001 and 2003, Argentina cycled through five presidents, each unable to pull the country out of the chaotic downturn. Hundreds of thousands emigrated.

In the April 2003 elections, another Peronista, Néstor Kirchner, won a five-year term. A relative unknown from the south, Kirchner took office with confidence and soon put his stamp on the government. He negotiated an extension of the country's foreign debt to gain some breathing space, yet refused to comply with the harshest policies demanded by the IMF. He received strong public support, and the economy gained some momentum after years of depression.

Kirchner also broke with Menem and other former presidents and allowed courts to prosecute decades-old cases against military officers accused of murder, torture, and other crimes from the Dirty War. Congress revoked the

**Figure 25.3** Presidents Dilma
Rousseff and Cristina Fernández
de Kirchner at a Mercosur
meeting in 2015. Courtesy
Wilsom Dias/Agência Brasil,
Wiki Commons.

amnesty law that protected them, and dozens of officers faced trials and possible incarceration. For a country that began the century in economic and social chaos and with the dark memory of the Dirty War still hovering over it, the leftist Kirchner received widespread acclaim for putting Argentina on a path to a brighter future.

Kirchner decided not to run for reelection in 2007. Instead, he backed his wife, Senator Cristina Fernández de Kirchner, who won by a wide margin. A lawyer and politician, Fernández stood tall and gained legitimacy for having opposed the military decades earlier. As a Peronist/nationalist, she called for economic rebuilding that included the expansion of the state's role in the economy. Even as the 2008 global economic crisis threatened, she managed to impose reforms that kept the economy growing. She tackled campaign finance rules, renegotiated the foreign debt, overhauled social security, legalized same-sex marriage, and increased the minimum wage, garnering widespread support. While foreign investors and large business and landowners resisted these nationalizing changes, Fernández remained popular and won reelection in 2011. Fernández's second term went less smoothly as the economy slowed. She rejected criticisms of her administration's actions while shrugging off demands for more transparency and inclusion. Less responsive to the populace than Peronism historically had been, Fernández lost public trust.

In November 2015, the remaining Peronistas took a blow when conservative Mauricio Macri, a business owner and soccer club president, was elected Argentina's first conservative president in many years. Some called this the first major defeat of the pink tide in South America. Macri won not only with a broad and moderately conservative platform, but also by including a liberal democratic message and preserving social rights. He took advantage of a society weary of the Kirchners' style and pledged that he would bring change while continuing popular social programs and state economic intervention. In doing so, Macri was able to distance the conservative right from its military allies and replant it firmly in the democratic field.

Macri actively promoted his agenda. Within weeks of taking office he decreased export taxes and currency controls and moved to end a dispute with foreign bondholders that had the country estranged in the international credit markets. And in mid-2016, ex-president Fernández was indicted for currency manipulation while in office. Argentina, in many ways, remains an enigma to those who analyze its history.

## Chile

Michelle Bachelet's supporters joyously celebrated her election to the presidency in Chile in March 2006. As the country's first female president, she represented an unprecedented victory for women's rights. Moreover, as the daughter of an air force general and Allende supporter who had been detained by the Pinochet regime and then died while in prison in early 1974, and as a victim of torture herself, she also represented a new age for Chile.

Since 1973, Chile had lived under the influence of Pinochet and his supporters, and Bachelet rose to challenge the conservative side of Chilean national life. She embodied all that Chile had become as it restored its democratic traditions after the divisions of the Allende-Pinochet years. She had spent the late 1970s in exile from the military regime and then returned to Chile in 1979 to continue her medical studies. She also completed military strategy studies in Washington, D.C., and in Chile. By the early 2000s, she was a rising star in the Socialist Party.

Bachelet (2006–2010, 2014–) took office after serving as a highly respected minister of health under her predecessor, Ricardo Lagos Escobar (2000–2006). Lagos was viewed as a sound manager of Chile's neoliberal policies. In the eyes of the international community, Chile was emerging as a model free-market developing nation, and Lagos did all that he could to maintain and improve that image. He also expanded his predecessor's social programs and further reduced poverty.

Bachelet won wide respect for firmness and compassion. She advocated justice for the victims of the Dirty War but also sought reconciliation between the armed forces and the left. She won election as the candidate of the center-left Concertación, a coalition that oversaw economic growth in the 1990s while expanding social spending.

## Women and Politics in the Twenty-First Century

Recent years have seen new levels of women's participation in politics in Latin America. Although wealthy white or mestizo men continue to dominate politics in what remain highly patriarchal societies, women have risen to distinction as heads of state. The elections of Rousseff in Brazil, Bachelet in Chile, and Fernández in Argentina reflect not just a leftist turn but also greater involvement of women in politics.

During the twentieth century, women all over the region struggled to gain constitutional and legal rights. By midcentury, most had gained the right to vote and most civil rights. The first Latin American country to give women the vote was Ecuador, in 1929; the last was Paraguay, in 1961. All of the constitutions in the Americas guarantee equality among their citizens, and only a few legal issues continue to discriminate against women, especially those surrounding divorce and reproductive rights. Many Latin American countries today have quotas in place requiring certain percentages of female candidates in elections. New efforts have been made to hire women for government and police jobs.

Moreover, a considerable proportion of women now work for wages and salaries. Some professions are primarily in the hands of women, such as nursing, K–12 education, and secretarial services. Women are also rising to take over management and supervisory positions in offices and schools, and many have become directors of commercial and financial firms. Nevertheless, in Brazil in 2010, just 0.5 percent of executives of large businesses were women.

While economic insecurity and migration have meant that single motherhood is on the rise among the region's poor, women are gaining more education and professional experience. After decades of moving into university classrooms and into the formal workforce, as well as organizing to challenge military governments, women were well placed to take on new roles when democracy returned to the region.

Most of these female leaders have been careful to avoid feminist language. They favor, instead, messages and policies that advocate equality for all. Bachelet nevertheless promoted women's rights as part of her agenda, including expanded access to birth control and sex education. She also included an unprecedented number of women as ministers in her cabinet. In a historic moment, ex-president Salvador Allende's daughter, Isabel Allende Bussi, who at the time was the president of the Chilean Senate, affirmed Bachelet in office.

Women have faced opposition simply by being female in what remains a man's world. Many women politicians, including Bachelet, Fernández, and Rousseff, were repeatedly accused of weakness and of lacking the intellectual heft and strength of character of their male counterparts. In 2016, Rousseff was impeached and Fernández was indicted. Nevertheless, the move of women into public life has confirmed the radical changes in women's lives in the twenty-first century.

But Bachelet also differed from her predecessors in office. She was younger, a professional rather than a career politician, and promised more mass participation in politics. Her campaign had an air of populism about it, and her slogan was Estoy Contigo (I'm with You). Her inclusive vision of politics was welcomed by a population weary of the empty rhetoric of prior Concertación leaders, who promised growth but paid little attention to indigenous, poor, and other marginalized groups, and that had witnessed a growth in the gap between the wealthy and the poor since the 1980s. She built upon her popularity by continuing the focus on economic growth but also by pairing it with a bigger social safety net. Health care, social security, and education all grew under her leadership, as she focused on shifting some of Chile's prosperity to the country's poorest.

Despite Bachelet's personal popularity, the Concertación coalition lagged in popular support, and the conservative Sebastián Piñera (2010–2014) replaced her in the presidency. Piñera recommitted Chile to the neoliberal policies that had shaped the economy since the 1970s. And there were protests. Students demanded free and universally accessible education. Copper miners engaged in a series of protests over Piñera's efforts to privatize the industry. But his changes were short-lived. After serving as the secretary general of the UN Entity for Gender Equality and the Empowerment of Women, Michelle Bachelet returned to Chile to win the 2013 elections. Her second term in office has not gone as smoothly as her first, however. Her public support has plummeted after a drop in global copper prices forced her to retreat from her reform promises, and her son and daughter-in-law were caught up in a corruption scandal.

## Peru

Peru's trajectory in the first decade and a half of the twenty-first century was considerably less anguished and conflicted than in some of the other Latin American states. This largely resulted from a very impressive export economy, especially of basic minerals and commodities such as copper, silver, gold, and food products like fruits and vegetables to traditional markets in Europe and the United States, as well as increasing percentages going to Asian buyers, especially China.

Culturally, Peru exploded on the global stage, especially the popularity of Peruvian cuisine in the world. Dishes such as *ceviche* and *anticuchos* have awakened more palates, especially among Americans, not only to the rich cuisine and vibrant multiculture but also to basic foods like quinoa, enhancing diets everywhere. In 2010 one of the most celebrated, prolific, and creative writers of the boom generation of Latin Americans, Mario Vargas Llosa, won the Nobel Prize for literature in recognition of his body of work, whose themes transcend Peru and Latin America.

**Figure 25.4** Peruvian president Ollanta Humala meeting with U.S. secretary of state Hillary Clinton in 2011. Courtesy U.S. Department of State, Wiki Commons.

Still, in a country where more than half the population lives below the poverty line, politicians have to grapple with tough economic and social realities. Plus, the sometimes bizarre machinations of politics, such as the fall of President Alberto Fujimori in 2000, keep things stirred up. The roll call of recent Peruvian presidents includes Alejandro Toledo (2001–2006), Alan García (2006–2011), Ollanta Humala (2011–2016), and Pedro Pablo Kuczynski (2016–). They span the style spectrum from old-style authoritarians, new leftists in the Chávez (Venezuela) model, and traditional defenders of the poor or the rich. They almost included ex-president Fujimori's daughter, Keiko Fujimori, whom Kuczynski only narrowly defeated in the 2016 runoff elections. Voters have usually chosen leaders with the ability to straddle the broad interests of its racially and culturally diverse population. While incidents of political violence have occurred in all presidential terms since 2001, Peru's commitment to the democratic process remains strong.

## GLOBALIZATION AND REGIONAL INTEGRATION

Neoliberalism brought forth a new era of globalization. World demand for agricultural and energy exports expanded the region's place in the global economy and brought new wealth to the region. In the past few decades, the region's GDP has doubled while its population has grown much more slowly, a notable gain even if it has come at the cost of continued reliance on exports of primary goods. Latin America's integration into the world economy, which began in earnest in the nineteenth century, was certainly enhanced by being very closely tied into affairs across the globe.

The United States sought to retain its influence in the region by fostering hemispheric solidarity among its leaders. It promoted cooperation on issues like tariff reduction, immigration, and narcotics suppression. George W. Bush, for example, sought the support and confidence of Latin Americans early in his administration (2001–2009). Indeed, President Bush's first international trip was to Mexico to meet President Vicente Fox Quesada, indicating his administration's commitment to good neighborliness. Despite rhetorical flourish, however, world events swept U.S. attention much further afield, toward the Middle East and Asia. For better or worse, Latin America has been left to forge its own international path in the twenty-first century.

Globalization has emerged to supplant waning U.S influence in the region. Leaders of the pink tide (Chávez et al.) promoted regional integration and unity in order to replace U.S. influence. They also criticized U.S. policy in the Middle East and built ties with China, Russia, and the OPEC nations. Brazil has taken a leading role in advancing such extra-hemispheric cooperation and has assumed leadership of South American nations, a position solidified by its rank among the largest economies in the world.

Political cooperation among leftist leaders across South America helped them survive domestic and foreign challenges to their power. Economic collaboration emerged soon after the region recovered from the 2001 recession. Since then, most Latin American countries have experienced modest growth of about 1.5 percent a year. This improvement resulted from more capital flowing in at lower rates, better terms of trade for exports, and better fiscal management by governments.

South American countries resisted pressure from the United States to extend NAFTA to the whole hemisphere in order to create a Free Trade Area of the Americas. Public opinion throughout the region broadly rejected the free-market policies that had prevailed in the 1990s, preferring to pursue social programs and economic equity. Only in Central America did governments accept a free-trade treaty with the United States.

Instead of falling in with U.S. wishes, a number of countries established their own trading alliances, such as Mercosur (Brazil, Uruguay, Paraguay, Argentina, Venezuela, and Bolivia), the Andean Community (Colombia, Peru, Ecuador, and Bolivia), and Caricom (fifteen Caribbean nations and dependencies). The upshot was greater trade freedom, more competitive prices for consumer goods, and broader markets for emerging businesses. By 2014 the combined trade in merchandise stood at nearly $2,400 billion in NAFTA,

$108 billion in Mercosur, and $21 billion in the Andean Community. These values had not changed much, however, during the preceding fifteen years.

Expanding businesses and markets around the world also challenged the historic dominance of the United States in the hemisphere. Firms from Australia, India, and China, among many others, now actively invest in mining and infrastructure projects in countries as varied as Bolivia, Brazil, Mexico, and Panama. The Chinese premier has visited Latin America a number of times since 2000 to signal China's commitment to building economic relations in the region. Significantly, China has promoted a global alliance of developing countries based on shared economic and diplomatic interests and respect for national sovereignty.

In 2015, however, twelve medium- and large-size nations approved a new trade agreement, called the Trans-Pacific Partnership (TPP), which aspired to set rules for the future of global commerce. Most of the nations included are in Asia, although China is not a member. Mexico, Peru, and Chile figured prominently in the TPP, which also included Canada. Much of the impetus for the TPP came from up-and-coming economies that feared stagnation in trade due to the collapse of the Doha (Qatar) round of World Trade Organization negotiations. They believed that competitors like China, the United States, and the EU might by-pass them in future deals. U.S. trade officials under President Barack Obama perceived an opportunity to help define trade terms, so they joined the effort and became important advocates. Soon after taking office, however, U.S. president Donald Trump withdrew the U.S., putting the agreement in limbo in early 2017.[3]

## CUBA AND PANAMA: A TALE OF TWO LIBERATIONS

These two small nations have unexpectedly shared similar destinies in the twenty-first century. Both managed to sever imperialist ties (Cuba from the USSR and Panama from the United States) and to launch new trajectories. Cuba survived the special period and restored its standard of living through economic adjustments and rapprochement with the United States. Panama burst forth as operator of the former U.S. canal and has achieved the highest growth rates in the hemisphere for several years.

Cuba's recovery depended on traditional activities like tourism, as well as new ones like the export of medical services. Countries sympathetic with Cuban socialism helped, especially Spain, Venezuela, and more recently Brazil. Even the United States opened its doors slightly by allowing exports of food and other basic goods. For its part, Cuba relaxed its autocratic system, anointed Raúl Castro as president in 2008, introduced market reforms in some sectors, and welcomed foreign investors as joint partners with Cuban firms.

Unquestionably the biggest change in Cuba's future came in December 2014, when Castro and U.S. president Barack Obama announced restoration of

**Figure 25.5** Presidents Raúl Castro and Barack Obama met and held discussions during the seventh Summit of the Americas, held in Panama in April 2015, captured in a White House photo. Courtesy U.S. Government.

diplomatic relations between the two nations. The road to normalize ties will continue to be rocky, due to a half-century of hostilities since the revolution, and the 2016 election of Donald Trump raised further doubts about future relations.

Meanwhile, Fidel Castro passed away in November 2016, marking the end of a tumultuous period in Cuban history. In a 1953 trial defending his revolutionary acts, Castro asserted, "History will absolve me." While we don't know for sure what history's final judgment will be, Castro certainly was a towering figure of Latin American and global history. His legacy is complicated. As summarized by the *Daily Telegraph* on November 26, 2016, Castro was "either praised as a brave champion of the people, or derided as a power-mad dictator."

Panama took over the canal in 1999 and put it on a profit-making course, so that excess revenues over expenses could fund improvements in the rest of the nation. They adopted a corporate management model that stressed efficiency, good relations with shippers, tolls based on value, and safety. Within five years, the canal produced a half-billion dollars for Panama, and by 2015 it reached a billion. Run by the independent Panama Canal Authority, it operates free of the political strife and corruption that seem endemic in the rest of the government.

Demand for more transits and larger capacity led managers to propose a new set of locks that would allow the canal to take ships 2.8 times larger than the old locks. This would accommodate a new generation of vessels, called neo-Panamax, and to triple cargo handled and toll revenues. Panamanians

**Figure 25.6** New Atlantic side Panama Canal locks, with gigantic sliding gates and recycling ponds on the right. The artificial Gatún Lake, through which ships transit most of the way, can be seen in the background. Courtesy Panama Canal Authority.

approved the plan in a 2006 plebiscite and work got under way in 2007. The new locks, opened in 2016, cost about $7 billion and rivaled the original U.S. construction in size and complexity. Despite their expanded capacity, the new locks use less water than the old ones, due to an ingenious system of recycling.

The success of canal operations and the cash flow it engendered contributed to rapid growth in Panama's GDP, in double digits in some years. The expansion project also stoked more economic activity from wages and local contracts. Finally, government and canal leaders pushed a broadened role for the nation in the global economy, which they refer to as the "hub of the Americas." In addition to moving ships between oceans, the canal provides ancillary services such as fuel and ship supplies, repairs, container marshaling, legal facilities, crew training, and intermodal (i.e., between maritime and rail) connections.

The "hub" goes beyond canal-related activities to include air transport through the main and auxiliary airports, dollar-based banking in the offshore financial sector, bonded manufacturing in the Colón Free Trade Zone, and super-fast fiber optic communications. Panama grew at the fastest rate of any country in the hemisphere during most of the 2010s, and its people polled as among the happiest on earth in some of those years. Panama has truly been a major success story following the U.S. turnover of the canal.

Politics kept pace with other progress, though not without heavy doses of graft. Each five-year election cycle, which observers found as open and honest as any in the region, ushered in another party. New presidents usually continued the mega-projects initiated by their predecessors, like new highways and bridges and the first rapid transit system in Central America. The government has been sorely challenged, however, to remedy the nation's highly unequal distribution of wealth and appalling educational underachievement. Elections to be held in 2019 will surely focus much attention on these continuing problems.

## URBANIZATION AND THE ENVIRONMENT

Latin America at the start of the twenty-first century is a world apart from where it was a century ago. Population growth, urbanization, industrialization, and the rise of mass consumer culture mean that most residents today live very different lives than their grandparents or even parents did. But development and growth have brought new challenges, especially for the environment. Water is often scarce, air pollution in the largest cities creates a permanent haze, and forests have been devastated, as industry, mining, and agriculture have stripped lands of their natural bounty.

The population of Latin America and the Caribbean grew quickly in the twentieth century, from 74 million people in 1900 to over 600 million by 2015. Close to 80 percent of the population in the region now lives in urban areas, with Mexico City and São Paulo among the largest cities in the world. This population growth, although now slowed by declining birthrates, and urbanization have been fed by rapid economic changes, fostered by factories, huge agro-industry, and aggressive new mining ventures.

Latin America's middle class has also expanded in the past century. Economic and job growth along with spending on social programs have encouraged this trend, and the middle class now is 30 percent of the population in the region. More children now attend school. They stay in school longer, and more women than ever are in the formal workforce. This growth varies across the region, with Brazil, Colombia, Chile, Costa Rica, and Peru seeing the largest increases in the middle class.

Together, this demographic boom, urbanization, and economic growth have created huge pressures on natural resources and the environment. Environmental problems have been made worse by the unequal distribution of wealth, an often ramshackle infrastructure, and weak regulations that exacerbate the impact of human activity on the environment.

Access to safe water has emerged as a defining issue of the twenty-first century. Ironically, Latin America has close to one-third of the world's fresh water. Moreover, its governments have been at the forefront in water management for the developing world, and from 1960 to the present, the percent of the population with direct access to water has risen from 33 percent to 85 percent. Yet the region also has vast arid spaces, for example, northern Mexico and the Andean altiplano, which, along with rapid urbanization, have led to unequal access to water, with rural areas and urban slums lacking safe water. Climate change and the privatization of water resources have exacerbated these effects, especially in places like Bolivia, leading to high prices and further inequality in access. Overall the poor have less water than others and they pay more than the wealthy for the water they do have.

The depletion of water sources has been accompanied by growing air pollution, especially in heavily industrial areas like Mexico City and São Paulo. Regulations have improved the situation somewhat, but environmental degradation caused by industrial pollution along the U.S.-Mexico border continues apace. Even though Latin America is a global leader in clean energy because of its reliance on hydropower, droughts caused by climate change and poor management put that in jeopardy and may lead to more reliance on fossil fuels.

Environmental diversity is at risk in Latin America. From the steppe-like altiplanos of Bolivia to the steamy jungles of the Amazon, the region contains more biodiversity than any other continent on earth, especially in the plant kingdom. The world received from the Americas major food staples like the potato and corn, pharmaceuticals like quinine and ipecac, unique animals like the rhea and the llama, and tropical plants running into the tens of millions of varieties. No wonder Charles Darwin received his inspiration for *On the Origin of Species* (1859) after studying South America. The region is a veritable laboratory for botany, zoology, biology, geology, and most other natural sciences.

Conservationists have long insisted on protecting the Amazon rainforest from clearing and burning, and with good reason. It is the world's largest tropical rainforest and contains 20 percent of the world's fresh water. Conservationists now understand how interconnected the many regional environments of the world are, and they warn against the loss of biological diversity. Lowland tropical forests on the west coast of Colombia, in Central America, on many Caribbean islands, and along Brazil's littoral have also been subject to a great deal of timber harvesting and clearing. Because those forests are less extensive than the Amazon, their ability to regenerate is limited. In all, Latin America contains approximately 70 percent of the world's remaining tropical rainforest.

Indigenous organizations have been some of the key allies of environmental groups in Latin America since 2000. From the water and gas wars of Bolivia to lawsuits against major oil companies in Ecuador, indigenous groups have challenged the environmental impact of large corporations and governments by raising political awareness and by linking degradation to land policies and a lack of autonomy that have hurt their communities. Their protests even helped to bring down governments in Bolivia and Ecuador. Between 1972, when the first Earth Day conference was held, and today, nations around the world, led by the UN and thousands of NGOs, have sought to decrease environmental degradation and "save the planet," as the slogan proclaims. Numerous meetings have been held, culminating in the 2015 UN Climate Change Conference in Paris. Delegates from 196 nations and eighty heads of state convened in order to assure that achievable climate change goals be formalized.[4]

Latin America plays a minor role in global warming compared to China, India, the United States, and Europe, yet it holds important keys to remediating it and also stands to suffer its consequences. Warming already endangers glaciers in the Andes and affects Antarctica, where several countries have territory. El Niño episodes subject many regions to either deluges or droughts. Such effects will certainly grow in the future.

Brazil, with its vast Amazon rainforest, plays a complex role in climate change. Sustained deforestation over the past century has removed thousands of kilometers of rainforest, whose carbon-absorbing and oxygen-producing characteristics have been lost. On the other hand, protecting the remaining forest promises to remediate adverse effects of global warming. And with the ninth largest economy in the world, Brazil has a significant influence on the climate in general.

Observers therefore paid special attention to President Dilma Rousseff's speech at the Paris conference. First, she noted a major decline in Amazon deforestation rates and pledged to continue protecting the region. She also announced her nation's attainment of 45 percent reliance on renewable energy and promised even higher targets. She committed her administration to reduce carbon emissions. With regard to the Paris Agreement under development, she urged that its measures be legally enforceable and that wealthy nations provide funding, technology, and training to help developing countries contribute to reductions in global warming. Latin America, it seemed, stood ready to play a positive role in environmental protection.

Other places are in jeopardy as well. Scientists worry about coastal reefs and deep marine life in the Caribbean and the Pacific trenches. Even remote mountainous settings have undergone drastic changes. Central Mexico and the Andean highlands have lost most of their original forest cover. And as scientists in temperate lands have discovered, loss of habitat leads to the loss of animal species.

Humans have adapted to the extremely diverse lands of Latin America, most of which are still inhabitable. But economic activity is harder to sustain in these landscapes. Haiti's mountains may never again be cultivable due to clearing and erosion. The barrier reef of Belize may never again produce shrimp. Farms in western Brazil may never again grow cereals due to leaching of the soils. And the Darien rainforest of eastern Panama may never again produce hardwoods due to over-logging. In short, human existence in these fragile environments may itself become impoverished because of land mismanagement.

### Tropical Deforestation

"The clearing of tropical forests across the Earth has been occurring on a large scale for many centuries. This process, known as deforestation, involves the cutting down, burning, and damaging of forests. The loss of tropical rain forest is more profound than merely destruction of beautiful areas. If the current rate of deforestation continues, the world's rain forests will vanish within 100 years, causing unknown effects on global climate and eliminating the majority of plant and animal species on the planet.

"Deforestation occurs in many ways. Commercial mining operations are major contributors to environmental degradation and deforestation. But most of the clearing is done for agricultural purposes—grazing cattle or planting crops. Poor farmers chop down a small area (typically a few acres) and burn the tree trunks—a process called Slash and Burn agriculture. Intensive, or modern, agriculture occurs on a much larger scale, sometimes deforesting several square miles at a time. Large cattle pastures often replace rain forest to grow beef for the world market.

"Commercial logging is another common form of deforestation, cutting trees for sale as timber or pulp. Logging can occur selectively—where only the economically valuable species are cut—or by clearcutting, where all the trees are cut. Commercial logging uses heavy machinery, such as bulldozers, road graders, and log skidders, to remove cut trees and build roads, which is just as damaging to a forest overall as the chainsaws are to the individual trees."

Gerald Urquhart, Walter Chomentowski, David Skole, and Chris Barber, "Tropical Deforestation," *Earth Observatory,* http://earthobservatory.nasa.gov/Features/Deforestation /tropical_deforestation_2001.pdf.

## MIGRATION AND VIOLENCE

Since independence, Latin Americans have been on the move, with vast migrations of people into and within the region creating dynamic, diverse, and unique cultures and societies. In the twentieth century, the migration of Latin Americans to the United States grew, in part encouraged by U.S. policy and economic demands. The Bracero Program, which brought Mexican and Puerto Rican workers to the United States, as well as the fact that Puerto Ricans have U.S. citizenship, encouraged the massive migration of people from these countries. While U.S. immigration enforcement has periodically attempted to slow the flow of migrants, many factors in both the United States and Latin America have continued to encourage it. Neoliberalism and globalization have accelerated migration, as people have left their communities for urban areas or abroad in search of jobs, education, or, increasingly in the twenty-first century, safety.

Neoliberal policies since the 1980s have led to disruptions in land and labor use that have pushed people to seek out new opportunities. Many have moved to urban areas, where jobs in both the formal and informal sectors are more plentiful. Today, for example, the majority of Peru's indigenous population now no longer lives in rural highland areas but rather in urban communities. Rural areas have been devastated by this emigration—emigration that has caused rural poverty, shrinking rural populations, and increasing rural-urban inequality. Urban areas have grown quickly as they have absorbed the migrants, who often settle in shantytowns with minimal public services. Others have migrated to free-trade zones in places like Mexico and the Dominican Republic, where foreign companies have built maquiladoras, or factories that provide jobs for Latin Americans and cheap consumer goods to the developed world.

By the same token, millions of Latin Americans have come to live in the United States, legally and otherwise. They swell the populations of some states, with over half of the U.S. Hispanic population concentrated in Florida, Texas, and California. About two-thirds of those of Hispanic origin come from Mexico, and about 10 percent from Puerto Rico. Those of Cuban, Salvadoran, Dominican, and Guatemalan origin are also well represented. After becoming part of the U.S. labor force and communities, many migrants do not return, choosing instead to raise families in the U.S. Today, the United States has the second-largest Hispanic population in the world, behind only Mexico.

Many who come to the United States do so with the intention of returning home after working for a few years. They hope to earn money to send remittances to their families, then take a cash stake home. This became especially important in the 1990s, when people migrated north to find jobs that could pay for their family needs back home. The financial crisis of 2008 hurt the flow of remittances, though by 2014 they had recovered. Mexico is by far the largest receiving country in Latin America, getting about $25 billion in remittances in 2015. It is followed by Guatemala, the Dominican Republic, El Salvador, and Colombia, each of which received about $4 to $6 billion from U.S. remittances in 2014. In countries like Guatemala, Honduras, Nicaragua, and El Salvador, remittances account for 10 to 15 percent of the GDP.

Most who come to the U.S. from Mexico and Central America are of lower-class background, and their money often goes to basic necessities like food, shelter, and clothing. Peru and Venezuela, however, send predominantly middle-class migrants who often work in low-wage jobs such as cleaning or construction to sustain middle-class lives for families back home, including private education, cars, and appliances.

People of Latin American descent are now the largest minority in the United States. In 2015, they accounted for about 17 percent of the total population, with about one-third born abroad. The growth of the Hispanic population has

**Figure 25.7** Shakira, the Colombian-born singer, has become a celebrity around the world. Courtesy Andrés Arranz, Wiki Commons.

slowed since 2000, in large part due to the post-2008 drop in immigration. But it continues to grow and is predicted to represent one-third of the U.S population by the middle of the twenty-first century.

Like Latin America itself, the ethnic and racial differences within the Hispanic population are notable, and their influence on U.S. society has been equally diverse. While immigrants work predominantly in the service sector, U.S.-born Hispanics have increasingly moved into professional jobs, even heading multinationals like Coca-Cola. They have also become sports stars, such as NFL quarterback Tony Romo and boxing champions Oscar de la Hoya and Julio César Chávez. And one, Sonia Sotomayor, became a member of the U.S. Supreme Court.

Hispanics have had an equally vast influence on U.S. culture. In the 1980s and 1990s, well-known performers like Gloria Estefan, Selena, and Ricky Martin broke ethnic barriers and enjoyed enormous followings. They, in turn, laid the groundwork for singers like Jennifer Lopez, Shakira, Pitbull, and Selena Gomez. In the first years of the twenty-first century, Mexican filmmakers burst onto the international scene with films like Alejandro González Iñárritu's film *Amores perros* (2000), Alfonso Cuarón's *Y tu mama también* (2001), and Guillermo del Toro's *Pan's Labyrinth* (2006). Some have gone on to direct major motion pictures, such as Cuarón's *Gravity* (2013) and *Harry Potter and the Prisoner of Azkaban* (2004), and Iñárritu's *The Revenant* (2015) and *Birdman* (2014), setting new standards in the industry. Actors like Sofia Vergara, America Ferrara, Salma Hayak, Gael García Bernal, and Benicio del Toro earn top salaries in the industry. Through music, film, and TV, they have introduced Latin rhythms and themes into U.S. culture, and their success has been as part of the U.S. mainstream. The Spanish-language conglomerate Univision now ranks as a top media company in the world.

More recently, violence in Latin America has played a prominent role in driving migration. People flee their rural homes in search of safety in cities and foreign countries. Colombia had some of the highest numbers of internally displaced people in the world as it fought its decades-long war with rebels and drug traffickers, though the recent peace agreement between the rebels and the government may slow or even halt the displacements.

Many migrants have ended up in cities that are unable to absorb them, and the lack of housing, education, and jobs has encouraged crime. Cities like Caracas, Mexico City, and São Paulo saw dramatic growth in crime after the 1980s. Corrupt local police forces do little to slow it. Local gangs and drug dealers move into the vacuums created by the lack of security, creating even more violence and disruption for families and communities.

In 2015, fifteen of the twenty countries with the highest murder rates in the world were in the circum-Caribbean region of Latin America. Much of the violence, which includes robberies, rapes, and assaults, is caused by economic insecurity, official corruption, rising transience, and the presence of great wealth. The drug trade plays a prominent role, with Central America, Mexico, and the Caribbean serving as key transit routes for moving drugs north from South America to lucrative U.S. markets. Since the 1990s the U.S. government has pumped billions of dollars of military aid into the region in an attempt to slow the trade. It has also invested in programs to encourage alternative crops to coca and alternative livelihoods for the coca farmers of Peru, Colombia, and Bolivia. The aid has not been successful in slowing the drug trade, though it has helped to militarize much of the region.

Insecurity is high in countries like Honduras, which had the highest murder rate in the world in 2015, followed in order by Venezuela, Belize, El Salvador, and Guatemala. This is driving a new wave of refugees who, under threats of extortion and assassination from local gangs and cartels, seek safety in the United States. Homicide rates have grown to the point that average life expectancy for men in places like Mexico and Honduras is dropping. In Mexico, in 2006 President Felipe Calderón launched a war on drug cartels that had gained control of nearly all cocaine entering the United States. Since that time, Mexico

**The Mara Salvatrucha, or MS-13**

The Mara Salvatrucha, or MS-13, street gang began in Los Angeles in the 1980s, drawing on the influx of Salvadorans fleeing civil war at home. Its members are predominantly Salvadorans, Hondurans, and Guatemalans. Considered one of the most violent gangs in the world, its members are routinely deported when released from U.S. prisons. This practice allowed MS-13 to establish cells across Central America and beyond. MS-13 members are known for their extensive tattoos, including on the face, and for their use of extreme violence. Their primary rivals are another gang known as Barrio-18, which many consider to be even larger and better organized.

Gang members' ties to both U.S. and Central American allies, combined with weak and corrupt law enforcement in Central America, have allowed them to move into the drug trade and to take over whole communities, which they govern with violence, extortion, and intimidation. MS-13 members work for groups such as the Sinaloa and Zeta drug cartels in Mexico, transporting and selling drugs and weapons, and committing kidnappings and murders. This has led to more violence and insecurity across the region, causing people to flee to escape their reach.

has seen a dramatic rise in violence, and more than 150,000 people have been killed or disappeared, most of them as part of the drug wars. Drug cartels and gangs have preyed on the climate of insecurity in the country, and their killings and abductions are often done in collusion with corrupt security forces paid to either assist or look the other way.

Displaced women and children have been especially hard hit by violence, but police have done little to stop gender-based violence. Economic insecurity caused by the loss of family members to violence has driven many from Mexico, Central America, and Colombia to cities or to the United States. Targeted by rebels, gangs, and cartels, femicide (the specific killing of women) and rape are now considered human rights abuses by organizations like Amnesty International. Migrants traveling from Central America through Mexico on their way to the U.S. have been especially targeted.

Migrants who make it to the United States often find safety from threats and extortion. And the United States has absorbed millions of Latin Americans, whether legally or illegally, who arrive for economic opportunity or to escape violence. But due to national security threats, U.S. immigration policy has become increasingly tough, and millions of migrants have been deported back to Mexico and Central America, despite rising numbers who face abduction and murder if they return home due to dangerous situations or torn-apart families. The November 2016 election of Donald Trump, who campaigned on building a wall along the Mexican border and on tightening immigration in general, threw the issue into even more doubt.

## RACE AND LGBT RIGHTS

No other region in the world has experienced such a radical mixing of peoples as Latin America. Its original inhabitants migrated from central Asia tens of thousands of years ago; over 12 million Africans were transported to the Americas as slaves; and tens of millions emigrated from Europe and the Middle East. Despite years of legal equality, however, race and ethnicity are still primary factors limiting access to wealth and opportunity across Latin America.

Indigenous and Afro-descendant people remain disproportionately poor. In Panama, 90 percent of the indigenous population lives below the poverty line, whereas just 30 percent of the non-indigenous population does. In Bolivia, Guatemala, Paraguay, Nicaragua, and Honduras, over 60 percent of the indigenous population is poor. And 67 percent of Afro-descendant Peruvians live below the poverty line as compared to only 23 percent of mestizos. In Brazil, those of European descent earn twice what Afro-descendant citizens do, an inequality captured in the 2002 Brazilian film *Cidade de Deus.* Access to services like health care and education, and especially higher education, remains a particular problem, even in countries that have put in place programs and policies to address race-based inequality.

The Afro-descendant population in the region is about 30 percent, though it is heavily concentrated in countries such as Brazil, Colombia, Cuba, and Venezuela. Since 2000, Afro-rights movements have emerged across the region to press for both recognition and rights. They are urging better enforcement of social inclusion laws and seeking to expand public knowledge about race-based discrimination and the African contribution to Latin American culture. In a triumph for local groups, for the first time in 2015, Mexico recognized its Afro-descendant population in the national census.

Similarly, LGBT rights became a prominent issue in the region in the new century. Legal protections vary widely, with countries such as Argentina and Uruguay allowing same-sex unions and others outlawing homosexuality completely. But antidiscrimination laws and legislation granting same-sex marriage rights or gender identity protections have passed in a number of countries in the region recently, including Mexico, Bolivia, Chile, Cuba, Colombia, Brazil, Uruguay, and Argentina. Rights groups have been more public and proactive in pressing for stronger protections. Gender identity laws now allow for people to legally change their gender in Argentina and Chile, for example.

Mexico has gone so far as to outlaw derogatory terms for gay people, termed hate speech, and it is now common to see same-sex couples strolling hand in hand down the streets of Mexico City.

## CENTENNIAL APPRAISALS

Latin American observers in the year 1800 clearly saw time accelerate. They had witnessed a revival of Spain's fortunes under the Bourbon dynasty. That led to increased exploitation of American subjects by agents of the king and the Pope. They noted the reorganization of Portugal's government under Prime Minister Pombal and its enforcement of new taxes and levies on Brazil. Many writers forecast that momentous changes would result from the independence of the thirteen British colonies in North America and the massive rebellion of Africans in Haiti. They believed that people of the Americas would no longer tolerate the yokes of colonialism and slavery. And they were right.

The late 1700s were truly the beginning of an age of revolution in all facets of life: political, economic, intellectual, religious, and social. Latin America was swept up in these changes. Following independence in the early nineteenth century, Latin Americans turned more deliberately outward to Europe and North America. Many educated Latin Americans traveled to England, France, and the United States in the middle and late nineteenth century and came back with new ideas, new fashions, and new models.

They predicted that Spanish and Portuguese Americans would emulate those other societies. In the area of material civilization, they foresaw the spread of industry to the Americas, resulting in major increases in the productivity of its economies. New knowledge available in the liberal arts, sciences, and engineering would permit Latin Americans to use more of their resources to raise their standards of living. Steam power, carbon steel, and high-grade ceramics would make life easier and more rewarding for people all over the world. International travel had become accessible to large numbers of well-to-do citizens, who could visit the far corners of the earth for business and study. And governments were listening more closely to the voices of their citizens, even those who labored with their hands and who expressed themselves in protests and riots.

Observers in the year 1900 could assess the outcomes of the multiple revolutions that had swept the Western world in the previous century. Most of the former Iberian colonies had become independent nations in the 1810s and 1820s. All took steps to end the slave trade and eventually abolished slavery itself. The new nations opened their borders and ports to foreigners, who brought manufacturing, new businesses, railroads, scientific instruments, books, and other innovations. National leaders took over from Europeans and forged new identities based on their own traditions and aspirations. Writers, painters, poets, sculptors, composers, and dramatists soon created national cultures for their homelands. These drew largely on European heritage and ignored indigenous or African traditions, at the time thought to be inferior. Leading citizens built cities, factories, ships, railroads, plantations, and monuments to reflect their coming of age.

The nineteenth century brought progress of a sort to Latin America. Exports of raw materials and food—nitrates, coffee, cacao, guano, sugar, hides, cereal, meat, nonferrous ores, industrial metals, timber, and much more—allowed Latin Americans to import the consumer goods thought to represent civilization in that era. Yet, these imports also harbored stowaway attitudes from Europe, like scientific racism, disdain for the poor, and individualistic materialism. These attitudes often clashed with centuries-old traditions in the region and produced conflict and upheaval. Class divisions were sharpened, poor people were uprooted from villages and stable hacienda life, and mass migrations brought in millions of outsiders and uprooted millions of indigenous people. By the year 1900, mass society, with all its promise and danger, appeared in the larger cities of Latin America.

Observers in the twenty-first century, looking back on the twentieth century, see an even more accelerated and tumultuous period of history. Revolutions that now mobilized those at the bottom—*los de abajo*—arose to challenge traditional elites. In Mexico, Bolivia, Cuba, and Nicaragua, guerrilla armies overthrew established governments. In other places, movements from below narrowly missed becoming full-blown revolutions. Governments in the hemisphere, usually led by the United States during the Cold War, collaborated to prevent disturbances to the existing order, especially by rebellions from below.

When the Soviet Union collapsed in the early 1990s, so did much of United States opposition to changes from below. Thus ended an overarching theme of the past hundred years, revolution versus the status quo. Revolutionaries of the left had claimed the high ground of social and economic justice, while the opposition usually resisted change and defended traditional moral, political, economic, and religious values. Revolutionaries and reactionaries alike wrapped themselves in the language of democracy and true republican values, recalling the origins of the republics in the early nineteenth century.

The spread of modern technology and modes of production continued, allowing several Latin American nations to become industrialized. Mexico, Brazil, Argentina, Chile, and Colombia have economies that balance mining, agriculture, ranching, and industry. Most governments provide a wide array of basic services to their citizens, even if those services are unevenly available.

Today, Latin American countries rank somewhere in the middle of the world's nations in terms of productivity and standards of living. Moreover, nations in Latin America have adopted digital technology with enthusiasm, with high rates of Internet usage and speeds that outpace that in some nations of the developed world. Classrooms from Chile to Mexico have computer labs and Internet access, where children learn interactively. E-commerce captures ever-larger shares of retail business, and the region's youths are savvy Internet and cell phone users. Facebook, Twitter, Instagram, WhatsApp, and YouTube have more penetration there than in the United States.

Latin American culture gained international stature during the twentieth century, and it continues to thrive in the twenty-first. Much of its success is owed to its originality, in that it often blends indigenous influences with the diverse traditions of the region's descendants from Africa, Europe, the Middle East, and Asia. Music, dance, film, and literature have all reached global recognition and profitability. Many nations excel in sports, especially soccer, baseball, tennis, and volleyball, and win recognition in the Olympics and especially the World Cup. Meanwhile, sophisticated film and television production developed in Mexico, Brazil, Argentina, and Chile after the middle of the century. Even hybrid cuisines from Latin America—from tacos and plantains to feijoada and enchiladas—spread to the United States and Europe. Latin America is truly part of the globalized world.

## Discussion Questions

What was the pink tide that took place in the first part of the twenty-first century and why did it occur?

What were the key characteristics shared by the leaders of the various countries that were part of the leftist turn? What were the differences between them?

In what ways have women's roles changed in the twenty-first century, and what is the impact in society and politics?

What has been the impact of globalization on Latin America? What has it meant for U.S. power in the region?

What has been the impact of population growth and economic growth on Latin America's environment and why is this important in terms of global climate change?

What is the connection between poverty, violence, and migration in Latin America and the United States?

## Timeline

| | |
|---|---|
| 1999–2013 | Hugo Chávez is president of Venezuela |
| 2003–7 | Néstor Kirchner is president of Argentina |
| 2003–10 | Lula da Silva is president of Brazil |
| 2006–10 | Michelle Bachelet is president of Chile |
| 2006–present | Evo Morales is president of Bolivia |
| 2007–15 | Cristina Fernández de Kirchner is president of Brazil |
| 2011–16 | Dilma Rousseff is president of Brazil |
| 2014–present | Michelle Bachelet is president for a second time in Chile |
| 2015 | Paris UN Climate Change Conference |

## Keywords

Andean Pact
Bolivarian Revolution
Caricom
climate change
globalization
Mara Salvatrucha (MS-13)
Mercosur

Movement toward Socialism (MAS)
multiculturalism
neoliberalism
Panama Canal expansion
pink tide
Trans-Pacific Partnership (TPP)

# Notes

## COLONIAL PROLOGUE

1. See John E. Kicza, ed., *The Indian in Latin American History: Resistance, Resilience, and Acculturation*, rev. ed. (Lanham, Md.: Rowman and Littlefield, 1999), especially the very useful introduction by Kicza.

## PART I. INDEPENDENCE AND TURMOIL

1. See Greg Grandin, *The Empire of Necessity: Slavery, Freedom, and Deception in the New World* (New York: Picador Books, 2014) for a brilliant and immensely readable study of this phenomenon.
2. Evelyn Cherpak, "The Participation of Women in the Independence Movement in Gran Colombia, 1780–1830," in Asunción Lavrin, *Latin American Women: Historical Perspectives* (Westport, Conn.: Greenwood Press, 1978), p. 222. Cherpak takes the quote from *Las fuerzas armadas de Venezuela en el siglo xix: Textos para su estudio*, 12 vols. (Caracas, 1963), 1:242.

## CHAPTER 1. BACKGROUND TO INDEPENDENCE

1. From Hugh Hamill Jr., *The Hidalgo Revolt: Prelude to Mexican Independence* (Gainesville: University of Florida Press, 1966), pp. 121–22.
2. *The Tupac Amaru and Catarrista Rebellions: An Anthology of Sources*, trans. Ward Stavig and Ella Schmidt (Indianapolis: Hackett, 2008), pp. xxvii, 9–10, 109–13. For more on the Túpac Amaru rebellion see Charles F. Walker, *The Tupac Amaru Rebellion* (Cambridge: Harvard University Press, 2014).
3. Jorge Basadre, "La promesa de la vida peruana y otros ensayos" (Lima: Mejía Baca, 1958), in R. A. Humphreys and John Lynch, eds., *The Origins of the Latin American Revolutions, 1808–1826* (New York: Knopf, 1965), p. 297.
4. Peter Wade, *Race and Ethnicity in Latin America*, 2nd ed. (London: Pluto Press, 2010), p. 27.

## CHAPTER 2. THE COMING OF INDEPENDENCE TO SOUTH AMERICA

1. David Bushnell, ed., *Simón Bolívar: El Libertador; Writings of Simón Bolívar*, trans. Frederick H. Fornoff (Oxford: Oxford University Press, 2003), p. 18.
2. John Lynch, *Simón Bolívar: A Life* (New Haven and London: Yale University Press, 2006).

3. Quoted in John Lynch, *The Spanish-American Revolutions, 1808–1826*, 2nd ed. (New York: Norton, 1986), p. 240, from Antonio Nariño's *La Bagatela*.
4. Sergio Serulnikov, *Revolution in the Andes: The Age of Túpac Amaru* (Durham: Duke University Press, 2013), pp. 139–41.
5. Lynch, *Spanish-American Revolutions*, p. 314.

## CHAPTER 3. THE INDEPENDENCE MOVEMENTS: ON TO VICTORY

1. *Colección documental de la independencia del Perú, Tomo XX: La Iglesia*, vol. 2, *La acción del clero*. Comisión Nacional del Sesquicentenario de la Independencia del Perú (Lima: [1974], pp. 143–44).
2. William R. Manning, *Diplomatic Correspondence of the United States Concerning the Independence of the Latin-American Nations*, vol. 1 (New York: Oxford University Press, 1925), p. 18. The letter from Monroe to John Adams, then in London, is dated December 15.
3. Quoted by John Lynch, *The Spanish-American Revolutions: 1808–1826*, 2nd ed. (New York: Norton, 1986), p. 209.
4. Ralph Lee Woodward Jr., *Central America: A Nation Divided*, 3rd ed. (New York: Oxford University Press, 1999), p. 92.
5. Bolívar quote from Lynch, *Spanish-American Revolutions*, p. 269.

## CHAPTER 4. THE AFTERMATH OF INDEPENDENCE

1. William R. Manning, *Diplomatic Correspondence of the United States Concerning the Independence of the Latin-American Nations*, vol. 2 (New York: Oxford University Press, 1925), pp. 1794, 1797.
2. Richard A. Warren, *Vagrants and Citizens: Politics and the Masses in Mexico City from Colony to Republic* (Lanham, Md.: SR Books, 2001).
3. Herbert S. Klein, *Bolivia: The Evolution of a Multi-Ethnic Society*, 2nd ed. (New York: Oxford University Press, 1992), pp. 109–11.
4. Rebecca Earle, "Rape and the Anxious Republic: Revolutionary Colombia, 1810–1830," in Elizabeth Dore and Maxine Molyneux, eds., *Hidden Histories of Gender and the State in Latin America* (Durham: Duke University Press, 2000), pp. 127–46. Also, Nara Milanich, "Women, Gender, and Family in Latin America, 1820–2000," in Thomas H. Holloway, ed., *A Companion to Latin American History* (Malden, Mass.: Blackwell, 2011), p. 462; and Sarah C. Chambers, *From Subjects to Citizens: Honor, Gender, and Politics in Arequipa, Peru, 1780–1854* (University Park: Pennsylvania State University Press, 1999).

5. Silvia Arrom, *The Women of Mexico City, 1790–1857* (Stanford: Stanford University Press, 1985), chapters 3–5; statistic on employment from p. 158.
6. Quoted in Magnus Mörner, *Race Mixture in the History of Latin America* (New York: Little, Brown, 1967), pp. 86–87.
7. Mörner, *Race Mixture*, pp. 87–88. From letter to Santander in 1826 upon being informed that Páez was in revolt.
8. Ibid., p. 88.
9. Quoted in John Lynch, *New Worlds: A Religious History of Latin America* (New Haven: Yale University Press, 2012), p. 114.
10. John Lynch, *The Spanish American Revolutions, 1808–1826,* 2nd ed. (New York: Norton, 1986), p. 342.
11. John Tutino, *From Insurrection to Revolution in Mexico: Social Bases of Agrarian Violence, 1750–1940* (Princeton: Princeton University Press, 1986), chapter 6.

## CHAPTER 5. THE SEARCH FOR POLITICAL ORDER: 1830S–1850S

1. From John Lynch, *Argentine Dictator: Juan Manuel de Rosas, 1829–1852* (Oxford: Clarendon Press, 1981); first selection, pp. 208–9; second selection, pp. 305–6. The first selection from Rosas to Juan José Díaz, Estancia San Martín, 3 March 1835, Adolfo Saldías, ed., *Papeles de Rosas* (2 vols., La Plata, 1904–1907), 1:134; the second selection from Sarmiento, *El Progreso,* 8 October 1844, *Obras de D. F. Sarmiento,* pp. vi, 118–19; *Obras selectas,* ed. Enrique de Gandia, *Juan Manuel de Rosas: Su política, su caída, su herencia* (Buenos Aires, 1944), 3:103–106.
2. Quoted in Hugh M. Hamill Jr., ed., *Dictatorship in Spanish-America* (New York: Alfred A. Knopf, 1965), p. 24.
3. Richard Alan White, *Paraguay's Autonomous Revolution, 1810–1840* (Albuquerque: University of New Mexico Press, 1978), p. 99.
4. Brian Loveman, *Chile: The Legacy of Hispanic Capitalism,* 3rd ed. (New York: Oxford University Press, 2001), p. 111.
5. John V. Lombardi, *Venezuela: The Search for Order, the Dream of Progress* (New York: Oxford University Press, 1982), p. 174.
6. Will Fowler, *Santa Anna of Mexico* (Lincoln: University of Nebraska Press, 2007).
7. Greg Grandin, *The Blood of Guatemala: A History of Race and Nation* (Durham: Duke University Press, 2000), pp. 100–108.

## CHAPTER 6. ORDER AND PROGRESS

1. Cosmes cited in Leopoldo Zea, "Positivism," in *Major Trends in Mexican Philosophy,* trans. A. Robert Caponigri (Notre Dame: University of Notre Dame Press, 1966), pp. 234–35. Zea quotes a periodical that Cosmes edited.
2. See Gregory T. Cushman's *Guano and the Opening of the Pacific World: A Global Ecological History* (New York: Cambridge University Press, 2013) for a wide-ranging study of the guano industry as an element in the ecological history of the world, relating guano and atomic bombs, for example, in provocative ways.
3. Quote from Leopoldo Zea, *The Latin-American Mind* (Norman: University of Oklahoma Press, 1963), p. 276.
4. Edward Telles and the Project on Ethnicity and Race in Latin America (PERLA), *Pigmentocracies: Ethnicity, Race, and Color in Latin America* (Chapel Hill: University of North Carolina Press, 2014), p. 17.
5. Ralph Lee Woodward, ed., *Positivism in Latin America, 1850–1900: Are Order and Progress Reconcilable?* (Lexington, Mass.: Heath, 1971), p. x.
6. Lawrence A. Clayton, *Grace: W. R. Grace & Co.: The Formative Years, 1850–1930* (Ottawa, Ill.: Jameson Books, 1985), p. 55, cites Jacinto Lopez's biography of Pardo, *Manuel Pardo* (Lima: Imprenta Gil, 1947).
7. Clayton, *Grace, W. R. Grace & Co.,* p. 55.

## CHAPTER 7. CITIZEN AND NATION ON THE ROAD TO PROGRESS

1. Letter from Mariquita Sánchez (María Sánchez de Thompson) to Juan Bautista Alberdi, Buenos Aires, January 16, 1851, in *Cartas de Mariquita Sánchez,* comp. Lara Vilasca (Buenos Aires: Ediciones Peuser, 1952).
2. Evelyn Cherpak, "The Participation of Women in the Independence Movement in Gran Colombia, 1780–1830," in Asunción Lavrin, ed., *Latin American Women: Historical Perspectives* (Westport, Conn.: Greenwood, 1978), pp. 219–20.
3. Fanny Calderón de la Barca, *Life in Mexico,* ed. Howard T. Fisher and Marion Hall Fisher (Garden City: Doubleday, 1966), pp. 286–87, quoted in June E. Hahner, ed., *Women in Latin American History: Their Lives and Views* (Los Angeles: UCLA Latin American Center Publications, 1976), p. 44.
4. Cynthia Jeffress Little, "Education, Philanthropy, and Feminism: Components of Argentine Womanhood, 1860–1926," in Lavrin, *Latin American Women,* p. 237.
5. Sylvia Arrom, "Changes in Mexican Family Law in the Nineteenth Century: The Civil Codes of 1870 and 1884," *Journal of Family History* 10, no. 3 (Fall 1985): 95.
6. Elizabeth Dore, "Property, Households, and Public Regulation of Domestic Life: Diriomo, Nicaragua, 1840–1900," in Elizabeth Dore and Maxine Molyneux, eds., *Hidden Histories of Gender and the State in Latin America* (Durham: Duke University Press, 2000), pp. 147–71.
7. From Francisco Pimentel in 1865, quoted in Luis Gonzales, Daniel Cosío Villegas, et al. *Historia moderna de Mexico,* vol. 3, *La república restaurada, la vida social* (Mexico, 1956), p. 151, in turn quoted in Michael C. Meyer, William L. Sherman, and Susan M. Deeds, *The Course of Mexican History,* 10th ed. (New York: Oxford University Press, 2013), p. 310.
8. Vincent C. Peloso, *Race and Ethnicity in Latin American History* (New York: Routledge, 2014), p. 118.
9. John Lynch, "The Catholic Church in Latin America, 1830–1930," in Leslie Bethell, ed., *The Cambridge History of Latin America,* 4:560; Jeffrey L. Klaiber, S.J., *Religion and Reform in Peru, 1824–1976* (Notre Dame: University of Notre Dame Press, 1977).

## CHAPTER 8. THE DEVELOPMENT OF NATIONS: MEXICO AND CENTRAL AMERICA

1. Greg Grandin, *The Blood of Guatemala: A History of Race and Nation* (Durham: Duke University Press, 2000).

## CHAPTER 9. THE DEVELOPMENT OF NATIONS: SOUTH AMERICA

1. Manuel Meliton Carbajal, "Parte oficial del Capitan de Fragata [Comander] don Manuel Meliton Carbajal, San Bernardo, Octubre 16, 1879," in *A la gloria del gran almirante del Perú*

*Miguel Grau,* Comisión Cultural del Centro Naval del Perú (Lima 1979), pp. 337–41.

2. Edward Telles and the Project on Ethnicity and Race in Latin America (PERLA), *Pigmentocracies: Ethnicity, Race, and Color in Latin America* (Chapel Hill: University of North Carolina Press, 2014), pp. 131–36.

3. Herbert S. Klein, *Bolivia: The Evolution of a Multi-Ethnic Society,* 2nd ed. (Oxford: Oxford University Press, 1992), p. 153.

4. Brian Loveman, *Chile: The Legacy of Spanish Capitalism,* 3rd ed. (Oxford: Oxford University Press, 2001), p. 232.

5. From Arthur P. Whitaker, *The United States and the Southern Cone: Argentina, Chile, and Uruguay* (Cambridge: Harvard University Press, 1976), p. 27.

6. David Rock, *Argentina, 1516–1987: From Spanish Colonization to Alfonsín* (Berkeley: University of California Press, 1987), p. 131.

7. Alexander Dawson, *Latin America since Independence: A History with Primary Sources* (New York: Routledge, 2011), p. 61.

8. James R. Scobie, *Argentina: A City and a Nation,* 2nd ed. (New York: Oxford University Press, 1971), p. 119.

9. John Charles Chasteen, *Heroes on Horseback: A Life and Times of the Last Gaucho Caudillos* (Albuquerque: University of New Mexico Press, 1995).

10. Luis Carlos Benvenuto, *Breve historia del Uruguay: Economía y sociedad* (Montevideo: Arca, 1981), pp. 80–81.

11. John Hoyt Williams, *The Rise and Fall of the Paraguayan Republic, 1800–1870* (Austin: Institute of Latin American Studies, 1979), chapter 13.

12. Sandra Lauderdale Graham, *House and Street: The Domestic World of Servants and Masters in Nineteenth-Century Rio de Janeiro* (Austin: University of Texas Press, 1992).

13. Donald Emmet Worcester, *Brazil: from Colony to World Power* (New York: Scribner, 1973).

## CHAPTER 10. INVENTING LATIN AMERICA

1. From *Selected Poems of Rubén Darío,* by Rubén Darío, trans. Lysander Kemp, ©1965, renewed 1993. By permission of the University of Texas Press.

2. Comisión Nacional de Homenaje a Sarmiento, *Sarmiento: Cincuentenario de su muerte,* 5 vols. (Buenos Aires: 1939), 1:140, quoted in William Rex Crawford, *A Century of Latin American Thought* (Cambridge: Harvard University Press, 1961), p. 38.

3. Quoted in Leopoldo Zea, *The Latin-American Mind* (Norman: University of Oklahoma Press, 1963), p. 57.

4. For more on Bello, see Rafael Caldera, *Andrés Bello: Philospher, Poet, Philologist, Educator, Legislator, Statesman,* trans. John Street (London: George Allen and Unwin, 1977).

5. Doris Sommer, *Foundational Fictions: The National Romances of Latin America* (Berkeley: University of California Press, 1993).

6. Jean Franco, *The Modern Culture of Latin America: Society and the Artist* (New York: Praeger, 1967), p. 7.

7. Euclides da Cunha, *Rebellion in the Backlands (Os sertões),* trans. Samuel Putnam (Chicago: University of Chicago Press, 1944), p. 130.

8. Da Cunha, *Rebellion in the Backlands,* pp. 128–29.

9. Ibid., pp. 54, 408.

10. This translation courtesy of Anne Fountain. It appeared in Romance Monographs, no. 56, *Versos Sencillos,* by José Martí (University of Mississippi, 2000).

11. Jaime Suchlicki, *Cuba: From Columbus to Castro,* 2nd ed. (Washington, D.C.: Pergamon, 1986), p. 77.

12. Franco, *Modern Culture of Latin America,* p. 50.

## CHAPTER 11. CHANGING WORLDS AND NEW EMPIRES

1. Secretary of State Richard Olney's message to Great Britain, July 20, 1895, quoted in Thomas G. Paterson, ed., *Major Problems in American Foreign Policy: Documents and Essays, Vol. 1: to 1914* (Lexington, Mass.: D.C. Heath, 1978), p. 246.

2. Josiah Strong, *Our Country,* ed. Jurgen Herbst (Cambridge: Belknap Press of Harvard University Press, 1963), p. 214.

3. James D. Richardson, ed., *A Compilation of the Messages and Papers of the Presidents, 1890–1897,* 10 vols. (Washington, D.C.: Government Printing Office, 1896–1899), 9:251, cited in Joseph Smith, *Illusions of Conflict: Anglo-American Diplomacy toward Latin America, 1865–1896* (Pittsburgh: University of Pittsburgh Press, 1979), p. 120.

4. Frelinghuysen to John F. Miller, March 26, 1884, cited in West to Granville, no. 116, April 16, 1884, in Public Records Office, *The Records of the Foreign Office, 1782–1939* (London: Her Majesty's Stationary Office, 1969), 5/1869, cited in Smith, *Illusions of Conflict,* p. 121.

## CHAPTER 12. EARLY POPULISM IN SOUTH AMERICA

1. Frederick Pike, *Chile and the United States, 1880–1962* (Notre Dame: University of Notre Dame Press, 1963), p. 179.

2. Julio César Jobet, *Temas históricos chilenos* (Santiago: 1973), p. 220.

3. Sandra McGee Deutsch, "The Catholic Church, Work, and Womanhood in Argentina, 1890–1930," in Gertrude M. Yeager, ed., *Confronting Change, Challenging Tradition: Women in Latin American History* (Wilmington, Del.: Scholarly Resources, 1994), p. 129.

## CHAPTER 13. DICTATORS OF THE CARIBBEAN BASIN

1. Special Correspondent, "Head of Revolution Tells Party's Aims," *New York Times,* September 1, 1929.

2. John J. Johnson, *Latin America in Caricature* (Austin: University of Texas Press, 1980); Frederick Pike, *The United States and Latin America: Myths and Stereotypes of Civilization and Nature* (Austin: University of Texas Press, 1992).

3. Burton J. Hendrick, ed., *The Life and Letters of Walter H. Page* (Garden City, N.Y.: Doubleday, Page, 1925), p. 188.

4. *Congressional Record,* 58th Congress, 8th session, p. 19.

5. Quoted in Thomas A. Bailey, *A Diplomatic History of the American People* (New York: Appleton-Century-Crofts, 1964), p. 477.

## CHAPTER 14. DIVERGENT PATHS TO MODERN NATIONHOOD: PANAMA, BRAZIL, AND PERU

1. Cited by permission of Eunice Mason.

2. Michael L. Conniff, *Panama and the United States,* 3rd ed. (Athens: University of Georgia Press, 2012).

3. Barbara Weinstein, *The Color of Modernity: São Paulo and the Making of Race and Nation in Brazil* (Durham: Duke University Press, 2015).

4. Edward Telles and the Project on Ethnicity and Race in Latin America (PERLA), *Pigmentocracies: Ethnicity, Race, and Color in Latin America* (Chapel Hill: University of North Carolina Press, 2014), p. 177.
5. Peruvian Nobel laureate Mario Vargas Llosa's *The Dream of the Celt* (London: Faber and Faber, 2012), a fictionalized biography of Roger Casement, an Irish diplomat who exposed the enslavement of the indigenous people in the Putumayo, devotes nearly a third of its narrative to the shocking revelations of abuse and death among Amazonian Indians.

## CHAPTER 15. EARLY REVOLUTIONARIES: MEXICO, BRAZIL, AND NICARAGUA

1. John Womack Jr., *Zapata and the Mexican Revolution* (New York: Knopf Doubleday, 2011), appendix B.
2. Adapted from John Dunn, *Modern Revolutions: An Introduction to the Analysis of a Political Phenomenon,* 2nd ed. (London: Cambridge University Press, 1989) p. xvi.
3. Crane Brinton, *Anatomy of Revolution,* 3rd ed. (New York: Vintage, 1965), pp. 198–202; see also Neill Macaulay, *The Sandino Affair,* 2nd ed. (Durham: Duke University Press, 1985), p. 57.
4. Macaulay, *Sandino Affair,* p. 57.

## CHAPTER 16. THE 1930S: YEARS OF DEPRESSION AND UPHEAVAL

1. J. Brosh to Foreign Office, July 9, 1932, Public Records Office FO 341/15849.
2. Jody Pavilack, *Mining for the Nation: The Politics of Chile's Coal Communities from the Popular Front to the Cold War* (University Park: Pennsylvania State University Press, 2011).
3. Josephus Daniels, "The Oil Expropriation," in Gilbert M. Joseph and Timothy J. Henderson, eds., *The Mexico Reader: History, Culture, Politics* (Durham: Duke University Press, 2002), p. 454.
4. Lauren (aka Robin) Derby, "The Dictator's Seduction: Gender and State Spectacle during the Trujillo Regime," in William H. Beezley and Linda A. Curcio-Nagy, eds., *Latin American Popular Culture since Independence: An Introduction,* 2nd ed. (Lanham, Md.: Rowman and Littlefield, 2012), p. 207.

## CHAPTER 17. LATIN AMERICA IN WORLD WAR II

1. From Aricildes de Moraes Motta, ed., *História oral do Exército na Segunda Guerra Mundial* (Rio de Janeiro: Biblioteca do Exército Editora, 2001), 5:310–22. Reprinted by permission.
2. The best source for these events is Frank D. McCann, *The Brazilian-American Alliance, 1937–1945* (Princeton: Princeton University Press, 1973).
3. Seth Garfield, *In Search of the Amazon* (Durham: Duke University Press, 2013).
4. Raúl Prebisch, *The Economic Development of Latin America and Its Principal Problems* (Lake Success, N.Y.: United Nations, 1950).

## CHAPTER 18. THE CLASSIC POPULISTS

1. "Algunas frases de Pepe Figueres," *Kalettal* (blog), https://kalettal .wordpress.com/2011/04/16/algunas-frases-de-pepe-figueres/.

2. Tad Szulc, *Twlight of the Tyrants* (New York: Holt, 1959).
3. Quoted in Robert M. Levine and John J. Crocitti, eds., *The Brazil Reader* (Durham: Duke University Press, 1999), pp. 222–24.
4. Edward Telles and the Project on Ethnicity and Race in Latin America (PERLA), *Pigmentocracies: Ethnicity, Race, and Color in Latin America* (Chapel Hill: University of North Carolina Press, 2014) pp. 179–80.
5. Daniel James, *Resistance and Integration: Peronism and the Argentine Working Class, 1946–1976* (Cambridge: Cambridge University Press, 1988), p. 33.
6. Daniel James, *Doña María's Story, Life History, Memory, and Political Identity* (Durham: Duke University Press, 2000).
7. Sandra McGee Deutsch, "Gender and Sociopolitical Change in Twentieth-Century Latin America," *Hispanic American Historical Review* 71, no. 2 (1991): 259–306.
8. Telles, *Pigmentocracies,* pp. 138–43.
9. See the opening section of chapter 13.

## CHAPTER 19. MEXICO SINCE WORLD WAR II

1. Adapted from John Womack Jr., *Rebellion in Chiapas: An Historical Reader* (New York: New Press, 1999), pp. 247–49.
2. The most authoritative source is Roderic Ai Camp, *Mexican Political Biographies, 1935–2009,* 4th ed. (Austin: University of Texas Press, 2011).
3. Susan Gauss, *Made in Mexico: Regions, Nation, and the State in the Rise of Mexican Industrialism, 1920s–1940s* (University Park: Pennsylvania State University Press, 2010).
4. Eric Zolov, *Refried Elvis: The Rise of the Mexican Counterculture* (Berkeley: University of California Press, 1999).

## CHAPTER 20. COLOMBIAN CONUNDRUM

1. Herbert Braun, *The Assassination of Gaitán: Public Life and Urban Violence in Colombia* (Madison: University of Wisconsin Press, 1985), p. 134.
2. U.S. Department of State, Office of the Historian, *Foreign Relations of the United States, 1948: The Western Hemisphere, vol. 9,* telegram, https://history.state.gov/historicaldocuments /frus1948v09/d22.
3. U.S. Department of State, Office of the Historian, *Foreign Relations of the United States, 1948: The Western Hemisphere, vol. 9,* telegram, https://history.state.gov/historicaldocuments /frus1948v09/d24.
4. Kate Paarlberg-Kvam, "The Key to Peace Is Ours: Women's Peacebuilding in Twenty-First Century Colombia" (Ph.D. diss., University at Albany, State University of New York, December 2016).

## CHAPTER 21. CARIBBEAN BASIN COUNTERCURRENTS

1. Jean-Robert Cadet, *Restavec: From Haitian Slave Child to Middle-Class American* (Austin: University of Texas Press, 1998), pp. 1–4.
2. Piero Gleijesis, *Shattered Hope: The Guatemalan Revolution and the United States, 1944–1954* (Princeton: Princeton University Press, 1992), chapter 3.
3. Gleijesis, *Shattered Hope,* chapter 13.

4. Ilja A. Luciak, "Gender Equality, Democratization, and the Revolutionary Left in Central America: Guatemala in Comparative Context," in Victoria González and Karen Kampwirth, eds., *Radical Women in Latin America: Left and Right* (University Park: Pennsylvania State University Press, 2001), pp. 193–94.

## CHAPTER 22. THE CUBAN REVOLUTION AND ITS AFTERMATH

1. Latin American Network Information Center, Castro Speech Data Base, http://lanic.utexas.edu/project/castro/db/1959/19590728.html.
2. Anna M. Fernández Poncela, "Nicaraguan Women: Legal, Political, and Social Spaces," in Elizabeth Dore, ed., *Gender Politics in Latin America: Debates in Theory and Practice* (New York: Monthly Review Press, 1997), pp. 36–51.
3. Margaret Randall, *Sandino's Daughters Revisited: Feminism in Nicaragua* (New Brunswick: Rutgers University Press, 1994).

## CHAPTER 23. THE NATIONAL SECURITY STATES

1. From *Velasco: La voz de la revolución; Discursos del presidente de la república general de División Juan Velasco Alvarado, 1968, 1969.* Colección Documentos Revolucionarios, Oficina Nacional de Difusión SINAMOS (Lima, 1972), pp. 43–44.
2. Lois Hecht Oppenheim, *Politics in Chile: Socialism, Authoritarianism, and Market Democracy,* 3rd ed. (Boulder: Westview Press, 2007), p. 59.
3. Lisa Baldez, "Nonpartisanship as a Political Strategy: Women Left, Right and Center in Chile," in Victoria González and Karen Kampwirth, eds., *Radical Women in Latin America: Left and Right* (University Park: Pennsylvania State University Press, 2001), p. 278.
4. Vincent C. Peloso, *Race and Ethnicity in Latin American History* (New York: Routledge, 2014), p. 166; and Amnesty International, "Chile, 'Extreme Cruelty': The Plight of the Mapuche Indians during the Years of Military Rule" (July 1992), AI Index: AMR 22/09/92.
5. Heidi Tinsman, *Buying into the Regime: Grapes and Consumption in Cold War Chile and the United States* (Durham: Duke University Press, 2014).

## CHAPTER 24. DEMOCRATIZATION AND CONFLICT IN THE LATE TWENTIETH CENTURY

1. R. Andrew Chestnut, *Born Again in Brazil* (New Brunswick: Rutgers University Press, 1997), pp. 87–88.

## CHAPTER 25. LATIN AMERICA IN THE TWENTY-FIRST CENTURY

1. Reprinted by permission. Nancy Alonso, *Closed for Repairs,* trans. Anne Fountain (Evanston, Ill.: Curbstone Press, 2007). Originally published as *Cerrado por reparación* (Havana: Ediciones Unión, 2002).
2. Edward Telles and the Project on Ethnicity and Race in Latin America (PERLA), *Pigmentocracies: Ethnicity, Race, and Color in Latin America* (Chapel Hill: University of North Carolina Press, 2014), pp. 22–24.
3. TPP: Made in America; The Transpacific Partnership, Executive Office of the President, Office of the United States Trade Representative, https://ustr.gov/tpp/.
4. Paris 2015 UN Climate Change Conference, http://www.cop21.gouv.fr/en/.

# Bibliography

## BIBLIOGRAPHY FOR PART I

Anna, Timothy E. *The Fall of Royal Government in Peru.* Lincoln: University of Nebraska Press, 1980.

———. *Forging Mexico: 1821–1835.* Lincoln: University of Nebraska Press, 1998.

———. *Spain and the Loss of America.* Lincoln: University of Nebraska Press, 1983.

Archer, Christon I., ed. *The Birth of Modern Mexico, 1780–1824.* Wilmington, Del.: SR Books, 2003.

———, ed. *The Wars of Independence in Spanish America.* Wilmington, Del.: Scholarly Resources, 2000.

Arrom, Silvia M. *The Women of Mexico City, 1790–1854.* Stanford: Stanford University Press, 1985.

Barman, Roderick J. *Brazil: The Forging of a Nation, 1798–1852.* Stanford: Stanford University Press, 1988.

Bethell, Leslie, ed. *The Independence of Latin America.* Cambridge: Cambridge University Press, 1987.

Bushnell, David. *Reform and Reaction in the Platine Provinces, 1810–1852.* Gainesville: University Press of Florida, 1983.

———. *The Santander Regime in Gran Colombia.* 2nd ed. Westport, Conn.: Greenwood Press, 1970.

———, ed. *Simón Bolívar: El Libertador; Writings of Simón Bolívar,* translated by Frederick H. Fornoff. Oxford: Oxford University Press, 2003.

Bushnell, David, and Neill Macaulay. *The Emergence of Latin America in the Nineteenth Century.* 2nd ed. New York: Oxford University Press, 1994.

Butler, Kathleen Mary. *The Economics of Emancipation: Jamaica and Barbados, 1823–1843.* Chapel Hill: University of North Carolina Press, 1995.

Cavaliero, Roderick. *The Independence of Brazil.* New York: St. Martin's Press, 1994.

Chambers, Sarah C. *Families in War and Peace: Chile from Colony to Nation.* Durham: Duke University Press, 2015.

Chasteen, John Charles. *Americanos: Latin America's Struggle for Independence.* Oxford: Oxford University Press, 2008.

Clissold, Stephen. *Bernardo O'Higgins and the Independence of Chile.* New York: Praeger, 1969.

Cussen, Antonio. *Bello and Bolivar: Poetry and Politics in the Spanish American Revolution.* Cambridge: Cambridge University Press, 1992.

Di Tella, Torcuato. *National Popular Politics in Early Independent Mexico, 1820–1847.* Albuquerque: University of New Mexico Press, 1996.

Dubois, Laurent. *Avengers of the New World: The Story of the Haitian Revolution.* Cambridge: Belknap Press of Harvard University Press, 2004.

Ferrer, Ada. *Freedom's Mirror: Cuba and Haiti in the Age of Revolution.* Cambridge: Cambridge University Press, 2014.

Fowler, Will. *Santa Anna of Mexico.* Lincoln: University of Nebraska Press, 2007.

Gaffield, Julia. *Haitian Connections in the Atlantic World: Recognition after Revolution.* Chapel Hill: University of North Carolina Press, 2015.

Geggus, David P., ed. *The Impact of the Haitian Revolution in the Atlantic World.* Columbia: University of South Carolina Press, 2001.

Graham, Richard. *Independence in Latin America: Contrasts and Comparisons.* 3rd ed. Austin: University of Texas Press, 2013.

Green, Stanley C. *The Mexican Republic: The First Decade, 1823–1832.* Pittsburgh: University of Pittsburgh Press, 1987.

Guardino, Peter. *The Time of Liberty: Popular Political Culture in Oaxaca, 1750–1850.* Durham: Duke University Press, 2005.

Halperín Donghi, Tulio. *Politics, Economics, and Society in Argentina in the Revolutionary Period.* Cambridge: Cambridge University Press, 1975.

Henderson, Timothy J. *A Glorious Defeat: Mexico and Its War with the United States.* New York: Hill and Wang, 2008.

———. *The Mexican Wars for Independence.* New York: Hill and Wang, 2010.

Humphreys, R. A., and John Lynch, eds. *The Origins of the Latin American Revolutions, 1808–1826.* New York: Knopf, 1965.

Hunefeldt, Christine. *Paying the Price of Freedom: Family and Labor among Lima's Slaves, 1800–1854.* Berkeley and Los Angeles: University of California Press, 1994.

Johnson, John J. *A Hemisphere Apart: The Foundations of United States Policy towards Latin America.* Baltimore: Johns Hopkins University Press, 1990.

Johnson, John J., and Doris M. Ladd, eds. *Simón Bolívar and Spanish American Independence, 1783–1830.* New York: Van Nostrand Reinhold, 1968.

Johnson, Lyman L. *Workshop of Revolution: Plebeian Buenos Aires and the Atlantic World, 1776–1810.* Durham: Duke University Press, 2011.

Kinsbruner, Jay. *Independence in Spanish America: Civil Wars, Revolutions, and Underdevelopment.* Rev. ed. Albuquerque: University of New Mexico Press, 2000.

Langley, Lester D. *The Americas in the Age of Revolution, 1750–1850.* New Haven: Yale University Press, 1996.

Lasso, Marixa. *Myths of Harmony: Race and Republicanism during the Age of Revolution, Colombia, 1795–1831.* Pittsburgh: University of Pittsburgh Press, 2007.

Lipsett-Rivera, Sonya. *Gender and the Negotiation of Daily Life in Mexico, 1750–1856.* Lincoln: University of Nebraska Press, 2012.

Lynch, John. *Caudillos in Spanish America, 1800–1850.* New York: Oxford University Press, 1992.

**653**

———, ed. *Latin American Revolutions, 1808–1826: Old and New World Origins.* 2nd ed. Norman: University of Oklahoma Press, 1994.

———. *San Martín: Argentine Soldier, American Hero.* New Haven: Yale University Press, 2009.

———. *Simón Bolívar: A Life.* New Haven and London: Yale University Press, 2006.

———. *The Spanish-American Revolutions, 1808–1826.* 2nd ed. New York: Norton, 1986.

Macaulay, Neill. *Dom Pedro: The Struggle for Liberty in Brazil and Portugal, 1798–1834.* Durham: Duke University Press, 1986.

Martínez-Alier, Verena. *Marriage, Class, and Colour in Nineteenth-Century Cuba.* 2nd ed. Ann Arbor: University of Michigan Press, 1989.

McFarlane, Anthony. *War and Independence in Spanish America.* New York: Routledge, 2008.

Murray, Pamela S. *For Glory and Bolívar: The Remarkable Life of Manuela Sáenz.* Austin: University of Texas Press, 2008.

Paquette, Robert L. *Sugar Is Made with Blood: The Conspiracy of La Escalera and Conflict between Empires over Slavery in Cuba.* Middletown: Wesleyan University Press, 1989.

Rodriguez O., Jaime E. *The Independence of Spanish America.* Cambridge: Cambridge University Press, 1998.

———. *The Origins of Mexican National Politics, 1808–1847.* Wilmington, Del.: Scholarly Resources, 1997.

Schultz, Kirsten. *Tropical Versailles: Empire, Monarchy, and the Portuguese Royal Court in Rio de Janeiro, 1808–1821.* New York: Routledge, 2001.

Serulnikov, Sergio. *Revolution in the Andes: The Age of Túpac Amaru.* Durham: Duke University Press, 2013.

Simpson, Lesley Byrd. *Many Mexicos,* 4th ed., revised. Berkeley: University of California Press, 1971 [1941].

Stevens, Donald F. *Origins of Instability in Early Republican Mexico.* Durham: Duke University Press, 1991.

Szuchman, Mark D., and Jonathan C. Brown, eds. *Revolution and Restoration: The Rearrangement of Power in Argentina, 1776–1860.* Lincoln: University of Nebraska Press, 1994.

Vincent, Theodore. *The Legacy of Vicente Guerrero, Mexico's First Black Indian President.* Gainesville: University Press of Florida, 2001.

White, Richard Alan. *Paraguay's Autonomous Revolution, 1810–1840.* Albuquerque: University of New Mexico Press, 1978.


## BIBLIOGRAPHY FOR PART II

Andrews, George Reid. *The Afro-Argentines of Buenos Aires, 1800–1900.* Madison: University of Wisconsin Press, 1980.

Arrom, Silvia M., and Servando Ortoll, eds. *Riots in the Cities: Popular Politics and the Urban Poor in Latin America, 1765–1910.* Wilmington, Del.: Scholarly Resources, 1996.

Barickman, Bert J. *A Bahian Counterpoint: Sugar, Tobacco, Cassava, and Slavery in the Reconcavo, 1780–1860.* Stanford: Stanford University Press, 1998.

Barman, Roderick J. *Citizen Emperor: Pedro II and the Making of Brazil, 1825–91.* Stanford: Stanford University Press, 1999.

———. *Princess Isabel of Brazil: Gender and Power in the Nineteenth Century.* Wilmington, Del.: Scholarly Resources, 2002.

Bauer, K. Jack. *The Mexican War, 1846–1848.* Lincoln: University of Nebraska Press, 1992.

Beattie, Peter M. *The Tribute of Blood: Army, Honor, Race, and Nation in Brazil, 1864–1945.* Durham: Duke University Press, 2001.

Bergad, Laird W., Fe Iglesias Garcia, and Maria del Carmen Barcia. *The Cuban Slave Market, 1790–1880.* Cambridge: Cambridge University Press, 1995.

Blakemore, Harold. *British Nitrates and Chilean Politics, 1886–1896.* London: Athlone Press for the Institute of Latin American Studies, 1974.

Blanchard, Peter. *The Origins of the Peruvian Labor Movement, 1883–1919.* Pittsburgh: University of Pittsburgh Press, 1982.

———. *Slavery and Abolition in Early Republican Peru.* Wilmington, Del.: SR Books, 1992.

Bunker, Steven. *Creating Mexican Consumer Culture in the Age of Porfirio Díaz.* Albuquerque: University of New Mexico Press, 2012.

Burns, E. Bradford. *The Poverty of Progress: Latin America in the Nineteenth Century.* Berkeley: University of California Press, 1980.

Calderón de la Barca, Frances. *Life in Mexico.* Reprint. Berkeley and Los Angeles: University of California Press, 1982.

Chasteen, John Charles. *Heroes on Horseback: A Life and Times of the Last Gaucho Caudillos.* Albuquerque: University of New Mexico Press, 1995.

Clayton, Lawrence A. *Grace: W. R. Grace & Co., the Formative Years, 1850–1930.* Ottawa, Ill.: Jameson Books, 1985.

Clegern, Wayne M. *Origins of Liberal Dictatorship in Central America.* Niwot: University Press of Colorado, 1994.

Conrad, Robert E. *The Destruction of Brazilian Slavery, 1850–1888.* 2nd ed. Melbourne: Krieger, 1993.

Costa, Emilia Viotti da. *The Brazilian Empire.* Chicago: Dorsey Press, 1985.

Costeloe, Michael P. *The Central Republic in Mexico, 1835–1846.* Cambridge: Cambridge University Press, 1993.

Dean, Warren. *Rio Claro: A Brazilian Plantation System, 1820–1920.* Stanford: Stanford University Press, 1978.

Deustua, Jose R. *The Bewitchment of Silver: The Social Economy of Mining in Nineteenth-Century Peru.* Athens: Ohio University Press, 2000.

Dumond, Don E. *The Machete and the Cross: Campesino Rebellion in Yucatan.* Lincoln: University of Nebraska Press, 1997.

Ferrer, Ada. *Insurgent Cuba: Race, Nation, and Revolution, 1868–1898.* Chapel Hill: The University of North Carolina Press, 1999.

Garner, Paul. *British Lions and Mexican Eagles: Business, Politics, and Empire in the Career of Weetman Pearson in Mexico, 1889–1919.* Stanford: Stanford University Press, 2011.

Gootenberg, Paul. *Between Silver and Guano: Commercial Policy and the State in Postindependence Peru.* Princeton: Princeton University Press, 1989.

Graham, Richard. *Britain and the Onset of Modernization in Brazil, 1850–1914.* Cambridge: Cambridge University Press, 1968.

———. *Patronage and Politics in Nineteenth-Century Brazil.* Stanford: Stanford University Press, 1989.

Graham, Sandra Lauderdale. *Caetana Says No: Women's Stories from a Brazilian Slave Society.* Cambridge: Cambridge University Press, 2002.

———. *House and Street: The Domestic World of Servants and Masters in Nineteenth-Century Rio de Janeiro.* Austin: University of Texas Press, 1992.

Gudmundson, Lowell, and Hector Lindo-Fuentes. *Central America, 1821–1871.* Tuscaloosa: University of Alabama Press, 1995.

Haber, Stephen, ed. *How Latin America Fell Behind.* Stanford: Stanford University Press, 1997.

Hale, Charles A. *The Transformation of Liberalism in Late Nineteenth-Century Mexico.* Princeton: Princeton University Press, 1991.

Hamill, Hugh, ed. *Caudillos: Dictators in Spanish America.* Norman: University of Oklahoma Press, 1992.

Hart, John Mason. *Empire and Revolution: The Americans in Mexico since the Civil War.* Berkeley: University of California Press, 2006.

Holloway, Thomas. *Immigrants on the Land: Coffee and Society in São Paulo, 1886–1934.* Chapel Hill: University of North Carolina Press, 1980.

Holt, Thomas C. *The Problem of Freedom: Race, Labor, and Politics in Jamaica and Britain, 1832–1938.* Baltimore: Johns Hopkins University Press, 1991.

James, Marquis, with an introduction by Lawrence A. Clayton. *Merchant Adventurer: The Story of W. R. Grace.* Wilmington, Del.: SR Books, 1993.

Jiménez de Wagenheim, Olga. *Puerto Rico: An Interpretive History from Pre-Columbian Times to 1900.* Princeton: Markus Wiener, 1997.

Leonard, Thomas M., ed. *United States-Latin American Relations, 1850–1903.* Tuscaloosa: University of Alabama Press, 1999.

Levine, Robert M. *Vale of Tears: Revisiting the Canudos Massacre in Northeastern Brazil.* Berkeley and Los Angeles: University of California Press, 1992.

Levy, Claude. *Emancipation, Sugar, and Federalism: Barbados and the West Indies, 1833–1876.* Gainesville: University Press of Florida, 1980.

Lewis, Paul H. *Political Parties and Generations in Paraguay's Liberal Era, 1869–1940.* Chapel Hill: University of North Carolina Press, 1993.

Lynch, John. *Argentine Caudillo: Juan Manuel de Rosas.* Washington, Del.: SR Books, 2001.

McCrea, Heather. *Diseased Relations: Epidemics, Public Health and State-Building in Yucatán, Mexico, 1847–1924.* Albuquerque: University of New Mexico Press, 2010.

Pang, Eul-Soo. *In Pursuit of Honor and Power: Noblemen of the Southern Cross in Nineteenth-Century Brazil.* Tuscaloosa: University of Alabama Press, 1988.

Peloso, Vincent C., and Barbara Tenenbaum, eds. *Liberals, Politics and Power: State Formation in Nineteenth-Century Latin America.* Athens: University of Georgia Press, 1996.

Pineo, Ronn F. *Social and Economic Reform in Ecuador: Life and Work in Guayaquil.* Gainesville: University Press of Florida, 1996.

Sanders, James E. *Contentious Republicans: Popular Politics, Race, and Class in Nineteenth-Century Colombia.* Durham: Duke University Press, 2004.

Sater, William F. *Chile and the War of the Pacific.* Lincoln: University of Nebraska Press, 1986.

Schoonover, Thomas D. *The United States in Central America, 1860–1911.* Durham: Duke University Press, 1991.

Scobie, James R. *Argentina: A City and a Nation.* 2nd ed. New York: Oxford University Press, 1971.

———. *Revolution on the Pampas: A Social History of Argentine Wheat, 1860–1910.* Austin: University of Texas Press, 1964.

Scott, Rebecca J. *Slave Emancipation in Cuba: The Transition to Free Labor, 1860–1899.* Princeton: Princeton University Press, 1985.

Slatta, Richard W. *Cowboys of the Americas.* New Haven: Yale University Press, 1990.

———. *Gauchos and the Vanishing Frontier.* Lincoln: University of Nebraska Press, 1983.

Sommer, Doris. *Foundational Fictions: The National Romances of Latin America.* Berkeley: University of California Press, 1993.

Stein, Stanley. *Vassouras: A Brazilian Coffee County, 1850–1900.* Cambridge: Harvard University Press, 1970.

Stern, Orin, et al., eds. *The Peru Reader: History, Politics, Culture.* Durham: Duke University Press, 2005.

Szuchman, Mark D. *Order, Family and Community in Buenos Aires, 1810–1860.* Stanford: Stanford University Press, 1988.

Tenenbaum, Barbara. *The Politics of Penury: Debts and Taxes in Mexico, 1821–1856.* Albuquerque: University of New Mexico Press, 1986.

Tinker Salas, Miguel. *In the Shadow of the Eagles: Sonora and the Transformation of the Border during the Porfiriato.* Berkeley: University of California Press, 1997.

Vallens, Vivian J. *Working Women in Mexico during the Porfiriato, 1880–1910.* Palo Alto: R & E Research, 1978.

Vanderwood, Paul J. *Disorder and Progress: Bandits, Police, and Mexican Development.* Wilmington, Del.: SR Books, 1992.

Voss, Stuart F. *On the Periphery of Nineteenth-Century Mexico: Sonora and Sinaloa, 1810–1877.* Tucson: University of Arizona Press, 1982.

Wasserman, Mark. *Capitalists, Caciques and Revolution: The Native Elite and Foreign Enterprise in Chihuahua, Mexico, 1854–1911.* Chapel Hill: University of North Carolina Press, 1984.

———. *Pesos and Politics: Business, Elites, Foreigners, and Government in Mexico, 1854–1940.* Stanford, CA: Stanford University Press, 2015.

Weinstein, Barbara. *The Amazon Rubber Boom, 1850–1920.* Stanford: Stanford University Press, 1983.

Wells, Allen, and Gilbert M. Joseph. *Summer of Discontent, Seasons of Upheaval: Elite Politics and Rural Insurgency in Yucatán, 1876–1915.* Stanford: Stanford University Press, 1996.

Whigham, Thomas. *The Paraguayan War.* Lincoln: University of Nebraska Press, 2002.

———. *The Politics of River Trade: Tradition and Development in the Upper Plata, 1780–1870.* Albuquerque: University of New Mexico Press, 1994.

Wolfe, Justin. *The Everyday Nation-State: Community and Ethnicity in Nineteenth-Century Nicaragua.* Lincoln: University of Nebraska Press, 2007.

Woodward, Ralph Lee, ed. *Positivism in Latin America, 1850–1900: Are Order and Progress Reconcilable?* Lexington, Mass.: Heath, 1971.

Woodward, Ralph Lee, Jr. *Rafael Carrera and the Emergence of the Republic of Guatemala, 1821–1871.* Athens: University of Georgia Press, 1993.

## BIBLIOGRAPHY FOR PART III

Albert, Bill. *South America and the First World War: The Impact of the War on Brazil, Argentina, Peru, and Chile.* Cambridge: Cambridge University Press, 1988.

Baud, Michiel. *Peasants and Tobacco in the Dominican Republic, 1870–1930.* Knoxville: University of Tennessee Press, 1995.

Bergquist, Charles. *Labor in Latin America.* Stanford: Stanford University Press, 1986.

Besse, Susan K. *Restructuring Patriarchy: The Modernization of Gender Inequality in Brazil, 1914–1940.* Chapel Hill: University of North Carolina Press, 1996.

Brown, Jonathan C. *Oil and Revolution in Mexico.* Berkeley and Los Angeles: University of California Press, 1993.

Brunk, Samuel. *Emiliano Zapata: Revolution and Betrayal in Mexico.* Albuquerque: University of New Mexico Press, 1995.

Buchenau, Jürgen. *In the Shadow of the Giant: The Making of Mexico's Central American Policy, 1876–1930.* Tuscaloosa: University of Alabama Press, 1996.

Calder, Bruce J. *The Impact of Intervention: The Dominican Republic during the U.S. Occupation of 1916–1924*. Princeton: Markus Wiener, 1984, 2006.

Dawson, Alexander. *Indian and Nation in Revolutionary Mexico*. Tucson: University of Arizona Press, 2004.

Diacon, Todd A. *Stringing Together a Nation: Cândido Mariano da Silva Rondon and the Construction of a Modern Brazil, 1906–1930*. Durham: Duke University Press, 2004.

Dosal, Paul J. *Doing Business with the Dictators: A Political History of United Fruit in Guatemala, 1899–1944*. Wilmington, Del.: SR Books, 1993.

Dunn, John. *Modern Revolutions: An Introduction to the Analysis of a Political Phenomenon*. 2nd ed. London: Cambridge University Press, 1989.

Dye, Alan. *Cuban Sugar in the Age of Mass Production: Technology and the Economics of the Sugar Central, 1899–1929*. Stanford: Stanford University Press, 1998.

Farnsworth-Alvear, Ann. *Dulcinea in the Factory: Myths, Morals, Men, and Women in Colombia's Industrial Experiment*. Durham: Duke University Press, 2000.

Greene, Julie. *The Canal Builders: Making America's Empire at the Panama Canal*. New York: Penguin, 2009.

Guy, Donna. *Sex and Danger in Buenos Aires: Prostitution, Family, and Nation in Argentina*. Lincoln: University of Nebraska Press, 1991.

Haber, Stephen H. *Industry and Underdevelopment: The Industrialization of Mexico, 1890–1940*. Stanford: Stanford University Press, 1989.

Hall, Linda B. *Oil, Banks, and Politics: The United States and Postrevolutionary Mexico, 1917–1924*. Austin: University of Texas Press, 1995.

Harpelle, Ronald N. *The West Indians of Costa Rica*. Montreal: McGill-Queen's University Press, 2001.

Hart, John Mason. *Revolutionary Mexico*. Berkeley and Los Angeles: University of California Press, 1987.

Helg, Aline. *Our Rightful Share: The Afro-Cuban Struggle for Equality, 1886–1912*. Chapel Hill: University of North Carolina Press, 1995.

Hernández, José M. *Cuba and the United States: Intervention and Militarism, 1868–1933*. Austin: University of Texas Press, 1993.

Hutchison, Elizabeth Quay. *Labors Appropriate to Their Sex: Gender, Labor, and Politics in Urban Chile, 1900–1930*. Durham: Duke University Press, 2001.

Joseph, Gilbert M., and Jürgen Buchenau. *Mexico's Once and Future Revolution: Social Upheaval and the Challenge of Rule since the Late Nineteenth Century*. Durham: Duke University Press, 2013.

Knight, Alan. *The Mexican Revolution*. 2 vols. Lincoln: University of Nebraska Press, 1986.

Lavrin, Asunción. *Women, Feminism, and Social Change in Argentina, Chile, and Uruguay, 1890–1940*. Lincoln: University of Nebraska Press, 1995.

Masterson, Daniel M. *The Japanese in Latin America*. Urbana: University of Illinois Press, 2004.

McCann, Frank D. *Soldiers of the Pátria: A History of the Brazilian Army, 1889–1937*. Stanford: Stanford University Press, 2003.

McCreery, David. *Rural Guatemala, 1760–1940*. Stanford: Stanford University Press, 1994.

McPherson, Alan. *The Invaded: How Latin Americans and Their Allies Fought and Ended U.S. Occupations*. New York: Oxford University Press, 2014.

Milanich, Nara B. *Children of Fate: Childhood, Class, and the State in Chile, 1850–1930*. Durham: Duke University Press, 2009.

Monteon, Michael. *Chile in the Nitrate Era*. Madison: University of Wisconsin Press, 1982.

Nunn, Frederick M. *Yesterday's Soldiers: European Military Professionalism in South America*. Lincoln: University of Nebraska Press, 1983.

Ortiz, Fernando. *Cuban Counterpoint*. 2nd ed. Durham: Duke University Press, 1995.

Pearcy, Thomas L. *We Answer Only to God: Politics and the Military in Panama, 1903–1947*. Albuquerque: University of New Mexico Press, 1998.

Pérez, Louis A., Jr. *Cuba under the Platt Amendment, 1902–1934*. Pittsburgh: University of Pittsburgh Press, 1986.

Poniatowska, Elena. *Soldaderas: Women of the Mexican Revolution*. El Paso: Cinco Puntos Press, 2006.

Porter, Susie. *Working Women in Mexico City: Public Discourses and Material Conditions, 1879–1931*. Tucson: University of Arizona Press, 2003.

Ruíz, Ramón Eduardo. *The Great Rebellion: Mexico, 1905–1924*. New York: Norton, 1980.

Salas, Elizabeth. *Soldaderas in the Mexican Military*. Austin: University of Texas Press, 1990.

Salisbury, Richard V. *Anti-Imperialism and International Competition in Central America, 1920–1929*. Wilmington, Del.: SR Books, 1989.

Schmidt, Hans. *The United States Occupation of Haiti, 1915–1934*. New Brunswick: Rutgers University Press, 1995.

Sippial, Tiffany A. *Prostitution, Modernity, and the Making of the Cuban Republic, 1840–1920*. Chapel Hill: University of North Carolina Press, 2013.

Smith, Stephanie J. *Gender and the Mexican Revolution: Yucatán Women and the Realities of Patriarchy*. Chapel Hill: University of North Carolina Press, 2009.

Solaun, Mauricio. *U.S. Intervention and Regime Change in Nicaragua*. Lincoln: University of Nebraska Press, 2005.

Stoner, K. Lynn. *From the House to the Streets: The Cuban Woman's Movement for Legal Reform, 1898–1940*. Durham: Duke University Press, 1991.

Topik, Steven C. *The Political Economy of the Brazilian State, 1889–1930*. Austin: University of Texas Press, 1987.

———. *Trade and Gunboats: The United States and Brazil in the Age of Empire*. Stanford: Stanford University Press, 1996.

Vanderwood, Paul. *The Power of God against the Guns of Government: Religious Upheaval in Mexico at the Turn of the Nineteenth Century*. Stanford: Stanford University Press, 1998.

Walter, Richard J. *Politics and Urban Growth in Buenos Aires, 1910–1942*. Cambridge: Cambridge University Press, 1993.

Weinstein, Barbara. *The Color of Modernity: São Paulo and the Making of Race and Nation in Brazil*. Durham: Duke University Press, 2015.

Wolfe, Joel. *Working Women, Working Men: São Paulo and the Rise of Brazil's Industrial Working Class, 1900–1955*. Durham: Duke University Press, 1993.

Womack, John, Jr. *Zapata and the Mexican Revolution*. New York: Knopf Doubleday, 2011.

## BIBLIOGRAPHY FOR PART IV

Andreas, Carol. *When Women Rebel: The Rise of Popular Feminism in Peru*. Westport, Conn.: Greenwood, 1985.

Bantjes, Adrian A. *As if Jesus Walked on Earth: Cardenismo, Sonora, and the Mexican Revolution*. Wilmington, Del.: Scholarly Resources, 1998.

Becker, Marjorie. *Setting the Virgin on Fire: Lázaro Cárdenas, Michoacán Peasants, and the Redemption of the Mexican Revolution.* Berkeley and Los Angeles: University of California Press, 1996.

Beezley, William H., and Linda A. Curcio-Nagy, eds. *Latin American Popular Culture since Independence: An Introduction.* 2nd ed. Lanham, Md.: Rowman and Littlefield, 2012.

Bliss, Katherine Elaine. *Compromised Positions: Prostitution, Public Health, and Gender Politics in Revolutionary Mexico City.* University Park: Pennsylvania State University Press, 2002.

Braun, Herbert. *The Assassination of Gaitán: Public Life and Urban Violence in Colombia.* Madison: University of Wisconsin Press, 1985.

Brennan, James P., ed. *Peronism and Argentina.* Wilmington, Del.: SR Books, 1998.

Brown, Jonathan C., ed. *Workers' Control in Latin America, 1930–1979.* Chapel Hill: University of North Carolina Press, 1997.

Buchenau, Jürgen. *Plutarco Elías Calles and the Mexican Revolution.* Lanham, Md.: Rowman and Littlefield, 2006.

Bulmer-Thomas, Victor. *The Political Economy of Central America since 1920.* Cambridge: Cambridge University Press, 1987.

Chesterton, Bridget. *The Grandchildren of Solano López: Frontier and Nation in Paraguay, 1904–1936.* Albuquerque: University of New Mexico Press, 2013.

Conniff, Michael L., ed. *Populism in Latin America.* 2nd ed. Tuscaloosa: University of Alabama Press, 2012.

———. *Urban Politics in Brazil: The Rise of Populism, 1925–1945.* Pittsburgh: University of Pittsburgh Press, 1982.

Cook, Maria Lorena. *Organizing Dissent: Unions, the State and the Democratic Teachers' Movement in Mexico.* University Park: Pennsylvania State University Press, 1996.

Delpar, Helen. *The Enormous Vogue of Things Mexican: Cultural Relations between the United States and Mexico, 1920–1935.* Tuscaloosa: University of Alabama Press, 1992.

Fraser, Nicholas, and Marysa Navarro. *Evita: The Real Life of Eva Perón.* New York: W. W. Norton, 1996.

French, John D. *The Brazilian Workers' ABC: Class Conflict and Alliances in Modern São Paulo.* Chapel Hill: University of North Carolina Press, 1992.

Garfield, Seth. *In Search of the Amazon.* Durham: Duke University Press, 2013.

Gauss, Susan. *Made in Mexico: Regions, Nation, and State in the Rise of Mexican Industrialism, 1920s-1940s.* University Park: Pennsylvania State University Press, 2010.

Horowitz, Joel. *Argentine Unions, the State, and the Rise of Perón, 1930–1945.* Berkeley: Institute of International Studies, 1990.

Humphreys, R. A. *Latin America and the Second World War.* London: Athlone Press for the Institute of Latin American Studies, 1981–1982.

Jones, Halbert. *The War Has Brought Peace to Mexico: World War II and the Consolidation of the Post-Revolutionary State.* Albuquerque: University of New Mexico Press, 2014.

Joseph, Gilbert M., and Timothy J. Henderson, eds. *The Mexico Reader: History, Culture, Politics.* Durham: Duke University Press, 2002.

Landes, Ruth, *The City of Women.* 2nd ed. Albuquerque: University of New Mexico Press, 1994.

Levine, Robert M. *Father of the Poor?: Vargas and His Era.* Cambridge: Cambridge University Press, 1998.

Longley, Kyle. *The Sparrow and the Hawk: Costa Rica and the United States during the Rise of José Figueres.* Tuscaloosa: University of Alabama Press, 1997.

Macias, Anna. *Against All Odds: The Feminist Movement in Mexico to 1940.* Westport, Conn.: Greenwood, 1982.

McCann, Frank D., Jr. *The Brazilian-American Alliance, 1937–1945.* Princeton: Princeton University Press, 1973.

Navarro, Aaron. *Political Intelligence and the Creation of Modern Mexico, 1938–54.* University Park: Pennsylvania State University Press, 2010.

Pavilack, Jody. *Mining for the Nation: The Politics of Chile's Coal Communities from the Popular Front to the Cold War.* University Park: Pennsylvania State University Press, 2011.

Pike, Frederick B. *FDR's Good Neighbor Policy.* Austin: University of Texas Press, 1995.

Potash, Robert A. *The Army and Politics in Argentina, 1928–1945.* Stanford: Stanford University Press, 1969.

Rath, Thomas. *Myths of Demilitarization in Postrevolutionary Mexico, 1920–1960.* Chapel Hill: University of North Carolina Press, 2013.

Sanders, Nichole. *Gender and Welfare in Mexico, The Consolidation of a Postrevolutionary State.* University Park: Pennsylvania State University Press, 2011.

Schaefer, Claudia. *Women, Art, and Representation in Modern Mexico.* Tucson: University of Arizona Press, 1992.

Schmidt, Hans. *The United States Occupation of Haiti, 1915–1934.* 2nd ed. New Brunswick: Rutgers University Press, 1995.

Senior, Olive. *Working Miracles: Women's Lives in the English-Speaking Caribbean.* Bloomington: Indiana University Press, 1992.

Sharpless, Richard E. *Gaitán of Colombia.* Pittsburgh: University of Pittsburgh Press, 1977.

Tamarin, David. *The Argentine Labor Movement, 1930-1945: A Study in the Origins of Peronism.* Albuquerque: University of New Mexico Press, 1985.

Torre, Carlos de la. *Populist Seduction in Latin America.* 2nd ed. Athens: Ohio University Press, 2010.

Tota, Antonio Pedro. *The Seduction of Brazil: The Americanization of Brazil during World War II,* translated by Lorena B. Ellis. Austin: University of Texas Press, 2009.

Vaughan, Mary Kay. *Cultural Politics in Revolution: Teachers, Peasants, and Schools in Mexico, 1930–1940.* Tucson: University of Arizona Press, 1997.

Walter, Knut. *The Regime of Anastasio Somoza, 1936–1956.* Chapel Hill: University of North Carolina Press, 1993.

Weinstein, Barbara. *For Social Peace in Brazil: Industrialists and the Remaking of the Working Class in São Paulo, 1920–1964.* Chapel Hill: University of North Carolina Press, 1996.

## BIBLIOGRAPHY FOR PART V

Alegre, Robert F. *Railroad Radicals in Cold War Mexico: Gender, Class, and Memory.* University of Nebraska Press, 2013.

Almeida, Anna Luiza Ozorio de. *The Colonization of the Amazon.* Austin: University of Texas Press, 1992.

Balfour, Sebastian. *Castro.* 2nd ed. London: Longman, 1995.

Bergquist, Charles W., et al. *Violence in Colombia.* Wilmington, Del.: SR Books, 1992.

Browder, John O., and Brian J. Godfrey. *Rainforest Cities: Urbanization, Development and Globalization of the Brazilian Amazon.* New York: Columbia University Press, 1997.

Brusco, Elizabeth E. *The Reformation of Machismo: Evangelical Conversion and Gender in Colombia.* Austin: University of Texas Press, 1995.

Camp, Roderic A. *The Making of a Government: Political Leaders in Modern Mexico.* Tucson: University of Arizona Press, 1985.

———. *Mexican Political Biographies, 1935–2009*. 4th ed. Austin: University of Texas Press, 2011.

Carey, Elaine. *Plaza of Sacrifices: Gender, Power and Terror in 1968 Mexico*. Albuquerque: University of New Mexico Press, 2005.

Castro, Daniel, ed. *Revolution and Revolutionaries*. Wilmington, Del.: SR Books, 1999.

Child, Jack. *The Central American Peace Process, 1983–1991*. Boulder: Lynne Rienner, 1992.

Clawson, Patrick L., and Rensselaer W. Lee III. *The Andean Cocaine Industry*. New York: St. Martin's Press, 1996.

Constable, Pamela, and Arturo Valenzuela. *A Nation of Enemies: Chile under Pinochet*. New York: Norton, 1991.

Cornelius, Wayne A. *Mexican Politics in Transition: The Breakdown of a One-Party-Dominant Regime*. San Diego: Center for U.S.-Mexican Studies, 1996.

Danner, Mark. *The Massacre at El Mozote*. New York: Vintage, 1994.

Davis, Diane E. *Urban Leviathan: Mexico City in the Twentieth Century*. Philadelphia: Temple University Press, 1994.

Dore, Elizabeth, ed. *Gender Politics in Latin America: Debates in Theory and Practice*. New York: Monthly Review Press, 1997.

Dosal, Paul J. *Comandante Che: Guerrilla Soldier, Commander, and Strategist, 1956–1967*. University Park: Pennsylvania State University Press, 2003.

Drake, Paul W. *Labor Movements and Dictatorships: The Southern Cone in Comparative Perspective*. Baltimore: Johns Hopkins University Press, 1996.

Drake, Paul W., and Eduardo Silva, eds. *Elections and Democratization in Latin America, 1980–1985*. San Diego: Center for U.S.-Mexican Studies, 1986.

Enríquez, Laura J. *Agrarian Reform and Class Consciousness in Nicaragua*. Gainesville: University Press of Florida, 1997.

Fleet, Michael, and Brian H. Smith. *The Catholic Church and Democracy in Chile and Peru*. Notre Dame: University of Notre Dame Press, 1997.

Garcia, Maria Cristina. *Havana USA: Cuban Exiles and Cuban Americans in South Florida, 1959–1994*. Berkeley and Los Angeles: University of California Press, 1996.

Gillespie, Charles Guy. *Negotiating Democracy: Politicians and Generals in Uruguay*. Cambridge: Cambridge University Press, 1991.

Gillingham, Paul. *Cuauhtémoc's Bones: Forging National Identity in Modern Mexico*. Albuquerque: University of New Mexico Press, 2011.

Gleijeses, Piero. *Shattered Hope: The Guatemalan Revolution and the United States, 1944–1954*. Princeton: Princeton University Press, 1992.

Goertzel, Ted G. *Brazil's Lula: The Most Popular Politician on Earth*. Boca Raton: BrownWalker Press, 2011.

———. *Fernando Henrique Cardoso: Reinventing Democracy in Brazil*. Boulder: Lynne Rienner, 1999.

González, Victoria, and Karen Kampwirth, eds. *Radical Women in Latin America: Left and Right*. University Park: Pennsylvania State University Press, 2001.

Gorriti Ellenbogen, Gustavo. *The Shining Path: A History of the Millenarian War in Peru*. Chapel Hill: University of North Carolina Press, 1999.

Gross, Liza. *Handbook of Leftist Guerilla Groups in Latin America and the Caribbean*. Boulder: Westview Press, 1995.

Gutierrez, David G., ed. *Between Two Worlds: Mexican Immigrants in the United States*. Wilmington, Del.: Scholarly Resources, 1996.

Guzmán Bouvard, Marguerite. *Revolutionizing Motherhood: The Mothers of the Plaza de Mayo*. Wilmington, Del.: SR Books, 1994.

Handy, Jim. *Revolution in the Countryside: Rural Conflict and Agrarian Reform in Guatemala, 1944–1954*. Chapel Hill: University of North Carolina Press, 1994.

Hemming, John. *Die if You Must: Brazilian Indians in the Twentieth Century*. London: Macmillan, 2003.

Hoyt, Katherine. *The Many Faces of Sandinista Democracy*. Athens: Ohio University Press, 1997.

Hunter, Wendy. *Eroding Military Influence in Brazil: Politicians against Soldiers*. Chapel Hill: University of North Carolina Press, 1997.

Iber, Patrick. *Neither Peace nor Freedom: The Cultural Cold War in Latin America*. Cambridge: Harvard University Press, 2015.

Johnson, Ollie Andrew, III. *Brazilian Party Politics and the Coup of 1964*. Gainesville: University Press of Florida, 2001.

Keck, Margaret E. *The Workers' Party and Democratization in Brazil*. New Haven: Yale University Press, 1992.

Kopinak, Kathryn. *Desert Capitalism: Maquiladoras in North America's Western Industrial Corridor*. Tucson: University of Arizona Press, 1996.

La Botz, Dan. *Democracy in Mexico: Peasant Rebellion and Political Reform*. Boston: South End Press, 1995.

Lesser, Jeffrey. *Negotiating National Identity: Immigrants, Minorities, and the Struggle for Ethnicity in Brazil*. Durham: Duke University Press, 1999.

Levitsky, Steven, and Kenneth M. Roberts. *The Resurgence of the Latin American Left*. Baltimore: Johns Hopkins University Press, 2011.

Loveman, Brian, and Thomas M. Davies Jr., eds. *The Politics of Antipolitics: The Military in Latin America*. 3rd ed. Wilmington, Del.: SR Books, 1997.

Lowenthal, Abraham F. *The Dominican Intervention*. 2nd ed. Baltimore: Johns Hopkins University Press, 1995.

Macaulay, Neill. *A Rebel in Cuba*. Micanopy, Fla.: Wacahoota Press, 1999.

Martinez, Oscar, ed. *U.S.-Mexico Borderlands*. Wilmington, Del.: SR Books, 1996.

Martínez-Fernández, Luis. *Revolutionary Cuba: A History*. Gainesville: University Press of Florida, 2014.

McCann, Bryan. *Hello, Hello Brazil: Popular Music in the Making of Modern Brazil*. Durham: Duke University Press, 2004.

McCormick, Gladys I. *The Logic of Compromise in Mexico: How the Countryside Was Key to the Emergence of Authoritarianism*. Chapel Hill: University of North Carolina Press, 2016.

McGuire, James W. *Peronism without Perón: Unions, Parties, and Democracy in Argentina*. Stanford: Stanford University Press, 1997.

McPherson, Alan L. *Yankee No!: Anti-Americanism in U.S.-Latin American Relations*. Cambridge: Harvard University Press, 2003.

Middlebrook, Kevin J., and Carlos Rico, eds. *The United States and Latin America in the 1980s*. Pittsburgh: University of Pittsburgh Press, 1985.

Morris, Stephen D. *Political Reformism in Mexico*. Boulder: Lynne Rienner, 1995.

Norden, Deborah L. *Military Rebellion in Argentina: Between Coups and Consolidation*. Lincoln: University of Nebraska Press, 1996.

Nunn, Frederick M. *The Time of the Generals: Latin American Professional Militarism in World Perspective*. Lincoln: University of Nebraska Press, 1992.

Oppenheim, Lois Hecht. *Politics in Chile: Socialism, Authoritarianism, and Market Democracy.* 3rd ed. Boulder: Westview, 2007.

Orme, William A., Jr. *Understanding NAFTA.* Austin: University of Texas Press, 1996.

Palmer, David Scott, ed. *Shining Path of Peru.* 2nd ed. New York: St. Martin's Press, 1994.

Pereira, Anthony W. *The End of the Peasantry: The Rural Labor Movement in Northeast Brazil, 1961–1988.* Pittsburgh: University of Pittsburgh Press, 1997.

Pérez-Stable, Marifeli. *The Cuban Revolution: Origins, Course, and Legacy.* 3rd ed. New York: Oxford University Press, 2011.

Place, Susan E., ed. *Tropical Rainforests: Latin American Nature and Society in Transition.* Wilmington, Del.: Scholarly Resources, 1993.

Potash, Robert A. *The Army and Politics in Argentina, 1962–1973.* Stanford: Stanford University Press, 1996.

Quirk, Robert E. *Fidel Castro.* New York: Norton, 1993.

Rabe, Stephen. *The Killing Zone: The United States Wages Cold War in Latin America.* New York: Oxford University Press, 2011.

Reich, Peter Lester. *Mexico's Hidden Revolution: The Catholic Church in Law and Politics since 1929.* Notre Dame: University of Notre Dame Press, 1996.

Rohter, Larry. *Brazil on the Rise: The Story of a Country Transformed.* New York: Palgrave Macmillan, 2010.

Romero, Luis Alberto. *A History of Argentina in the Twentieth Century.* University Park: Pennsylvania State University Press, 2002.

Rubenstein, Anne. *Bad Language, Naked Ladies and Other Threats to the Nation: A Political History of Comic Books in Mexico.* Durham: Duke University Press, 1997.

Schlesinger, Stephen, and Stephen Kinzer. *Bitter Fruit: The Story of the American Coup in Guatemala.* Revised and expanded. Cambridge: DRCLAS, 2005.

Schneider, Ronald M. *Brazil: Culture and Politics in a New Industrial Powerhouse.* Boulder: Westview, 1996.

Schutte, Ofelia. *Cultural Identity and Social Liberation in Latin American Thought.* Albany: State University of New York Press, 1993.

Sigmund, Paul E. *The Overthrow of Allende and the Politics of Chile, 1964–1977.* Pittsburgh: University of Pittsburgh Press, 1978.

Skidmore, Thomas E. *The Politics of Military Rule in Brazil, 1964–1985.* New York: Oxford University Press, 1988.

Smith, Louise, and Alfred Padula. *Sex and Revolution: Women in Socialist Cuba.* New York: Oxford University Press, 1996.

Spooner, Mary Helen. *Soldiers in a Narrow Land: The Pinochet Regime in Chile.* Berkeley and Los Angeles: University of California Press, 1994.

Stephen, Lynn. *Women and Social Movements in Latin America: Power from Below.* Austin: University of Texas Press, 1997.

Stokes, Susan C. *Cultures in Conflict: Social Movements and the State of Peru.* Berkeley: University of California Press, 1995.

Tinsman, Heidi. *Buying into the Regime: Grapes and Consumption in Cold War Chile and the United States.* Durham: Duke University Press, 2014.

Vanden, Harry E., and Gary Prevost. *Democracy and Socialism in Sandinista Nicaragua.* Boulder: Lynne Rienner, 1992.

Walker, William O., III, ed. *Drugs in the Western Hemisphere.* Wilmington, Del.: SR Books, 1996.

Wickham-Crowley, Timothy P. *Guerrillas and Revolution in Latin America.* Princeton: Princeton University Press, 1992.

Winn, Peter. *Weavers of Revolution: Yarur Workers and Chile's Road to Socialism.* New York: Oxford University Press, 1989.

Womack, John, Jr. *Rebellion in Chiapas: An Historical Reader.* New York: New Press, 1999.

Wood, Bryce. *The Dismantling of the Good Neighbor Policy.* Austin: University of Texas Press, 1985.

Wright, Thomas C. *Latin America in the Era of the Cuban Revolution.* Westport, Conn.: Praeger, 1991.

Zolov, Eric. *Refried Elvis: The Rise of the Mexican Counterculture.* Berkeley: University of California Press, 1999.

## GENERAL BIBLIOGRAPHY

Aguilar Camín, Héctor, and Lorenzo Meyer. *In the Shadow of the Mexican Revolution.* Austin: University of Texas Press, 1993.

Andrews, George Reid. *Afro-Latin America, 1800–2000.* New York: Oxford University Press, 2004.

Atkins, G. Pope. *Latin America in the International Political System.* Boulder: Westview, 1995.

Atkins, G. Pope, and Larman C. Wilson. *The Dominican Republic and the United States.* Athens: University of Georgia Press, 1997.

Bethell, Leslie, ed. *The Cambridge History of Latin America.* 12 vols. Cambridge: Cambridge University Press, 1984–2008.

Blasier, Cole. *The Hovering Giant: U.S. Responses to Revolutionary Change in Latin America, 1910–1985.* Rev. ed. Pittsburgh: University of Pittsburgh Press, 1985.

Boyer, Christopher R. *A Land between Waters: Environmental Histories of Modern Mexico.* Reprint. Tucson: University of Arizona Press, 2014.

Brown, Jonathan. *Cuba's Revolutionary World.* Cambridge: Harvard University Press, 2017.

Bulmer-Thomas, Victor. *The Economic History of Latin America since Independence.* 3rd ed. Cambridge: Cambridge University Press, 2014.

Burns, E. Bradford, ed. *Latin America: Conflict and Creation; A Historical Reader.* Englewood Cliffs, N.J.: Prentice Hall, 1993.

Bushnell, David. *The Making of Modern Colombia.* Berkeley and Los Angeles: University of California Press, 1992.

Camp, Roderic Ai. *Politics in Mexico: Democractic Consolidation or Decline?* 6th ed. Oxford: Oxford University Press, 2013.

Clayton, Lawrence A. *The Bolivarian Nations of Latin America.* Arlington Heights, Ill.: Forum Press, 1984.

———. *Peru and the United States: The Condor and the Eagle.* Athens: University of Georgia Press, 1999.

Coatsworth, John H., and Alan M. Taylor, eds. *Latin America and the World Economy since 1800.* Cambridge: Harvard University Press, 1999.

Collier, Ruth Berins, and David Collier. *Shaping the Political Arena: Critical Junctures, the Labor Movement, and Regime Dynamics in Latin America.* South Bend: University of Notre Dame Press, 2002.

Collier, Simon, and William F. Sater. *A History of Chile.* 2nd ed. Cambridge: Cambridge University Press, 2004.

Collier, Simon, Thomas E. Skidmore, and Harold Blakemore, eds. *The Cambridge Encyclopedia of Latin America and the Caribbean.* 2nd ed. Cambridge: Cambridge University Press, 1992.

Conniff, Michael L. *Panama and the United States.* 3rd ed. Athens: University of Georgia Press, 2012.

Conniff, Michael L., and Thomas J. Davis, eds. *Africans in the Americas: A History of the Black Diaspora.* Reprint. Caldwell, N.J.: Blackburn Press, 2002.

Conniff, Michael L., and Frank McCann, eds. *Modern Brazil: Elites and Masses in Comparative Perspective.* 2nd ed. Lincoln: University of Nebraska Press, 1991.

Crawley, Eduardo. *A House Divided: Argentina, 1880–1980*. London: C. Hurst, 1984.

Cushman, Gregory T. *Guano and the Opening of the Pacific World: A Global Ecological History*. New York: Cambridge University Press, 2013.

da Cunha, Euclides. *Backlands: The Canudos Campaign*, translated by Elizabeth Lowe. New York: Penguin, 2010.

Davis, Darien. *Beyond Slavery: The Multilayered Legacy of Africans in Latin America and the Caribbean*. Lanham, Md.: Rowman and Littlefield, 2006.

Dore, Elizabeth, and Maxine Molyneux, eds. *Hidden Histories of Gender and the State in Latin America*. Durham: Duke University Press, 2000.

Eakin, Marshall C. *Brazil: The Once and Future Country*. New York: St. Martin's Press, 1997.

Euraque, Dario. *Reinterpreting the Banana Republic: Region and State in Honduras, 1870–1972*. Chapel Hill: University of North Carolina Press, 1996.

Ewell, Judith. *Venezuela: A Century of Change*. Stanford: Stanford University Press, 1975.

———. *Venezuela and the United States*. Athens: University of Georgia Press, 1996.

Fausto, Boris. *A Concise History of Brazil*. Cambridge: Cambridge University Press, 1999.

Fick, Carolyn E. *The Making of Haiti: The Saint Domingue Revolution from Below*. Knoxville: University of Tennessee Press, 1990.

French, William E., and Katherine Elaine Bliss. *Gender, Sexuality and Power in Latin America since Independence*. Lanham, Md.: Rowman and Littlefield, 2006.

Galván, Javier. *Latin American Dictators of the 20th Century: The Lives and Regimes of 15 Rulers*. Jefferson, N.C.: McFarland, 2012.

Grandin, Greg. *The Blood of Guatemala: A History of Race and Nation*. Durham: Duke University Press, 2000.

———. *Empire's Workshop: Latin America, the United States and the Rise of the New Imperialism*. New York: Metropolitan Books, 2006.

Green, James N. *Beyond Carnival: Male Homosexuality in Twentieth-Century Brazil*. Chicago: University of Chicago Press, 1999.

Hahner, June E. *Emancipating the Female Sex: The Struggle for Women's Rights in Brazil, 1850–1940*. Durham: Duke University Press, 1990.

Hamill, Hugh M., ed. *Caudillos: Dictators in Spanish America*. Norman: University of Oklahoma Press, 1992.

Henderson, James D., Helen Delpar, Maurice P. Brungardt, and Richard N. Weldon. *A Reference Guide to Latin American History*. New York: M. E. Sharpe, 2000.

Huber, Evelyne, and Frank Safford, eds. *Agrarian Structure and Political Power: Landlord and Peasant in the Making of Latin America*. Pittsburgh: University of Pittsburgh Press, 1995.

Jaquette, Jane S., ed. *The Women's Movement in Latin America*. Boulder: Westview, 1994.

Johnson, John J. *Latin America in Caricature*. Austin: University of Texas Press, 1980.

Keith, Robert G., ed. *Haciendas and Plantations in Latin American History*. New York: Holmes and Meier, 1977.

Kicza, John E. ed. *The Indian in Latin American History: Resistance, Resilience, and Acculturation*. Rev. ed. Lanham, Md.: Rowman and Littlefield, 1999.

Kinsbruner, Jay, and Erick Detlef Langer, eds. *The Encyclopedia of Latin American History and Culture*. 2nd ed. Menlo Park, Calif.: Cengage-Gale, 2008.

Klein, Herbert S. *Bolivia: The Evolution of a Multi-Ethnic Society*. 2nd ed. Oxford: Oxford University Press, 1992.

———. *A Concise History of Bolivia*. 2nd ed. Cambridge: Cambridge University Press, 2011.

Knight, Franklin W. *The Caribbean: The Genesis of a Fragmented Nationalism*. 3rd ed. Oxford: Oxford University Press, 2011.

Krauze, Enrique. *Mexico: Biography of Power: A History of Modern Mexico, 1810–1996*. New York: Harper, 1997.

Leonard, Thomas M. *Central America and the United States: The Search for Stability*. Athens: University of Georgia Press, 1991.

Levine, Robert M., and John J. Crocitti, eds. *The Brazil Reader: History, Culture, Politics*. Durham: Duke University Press, 1999.

Lombardi, John V. *Venezuela: The Search for Order, the Dream of Progress*. New York: Oxford University Press, 1982.

Longley, Kyle. *In the Eagle's Shadow: The United States and Latin America*. Malden, Mass.: Wiley, 2009.

Loveman, Brian. *Chile: The Legacy of Spanish Capitalism*. 3rd ed. Oxford: Oxford University Press, 2001.

Lynch, John. *New Worlds: A Religious History of Latin America*. New Haven: Yale University Press, 2012.

MacLachlan, Colin M., and William H. Beezley. *El Gran Pueblo: A History of Greater Mexico*. New York: Pearson, 2003.

Maingot, Anthony P. *The United States and the Caribbean: Challenges of an Asymmetrical Relationship*. Boulder: Westview, 1994.

Meyer, Michael C., William L. Sherman, and Susan M. Deeds. *The Course of Mexican History*. 10th ed. New York: Oxford University Press, 2013.

Miller, Francesca. *Latin American Women and the Search for Social Justice*. Hanover: University Press of New England, 1991.

Moya Pons, Frank. *The Dominican Republic: A National History*. Princeton, NJ: Markus Wiener, 2010.

Murray, Pamela S. *Dreams of Development: Colombia's National School of Mines, 1887–1970*. Tuscaloosa: University of Alabama Press, 1997.

Navarro, Marysa, and Virginia Sánchez Korrol. *Women in Latin America and the Caribbean: Restoring Women to History*. Bloomington: Indiana University Press, 1999.

Nicholls, David. *From Dessalines to Duvalier: Race, Colour, and National Independence in Haiti*. Rev. ed. New Brunswick: Rutgers University Press, 1996.

Palacios, Marco. *Between Legitimacy and Violence: A History of Colombia from 1875 to 2002*. Durham: Duke University Press, 2006.

Palmer, David Scott. *Peru: The Authoritarian Tradition*. New York: Praeger, 1980.

Peloso, Vincent C. *Race and Ethnicity in Latin American History*. New York: Routledge, 2014.

Pérez, Louis A., Jr. *Cuba and the United States: Ties of Singular Intimacy*. 3rd ed. Athens: University of Georgia Press, 2003.

———. *Cuba: Between Reform and Revolution*. 5th ed. Oxford: Oxford University Press, 2014.

———. *On Becoming Cuban: Identity, Nationality and Culture*. Chapel Hill: University of North Carolina Press, 1999.

Pike, Frederick B. *The United States and Latin America: Myths and Stereotypes of Civilization and Nature*. Austin: University of Texas Press, 1992.

Plummer, Brenda Gayle. *Haiti and the United States*. Athens: University of Georgia Press, 1992.

Raat, W. Dirk. *Mexico and the United States: Ambivalent Vistas*. 4th ed. Athens: University of Georgia Press, 2010.

Randall, Stephen J. *Colombia and the United States*. Athens: University of Georgia Press, 1992.

Richardson, Bonham C. *The Caribbean in the Wider World, 1492–1992*. Cambridge: Cambridge University Press, 1992.

Rock, David, *Argentina, 1519–1987: From Spanish Colonization to Alfonsín*. Berkeley: University of California Press, 1987.

Rodó, Jose Enrique. *Ariel*. Austin: University of Texas Press, 1988.

Rodríguez, Linda A., ed. *Rank and Privilege: The Military and Society in Latin America*. Wilmington, Del.: SR Books, 1994.

Rouquié, Alain. *The Military and the State in Latin America*, translated by Paul E. Sigmund. Berkeley and Los Angeles: University of California Press, 1993.

Sater, William F. *Chile and the United States*. Athens: University of Georgia Press, 1990.

Schodt, David W. *Ecuador: An Andean Enigma*. Boulder: Westview Press, 1987.

Schoultz, Lars. *Beneath the United States: A History of U.S. Policy toward Latin America*. Cambridge: Harvard University Press, 1998.

Shepherd, Verene, Bridget Brereton, and Barbara Bainley. *Engendering History: Caribbean Women in Historical Perspective*. New York: St. Martin's Press, 1995.

Skidmore, Thomas E. *Brazil: Five Centuries of Change*. 2nd ed. New York: Oxford University Press, 2010.

Smith, Peter. *Talons of the Eagle: Latin America, the United States and the World*. 3rd ed. New York: Oxford University Press, 2007.

Stone, Roger D. *Dreams of Amazonia*. Rev. ed. New York: Penguin, 1992.

Telles, Edward, and the Project on Ethnicity and Race in Latin America (PERLA). *Pigmentocracies: Ethnicity, Race, and Color in Latin America*. Chapel Hill: University of North Carolina Press, 2014.

Torres Rivas, Edelberto. *History and Society in Central America*. Austin: University of Texas Press, 1993.

Vanden, Harry E., and Gary Prevost. *The Politics of Latin America*. 5th ed. Oxford: Oxford University Press, 2014.

Vinson, Ben, and Matthew Restall. *Black Mexico: Race and Society from Colonial to Modern Times*. Albuquerque: University of New Mexico Press, 2009.

Wade, Peter. *Race and Ethnicity in Latin America*, 2nd ed. London: Pluto Press, 2010.

Warren, Richard A. *Vagrants and Citizens: Politics and the Masses in Mexico City from Colony to Republic*. Lanham, Md.: SR Books, 2001.

Weber, David J., and Jane M. Rausch, eds. *Where Cultures Meet: Frontiers in Latin American History*. Wilmington, Del.: SR Books, 1994.

Woodward, Ralph Lee, Jr. *Central America: A Nation Divided*. 3rd ed. Oxford: Oxford University Press, 1999.

Wright, Winthrop R. *Café con leche: Race, Class, and National Image in Venezuela*. Austin: University of Texas Press, 1990.

Zanetti Lecuona, Oscar, and Alejandro Garcia. *Sugar and Railroads: A Cuban History, 1837–1959*. Chapel Hill: University of North Carolina Press, 1998.

# Glossary

**26th of July Movement:** Cuban revolutionary movement; name taken from Castro's failed assault on the Cuban army's headquarters in Santiago on July 26, 1953.

**abertura/apertura:** political opening or restoration of democracy by military government.

**abolition:** the end of slavery.

**Adams-Onís Treaty:** 1819 treaty (ratified in 1821) by which Spain ceded Florida to the United States; the U.S. also gave up claims to Texas, acquired Spain's claim to the Oregon Territory north of the Forty-Second Parallel, and paid Spain $5 million; also called the Transcontinental Treaty.

**Age of Reason:** also called the Age of Enlightenment or the Age of Democratic Revolution. Period during which the Wars of Independence were inspired, underpinned by ideas like popular sovereignty, that all people are created equal in nature, and that all people possess equal rights.

**Alamo, The:** mission in San Antonio; site of an uprising of Texans, ultimately overwhelmed and put down by General Santa Anna. Execution of prisoners at this event served to bolster American support of Texas.

**Alianza Popular Revolucionaria Americana (APRA):** a leftist, but not communist-inspired, anti-imperialist organization founded by Victor Raúl Haya de la Torre in Mexico City in 1924.

**Alliance for Progress:** program created by President John F. Kennedy to strengthen economic cooperation and mutual security among the republics of the Americas; responded directly to Fidel Castro's revolution.

**anarchists:** activists, often workers, who opposed all forms of organized government.

*Ariel:* Uruguayan book in which José Enrique Rodó pictured Latin America as a land where spiritual harmony, ethics, and aesthetics still prevailed, whereas the United States was given to materialism and governed by the mundane priorities of the present, with little or no sense of the past or future.

**Army of the Andes:** army fashioned by General José de San Martín, made up of five thousand mostly Argentines and Chileans, including black slaves who were promised freedom in return for service in the cause of Latin American independence.

**Association of Nicaraguan Women Luisa Amanda Espinoza (AMNLAE):** group created soon after the Sandinistas took power in 1979 to replace the Association of Women Confronting the National Problem; challenged sexist policies, thinking, and practices.

**Association of Women Confronting the National Problem (AMPRONAC):** group created in 1977 that promoted women's and human rights in the face of the repressive Somoza regime; its goal was to make women central actors in the social and political reform of the country.

**Audiencia:** judicial court in Spanish American colonies that possessed both judicial and legislative authority.

**austerity:** measures to cut public spending, including on welfare programs; often conditions attached to loans.

*Aves sin nido:* written by Clorinda Matto de Turner, *Birds without a Nest* was the first Indianist, or *indigenista,* novel. Its forthright description of the plight of Indians earned Turner the contempt of both the Catholic Church and the Peruvian elite.

**aviadores:** merchants who sold goods and loaned money to rubber tappers along the Amazon tributaries.

**banana republic:** epithet used to describe nations of the Caribbean Basin during the 1910s-1920s, suggesting they were not genuine nation-states.

**barriadas:** shantytowns in and around major cities in Latin America.

**Battle of Ayacucho:** 1824 battle led by General Antonio José de Sucre that effectively ended Spanish power on the South American continent and secured the independence of Peru.

**Bay of Pigs invasion:** failed U.S.-led attempt by Cuban exiles to overthrow Fidel Castro with an invasion of Cuba at the Bay of Pigs in April 1961.

**Bogotazo:** outpouring of grief and anger from Bogotá's poor, who rioted and looted for days after Jorge Eliécer Gaitán's assassination.

**Bolivian Constitution of 1826:** constitution providing for a president for life who controlled the army, guarantees of civil rights, an independent judiciary, and ministers answerable to the national legislature.

**bossa nova:** a jazz-influenced version of Brazilian samba music popular since the 1960s.

**Boyacá:** location of royalist defeat by Simón Bolívar–led army.

**bracero:** Mexican worker in the U.S. with a temporary visa.

**Bracero Program:** program lasting from 1942 to 1964 involving special U.S. entry visas for Mexican workers (and later others) to harvest crops and work in specific industries for limited periods of time.

**Brasília:** new capital city of Brazil; became the centerpiece of Juscelino Kubitschek's administration.

**Brazilian Expeditionary Force (FEB):** over twenty-five thousand men and women who went to fight alongside the Americans and Allies in Italy during WWII.

**cabildos:** city councils; cabildos abiertos were open town meetings to deal with crises, largely associated with the early Wars of Independence period. The term "cabildo" refers not only to the elected officials themselves—the alcaldes and regidores—but to the physical building where the council met.

**caciques:** regional or local leaders whose origins pre-date the Spanish conquest of the Caribbean, where caciques were native Indian chieftains. In the modern era, the term carries many meanings, all implying a leadership role in the community, region, or even nation. *See* caudillo.

**café com leite:** Portuguese for "coffee with milk"; slang for informal arrangements between 1889 and 1930 for Brazilian presidents to alternate from the states of São Paulo (major coffee-growing region) and Minas Gerais (a dairy state).

**café con leche:** Spanish for coffee with milk; slang for mulattoes in Venezuela, with light skin color.

**campesino:** peasant farmer.

**Candomblé:** a syncretic religion originally created by slaves in Brazil that blends West African religious beliefs with elements of Catholicism.

**Caribbean Basin Initiative (CBI):** a development program launched by U.S. president Ronald Reagan in 1983 that offered low tariffs and investment money in exchange for cooperation with U.S. policy aims in the Caribbean Basin.

**Caribbean Legion:** movement that tried to rid the Caribbean Basin of dictators in the mid-twentieth century.

**Caricom:** trading alliance established in 1973 among fifteen Caribbean nations and dependencies.

**Cartagena Manifesto:** document penned by Simón Bolívar calling for unity above all other considerations in the event of Venezuelan independence. Argued for centralism rather than federalism; it postponed questions of constitutionality, popular elections, and representative government.

**Carter-Torrijos Treaties:** 1977 treaty pledging the U.S. and Panama to a gradual transfer of operations until December 31, 1999, when Panama would take full possession of the canal.

**caudillo:** a strongman in Latin American politics and society possessing autocratic qualities; caudillos came to power and governed through the force of their personality, and could rule at all levels, from local or regional caudillos to national leaders such as Juan Manuel de Rosas of Argentina.

**centrales:** sugar-refining complexes, including factories and estates that were created by combining older mills and farms for greater efficiency. Built after the 1880s, most often associated with the modernization of the industry in Cuba.

**centralists:** those who supported the concentration of power in the central state and often fought against those seeking decentralized government in the decades after the Wars of Independence. *See* federalism.

**Chaco War:** war precipitated by Bolivia's invasion of Paraguay in 1932 over disputed scrubland believed to contain oil.

**cholo:** Hispanicized or urbanized indigenous person in the Andes who moves to an urban setting and works, dresses, and acts like the mestizo/ white society. Can also refer to a lower-class mestizo.

**chusma:** masses of mostly poor people, especially used by Ecuador's Velasco Ibarra. Sometimes means "mobs."

**científicos:** Mexican positivists from the era of Porfirio Díaz (1876–1911).

**Cinco de Mayo:** Mexican celebration of the Battle of Puebla on May 5, 1862.

**Clark Memorandum:** 1928 U.S. State Department memorandum arguing that the U.S. should not automatically send troops into civil conflicts in Latin America, even when U.S. citizens and property were endangered.

**Clayton-Bulwer Treaty:** signed between the United States and Great Britain in 1850, resulting from British efforts to keep Americans from dominating the site of a transisthmian canal across Central America.

**comandante:** military commander.

**compadrazgo:** godfather/godmother relations, ritual kinship.

**Confederation of Mexican Workers (CTM):** labor organization that became a main source of President Lázaro Cárdenas's support in the 1930s and a pillar of PRI support for decades after.

**Congress of Angostura:** Congress where Venezuela and Colombia were declared independent as one nation, Gran Colombia, in 1819.

**Congress of Panama:** Bolívar's 1826 attempt to bring Latin American nations together to defend their interests and solve common problems.

**Conquest:** the subjugation of the indigenous population by Spanish and Portuguese explorers, warriors, and missionaries from Europe.

**Conquest of the Desert:** Argentine campaign in which President Julio Argentino Roca definitively broke Indian resistance, taking over fifteen thousand captives and slaughtering another thousand. He also secured the south of Argentina for white settlers, making Argentina's claims to Patagonia more secure against Chilean aspirations.

**conquistador:** Spanish conqueror from the era of discovery and conquest.

**conservative:** ideology aligned with traditional power structures such as church and monarchy.

**constitutional monarchy:** a king or queen whose powers are circumscribed and delineated by a constitution whose laws he or she must obey.

**Constitution of 1917 (Mexico):** declared that the state would confiscate landholdings in excess of certain sizes; institute the ejido system of communal land ownership; nationalize all subsoil mineral, water, and hydrocarbon rights; nationalize all religious property and prohibit public displays of faith; decree universal free education; and provide extensive rights for workers.

**Contras:** counterrevolutionary military force, supported by the United States in the 1980s, dedicated to overthrowing the Sandinista government of Nicaragua.

**copper:** Chilean mineral product that overtook nitrates as leading export in the 1920s; also mined in significant quantities in Peru, Mexico, and other countries; a leading commodity export from Latin America.

**coronéis:** in Brazil, rural bosses ("colonels"); from National Guard commissions distributed liberally in the nineteenth century.

**Cortes:** Spanish parliament.

**counterrevolution:** Spanish counterattacks during the Latin American Wars of Independence. Also any counterrevolutionary movement.

**coup d'etat:** (*golpe de estado* in Spanish); literally, a blow to the state. The overthrow of a government outside the normal, usually constitutional, provisions for transitions in political power.

**Creole:** a person of Spanish descent born in the Americas (*criollo* in Spanish).

**cristeros:** devout Catholics who rebelled in the late 1920s against the secularizing tendencies of the Mexican government.

**Cuba Libre:** 1890s nationalist slogan for ending the Spanish colonial regime; articulated the idea of a Cuban nation with equality for all born on the island, regardless of race.

**Cuban Missile Crisis:** October 1962 international confrontation when the United States challenged the USSR over its nuclear missiles being installed in Cuba.

**Cuban Revolutionary Party:** party formed in 1892 by José Martí.

**debt peonage:** a type of forced labor in which an employer forces people to work in order to pay off their debt.

**Democratic Spring:** ten-year period following the 1944 presidential election of Juan José Arévalo, the fairest election in Guatemalan history to that point.

**dependency theory:** theory from the mid-twentieth century that developing nations (the periphery) were held back by industrial countries (the center) by the latter's control of capital and technology.

**descamisados:** the poor, from Spanish word for shirtless persons; used most often in Argentina. *See* chusma.

**dictablanda**: literally, "soft dictatorship," such as that of Getúlio Vargas in Brazil.

**diffusion theory:** theory from the 1950s that investments, culture, technology, and immigrants to Latin America had a positive effect on development; held that the benefits of progress and modernization spread to Latin America like ripples on a pond, from centers in Europe and North America.

**Dirty Wars:** campaigns of surveillance, torture, kidnapping, rape, and murder of leftists in various military regimes in the 1970s and 1980s.

**ejidos:** traditional communal lands in Mexico used by mestizos and indigenous people, legalized and guaranteed under the 1917 Constitution but reformed in 1992.

**enclave sector:** sector of the economy controlled by foreign investment and focused on production for export; separated from the rest of the economy, with profits largely sent abroad.

**Enlightenment:** period undergirded by ideas of reason and progress, secularism, and scientific investigation in medicine, botany, and agriculture; sometimes labeled Age of Reason; helped to inspire independence movements in Latin America.

**Estado Novo:** Getúlio Vargas's dictatorship, imposed on Brazil in response to failed communist-led revolt, formalized with a constitution in 1937.

**estancia:** large pastoral estate or cattle ranch in Argentina and other countries.

**estancieros:** Argentine ranch owners.

**FARC:** The Revolutionary Armed Forces of Colombia (FARC), founded in 1964 by peasant leaders working with the Communist Party; became the most powerful guerrilla group in the nation.

**favelas:** Brazilian shantytowns in major cities, especially Rio de Janeiro.

**fazendas:** large landed estates in Brazil.

**fazendeiros:** estate owners in Brazil.

**federalism:** system of government combining state-level governments with a central governing body, with a preference for decentralized government. *See* centralists.

**Federation of Cuban Women:** Castro-created group intended to incorporate women into the political and social life of the country.

**feminism:** position that women deserve the same rights and privileges as men.

**foco:** a small guerrilla group that used armed struggle to build, or focus, popular support for a more widespread insurrection ; characteristic of the guerrilla warfare developed by Ernesto Che Guevara.

**fueros:** corporate privileges enjoyed by certain groups, especially the military and clergy.

**gachupines:** peninsular Spaniards.

**Gadsden Purchase:** $10 million U.S. purchase of land in southern Arizona and New Mexico from Mexico in 1853, intended to facilitate a southern transcontinental railroad route.

**gamonales:** rural bosses.

**gauchos:** cowboys of the pampas of Argentina and Uruguay.

**globalization:** increasing integration and interdependence of economies and cultures around the world.

**Good Neighbor policy:** U.S. non-intervention policy toward Latin America launched by Franklin D. Roosevelt in the early 1930s.

**grandeza:** a nationalist vision of Brazilian "greatness" that shaped development and politics from the 1950s to the 1970s.

**Granma:** yacht the Castro brothers used to launch a failed invasion of Cuba in 1956.

**grano de oro:** "grain of gold"—the coffee bean.

**Green Revolution:** financing of irrigation, fertilization, herbicides, and hybrid seeds to promote commercial-scale agriculture in Mexico and elsewhere.

**Grito de Dolores:** literally, the 1810 cry or shout of Dolores, in the village where the priest Miguel Hidalgo began the Mexican War of Independence, with his call to arms and revolution.

**Grito de Ipiranga:** Prince Pedro's 1822 declaration of Brazilian independence.

**guajiro:** peasant farmer; term typically used in Cuba and Puerto Rico.

**guano:** seabird dung; sold to U.S. and European farmers as fertilizer. Profits from guano exports drove Peru's modernization process in the nineteenth century.

**Guardia Nacional:** National Guard; many were created by the United States in Caribbean and Central American nations to promote stability and order.

**Guggenheim family:** Americans who developed one of the most prosperous mining empires in Mexico.

**gunboat diplomacy:** method of maintaining U.S. control over Caribbean nations via naval threats and occupation.

**hacendados:** hacienda owners.

**hacienda:** large, landed estate in Spanish America.

**Haitian Revolution:** African slave rebellion in 1791, led by Toussaint L'Ouverture, that produced the first independent nation-state in Latin American in 1804.

**huasos:** Chilean cowboys.

**Iberia:** referring to Spain and Portugal, which comprise the Iberian Peninsula.

**imperialism:** assertion of control by more powerful countries over large territories and empires around the world, using military force and economic measures.

**import substitution industrialization (ISI):** state-led economic growth strategy popular from the 1930s to the 1970s that promoted domestic industrialization to replace foreign imports.

**indentured servants:** persons who signed contracts to work in the Americas whose passages and expenses were paid with discounts from their wages.

**indigenismo:** Indianism; a largely twentieth-century movement to restore the indigenous people to prominence in history and culture.

**Indio:** term that people use in the Dominican Republic to self-identify as Spanish-descendant as opposed to Afro-descendant.

**individualism:** philosophy favoring individuals' freedom of action and will.

**infamous decade:** 1930s in Argentina, when the Agustín Pedro Justo regime suppressed labor strikes.

**inquilinos:** Chilean tenant farmers.

**International Monetary Fund (IMF):** organization created in 1945 with close to two hundred member countries that fosters monetary, trade, economic, and financial growth and cooperation around the world.

**Islas Malvinas:** the Falkland Islands, located off the coast of Argentina; occupied by Argentina in the 1820s, but seized by a U.S. naval vessel and turned over to British forces in 1833. Since then their status has been disputed by Argentina and Great Britain.

**Jamaica Letter:** a description written by Bolívar in exile of the nature of the Venezuelan people, championing a strong central government.

**junta:** a committee; term often applied to governments that come to power through a coup or revolution.

**Krausismo:** German philosophy that became popular among Latin American intellectuals and teachers in the early twentieth century to challenge positivism. In Latin America, it favored social unity over individualism and promoted education, culture, and ethical behavior over materialism. *See* individualism.

**ladinos:** in Central America, persons of mixed or Hispanicized culture and race.

**Lake Maracaibo:** center of Venezuelan oil production.

**La Onda:** Mexican counterculture movement in the 1960s that defended freedom and justice in the face of decades of corruption, fraud, and state violence.

**La Reforma:** movement in Mexico in the 1850s and 1860s in which liberals imposed major changes in land ownership and religious practice.

**latifundia:** large, landed estate in Spanish America.

**La Violencia:** widespread partisan violence in Colombia during the 1950s and 1960s, after the assassination of Jorge Eliécer Gaitán; ultimately claimed over a quarter of a million lives.

**Law of the Free Womb:** the Rio Branco Law, passed in Brazil in 1871, was enacted to free all children born of slave mothers, upon reaching twenty-one years of age.

**Ley Juárez:** 1855 Mexican law that stripped military and ecclesiastical tribunals of their right to try all cases—civil or criminal—involving officers and clergy, throwing them into the regular judicial system.

**Ley Lerdo:** 1856 Mexican law that forced civil and religious corporations such as the Catholic Church to sell off their properties.

**liberal:** nineteenth-century political philosophy valuing individual freedoms, including economic, personal, religious, and political.

**llaneros:** Venezuelan cowboys of the nineteenth-century

**llanos:** prairies and plains of southern Venezuela and Colombia.

**Lost Decade:** the 1980s, when Latin American economies stagnated and sometimes shrank painfully.

**M-19:** Colombian guerrilla movement arising in the 1960s that declared itself to be the armed wing of the National Popular Alliance, or ANAPO.

**machismo:** concept associated with masculine virility, strength, and power; male dominance.

**magical realism:** literary style of Latin American writers that emerged after the 1940s, in which fantastic events were portrayed realistically.

**manifest destiny:** widespread belief in the 1840s and 1850s that the United States was destined to spread across North America, regardless of other peoples or national territories existing there. Reached a peak in the Mexican-American War.

**maquiladora:** a bonded manufacturing plant, usually along the U.S.-Mexico border, that assembles components from abroad and exports finished products, usually to the United States.

**Mara Salvatrucha (MS-13):** a street gang begun in Los Angeles in the 1980s that drew members from young Salvadorans fleeing civil war at home.

**mariachi:** a typical musical group in Mexico specializing in popular songs from the countryside.

**marianismo:** special worship of the Virgin Mary; stresses obedience, loyalty, docility, and faithfulness in women. Often thought of as the counterpoint to machismo.

**Maximato:** the 1928–1934 period when Plutarco Elías Calles dominated Mexican politics.

**mazorcas:** gangs of thugs who enforced Juan Manuel de Rosas's rule in Argentina in the 1830s and 1840s; by extension, pro-Perón bands in the 1950s.

**Medellín cartel:** major Colombian drug cartel, headed by Pablo Escobar.

**Mercosur:** a common market of countries in South America formed in 1991.

**Mesoamerica:** Middle America, comprising southern Mexico and portions of Guatemala, El Salvador, and Honduras.

**mestizo:** a person whose parents were of European and indigenous ancestry during the colonial period; later, this term came to mean someone of mixed racial and ethnic heritage.

**Mexican-American War:** war provoked by the United States in 1846 that resulted in Mexico losing half of its territory in 1848.

**militarism:** system of rule by military authority, rather than by obedience to the constitution and law.

**Minas Gerais:** one of the major Brazilian states, in territory and population.

**mita:** Indian tribute labor, by the forced recruitment of indigenous laborers by Spanish colonial businessmen and administrators to work in the mines and other economic enterprises of the viceroyalty of Peru. Revived in the 1920s in Peru when Indians had to provide free labor for public works.

**modernismo:** a late nineteenth- and early twentieth-century literary movement closely identified with the beginnings of a true Latin American literature. Emerging from European romanticism, its goal was to make the form and content of both prose and poetry true to national cultures as well as to challenge imported naturalism and Western materialism.

**Monroe Doctrine:** U.S. doctrine announced in 1823 by President James Monroe espousing the noncolonization principle—that the Americas were closed to further colonization or recolonization by European powers—and that American continents and political systems differed from their European counterparts.

**Montoneros:** Argentine urban guerrilla group, active during the 1060s and 1970s.

**Mothers of Plaza de Mayo:** *las madres* (the mothers) of missing persons, who paraded weekly in Buenos Aires's Plaza de Mayo beginning in 1977 to demand news of their disappeared loved ones during the Dirty Wars. *See* Dirty Wars.

**mulatto:** a person born of a white and a black parent. *See* pardo.

**Nacional Financiera:** national development bank, formed in Mexico in 1934.

**NAFTA:** North American Free Trade Agreement; customs union treaty between Mexico, the United States, and Canada that came into force in 1994.

**narcotraffickers:** people who illegally traffic narcotics across borders in the Americas.

**Natal air base:** Brazilian air base loaned to U.S. forces during World War II. Major air base for flights to and from the war fronts in Africa, Asia, and Europe.

**National Front:** term for government by collaboration between parties; 1958–1974 bipartisan arrangement in Colombia intended to diminish political conflict by bringing the two major parties into a power-sharing arrangement. *See* La Violencia.

**nationalization:** government expropriation of private companies and other economic enterprises, sometimes with compensation for prior owners.

**National Liberation Army:** Colombian urban-based, communist guerrilla force that emerged in the 1960s out of discontent with traditional party politics; has been a force ever since.

**National Security Doctrine:** military role assumed by Brazil's army in the 1950s, generated at the Superior War College in response to the Cold War and perceived internal threats to Brazil's peace and security. Similar doctrine adopted by other military regimes in South America.

**Negritude:** mid-twentieth-century literary and intellectual movement that recognized the importance of African cultural heritage in the Atlantic World, including the Americas.

**neocolonialism:** use of indirect, nonmilitary power, such as economic or diplomatic, to control other countries, sometimes though not always former colonies.

**neoliberalism:** a set of policies that emerged in the 1980s and 1990s that prescribed freer trade, privatization of public enterprises, and less government spending, and which dismantled decades-old intervention and regulation by public agencies.

**neopopulism:** a 1980s revival of populist political strategies from the mid-twentieth century, drawing upon charismatic leadership, mass media campaigns, promises of reforms, and evocation of the common people's interests.

**New World:** North and South America, including the Caribbean. In effect, all of the Americas, which were unknown to the early European explorers.

**nitrates:** mineral fertilizer and important export commodity that caused conflict among Peru, Chile, and Bolivia leading up to the 1879–1883 War of the Pacific. Also used to manufacture explosives.

**norteños:** Mexicans from northern states.

*Nunca mais:* *Never Again,* a chronicle of the tortures and deaths that occurred under Brazilian military rule in the 1970s, assembled secretly by the archdiocese of São Paulo.

**Oncenio:** the eleven-year administration of President Augusto B. Leguía of Peru, 1919–1930.

**Operation Condor:** code name for CIA-assisted program wherein Southern Cone military governments in Brazil, Argentina, Chile, Bolivia, Paraguay, and Uruguay collaborated to crack down on leftists in the region. *See* Dirty Wars.

**Operation Just Cause:** December 1989 military invasion of Panama authorized by President George H. W. Bush to arrest Colonel Manuel Antonio Noriega for prosecution in Florida on drug charges.

**Order and Progress:** slogan embodying nineteenth-century ideology of positivists throughout Latin America; in general, to have the economic progress one needed to have political order.

**Organization of American States (OAS):** association established by the nations of the Americas in 1948 to promote regional diplomacy and cooperation; successor to the Pan-American Union (1910–1948).

**pampas:** plains of Argentina and southern Brazil, where cattle and agriculture thrive.

**Panama Canal:** transisthmian waterway through Panama allowing ships to pass between the Pacific and the Atlantic Oceans, completed by the United States in 1914 and turned over to Panama in 1999.

**Pan-American Highway:** first conceived in the 1920s and 1930s; became important during World War II to connect the United States with Latin American allies. Today most nations have connections to the highway.

**Pan-Americanism:** idea that nations of the Western Hemisphere share many historical legacies and common interests, to be pursued diplomatically as equal nations.

**pan o palo:** literally "bread or stick"; system under Porfirio Díaz where peace and stability were maintained by a combination of rewards and intimidation. *See* Order and Progress.

**parceiros:** nineteenth-century Brazilian tenant farmers.

**pardo:** a person born to a white and a black parent; the term is used interchangeably with "mulatto."

**Parián riot:** 1828 Mexico City riot where thousands of lower-class residents looted luxury shops in the city center after days of political protests against the country's president.

**Paris UN Climate Change Conference:** 2015 meeting of delegates from 196 nations and eighty heads of state convened to assure that achievable climate change goals be formalized.

**patria:** fatherland, homeland.

**patriarchy:** system where males hold primary leadership roles, social privilege, moral authority, and control over wealth and property.

**patriots:** those who fought against Spain in the Latin American Wars of Independence.

**patronage:** favors given by politicians (patrones) to protect, defend, and provide for the welfare of their soldiers and followers in return for their loyalty and support.

**Patronato Real:** treaty between the Spanish crown and the Roman Catholic Church that gave the crown the right to exercise effective control over the church in the Spanish-American colonies, such as founding churches, appointing clerics, and collecting the tithe. The Padroado Real was a similar arrangement with Portuguese monarchs.

**Pax Britannica:** a period of British preeminence in world affairs, roughly from 1815 until World War I.

**Pemex:** Petróleos Mexicanos, a government corporation created in 1938 to administer oil production, refining, and distribution; the state-owned petroleum industry of Mexico.

**peninsular:** a Spaniard in the Americas who was born in Spain as opposed to a child of Spanish descent born in the Americas. *See* Creole.

**peón:** a Latin American peasant. Typically they were persons tied to the land by tradition and various institutions, some formal and some informal; some synonyms are *campesino* and *guajiro* (especially in Cuba), among other regional variations.

**Peronist Women's Party:** Argentine party founded by Evita Perón after women won the right to vote in 1947.

**personalism:** *personalismo* in Spanish; forming networks of allies and supporters—whether in government or business—based on personal connections rather than affinities such as merit, titles, and accomplishments.

**Peru-Bolivia Confederation:** 1836–1838 union of Peru and Bolivia that went to a brief war against Chile and dissolved after defeat.

**Petrobras:** state-owned oil company in Brazil.

**pink tide:** series of leftist political victories across Latin America in the late twentieth and early twenty-first centuries.

**Plan Colombia:** a U.S. military and diplomatic aid initiative launched in the late 1990s aimed at combating Colombian drug cartels and left-wing insurgent groups.

**Plan de Ayutla:** a 1854 plan to remove Antonio López de Santa Anna as dictator of Mexico; the plan also led to the calling of a constituent assembly to draft a federal constitution, setting in motion the conflict that led to the 1857–1860 War of the Reform.

**Plan de Iguala:** 1821, also known as the Plan of the Three Guarantees; called for the restoration of the church and all its rights and privileges, independence of Mexico under a constitutional monarchy, and equal treatment of all citizens.

**Plan de San Luis Potosí:** a document written in San Luis Potosí, Mexico, in 1910, by presidential candidate Francisco Madero; it called for an end to the dictatorship of Porfirio Díaz and for a popular uprising that ushered in the Mexican Revolution.

**Plan de Tuxtepec:** 1876 declaration by Porfirio Díaz calling for "No Reelection" of presidents; led to the presidency of Porfirio Díaz (known as the Porfiriato) from 1876 to 1911.

**Platt Amendment:** 1901 amendment to the U.S. military appropriations bill, later adopted in the Cuban Constitution, which was a precondition for the withdrawal of U.S. troops. It allowed the United States certain rights in Cuban affairs, rendering Cuba a de facto protectorate of the United States.

**popular sovereignty:** principle that the ultimate authority of the state resides in the people.

**Popular Unity:** a broad coalition of center and leftist parties that backed Salvador Allende in Chile's 1970 presidential election.

**populism:** political style throughout Latin America in the twentieth-century, in which charismatic leaders formed multiclass movements, exploited new communications media, and generally promised better standards of living to the masses.

**Porfiriato:** period when Porfirio Díaz governed Mexico, 1876–1911.

**porteños:** citizens of the port city of Buenos Aires.

**positivism:** a philosophy rooted in the idea that society operates according to general laws grounded in empirical science and reason. In Latin America, it stressed order and progress, and had large upper-class followings in the late nineteenth century. *See* Order and Progress.

**precursors:** leaders who, like Francisco de Miranda of Venezuela, preceded and spearheaded independence movements of the 1810s.

**Prestes Column:** 1924–1927 Brazilian guerrilla march led by Luis Carlos Prestes.

**privatization:** political and economic strategy in the 1980s and 1990s that put government-owned enterprises up for sale to domestic or foreign investors. *See* neoliberalism.

**racial democracy:** concept popularized by Brazilian writer Gilberto Freyre that blurred ethnic and racial distinctions and asserted that a racial democracy of sorts prevailed in Brazil.

**Radical Party:** this party, founded in Argentina as a protest movement in 1891, is the oldest Argentine party in existence and has embraced a generally moderate, liberal political philosophy.

**ranchera:** popular music in Mexico that dates from the early twentieth century.

**rancheros:** small-scale farmers and ranchers in Mexico.

**reconcentración:** military policy during the Cuban-Spanish-American War of 1898 by which Spain forced the rural population into camps and towns to prevent them from aiding rebels.

*Rerum Novarum:* Pope Leo XIII's 1891 encyclical calling for improved conditions for the working class.

**resguardos:** Indian communities of Colombia that owned their land collectively.

**Revolution on the March:** Alfonso López's popular program in 1934–1936 asserting that the Colombian federal government had to address pressing social needs and enact far-reaching reforms.

**Rio de la Plata:** river and estuary formed by the confluence of the Paraná and Uruguay rivers.

**Roca-Runciman Treaty:** 1933 pact between Argentina and Great Britain extending favorable terms of trade with Great Britain during the depths of the Great Depression.

**Roman Catholic Church:** the principal religious branch of Christianity in Latin America, closely allied with the Spanish monarchy before independence.

**Roosevelt Corollary:** corollary to the Monroe Doctrine, announced in 1904 by President Theodore Roosevelt, that rejected European intervention in Latin America and asserted that the United States would instead settle European disputes in the region; it served as a justification for U.S. imperialism in the Caribbean Basin for three decades.

**Rosistas:** supporters of the Argentine caudillo Juan Manuel de Rosas.

**Royalists:** Spanish forces during the Wars of Independence throughout Latin America.

**rurales:** rural police force created by Porfirio Díaz in Mexico.

**samba:** Brazilian music and dance with African roots that today embodies Brazilian identity.

**Sandinismo:** Augusto Sandino's creed and style of rebellion, refusing to cooperate with any election held while U.S. forces still occupied Nicaragua in the 1920s through the early 1930s; later employed by Nicaraguan revolutionaries who came to power in 1979.

**Sandinistas:** Nicaraguan guerrilla movement that overthrew Anastasio Somoza in 1979; took its name from Augusto Sandino, whose guerrillas had stymied both Nicaraguan and U.S. armies.

**São Paulo:** capital city of the state of São Paulo— the most populous, powerful, and wealthy in Brazil.

**secularism:** the principle of separating government institutions and persons from religious ones.

**sertão:** Brazil's dry, inhospitable backlands.

**Shining Path:** Sendero Luminoso, a violent, Marxist revolutionary movement in Peru from the 1970s through the early 1990s.

**sierra:** mountain range.

**social Darwinism:** interpretation drawn from the writings of Charles Darwin on evolution asserting that natural selection resulted in survival of the fittest among people, just as in plants and animals; largely a racist justification for white supremacy.

**soldaderas:** female fighters and camp followers during the Mexican Revolution.

**Southern Cone:** a region comprised of Argentina, Bolivia, Chile, Paraguay, and Uruguay.

**spiritual socialism:** Juan José Arévalo's progressive ideas and political philosophy, expressed when he served as president of Guatemala from 1945 to 1951.

**Stabilizing Development:** slogan of Mexican president Miguel Alemán (1946–1952) indicating his strategy to deemphasize social reforms in favor of private enterprise and foreign investment.

**Suez Canal:** canal in Egypt connecting the Red and Mediterranean Seas, completed in 1869 by the French entrepreneur Ferdinand de Lesseps—the man who tried, and ultimately failed, to build the Panama Canal in the 1880s.

**syncretized religion:** in the Latin American context, where indigenous or African customs, beliefs, and forms of worship were integrated into Christian practices, and vice versa, producing unique hybrid religions.

**syndicalists:** radical labor unionists who, often allied with anarchists, sought to destroy all government in the late nineteenth and early twentieth centuries.

**technocrat:** a government functionary with technical education or knowledge who attempts to develop policy and plans based on technological expertise.

**tenentes:** rebel officers and cadets in Brazil who fought against the government from 1922 to 1930 and then served in Getúlio Vargas's presidential administration.

**tenentismo:** political and revolutionary ideology of the Prestes Column; began as grievances over political corruption and gradually expanded into a broad call for social, economic, and political reform.

**Ten Years' War:** 1868–1878 war led by Cubans to achieve independence from Spain and freedom for Afro-descended slaves.

**tienda de raya:** a general company store located on a Mexican hacienda complex.

**Tlatelolco Massacre:** massacre of hundreds of student protesters by government forces in Mexico City on the eve of the 1968 Olympic games held there.

**Tontons Macoutes:** Haitian paramilitary agents and mythical bogeymen; myths that they had turned thousands of people into zombies enhanced the power and awe that Papa Doc Duvalier, longtime dictator of Haiti (1957–1971), had over Haitians.

**Trans-Pacific Partnership:** proposed 2016 trade agreement among twelve nations that aspired to set modern and efficient rules for global commerce; prominent members include Mexico, Peru, Chile, and Canada, as well as a number of Asian countries.

**Treaty of Ancón:** signed in 1883, treaty ending the War of the Pacific (1879–1883).

**Treaty of Guadalupe Hidalgo:** signed in 1848, treaty ending the Mexican-American War and stripping Mexico of its claims to Texas, as well as immense territories between New Mexico and California.

**tribute:** a form of tax paid by indigenous people to landowners or the local authorities; could be in goods, money, or labor.

**ultramontanism:** viewpoint emphasizing the infallible powers of the Pope and his universal authority.

**UNAM:** National Autonomous University of Mexico; originally sited in the buildings of its colonial predecessor, it was reorganized in 1910 and gained its modern campus in the 1950s.

**unitarios:** political party based in the city of Buenos Aires that favored centralized rule in Argentina.

**United Fruit Company (UFCO):** formed in Boston in 1899 by combining several other companies; came to dominate banana and other fruit exports from Latin America; perceived as representing U.S. imperialism in the region; symbolized the widespread dominance of Central America by the United States.

**United Self-Defense Forces of Colombia:** a Colombian paramilitary and drug-trafficking organization that from 1997 to 2006 fought against the rebels.

**U.S.S. *Maine:*** U.S. naval ship that exploded in Havana harbor, Cuba, in February 1898, with heavy loss of life; although it was later determined that the explosion was caused by an internal accident, at the time the Spanish were blamed and this helped precipitate the U.S. war on Spain for Cuban independence.

**Walker invasion:** William Walker, an American, was invited to assist Nicaraguan liberals in their struggles against conservatives; Walker and a small band of mercenaries took over Nicaragua from 1856 to 1857, legalized slavery, made English the official language, and attracted

American adventurers, called filibusters, to the country.

**War of the Pacific:** 1879–1883 war caused by competition among Chile, Bolivia, and Peru over the guano and nitrate riches along the rugged coastal desert shared by all three countries.

**War of the Reform:** 1857–1860 war between Mexican liberals and conservatives, triggered in part by the passage of the Ley Juárez and Ley Lerdo.

**War of the Triple Alliance:** Also known as the Paraguayan War, 1864–1870, between Paraguay and a coalition of its neighbors: Argentina, Brazil, and Uruguay.

**War on Drugs:** multifaceted U.S.-led programs intended to slow down the drug trade from Latin America to the United States.

**Wars of Independence:** movements against colonial powers across Latin America. Ideologically born in the Age of Enlightenment, they were driven by diverse economic, ethnic, and nationalistic motives.

**Washington Conference:** the first major inter-American conference, held in Washington, D.C., in 1889–1890; gave official expression to deepening relations between the American nations at the end of the nineteenth century. Periodic conferences evolved into the permanent Pan-American Union (1910–1948). Also known as the First International American Conference.

**Washington Consensus:** the 1990s neoliberal policies promoted in Latin America by the International Monetary Fund, the World Bank, and the United States.

**West Indian:** people from the West Indies islands of the Caribbean; also called Antilleans.

**W. R. Grace & Co.:** major U.S. trade and shipping firm operating in Latin America beginning in the mid-nineteenth century.

**yellow press:** a type of journalism reporting false or grossly exaggerated versions of events. Originated during the Cuban-Spanish-American War of 1898, as practiced by competing newspaper moguls Joseph Pulitzer and William Randolph Hearst. Labeled "yellow" because of "flamboyant" and "colorful" headlines, often in yellow to catch readers' attention.

**zambo:** child of a black and an indigenous parent.

**Zapatistas:** revolutionaries in the southern state of Chiapas, Mexico, that launched a rebellion in 1994 and took their name—the Zapatista Army of National Liberation (EZLN)—from the followers of Emiliano Zapata during the Mexican Revolution.

**Zimmerman telegram:** telegram by the German diplomat Arthur Zimmerman in early 1917. Intercepted by Great Britain, it urged Mexico to ally with Germany in the event that the United States entered World War I in return for German support in the recovery of Mexican lands lost to the U.S. in the Mexican-American War.

# Index